CISTERCIAN STUDIES SERIES: NUMBER TWO HUNDRED TEN

JAMES FRANCE

MEDIEVAL IMAGES OF SAINT BERNARD OF CLAIRVAUX

JAMES FRANCE

Medieval Images of Saint Bernard of Clairvaux

CISTERCIAN PUBLICATIONS
Kalamazoo, Michigan

The work of Cistercian Publications is made possible in part by support from Western Michigan University to The Institute of Cistercian Studies.

Library of Congress Cataloguing in Publication Data

France, James.
Medieval images of Saint Bernard of Clairvaux / James France.
p. cm. — (Cistercian studies series ; no. 210)
Includes bibliographical references.
ISBN-13: 978-0-87907-310-7
ISBN-10: 0-87907-310-1
1. Bernard, of Clairvaux, Saint, 1090 or 91–1153—Art.
2. Christian art and symbolism—Europe—Medieval, 500–1500.
I. Title. II. Series.

N8080.B474F73 2006
704.9'4863—dc22

2006100431

Printed in the United States of America

CONTENTS

TABLE OF ILLUSTRATIONS

TABLE OF ABBREVIATIONS

Adv	Bernard of Clairvaux, Advent Sermon / *Sermo in adventu Domini*
Apologia	Bernard of Clairvaux, *Apologia ad Guillelmum abbatem / Apologia to Abbot William of Saint Thierry*
Dialogue	Caesarius of Heisterbach, *Dialogus miraculorum* (ed. J. Strange)
EM	*Exordium Magnum,* attributed to Conrad of Eberbach (ed. B. Griesser)
Ep	*Epistola* / Letter
LA	*Legenda Aurea / The Golden Legend* of Jacobus de Voragine
PL	J.-P. Migne, Patrologia cursus completus, series Latin
SBOp	*Sancti Bernardi Opera,* edd. J. Leclercq, H. M. Rochais, C. H. Talbot. 8 volumes. Rome: Editiones Cistercienses, 1957–1977.
VP	*Vita Prima Bernardi* / The First Life of Bernard

AN INTRODUCTION

THE MEDIEVAL ICONOGRAPHY OF BERNARD OF CLAIRVAUX

THIS STUDY of the medieval iconography of Saint Bernard of Clairvaux (1090–1153) covers the period from the twelfth century to the end of the Middle Ages, around 1530, and encompasses all of western Christendom and all media. The largest group of images are miniatures in illuminated manuscripts; these are also the only ones covering the whole period. They begin with the earliest known image of Bernard, from *c.* 1135—apart from the 'portrait' on his seal matrix dated 1151, the only known image from his lifetime. Apart from its age and the fact that it is one of the only two images known of him prior to his death in 1153, this figural representation of the saint on his seal is important in that it contradicts the traditional view that Bernard was at best indifferent and at worst inimical to the visual arts.

Paintings are largely represented in the form of altarpieces or parts of altarpieces, such as wings of triptychs. They were at first prohibited by the Cistercians as being both extravagant and distractive, and are generally found only from the fourteenth century onwards. For the same reason, the earliest representations of Bernard in illuminated manuscripts are not of cistercian but of benedictine origin, and the cistercian prohibition against figural representations also meant that Bernard was not portrayed either in sculpture or in glass until the fourteenth century. Bernardine images in woodcuts, either as single sheets or as illustrations in books, belong to the period of printing from the second half of the fifteenth century onwards. A small number of images in other media—engravings on metal, tin-alloy pilgrim badges, and embroidery—all belong to the late Middle Ages.

The iconography of Bernard is a subject which has until now not received a global treatment. The only studies to date are devoted either to particular regions or to themes. I will not attempt to give a complete overview of all bernardine images, and I have been concerned not with artistic style—for that is the proper preserve of the art historian, upon which I am not qualified to encroach—but with content. The images tell us not so much about their subject—for in this respect the literary sources and especially Bernard's own works are supreme—as about Bernard's clients and their artists. Earlier conceptions of what in German has been called his *Rezeption*—the way he was used, especially in his role as model and intercessor—and the way his *Nachleben* changed and developed in the course of the Middle Ages from his day and until the sixteenth century may be supplemented and revised as a result of an analysis of all the material. A number of factors contributed to the dissemination of knowledge of the different saints, and, similarly, their relative appeal and popularity fluctuated from region to region and from century to century and were subject to a variety of circumstances. A closer look at Bernard in relation to other saints forms an important part of the study.

The significance of Bernard can be understood only in the context of his connection with the Cistercian Order whose most illustrious member he became. His enormous impact on its later growth has often, but wrongly, been responsible for giving him credit for its inception, an event which took place fifteen years before his arrival in 1113. In 1098 twenty-one monks with Robert as their abbot left the benedictine abbey of Molesme and settled in a heavily wooded place described as one of 'horror and vast solitude'[1] in a text borrowed from Deuteronomy (32:10), then known as the 'New Monastery' and later named Cîteaux. The monks wished to leave the 'old' ways of traditional monachism with its elaborate liturgy and replace it with a 'new' and stricter inter-

[1] *Exordium Cistercii* 1; Waddell 1999, 179 & EM 1.13; Griesser 1961, 65.

pretation of the Rule of Saint Benedict and to emphasize the simplicity and withdrawal from the world which, *inter alia,* included putting a stop to the admission of children and the reinstatement of manual labour. New elements included the introduction of lay brothers, whose work on the Order's outlying granges enabled the monks to reside in the cloister as the Rule demanded, and whose admission opened up the religious life to a generally lower class than had previously been able to enter the cloister.

The move represented only one of many attempts in the late eleventh and early twelfth centuries of monastic renewal and reform based on apostolic models. The state of monastic turmoil is reflected in Robert's own career. He had already relinquished or abandoned the office of superior four times before making a fifth, and final, move by returning to Molesme after a short time at Cîteaux. He was succeeded by the prior Alberic, who ruled until 1108, and was followed by the Englishman, Stephen Harding (1108–1134), under whom Bernard and his friends entered the monastery. The seed which was, in the words of the early thirteenth-century cistercian writer Caesarius of Heisterbach, 'to grow and expand and extend its branches from sea to sea'[2] may be traced back to Stephen's abbacy. Growth had already been such before the arrival of Bernard that the abbot of Cîteaux had found it necessary to send out a group of monks to found a new monastery at La Ferté, and plans were already under way for another foundation at Pontigny.

The most salient events in the sixty-three years of Bernard's life are recorded in two short passages by two of the three authors of his contemporary biography, the so-called *Vita Prima*. His friend, William of Saint Thierry, writes:

> In the year of the Lord's Incarnation 1113, the fifteenth year from the founding of Cîteaux, when he was twenty-three years old, the servant of God Bernard entered that house with more than thirty companions. Thus he submitted his neck to the gentle yoke of Christ, under the Abbot Stephen.[3]

[2] Caesarius of Heisterbach 1929, 6.

[3] VP 1.4.19; PL 185:227-228: *Anno ab incarnatione Domini millesimo centesimo decimo tertio, a constitutione domus Cisterciensis quindecimo, servus Dei Bernardus annos natus circiter tres et viginti Cistercium ingressus, cum sociis amplius quam triginta, sub abate Stephano, suavi jugo Christi collum submissit.*

William did not want his account of Bernard's life to be published before his death, for Bernard 'would have found it unbearable to suffer such praise'.[4] William, however, died before Bernard, and the *Life* was continued by Arnold of Bonneval who wrote the second book. He was followed by Geoffrey of Auxerre, Bernard's secretary and travelling companion, who wrote a further three books. It is Geoffrey who records Bernard's death on 20 August 1153:

> It was hardly the hour of Terce when . . . that great light of his age, holy (and indeed blessed) Bernard was led by Christ from the body of death into the land of the living. No longer with those who wept at his departure, he was now with the rejoicing throng of those who have gone before him into the dwelling of the saints in heaven and of the choir of angels.[5]

With these words Geoffrey anticipated the official recognition of Bernard's sainthood by the Church twenty-one years later, when he was canonized by Pope Alexander III in 1174. According to custom his feast was observed on 20 August, thought of not so much as the day of his death as the day he was born into eternal life, when, in the words of Geoffrey, 'he had exchanged death for life, and the light of faith for the fulfilled vision'.[6]

Bernard was born to pious parents who belonged to the lower nobility of a military class. One of the first stories in the *Vita Prima* is how Bernard's mother had a dream while expecting him: she had within her a white dog which, she was told, would be a guardian of God's household and 'bark on its behalf at the great enemies of the faith' and that he would become a great preacher.[7] The way in which he was marked out even before his birth satisfies one of the proofs of sanctity and forms a relatively common component of the legendary lives of saints. Not

[4] VP 1 Preface; PL 185:226.

[5] VP 5.2.13; PL 185:359: *Hora autem diei pene tertia singularis lucerna suae generationis, sanctus ac vere beatus abbas Bernardus, a corpore mortis in terram viventium feliciter Christo duce migravit, ex filiorum circumstantium et inter graves singultus ac lacrymas uberes utcumquepsallentium choro ad multorum, quos ipsae praemiserat, caetus transiens laetabundos, ad sanctorum cuneos gratulentes, ad obvia agnima angelorum.*

[6] VP 5.2.13; PL 185:359.

[7] VP 1.1.2; PL 185:227-228.

unnaturally the scene itself or simply the inclusion of a small dog in Bernard's presence was to form a favourite topic of his iconography. Bernard's mother prepared him for his future life by sending him to school with the canons of Saint Vorles at Châtillon some fifty miles north of his birthplace at Fontaine. The strength of his vocation and his charismatic nature were such that he soon gathered a group of friends and relatives around him who, having decided to dedicate themselves to a life in religious community, chose Cîteaux as the monastery in which they wished to live out their vocation.

After having been a monk for only two years at Cîteaux, Bernard was sent by Stephen Harding with a group of monks to found Clairvaux, and in the same year (1115) another daughter house at Morimond was founded. Under Stephen Harding, guidelines defining the relationship between the new monasteries and Cîteaux were gradually drawn up, guaranteeing the unity of observance and discipline. As a result, the Cistercian Order may be said to have arisen, the first fully-fledged monastic Order in the medieval church. The four 'elder daughters' of Cîteaux—La Ferté, Pontigny, Clairvaux and Morimond—came to enjoy within the fledgling Order a special status whereby each, together with Cîteaux, headed a 'filiation' or 'line' of new foundations which made up the cistercian family. Each abbey was to be visited annually by the abbot of its mother-house, and all abbots were to meet each year at Cîteaux for General Chapter. Stephen was responsible for sowing the first seeds of new foundations and has been credited with the foresight of initiating the machinary, with the twin planks of visitation and annual General Chapter, which guaranteed the desired degree of uniformity, but it was the entry of Bernard which heralded the phenomenal growth of what became the Cistercian Order, and particularly that of his own Clairvaux filiation. The pressure of numbers resulting from an influx of recruits was so great that the setting up of new monasteries became inevitable. Monasteries sprang up in the wake of Bernard's travels, many of them existing communities which were then affiliated with the Cistercians. Walter Map, later in the century, records that Bernard 'used to have carts driven round through the town and castles, in which to carry off his converts to the cloister'.[8] Other monasteries were the outcome of Bernard's network of friends; Saint Malachy

[8] Quoted from James 1983, 79.

brought the Cistercians to Ireland and Archbishop Eskil of Lund was influential in the spread of the order in Scandinavia. No less than sixty-eight daughter houses were founded during Bernard's lifetime. In time the Clairvaux filiation—its daughter-houses and their offspring—reached the staggering total of three hundred fifty-six monasteries, spanning from Norway in the North to Sicily in the South and from Poland and Hungary in the East to Ireland and Portugal in the West.

It is not just to Clairvaux and its cloister that we must look for the way Bernard influenced the course of events in the first half of the twelfth century. His intervention in the papal schism of 1130–1138 resulted in the recognition of Innocent II as the legitimate pope. He saw to it that the teachings of Abelard and Gilbert of Poitiers were condemned. One of his former disciples at Clairvaux was elected pope as Eugene III in 1145. Bernard preached the Second Crusade at Vezelay; he preached against heresy in the South of France, defending orthodoxy and countering Catharism. He mediated in a number of conflicts, and he intervened in several disputed episcopal elections. These and other forays into the Lord's vineyard he conducted both by the pen and by extensive travels. It has been estimated that he was absent from Clairvaux for approximately a third of the time. He justified his involvement in the affairs of the wider Church by what he perceived to be the need to defend it against its foes, both internal and external, 'the little foxes that spoil the vines', as he called them at the opening of his Sermon 64 *On the Song of Songs.*[9] He shared the current theory that the temporal and the spiritual cannot be separated. In his treatise *On Consideration,* counselling his former disciple Eugene III, Bernard developed the famous image of the two swords by writing:

> Both swords, that is, the spiritual and the material, belong to the Church; however, the latter is to be drawn for the Church and the former by the Church. The spiritual sword should be drawn by the hand of the priest; the material sword by the hand of the knight, but clearly at the bidding of the priest and at the command of the emperor.[10]

[9] SBOp 2:166.

[10] *De consideratione* 4.7; SBOp 3:454: *Uterque ergo Ecclesiae, et spiritualis scilicet gladius, et materialis, sed in quidem pro Ecclesia, ille vero et ab Ecclesia exserendus; ille sacerdotis, is militis manu, sed sane ad nutum sacerdotis et iussum imperatoris.*

In one letter he pleaded to be relieved from non-monastic duties, 'may it please you to bid the noisy and importunate frogs keep to their holes and remain contented with their ponds'.[11] He was only too aware of the tensions created by the inconsistency between his monastic profession and his activity in the world and he made frequent references to the pain this caused him. He likened himself to an 'unfledged nestling', exposed to winds and tempests. He acknowledged the dilemma when he gave himself the well-known title, 'chimaera of my age', for 'having kept the habit of a monk but long abandoned the life'.[12] Such was his reputation that he was offered five bishoprics: Genoa, Châlons, Milan, Langres, and Reims; all of which he refused. The *Vita Prima* relates how he was constantly pursued as a most worthy candidate for high ecclesiastical office, but always declined, although, having avoided the 'honours of the world, he has not missed out on the authority that belongs to such honours'.[13] His involvement outside the cloister in all the most important issues of the early twelfth century was by no means always a success, and it is as a towering monastic figure in an age when the new reformed monastic orders represented a model close to the sanctity of the early Church that Bernard is best remembered. In the words of the greatest modern Bernard scholar, Jean Leclercq, he

> had an acute sense of observation, a vivid imagination, an exceptional capacity for feeling and he was easily moved, a burning heart, generous in charity, passionate in disputation.[14]

He is best revealed by the authentic texts of his own works, not least the hundreds of letters he addressed to a large variety of people. Many of these are illustrated with images which reveal him as the father and teacher of his monks, and indeed monks and nuns everywhere. Much of what he wrote he did at the request of others: *The Steps of Humility* he wrote for his cousin Godfrey; his *Apologia* for William of Saint Thierry, to whom he also dedicated the *On Grace and Free Will*. Other works were similarly requested by or addressed to others: *On the Love of God*

[11] Ep. 48; SBOp 7:139.
[12] Ep. 12; SBOp 7:62, and Ep. 250; SBOp 8:147.
[13] VP 1.14.69; PL 185:265.
[14] Leclercq 1976, 16.

to Cardinal Haimeric, Chancellor of the Roman Church; to the Templars the treatise *In Praise of the New Knighthood;* to the benedictine monks of Chartres *On Precept and Dispensation* (Bernard's commentary on the Rule of Saint Benedict); to the Irish monks a *Life of Saint Malachy;* and his final work, *On Consideration,* Bernard's counsel to Pope Eugene III. His literary output was not vast but, steeped in the Bible, the Fathers, and the liturgy, he developed a mystical theology based on his own experience which was to have a profound effect throughout the Middle Ages and which outlived his reputation as a man of action.

Bernard's stature is acknowledged by all modern commentators. His classic nineteenth-century biographer, Abbé Vacandard, whose work has not been superseded, calls him 'the last of the Fathers, he is as great as the greatest', quoting the benedictine scholar Jean Mabillon (*ultimus inter Patres, primus certe non impar*).[15] According to another authority, Watkin Williams,

> There have been perhaps few instances of one man playing so important a part over, speaking relatively, so large an area of Western civilization.[16]

The great monastic historian, David Knowles, refers to Bernard as 'one of the small class of supremely great men whose gifts and opportunities have been exactly matched'. He adds:

> It is difficult to name any other saint in the history of the Church whose influence, both on the public life of the epoch and on the consciences of a multitude of individuals, was during his lifetime so profound and so pervasive.[17]

Louis Bouyer has expressed Bernard's contribution to the Cistercian Order in the following terms:

> It is undeniable that after its slow and painful beginnings the sudden brilliance of Cîteaux was due to St Bernard more than

[15] Vacandard 1927, 2:557, quoting PL 182:26.
[16] Williams 1935, XI.
[17] Knowles 1969, 77 and Knowles 1940, 217.

> anyone else. Moreover, no one contributed more than he to shaping, nor marked so deeply with his personal character, the spiritual tradition which remains the great Cistercian heritage . . . Indeed, his personality seems as exceptional as the course of his life.[18]

The great critic of monasticism, C. G. Coulton, refers to him in these terms: 'Few men ever brought to the service of an ideal, chosen so early and unflinchingly, a nobler combination of qualities'.[19] More recently, the Cistercian and historian, Louis Lekai, called him the 'man of the century' who 'played an unrivaled role in the direction of European politics for three long decades',[20] while Brian McGuire, in the collection of studies appositely entitled *The Difficult Saint,* claims that 'he dominated the second quarter of the twelfth century'.[21] Bernard himself referred to his dominant position at the height of his career in a letter to Eugene III in these terms: 'It is said that you are not the Pope but in fact I am: those who have business to conduct come to me from all sides'.[22]

Although Bernard's pivotal role throughout Christendom in the second quarter of the twelfth century is beyond doubt, he was not the only giant on the european stage at the time and his interventions in the key events were by no means always a success. Among those who shared the limelight may be counted the great abbots Peter the Venerable of Cluny and Suger of Saint Denis, the scholar Peter Abelard and the monk William of Saint Thierry. The question arises—and it forms a central part of this study—why is it that Bernard was so extensively and variously depicted in a way that few other medieval figures have been, whereas there are virtually no images of these men or any other of Bernard's contemporaries? The earlier medieval images were, as all art at the time, anonymous. Artists were thought of as craftsmen on a par with scribes or carpenters. These unknown artists later gave way to the named practitioners of 'high art' and Bernard formed a subject much in demand among their patrons. The large number of late medieval and

[18] Bouyer 1958, 15.

[19] Coulton 1923–1950, 1:285.

[20] Lekai 1977, 34 and 48.

[21] McGuire 1991, 17.

[22] Ep. 239; SBOp 8:120: *Aiunt non vos esse papam, sed me, et undique ad me confluunt qui habent negotia.*

early modern artists who depicted him provides ample testimony of the quite extraordinary interest in Bernard which persisted after his lifetime. Among the more famous can be listed Fra Angelico da Fiesole (1387–1455), Giovanni di Paolo (*c.* 1403–1482/3), Filippo Lippi (1406–1469), Jean Fouquet (*c.* 1416–1480), Filippino Lippi (1457–1504), Perugino (*c.* 1450–1523), Jan Provoost (*c.* 1465–1529), Albrecht Dürer (1471–1528), Jean Bellegambe (active 1504–1534), Hans Holbein (1497–1543), El Greco (Domenico Theotocopoulos) (1541–1614), Francisco Ribalta (1550–1628), Bartolomé Estebàn Murillo (1618–1682), and Francisco de Goya (1746–1828).

The great majority of the nine-hundred sixty-four images recorded in the Catalogue (attached in the form of a CD-ROM) are by unnamed artists and belong to the period before the advent of portraiture in the fifteenth century—that is, images representing a true likeness with individualized features bearing a physical resemblance and achieved by the artists by the sittings of their subjects. Before then the viewer relied on a number of widely-recognized shorthand codes to identify the persons whom the artists were portraying. Although the iconography of Bernard offers plenty of examples of the arbitrary ways in which artists have chosen to represent him, the chief means of recognizing him are nevertheless his portrayal as the cistercian monk he became when he entered Cîteaux in 1113, as the abbot he became after moving to Clairvaux in 1115, and as the saint he officially became when he was canonized in 1174. The three signs of recognition—the so-called attributes—are the habit as a Cistercian, the emblems of abbatial office—the crozier and the book representing the Rule whereby the abbot governs, and the halo as a token of sainthood. These will all be discussed.

In a number of late medieval images of Bernard a marked difference exists from one to the next in the way he is portrayed, and yet the features are so individualized that there is no doubt that they represent real people. They are usually elderly and often rather portly figures and represent portraits of donor abbots in the guise of Bernard. They are depicted not as the austere, emaciated saint in a shabby habit, but as the *grand seigneur* which the cistercian abbot had become, dressed in the late medieval cowl with separate *cappa* and full sleeves and carrying a costly and elaborate crozier.

Although no 'portraits' of Bernard exist, there is a remarkably detailed literary portrait in the *Vita Prima* written by his secretary and biographer,

Geoffrey of Auxerre; a rare thing as early as the twelfth century. In addition, a few other contemporary texts hint at Bernard's appearance. These literary sources gave rise to a strand which, after a long chain of intervening examples, developed into the post-medieval so-called *Vera Effigies* (True Likeness). This may be contrasted with the recent reconstruction of Bernard's appearance based on the latest forensic techniques.

Parallel to the question 'why' are those of 'how' and 'when'. In what way was Bernard portrayed? Who were the artists and who were their audience? What are the different themes? What was their relative popularity? When did they arise and what were their sources? Why were some very popular in certain regions and virtually unknown in others? Was there a development in images of Bernard from the twelfth to the early sixteenth century and, if so, what does it tell us about the way Bernard was perceived in cistercian, religious, and lay circles? Were new facets added to Bernard in his iconography in the way this happened in the literary tradition? Does the way he was portrayed tell us anything about the use made of him in his cult as a saint? Can we discern anything in his iconography which relates to the general cult of saints?

PREVIOUS STUDIES OF BERNARDINE ICONOGRAPHIC THEMES

In an attempt to answer some of these questions I became aware of the fact that no overall study existed and that a pre-condition for this—a comprehensive Catalogue—was not available, although the need for such a tool had been expressed more than once and tentative attempts at establishing such a research tool had previously been mooted. In 1927 the Cistercian Tibertius Hümpfner published a small booklet.[23] In a short foreword he claimed to have been acquainted with almost a thousand Bernard images—undoubtedly, like most of the illustrations, overwhelmingly post-medieval—but said that his small publication was only an attempt at a beginning of what he hoped would herald a complete iconography of Saint Bernard, as far as this was possible: 'Vorlegendes Werk ist nur ein Versuch, es soll hiermit der Anfang gemacht werden, eine möglichst vollständige Ikonografie des hl. Bernhard

[23] Hümpfner 1927.

anzubahnen'. Nothing further was published, but similar sentiments have subsequently been expressed. The foreword to the beautifully-produced volume on the Bernard cycles by Arno Paffrath—*Bernhard von Clairvaux—Leben und Wirken—dargestellt in den Bilderzyklen von Altenberg bis Zwettl*[24]—refers to the suggestion by a Cistercian, Dr Hermann Watzel from Heiligenkreuz in Austria, in a letter dated 17 April 1979, that 'a Group or Committee be set up in order to assemble a bernardine iconography at least for German-speaking lands': 'eine Gruppe oder ein Komitee zusammentreten solle, um eine Ikonographia Bernardina wenigstens für den deutschen Sprachraum zu erstellen'.[25] Paffrath adds that the suggestion deserves to be acted upon, especially in view of the forthcoming celebration in 1990 of the nine-hundredth anniversary of Bernard's birth, and he ends by offering his work as a stimulation towards this end.

The lack of such an apparatus and the need for it has been expressed again more recently. In an article entitled 'The Various Saint Bernards' published in 1992, the great Bernardine scholar Jean Leclercq refers to the iconography of Bernard by writing: 'In the not too distant future we shall have a complete inventory of the innumerable representations of Saint Bernard'.[26] Sadly, Jean Leclercq died in the following year and it has not been possible to ascertain what he was referring to, but at any rate no such inventory has been compiled. In his study on Bernard in Dante's Divine Comedy—*Dante and the mystical tradition—Bernard of Clairvaux in the Commedia Divina*[27]—Steven Botterill writes: 'As yet, there is no detailed iconographical catalogue of manuscripts of Bernard, still less one that deals with portrayals of him in manuscripts of works by other authors'.[28] In 1997 Franz Posset, in an article in the *Lutheran Quarterly* entitled 'St Bernard of Clairvaux in the Devotion, Theology, and Art of the Sixteenth Century', asserted that 'There is no comprehensive study on the Bernard iconography'.[29]

Previous studies have on the whole been limited and sporadic, and they have all suffered from being based on a less than complete collec-

[24] Paffrath 1984.
[25] Paffrath 1984, 25.
[26] Leclercq 1992, 30.
[27] Botterill 1994.
[28] Botterill 1994, 50.
[29] Posset 1997, 314.

tion of material. Hümpfner's booklet from 1927 is only worth a mention because it was the first modern publication devoted to the subject. In it ninety-six bernardine images are reproduced, but only ten of these are medieval and only one manuscript miniature is represented. The text, limited to four pages altogether, lists sixty-nine towns in which Hümpfner had knowledge of Bernard images, but again most are probably post medieval. Since then a number of more substantial thematic and regional studies have appeared.

The Lactatio *theme*

The most popular of all bernardine themes, the *Lactatio*—Mary offering Bernard milk from her breast—, has been the subject of more studies than any other bernardine image. In the earliest, an article in *Cîteaux* in 1956, L. Dewez and A. van Iterson refer to passages in Bernard's works which might have inspired the legend as well as to earlier parallel examples.[30] They make the point that the *Lactation* was, first and foremost, an iconographical theme of iberian origin and they describe a number of variants, such as half figures and statues that come alive, and provide illustrations of a number of examples. J. Berlioz, in an important article in 1988, also in *Cîteaux,* balanced their work by pointing to an early fourteenth-century literary source, a manual of christian instruction based on *exempla* and entitled *Ci nous dit* from its opening words.[31] Berlioz advances a number of factors relating to Bernard's spirituality as contributing to the rise of the theme. Although earlier literary versions connected with other recipients are known, he points out, no other similar images of the subject have been recorded. The lactation scene he describes (MA042)—one of four pictures devoted to Bernard—is the only known image of Bernard obtaining Mary's milk direct from sucking her breast.

Two other near-contemporary literary versions of the lactation form the subject of two further studies. In *The Difficult Saint,* published in 1991, Brian McGuire presents a hitherto unknown version found in a norse collection of marian stories called *Mariu Jartegnir* (Mary's Miracles).

[30] Dewez & Iterson 1956, 165–189.
[31] Berlioz 1988, 270–283.

This is thought to be from the first quarter of the fourteenth century and is likely to derive from an unidentified latin source.[32] The author traces the growth of the image and sets it within the context of the pre-bernardine legendary material as well as the catalan iconographic examples. He also points to thirteenth-century cistercian visionaries in the Low Countries and the link their spirituality had to physical sustenance, and to the late medieval popularity of Bernard as a saint for ordinary people. The third literary version is also referred to by McGuire and also forms the subject of a longer study by P. Arabeyre in the 1993 collection of bernardine studies entitled *Vies et légendes de Saint Bernard* (1993).[33] According to him the crypt of the church of Saint Vorles at Châtillon-sur-Seine, which had been the scene of Bernard's childhood vision of the Nativity,[34] had a statue of the black Virgin from which Bernard is said to have received three drops of milk. The lactation scene was later depicted on the wall of the chapel.[35] The same volume contains another study of the iconography of the *Lactation* by Cécile Dupeux, which is preceded by a short survey of the general iconography of Bernard. In it she mistakenly refers to Bernard's seal as the earliest known bernardine image and to the well-known pen and ink *Andachtsbild* of Bernard and a nun at the foot of the cross as an example of an *Amplexus* image,[36] which it is not. She then introduces the interesting idea of the intercessional significance of lactation scenes with donor portraits of abbots in the guise of Bernard. A famous phrase by Arnold of Bonneval containing the intercessional idea of the Virgin before the Son and the Son before the Father, which was for a long time attributed to Bernard, formed the subject of a number of pictorial representations.[37] The remarkable concentration in the last quarter of the fifteenth century of lactation images in the regions of Flanders, the Low Countries, and the Rhineland is seen by Dupeux as Bernard's influence on ideas connected with the 'Brautmystik' of the Rhineland and Ruysbroek's *Devotio moderna*. She mentions the italian variant known as the *Doctrina* and a curious example from Savoy which contains elements from both themes.

[32] McGuire 1991, 189–225.
[33] Arabeyre 1993, 173–197.
[34] VP 1.2.4; PL 185:229.
[35] Illustrated in Berlioz 1990, 49.
[36] Dupeux 1993, 152–166.
[37] *De Laudibus B. Mariae Virginis;* PL 189:1726.

The Amplexus *Theme*

The *Amplexus*—Christ's descent from the Cross to embrace Bernard—is studied by McGuire in another chapter in *The Difficult Saint*.[38] He traces the way the theme changed in the last medieval centuries to suit changing needs, and the way the image of Bernard was still alive and important right up to the end of the Middle Ages. Using the *Amplexus* carving on the altarpiece at Esrum abbey in Denmark as an example, the author notes the change from the way Bernard received the embrace of Christ passively in the original twelfth-century account to his active initiative in taking hold of the figure of Christ which is falling onto him as in a Deposition scene. The iconography of this motif is the subject of an article by Franz Posset in *Cistercian Studies Quarterly* from 1998.[39] He is mistaken in giving the *Vita Prima* as its source and wrongly states that 'McGuire gives the false impression that this story is found first in Herbert's *Book of Miracles*'.[40] In referring to the forerunners of the story he is mistaken in claiming that the figure being embraced by Christ in an Anglo-Norman *Manuel des Péchés* composed *c.* 1260 is Saint John Gualbert, when in fact it represents the knight in the story it illustrates. He describes a number of examples from the earliest—dated *c.* 1320, a miniature in a Gradual from the nuns' abbey of Wonnental—and points to the rapid increase of the image with the invention of woodcuts and the advent of printing. He points to two types: those which are less faithful to the original story in that they are set out of doors, as if Bernard were present at Golgotha and which are represented by the earliest examples; and those which take place in a church before an altar in accordance with the literary source and which are frequently represented in later woodcuts.

The Chained-Devil Theme

Apart from the *Amplexus* and the *Lactatio* and its italian variant, the *Doctrina,* the only other theme in the iconography of Bernard which became widespread in the late Middle Ages, and for which there is no literary source,

[38] McGuire 1991, 227–249.
[39] Posset 1998, 289–314.
[40] Posset 1998, 293.

is that of Bernard with the devil on a chain. It was particularly common in Books of Hours, where it was used to illustrate the so-called *Verses of Bernard,* which consisted of the opening lines of seven or sometimes eight psalms, and was often introduced by a description of the legend. The daily recitation of these *Verses* was believed to ensure salvation, but their identity was known only to the devil. Bernard got round the dilemma by reciting the whole psalter, whereupon the devil relented and divulged the verses in question. The iconography of the theme belonged exclusively to the laity and, unlike the other motifs, there are no examples of cistercian origin. Like the other themes, the motif was used as an easy means of identification and supplemented the basic attributes of monastic habit, crozier, and halo, and, like them, may be described as a 'scene-attribute'. The chapter 'Bernard and the Devil' forms the first study of the theme as well as of the associated *Verses of Bernard.*

In addition to the thematic studies there are a number of regional surveys. In 1953 the Cistercian Rafael M. Durán published his *Iconografía Española de San Bernardo.*[41] He refers to episodes in Bernard's life recorded in the *Vita Prima* and gives examples of their portrayal in the spanish iconography of Bernard. He provides further examples of the *Lactatio* and the *Amplexus.* In describing the earliest known Bernard altarpiece, dated *c.* 1290 from Palma, he wrongly identifies one of the four scenes from the life of Bernard as Saint Malachy appearing to Bernard whereas it is in fact Christ who appears to assure Bernard that his friend Malachy is a saint, a scene based on Geoffrey of Auxerre's account in the *Vita Prima,* and one which appears again in the Montblanch retable dated 1348. A number of scholars have since followed Durán and repeated his mistake. The text is followed by one hundred illustrations, but only forty-three of them are medieval, and of these there is only one example of a manuscript miniature.

Other Studies

Laura Dal Prà has devoted three studies to Bernard's iconography in Italy.[42] In an article published in 1990, she refers to the initial phase when Bernard was shown as a teacher and guide of his monks in a form much

[41] Duran 1953.
[42] Dal Prà 1990 & 1991, and Florence 1990.

influenced by byzantine art. She outlines the development whereby his image was popularized, various themes emerged, and episodes from his life drawn from the *Vita Prima* were used to satisfy a variety of needs. She notes the influence on the iconography of Bernard by the growth in the cult of the Virgin in the later medieval centuries. In the introduction to the catalogue from an exhibition held in Florence in 1990, *Bernardo di Chiaravalle nell'arte italiana,* she reviews the various themes in Italy, among them scenes from Bernard's life, Bernard in the presence of Mary, especially in altarpieces, images of the *Lactatio* which reached Italy only after the Middle Ages, and the italian variant of the *Doctrina*—the vision of Mary Bernard experienced while writing and whereby he received the skill to teach and preach. She also refers to images of Bernard with the devil on a chain, which in Italy were not associated with the *Verses of Bernard* or Books of Hours but were merely used as a means of identification in statues, glass, and *Doctrina* images. Most interesting is the way Dal Prà shows how Bernard's reputation in Italy in the later medieval period had grown to the extent that his image was used in defence of the doctrine of the Immaculate Conception, in spite of his well-known opposition to this teaching during his lifetime. In *Iconografia di San Bernardo di Clairvaux in Italia La Vita,* published in 1991, Laura Dal Prà surveys the italian Bernard cycles, which include three medieval examples, and describes each image and gives the literary source.

Dante's choice of Bernard as his guide in the last three cantos of the *Paradiso,* immediately before reaching his destination, and the influence on him of the role of Bernard in marian devotion, is brilliantly evoked in Steven Botterill's *Dante and the Mystical Tradition—Bernard of Clairvaux in the Commedia.*[43] He does not deal with the iconography of Bernard in *The Divine Comedy,* but examples are given in Peter Brieger, Millard Meiss, and Charles S. Singleton, *Illuminated Manuscripts of the Divine Comedy.*[44]

Arno Paffrath's *Bernhard von Clairvaux* (1984) contains lavishly illustrated examples, mostly in colour, of all images from Bernard cycles in German-speaking lands along with full descriptions, literary sources, inscriptions, and a list of similar images.[45] Although most of the cycles

[43] Botterill 1994.

[44] Brieger, Meiss, & Singleton 1969.

[45] Paffrath 1984.

are post-medieval, Paffrath includes the most extensive of all cycles, the glass panels from the former cloister of Altenberg. He supplies a plan of the cloister, showing the original position of the panels, and, as far as is possible, lists the panels representing scenes from the life of Bernard chronologically. Paffrath also describes the glass from Saint Apern nuns' abbey, the altarpieces from Neuberg and Zwettl in Austria, and the reliquary from Saint Urban in Switzerland. A useful map shows Bernard's journeys, from which many of the Altenberg scenes are drawn. Although useful as a reference work, the book is basically a catalogue of images which fails to view Bernard in an historical context. A sequel by Arno Paffrath entitled *Bernhard von Clairvaux 2* appeared in 1990, and covered a selection of italian altarpiece paintings, german paintings, glass, and sculpture, and manuscript illuminations from German-speaking lands with text by the Cistercian Gabriel Hammer.[46] Again, the images are fully described and illustrated in colour, but there is little attempt at an historical interpretation.

Two articles by Jean-Claude Schmitt deal with the iconography of Bernard in a general way. One is published in the magnificent catalogue of the exhibition held in Paris in 1990, *Saint Bernard et le Monde Cistercien,* one of a number held to mark the nine-hundredth anniversary of Bernard's birth.[47] Schmitt's work is of considerable interest despite the fact that he opens it by wrongly stating that there is no image of Bernard produced during his lifetime. Schmitt refers to the literary portrait and the way this may have influenced the *Vera Effigies* tradition. He goes on to ask the question of how to recognize Bernard, and states that the attributes were less precise in the twelfth century and became clearer as time went on. The great richness of Bernard's iconography is testified by the variety of the narrative images and the scene-attributes. In another article—in *Bernard de Clairvaux—Histoire, Mentalités, Spiritualité*—Schmitt raises the question of the relationship of the Bernard of images to the historical Bernard. He refers to inscriptions and attributes as a means of identification, as well as to the later use of scene-attributes, and gives examples of all of these.[48] He concludes, as we shall see, that there was never a true 'portrait', there are only 'effigies', for

[46] Paffrath 1990.
[47] Schmitt 1990, Paris 1990 149–163.
[48] Schmitt 1992, 639–657.

these images appeared only in the fourteenth century, and Bernard was portrayed in an almost infinite variety of ways.

THE PRESENT STUDY

The first step in the present study was to compile a comprehensive Catalogue of the kind that has not previously existed. This has provided the material upon which it has become possible to answer some of the questions posed above. Material for the Catalogue, attached at the back of the book in the form of a CD-ROM, has been gathered from a large variety of sources, beginning with all the iconographical studies referred to above. A very useful listing of all medieval manuscripts containing images of Bernard was compiled by Jean Leclercq, using the 1444 bernardine manuscripts he consulted during the preparation of his critical edition of Bernard's works. The list was published in *Analecta Sacri Ordinis Cisterciensis* in 1953 and consists altogether of fifty-seven important, mostly early, examples. This formed the nucleus of the present Catalogue. The standard work on medieval service books by Abbé V. Leroquais has been another important source of information,[49] as has the catalogue of an exhibition in Dijon in 1953, *Saint Bernard et l'Art des Cisterciens*.[50] The Dijon Catalogue lists twenty-five images in medieval manuscripts, twenty-two in paintings, ten in printed books, ten in sculpture, and three in glass, all medieval. The catalogue of a 1990 Florence exhibition contains thirty illustrations, with full descriptions, of medieval images, many of them manuscript miniatures, along with the many illustrations to Laura Dal Prà's article;[51] and the 1990 Paris exhibition catalogue has numerous illustrations both in the catalogue section as well as in a number of articles.[52] A landmark study is George Kaftal's *Iconography of the Saints in Italy* in four volumes, which includes a comprehensive catalogue of bernardine images in italian art.[53] Another resource which has been used is the Index of Christian Art at Princeton University, the largest archive of medieval art in the world.

[49] Leroquais 1924, 1927, 1934, and 1940–1941.
[50] Dijon 1953.
[51] Florence 1990.
[52] Paris 1990.
[53] Kaftal 1952, 1965, 1978, 1985.

Much material has been gleaned from library catalogues, especially those published in the recent past which, on the whole, give iconographic data and sometimes have an iconographic index, as well as from museum catalogues. References to other images have been found in art historical dictionaries, such as Karl Künstle *Ikonographie der Heiligen,*[54] Louis Réau *Iconographie de l'Art Chretien,*[55] H. Aurenhammer *Lexikon der Christlichen Ikonographie,*[56] and E. Kirschbaum & W. Braunfels *Lexikon der Christlichen Ikonographie.*[57] I have also travelled extensively and seen many of the images *in situ* in large numbers of libraries, museums, and churches in many countries throughout Europe.

A databank has been created containing all known medieval images of Bernard in all media. It consists of nine hundred sixty-four examples from all over the world. Although comprehensive, it is not, and never could be, complete. There are many images tucked away in private collections, particularly in Books of Hours, as well as in single sheets cut out from medieval manuscripts. A number listed in the Catalogue are only known from manuscripts which have been sold at auction in the last half century, and which were photographed and recorded before usually being 'lost' again into private ownership.

An interpretation of the visual tradition of Bernard and its development is based on asking a series of questions in a structured way according to three main criteria: chronological, geographic, and thematic.

The earliest images of Bernard celebrate him in the form of traditional author 'portraits'. The way in which the monastic Bernard, the abbot and teacher, as portrayed in the intimate pictures of the twelfth century, becomes the master of the schools in late medieval representations is traced. The significance of the choice of events from Bernard's life to changing religious needs is examined. The way in which Bernard grew with the increase in the cult of Mary in the later medieval centuries is charted. The importance of women and the late medieval conception of the family is reflected in the tenderness with which Bernard is portrayed in the presence of Mary.

[54] Künstle 1926.
[55] Réau 1955–1959.
[56] Aurenhammer 1959–1967.
[57] Kirschbaum & Braunfels 1968–1976.

By looking at the whole of Europe one gets a fuller sense of bernardine reception than has previously been possible. Regional differences in the way Bernard was viewed by artists reflect various fashions and tastes in devotional practices.

The different themes covered are narrative pictures, both single scenes from Bernard's life in manuscripts or series of pictures in the form of cycles in a number of media, as well as the so-called scene-attributes which are used either to make an important point or merely as a means of identification in addition to the conventional attributes. The *Amplexus*—Bernard receiving the embrace of Christ—is the only truly bernardine theme in that it is based on a story that goes back to Bernard's lifetime, and yet its first iconographic expression dates only from the first half of the fourteenth century and it was extensively popularized only towards the end of the Middle Ages and was almost exclusively a german cistercian motif. The *Lactatio*—Mary offering Bernard milk from her breast—was the most popular of all bernardine themes and, unlike the *Amplexus*, the earliest known versions were to be found, not in a literary, but in a pictorial form, with the first known examples in catalan altarpieces. It was equally widespread in the iconography of the Cistercians, of other religious Orders, in secular churches, and among the laity. After Spain, its popularity was greatest in the Low Countries, Flanders, and the upper Rhine, prime religious centres to whose needs on private devotion and meditation, with the accent on the interior life, it responded. Instead of Mary feeding Bernard physically, in the italian variant, the *Doctrina*, she gives him verbal and intellectual nurture. Because of this, and the marian connection generally, and his particularly strong cult in Florence, Bernard was immortalized by Dante in his *Commedia Divina*, in which the saint plays a pivotal role.

The last scene-attribute, Bernard with the devil on a chain, is particularly associated with the so-called *Verses of Bernard* and formed a relatively common illustration of these in Books of Hours; it is the only one of the scene-attributes never found in a cistercian context. Although it has been mentioned in several of the studies cited, it has not previously been examined in any depth.

The last theme covered is that of the cult of Bernard and his place in the constellation of saints as represented in medieval art. It is my belief that the comprehensiveness of the material, and its accessibility in the form of a database, has made a more accurate and wide-ranging assessment possible.

Images—many of them not previously reproduced—have been scanned either from photographs obtained from libraries or museums or from reproductions in books, and then have been inserted into the databank.

Until very recently it has, of course, not been possible to analyse material in such detail and, as far as I know, this is the first electronic database covering the iconography of any saint. Just as the computerization of all the words of Bernard's works has greatly facilitated their study and interpretation, so the iconographic database provides objective material upon which the images may be assessed and the danger of interpreting them to suit a particular viewpoint avoided. My approach has been the same as that employed by previous scholars of hagiographic images, but the data may now be manipulated with a flexibility which was hitherto impossible. It enables one to assess the development of Bernard's iconography from the twelfth century to the end of the Middle Ages and to distinguish the different uses to which his images were put in monastic and lay circles. In addition, the genesis of various themes, their relative popularity as well as regional variations, may be identified with a new degree of accuracy. As the saying goes, 'numbers do not lie'. To the inter-disciplinary study of Bernard, encompassing his iconography in which the relationship between text and images is frequently expressed, statistics may now be added. It becomes possible not only to draw on images as a source of information, but, as a result of a quantitative analysis of the total iconographic corpus, to derive a deeper understanding of their meaning.

The inclusion of examples from all over Europe has only been made possible through the help of numerous institutions, libraries, museums, and monasteries as well as to individual photographers, including my daughter, Tessa. I owe a special debt to the staff of the Bodleian Library and the Sackler Library at The Ashmolean Museum, Oxford, where most of the research was done. Any study of this kind inevitably requires money, and I offer my profound thanks to the British Academy for generous grants in three successive years which enabled me to view many of the images throughout Europe and to visit the Index of Christian Art at Princeton, New Jersey. Their financial support and further grants from the Abbeys of Gethsemani, Kentucky, and Westmalle, Belgium, also made it possible to obtain photographs and permission to reproduce the various images. I am also indebted to a number of individuals for drawing my attention to images of whose existence I would not otherwise have been aware: especially Wolfgang Brandis, Thomas Coomans, Fr Gabriel Hammer OCist, Peter Kidd, Terryl N. Kinder, Jos Koldeweij, Christine Kratzke, Henrike Lähnemann, James Marrow, Franz Posset, Hans-Walter Stork, and David H. Williams. I am particularly grateful to Dr Annette Zurstrasse of the Altenberg Domverein for allowing me to reproduce the many stained glass panels from Altenberg and Saint Apern as well as other images in the two beautiful volumes by Arno Paffrath published by the Domverein. I owe an especial thanks to Fr Hilary Costello OCSO for his help in deciphering and identifying the text of a number of inscriptions and for his expert guidance in matters relating to the monastic liturgy and cistercian custom. I have also benefited from the knowledge of different specialists, among them Peter Botterill, T. A. Heslop, Peter Hoegger, Christopher Holdsworth, Dörthe Jakobs, Martin Kauffmann, Andrea G. Pearson, and Fr Chrysogonus Waddell OCSO. To them, and for the support and encouragement of others including Abbot Thomas X Davis OCSO, Colum Hourihane, and Nigel F. Palmer, I owe a debt of gratitude. Not least, I am greatly indebted to John Frederiksen without whose help in setting up the database and producing the CD-ROM, as well as his patience in sorting out the numerous problems that arose along the way, the project would never have been completed. The same may be said of my supervisor, Brian Patrick McGuire, much of whose work on Bernard has inspired me to pursue this study of whether and how Bernard's iconography may add to our global understanding of this towering medieval figure. I have greatly benefited from his expert advice, and his constant support and encouragement has been invaluable. Finally, I owe immense gratitude to the Department of History and Social Theory at Roskilde University in Denmark, to which this work was originally submitted as a Ph. D dissertation, and at which it was defended in 2002, for allowing me to submit my dissertation, and to my examiners Dr Michael Harbsmeier, Dr E. Rozanne Elder, and Dr Tore Nyberg, whose wise comments have led to a number of improvements. I am particularly fortunate in having Dr Elder as my editor as well; her careful scrutiny of the manuscript and many perceptive suggestions and corrections have been a great bonus.

James France

Blewbury
1 March 2005

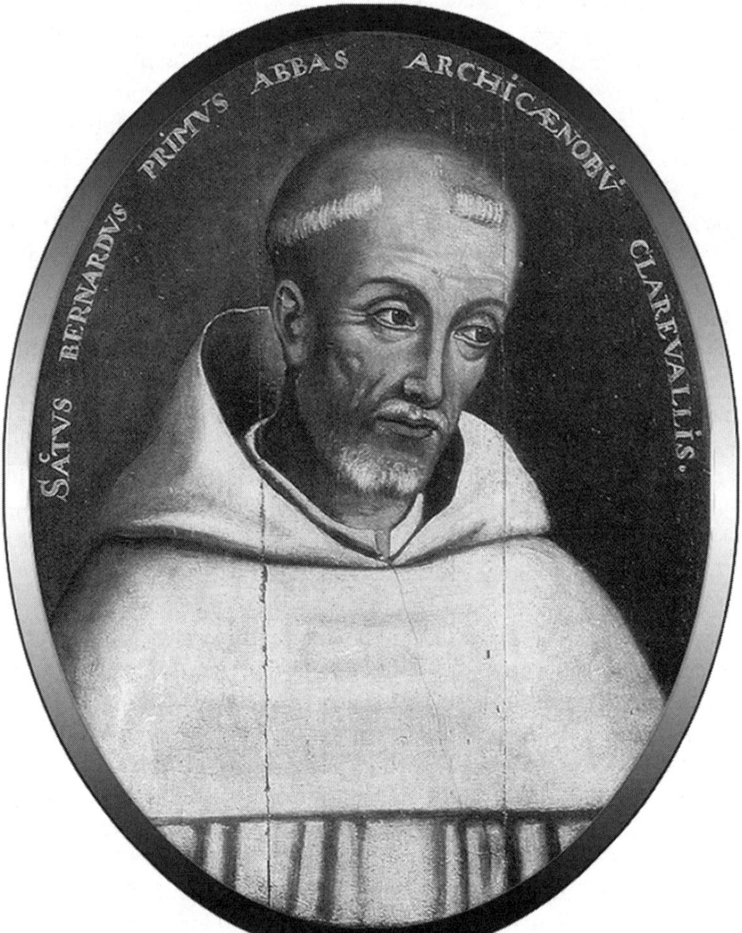

Figure 1: *Vera Effigies:* a late sixteenth-century bust of Saint Bernard.

ONE

THE LITERARY PORTRAIT AND THE *VERA EFFIGIES*

THE LITERARY PORTRAIT

Literary portraits from the twelfth century are extremely rare, and yet two remarkably detailed ones of Bernard by those who knew him best have survived. The first reference to Bernard's appearance was made during his lifetime by his friend and biographer, William of Saint Thi erry, in the first book of the *Vita Prima*. According to this 'his physique was elegant, he was good-looking, his manners delightful'.[1] A much more detailed description, which is thought to have influenced the iconographical tradition, is found in the third book of the *Vita Prima*. There his other biographer, his secretary, Geoffrey of Auxerre describes both Bernard's physique and the way it was shaped by his inner qualities and delicate health:

[1] VP 1:3:6; PL 185:230: *eleganti corpore, grata facie praeeminens, suavissimis ornatus moribus. . . .*

> A certain refinement in his appearance was spiritual rather than physical. His face shone brightly in a way that was not earthly but heavenly. His eyes revealed an angelic purity and a dove-like simplicity radiated from him. His inner beauty was so great that it revealed itself clearly in his outward appearance. He had an air of inner purity full of grace. His body was very thin, and he seemed gaunt with a complexion so pale that there was hardly any colour on his cheeks. . . . His hair was a light auburn. His beard was reddish, and towards the end of his life flecked with white. He was of average, or perhaps a little above average, height. He was like something precious contained in a fragile vessel, a vessel at times almost broken. He was afflicted with various debilitating infirmities.[2]

A further small detail regarding Bernard's appearance is contained in a story in the *Exordium Magnum*.[3] During Bernard's visit to Toulouse to counter the heresy of Henry of Lausanne, a partisan of Henry commented on the difference between his master's and Bernard's horses; to this Bernard replied that they would not be judged by the necks of their horses but for their own, pointing to his neck and asking which was the fatter, Henry's or his. Conrad of Eberbach writes: 'Saying this, he threw back his hood and bared his head to his shoulders, displaying his long and slender neck. This was thin and emaciated, but by heaven's grace it was as white and beautiful as that of a swan'. The story is depicted in one of the early sixteenth-century glass panels from the former

[2] VP 3:3:1. PL 185:303: *Apparabat in carne ejus gratia quaedam, spiritualis tamen potius quam carnalis.In vultu claritas praefulgebat, non terrana utique, sed caelestis: in oculis angelica quaedam puritas, et columbina simplicitas radiabat. Tanta erat interioris ejus hominis pulchritudo, ut evidentibus quibusdam indiciis foras erumperet, et de cumulo internae puritatis et gratiae copiosae perfusus homo quoque exterior videretur. Corpus omne temissimum, et sine carnibus erat, ipsa quoque subtillissima cutis ingenis modice rubens. . . . Caesarius ex flavo colorabatur et candido. Barba subrufa, circa finem vitae ejus respersa canis. Statura mediocritatis honestae, longitudini tamen vicinior apparabat. Alias autem thesaurus iste in vase fictili erat, contrito penitus et undique conquassato. Laborabat siquidem caro ejus multicibus infirmitatum in commodis, ut in eis virtus animi perficeretur.*

[3] EM 2:17 (Griesser 1961, 110–111): *Hoc itaque dicto caputium exuit et capite denudato usque ad humeros apparuit ipsius collum, ut erat productum et gracile; quod quamvis esset carnibus exesum et tenue, erat tamen ex dono caelesti pulchrum et candidum nimis sicut collum oloris.*

cloister of Altenberg in the Rhineland (GL31). On the left Bernard pulls down his hood while pointing to Henry's partisan. Bernard's horse is in the centre and the dialogue is indicated by the text on scrolls.

Prominent among the episodes which William of Saint Thierry recorded of Bernard as a young man before he entered the monastery at Cîteaux are three which deal with the way Bernard withstood the temptations of the flesh. Their inclusion were no doubt intended primarily to satisfy one of the main claims to sanctity, the ability to remain chaste, and thereby comply with the demands of hagiographical convention. Yet, at the same time, they testify to the way Bernard's good looks as a young man attracted the attention of the opposite sex.

All three chastity stories are represented in early sixteenth-century stained glass panels from the former cloister of the cistercian abbey of Altenberg in the Rhineland. The first refers not to his appeal to women but rather to his feelings for them. On one occasion Bernard found his gaze dwelling on a young lady for rather too long; as a result he blushed, ashamed of himself, and leapt into a pool of freezing water up to his neck until 'he was cooled down from the heat of carnal longing'.[4] The event was depicted in glass that was destroyed during the Second World War (GL04). The second account records how Bernard was able to ignore the advances of a naked girl who had climbed into his bed.[5] She is depicted in the bed in which Bernard has yielded her the space, turned round and gone to sleep. She eventually gave up, and on the right she is seen leaving the scene (GL05). The third story tells of an occasion when Bernard lodged with a certain matron with some companions. Bernard is described as being handsome in looks (*decorum aspectu*) and the woman 'was captured by the snare of her eyes and burning with desire for him'. She made three attempts to invade his bed, each of which he managed to thwart by shouting 'Robbers, Robbers' thereby frightening her away and alerting his companions who instigated a search. When asked the next day about the imaginary thieves, Bernard confirmed that there had been a robber for 'our hostess was out to deprive me of what is most precious to me in this life, my incomparable treasure, my chastity!'[6] The story is depicted in two halves. On the left

[4] VP 1:3:6 (PL 185:229-30): *a calore carnalis concupiscentiae totus refriguit.*
[5] VP 1:3:7 (PL 185:230-1).
[6] VP 1:3:7 (PL 185:230-1).

Bernard is sitting with two companions at a table laden with food and drink. Bernard, on the right, is dressed in red and with a white cap, being eyed by his landlady standing in a doorway on the far left. On the right Bernard is shown lying in bed with a woman approaching. The scroll reads: 'Latrones, latrones' (Robbers, robbers) (GL06). The nuns' cloister of St Apern in Cologne had a panel with almost the identical scene: it also consisted of two halves separated by a column, the scene on the left is also of Bernard and his companions at table being observed by their landlady, and, on the right, Bernard is again shown lying in bed and again the scroll reads 'Latrones, latrones' is repeated. ▶ *Colour plate 1* (GL78)[7] The main difference between the two is that while the landlady in the Altenberg panel is depicted approaching Bernard, in the Saint Apern panel she is shown on her way out as a result of Bernard's screaming. Strangely, while the panel illustrates the third story, the text in the top right corner refers to the second:

> When once the saint discovered a girl, who had got naked into his bed at the instigation of the devil, he yielded to her the part of the bed which he had occupied, and, resting on the other side, went to sleep. After she had made him bleed by worrying him with her nails, and he had continued motionless, she blushed with shame, arose, and fled away.[8]

The writer has embellished the account in the *Vita Prima* by expanding the *palpitans* and *stimulans* of the original text to action which caused blood to be drawn.

Two of the stories, those of eyeing a young woman and of resisting the advances of another who climbed into his bed, have been combined and are depicted in one of the eight images of Bernard in a Legendary

[7] The Saint Apern panel is now in the small village church of Saint Leonard in Marston Bigot, Somerset, England. It is little-known and is the only extant window from the Altenberg and St Apern cycles not described or illustrated in Arno Paffrath, *Bernhard von Clairvaux—Leben und Wirken—dargestellt in den Bilderzyklen von Altenberg bis Zwettl.* The author was evidently not aware of its existence: in his description of the Altenberg window he states that no comparable representation of this theme exists (p. 43).

[8] *Cum aliquando puellam quondam nudam instinctu demonis in lectu in iniectam beatus facteret, partem ei lectuli quam occupaverat concessit, immissusque in latus alterum obdormivit. Quum multiquam eum provocando unguibus cruentasset, illeque immobile pertitisset, erubuit illa surgenque aufugit.*

illustrated by Nicolas of Bologna dated 1330–1340 and featuring the lives of fifty-one saints (MA247). The upper part of the picture shows Bernard in bed next to a woman, both of them covered by a bedspread. Below a naked Bernard lies in a bath of icy water. According to the caption it shows 'How he lay with his sister and, secretly rising up, placed himself in the water so that fornication might be prevented'.[9] This reference to a potentially incestuous relationship with his sister Humbeline is not warranted by any of the literary sources. It is not to be found in any of the *Lives* or in the *Legenda Aurea* and appears to be the invention of the artist, who perhaps inserted it for greater effect.

Even more prominent in William's account of Bernard's life than the 'chastity stories' is the recurring theme of his excessive asceticism and the way he neglected his health, a habit which must have enormously influenced his appearance. Fasts and abstinence even to the point of self-destruction were a sign of contempt for the world and formed another common mark of sainthood. William records how

> Eating is an activity to which, even to this day, he is rarely drawn by an appetite for enjoyment, but only by pure fear of collapse. Indeed, as mealtime approaches, before ever he eats a thing, he is already sated by the mere remembrance of food. He approaches the taking of food as he would a torment.[10]

A little further on William tells of how Bernard would eat food which the healthiest would not touch even if they were extremely hungry, and how he mistakenly ate blood instead of butter and drank oil instead of water.[11] The story of Bernard absentmindedly drinking oil while concentrating on the things of the spirit is depicted in a drawing by Hans Holbein in the margin of the *Praise of Folly* by Erasmus of Rotterdam (DR02).[12] In view of the fact that William was writing with the

[9] *Quomodo jacebat cum sorore sua et occulte surgens posuit se in aquam ut fornication sibi non evenitur.*

[10] VP 1:4:22 (PL 185:239), trans. Martinus Cawley: *Porro ad comedendum usque hodie vix aliquando voluptate trahitur appetitus, sed solo timore defectus. Etenim comesturus, priusquam comedat, sola cibi memoria satiatus est. Sic accedit ad sumendum cibum, quasi ad tormentum.*

[11] VP 1:7:33; PL 185:247.

[12] See p. 302.

intention of securing Bernard's canonization, it is surprising that he reprimanded Bernard for going too far, even though he appreciated the effect it had in fostering his cult: 'Even if the exaggeration in his holy fervour deserves reproof, his very excess is widely revered among devout souls'.[13] An inadequate diet and exaggerated fasting broke Bernard's health and, above all, affected his digestion. His vomiting in choir became so persistent that he was first given a spittoon next to his place and then asked by the brethren to leave, and William laments that, as a result, the monks had to forego his company altogether.[14] He goes on to describe how Bernard

> once felt sick and as it were a river of phlegm flowed constantly from his mouth. Exhausted in body his strength began to fail. After some time his condition became so severe that his sons and his friends came together to perform the last rites.[15]

The scene is depicted in one of the surviving windows from the nuns' abbey of Saint Apern in Cologne (GL62). It shows Bernard on his sick bed surrounded by the community, his hands folded and his eyes closed. To remove any doubt as to the identification, he has a crozier under his arm. The abbot carrying a crozier in the centre of the scene is probably William of Saint Thierry who says that he was present.[16] The artist has not got it quite right, for he shows William as a Cistercian abbot whereas he was in fact a Benedictine abbot before he became a simple Cistercian which he remained for the rest of his life. A monk on the left with his hood over his head holds his hands to his mouth and nose as if the smell is overpowering. There is an almost identical panel made in the same Cologne workshop which used to adorn the cloister of the monks at Altenberg (GL18).

[13] VP 1:8:41 (PL 185:251): *Porro si nimietas in eo reprehenditur sancti fervoris, habet certe apud pias mentes excessus iste reverentiam suam.*

[14] VP 1:8:40; PL 185:250.

[15] VP 1:12:57; PL 185:258: *Infirmabatur aliquando Homo Dei, et velut rivulus quidam phlegmatis incessanter ab ejus ore fluebat. Unde exhausto corpore usquequaque deficiens, paulo minus ad extrema devenit. Convenerunt itaque filii et amici ejus velut ad exsequias tanti Patri.*

[16] VP 1:7:32; PL 185:246.

William of Saint Thierry also refers to Bernard's appearance when he contrasts it unfavourably with the monk who accompanied him on his visit to the bishop of Châlons-sur-Marne, William of Champeaux, to seek his episcopal blessing as the newly appointed abbot of Clairvaux. He describes Bernard as 'a young man, emaciated in body, and looking half-dead, wearing a disgracefully shabby habit, while behind him was an older monk, big in stature, robust, and good-looking. Some were laughing at him, others mocked him'.[17] In spite of this difference between the two, when asked which was the abbot, the bishop had no difficulty in identifying Bernard as the 'Servant of God'. The state of his dress conforms to Bernard's dictum that he and his monks were clothed in 'rags and tatters', a claim which gave rise to Bernard being included among the wolf-monks in the satirical beast-epic, *Ysengrinus,* under the title of 'that rag-wearer from Clairvaux'.[18]

In picking out Bernard, William of Champeaux detected in him some of the characteristic signs of sainthood: the presence of a certain energy or *virtus* which expressed itself through the body, the face being a reflection of the soul.[19] This was the 'inner beauty' referred to by Geoffrey of Auxerre which 'revealed itself in his outward appearance'. The Office for Bernard's feast, the celebration of which was ordered by the General Chapter in 1175,[20] mentions his physical appearance in the same terms. The First Responsary of the first Nocturn for Vigils refers to the way his outward appearance was shaped by his inner qualities of harmony and order:

> The first virtue [to be noticed] in this holy man was the harmony of his bearing; always his manner was composed and uniform, so that nothing might appear to him to give offence to those beholding him. Everything about him was

[17] VP 1:7:31; PL 185:245: *juvenis exesi corporis et moribundi, habitu quoque despicabilis, subsequente monacho seniore, et magnitudine et robore corporis eleganti, aliis ridentibus, aliis irridentibus. . . .*

[18] *Apologia ad Guillelmum Abbatem* 1:1 (SBOp 3:81): *in pannis et semicinctiis.* The description of Bernard in the *Ysengrinus* is in Mann 1987, 15.

[19] For this, see Vauchez 1997, 423–425.

[20] *Statuta* 1:82 (1175:2): *De sancto Bernardo proprium officium et due misse et fratres laborent.*

> well-ordered, everything bore the mark of virtue, and was a model of perfection.[21]

The image of Bernard appeared more frequently in the opening initial *P* of this responsary (in Latin: *Prima virtus viri sancti*) than anywhere else in antiphonaries. It was probably chosen to open the series because of the incipit 'The first'. Eleven examples have been recorded in this study. Among them is one from the first half of the thirteenth century from the Cistercian nuns' abbey of Arouca. In this the standing figure of Bernard in a greyish cowl with his hood partially over his head is depicted in the upper half of the initial *P*. ► *Colour plate 7* (MA414). He is pointing in a teaching mode. Another example dated *c.* 1300 is from the Cistercian abbey of Morimondo in northern Italy (MA291).[22] The three-quarter length bearded figure of Bernard with a red halo is depicted within the blue initial *P* decorated with white against a rosa background. He stands on the right wearing a white cowl and carrying a rosa book with clasps in his left hand, while his right hand is raised in blessing a group of seven tonsured monks in white habits on the left. This compares closely with another earlier historiated miniature from the same abbey, a Homiliary from the second half of the thirteenth century (MA292).

The text of the First Responsary 'is the closest this Office gives us to a "photograph" of the saint' in the opinion of the cistercian liturgiologist Chrysogonus Waddell.[23] As it transpires, however, the source for the text is the Office for Bernard's friend, Saint Malachy, with the substitution of *viri sancti* for *Malachiae*. This office, in turn, is based

[21] *Prima virtus viri sancti*
habitus corporis sui,
quod ita composite
et uno semper modo agebat,
Ut nil appareret in eo
quod posset offendere intuentes.
Totum in eo disciplinatum,
totum insigne virtutis,
perfectionis forma.

The translation is from Waddell 1992, 392. For what follows, see also Waddell 1992, 381–426 and particularly 415–416.

[22] The others are MA035 from the late twelfth century; MA047, MA104, MA106, MA212, MA070, and MA414 from the thirteenth century; MA220 from the fifteenth century; and MA015 from the early sixteenth century.

[23] Waddell 1992, 415.

on Bernard's own *Life of Malachy*, so that, indirectly, Bernard was himself the author of part of his Office! Bernard's description of Malachy has been adapted to refer to himself:

> His life and way of life showed forth his beauty and courage and purity, and he carried himself outwardly in so modest and becoming a manner that there was nothing in him which could displease those who saw him. . . . Was there anything in his walk, his appearance, his bearing, or his countenance that was not edifying? . . . He kept himself under strict discipline, totally marked with virtue, the model of perfection. . . .[24]

The way in which inner spiritual qualities express themselves through the body is something to which Bernard referred elsewhere in the lyrical words of Sermon 85 on the Song of Songs:

> But when this beauty and brightness has filled the inmost part of the heart, it must become outwardly visible, and not be like a lamp hidden under a bushel, but be a light shining in darkness, which cannot be hidden. It shines out, and by the brightness of its rays it makes the body a mirror of the mind, spreading through the limbs and senses so that every action, every word, look, movement and even laugh (if there should be laughter) radiates gravity and honour.[25]

The authors of the *Vita Prima* were not alone in commenting on Bernard's appearance. The way in which this inner light shone through

[24] *Vita Malachiae* 19:43 (SBOp 3:348)—trans. Meyer 1978, 57: *Ut enim taceam interiorem hominem eius, cuius pulchritudinem, fortitudinem, puritatem satis indicabant mores ipsius et vita, ipsum exteriorem ita uno semper modo, ipsoque modestissimo et decentissimo gessit, ut nil prorsus appareat in eo, quod posset offendere intuentes Immo quid non aedificare in eius incessu, aspectu, habitu, vultu? . . . Totum in eo disciplinatum, totum insigne virtutis, perfectionis forma.*

[25] Song of Songs 85:11 (SBOp 2:314): *Cum autem decoris huius claritas abundantius intima cordis repleverit, prodeat foras necesse est, tamquam lucerna latens sub modio, immo lux in tenebris lucens, latera nescia. Porro effulgentem et veluti quibusdam suis radiis erumpentem mentis simulacrum corpus excipit, et diffundit per membra et sensus, quatemis omnis inde reluceat actio, sermo, aspectus, incessus, risus, si tamen risus, mixtus gravitate et plenus honesti.*

Bernard's bedraggled looks was commented on by the Benedictine abbot Wibald of Stavelot in a letter dated 1149:

> That good man stayed a long time in the desert fasting until he was quite pale. It also gave him an aura of spiritual beauty, so that even before he spoke people were attracted merely by looking at him.[26]

That Bernard was endowed with an extraordinary charisma there can be no doubt. A number of other references to the magnetism of his personality may be cited. According to William of Saint Thierry, when he preached to the germanic peoples, who were not able to understand his language, these listened more intently to his voice than to the interpreter who spoke after him, and his words moved them to tears.[27] William records how, when Bernard was around 'mothers hid their sons, wives kept their husbands home, and friends removed their friends'.[28] The threat they felt is graphically recorded by Walter Map: Bernard 'used to have carts driven round through the town and castles, in which to carry off his converts to the cloister'.[29] One may be tempted to think that such stories represent merely pious hagiographical rhetoric, but the growth of the Clairvaux family of monasteries during Bernard's lifetime was little short of miraculous and tells us otherwise. Only three years after Clairvaux itself was founded a group of monks was sent out to settle at Troisfontaines in the diocese of Châlons sur Marne north of Clairvaux and a year later another group founded Fontenay in the diocese of Autun south of Clairvaux.[30] According to the *Exordium Magnum* there were at one time ninety novices at Clairvaux.[31] Geoffrey of Auxerre claims that Clairvaux had 'close to seven hundred souls dwelling there and serving God'.[32] The pressure of numbers resulting from the

[26] Ep 147 (PL 189:1255): *Siquidem vir ille bonus longo eremis qualore et jejuniis ac pallore confectus, et in quamdam spiritualis formae tenuitatem redactus, prius persuadet visus quam auditus.*

[27] VP 3:3:7; PL 185:307.

[28] VP 1:3:15; PL 185:235: *Matres filios abscondebant, uxores detinebant maritos, amici amicos avertebant. . . .*

[29] James 1983, 79.

[30] Donkin 1978, 21–29.

[31] EM 6:10; Griesser 1961, 366.

[32] VP 5:3:20; PL 185:363.

influx of recruits made the setting up of new monasteries inevitable. No less than sixty-eight daughter houses were founded in Bernard's lifetime. Eventually the Clairvaux filiation reached a total of three hundred fifty-six monasteries, as compared with one hundred nine under Cîteaux and two hundred fourteen under Morimond.[33]

VERA EFFIGIES

Genuine portraiture in the modern sense, investing the subject with individual character, was unknown until the late Middle Ages. In most cases artists would not have been acquainted with their subjects, and the idea of sitting for a 'portrait' was unheard of in the twelfth century. For identification artists relied on the use of attributes, often aided by an identifying inscription.[34] And yet the literary portraits of Bernard gave rise to an oral tradition and that in turn may have led to one strand which, after a long chain of intervening examples, developed into the *Vera Effigies* (True Likeness) portraits. These came to be commonly displayed in abbeys in the sixteenth and seventeenth centuries and have subsequently become the standard way of representing Bernard.

Recently this stereotype has been challenged by the work of the Ukrainian forensic reconstruction expert Sergei Gorbenko. The remains of Bernard's skull preserved at Troyes were subjected to the latest scientific techniques resulting in what is claimed as the most accurate likeness ever created. The reconstructed bust is now on display in the cathedral at Troyes.[35] The result is surprising in that it is quite unlike the *Vera Effigies* model and does not resemble any of the earlier representations of Bernard. Bernard's head is square, his forehead pronounced, his cheekbones high, his nose is prominent and he has a wide mouth.

The prototype for the *Vera Effigies* pictures was a late sixteenth-century bust which once hung in the monks' refectory at Clairvaux and which assumed the grand title of *Vera Effigies*.[36] *Fig. 1.* Now in the Treasury of Troyes cathedral, it was one of eight portraits of early illustrious

[33] Donkin 1978, 28.

[34] See Chapter 2.

[35] It is illustrated in Aubé 2003, 639.

[36] As it is not medieval it is not included in the database of images, but it is illustrated in colour in *Bernard de Clairvaux—Histoire, Mentalités, Spiritualité* 1992, facing 704.

members of the Order, seven of which remained at the abbey of Cîteaux. Comparable engravings by André Thevet from 1584 and by Antonio Tempesta from 1587 were probably based on the 'portrait',[37] and in the classical bernardine iconographical study by Tiburtius Hümpfner the reproduction of the Clairvaux *Vera Effigies* is followed by six more almost identical post-medieval images.[38]

Painted in oil on wood within an oval medallion, Bernard appears in the *Vera Effigies* much as he is described by Geoffrey of Auxerre and others: a thin face and pale complexion, whitish hair and beard, and with a meditative expression. His head is inclined to the right, he has a large cranium emphasizing his great mental powers, and a tuft of hair in the middle of his brow is flanked by two gaps in his monastic tonsure or crown. This small feature, in itself quite unimportant, nevertheless appears in too many Bernardine images for it to be a coincidence and it seems to have been as much one of his physical characteristics which came to make up his attributes, much as did his beard.[39] Although in itself only a tiny detail, the break in his tonsure does point to a common source for one strand in the iconography of Bernard. Around the edge of the *Vera Effigies* an inscription reads SA[N]CTUS BERNARDUS PRIMUS ABBAS ARCHICAENOBII CLAREVALLIS (Saint Bernard first abbot of the archabbey of Clairvaux).

The *Vera Effigies* had an immense influence on the way Bernard has subsequently been represented. It has dominated his post-medieval iconography to the extent that any deviation from it would confuse viewers in the same way as would portrayals of Christ without a beard. Although the Clairvaux *Vera Effigies* is dated to the late sixteenth century, its distinctive attributes nevertheless indicate it as having medieval roots. Its evolution has been traced back to the statue of Bernard which was later placed on his tomb in the church at Clairvaux. This is either the late fourteenth-century statue—one of the first representations of Bernard in sculpture—or one on which this surviving statue is

[37] Paris 1990, 282.

[38] Hümpfner 1927, ill. 1–7 & 9.

[39] Examples include SC04, MA024, and PA106. Of the total of 930 the 'tuft' appears in 145. Bearing in mind that it is not found in any of the late medieval glass cycles and that in very many images it is not possible to see the tonsure (for example when the hood is over the head), this figure is sufficiently high to allow us to conclude that the presence of the 'tuft' is no mere coincidence.

modelled (SC04). It corresponds exactly to a description of the one that adorned Bernard's tomb: his head inclined to the right, as was common in later representations, and it shows him with the usual break in his tonsure with the central tuft of hair. Carved in sandstone, it shows traces of polychrome and measures eighty centimetres in height. Bernard is carrying a model of a church in his left hand, while his right hand, in which he would have been carrying a crozier, is missing. He is dressed in a cowl with his hood partially over his head. This is the most famous and first recorded image of Bernard as a founder of monasteries, first and foremost of Clairvaux, but, with the model he is carrying, may also be symbolic of him as the initiator of a larger number of monasteries than perhaps any other person before or since.

Sculptures were prohibited in early cistercian legislation. Bernard's own, well-known objection to art in monastic enclosures was expressed in the following General Chapter injunction:

> We forbid sculptures and paintings in our churches or in any place in the monastery, because while one's attention is directed to such things, the advantage of good meditation or the discipline of monastic seriousness is often neglected.[40]

For a long time this restriction was adhered to and there were no statues in Cistercian churches, not even of Bernard. Although the Clairvaux statue was among the early deviations from this, there are a number of examples that pre-date it. Thought to be the earliest stone statue of Bernard is a carved figure on the exterior of the northeastern corner of the West Tower of Freiburg Cathedral (SC01). Dating from *c.* 1280, it commemorates Bernard's visit to Freiburg on 3 and 4 December 1146 following his decision after his visit to Frankfurt am Main not to return straight to Clairvaux, but to accept Bishop Hermann of Constance's invitation to preach the Crusade in Switzerland. The oldest known statue of Bernard in a Cistercian church is at Amelungsborn in Lower Saxony (SC08). It is in red limestone from about 1350 and is placed high above the celebrants' sedilia in the abbey church. Another early statue, carved in polychrome wood, is at the cistercian abbey of Val-Dieu in Belgium,

[40] Waddell 1999, 464.

but while the head dates from the first half of the fourteenth century, the rest is post-medieval (SC20).

There were two other links in the *Vera Effigies* chain. One was a silver-gilt bust-reliquary, one of two commissioned in 1332 by Abbot Jean d'Aizanville of Clairvaux (1330–1345) to contain the skulls of Bernard and Saint Malachy. The austrian monk Joseph Meglinger saw the Bernard reliquary in 1667 and was struck by its resemblance to Geoffrey of Auxerre's literary portrait. From this he concluded that there was a reliable tradition behind the portrait.[41] The other link was a silver-gilt statue which, like the reliquary, perished during the French Revolution. It carried the inscription 'The true likeness of Lord Bernard, life size, from the sculpted prototype which is to be found at Clairvaux', and was the paradigm for paintings which found their way to six different austrian abbeys including Heiligenkreuz and Zwettl.

Among the images which may belong to the antecedents of the *Vera Effigies*, and may have had as their source the statue once over Bernard's tomb, is the well-known painting of the standing figure of Bernard from the Clairvaux altarpiece from the second half of the fifteenth century. Almost always reproduced on its own,[42] this 'portrait' is in fact only the lefthand panel of a larger retable (PA092). The central scene shows Christ's Baptism by John, witnessed by two angels and, above, God the Father with the dove representing the Holy Spirit. This panel is flanked by the two standing figures: Bernard on the left and, on the right, Saint Malachy, Bernard's great friend who died at Clairvaux in 1148 and was buried in the church near Bernard. They are both painted against a rich golden damask cloth. Archbishop Malachy is wearing a cope and mitre. In his left hand he carries the cross of an archbishop and in his right hand he holds an open book. In contrast to his colourful and costly vestments is the plain white cowl worn by Bernard. This is pulled up slightly to reveal the white tunic and black scapular of the Cistercian habit beneath. He carries a crozier and has a book under his right arm, and, like the statue over his tomb, he holds a model of a church with both hands, indicating his role as founder both of Clairvaux and of its numerous daughter-houses. As in the tomb statue, he has his hood

[41] PL 185:1743.

[42] For example in Paris 1990, 59; Dijon 1953, ill. 14; Hümpfner 1927, 12; Berlioz 1990, 114; and Leclercq 1976, 8.

partially over his head, which is similarly inclined to the right, there is the same central tuft and break in his tonsure; he is pale and thin and has an austere air about him.

Although much earlier than the paintings in the austrian abbeys, there is a remarkable resemblance between the *Vera Effigies* and the image of Bernard in one of the earliest manuscripts from the austrian abbey of Zwettl dated 1175–1176 (MA002). It is tempting to see in this a connection between the literary portraits and the *Vera Effigies,* but this is pure speculation and almost certainly a coincidence. The chain appears to have been broken and, although it may have been kept alive by oral tradition, there are not enough links at regular intervals in the form of extant images to establish a convincing connection between the twelfth-century literary portraits and the post-medieval *Vera Effigies*.

There are, however, four other images which bear a striking resemblance to the *Vera Effigies* model. Two of these appear together on the same folio in the life cycle of Saint Hedwig of Silesia known as the Schlackenwerther or Hedwig Codex which was completed in 1353 in the court atelier of Ludwig I of Liegnitz and Brieg. It contains sixty-one illustrations including two of Bernard which decorate his Sermons (MA024). Above, a tonsured, bearded, and nimbed Bernard in a greyish habit is shown writing at an adjustable desk against which his crozier is leaning. Below he is shown pointing to an open book which he holds in his left hand while addressing five monks at his feet, two of them with their hoods partially over their heads, one pointing to Bernard and another looking at him attentively. Both images are remarkably like the *Vera Effigies:* the upper one in particular depicts him in much the same position, whereas in the image below he is shown in a frontal position. Although the beard, thin face, large cranium, break in the tonsure and central tuft all manifest an unmistakable similarity, the significance of these attributes may be questioned as other figures are represented in an almost identical way elsewhere in the manuscript. The seated figure of Abbot Günther of Lubiaz (Leubus), portrayed elsewhere in the manuscript, is virtually indistinguishable from the 'portrait' of Bernard.[43] The same abbot, or another monk, appears again on another folio as the celebrant at Hedwig's burial looking, once more,

[43] Illustrated in Gottschalk 1967, ill. 30 (black & white) and facing p. 87 (colour).

exactly the same.[44] Another image with a distinct resemblance to the *Vera Effigies* occurs in an early thirteenth-century manuscript from the benedictine scriptorium of Saint Augustine's, Canterbury, in which Bernard is shown writing with the blessing hand of God appearing from a cloud (MA044). Finally, the same characteristics of a beard, a large cranium and tilted head appear in a glass panel dated *c.* 1320 from the swiss cistercian abbey of Kappel (GL73).

In one respect the twelfth-century literary tradition did *not* influence Bernard's iconography: references to his untidy dress were not reflected in the way artists chose to portray him. The worn and threadbare habits of cistercian monks depicted in the Cîteaux *Moralia in Job* manuscript from 1111 probably represented quite faithfully the way Bernard looked,[45] but it was apparently not considered a suitable way of showing a sainted abbot. For some such shabbiness did not fit the idealized image appropriate for a saint, while others, like the onlookers when Bernard was introduced to William of Champeaux, might have been tempted to laugh at rather than venerate him.

In the great majority of the nine hundred sixty-four recorded images of Bernard no attempt has been made to invest him with a particular look dictated by either literary or oral tradition. As mentioned above, portraiture in the modern sense was unknown until the late Middle Ages. Up till then artists were content to base the identification of their portrayals on rules that had evolved over time.[46] Evidence of this is not hard to find. The artist of the Hedwig Codex was quite happy for Bernard and Abbot Günther to look the same and to rely on the context in which they were shown and the text describing the scene, as well as the halo or absence of a halo, to differentiate between them. An early thirteenth-century manuscript of Bernard's Sermons from the english abbey of Buildwas depicts Bernard within the initial *H(odie)* introducing Sermon One for Advent (MA061). He is shown in a frontal position, dressed in a white cowl and seated on a stool with a cushion. He has a crozier in his right hand and his left hand is raised in blessing. The initial is red and blue, decorated with white dots, against a pinkish-brown background decorated with white circles and dots. The figure of Bernard is copied

[44] Illustrated in Gottschalk 1967, 44 (black & white).
[45] Illustrated in France 1998, ill. 45, 134 & colour pl. 24.
[46] For this, see Chapter 2.

from an earlier Buildwas manuscript, that of a late twelfth-century manuscript of Hugh of Fouilloy's *De Claustro* where an identical figure of an abbot is found in a drawing of the *Wheel of True Religion*.[47] The artist had no problem with using this picture of an anonymous abbot as his model for portraying Bernard.

The same disregard for differentiating facial features appears clearly in many of the examples in which Bernard appears together with Saint Benedict. In the early fourteenth-century carving on the oak choir stalls at Doberan they are depicted virtually as twins. Both are nimbed, both carry croziers and books, and, because both are carved in natural wood it is not possible to tell them apart, except that the figure on the right has a 'tuft' and may therefore represent Bernard. ▶ *Fig. 18* (SC15). The carvings of the two saints in natural wood on the choir stalls at the abbey of Hauterive (SC18) are also virtually identical, but the two figures at the abbey of Zinna (SC23) are painted and it is therefore possible to distinguish between them by the colour of their habits. They are otherwise identical in every respect. The same applies in the case of the centre of an altarpiece commissioned by Abbot Wolfgang Oertl (1495–1508) for his private chapel at Zwettl (SC05).[48] Here the carved central figures of the enthroned Virgin and Child are flanked by those of Bernard and Benedict, all of them gilt with flesh-coloured faces and hands. The two wings were painted by Jörg Breu to show eight scenes from the life of Bernard (PA038-045). The gilt figures of Bernard and Benedict are once again presented as virtual twins, and the identification of each rests on the addition of a small attribute which is not normally needed when they are portrayed in their white and black habits. On the left Bernard stands carrying a crozier and looking down on an open book which he holds in his hands. Benedict is also shown carrying a crozier, but in his left hand he has a closed book upon which are a beaker and a snake, the traditional attribute by which he was sometimes identified. It recalls the episode in Gregory's *Dialogue* when Benedict blessed a cup containing poison as a result of which it shattered and a serpent emerged.[49] The inclusion of this attribute was not common when the two saints are depicted together. Among other numerous examples of Bernard and

[47] Illustrated in Sheppard 1997, ill. 29.
[48] Among other examples are MA094, MA019, GL75, GL76, and PA036.
[49] Dial. II, ch. 3; PL 66:136.

Benedict portrayed in an almost identical way are the glass panels from the cloister of the nuns' abbey of Wienhausen (GL75), the full-page miniature in William of Tournai's *Flores Sancti Bernardi* (MA094), and a full-page miniature in a catalan Book of Hours (MA083).

The total medieval reliance on attributes at the expense of 'portraiture' is best demonstrated by a miniature in an english manuscript from the second half of the fourteenth century (MA177). Its two hundred seventy-one images in water colour with accompanying text are a kind of visual litany of the saints shown with their attributes. One folio has on the left a tonsured and nimbed figure in a pale brown cowl with a red book in the right hand and a crozier in the left. The inscription above tells us that it represents both Bernard and Benedict: *Sancte Bernarde ora pro nobis, Sancte Benedicte ora pro nobis* (Saint Bernard, pray for us, Saint Benedict, pray for us). As their attributes are the same, the artist has decided that it was not necessary to draw two figures. The figure on the right is Saint Francis, wearing the characteristic knotted cord round his waist.

The considerable difference from one to the next in the way Bernard is portrayed in many late medieval images tells us that these were real portraits, not of Bernard, but usually those of the commissioning abbot who is portrayed in the guise of Bernard. They are particularly to be found in late fifteenth and early sixteenth-century images of Bernard receiving the Virgin's milk, the so-called *Lactatio Bernardi*. The identification of the sitter with Bernard was not only flattering, but also associated him with the intercessional significance of the scene as a sharer of the grace bestowed on Bernard by Mary. The identity of a number of these alter Bernards is known, including Denis van Zeverdonck of Villers (1524–1545) (PA073), Peter van Onderberghen of Les Dunes (1509–1515) (PA077), and Jean van Deynse, twenty-sixth abbot of Baudeloo (PA132). They are often shown as portly figures of high social standing carrying elaborate and precious croziers. They no doubt welcomed the identification with Bernard but they almost certainly also relished being portrayed as important prelates as much as Bernard would have abhorred it. A good example of one of these late medieval abbots is contained in the report which described an early nineteenth-century excavation of the abbot's lodgings at the english abbey of Whalley. It refers to such a donor portrait in painted glass:

> I have what was meant for a portrait of Bernard in painted glass, preserved out of the wreck of the long gallery at Whalley,

but it is only appropriated by the crozier, the glory, and the white Cistercian gown; for the man who sat for this picture must have been a plump and jovial monk of later days, not the pale and meagre saint much attenuated by the discipline, and more by the disease of fasting. For Bernard was long afflicted by a constriction of the oesophagus. How happy for himself that he thought abstinence a duty![50]

[50] Whitaker 1806, 108.

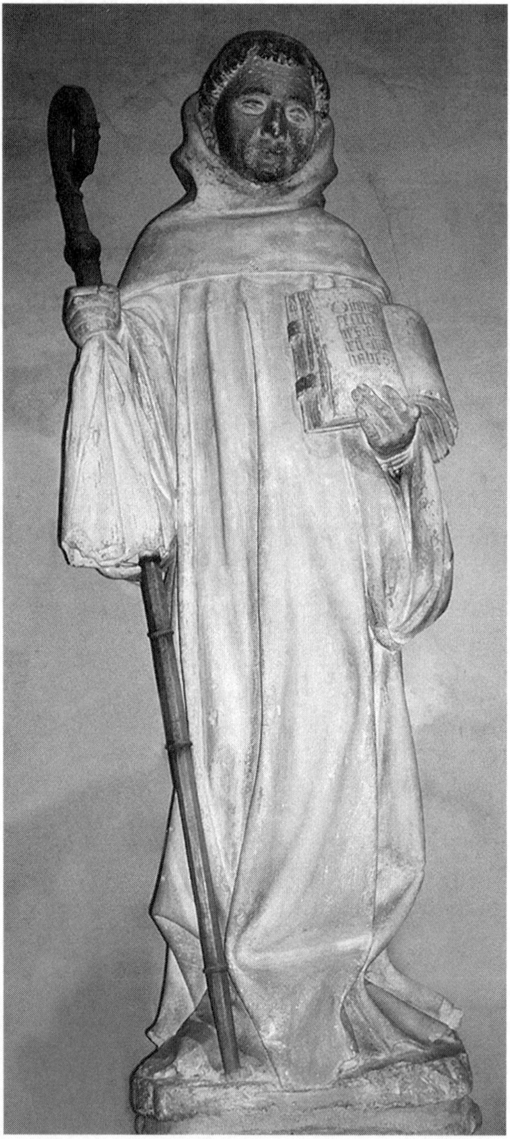

Figure 3: The church of Fontaine-les-Dijon: polychrome stone statue, *c.* 1470 (SC26).

TWO

THE PRINCIPAL ATTRIBUTES OF SAINT BERNARD

UNTIL THE EMERGENCE of portraiture artists had recourse to a number of widely-recognized shorthand codes to identify the persons they were portraying. Crowns denoted kings, halos saints, mitres bishops, palms martyrs, and so on. These are the subject's 'attributes'—from the Latin *attributum* or *ad-tribuere* (to assign or give to a person)—the conventional symbols used to allow onlookers to identify the person, but not sign inherent to him or her. They have been described as 'heraldic hagiography'.[1]

How do we recognize Bernard in medieval iconography? The chief 'attributes' are his portrayal as the *monk* he became when he entered Cîteaux, probably in the spring of 1113; as the *abbot* who founded Clairvaux in 1115; and as the *saint* he was officially declared when canonized in 1174. The three—the habit as a Cistercian, the mitre and crozier, marks of abbatial office, and the nimbus, the token of

[1] In Réau 1955–1959, 1:417. Réau distinguishes between 'characteristics' which he defines as both physique and dress, and 'attributes' which are other signs of recognition added to the person (for this, see Réau 1955–1959, 1:416-430). I have chosen to include dress as one of the attributes.

sainthood—indicate a cistercian-abbot-saint, but they do not identify Bernard specifically. In the twelfth and thirteenth centuries only such generic attributes existed, and only later, as will emerge in the following chapters, were the saints invested with one or more individualised attributes whereby they could be positively identified.

Until then, the identity of Bernard could only be established for certain in one of two ways. First, the context in which his image appears: an author portrait at the beginning of one of his works (MA044, MA168, MA036)—or of pseudo-Bernard works like, for example, the *Verses* (MA095, MA097, MA296, MA355)—; an abbot saint within a cistercian setting (GL75, MA094, PA010), as in cistercian Missals and Antiphonaries (MA002 & MA104); a figure in copies of the *Vita Prima* (MA001, MA026, MA119, MA120), at the beginning of the chapter devoted to him in the *Legenda Aurea* (MA161), and in the last cantos in Dante's *Divine Comedy* (MA065, MA073, MA192). Second, it was quite common to establish the subject's identity beyond doubt by including an inscription of his name, either above or below his portrait—as in a thirteenth-century manuscript of his Sermons (MA168), a late fifteenth-century cupboard door from Sweden (PA035) or a manuscript from Heilsbronn (MA071); or—as in the Heisterbach retable (PA010)—contained within the halo.

AS A MONK

Walter Daniel, Saint Aelred of Rievaulx's biographer, says in a letter 'I wear the habit of a monk, I am tonsured, I am cowled'.[2] The tonsure and the cowl were the hallmark of the monk. Unlike the other principal attributes associated with Bernard—those that denote him as an abbot and a saint—he is virtually always depicted with the monastic tonsure, and it has not therefore seemed necessary to include this as one of the keywords in analyzing the iconographic material.

The Tonsure

The monastic tonsure was also known as the monastic crown or *corona*. It represented Christ's crown of thorns or His royal priesthood. The

[2] Powicke 1950, 7.

loss of hair signifies an act of deprivation symbolic of a penitential life, a setting apart and a form of consecration.

Two types of tonsure existed: the more common—and the one almost universally adopted from the early thirteenth century until the end of the Middle Ages and beyond—consisted of a narrow horizontal band of hair approximately one inch wide which formed a circle around the head above the ears; the rest of the head was shaven, above and below this band. The other form consisted of shaving a large circular area at the top of the head with the rest of the hair left unevenly long lower down, sometimes even covering the ears.

Examples of the first tonsure in the iconography of Bernard are numerous. It may be clearly seen in the glass panel (GL77) from the second half of the fourteenth-century pilgrimage church of Strassengel, which belonged to the austrian cistercian abbey of Rein; it features the standing figure of a nimbed Bernard in a white cowl and carrying a crozier. ▶ *Colour plate 2.* Although most of the portrayals of monks at work in the famous Cîteaux *Moralia* manuscript show them with true crowns of the first type, the great majority of twelfth-century representations, such as for example those from the scriptoria of the great Austrian abbeys, belong to the second category. This is true of all the early images of Bernard, beginning with the earliest of all, the manuscript of *The Steps of Humility* from the benedictine abbey of Saint Augustine, Canterbury, dated before 1135 (MA006). This is how Bernard is represented in a very early version of his Sermons in the vernacular, dated either to the end of the twelfth century or the early thirteenth century (MA040). He is seated with his head bowed writing at a desk, holding a pen in his right hand and a knife in his left. He has a short beard and a circular area at the top of his head is shaven while his hair is long at the sides and back. Unusually, he is shown wearing a blue tunic with white dots. His tunic has ample sleeves and a shawl is draped over his left shoulder and lap. Other examples of this second tonsure include the manuscript of Aelred of Rievaulx's *Mirror of Charity,* in which both Bernard and Aelred are featured with long hair (▶ *Colour plate 3*), the image of Bernard in eucharistic vestments which appears in a late twelfth-century manuscript of the *Vita Prima* (MA026); and an early thirteenth-century manuscript of Bernard's *Sermons on the Song of Songs* from the german premonstratensian abbey of Weissenau (MA168). This last also provides us with one of numerous examples of

Bernard being identified by name: the inscription above him reads *Sanctus BERNHARDUS abbas*. An unusual late example of this type of tonsure is a fragment of glass from the nuns' abbey of Saint Apern, Cologne, dated *c.* 1525 (GL68). This shows a youthful Bernard with longish hair at the back and the shaven top of his head.

The Habit

The other distinguishing feature of the monk is the habit, the origin of which goes back to roman times. It consists of a tunic, which was the standard roman garment, the scapular, which was worn for work to protect the tunic very much like an apron, and the cowl or *cuculla,* which was originally a simple head cover to provide protection against rain and the heat of the sun and which was worn by the poorest members of society, notably slaves. The hood was later attached to a garment which covered the rest of the body, the *vestis cum cuculla* (robe with cowl) and in time this garment was abbreviated to *cuculla* (cowl), the distinctive monastic garment.[3]

The early cistercian texts have only two short statements regarding dress: under the heading 'Of clothing' the General Chapter *Capituli*—edited by Bernard's disciple Raynard from Clairvaux, who after Guy's short abbacy at Cîteaux succeeded to that office in 1134/1135—laid down that 'Clothing is simple and ordinary—no fur garments and undergarments of wool or linen, but such, in a word, as described by the Rule'.[4] The General Chapter *Instituta,* under the heading 'Of various types of clothing', refer to 'Those who are clothed in soft garments are in the houses of kings', a quotation from Mt 11:8 which Bernard himself used in a famous letter to his nephew, Robert, who had abandoned the austerities of life at Clairvaux in favour of the easier life at Cluny.[5] The *Instituta* chapter continues: 'Those sorts of things ill become a monastery. Let us put aside soft garments, and from now on let no one make use of . . . finely woven kinds of cloth, whether new or old'.[6]

[3] For the monastic habit, see France 1998, 72–82.
[4] Waddell 1999, 459.
[5] Ep 1, SBOp 7:9-10.
[6] Waddell 1999, 491.

The *Exordium Parvum* says that the monks who came from Molesme rejected 'whatever offended against that [Saint Benedict's] Rule: namely, coats, fur garments, linen shirts, hoods, too, and drawers. . . . Having therefore put off the old man, they were rejoicing to have put on the new'.[7] And in his letter Bernard asks his cousin:

> Does salvation rest rather in soft raiment and high living than in frugal fare and moderate clothing? If warm and comfortable furs, if fine and precious cloth, if long sleeves and ample hoods, if dainty coverlets and soft *woollen* shirts make a saint, why do I delay and not follow you at once? But these things are comfort for the weak, not the arms of fighting men.[8]

The succinctness of early cistercian legislation regarding dress is totally consistent with the lack of detailed regulations in the Rule. In Chapter 55, on 'The Clothes and Shoes of the Brethren', Benedict gives general guidelines. He enumerates the clothing each monk is to possess rather than defining the individual items.[9] A story in the *Liber Visionum et Miraculorum* compiled by Prior John of Clairvaux in the 1170s indicates that this injunction in the Rule was still being strictly adhered to. After the death of one of the monks it was discovered that he had had one tunic more than was allowed according to the law of the Order (*lex ordinis*).[10] The monks were concerned as to how they should deal with this as there was no indication that the monk had confessed before he died, and in the end they consulted a visiting bishop who belonged to the Order.

The early Cistercians may not have been very explicit as to the details of monastic dress, but they were clear as to what they found unacceptable in the clothing of their monastic contemporaries. They objected to cowls made of cloth of high quality which in the course of time had become very ample with long full sleeves and a copious hood. This is what Bernard referred to in his virulent attack in the *Apologia,* in which he devoted a whole chapter to 'On Costly and Ostentatious Clothing':

[7] Waddell 1999, 434.
[8] Trans. James 1953, 8.
[9] Rule 55; trans. McCann 1976, 60–61.
[10] Quoted in McGuire 1998, 118–119.

> Today's religious is less concerned with keeping out the cold than with cutting a good figure, so he is after refinement rather than serviceability, and seeks, not the cheapest article, as the Rule prescribes, but the one that can be displayed to best advantage. . . . I do not think that they would have bothered overmuch with the quality, colour and style of their clothes. . . . Knight and monk today cut cloak and cowl from the same bolt. There isn't a secular dignitary—no, not a king, nor the emperor himself—who would turn up his nose at our clothing. . . . Soft clothing is a sign of moral flabbiness.[11]

What emerges from the early Cîteaux texts and Bernard's comments on the monastic habit is an insistence on simplicity and poverty rather than uniformity of style or colour. The best examples of this are the famous pictures of monks at work in the *Moralia* manuscript dated 1111, in which they are depicted in a motley of tunics and scapulars, the sleeves and bottoms of which are frayed and worn.[12] These are the clothes Bernard referred to as 'rags and tatters', and which in turn prompted the satirist's description of him as 'that rag-wearer from Clairvaux'.[13]

Bernard's strictures against 'soft raiment' were directed against the black monks and especially those of Cluny and its dependencies. And yet, as part of the general relaxation of early austerity and one of the symptoms of later decline, the cistercian habit was to undergo a development similar to that which had taken place among Benedictines before the cistercian reform; and this, in time, was to make them indistinguishable from other monks in clothing as in so many other respects.

The simple one-piece cistercian cowl was gradually replaced by a two-piece garment in the cluniac style. The robe became more capacious, the sleeves wider, and the separate cape with attached hood more ample in its cut. There are numerous examples of this in the later iconography of Bernard. They include a full-page miniature in a Book of Hours from around 1500, in which the standing figures of Saint Benedict on the left and Bernard on the right are depicted in black and white cowls respec-

[11] *De vestitu superfluo vel superbo*, SBOp 3:101-102; trans. Matarasso 1993, 53–54.

[12] See, for example, the miniature of two monks splitting a log in France 1998, colour plate 24.

[13] SBOp 3:81; trans. Rudolph 1990, 81. The description of Bernard in the *Ysengrinus* comes from Mann 1987, 15.

tively (MA083). The separate cape with hood can be clearly seen, the sleeves go nearly to the ground, and the robe itself falls in folds trailing along the ground. Bernard is also portrayed in a very full cowl with wide sleeves and separate cape and hood kneeling in front of the Virgin in a full-page *Lactation* scene from a manuscript of the devotional work *Manuale pietatis* painted in Antwerp around 1524 (MA115). The extravagance of these elegant garments is in sharp contrast to the simplicity and austerity of earlier cowls with their modest attached hoods and tight, narrow sleeves such as appear in the Weissenau *Sermons on the Song of* Songs (MA168) as well as in all early bernardine images. Likewise, in the Flores *Bernardi* manuscript from Canterbury Bernard is depicted wearing the earlier simple cowl while the sleeves of Saint Benedict's cowl, by contrast, are much fuller (MA094).

Of the nine-hundred sixty recorded medieval images of Bernard it is possible to distinguish between the old and the new style cowls with a high degree of certainty in six-hundred one cases. Of these, seventy-one are representative of the old and five-hundred thirty of the new style; and an analysis of these, arranged in chronological order, enables us to establish the period of gradual transition between the two styles.

The old type is found in all early images and only six of the seventy-one date from later than the middle of the fourteenth century. Among the late examples of the one-piece cowl are the famous statue of Bernard as the founder of Clairvaux from the end of the fourteenth century (SC04); a full-page miniature in a fifteenth-century manuscript of Bernard's Sermons and Letters from the premonstratensian abbey of Tongerloo (MA156); and a miniature in a Cistercian Hymnal from the abbey of Settimo in Florence dated *c.* 1440–1450 (MA266). In this last, Bernard is kneeling within the initial B of *Bernardus doctor inclitus,* the hymn for his feast, which is indicated by the text on the previous folio: *In festo patris nostri Bernardi*. In front of him is an open book on a lectern. A smaller Virgin in blue appears in a red cloud on a blue sky above in what is a *Doctrina* image.[14] The cut of the cowl in these late examples may also well be due to the artists' lack of familiarity with the cistercian habit.

The much larger number of new-style two-piece cowls includes all images from the fifteenth century onwards; of the five-hundred thirty

[14] See Chapter 9.

images, only forty-six represent the fourteenth century, and of these none are from before the second quarter. The two oldest recorded are from Catalonia. The two-piece cowl may be clearly seen in the half-figure of Bernard on the predella of a Saint Peter altarpiece by Ramon de Mur (before 1402–1435) from Bera, the centre of which features Saint Peter with the keys and wearing a papal tiara (PA027). The predella consists of the figure of Christ in the centre flanked by three saints on either side, each under a trifoliate arch. They are all nimbed, and Bernard is portrayed in a white cowl and carrying a golden crozier in his right hand. The other catalan example is the carved stone altarpiece from 1348 in the church of Saint Mary in Montblanch dedicated to Saint Barnabas and Saint Bernard. In the centre are the carved standing figures of the two saints: on the left Bernard, nimbed and bearded, with a crozier with sudarium attached in his right hand and a book in his left (SC43). The central figures are flanked by four scenes from the life of each of the two saints. ▶ *Fig. 9* (SC39-SC42). The new-style cowl may be clearly seen in the central figure as well as in some of the scenes.

Although all late medieval cowls were two-piece, they were not always extremely ample or particularly wide-sleeved. The iconographical material allows us to date the transition from the old to the new style of cowl to the first half of the fourteenth century, although somewhat earlier examples are known from literary sources. In 1269 the General Chapter decreed that members of the Order should guard against 'strangeness of clothing and that the cowl and the sleeves of the cowl are not to be too long but are to be measured according to the decree of our rule'.[15] The new style is known to have been introduced at the english abbey of Beaulieu before *c.* 1270, when the Account Book lists both cowls and *caputia* (capes with hoods).[16]

Under the cowl Cistercians wore a white tunic and dark—at first brown and later black—scapular, an apron-like garment covering the shoulders and extending in front and back below the knees and fitted with a hood. In the course of time the scapular was the subject of a development similar to that of the cowl: it became longer and consisted of two garments. Bernard is only rarely depicted in tunic and scapular alone, and as all sixty-nine known examples of this are late medieval,

[15] *Statuta* 2:69 (1269:4).
[16] Hockey 1975, 219.

they all show him in the two-piece scapular. This may be seen in a Book of Hours from Lorraine dated *c.* 1470, where Bernard is shown kneeling on a road at the beginning of the text of the Seven Verses (MA206). He is wearing a white tunic and over it a long black scapular with separate cape which covers his chest and with hood attached.

Concern at the relaxation of the early austerity as regards dress was still being expressed in 1419, when the abbot of Cîteaux, John of Marigny (1405–1428), wrote to the abbot of Poblet in Catalonia, who was vicar and visitor of all spanish houses. John refers to the 'extravagance of habit both as regards its material and cut, the cowls are excessively long, the sleeves too broad, the separate capes (*cappa*) with their hoods—both of the cowl and the scapular—too ample', and he contrasts this with what Bernard and the Fathers of the Order wore, for they had been careful that 'nothing appeared in them that could offend those looking on'.[17]

There is no reference to the colour of the monastic habit either in the Rule or in the early cistercian texts. The earliest mention of the change from the black, which in the course of time had been adopted by the Benedictines, to the white with which the Cistercians became identified, occurs in a letter from the abbot of Cluny, Peter the Venerable, to Bernard.[18] According to legend the Virgin is said to have appeared to the second abbot of Cîteaux, Alberic (1099–1108), and miraculously changed the habit from black to white. Although this story appears to have its origin in the fifteenth century, the change must have occurred soon after the foundation of Cîteaux, for the earliest portrayal of a cistercian monk, which adorns the large initial *I* of the famous opening words of Saint John's Gospel in Stephen Harding's Bible, completed in 1109, shows him in a white cowl.[19]

Similarly, Bernard is depicted in white in the earliest image of him known, painted in Canterbury before 1135 and the only one from his lifetime (MA006). He also appears in white in the large opening initial *I* which introduces Bernard's treatise, *The Steps of Humility and Pride* in the oldest collection of the works of Bernard, a three volume set, compiled at the benedictine abbey of Anchin and the work of one scribe, Siger (MA028).

[17] Quoted in Duran 1950, 29–30.
[18] Constable 1967, 1:368.
[19] Illustrated in Zaluska 1989, Planche 1.

The contrast between the colours came to play an important part in the later polemics. Writing in 1135, the black monk Orderic Vitalis said of the Cistercians:

> They specially favour white in their habit and thereby seem remarkable and conspicuous to others. Black represents humility in many places in Holy Scripture; therefore up to now monks in their devotion have chosen to wear that colour.[20]

The Cistercians interpreted the change in colour quite differently. A General Chapter Statute from 1350 speaks of 'the white habit which is a sign of purity and interior cleanness',[21] and Aelred of Rievaulx's biographer, Walter Daniel, records how before entering Rievaulx Aelred had heard tell of

> wonderful men, famous adepts in the religious life, white monks by name and white also in vesture. For their name arose from the fact that, as the angels might be, they were clothed in undyed wool spun and woven from the pure fleece of the sheep.[22]

The reason for the colour change was economic; undyed wool was cheaper than dyed. The use of dyed wool was specifically prohibited by the General Chapter in 1181 in these words: 'Dyed and modish wools are utterly excluded from our Order'.[23] Being made of undyed and unbleached wool, the colour of the habit could range, like that of sheep, from whitish, a creamy yellow, pale brown or grey to a dark brown or almost black. Orderic Vitalis recognized this when he said that the Cistercians are 'clothed in white or other distinctive habits', and in the Benedict XII's Constitution *Fulgens sicut stella* of 1335, the colour of the habit was described as white or brown.[24] The range of colours gave rise to the Cistercians sometimes also being known as 'grey monks'.[25]

[20] Chibnall 1969–1980, 4:311.
[21] *Statuta* 3:517 (1350:3).
[22] Powicke 1950, 10.
[23] *Statuta* 1:89 (1181:11).
[24] Chibnall 1969–1980, 4:327; *Statuta* 3:423.
[25] The description occurs, for example, in the twelfth-century text *Dialogue between a Cluniac and a Cistercian* in which the Cluniac author accuses the Cistercians in these

The colour of the cowl may be discerned in seven of the twelfth-century images of Bernard. In four of these Bernard is depicted in white (MA006, MA028, MA035, MA119), whereas in the remaining three his cowl is grey or bluish grey (MA004, MA025, MA040). While he is shown in white in the Anchin manuscript of *The Steps of Humility and Pride*, another manuscript from the same scriptorium, also from the third quarter of the twelfth century—Aelred of Rievaulx's *Mirror of Charity*—shows Bernard in a grey cowl handing his letter to Aelred, who is depicted on the opposite folio. ▶ *Colour plate 3* (MA004). Of the forty-nine thirteenth-century manuscripts in which the colour of the habit may be ascertained, Bernard is portrayed in a white cowl in twenty-five while he is shown in black, grey or brown in twenty-four cases. Surprisingly, by this time the so-called 'white monks' were almost as frequently dressed in darker coloured cowls as in white. Yet in 1269 the General Chapter insisted that 'monks should everywhere wear a white cowl in the cloister and in the morning hours in choir, especially in lands and places where they can be reasonably procured', suggesting that they could wear darker cowls for travelling. In spite of this and the repetition in 1270 that 'monks and abbots use white cowls in the cloister uniformly throughout the whole Order', grey and brown cowls seem to have been equally popular.[26] One of many examples of grey may be seen in a miniature of Bernard and Saint John the Evangelist in a Gradual for the german cistercian nuns' abbey of Seligenthal (MA164).

From the middle of the fourteenth century onwards black gradually replaced grey/brown as the most popular colour for cowls. A statute from 1350 decreed that, while white should be kept for divine service, monks should 'be able to use black cowls at the time of eating both in the infirmary and in the convent where they can use them freely lest they should soil the white and dirty them while eating'.[27] In 1469 the General Chapter noted that: 'In some monasteries in parts of Germany this uniformity is badly observed, as in many places the abbots and monks of the German nation put on grey cowls contrary to what was ordained', and they are ordered to wear either white or black.[28] And yet

words: 'the grey monks are always on the move' (*Dialogue* 3:50; trans. Idung of Prüfening 1977, 137).

[26] *Statuta* 2:69 (1269:4) & 3:79-80 (1270:1).

[27] *Statuta* 3:517 (1350:3).

[28] *Statuta* 5:251-2 (1469:64).

it is precisely in Germany that Bernard is depicted in a large number of late medieval *Amplexus* images wearing a black cowl.[29] Among the many examples are the wing of an altarpiece from the augustinian church in Nuremburg, painted in 1487 (PA009), and a panel from a triptych of the Mass of Saint Gregory, painted in 1480/1485 for the benedictine nuns of Saint Agatha in Cologne (PA017).

The frequency with which Bernard is portrayed wearing a black or dark grey cowl in fifteenth- and sixteenth-century iconography must have seemed puzzling to those who were used to thinking of the Cistercians as the 'white monks'. It is therefore probably no coincidence that a number of artists chose to show Bernard holding up the black cowl with one hand just sufficiently for the white tunic to show underneath. Thirty-two instances of this device have been located, making the identification of Bernard as a cistercian monk considerably clearer (MA015, MA029, PA006, PA010). One of these is found in a Prayer Book in Flemish from *c.* 1480, in which, within the initial *O* of *O heere ih[u]s* the standing figure of Bernard is shown trampling on the devil. He holds a crozier in his right hand and a book in his left with which he also holds up his black cowl, thus revealing the white tunic underneath (MA155). In another example from around the same time, the two figures of Saint Benedict and Saint Bernard are painted on the doors of a cupboard originating in northwestern Germany but now in a church in Sweden (PA035). They are identified by their names below; they each carry a crozier and a book, and they are both wearing black cowls, but, significantly, while Benedict's cowl goes to the floor all round, Bernard's is held up on his right and his white tunic is deliberately clearly displayed.

Out of a total of nine-hundred sixty images, the colour of the cowl may be ascertained in six-hundred fifty-eight. Of these four-hundred fifty-three show white cowls while two-hundred five are grey/brown/black. The number of instances in which Bernard is portrayed in non-white is really quite remarkable, especially considering that the figure for white cowls includes sixty-nine of the Altenberg and Saint Apern stained glass panels from the early sixteenth century. If these are deducted, the white cowl appears in only slightly more than a third of the total. The conclusion is that, despite the cistercian nickname, it is by no

[29] See Chapter Seven.

means safe to assume that the white cistercian cowl is invariably one of the attributes by which images of Bernard may be identified.

A further complication in the use of the colour of the habit as a means of identification in the case of the iconography of Bernard arises in Italy. There the semi-eremitical camaldolese monks, named after Camaldoli, near Arezzo, founded by Saint Romuald (*c.* 950–1027) and following the Rule of Saint Benedict, adopted the white habit; and in images of camaldolese origin Saint Benedict is invariably portrayed in white. It is therefore not safe to identify images of white-cowled figures which incorporate the traditional bernardine attributes, as representing Bernard without having other corroborative evidence. It is, for example, impossible to be sure whether or not the half-length bearded figure in a white cowl with the hood over the head and carrying a crozier and a book which is featured in a miniature cut out of a mid-fifteenth-century Italian Antiphonary, represents Bernard (MA216). It is just as likely to be Saint Romuald or Saint Benedict.[30] A fourteenth-century florentine painting by Agnolo Gaddi of the *Madonna Enthroned with Saints and Angels* has both Benedict and Bernard, identified by inscriptions (PA070). Flanking the central figure of the Virgin and Child are, on the left, Saint Andrew and Saint Benedict—unusually depicted in a white cowl but identified by the inscription *S Benedictus Abbas* and the opening words of his Rule (*Ausculta O Fili precepta*) on the book he holds. On the right are Bernard, also depicted in a white cowl with the inscription *S Bernardus Doctor* below, and Saint Catherine.

AS AN ABBOT

In the first chapter of the Rule Saint Benedict defined three different categories of monks, distinguishing between those who live under a rule and an abbot, and those who live without a shepherd and in their own sheepfold.[31] He developed the theme of the abbot as shepherd in three further chapters.[32] Like the Good Shepherd of Luke 15:4-5, the

[30] Another example is one of three panels painted by Carlo Crivelli representing an abbot saint in a white cowl, again either Benedict or Bernard (PA005).

[31] Rule 1; trans. McCann 1976, 5.

[32] Rule 2, 27 and 64; trans. McCann 1976, 6–9, 36 and 70–72.

abbot must be flexible and adaptable and 'act with prudent moderation, lest being too zealous in removing the rust he break the vessel . . . let him so temper all things that the strong may still have something to long after, and the weak may not draw back in alarm'.[33] The pastoral theme was the inspiration behind a fine full-page miniature in an early manuscript from the french abbey of Clairmarais illustrating Hugh of Fouilloy's treatise *Shepherd and Sheep,* dated *c.* 1200–1210.[34] On the left, Christ the Good Shepherd holds the top of a pastoral staff, the bottom end of which is grasped on the right by a tonsured figure in a brown habit, the unworthy shepherd. Below them are figures in two lines. Beneath Christ is the good line: a ram, ewes, and lambs guarded by an alert shepherd with an attentive dog. Below the abbot is the bad line: billy goat, nanny goats, kids and a negligent shepherd accompanied by a drowsy dog.

The Staff or Crozier

The pastoral nature of the abbatial office is symbolized by the staff or crozier with which abbots were invested at their blessing by the bishop and which was the emblem *par excellence* of their authority. The act of being granted and accepting the staff was what legitimized the foundation of Cîteaux, the 'New Monastery', as it was then called. According to the *Exordium Cistercii,* in 1098:

> they found a desert place and began building it into an abbey. That aforesaid Robert received the pastoral staff from the bishop of that diocese, that is, of Chalon; and the others bound themselves to stability under him in the same place.[35]

At first the abbot's staff was a simple wooden shepherd's crook. Conrad of Eberbach described the staff carried by Stephen Harding, Bernard's abbot:

[33] Rule 64; trans. McCann 1976, 71–72.
[34] Illustrated in France 1998, colour plate 11.
[35] *Exordium Cistercii* II; trans. Waddell 1999, 401.

> He was a pastor of great humility, not interested in worldly things. He hated all display of pride. This is sufficiently indicated by the pastoral staff which he used to carry in procession on feast days and which seems to be not dissimilar to the common staffs which old men and the sick lean on.[36]

The early simple staff developed into the elaborately decorated crozier of late medieval bishops and abbots. Among Cistercians, this reflects the same relaxation of the original austerity which marked the gradual change in the monastic habit, and this evolution may be seen in the iconography of Bernard. When Conrad of Eberbach, writing in the early thirteenth century, commented on the simplicity and almost plainness of Stephen Harding's pastoral staff, he was clearly contrasting it with the more intricate designs that were becoming the fashion in the early thirteenth century when he was writing and which were to end in the ornate croziers of the late Middle Ages and the Renaissance.

By the mid twelfth century a plain spherical knob was added between the curved crook-head and the straight staff, and this is how the staff is depicted in all early images of Bernard: in the opening initial *I* in the manuscript of the *Steps of Humility and Pride*, dated *c.* 1165 (MA028); in the other Anchin manuscript from around the same time, Aelred of Rievaulx's *Mirror of Charity*, ▶ *Colour plate 3* (MA004); in the *Vita Prima* manuscript from Zwettl, dated *c.* 1189 (MA001); in another late twelfth-century *Vita Prima* manuscript, ▶ *Fig.* 6 (MA026); in the early thirteenth-century manuscript from Weissenau of Bernard's *Sermons on the Song of Songs* (MA168); and in a late twelfth-century or early thirteenth-century Antiphonary from the Austrian abbey of Heiligenkreuz (MA021).

The same may be clearly seen in a half-length drawing of Bernard in a mid-thirteenth-century *Universal Chronicle* which may have been written at the english benedictine abbey of Glastonbury (MA307). There Bernard is depicted with the hood of what is clearly the old-style one-piece cowl partially over his head and carrying the primitive type of crozier with a small knop between the curved upper part and the staff. This design, which allowed the crozier to be made in two halves and therefore of two different materials, may be clearly seen in the two early *Vita Prima* manuscripts (MA001 and MA026). In the first, from

[36] EM 1:27; Griesser 1961, 84.

Zwettl, the upper part—the crook or volute—is drawn with a single line whereas the lower staff consists of two parallel lines; in the second, the upper part is gold while the lower staff has transverse stripes. It may also be seen in two later examples (MA224 and MA226), in which the croziers are shown having gold crooks and brown, presumably wooden, staffs.

The next, small, development in the design of the pastoral staff was the appearance of a simple foliate ending on the crook, often in the form of a trefoil. This is how Bernard's staff appears *c.* 1320–1330, in a manuscript of the Sermons by Abbot Konrad von Brundelsheim of Heilsbronn (abbot 1302–1306 and again 1317–1321) (MA071). A miniature in the lower margin shows a lady kneeling with her hands clasped in prayer; a scroll rising from them carries the inscription 'Pray for me, blessed Bernard'. Before her is the standing figure of Bernard in a grey cowl, identified by the inscription above his blue halo; *S.Bernardus.* The crozier in his right hand consists of a brown staff separated from the by a green knob with a single green leaf at the end of the crook.

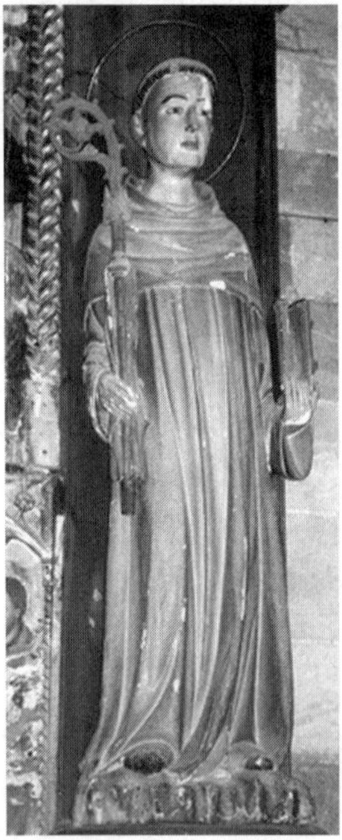

Figure 2

Another minor development in design occurred when the crook terminated in two trefoils, one going inwards and one outwards. This type is represented by the fourteenth-century glass panel from Strassengel, in Austria, in which Bernard holds a two-piece crozier, the crook of which has two foliate endings. ▶ *Colour plate 2.* Other examples occur in the carving from the choir stalls at Doberan (▶ *Fig. 18*) and the stained glass panel from Wienhausen; there again the crozier consists of a white staff with an upper golden foliate crook (GL75). This more elaborate style was followed by croziers not just with leaves within the volute but also with buds or crockets on the outside of the crook. Examples of this type include the statue of Bernard in the Montblanch altarpiece (▶ *Fig. 9*), the polychrome statue from the Catalan abbey of Santes Creus, ▶ *Fig. 2* (SC45), and the earliest known representation of the *Amplexus,* which is found in a Gradual from the women's abbey of Wonnental dated the first half of the fourteenth century (MA059); a folio from the *Hedwig Codex* completed in 1353, which has two scenes with Bernard, in each of which he carries a crozier (MA024); and a late thirteenth-century manuscript of Bernard's Sermons from the nuns' abbey of Nizelles, in which he is portrayed blessing a group of kneeling nuns (MA036). In each of these, the crozier has two foliate endings, one inward and one outward, and crockets on the outside of the crook.

The last and most elaborate design, and the one which symbolized the gradual transformation of the abbot from being the spiritual father and shepherd of his monks to being a *grand seigneur,* combined the extravagant decoration of the inside of the volute and exterior crockets with an elaborate elongated section, usually of architectural design, separating the crook from the staff and thus replacing the simple spherical knop. This is the kind of crozier depicted in the magnificent grisaille miniature by Jean le Tavernier in the *Book of Hours of Philip of Burgundy* from 1454. Within a border of foliate decoration Bernard is portrayed standing in a chamber. He holds a book in his left hand and with his right hand he carries a crozier of the latest ostentatious design (MA129). The same late medieval type of crozier appears in a triptych in which the *Coronation of the Virgin* forms the theme of the central panel while on each of the wings the scene is witnessed by twenty-three saints, among them Bernard in a white cowl (PA106).[37] He is carrying a crozier richly decorated with figures under trifoliate arches separated by columns forming the elongated section below the volute. The volute itself has the usual foliate endings and exterior crockets, and within it is a representation of Bernard himself in the form of a *Lactation* scene, which is what enables us to identify the figure as Bernard. Other elaborate croziers are featured in a fifteenth-century manuscript of Bernard's Sermons (MA156), in an early sixteenth-century Book of Hours (MA136), and in the Heisterbach altarpiece from the middle of the fifteenth century (PA010).

The most extreme examples of the over-elaborate late medieval crozier are those featured in a series of small painted panels of the *Lactation* scene which are, almost all, of identical composition. Of

[37] For the whole triptych, see PA069.

Flemish or Lower Rhenish origin, they date to the late fifteenth or early sixteenth century. They all consist of half figures of the Virgin baring her breast and a kneeling Bernard in a room with a landscape in the background visible through a window, and on the sill in the foreground the naked Christ Child. A well-fed Bernard, verging on the corpulent, has his hands folded in prayer while his precious and heavy crozier leans against his shoulder. These include the painting by the Lower Rhine Master dated *c.* 1478 (▶ *Colour plate* 9), another by Joos van Cleeve from *c.* 1480 (PA052), and at least five other known *Lactation* paintings (PA051, PA072, PA073, PA076, PA105). A close scrutiny of them reveals that, whereas they share a common design, there is a distinct difference as regards the features of Bernard, which are clearly individualized and—as we mentioned earlier—represent portraits of contemporary figures, namely the abbots who commissioned the paintings.

The complexity of late medieval croziers was enhanced by their often being fitted with a *sudarium* or *vexillum*. This piece of cloth was attached to the staff below the crook and had the dual function of protecting the precious metal against being tarnished by perspiration and of avoiding the cold touch of metal. It may be seen, for example, in the Philip of Burgundy Book of Hours image (MA129) and also in the only remaining part of the crozier of the fifteenth-century polychrome stone statue of Bernard from Fontaine-les-Dijon attributed to Antoine le Moiturier (the wooden crozier is a modern addition) ▶ *Fig. 3* (SC26). It is also visible in a statue from the second quarter of the fourteenth century in Tarragona in which the top part of the crozier is missing (SC46). Both croziers held by Bernard and Benedict in the gilt altar from the Austrian abbey of Zwettl have a sudarium attached (SC05).

Of the total of nine-hundred sixty recorded representations of Bernard, he is depicted carrying a crozier in four-hundred fifty-eight cases. If we allow for images of him as a youth, as a novice, and as a simple monk—in which the inclusion of a crozier would not have been appropriate—as well as for a number of cases where only fragments remain or a detail is shown, this still leaves a large number of images in which the artist has chosen to portray him without this badge of office. These form two broad categories.

The crozier is often missing when Bernard is engaged in an activity where holding it would not be appropriate as, for example, when saying

Mass—as in the early Zwettl Missal (MA002) or offering the Host to Duke William of Aquitaine in scenes of the duke's conversion as in the Maulbronn altarpiece (PA058)—, when he is engaged in harvest work (GL61 or PA040), or when he is writing or teaching. A miniature in a 1455 manuscript of the *Mirror of History* by Vincent of Beauvais has a nimbed Bernard in a white cowl sitting at a desk, writing on a roll of parchment which he holds with his left hand (MA196). An inkwell and another open book lie on the table and two more books and a piece of parchment with writing on it lie on a shelf on the wall. This miniature marks the beginning of the section listing Bernard's works. Occasionally Bernard has his crozier with him even in scenes of him writing, as happens in the *Flores Bernardi* manuscript from Canterbury, where it is propped up against his chair, thereby emphasizing the identification (MA044).[38]

The other category in which the crozier is sometimes, although by no means always, missing consists of images of the scene-attributes: *Amplexus* images, beginning with the oldest known example, from the nuns' abbey of Wonnental (MA059); and in late medieval woodcuts (EN14, EN17).[39] Whereas almost all late medieval paintings of the *Lactatio* show Bernard with his crozier, there are a few where this is missing (MA084, MA099, & MA133).[40] In the *Verses* of Bernard the omission is quite common (MA146, MA170, MA180, MA182, MA138, MA187).[41] In *Doctrina* scenes the crozier only very rarely appears.[42] There is, for example, no crozier in a fifteenth-century miniature in which Bernard is kneeling at a desk placed in a verdant wooded landscape (MA012). He is writing in a book while at the same time looking up at the Virgin, who appears in a mandorla in the sky flanked by two angels. In the florentine tradition Bernard is likewise depicted without a crozier in all known representations in the last few cantos of *Paradiso* of Dante's *Divine Comedy* (EN08, MA063, MA065, MA073, MA080, MA192).

[38] Other examples of images of him writing in which the crozier is omitted include the twelfth-century manuscript of Sermons (MA040), the late thirteenth-century manuscript of *On Precept and Dispensation* (MA051), and the fourteenth-century manuscript of pseudo-Bernard *Meditations* in French (MA018), MA208 and PA014; and of him teaching PA057, MA197 and MA198.

[39] See Chapter Seven.

[40] See Chapter Eight.

[41] See Chapter Eleven.

[42] See Chapter Nine.

One can only speculate as to why, in these particular cases, the artists chose to depict Bernard without the conventional attribute of a crozier. Perhaps some of the scenes were considered too sacred and Bernard too preoccupied by the presence of Christ or the Virgin for it to have seemed appropriate for him to be invested with this mark of his authority. Alternatively, the viewer may likely have been considered sufficiently familiar with the scene to be able to identify Bernard and its inclusion was therefore thought unnecessary.

The Book : The Rule of Saint Benedict

Equally as important as the crozier as an attribute whereby Bernard may be identified is the book he carries, the *Rule of Saint Benedict*. Fidelity to the Rule was the *leitmotiv* of the cistercian reform programme. The insistence of the founding fathers on a more literal observance of its precepts triggered the departure of the reforming party from Molesme, and the early texts are peppered with references to the Rule. At Molesme 'they still fell short of their desire and purpose to observe the Rule they had professed',[43] and there they 'often used to speak of, complain about, grieve over the transgression of the Rule of the blessed Benedict, Father of monks'.[44] They promised 'to order their life under the custody of the Holy Rule of our Father Benedict'.[45] In a letter, the papal legate, Archbishop Hugh of Lyon, referred to the early monks' wish 'to adhere more strictly and perfectly to the Rule of the most blessed Benedict, which till then you have observed lukewarmly and negligently in that monastery'.[46]

Other, outside, commentators noted the pivotal part the Rule played in the cistercian story. Writing in 1130, the Benedictine Orderic Vitalis described the reforming community as endeavouring 'to carry out a literal observance of the Rule of Saint Benedict'.[47] The chronicler Wil-

[43] *Exordium Cistercii* 1; trans. Waddell 1999, 400. The *Capitula* lay down that, as regards the buildings, they must 'live there in keeping with the Rule', that the Rule 'be understood in only one way, and observed in only one way', that their clothing be 'as described by the Rule', that 'according to the Rule' a monk should not live outside the cloister (see Waddell 1999, 408–410).

[44] *Exordium Parvum* 3, trans. Waddell 1999, 421.

[45] *Exordium Parvum* 1, trans. Waddell 1999, 418.

[46] *Exordium Parvum* 2, trans. Waddell 1999, 419.

[47] Chibnall 1969–1980, 3:338-339.

liam of Malmesbury asserted that they left Molesme where they were not able to follow 'the purity of the Rule' and he pointed to the importance the Cistercians attached to this by saying, 'So intent are they on their Rule, that they think no jot or tittle of it should be disregarded'.[48] Writing in the 1140s, the augustinian canon Philip of Harvengt noted that 'the Rule of Benedict recovered in our times the truth of the letter'.[49]

The Rule was one of the books which every cistercian abbey was bound to possess.[50] Every day one of its seventy-three chapters was read aloud in the room which was therefore known as the Chapter House, and the reading was followed by a commentary by the abbot. The monastery was to be governed by the abbot according to the Rule and therefore 'abbots who show contempt for the Rule' were to be warned four times and, if they did not amend their ways, they were to be deposed.[51]

The centrality of the Rule in western monasticism explains its traditional inclusion in the iconography of Saint Benedict and its subsequent presence as one of the principal attributes of all benedictine abbots, including Bernard. Because of its importance in the cistercian reform, it lies at the heart of the cistercian cult of Saint Benedict. Bernard is portrayed carrying the Rule in two hundred seventy-six recorded images, or nearly thirty percent of known images (excluding those which are thought to represent the psalter or his own works). Reasons for its omission are often the same as those for not showing the crozier: scenes in which its inclusion would not seem appropriate and images which include scene-attributes. Although the Rule is less often shown than the crozier, Bernard is almost always portrayed carrying both in images in which he is shown standing and on his own or in companion images with Saint Benedict (as in the examples already mentioned). This rule of thumb applies, for example, to statues of Bernard, like the early one from Amelungsborn (SC08), where he is shown carrying both book, held up in an eye-catching fashion, and crozier. He is also frequently portrayed with both in manuscripts, as in a full-page miniature

[48] William of Malmesbury 1847, 349.

[49] Philip of Harvengt, *De institutione clericorum*, 4:125, PL 203:836-7; trans. Constable 1985, 43.

[50] *Capitula* X, trans. Waddell 1999, 409.

[51] *Carta Caritatis Prior* IX, trans. Waddell 1999, 447–448.

in a fifteenth-century manuscript of his Sermons from the premonstratensian abbey of Tongerloo (MA156).

Most powerful of all are the images of Bernard in a frontal position with both book and crozier prominently featured. Among these is the central portrait in the altarpiece from the Templars' Church in Palma, painted in 1290 by the Catalan painter known as the Palma Master, ▶ *Colour plate 5* (PA011). Here the large figure of a nimbed and tonsured Bernard in a white cowl carries both a red book and a crozier with attached *sudarium* in his left hand while his right hand is raised in blessing. In a florentine altarpiece from *c.* 1430 (PA114), he is presented as someone with great authority. His figure, in a frontal position, is flanked by six scenes depicting episodes from his life. The placement of the bright red *Rule* against the white cowl at the very centre of the picture tells us, with an emphasis that is unparalleled in bernardine iconography, that it is from the Rule that he derives his authority.

The Mitre

The cistercian departure from the early ethos of simplicity and restraint, which showed itself in the development in the design both of the habit and of the crozier, was also marked by abbots assuming outward signs of a status equivalent to that of bishops. Bernard had warned against the 'temptation with which the devil assails men in religious life: to covet the fame of a bishop's status',[52] and yet it was inevitable that, as notable landowners, abbots should emerge as social equals with their episcopal and secular counterparts. At the same time abbots had gradually come to enjoy privileges of exemption from episcopal jurisdiction, another development fiercely opposed by Bernard.[53] In recognition of their status, abbots received papal grants of *pontificalia* whereby they were given the right to use a number of episcopal *insignia* and vestments, notably the mitre, which had formerly been forbidden them, and they received many of the powers normally reserved for bishops.[54] Although many

[52] *On the Song of Songs*, 12.9. SBOp 1:66; Bernard of Clairvaux 1971, 1:85.

[53] Lekai 1977, 68.

[54] The *insignia* are listed and the dates of grants to a number of english black monk houses in Knowles 1940, 711–712.

benedictine abbots had long enjoyed such privileges, cistercian abbots first received them in the fourteenth century, beginning with the great royal catalan abbeys of Poblet and Santes Creus in Catalonia in 1336–1337. Surprisingly, Cîteaux itself was not invested until 1380.[55]

Of the recorded images of Bernard, he is depicted with a mitre in only forty-seven. Over half of these are found in late medieval woodcut representations of the *Amplexus,* in which the mitre is most often placed on the ground (EN15). In others, the mitre is either carried by an angel (EN33), placed near an altar or behind Bernard (EN13, EN16), or floating in the air (EN17). In these images the mitre is often accompanied by the coat of arms of Clairvaux. Among these is a woodcut attributed to Albrecht Dürer, one of sixty-three depicting saints in the *Salus animae,* a devotional book printed in Nuremberg in 1503. ▶ *Fig. 4* (EN36) Other *Amplexus* images (MA191, MA219), as well as a single *Doctrina* image (MA132), incorporating the mitre, are found in manuscripts. Bernard is only very rarely depicted wearing a mitre. The earliest known example is in a manuscript of the *Golden Legend* in French dated *c.* 1340 (MA161), in other words contemporary with the very first grants of *pontificalia* to the Cistercians. In this manuscript, at the opening of the section on Bernard, he is shown standing in a raised wooden pulpit looking down and pointing to a group of at least twelve monks with their hoods over their heads. He, like the monks to whom he is preaching, is wearing a grey cowl, and on his head he has a white mitre with blue decoration against a golden halo. He is shown in much the same way in a late fifteenth century manuscript from the austrian abbey of Stams: in an historiated initial the half-figure of Bernard is portrayed in a red mitre and a grey cowl, carrying a crozier in his right hand and a red book in his left (MA057). In both images the artist has included the mitre as one of the attributes to establish Bernard's identity, but at the same time he shows a lack of familiarity with monastic

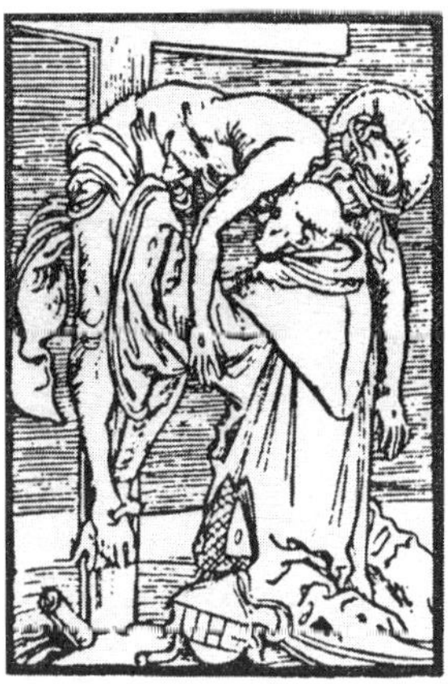

Figure 4

[55] For this, see France 1998, 116–118.

custom, for the mitre formed part of the liturgical vestments and would not have been worn with the cowl. This error may seem surprising in a manuscript belonging to a cistercian abbey, but in the late Middle Ages cistercian manuscripts quite commonly had their origin outside the monastic scriptorium.

In two other manuscripts Bernard is more correctly portrayed according to late medieval fashion, but nonetheless at total variance with Bernard's own view of the abbatial office. In a late fifteenth-century cistercian Missal, one of one hundred thirty-six historiated initials—the one marking Bernard's feast with the initial *I*(*n medio ecclesie*)—Bernard is portrayed sitting on a stool wearing a red cope with gold edging over a white alb and a red mitre, and blessing a cistercian monk in a white cowl kneeling before him (MA190). A *Book of Hours* from *c.* 1450 has a full-page miniature with Bernard introducing the *Seven Verses* of Bernard (MA157). He is shown in the way usual to these Verses: holding, in his right hand, a devil on a chain and a crozier in his left hand. However, he is depicted nimbed, with long curly hair, and, uniquely, in full pontifical vestments consisting of a white mitre, blue chasuble, rosa dalmatic, and white alb. Here again the artist has followed contemporary practice and utilized attributes at odds with the twelfth-century literary and pictorial tradition.

In some images Bernard is depicted with five mitres, and these carry a totally different meaning. They refer to the story in the *Vita Prima* which tells of how he was constantly pursued as the most worthy candidate for high ecclesiastical office, but always declined, even though, having avoided the 'honours of the world, he has not missed out on the authority that belongs to such honours'.[56] He is said to have refused five bishoprics: Genoa (1133?), Châlons (before 1135), Milan (1135), Langres (1138), and Reims (1139). The five mitres at the feet of the cross in an *Amplexus* scene from the inside wing of a triptych dated *c.* 1500, which may have come from the german abbey of Heisterbach, refer to these five rejected elections (PA020). In this scene, Christ, with his arms detached from a raised crucifix, is being supported by the kneeling Bernard. A cistercian monk carrying a book looks on. Bernard's refusal is also featured in one of the glass panels from Altenberg (GL30).

[56] VP 1.14.69; PL 185:265: *Sed cum hoc modo mundi hujus fugit honorem, omnium honorum non effugit auctoritatem.*

He is shown on the left carrying his crozier and book, with five mitres at his feet. Facing him on the right are five noblemen, each representing one of the cities that sought him as their bishop. One of them carries a mitre and his scroll reads: 'We pray and beseech Your Holiness to take on the cure of our souls'.[57] Two of the noblemen turn to a monk who is carrying a bull from which five seals are hanging and in which the pope absolved Bernard from accepting the offers. For this the monks of Clairvaux were grateful, for, according to the scroll: 'We have compared the precious stone to all things on offer in the world. If we are deprived, o precious stone, of our expectation we have all been ill provided for'.[58] Bernard points to the mitres at his feet and says: *Ego non sum meus, sed fratrum meorum servitio deputatus* ('I do not belong to myself, but am deputed to the service of my brethren'). Bernard's refusal of the episcopal office also forms the subject of one of the nine frescos showing scenes from his life; dated 1482, they appear in the Chapel of Saint Bernard at Pamparato in Italy (WA15). Accompanied by a monk with his hood over his head, the nimbed figure of Bernard stands holding a red book in his left hand while his right hand is raised to indicate his refusal of the two italian bishoprics of Genoa and Milan, the two mentioned in the *Golden Legend*. These are indicated by the two kneeling figures, each carrying a mitre. The inscription tells the story: COMO FURENO APRESENTATE DUE MITRE CHE NON VOSE ACEPTARE.

AS A SAINT

The Nimbus or Halo

The nimbus, or halo, as it is more commonly known, is the emanation of light surrounding a figure. It had its origin in the polytheistic cults of the graeco-roman world, and a fitting definition was given by Servius:

> Shining forth from a cloud, with the brightness of a storm-cloud. For there is a gleaming light with which the heads of

[57] *Petimus et Sanctitatem vestram oramus, nostrarum suscipere curam animarum.*
[58] *Nos venditis omnibus mundanis pretiosam marginatam comparavimus. Si privati, Marginata, exspectationi nostrae male provisum est.*

> the gods are surrounded; and this is also how they are usually depicted.[59]

When it was originally adopted by the early Christians its use was reserved to denote Christ. This is how he is depicted in catacomb frescos from the second and third centuries, and from this time on he is rarely portrayed without the nimbus. From the fifth century its use was extended to the martyrs and then to other saints, as at Ravenna. To differentiate between Christ and the saints, a cross was added to Christ's nimbus, and from the sixth century onwards the use of the cross-nimbus to denote Christ was widespread. By this time the plain nimbus had become the universal attribute of the saints.[60]

The earliest Christians to be recognised as saints were the martyrs. As they had given their lives for their faith there could be no doubt as to their heavenly reward. By popular acclaim the honour was extended to others whose lives were marked by outstanding virtue, and, although the demand continued to come from below, the growing power and prestige of the pope from the eleventh century onwards meant that the official recognition of sainthood became reserved to the papacy; for Bernard this occurred at his canonization in 1174.[61] The halo at first took the form of a flat circular disc. It was often depicted as golden to suggest bright gleaming light and is therefore also occasionally referred to as the aureole from the Latin *aurea*. Sometimes they are coloured—usually blue or greenish blue to signify the sky, or red, orange, or yellow to suggest brightness.

Although there was no doubt in cistercian circles as to Bernard's sanctity, the artists responsible for the three surviving miniatures painted before his canonization have observed the iconographical convention by not investing him with the nimbus (MA006, MA028, MA004).

The earliest known image of Bernard depicted nimbed, and one of the earliest of all Bernard images, dated 1175–1176—only a year or two after Bernard's canonization—is found in a Missal from the scriptorium at the austrian abbey of Zwettl (MA002). His halo is blue, as is the halo

[59] Quoted in Kirschbaum & Braunfels 1968–1976, 3:323.

[60] For this see Réau 1955–1959, 1:423.

[61] For a short survey of the process, see the introduction to David Hugh Farmer, *The Oxford Dictionary of Saints*, especially XX-XXII.

shown in the Gradual from the nuns' abbey of Seligenthal dated 1260 (MA164), in an Antiphonary from the portuguese nuns' abbey of Arouca, dated the first half of the thirteenth century (▶ *Colour plate 7*), in a late thirteenth-century manuscript of Bernard's Sermons (MA023), and in the manuscript of Abbot Konrad von Brundelsheim's Sermons from Heilsbronn dated *c.* 1320–1330 (MA071). Another early manuscript, a copy of Bernard's *Sermons on the Song of Songs* from the benedictine scriptorium of Liesborn and dated *c.* 1180, shows Bernard with a greenish-blue nimbus within the opening initial *V(obis fratres)* of Sermon One (MA025). A slightly later copy of the *Sermons on the Song of Songs* has Bernard with a green nimbus with white outline and decorated with small white circles (MA168). The earliest known examples of bernardine gold halos are in the late twelfth century manuscript of the *Vita Prima* (MA026) and, from around the same time, a manuscript of Bernard's Sermons in which he is shown seated with head bowed and writing at a desk with a pen in his right hand and a knife in his left (MA040). Numerous others followed (*e.g.* MA155, MA116). In the course of time, instead of being a plain gold disc the nimbus was decorated, either stippled or broken up in other ways (PA094, MA156, PA031, PA028).

One way of making a composition more informative was to include an inscription within the gold nimbus. An early sixteenth-century glass panel from a Cologne workshop depicting a *Lactation* scene (GL69) has the traditional words of these scenes—*Monstra te esse matrem*—inscribed around Bernard's halo. Inscriptions used to provide a means of identification include two works of the Cologne School: the magnificent Heisterbach retable from *c.* 1450, in which Bernard is featured together with Saint Benedict and the apostles and is identified by the inscription *sanctus bernardus* around the edge of the gold nimbus (PA010); and the *Lactation* scene painted by the Master of the Life of Mary between 1470–1475 (PA021). In yet another example, part of a predella painted *c.* 1480 by Derick Baegert (PA016), and now in the Rheinisches Landesmuseum in Bonn, Bernard is identified by the inscription *S bernardus abbas* painted within his halo. The scene has two half-figures: Bernard, in a greyish brown cowl; and Saint Quirinus of Neuss. Bernard has a crozier under the left arm while, with both hands, holding an open book with red binding from which he is reading. A further fragment, now in the museum in Dortmund, features Saints

Cornelius, Hubert, and Anthony the Hermit, who, with Quirinus, were known in the Cologne and Trier regions from the thirteenth century on as the 'four marshals'. The addition of Bernard suggests that the predella was from a cistercian church.

Sometimes the nimbus became smaller and less pronounced. This was achieved by the gold fill being applied to appear transparent within a gold ring (MA115), by delicate filigree decoration with dots within a gold ring (PA075), by a simple gold ring (MA083 & MA206), or by a ring of gold dots (MA226).

In the early fifteenth century the flat nimbus was finally replaced by a discus-like circle drawn in perspective at an angle behind the head and following its movements. This is how it was represented by Botticelli and Perugino,[62] and this is how Fra Bartolommeo treated it in his *Doctrina* painting, in which the halo behind Bernard's head is at an angle and, like that of the other figures, consists of a very fine oval ring (PA026).

Of the nine-hundred sixty recorded portrayals of Bernard, he is nimbed in six hundred forty-three, nearly sixty-seven percent of them. The obvious limitations imposed by three-dimensional images means that of the thirty-four recorded free-standing sculptures of Bernard, the halo appears in only one; the polychrome statue of Bernard from the early fifteenth-century retable which originally came from the Catalan abbey of Santes Creus, ▶ *Fig.* 2 (SC45), has a simple thin gilt ring attached to the back of the sculpted head. Otherwise haloes are omitted from statues for much the same reasons for which either the crozier or the book of the Rule are left out: the images contain other means of identification, notably some scene-attribute.[63] Yet the nimbus is almost always included in pictures where Bernard is shown as a standing figure on his own. Unlike the other scene-attributes, Bernard is almost always portrayed nimbed in *Doctrina* images, a single exception being the painting by Dominico Puligi from *c.* 1520 (PA086). The reason for its omission in late medieval *Lactatio* scenes may also be connected with the frequency with which the representation of Bernard is at the same time a portrait of a contemporary cistercian abbot (PA052).

[62] For the development in the design of the nimbus, see Kirschbaum & Braunfels 1968–1976, 3:323-332.

[63] In the following *Amplexus* pictures, for example, Bernard appears without a halo: PA060, EN13, MA191, PA009, PA079, PA081, GL083, EN36, MA131.

OTHER ATTRIBUTES

Model of Church

The traditional way of portraying the founder of a church is to show him carrying a model of his church. This is, for example, how Saint Amand and Saint Trond, the founders of benedictine monasteries named after them, are depicted in an early sixteenth-century triptych by Jean Bellegambe in which Bernard is also portrayed (PA107). Considering that Bernard was the founder and initiator of a larger number of monasteries than perhaps any other single person before or afterwards, it is surprising that there are not more images commemorating him in this role. Only three have been recorded: the famous statue which adorned his tomb at Clairvaux (SC04); the well-known painting of him on the Clairvaux retable from the second half of the fifteenth century (PA092); and a full-page miniature in a Book of Hours from *c.* 1500 (MA358). The Office of the Virgin in this last is according to the Use of the diocese of Langres, and its calendar contains many feasts of special significance there, including Saint Mammes, its patron saint. In this Book of Hours, Bernard is depicted standing on a multi-coloured tiled floor in a panelled chamber. He is wearing a black cowl with gold edging and has the hood over his head. In his right hand he carries a model of a church and in his left a golden crozier. The border consists of stylized leaves and flowers and has a scroll below Bernard with the inscription ORA PRO NOBIS BEATE BERNARDE ('Pray for us, Blessed Bernard'). The abbey of Clairvaux was in the diocese of Langres, and, significantly, all three known representations of Bernard with a church model refer more to Clairvaux than to his role as the initiator of a large and widespread family of monasteries.

Dog

While expecting Bernard, his mother Aleth had a dream that she carried within her a barking dog with a white coat and a reddish back. Frightened, she consulted a holy man who reassured her:

> There is no need to be afraid, for this foretells nothing but good. You are to be the mother of a wonderful dog who is destined to be the guardian of God's household. He will bark on its behalf at the great enemies of the faith. He will become a great preacher, and, like a good dog, the healing grace of his tongue will cure many of countless illnesses.[64]

Not surprisingly, this is one of the best known stories from the *Vita Prima*. It is not only a good story which combines human interest with humour, but it contains one of the characteristics of saints' *Vitae,* the divine imprint which marked him out even from before his birth, and it satisfies one of the proofs of sanctity which has been described as *fama sanctitatis,* reputation for holiness.[65]

Although there are only a few visual representations of Aleth's dream (GL01, MA054, SC39), there are a further twenty-three recorded images in which the story itself is not depicted but is alluded to by showing a small dog accompanying Bernard. In this way the dog became one of the minor attributes by which Bernard may be identified. A small white dog appears, for example, in seven of the eight panels with scenes from the life of Bernard painted by Jörg Breu in 1500 on the wings of the Zwettl altarpiece (PA038-043 & PA045). One of forty-two leaves cut out of an Antiphonary from Mainz, dated the last decade of the fifteenth century, has a large historiated initial *P* with acanthus decoration in *Prima virtus viri sancti,* the first Responsary of the first Nocturn from Vigils on the feast of Bernard (MA233). A nimbed and standing Bernard is shown holding a red crozier with a gold volute in his left hand and a grey book with clasp in his right. The artist has used considerable license in showing Bernard in a rosa cowl against a gold background, but he has been unusually accurate in depicting at Bernard's feet the dog exactly as described in both the *Vita Prima* and the *Legenda Aurea,* that is, white with a reddish back, thereby revealing a close knowledge of the literary source. A similar dog appears at the top of the border on the right hand side.

[64] VP 1.1.2; PL 185:227-228: *Ne timeas, bene res agitur, optimi catuli mater eris, qui domus Dei custos futurus, magnos pro ea contra inimicos fidei editurus est latratus. Erit enim egrerius praedicator, et tanquam bonus canis, gratia linguae medicinalis in multis multos morbos curaturus est animarum.*

[65] Vauchez 1997, 144.

The Arms of Clairvaux

The coat of arms of Bernard's family was later adopted by Clairvaux and appears in forty-five of the nine hundred sixty recorded bernardine images. Like the mitre, the arms are usually shown at Bernard's foot and are always in late medieval images. The earliest known example is the *Amplexus* image by Jerg Haspel from *c.* 1430–1440 (EN16). Most are from the late fifteenth or early sixteenth century. The arms consist of a black shield with a diagonal band of red and white (or silver) checks, usually going from top left to bottom right, although in a number of cases this is reversed. In heraldic parlance this design is described as 'Gules, a bend countercompony, Sable and Argent'. Nineteen of the forty-five recorded examples are engravings, and the same number, but not always the same examples, are *Amplexus* images. Among them is a miniature (MA326) in a Missal made *c.* 1525 for an unknown cistercian abbey by the leading Nuremberg illuminator Nikolaus Glockendon (+1533/34) whose monogram *NG* is found on another folio. Christ's lifeless-looking body is supported by Bernard, wearing a black cowl. Christ's head is partially obscured by Bernard's. Behind Bernard are the arms of Clairvaux surmounted, as was not uncommon, by a mitre. Bernard's crozier lies on the ground. Next to the miniature is a large initial *I(n medio ecclesie)* from the beginning of the Mass for the feast of Saint Bernard. The initial has the shape of a tree trunk whose branches extend to form the decoration of the border. Other examples of the arms of Clairvaux surmounted by a mitre occur in the Dürer woodcut from 1503 (▶ *Fig. 4*) and as one of a large number of woodcuts of saints by Hans Baldung Grien in the *Hortulus animae* printed in Strasbourg in 1512 (▶ *Fig. 11*).

Occasionally, when Bernard is depicted with another cistercian abbot, the arms of Clairvaux are shown together with those of the other abbey. An example is found in a Gradual from Salem in southern Germany dated 1463, commissioned by Abbot Ludwig Oschwald (1458–1471) (MA330). Within an unusually large historiated initial *A(d te levavi)* from the first Sunday in Advent, an abbot in a black cowl, with hands clasped in prayer, kneels before a nimbed Bernard in a white cowl. The abbot is mitred and carries a crozier under his arm. Bernard has a crozier in his right hand and his left hand is raised in acknowledgement of the abbot. The arms of Clairvaux and those of Salem—a white dove against a blue background—are at their feet.

Medieval artists had no means of knowing what their subjects looked like. A code gradually emerged to facilitate the identification of the figures they painted. Biblical scenes and the lives of saints formed the most common subject matter. Identification was aided by the emergence of iconographical emblems associated with the individual saint, for example the keys for Saint Peter or the wheel for Saint Catherine of Alexandria. Saint Bernard was represented by the (usually white) habit he wore as a cistercian monk, the crozier and the book—the *Rule of Saint Benedict*—he carried as an abbot, and the halo with which he was invested following his canonization in 1174. His attributes included a small dog, referring to the story of his mother's dream; a model of a church, alluding to his foundation at Clairvaux or to the large number of monasteries for which he was responsible; and the coat of arms of Clairvaux, often surmounted by the mitre with which abbots were invested in the later Middle Ages. Lest any doubt remain, positive identification was sometime achieved by the inscription of Bernard's name.

As the medieval centuries unfurled there was a marked development in the way Bernard was portrayed. In the twelfth century he had invariably been shown wearing the primitive cowl which conformed to the simplicity and poverty enjoined by the early Cîteaux texts.[66] In later medieval images Bernard is usually depicted in an ample two-piece cowl with full sleeves and copious hood, the very kind he had virulently attacked in the chapter devoted to 'On Costly and Ostentatious Clothing' in his *Apologia*.[67] The gradual relaxation of the early austerity also manifested itself in Bernard's abbatial attributes. The simple wooden shepherd's crook was gradually transformed into a costly and elaborate golden crozier, and since, from the middle of the fourteenth century abbots had the right to use a number of episcopal *insignia* and vestments, including the mitre, these too were included. Although Bernard had warned against the temptation 'to covet the fame of a bishop's status',[68] he was, ironically, often portrayed in accordance with late medieval fashion as the powerful prelate which cistercian abbots had by then become.

[66] Waddell 1999, 434, 459, 491.
[67] SBOp 3: 101-2; trans. Matarasso 1993, 53–54.
[68] SBOp 1:66.

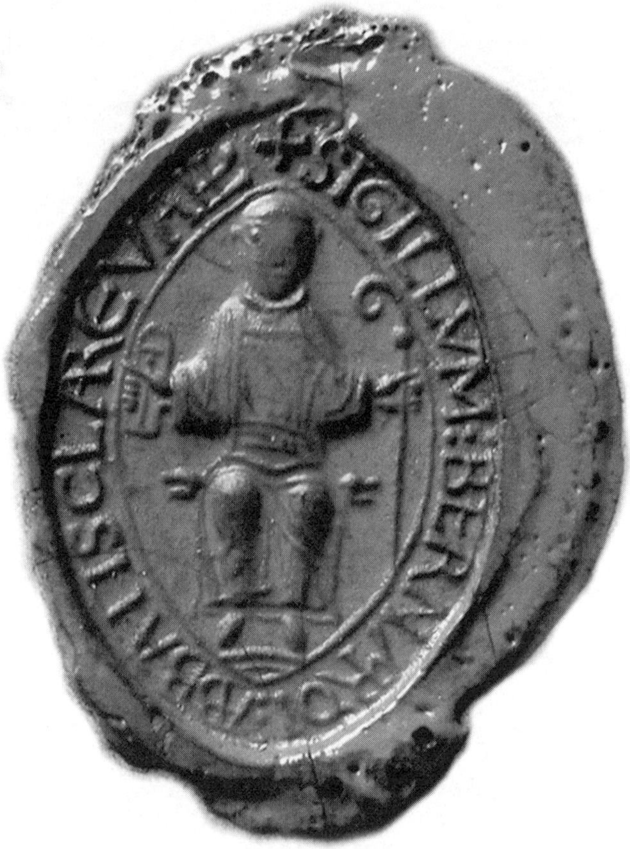

Figure 5: Impression from the matrix of Bernard's abbatial seal (VA17)
Copyright: Society of Antiquaries of London.

THREE

THE EARLIEST IMAGES: THE TWELFTH CENTURY

THERE APPEARS TO BE a good deal of confusion as regards the earliest image of Bernard. According to an authority on bernardine iconography, Jean-Claude Schmitt, 'no image produced during [Bernard's] lifetime has been preserved';[1] this view has been repeated in a recent reference work: 'no contemporary portrait of Bernard survives'.[2] These assertions are in line with a traditional view.[3] The lack is the more remarkable in that we have a full-page miniature of Bernard's abbot at Cîteaux, Stephen Harding, painted in 1124, during Stephen's lifetime, which is authenticated by the inclusion of his name.[4] That a contemporary image of Bernard does in fact exist in the form of a miniature in a manuscript dated before 1135, was first noted by Jean Leclercq in 1955,[5] and acknowledged in the *Lexikon der Christlichen Ikonographie*

[1] Schmitt 1990, 149.
[2] Duchet-Suchaux & Pastoureau 1994, 62.
[3] For example, Künstle 1926, 128, and Réau 1955–1959, 3:211.
[4] Illustrated in France 1998, colour plate 5.
[5] Leclercq 1955, 145.

(1968–1976).[6] This miniature has recently been described as 'the only known image from Bernard's lifetime'.[7] The same claim has been made for Bernard's seal, which has been described as 'the earliest preserved representation . . . the frontal portrait of Bernard enthroned on the seal matrix from 1151'.[8] The possibility that this seal is not authentic has also been made, in which case the honour is said to go to the image in the manuscript of Bernard's *Sermons on the Song of Songs* from Zwettl (MA342). In 1992, Jean-Claude Schmitt made the same claim for the seal, despite having earlier subscribed to the theory that there is no contemporary image of Bernard. Yet he also added the reservation as to its authenticity: 'the oldest "image" of Saint Bernard, the only one to have been produced during his lifetime, is not what is usually thought of as a work of art, but a seal'.[9]

In this chapter an attempt will be made to unravel these contradictory statements and to answer the question of what, if any, extant images of Bernard survive from his lifetime and his century. If the authenticity of the seal is accepted, there are thirteen known representations of Bernard dated to the twelfth century. Twelve of these are in illuminated manuscripts: one from Bernard's lifetime, two more from the period between his death in 1153 and his canonization in 1174, and a further nine from the last quarter of the twelfth century.

THE SEAL

In his 1335 reform constitution *Fulgens sicut stella,* the cistercian pope Benedict XII instituted a conventual seal for the Cistercians. This was to be round, made of copper, and bear an image of the Virgin Mary.[10] In the twelfth century each cistercian abbey employed its abbot's seal for the business of the house. In contrast to the Benedictines, the Cistercians did not at first have a common house or conventual seal.[11] If the pastoral staff was the emblem of the abbot's spiritual authority, then

[6] Kirschbaum & Braunfels 5:372.
[7] France 1998, 36.
[8] Aurenhammer 1959–1967, 332.
[9] Schmitt 1992, 640.
[10] *Statuta* 3:437 (1335:2).
[11] On cistercian seals, see Heslop 1986, Clay 1928, and Williams 1998, 108–111.

the abbatial seal represented his temporal rule. It provided him with the means whereby he administered the monastery's business. The possession of crozier and seal distinguished the abbot from the monks in his care. His seal was the tool he employed in authenticating all official transactions. The importance attached to the seal is reflected in the detailed provisions in the statutes of the General Chapter as to its design and use.[12] The greater the authority vested in the cistercian abbot as the sole user and guardian of the only official seal matrix—that is, the die from which an impression was made in wax—made it that much more important to guard against misuse.

Bernard's first seal, which is known from three extant impressions, followed the usual shape and design of early cistercian abbatial seals. It was pointed oval, or so-called *vesica piscis* from the most ancient emblem of Christ, the form based on the intersection of two segments of circles.[13] It depicted a cowled forearm from the right holding a crozier without a figure and with the legend + SIGNUM.ABBATIS.CLAREVALLIS.

Like many early abbatial seals *SIGNUM* was used rather than the later *SIGILLUM*. One of the impressions has been dated 1115,[14] probably for no better reason than that it is thought to be Bernard's first seal and that he became abbot in that year.[15] Elsewhere it is dated more realistically to 1146 and 1127–1147 respectively.[16] Another impression is attached to a charter in favour of the abbey of Saint Victor and is dated 1144.[17] The third is attached to a document in Ghent and is not dated.[18]

Bernard refers to the fate of this seal matrix in a letter dated 1151/1152 to his old disciple from Clairvaux, Bernardo Pignatelli, now Pope Eugene III, in which he complains of being in danger from false brethren:

[12] Details of statutes relating to seals are given in Heslop 1986, 282–283.

[13] Pedrick 1902, 26.

[14] The date is given in Walford & Way 1857 in the caption to illustration facing p. 48; and Paris 1990, 264.

[15] H. 675 Auxerre, Archives départementales (Yonne); PL 185:1747.

[16] Schmitt 1992, 641; and Pontigny 1999, 106.

[17] It is now in Archives nationales, Paris, L 888A No 75; Douët-d'Arcq 1868, 3:73 (No 8645).

[18] Ghent, Archives, reproduced in PL 185:3-4.

> Many forged letters have gone out under a forgery of my seal. And, what I fear may have happened, these forgeries are said to have reached even you. This is why I have rejected my old seal and am, as you see, using a new one for the future, containing both my image and name.[19]

Bernard asks the pope no longer to accept the 'old' seal, except in the case of a letter he had given to the bishop of Clermont and sealed before the new one was made. In another letter to Eugene Bernard tells him of how his secretary, Nicholas, had fled

> leaving behind him foul traces. . . . When he left there was found on his person, besides books, money and much gold, three seals, one his own, the other the prior's, and the third mine, not the old one, but the new one which I was obliged to have made on account of his cunning and frauds.[20]

Bernard goes on to say that it was Nicholas he had had in mind when he had previously written to the pope of 'false brethren'.

We know from Bernard's two letters that he was obliged to discontinue using the old seal and to have a new one made and that, had Nicholas not been searched before he left, Bernard would also have lost his new seal. From this it is clear that Bernard's motivation in deciding to include 'both my image and my name' (*continente et imaginem nostram et nomen*)[21] was first and foremost security. He had learned from experience that the utmost care was needed in storing and using his seal, an issue which dictated a number of General Chapter statutes

[19] Ep 284; SBOp 8:199; trans. James 431. The dating is from the new edition of James 1998, 548, taken from the italian edition, ed. F. Gastaldelli 1987: *Periclitati sumus in falsis fratribus, et multae litterae falsatae sub falsato sigillo nostro in manus multorum exierunt, et, quod magis vereor, etiam usque ad vos dicitur falsitas pervolasse. Hac necessitate abiecto illo, novello quod cernitis de novo utimur, continente et imaginem nostram, et nomen.*

[20] Ep 298; SBOp 8:214; trans. James 435–436. Gastaldelli's dating to 1152 (after May) is in James 1998, 548: . . . *exiit autem foeda post se relinquens vestigia. . . . Praeter libros, denarios et aureos multos, in ipso exitu eius inventa sunt super eum sigilla tria, unum eius proprium, alterum prioris, tertium nostrum, ipsumque non antiquum, sed novellum, quod et ob ipsius dolos et furtivas subreptiones mutare nuper coactus fueram.*

[21] Ep 284; SBOp 8:199.

on seals.[22] At the same time his decision to incorporate his *imaginem* as well as his *nomen* is a powerful indicator that he was not the iconophobe that he has often been made out to be.

A matrix which includes both Bernard's image and name, and therefore corresponds to the seal he described in the letter to the pope as a replacement for the earlier seal, is today found in the Musée des Antiquités in Rouen, ▶ *Fig. 5* (VA17). In a letter to the Permanent Secretary of the Academy of Inscriptions dated 16 August 1837, the then-director of the Rouen Museum, Achille Deville, describes the matrix, and continues:

> The effigy and name of S. Bernard are engraved on it: its shape and execution correspond exactly with the style of the time when S. Bernard informs us that he had had it made; it has in every way all the marks of genuineness that can be wished for.[23]

He then explains how the Museum acquired it: it was bought from the Collegiate Church of Saint Cyr in Issoudun, which was in some way connected with Clairvaux, by a merchant who then sold it to a retired officer who donated it to the museum.

The matrix is pointed oval and made of copper, four centimeters long and three centimeters wide.[24] The legend around the edge reads: + SIGILLUM : BERNARDI : ABBATIS : CLAREVALL', and not the more usual, less personal SIGILLUM ABBATIS CLAREVALL'. Unusually, the punctuation between the words is not double but triple point. The 'd' in Bernard is of uncial form while most of the letters are square. The 'e' of Clarevall' is also uncial, although the same letter in 'Bernard' is square. There are three instances of letters conjoined: AR in *Bernardi* and in *Clarevall'*, and AB in *Abbatis*. Within the legend, a tonsured Bernard is shown wearing a cowl—and not, as is sometimes stated,[25] sacerdotal vestments. His frontal figure is seated on a faldstool, the arms of which terminate in a serpent's or lion's head. The frontal position and the faldstool—the official seat of prelates—underline the abbot's authority in cistercian governance.

[22] For this, see Williams 1998, 108–111.
[23] The letter is printed in full in Eales 1889, 2:457-459. See also PL 185:1745-1748.
[24] Rouen, Musée des Antiquités de la Seine-Maritime, Inv. 152.
[25] *Bernard de Clairvaux* 1953, 325.

It was precisely by the imposition of his seal that Bernard exercized his authority. The matrix depicts him holding in his right hand—which in the waxen impression becomes his left—another symbol of his authority, a very simple pastoral staff of the earliest design with the crook turned inwards. The crook and the staff are separated by a circular knob. In his left hand, which becomes his right in the impression, he holds what has been described as 'an object of singular aspect, which has given rise to various conjectures' and 'an object which the roughness and minuteness of the work make it difficult to recognize'.[26] It has been referred to in almost as many different ways as the number of scholars who have described it: Mabillon said it was a book;[27] others, 'without doubt a book',[28] a book or roll,[29] a tablet or roll,[30] a church-door divided into two parts by a column surmounted by a capital,[31] an hour-glass, and 'an object of singular aspect'[32]—a *tabula pacis* or pax-board. It is, in fact, none of these things; it is, as T. A. Heslop has pointed out, a writing-tablet in the form of an arch-topped diptych and stylus—a design which occurs on a number of seals.[33] One end of the stylus is pointed, to be used to write in the wax, while the other end, which was used to erase by smoothing out the wax, is flat. As Bernard refers to the use of this seal on letters, and as letters, unlike charters, were written on waxen tablets, it is quite possible that this seal was primarily intended for authenticating his correspondence, and not for official documents of the abbey.

A similar and equally powerful expression of Bernard's authority can be seen in a full-page miniature in a manuscript (MA022) produced in the important scriptorium of Altzelle during the abbacy of Ludeger, who died sometime after 1234. It depicts Bernard in the same authoritative way, sitting in a frontal position on a faldstool with arms terminat-

[26] Walford & Way 1857, 50–52, and Eales 1889, 458.

[27] PL 185:1745-1748.

[28] Schmitt 1992, 642.

[29] Birch 1887–1890, 5:257.

[30] Paris 1990, 265.

[31] Eales 1889, 2:458.

[32] Walford & Way 1857, 50–52, where it is called a pax-board, and where it is also said that the man who sold the matrix called it an hour-glass and that the man who bought it also thought it was the door of a church.

[33] Heslop 1986, 268, suggests that it was not primarily a charter seal which may be why it names Bernard.

ing in the traditional animal heads and feet in claws. Unlike the seal matrix cast during his lifetime, however, this post-canonization image shows him nimbed. Dressed in sacerdotal vestments, he holds a crozier in his right hand, again with the crook turned inwards, but in his left hand he holds, not the tablet and stylus of a writer of letters, but a book denoting his *Sermons on the Song of Songs*, the text of which follows the illuminated page.

Original seal matrices as early as Bernard's have been described as 'of considerable rarity',[34] and the standard work on french seals also refers to the authenticity of Bernard's seal as 'doubtful'.[35] This assessment is perhaps influenced by the fact that although three impressions of Bernard's first seal are known, none of the second seal has survived. It has been claimed that 'a seal in white wax representing Saint Bernard in sacerdotal dress and holding a book in his right hand and in the other a crozier' was appended to a charter which is said to be in the Archives Nationales, but an inspection at the Archives reveals that, although the document is there, no seal is attached.[36] Although it is no longer there, the Maurist Jean Mabillon referred to the seal with name and effigy as being attached to a charter resolving a dispute between the two parisian abbeys of Sainte Genevieve and Saint Victor, an indication that such a seal was there in the seventeenth century. A combination of these two factors—the rarity of the matrix and the absence of impressions—may have contributed to the theory advanced by Michel Pastoureau that the matrix is not original but produced in the eighteenth century. In his recent appraisal undertaken for the Rouen Museum he gives five reasons for coming to this conclusion, three of them mentioned in the Catalogue of the Paris Saint Bernard Exhibition in 1990:[37]

1. It is too small for an abbatial seal of the sacerdotal [*sic*] type showing the prelate seated

[34] Walford & Way 1857, 50–52.

[35] Douët-d'Arcq 1868, 3:73 (No 8644): 'douteux'.

[36] The claim is made in *Bernard de Clairvaux* 1953, 325. The seal is said to be appended to charter, Archives nationales, K 23, n. 20. 3, the text of which is in PL 182:720. I am grateful to Emmanuel Rousseau, Conservateur at the Archives, who informs me that there is no known impression of Bernard's second seal.

[37] Paris 1990, 265. I am grateful to the present curator of the Rouen Museum, Evelyne Poirel, for sending me a copy of Pastoureau's report.

2. The type is in itself suspect in that twelfth-century abbatial seals are of the hand-and-staff type or show the abbot as a half-figure
3. The inclusion of the abbot's name is impossible in the twelfth century and is not found until the thirteenth or fourteenth century
4. The form of the letters and abbreviations is somewhat strange for the mid-twelfth century—the engraving is hesitant
5. The metal itself and its patina, and the absence of a means of holding the matrix all point to a forgery.

Although, as we saw above, these objections to the authenticity of the matrix have in recent times been responsible for the view that it is not genuine, the failure of any mention by the critics of Bernard's letter 354, with its specific reference to the inclusion on his seal of both his image and his name, seems strange and calls for a reappraisal.[38] Two further reasons may be advanced as to why the inclusion of Bernard's own personal name is not impossible in the twelfth century.

First, the inclusion of the abbot's name is not unique, but is also known from the almost contemporary abbatial seal of Longpont dated 1153. This consists of the standing figure of an abbot with a book in his right hand and a crozier in his left and the abbot's name, Gerard, in the legend: + SIGILLV. GIRARDI ABBATIS LONGIPONTIS.[39] Second, even if including the abbot's name is exceptional, we know from a General Chapter statute from 1200—the earliest legislation on seals—that a variety of abbatial seals existed and that the purpose of the legislation was to impose some uniformity.[40] Bernard's seal may well have been an example of one of the unacceptable types, and in future only two designs were to be allowed: either the original hand-and-staff, or a simple effigy of

[38] I am most grateful to Christopher Holdsworth for having suggested this need for a fresh look, not least as I have previously accepted the Pastoureau theory (France 1998, 35).

[39] Douët-d'Arcq 1868, 3:95 (No 8801).

[40] *Statuta* 1:251-2 (1200:15): *Quia in sigillis Ordinis quaedam discordia invenitur, et quamdam videtur inducere novitatem, praecipitur quatenus amodo in sigillis nulla discrepantia habeatur; sed sola et simplici effigie cum baculo, vel sine effigie cum manu et baculo annotetur.*

the abbot holding his crozier. To this may be added that permission to include the abbot's name was only introduced in the Reform Constitution of 1335, and that it would therefore have been exceptional at any time prior to that date.[41]

Although the chief objection to Pastoureaux's theory—the presence of the image and personal name—has been removed, others remain. The opinion that the seal is too small to be genuine is strange, given that it is almost exactly the same size as the majority of early cistercian abbatial seals; there are some even smaller, both of the hand-and-staff and the effigy types.[42] Cistercian abbatial seals were not only more modest in size than benedictine seals but were of such uniform size (around four centimeters in length, as Bernard's second seal) that it has even been suggested that this might be due to an unrecorded instruction.[43]

The lettering forms—including the ligatures AR and AB, the terminal abbreviation, the alternation between square and uncial, and the lack of separation or punctuation between ABBATIS and CLAREVALL—are all consistent with scribal practice at the middle of the twelfth century.[44] The lack of a suspension loop is surprising but, according to T. A. Heslop, this may have been filed off to make the matrix a more collectable object; as regards the metal we have no means of knowing on what basis any particular alloy would have been used.

That Bernard's matrix corresponds to Bernard's own description and that the features of size, design, inclusion of name, and style of lettering can all be paralleled in the twelfth century, suggest that there are no serious grounds for questioning its authenticity. It is of course possible that a forger worked from Bernard's description in his letter, but, as Heslop has pointed out referring to the peculiarities of the lettering, these 'are not features I would expect a forger to get right unless he was working close to the supposed date or from an original of that date'. Pastoureau argues that the matrix was made in the eighteenth century, and, if it is not genuine, it is most likely a copy of the original. In either

[41] *Statuta* 3:415.

[42] For example, hand-and-staff type: Bernard's first seal (3.5 cm), Llantarnam (3.0 cm), Neath (3.0); effigy type: Mortemer (3.4 cm), Nydala (3.5).

[43] Williams 1998, 109.

[44] I am most grateful to T. A. Heslop for this information and what follows, which is contained in a letter of 29 February 2000.

event, somehow its existence makes Bernard seem closer to us, and it is of considerable interest as it represents one of the only two images from Bernard's lifetime.

THE EARLIEST IMAGE

The earliest known image of Bernard (MA006) is, surprisingly, neither cistercian nor french. Appropriately, he is depicted in a manuscript of his first treatise, *The Steps of Humility and Pride* (*De gradibus humilitatis et superbiae*), a pastoral work in which Bernard the monk is addressing his fellow monks on monastic virtues.[45] The illuminated manuscript dates from before 1135 and was written in the scriptorium of the benedictine abbey of Saint Augustine at Canterbury.

This little-known earliest image of Bernard has him sitting at a desk writing. He is shown in profile, the conventional way of depicting the evangelists, which in turn was based on late Antique author portraits. He is depicted against a gold background as a young monk, tonsured but with longish hair at the back. In his left hand he holds a knife which is placed on the open book before him. Also known as a *rasurium,* this knife was used to erase errors, to sharpen the pen, and to steady the parchment. In his right hand he holds a pen.[46] He is not shown carrying a crozier, but there is nothing unusual in this as the crozier is often missing when he is engaged in an activity where this would not be appropriate as, for example, here when writing or when celebrating Mass. He is portrayed within the initial *R(ogasti me, frater G[aufride], quatinus ea que de gradibus humilitatis coram fratribus locutus fueram, pleniori tibi tractatu dissererem)*, the opening words of the preface to the treatise, in which he states how he came to write it: 'You asked me, Brother G[odfrey], to write out at greater length the sermons I gave to the brethren on the Steps of Humility'.[47] The letter is in red, blue, and green ink, the lower half consisting of intertwining green and blue foliage with one complete dragon and the heads of two others.

[45] SBOp 3:13-59, trans. Conway 1980, 25–82.

[46] This is barely visible, and I have therefore previously mistakenly seen it as his hand raised in blessing (France 1998, 35).

[47] SBOp 3:16; Bernard of Clairvaux 1980, 28.

Bernard's discourses on the degrees of humility, which he had delivered to the monks at Clairvaux, had made a deep impression on Godfrey who asked Bernard to put them into writing. Godfrey de la Roche-Vanneau was a cousin of Bernard who had entered Cîteaux with him, had gone with him when Clairvaux was founded, became first abbot of the daughter-house of Fontenay in 1119, and resigned in 1126/27 to return to Clairvaux, where he became prior, probably an even more than usually responsible position in view of Bernard's frequent absences. That his duties weighed on him is suggested in a letter Bernard wrote to him from Rome in 1138, at the end of a prolonged absence during the Anacletan schism: 'Now nothing remains to keep me here any longer, and I can change "I will come" for "I am coming", as you have been imploring me to do'.[48] At Bernard's instigation he was elected bishop of Langres around 1138. He resigned in 1162–1163 and returned to Clairvaux where he died a few years later.[49]

In the *Vita Prima* Geoffrey of Auxerre described *The Steps of Humility and Pride* as Bernard's 'first work' (*primum opus illius*),[50] and Bernard himself places it first in the list of his writings which he gives in Letter 18, dated 1126.[51] It was in fact composed in 1119, after Godfrey had been elected abbot of Fontenay, but it contains material which he had heard while still at Clairvaux, and it shows Bernard's solicitude for one of the daughter-houses for which he was responsible.[52] It may well have been one of the books Bernard referred to when, in Letter 74 (1125–1131), he asked that Abbot Reynald of Foigny, the third daughter-house of Clairvaux, 'please return as soon as you can those books of mine which you borrowed',[53] presumably so that they could be copied. The Canterbury manuscript from before 1135 is evidence that the popularity and early dispersion of Bernard's first work was not limited to

[48] Ep 317; SBOp 8:250; trans. Scott James 1953, 217: *Facio quod imperastis: 'Veniam' vertimus in 'venio'.*

[49] Veyssière 2000, 57.

[50] VP 3.8.29; PL 185:320.

[51] Ep 18; SBOp 7:69; trans. James 1953, 54: *Et ut sciatis quid petatis, scio me scripsisse libellum qui inscribitur DE HUMILITATE, et quattuor homilias IN LAUDIBUS VIRGINIS MATRIS, . . . necnon et APOLOGIAM.*

[52] For the dating, see Holdsworth 1994, 34–35, who suggests that it may have been a kind of farewell present when Godfrey went to Fontenay.

[53] Ep 74, SBOp 7:181; trans. James 1953, 108: *opuscula mea quae habes.*

the houses of the Clairvaux filiation, or even the wider cistercian family, but had now reached the english Benedictines.

TWO MORE PRE-CANONIZATION IMAGES

There are two known images of Bernard from the period between his death in 1153 and his canonization in 1174. One of them (MA028) is found in the oldest collection of his works, which was compiled at the benedictine abbey of Anchin (Nord, France) in *c.* 1165, little more than a decade after his death—further evidence of the early and widespread dispersion of Bernard's writings even outside the Cistercian Order. The manuscript consists of three volumes and was the work of one hand, the monk Siger, who is represented near the beginning of Bernard's Letters in a large initial *B(ernardus abbas)* and identified by the inscription above, *Suregis,* an anagram of *Sigerus.*[54] Siger is depicted sitting within the initial which he is in the process of drawing. The same manuscript contains another copy of *The Steps of Humility and Pride,* but in a revised version which begins not with the Preface explaining the reason for writing the treatise, as was the case with the Canterbury manuscript, but with a *Retractatio.* This is really an explanatory postscript or *erratum* in which Bernard explains how he had erred by quoting the Bible from memory and included a misquotation of which he had become aware only 'long after I wrote the booklet and it had been copied by many people' (*multo post quam a me idem libellus editus et a pluribus iam transcriptus fuit*)[55]—further evidence from Bernard himself of the early diffusion of his treatise. Strangely to us, although consistent with twelfth-century practice, the *Retractatio* is placed before the Preface and introduces *The Steps of Humility and Pride* with a large miniature in which Bernard is depicted. It extends the full length of the folio, forming the opening initial *I(n hoc opusculo, cum illud de Evangelio, quod Dominus ait, diem ultimi iudicii se nescire, ad aliquam sententiam confirmandam atque roborandam proferrem in medium, improvide quiddam apposui, quod in Evangelio postea deprehendi*): 'In

[54] The dating is given by Leclercq in SBOp 3:XXX. The initial *B(ernardus)* with the image of Siger is on f 4v and is illustrated in Escallier 1852, facing 111.

[55] SBOp 3:15. For this, see Holdsworth 1994, 35.

the course of this little work I have referred in support of one of my opinions to that passage of the Gospels where our Lord says that he does not know the day of the Last Judgment. I quoted, as I thought, the text and then found that it was not in the Gospel at all'[56]

In *The Steps of Humility* Bernard comments on the longest chapter of the Rule.[57] Humility is the monastic virtue par excellence, and the monks' model is Christ. The way to attain truth is by the road of humility by the twelve steps enumerated by Benedict, and the reward at the end of the road is charity. Bernard interprets the Rule in the light of his own experience, but instead of examining what happens on the way up he chooses to travel down the degrees of pride in what has been described as a 'retro-tour of Saint Benedict's steps of humility, with all the fun that seeing things in reverse can bring'.[58]

The large initial in the Anchin manuscript consists of a ladder, the one Jacob saw in a dream stretching from earth to heaven (Gen 28:12), a fragile connection on which the angels of God move up and down, and a reminder that faith is a precarious commitment. Not only is it easy to fall off, but it is only possible to reach the summit one step at a time. In the words of Bernard: 'No one reaches the summit immediately: the top rung of the ladder is grasped by ascending, not by flying'.[59] This accords with the kernel of Benedict's teaching contained in the famous definition of a monastery as 'a school of the Lord's service',[60] heaven being the reward for a long apprenticeship in humility.

The two sides of the ladder—representing the body and the soul—are painted silver, while the twelve rungs—indicating the twelve degrees of humility, the stages on the road to salvation—are gold. The angels on the left are ascending by humility, while those on the right are descending by self-exaltation. The angel on the top right is falling from the highest rung because of his pride. He represents Lucifer, the highest of the fallen angels, to whom the words on the scroll which he holds are always attributed: 'I will place my seat to the north, and I will be like the most high' (Is 14:13-14: *Ponam sedem meam ad aquilonem,*

[56] SBOp 3:15.

[57] Rule 7, trans. McCann 1976, 16–22.

[58] Kline 1992, 169.

[59] *Sermo 1 In natali Sancti Andreae,* SBOp 5:433: *Nemo repente fit summus: ascendendo, non volando apprehenditur summitas scalae.*

[60] Rule Prologue, trans. McCann 1976, 4.

et ero *s[imilis] a[ltissimo]*). The devil at the foot of the ladder has an axe in his right hand; with the other he grabs the hair of a falling angel. At the bottom within the top half of a semi-circle, Jacob is shown awakening. He holds a scroll which reads, 'Truly this is a holy place'. (Gen 28:16: *Vere locus iste sanctus est*). At the top Christ is depicted on a gold ground within the lower half of a semi-circle, symbolizing heaven, the goal to be reached at the summit. He is shown blessing those who, having followed the way, have now reached the Truth. This very benedictine theme occupied a central position in the teaching of Bernard, so it is not unexpected that here Christ is flanked by the half-figures of two monks, Benedict on the left in a brown habit seen writing his Rule, and Bernard on the right in a white habit carrying a book in his right hand and a primitive crozier in his left. The book carried by Bernard is traditionally the Rule, but in this instance it may also represent his own treatise. This is perhaps the most outstanding of all medieval images portraying Bernard. It is not only superb artistically, but is a masterpiece of pictorial theology.

The other pre-canonization image of Bernard also comes from the benedictine scriptorium at Anchin, ▶ *Colour plate* 3 (MA004). Like the previous two images, it is a historiated initial marking the opening of one of Bernard's own works, in this case the letter he wrote to Aelred of Rievaulx, asking him to write down his thoughts on the excellence of charity 'so that we may see in what you write, as if in a mirror, what charity is, how great sweetness there is in the possession of it, how much heaviness and sorrow there is in cupidity which is the contrary of it'.[61] It begins with the same theme of humility as the two previous examples: *E(st quidem sanctorum virtus permaxima humilitas, sed si vera, sed si discreta*): 'The great virtue of the saints is humility, but a sincere and discreet humility'.

Bernard had met Aelred in 1141, when, as a young monk of thirty-two, Aelred had been entrusted by his abbot with leading a mission to Rome in connection with the disputed episcopal election at York. Aelred's abbot was the Englishman William, who had been one of Bernard's

[61] Ep 523, SBOp 8:489 / Aelred of Rievaulx 1971, 3–4; trans. James 1953, 247: . . . *et quid sit caritas, quanta in ea dulcedo, quanta in cupiditate eius contraria sentiatur oppressio, postremo qualis in eius usu sit discretio, in opere tuo quasi in quodam speculo annotare non differas.*

disciples at Clairvaux before being sent back to his own country to found Rievaulx. The strong impression Aelred made on Bernard is revealed in the letter Bernard wrote to the pope in support of Aelred and his companions:

> These men whom you see before you are true, honest, and God-fearing. . . . Let your eyes rest upon these weary and poor men for not without reason have they come to you from afar, undismayed by the great distance, the dangers of the sea, the snows of the Alps and, being poor men, the great expense of such a journey.[62]

Bernard ordered Aelred to write something to assuage the fears of those embarking upon a monastic career. He reveals that Aelred had advanced the customary excuse of unworthiness, stating that he was 'ignorant of grammar . . . almost illiterate' (*minus grammaticum, immo pene illitteratum*)—a wild exaggeration—and that he had 'come to the desert, not from the schools, but from the kitchen' (*qui de coquinis, non de scholis, ad eremum veneris*), a reference to his service as steward at the court of King David of Scotland. Aelred's plea had the opposite of its purported intention. According to Bernard his excuses

> serve rather to inflame than extinguish the spark of my desire, because knowledge that comes from the school of the Holy Spirit rather than the schools of rhetoric will savour all the sweeter to me,

for Aelred would

> be able to strike something out of those rocks that you have not got by your own wits from the bookshelves of the schoolmen, and that you will have experienced sometimes under the

[62] Ep 347; SBOp 8:290; trans. James 1953, 262: *His quos videtis, viri sunt simplices et recti ac timentes Deum. . . . Ponite, quaeso, oculos vestros super fatigatos pauperes, quia non sine causa de longe ad vos veniunt, nec longa terrarum spatia, nec maris periculum, nec Alpium nives, nec sumptus grandis viae, cum pauperes sint, reputantes.*

shade of the tree during the heats of midday what you would never have learned in the schools'[63]

Bernard's wish expresses what was in fact to be Aelred's genius: his ability to draw on his own experience for the benefit of his novices, and, later as abbot, for the whole community in his care.

Bernard acknowledged the humility contained in Aelred's excuse, but he may have harboured the thought he had expressed in a letter to another abbot: 'Barren modesty is not acceptable nor is humility praiseworthy when it is not in accordance with the facts'.[64] To get his way Bernard invoked the primacy of obedience as laid down in the Rule when he asked Aelred, 'Where is the humility in refusing to consent to my wishes?'[65]

As a concession to Aelred's feelings, Bernard ordered that his letter be placed at the beginning of Aelred's work, and he even gave it its title 'so that whatever in the *Mirror of Charity* (for that is the name I give it) should displease the reader shall be imputed to me who have commanded it and not to you who have obeyed by writing it'.[66]

This explains the image of Bernard and the inclusion of his letter in Aelred's *Mirror of Charity,* which he began to write when he was made novicemaster upon his return from Rome and continued after being elected abbot of Rievaulx's daughter-house Revesby in 1143. The treatise was described by his disciple and biographer, Walter Daniel, as 'in my judgment the best of all his works' which 'in three books . . . contains as good a picture of the love of God and one's neighbour as a man

[63] Ep 523, SBOp 8:487; trans. James 1953, 246–247: *qua desiderii mei scintillam augeri potius sentio quam extingui, cum dulcius mihi debeat sapere, si id proferas quod non in cuiuslibet grammatici, sed in schola Spiritus Sancti. . . . aliquid tibi de rupibus illis excuderis, quod sagacitate ingenii de magistrorum scriniis non tulisses, et nonnumquam tale aliquid in meridiano fervore, sub umbris arborum senseris quale numquam didicisses in scholis.*

[64] Ep 201; SBOp 8:60; trans. James 1953, 339: *Nam nec sterilis verecundia grata est, nec humilitas praeter veritatem laudabilis.*

[65] Ep 523, SBOp 8:486; trans. James 1953, 246: *Numquid humilitatis est non acquiescere?*

[66] Ep 523; SBOp 8:488; trans. James 1953, 247: *Ut quidquid in SPECULO CARITATIS—hoc enim libro nomen imponimus—lectori displicuerit, non tibi, qui parueris, sed mihi qui invitum coegerim, imputetur.*

can see of himself in a mirror'.[67] Walter Daniel's assessment is one shared and reiterated by a number of modern Aelred scholars.[68]

Bernard is depicted at the top of the left-hand folio sitting within the golden opening initial, *E(st quidem sanctorum . . .)*, of his letter to Aelred. He has a pastoral staff of the primitive, simple variety in his right hand. In his left hand he has a scroll, presumably with the text of his letter to Aelred, which follows the image. Two fingers of the same hand are raised in blessing. He is tonsured but, as in many early images, his hair is longish at the back, and, in the tradition of the *Vita Prima*, he is lightly bearded. His cowl is light grey with the hood perched at the back of his head, and the tunic below is pale brown. The absence of a halo suggests that the manuscript pre-dates his canonization in 1174.

Bernard is facing right and looking down to the seated figure on the lower, far right half of the far right of the opposite folio, a young man holding a long scroll, identified by the words above his head, *Ailred mo(nachus)*—'the monk Aelred'. He is wearing a white cowl with his tonsured head partially covered by his hood. He is sitting within the initial *V*, the opening words of the treatise's Prologue on humility which echo the beginning of Bernard's letter: *Vere sanctorum vera et discreta humilitas virtus est: mea autem et mei similium defectus virtutis*, 'Genuine and discreet humility is indeed the virtue of the saints whereas mine and that of others like me is a lack of virtue'.[69] Above the initial the words INCIPIT PROLOGUS, with alternate letters in red and green, alerts us that the Prologue to the work follows.

This picture of Aelred, the oldest known of him, is usually featured on its own, while that of Bernard has virtually never been reproduced in spite of its being among the earliest known. Yet the true iconographical significance of the image of Aelred is revealed only when seen in relation to the figure of Bernard at the top of the facing folio. The position of Aelred on the folio is most unusual, but it is crucial to a proper interpretation of the

[67] Powicke 1950, 25–26: *Scripsit eciam tres libros secundum iudicium meum pre omnibus quos scripsit laudabiles, quos vocavit speculum caritatis, eo quod opus illud sic in se contineat imaginem Dei amoris et proximi, sicut in speculo ymaginem considerantis constat peruideri.*

[68] Thus Powicke 1950, LIX: 'The *Speculum Caritatis* is Aelred's finest work'; Squire 1969, 27–28: 'As an introduction to Aelred's talents as a writer . . . nothing more complete exists'; and McGuire 1994, 41: ' The *Mirror of Charity* became the most complete and profound work of Aelred's authorship'.

[69] Aelred of Rievaulx 1971, 5; trans. Connor 1990, 73.

connection between the two images. Only by relegating the three letters following the initial *U* to the following line has the artist been able to achieve the proper balance between this and the facing picture of Bernard. Aelred is facing left, his eyes directed upwards and meeting those of Bernard. Aelred's scroll represents either the letter from Bernard, written above, or his own work which follows. Bernard, in a position of authority as the great abbot of Clairvaux, is looking down on his subordinate, while the young monk whom he is ordering to write a treatise is literally looking up to Bernard in reverence. The juxtaposition of the two figures facing each other perfectly illustrates their relationship.

NINE MORE TWELFTH-CENTURY IMAGES

Nine images of Bernard from the quarter century following his canonization have been recorded: four introducing his biography in manuscripts of the *Vita Prima;* three as illustrations of his own works; and two adorning the pages of service books. The provenance of eight of these is either known for certain or can be reasonably surmised: five are thought to have belonged to cistercian houses and three to benedictine.

The earliest known image of a nimbed Bernard comes from the austrian abbey of Zwettl and is dated 1175–1176, only a year or two after his canonization (MA002). As in a number of other early images (MA023, MA025, MA071, MA164), Bernard's halo is blue. Bernard stands to the left of an initial *T(e igitur)*, the beginning of the Canon of the Mass, before an altar at which he is celebrating Mass. With his head inclined, his thin face and large cranium, a beard and a drooping moustache, the figure shows a distinct similarity to the way he was described by Geoffrey of Auxerre and to the later *Vera Effigies* tradition.[70] He is wearing an alb, a stole, and a simple chasuble. In his left hand he holds a chalice which he blesses with his right hand. The Host lies on the altar. The scene is blessed by the hand of God which comes down from above. The right of the initial *T* is decorated with scrollwork. The other late twelfth-century bernardine image in a service book is found in an antiphonary from a flemish cistercian women's house, the

[70] For this, see Chapter One.

earliest known portrayal of Bernard with nuns and the only one from the twelfth century, ▶ *Fig. 10* (MA035).

Vita Prima *Images*

One of the four late twelfth-century *Vita Prima* miniatures, showing a standing Bernard, adjoins the opening of the Preface to Book One by William of Saint Thierry, ▶ *Fig. 6* (MA026). The text is introduced by a large initial S. Framed by a narrow building with a pitched roof, which resembles a sentry box, Bernard is dressed in eucharistic vestments, an alb, a brown stole, and a blue chasuble with white spots. His halo is brown, he is bearded, and his tonsure is of the variety often found in early images, consisting of a circular shaven patch at the top of the head but with longish hair at the back. In his left hand he holds a crozier of the early design with a simple golden volute separated from the staff by the circular knob and is decorated with brown bands. His right hand is raised in blessing. The text alongside begins with a five-line blue initial *S*(*cripturus vitam servi tui ad honorem nominis tui prout dederis domine deus*): 'It is my aim to write the life of your servant and thereby give honour and praise to your Name'. The manuscript was probably from a cistercian abbey, possibly german or flemish.[71]

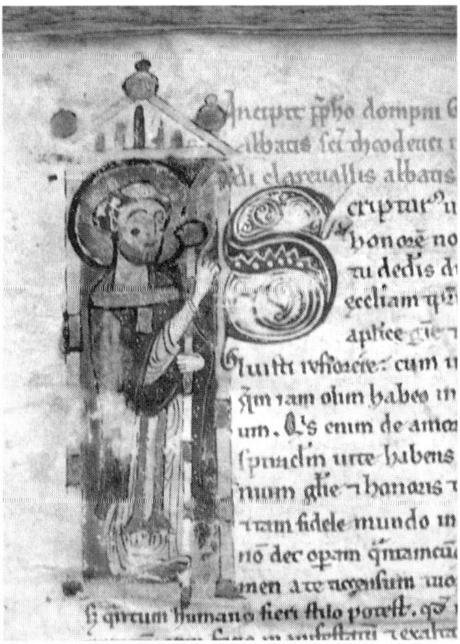

Figure 6

Roughly contemporary with this image is another one from Zwettl which appears in a composite manuscript, dated *c.* 1189, containing the

[71] Morson 1954, 30–34 & 214–221.

Vita Prima (MA001). Here a youthful Bernard is represented in the upper half of the initial *B(ernardus)*—the opening word of Book One, which goes on to announce his birth at Chatillon in Burgundy of illustrious parents. He is again depicted wearing a chasuble. The figure in the lower half of the initial represents the author, William of Saint Thierry, and is the only early medieval 'portrait' of Bernard's great friend and biographer. In another austrian manuscript, a composite which has the *Vita Prima* on folios 40v to 105r—*Vita S. Bernardi abbatis Claraevallensis in V libros* (MA327)—Bernard is again depicted in the upper half of the same opening initial to Book One, but this time alone. It is dated either late twelfth or early thirteenth century. A very large initial *B* in delicate blue and red, covering approximately three-quarters of the height of the folio, has intricate scrollwork within. The clefts in the initial on the right are connected by means of clasps decorated with the motif of five nails, a feature found in a number of early austrian and slovenian manuscripts.[72] The rest of the word (*ernhardus*) in red ink is placed vertically on the side. The three-quarter figure of Bernard in a frontal position is very discreetly included in the upper half of the initial, the inside decoration of which is dominated by the intertwining tendrils. He is nimbed and bearded and has the primitive tonsure with longish hair to the back. He carries a simple crozier in his right hand while his left hand is raised in blessing.

The fourth late twelfth-century *Vita Prima* image (MA119) is the only known medieval miniature to adorn one of the later books and not the Preface or Book One. The opening initial *I(nnumeris)* to Book Three contains an image of a standing monk, tonsured and bearded, in a white cowl who may represent Bernard, but, as he is neither nimbed nor carries a crozier, may equally well be the author, Geoffrey of Auxerre.

Images in Bernard's Works

One of three late twelfth-century images illustrating Bernard's own works appears in a manuscript from the german benedictine abbey of Liesborn and is dated *c.* 1180, only a few years after Bernard's canonization (MA025); it provides further proof of the early dispersion of his writings even outside the Order. Bernard is depicted within the opening initial *V* of Sermon One

[72] For this, see Ziegler 1985–1992, Walliser 1969, Galob 1994.

on the Song of Songs: *Vobis, fratres, alia quam aliis de saeculo, aut certe aliter dicenda sunt:* 'The instructions that I address to you, my brothers, will differ from those I should deliver to people in the world'.[73] The rest of the opening two words (*obis fratres*) is placed vertically alongside the initial *V*. Quoting Saint Paul, Bernard goes on to say that monks should be taught not in the way of philosophy but in the way the Spirit teaches, and that for the spiritually enlightened a more nourishing diet is appropriate, namely, the bread of Solomon's *Song of Songs*. Begun in 1135, Bernard's eighty-six *Sermons,* the last of which remained unfinished when he died on 20 August 1153—creating what Jean Leclercq called his 'unfinished symphony'—are both a theological and literary masterpiece.

The initial *V* at the opening of the text forms a dragon, which, along with images of smaller animals, is contained within a red and blue frame. The swirling bodies leave two circular areas open. In the upper circle the bust of a figure with a blue halo and a simple pastoral staff in his left hand is identified by the inscription above: *Bernhardus abbas*. His right hand holds a curved scroll across his body which reads, *Obedite propositis vestris* ('Obey them that have rule over you', Heb 13:17), a quotation which found its way into three of his works[74] and which, denotes his authority as abbot. The dictate is addressed to six monks gazing at Bernard in awe from within the lower circle, formed by the dragon's tail.

The Sermons were translated into French even before Bernard's canonization, the earliest evidence of the penetration of Bernard's teaching into lay society. An image in the form of an author portrait showing a long-haired Bernard sitting at a desk writing adorns the opening of a French version of Sermon One in a late twelfth-century manuscript (MA040).

The third image of Bernard illustrating his works appears in a late twelfth- or early thirteenth-century manuscript from the cistercian abbey of Kaisheim in Germany (MA020). It contains his well-known treatise *De consideratione,* 'On Consideration'. Consisting of five books, it was addressed to a former disciple at Clairvaux, Bernardo Pignatelli, a native of Pisa who had later returned to Italy to found the abbey of Saint Vincenzo and Saint Anastasio outside Rome and who in 1145 was

[73] SBOp 1.1.3; Bernard of Clairvaux 1971, 1.1.

[74] The three references are: *Sermones de diversis* 92 (SBOp 6/1:348), *Sententiae* 81 (SBOp6/2:118); and Ep. 242 (SBOp 8:129).

elected pope, taking the name Eugene III.[75] This was Bernard's last work and dealt with the duties of a pontiff. He wrote the first book in 1148 and completed the fifth in 1152. In writing to congratulate the new pope, Bernard had already adopted the tone which he was to develop in his *De consideratione*. Although he acknowledged that 'my son Bernard has been promoted to be my father Eugene' (*filius meus Bernardus in patrem meum Eugenium*), he reminded the new pope that it was he who 'begot you in the Gospel' (*per Evangelium te genui*) and that the pope is 'not to be served but to serve' (*non ministrari, sed ministrare venisse*).[76] He goes on to describe the election as God 'raising up the poor man out of the dust, the beggar from his dung-heap to sit among princes and reach the honour of a throne' (*Digitus Dei est iste, suscitans de pulvere egenum et de stercore erigens pauperem, ut sedeat cum principibus et solium gloriae teneat*).[77] As pope, Eugene devoted himself to raising the standard of clerical and monastic observance and he never discarded his cistercian habit or mitigated his monastic lifestyle. Although he had been nurtured by Bernard, as pope he was scrupulous in acting independently.

In a full-page miniature introducing the treatise in the Kaisheim manuscript Eugene is portrayed together with Bernard. It is a pen and ink drawing in brown, green, and red, and contains a good deal of text, some of it on scrolls. In the upper half Mary sits enthroned with the Child—both identified by their names above (*maria* and *Ihesus*)—and they are flanked by two kneeling noblewomen, named benefactresses of Kaisheim. Below them two bearded figures, dressed in robes resembling roman togas and wearing headdresses resembling primitive mitres, are sitting on stools under two round arches supported by columns surmounted by capitals. The two figures are identified by names next to their heads as Eugene, on the left, and Bernard, on the right. Around the arch over Bernard, the legend reads, 'This is Abbot Bernard redolent with the lovely perfume of his works and the rich fragrance of his virtue' (*Hic est Bernardus abbas redolens quasi nardus / Verborum flore vario virtutis odore*). The scroll which he holds proclaims that he is handing his treatise to the pope, "O, Eugene, as pope you are a father and not a son, receive this writing and listen to an old man' (*Mi pater Eugeni quia*

[75] SBOp 3:393-493.
[76] Mt 20:28 & Mk 10:45.
[77] Ep 238; SBOp 8:116; trans. James 1953, 277.

papa sed ordine fili / Auscultando seni suscipe vota stili). The legend above Eugene reads, 'Here is the chief prince of the Church yet a pupil of Clairvaux who, listening intently, takes in what Bernard is writing to him' (*Hic presul summus sed clarevallis alumnus / Aure patente bibit que Bernhardus sibi scribit*). The scroll held by Eugene proclaims, 'Wonderful harpist of the Holy Spirit singing songs of wisdom, I drink attentively from the pleasing goblet of your words' (*Pneumatis egregie cytharista fluenta sophye / Aure bibo vigili pocula grata stili*).[78]

The Kaisheim drawing, although artistically highly accomplished, is rare in its complexity for a work from a cistercian scriptorium. The representation of Bernard is most unusual in that he is not shown with any of his traditional attributes. He does not appear in the distinctive monastic cowl, he is not nimbed, and he does not carry a crozier or a book. He is not normally depicted wearing a headdress except occasionally a simple skullcap or, very occasionally in later representations, a mitre. Nor is Eugene portrayed in the way usual for a pope and is not wearing a primitive tiara. They are both seated on stools at the same level, which does not suggest the difference in status between pope and abbot. We are able to identify Bernard and Eugene only by the text on the scrolls and by the placement of the image at the opening of the treatise Bernard wrote for the pope.

SUMMARY OBSERVATIONS

A close look at the twelfth-century portrayals of Bernard has revealed a number of peculiarities compared with later images. First, although he is depicted carrying a book (the Rule) in some twenty-eight percent of the images recorded, this abbatial attribute is included in only one of the early images, the large initial *I* at the opening of *The Steps of Humility* (MA028), and there the book is as likely to represent Bernard's treatise as the Rule. Although the crozier, the other abbatial attribute, is featured in several of the early images (MA004, MA025, MA026, MA028, MA327), the book appears only in the thirteenth century (MA346), with the one exception mentioned above. The reason for this may be that its inclusion seemed less appropriate when he is engaged in writing or celebrating Mass than when he is merely shown as a single standing figure.

[78] The text of the scrolls is given in Leclercq 1953, 43–44.

The absence of the book may also, however, be connected with the second peculiarity of the early images: the abnormally large number of instances in which one of Bernard's hands is raised in blessing (MA001, MA002, MA004), a convention by which artists symbolized Bernard's solicitude for his monks. This occurs even in the *Vita Prima* image of him as a standing figure, ▶ *Fig. 6* (MA026).

Third, Bernard is depicted wearing eucharistic vestments in three of the images (MA001, MA002, MA026), an unusually large number considering that he is only portrayed in this way in twenty-nine out of the nine hundred sixty recorded images. It testifies to the importance the early Cistercians attached to the exercise of abbatial authority through priesthood. Among their duties the *Ecclesiastica Officia* or *Usages* listed celebrating Mass on all major feast days and hearing the monks' confessions, both of which required priestly ordination.[79]

Fourth, and paradoxically, none of the three earliest images of Bernard (MA004, MA006, MA028) were of cistercian origin but were produced in benedictine scriptoria. Five of the nine further images from the last quarter of the twelfth century were likewise not cistercian; two of them were benedictine (MA025, MA327), one premonstratensian (MA119), and two of unknown provenance. This is consistent with what we know of Bernard's attitude to art in a monastic context. His celebrated diatribe in his *Apology* to William of Saint Thierry against 'a fantastic conglomeration of beauty misbegotten and ugliness transmogrified',[80] has traditionally been seen as addressed to the abbey of Cluny in particular and to refer to what he considered the excesses of its cloister carvings. Conrad Rudolph[81] argues, however, that it was also aimed at the exuberance of the Cîteaux manuscript illuminations created under Bernard's former abbot, Stephen Harding and represented by his magnificent Bible and *Moralia in Job* manuscripts.[82] Bernard regarded all types of decoration as extravagant and distracting, and therefore inappropriate for monks. That he was against the admission of the decorative arts into the monastery is beyond doubt, but this does not mean that he was the enemy of art, as he has sometimes been portrayed, or an iconoclast. He is, for example, known to have pos-

[79] *Ecclesiastica Officia* 110, Griesser 1956, 270.

[80] *Apologia* 29, SBOp 3:106: *mira quaedam deformis formositas ac formosa deformitas?*; Matarasso 1993, 57; CF 1:66.

[81] Rudolph 1990.

[82] Dijon, MSS 15, 168–170 & 173.

sessed a lavishly illuminated Bible (admittedly not produced at Clairvaux, but a gift),[83] and, above all, it was he who, most unusually, chose to be represented by his own image in his second seal (▶ *Fig.* 5).

When Stephen Harding died, he was succeeded, after a short interregnum, by Raynard de Bar (1134/5–1150). He was a monk of Clairvaux and one of Bernard's disciples, and Bernard was now able to extend to Cîteaux the policy of restraint which he had enforced at Clairvaux. Under Bernard's influence, geometric patterns and interlace, sometimes accompanied by simple vegetative designs, became the decorative norm for which the Cistercians became famous. Austerity was applied equally to the carvings of corbels and capitals, to the Order's distinctive grisaille glass, and to the modest initials which adorned their manuscripts. Capitular regulations included one in the Instituta dealing with manuscript illumination and stained glass:

> Of [initial] letters and glass windows. [Initial] letters are to be of one colour, and without pictorial representation. Glass windows are to be clear, without crosses and pictures.[84]

This forms part of a series of statutes significantly edited by Raynard le Bar, which has been dated to *c.* 1147.[85] For some decades cistercian manuscripts were noted for a soberness and lack of decoration conforming to bernardine ideals, but in the long run the appeal of representations of the human form was too great and the legislation became a dead letter. Cistercian manuscript illumination became indistinguishable from what could be found elsewhere. The earliest known examples of a deviation from the cistercian ideal of simplicity come, significantly, from abbeys far removed from the burgundian cradle lands of the Order, from Zwettl and Heiligenkreuz in Austria, and from Stična in Slovenia. The earliest of all is the Zwettl Missal from 1175–1176 (MA002).[86] Paradoxically, the initial success in enforcing the bernardine policy of austerity in book illumination explains the earlier appearance of images of Bernard in benedictine than in cistercian manuscripts.

[83] For this and other examples of illumination at Clairvaux, see Dodwell 1954, 109.

[84] Waddell 1999, 491: *De litteris et vitreis. Litterae unius coloris fiant, et non depictae. Vitreae albae fiant, et sine crucibus et picturis.*

[85] Waddell 1999, 453. For legislation on art and architecture, see Norton 1986, 315–393.

[86] See Ziegler 1985–1992, Walliser 1969, and Galob 1994.

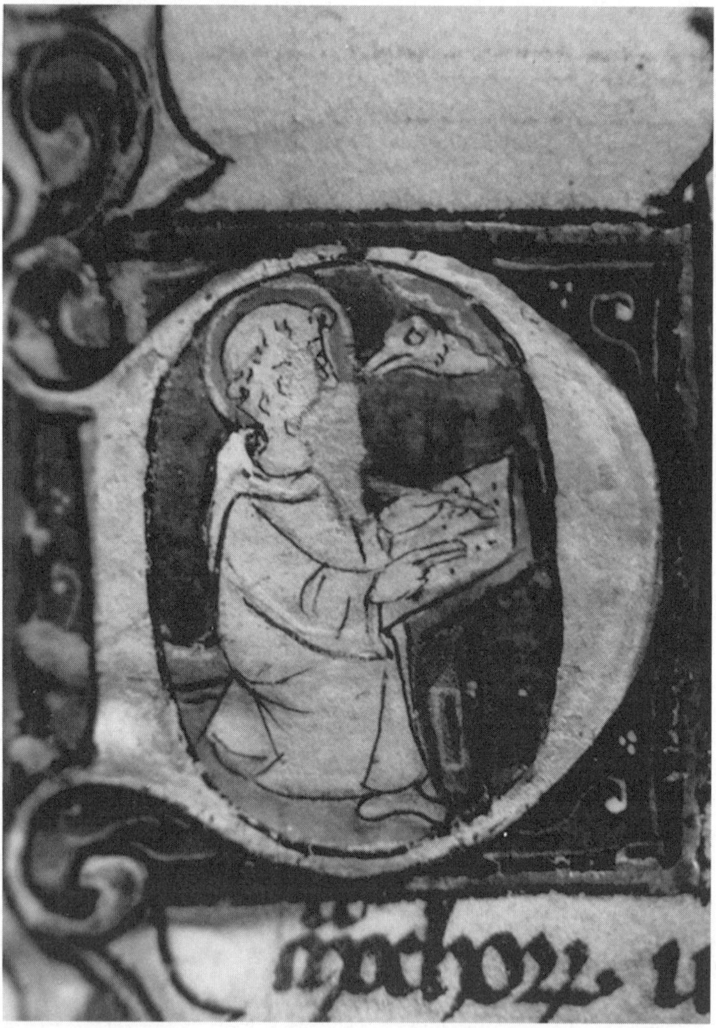

Figure 7: Bernard writing under the inspiration of the Holy Spirit, from a thirteenth-century french manuscript (MA051).

FOUR

IMAGES OF BERNARD: MONK AND ABBOT

AS MONK

WHEN BERNARD ENTERED CÎTEAUX with his uncle, his brothers, his cousins and his friends—'more than thirty companions' (*cum sociis amplius quam triginta*)—he 'submitted his neck to the gentle yoke of Christ, under the Abbot Stephen' (*sub abbate Stephano, suavi jugo Christi collum submisit*).[1] His whole life until that moment had, according to William of Saint Thierry, been a preparation for this: his mother's vision that he would become a guardian of God's house, her insistence on nursing him and his brothers and sister at her own breasts, the way she gave them a diet more suited to hermits in the desert than to noblemen in their palace, his education with the canons, and, finally, the quasi-monastic communal life he and his companions lived for six months at Châtillon before entering Cîteaux. In the best tradition of medieval hagiography Bernard seemed to have been predestined for the monastic life, and yet it was only upon his *conversio*—his entry into religious life—that God bestowed on him the grace reserved for

[1] VP 1.4.19; PL 185:237.

those who live in God's house and which enabled him to 'live an angelic life on earth' (*vitam angelicum gerens in terris vixit*).[2]

There are a number of iconographical examples of this pivotal event in his life. Among them is an early fourteenth-century miniature in the vernacular exemplum collection known from the opening words as *Ci nous dit;* this has a scene on the left of a nimbed Bernard accompanied by a monk being received by Stephen Harding who stands at the gate of Cîteaux; the right of the miniature has an unrelated *Lactatio* image (MA042). Other illustrations of this important moment include one of the glass panels from the Altenberg cloister (GL07), and one of the eight scenes in the altarpiece painted in 1500 by Jörg Breu for the austrian abbey of Zwettl (PA039). After the year as a novice prescribed by the Rule, Bernard made his vows of stability, conversion of manners, and obedience, and was clothed in the monastic habit.[3] The scene is depicted in a late fifteenth-century manuscript of the *Speculum Historiale* (MA089) and in one of the panels of the Neuberg altarpiece painted in 1518 (PA098).

Even as a novice Bernard was said never to spare himself any hardship. In later years his advice to those who were impatient to enter the monastery was:

> If you are in a hurry to come to what lies within, before you enter you must leave outside the bodies which you have brought from the world, for only hearts and minds may come in, since the flesh will not help you.[4]

And yet, most unusually, one of the few stories from the brief period Bernard spent as a novice tells of an occasion when he failed to live up to the high standard he had set for himself. William of Saint Thierry reveals that Bernard was reprimanded by his abbot—a rare example of a hagiographer portraying a saint as less than perfect.[5] He had failed, once, to recite the seven penitential psalms he had promised to say daily after Compline for the repose of the soul of his mother. His

[2] *Ibid.*

[3] Rule 58; trans. McCann 1976, 62–64.

[4] VP 1.4.20; PL 185:238: *'Si ad ea quae intus sunt festinatis, hic foris dimittite corpora quae de saeculo attulistis: soli spiritus ingrediantur, caro non prodest quidquam'.*

[5] VP 1.4.19-20; PL 185:237-238.

youthful negligence was noted by Stephen Harding, who rebuked him, and Bernard, confessing his transgression, threw himself at Stephen's feet. The event is featured in a glass panel from Altenberg which contains three scenes in which the story unfurls in three episodes—an old device in narrative iconography in which the unfolding of time is handled by a sequence in which the chief character reappears in a succession of scenes (GL08). As in a number of Altenberg panels, the viewers' ability to understand the story is aided by the inclusion of scrolls with text as well as an abbreviated version of the whole story at the foot of the panel. In this medieval forerunner to the strip cartoon, scrolls or banderoles take the place of modern 'bubbles'. In the middle, Bernard is seen praying in a distant dark church before the Blessed Sacrament. The banderole, which cites Psalm 6:1, reads 'O Lord, do not reprove me in your anger' (*Domine, ne in furore tuo . . .*), tells us that he is reciting one of the penitential psalms for his mother. On the left of the panel he is sitting with a closed psalter on his knee. Above him, the scroll reads, 'O Bernard, O Bernard, for what have you come?' (*Bernarde, Bernarde, ad quid venisti?*), words he often addressed to himself as a spur to steadfastness.[6] A fellow monk looks at him, his left hand over his breast indicating his inability to help. On the right we see the climatic moment when Stephen asks him, 'Brother Bernard, what are you doing leaving aside those psalms you should have said today, or whom have you delegated to say them?' (*Frater Bernarde, ubinam quaeso illos psalmos tuos hesterna die dimisisti? Aut cui eos commendasti?*). Bernard kneels down before his abbot, his hands over his face in shame, begging for pardon. He exclaims, 'O Lord, my God, how has this matter come out in the open which was known to my conscience alone?' (*Domine Deus, quomodo palam factum est verbum istud, de quo mihi soli conscius eram?*).

The same story is depicted very differently as a single scene in one of the panels from the cloister of the nuns' abbey of Saint Apern in Cologne (GL60). In this Bernard is shown being reprimanded publicly in the presence of six other novices. The scene is anachronistic in that novices at the time did not have their own habit but wore secular clothing, as may be seen in the famous picture in the Cîteaux *Moralia in Job*

[6] VP 1.4.19; PL 185:237.

manuscript which shows a young nobleman novice at the top of a tree that is about to be felled by one of the monks.[7]

Only from the second half of the twelfth century—that is, from the earliest known redaction of the Ecclesiastica Officia in which cistercian daily life was regulated in the minutest detail—were novices required to wear 'the same habit as the monks except for what is the special monastic item',[8] in other words, except for the cowl. Thereafter, instead of the cowl they wore a sleeveless mantle with hood or pelisse (*cappam et mantellam vel pelles habeat*) which was normally white, the same as the cowl. That is how the late medieval artist chose to represent the novices in the Saint Apern glass. They are shown wearing sleeveless mantles while Stephen, sitting in the centre of what looks like the chapter house, wears the monastic cowl. Stephen's gaze is directed at Bernard who in his embarrassment is looking down. Significantly, although Stephen is the central figure depicted in a position of authority, he is not nimbed while Bernard is. Although the design, colouring, and size of the Altenberg and Saint Apern panels are very similar, their composition is quite different, and indicates the input of the commissioning monastery and of the different briefs given to the glaziers.

AS ABBOT

After his profession Bernard was a simple monk of Cîteaux for little more than a year. Not surprisingly, there is no pictorial record of this period. His appointment by Stephen as abbot of the new monastery of Clairvaux in Champagne at the young age of twenty-five is, however, represented by another Altenberg panel which shows him being handed the crozier as a symbol of his authority (GL10). It is as abbot that Bernard is depicted in the majority of the recorded images: wearing the monastic cowl and carrying the pastoral staff and often also a book representing the Rule.

The manner in which he discharged his abbatial duties was almost totally ignored by his biographers. Only a few stories show him as abbot, in contrast to the lively way in which Walter Daniel describes

[7] Illustrated in France 1998, ill. 45.

[8] *Ecclesiastica Officia* Chapter 102; Griesser 1956, 264: *hisdem pannis induatur excepto habitu monachili. . . .*

what life was like at Rievaulx under Aelred and the way he dealt with his monks. In Bernard's *Life* there is nothing to compare with the story of how twenty or thirty monks at a time would gather round Aelred's bed in the hut built for him during his illness and how they 'walked and lay about his bed and talked with him as a little child prattles with its mother. . . . He did not treat them with the pedantic imbecility habitual in some silly abbots'.[9]

By contrast, William of Saint Thierry, a great friend of Bernard and the author of the first book of the *Vita Prima,* says surprisingly little about what life was like under him as abbot. He has plenty to say about Bernard's interior life, his mortification of the senses, his asceticism, his frail health and his problem with manual labour, and he writes as well of their time together at Clairvaux in what he refers to as its 'golden age'.[10] William tells us that 'when free from such work or toil, Bernard was inevitably at prayer or at reading or at meditation',[11] and only rarely does he let us see the abbot interacting with his monks. On the other hand, he does emphasize Bernard's exceptional ability to attract recruits, evidence of which is corroborated by the number of colonies of monks sent out from Clairvaux to establish new monasteries within a few years of its foundation, and the information contained in the *Exordium Magnum* that there was at one time ninety novices at Clairvaux.[12] The bright future that lay before them, William records, had been revealed to Bernard in a vision when

> suddenly he saw all around him, coming down from the neighbouring hillsides to the valley below, a multitude of people: variously garbed, of varied walks of life, and so numerous too that the whole valley could not contain them.[13]

The vision is illustrated in one of the Altenberg panels (GL11).

[9] Powicke 1950, 40.

[10] VP 1.4.20-34; PL 185:238-241. VP 1.7.33-35; PL 185:246-248: . . . *Clarae-Vallis aurea saecula. . . .*

[11] VP 1.4.24; PL 185:241: *Feriatus autem ab hujusmodi labore vel opere, jugiter aut orabat, aut legebat, aut meditabatur.*

[12] EM 6.10; Griesser 1961, 366.

[13] VP 1:5:26 (PL 185:242): *vidit undique ex vicinis montibus tantam diversi habitus et diversae conditionis hominum multitudinem in inferiorem vallem descendere, ut vallis ipsa capere non posset.*

William also provided an example of Bernard's amazing ability to attract swarms of converts: a group of knights once called at the abbey on their way to a tournament. It being then close to Lent Bernard begged them to lay down their arms, but they refused. Bernard summoned a monk to bring some beer, which he blessed before offering it to them. They were at first reluctant to drink, fearing the effect the power of God might have on them, but they gave in. Shortly after leaving, they talked among themselves and all turned back to offer themselves 'for the knighthood of the Spirit'.[14] Some of them, William wrote, are still serving while others have gone to their rest.

The episode is depicted in a painting from the german nuns' abbey of Günterstal (PA018). It shows Bernard on the right in a black cowl carrying a crozier. He is identified by his name inscribed in his halo and the arms of Clairvaux at his feet. With his right hand he blesses the beer which is held in one hand by a dismounted knight who in the other holds his feathered cap. A monk in a white cowl with his hood over his head stands behind Bernard in a doorway, holding a large jug of beer. A scroll by Bernard announces in old German *Trincken das drauff eiuer selen heil* ('Drink this up that your souls may be healed'); and that over the knight reads: *Lob und er sagen wier heiliger vatter von dier* ('Praise and honour we pay to thee, O Holy Father'). The inscription in Latin at the bottom reads: *Anno domini 1506 facta e[st] hec tabu[la] a venerabili[ssima] do[mi]na agnes de tissli[n]ge[n] minima abbatissa huius monastery* ('in the year of Our Lord 1506 this panel was made by the most venerable Lady Agnes von Tusslingen, unworthy abbess of this monastery'). The story found its way into the *Legenda Aurea,* but there the knights have become students, and, adjusting the story to his italian readers, James of Voragine has changed the beer to wine.[15]

Concomitant with stories of recruitment are those which reveal Bernard's solicitude for the perseverance of his monks. On one occasion Bernard lent money to a monk who in his previous life had been a gambler and had decided to return to the world, knowing that both he and the monk would lose the money but that at the same time it would ensure his return to the monastery (GL39, VA04). The letter Bernard wrote to his relative Robert, who had left Clairvaux for Cluny, seethes with Bernard's passion

[14] VP 1.11.55; PL 185:257: *spirituali militiae. . . .*
[15] LA 220.

to draw him back from an easier life.[16] William of Saint Thierry records a miraculous event surrounding its writing. To ensure privacy Bernard decided to take his secretary, William, later abbot of Rievaulx, outside to dictate the letter. Rain began to pour down and the scribe wanted to stop, but Bernard ordered him to continue. Neither the letter nor the monks got wet, for, as William of Saint Thierry put it, 'charity dictated the letter and charity conserved the text'.[17] As a result of this miracle this letter was ranked first in the volume of Bernard's collected letters. The scene is depicted within the initial *B(ernardus)* at the opening of the chapter on Bernard in a manuscript of the *Legenda Aurea* from 1446 (MA142). The figure on the left, wearing a cap, is writing and must therefore be Bernard's secretary while the smaller figure on the right with his hood over his head must be Bernard. The difference in scale is unusual in that Bernard is depicted as smaller than one of his monks; this suggests a mistake by the artist. The remoteness of the scene is indicated by the rocks in the background. The initial is decorated with acanthus leaves.

Although William of Saint Thierry provides little anecdotal material of how Bernard related to his monks, Bernard's primary task of ensuring the salvation of those for whom he was responsible is well documented by two stories. One tells of a wretched monk who, a few days after he died, appeared to Bernard, who detected the torment he was suffering on account of his lack of compassion in life. Bernard prayed for him incessantly for several days, joined by a number of brothers he knew to be particularly holy, until it was revealed to him that the monk had been freed.[18] The other tells of a monk whom Bernard had barred from receiving Communion but who, fearing on a major feast day that he would be noticed, nevertheless went up to Bernard to receive the host.[19] Bernard did not refuse him the host, but the monk was unable to swallow it and, trembling with anxiety, kept it in his mouth. He was forced to reveal his plight to Bernard who reproved him and gave him absolution; from then on he had no trouble receiving the Sacrament.

Book 2 of the *Vita Prima,* written by the benedictine abbot Arnold of Bonneval, is devoted entirely to events outside Clairvaux and largely

[16] Ep 1; SBOp 7:1-11.
[17] VP 1.11.50; PL 185:255.
[18] VP 1.10.46; PL 185:253-254.
[19] VP 1.11.51; PL 185:256.

to Bernard's involvement in the papal schism between 1130 and 1138. It tells us nothing about life at Clairvaux or Bernard as abbot. Geoffrey of Auxerre, Bernard's secretary who wrote Books 3 to 5 of the Vita Prima, knew him better than anyone and recorded a far larger number of miraculous episodes than did the two other biographers and yet he too has little to say about Bernard as abbot. He followed Bernard on his travels around Europe and describes many events which occurred outside Clairvaux. It has been observed that eighty percent of the very much larger number of Bernard's miracles recorded by Geoffrey than by the other two biographers took place away from Clairvaux.[20]

The *Exordium Magnum* written by Conrad of Eberbach near the end of the twelfth century is more revealing of Bernard's relations with his monks than is the earlier *Vita Prima*. Here again, the way Bernard enlisted new members for the community is illustrated by the story of a convicted prisoner whose reprieve Bernard obtained so that he might join him at Clairvaux and thus transform himself 'from wolf to lamb, from robber to lay brother' (GL20).[21] Of all the stories that deal with Bernard the abbot, the most poignant is perhaps the one about a monk who had lost his faith in the Real Presence. Found only in the *Exordium Magnum*,.[22] it forms a parallel to the eucharistic story told by William of Saint Thierry. In one of the Altenberg glass panels this monk is shown on the left in a double scene, being brought before Bernard by two of his fellow monks (GL14). In the text above him he expresses his lack of faith: 'No statement can induce me to believe that the bread and wine on the altar are the true body and blood of Christ, and for that reason I know that I shall go to hell' (*Ego nullis assertionibus ad hoc potero induci, ut panem et vinum, quae in altari proponuntur, credam verum esse corpus et sanguinem Christi, et propterea scio me in infernum descensurum*). Instead of condemning him, Bernard ordered him in the name of obedience to receive the Sacrament on Bernard's own faith. Bernard's scroll reads: 'The piety of Clairvaux descend to hell? God forbid! If you do not have faith, I order you, on the strength of obedience, to receive Communion on my faith!' (*Pietas e Clarevalle in in-*

[20] Holdsworth 1990, 89.

[21] EM 2.15; Griesser 1961, 109: *de lupo faciens agnum, de latrone conversum.*

[22] EM 2.6; Griesser 1961, 102: *De monacho, quem Sacramentis Altaris fidem non adhibentem iussit Pater Sanctus communicare fide sua.*

fernum descendet? Absit! Si tu fidem non habes, per virtutem obedientie precipio tibi: vade, communica fide mea!). In other words, if you go to hell, then 'the *pietas* of Clairvaux goes to hell', which is anathema. On the right the monk is seen receiving Communion from Bernard. The story demonstrates the lengths to which Bernard would go to secure the salvation of his monks.

These few examples of iconographic portrayal of the way Bernard functioned as abbot match the scantiness of the literary material. There are, however, many images of him portrayed as a writer of texts intended primarily for the benefit of his monks and as a teacher who used a number of these texts in preaching to them. William of Saint Thierry pays tribute to Bernard's powers of teaching and preaching when he says that

> full of that Spirit by whom all Scripture was divinely inspired, he has been doing what the Apostle says, making confident, practical, daily use of its pages for teaching, for convincing, for reproach. And so when he preaches the Word of God, he makes every text he propounds so understandable and enjoyable, so forceful and moving, that anyone of any learning, be it worldly learning or spiritual, is in wonderment at the words of grace proceeding from his mouth.[23]

In this way Bernard followed the precept of Saint Benedict that the abbot be 'learned in the divine law, so that he may have a treasure of knowledge whence he may bring forth things new and old'.[24] There is quite a large number of images which show Bernard in his role of writer/teacher/preacher, many of them chosen to illustrate manuscripts of his works.

AS WRITER

The way in which Bernard influenced the course of events by his writings is encapsulated in one of the Altenberg glass panels, the only scene which is not based on any of the literary sources (GL56). Here, standing

[23] VP 1.24; PL 185:240.

[24] Rule, Chapter 64; trans. McCann 1976, 71.

at the centre behind a table on which are a number of his books, sermons, and letters, Bernard is acknowledged as the great writer. Among the books his *De gratia et libero arbitrio* (On Grace and Free Will) and a volume of sermons may be identified, and on the right a kneeling Templar carries a copy of his *De laude novae militiae ad milites templi* (In Praise of the New Knighthood). On the shelf below the table a volume of his Letters may be seen. Bernard is surrounded by the recipients, first and foremost Pope Eugene III, a former disciple from Clairvaux, to whom he is handing his treatise *De consideratione* (On Consideration). There too are his cousin Godfrey, for him he wrote *The Steps of Humility;* and William of Saint Thierry,[25] for whom he wrote the *Apologia* and to whom he also dedicated the *On Grace and Free Will;* Cardinal Haimeric, Chancellor of the Roman Church, to whom he addressed *De diligendo deo* (On the Love of God), the Templars with their treatise; the Benedictines of Chartres with *De praecepto et dispensatione* (On Precept and Dispensation), and Irish monks with a *Life of Saint Malachy.* A scroll above Bernard's head has him saying to the pope 'Expel simony from the Church' (*Expelle symoniam de Ecclesia*), to which the pope's reply on another scroll is, 'Expel listlessness from the Cloister' (*Expelle tu inertiam de Claustro*). The inscription below the scene reads 'He wrote many books, sermons, and three hundred fifty letters, to four popes, cardinals, bishops, kings, princes, and many others' (*Scripsit multos Libros, Sermones et Epistolas CCCL, ad quattuor summos Pontifices, Cardinales, Episcopos, Reges, Principes, Abbates et plures alios*).

Some of the earliest images of Bernard, as we mentioned above, are based on the traditional way of depicting the evangelists, which in turn derives from late antique author portraits. He is shown in profile sitting at a desk writing with a pen in his right hand and a knife in the left. This is how he is portrayed in the earliest known image, the manuscript of *The Steps of Humility* from Canterbury (MA006) and in the late twelfth-century translation of his Sermons into the vernacular (MA040). Eight of the eleven known images of Bernard writing, up to the beginning of the fifteenth century, appear in manuscripts of his own works. This indicates that author portraits were one of the conventional ways of decorating manuscripts. None of the fifteenth and sixteenth century

[25] The abbot supposedly represents William of Saint Thierry, who was at the time of the writing a benedictine abbot and he was never a cistercian abbot.

images of Bernard writing, however, are author portraits. The majority of them are *Doctrina* images indicating that the skill of writing was transmitted to Bernard in a vision by the Virgin.[26]

In the later Middle Ages Bernard was sometimes portrayed much in the same way as Jerome, that is, as the prolific writer enclosed in his study, concentrating on his work and surrounded by his books. This is how he is shown in a manuscript, dated 1455, of the *Speculum Historiale* by Vincent of Beauvais, in which the miniature illustrates the section in which Bernard's works are listed (MA196). A similar scene is depicted in another manuscript of the *Speculum Historiale* from the late fourteenth century (MA260). A nimbed Bernard wearing a cap is sitting on a high-backed chair writing in a book on his lap. The number of books lying on a tall desk in the middle of the room and six further volumes seen on a high shelf in the background attest to Bernard's great literary output. He is identified by the inscription above his head, *s.bernard*, in the same way as he is in another miniature in the same manuscript which shows Bernard and his brothers being received at Cîteaux by Stephen Harding (MA089).

Although the majority of early bernardine manuscripts were decorated with author portraits, Bernard is portrayed in other ways in a great number of the seventy-five recorded miniatures decorating his works. Some show him writing under the inspiration of the Holy Spirit. A french manuscript of unknown provenance from the second half of the thirteenth century contains the Rule of Saint Benedict and Bernard's 'On Precept and Dispensation' (*De praecepto et dispensacione*), his commentary on the Rule. At the opening of Bernard's treatise there is a diminutive historiated initial *D(omino abbati Columbensi)*.[27] The letter contains the nimbed and tonsured figure of Bernard in a white cowl, ▶ *Fig. 7* (MA051). He is sitting at a desk on which is an open book in which he is writing. He has a pen in his right hand and a knife in his left. Close to his face is the beak of a white bird, as if feeding him the words which he is writing down. In the iconography of the saints the dove was the attribute of the Evangelists and the Doctors of the Church, especially Saint Gregory the Great, into whose ear the Paraclete spoke. By this device Bernard was represented as a new Evangelist and associated him

[26] See Chapter Nine.
[27] SBOp 3:253.

with the Fathers with whose teaching he was imbued and 'the last' of whom he himself became.[28] The source of the image may also be sought in William of Saint Thierry's description of Bernard's charisms, which included those of wisdom and knowledge, which William drew from Saint Paul's famous reference to the gifts of the Spirit.[29]

Bernard is again portrayed as writing under divine inspiration in an english manuscript dated the third quarter of the thirteenth century. In addition to five bernardine images illustrating his *De consideratione,* it has a sixth image of him at the opening of the text headed *Bernardus super cantica* in red ink (MA288). In fact, what follows turns out to be an introduction to Origen's First Homily on the Song of Songs, which begins with the initial *S(icut* [normally given as *Quomodo*] *didicimus per Moysen esse quaedam non solum sancta, sed et 'sancta sanctorum', et alia non tantum sabbata, sed et 'sabbata sabbatorum', sic nunc quoque docemur scribente Solomone esse quaedam non solum cantica, sed et 'cantica canticorum'):* 'As we have learned from Moses that some places are not merely holy, but holy of holies, and that certain days are not sabbaths simply, but are sabbaths of sabbaths; so now we are taught further by the pen of Solomon that there are songs which are not merely songs, but SONGS OF SONGS'.[30] This is one of many examples of the writings of others being ascribed to Bernard, and of the attribution being responsible for the artists' choice of subject. The 'author' portrait here has a bearded Bernard in a white cowl seated at a desk writing on a long length of parchment, a pen in his right hand and a knife in his left. In front of his face is a dove representing the Holy Spirit inspiring his writing.

The theme of divine inspiration is not confined to manuscripts of Bernard's works but also appears in a Gradual from the second quarter of the fourteenth century. Written in the cistercian scriptorium of Settimo in Florence by the monk Vincentio Monoculo, it is decorated with many miniatures of saints. The folio containing the Introit for Bernard's feast shows a decorated initial *I(n medio ecclesie*); an image of Saint John Evangelist is next to it, and beneath it a circular medallion within which Bernard is seated, enclosed in a round chair, writing on a piece of parchment with a pen in his right hand and a knife in his left (MA265).

[28] Réau 1955–1959, 3:2:610. Kirschbaum & Braunfels 1968–1976, 6:432.
[29] VP 1.8.42; PL 185:252, referring to 1 Corinthians 12:7-11.
[30] Origen, Homily 1 on the Song of Songs; Sources Chrétiennes 37:64.

The Holy Spirit in the form of a small white dove hovers close to his face, dictating what he is to write down.

Divine guidance and inspiration in Bernard's writing was also suggested by showing the blessing hand of God coming out of a cloud from heaven. An example of this is found in a large, almost full-page, miniature in an early thirteenth-century manuscript of *Flores Bernardi,* a florilegium containing extracts from Bernard's works, which comes from the benedictine scriptorium of Saint Augustine's, Canterbury (MA044). In blue, green, and red pen and ink a tonsured and bearded Bernard with a large cranium, reminiscent of the *Vera Effigies,* is portrayed seated on a high chair at a lectern, writing in a book in the characteristic medieval way, that is, holding a pen in his right hand and a knife in his left. He does not hold his crozier which leans against his seat. It has been included as one of the attributes whereby he is identified. Two smaller monk-pupils, one of them looking up and the other reading from an open book he holds in both hands, are seated at Bernard's feet. Their smaller scale indicates their importance relative to the saint. Divine approval and the imparting of grace are indicated by the presence in the upper right hand corner, not of the dove but of the hand of God.

Another way artists denoted Bernard's authorship was by portraying him pointing to the text, thereby claiming it as his work. An example of this is found in a late thirteenth-century manuscript of Bernard's *Sermons,* ▶ *Colour plate 4* (MA319), from the polish abbey of Bledzow, founded in 1282 from Dobrilugk. The standing figure of a bearded Bernard with the hood of his dark grey cowl over his head is depicted within the initial *C(onsidero laborem)* at the beginning of the Prologue of his *Sermon on Psalm 90 Qui habitat,* as expressed by the text in red at the head of the folio. Bernard's right hand is lifted up, pointing to a scroll within the initial which has the opening words of the psalm *Qui habitat in adjutorio altissimi* ('He who dwells in the secret place of the most High').[31] Bernard's white tunic shows under the grey cowl. Above the miniature he is identified by the inscription in red ink *Sanctus Bernhardus.* By contrast, in a manuscript from the third quarter of the fifteenth century which belonged to the regular canons at Utrecht (MA224), Bernard is depicted as a three-quarter length figure in a grey

[31] Quoted at the beginning of the sermons in SBOp 4:383.

cowl and with a crozier in his right hand and a book in his left within the same initial *C(onsidero laborem)*.

The device of having a figure point to the text to suggest authorship is also found in a late fourteenth-century italian manuscript of the *De consideratione* (MA245). A fine drawing in brown ink of a half-figure of Bernard in profile is contained within the rosa opening initial, against a blue background, *S(ubit animum dictare aliquid, quod te, Papa beatissime Eugeni, vel aedificet, vel delectet, vel consoletur)*: 'It has occurred to me to write something which might edify, delight or console you, Blessed Father Eugene',[32] the opening words of the Preface to *De consideratione*. Bernard's right hand is raised with the index finger pointing to the text he wrote for his old disciple from Clairvaux who was elected pope in February 1145 and remained in office until his death on 8 July 1153, a few months before Bernard himself died. This treatise in five books written over four to five years is Bernard's last work. Part of it was sufficiently advanced by 1149 to allow Nicholas of Clairvaux to refer to it in a letter to Peter the Venerable, but it was only finished shortly before Bernard's death.[33]

Although written for Eugene III, *De consideratione* was much prized by many of his successors, even down to modern times. Pope John XXIII used to have it read to him at mealtimes and commented that

> nothing more suitable and useful for a poor pope like myself, and for any pope at any time. Certain things which did not redound to the honour of the Roman clergy in the twelfth century still survive to-day. Therefore 'one must watch and correct', and bear in patience.[34]

Although he addressed it to the pope, Bernard wrote the treatise as much as an abbot as a servant of the wider Church. The tension which he described as inherent in the cistercian pope's role as a monk and an administrator was one that Bernard acknowledged as similar to the conflict in his own life between his responsibilities in the cloister and his involvement in the affairs of Church and state. The dilemma he

[32] SBOp 3:393; trans. Bernard of Clairvaux 1976, 23.
[33] See the introduction to *De consideratione* in SBOp 3:381-91.
[34] Pope John XXIII, *Journal of a Soul*, 298.

experienced gave rise to the well-known title he gave himself, 'chimaera of my age' (*Chimaera mei saeculi*).[35] Although the provenance of this italian manuscript is not known, manuscripts of *De consideratione* were commonly found in monastic libraries. A late twelfth-century manuscript from Kaisheim (MA020), with the strange full-page miniature of the abbey's two benefactresses and the seated figures of Bernard and Eugene III, has been described above.[36] There are five known examples from British Cistercian libraries.[37] The broad interest in this work which, because of Bernard's severe criticism of the Roman Curia was later used by the followers of Wycliffe, Luther, Calvin, and other reformers in polemical writings against the papacy, ensured its dispersion beyond monastic circles. There are at least seventy manuscripts in existence.

Among these, two contain more images of Bernard than does any other bernardine manuscript (MA 234-240 and MA 283-288). In both he is represented in historiated initials to the Preface and to Books 2 to 5. Instead of being identified by pointing to his text, Bernard is depicted as presenting his treatise to the recipient, Eugene III, much as in one of the earliest bernardine images he is portrayed as handing his Letter 523 to Aelred of Rievaulx, who is shown receiving this on the facing folio. ▶ *Colour plate 3*. One of these *De consideratione* manuscripts is dated to the third quarter of the thirteenth century and, while its origin is not known, it was presented to the Franciscans in York (MA283). The main text is preceded by Bernard's dedicatory letter to the pope. In the same opening initial to the Preface *S(ubit animum)* as in the fourteenth-century italian version (MA245), a bearded Bernard in a white cowl is seated, facing the pope who is also seated. Bernard hands a long piece of parchment containing the treatise to the pope with his right hand while pointing to him with his left. The pope is wearing a rosa chasuble and the conical type of headgear in which popes were depicted before the tiara was used. The red letters above the initial announce the beginning of the first book, but a marginal rubric tells us that we have here the Preface.

The other richly illustrated *De consideratione* manuscript (MA 234) is, as one would expect, one of a number of copies in the Vatican Library.

[35] Ep. 250; SBOp 8:147; trans. James 1953, 402.
[36] See above, pages 75–77.
[37] Bell 1992, 45.

This particular manuscript was commissioned by Pope Nicholas V in 1452. As in the English manuscript, the red letters above the first miniature announce the opening of Book 1 whereas the large blue initial *S*(*ubit animum*) in fact opens the Preface and not the first book, as is the case in the earlier english copy (MA283). Within the initial a nimbed Bernard in a white cowl kneels and hands a red book containing his treatise to Eugene, who is seated, dressed in a red cope edged with gold and fastened by a clasp in the front. On his head he has the later traditional papal tiara, the triple crown. He accepts the book with his left hand and with his right hand blesses Bernard. The scene is witnessed by a number of clerics shown against a gold ground. The lower margin of the folio has the keys of Peter surmounted by a tiara, the name of Nicholas V and the date 1452. There is a marked difference in the way the two figures are portrayed in the two miniatures: the simple dialogue between them in the english manuscript is replaced in the italian miniature two centuries later by a formal encounter between a magnificently attired pope and the submissive, kneeling figure of one of his subjects.

In Book 2 of the treatise Bernard refers to the failure of the Second Crusade which, he claims, was brought on by the sin of man, and he stresses the importance of consideration. In both manuscripts the miniatures are contained within the opening initial *M*(*emor promissi mei*)—'I remember the promise I made to you such a long time ago'.[38] In the english manuscript (MA284) both figures are seated. Eugene, in the left half of the initial, is dressed as at the prologue in a chasuble and the conical hat. On the right side the bearded Bernard in a white habit looks at Eugene, to whom he hands his work with the right hand while gesturing with his left. Eugene accepts it with his left hand while raising his right hand to point at Bernard. The later italian manuscript (MA235) has the two figures placed in the same way, one in either half of the initial *M*, but both are standing. On the right Eugene stands dressed as before but now wearing white gloves, each with a red spot. He holds the red book which Bernard has handed to him. On the left a nimbed Bernard looks downward, reading from an open book—his treatise.

Book 3 of *De consideratione* is devoted to the state of the Church and a survey of abuses, and in it Bernard urges the pope to consider whether discipline is being observed and the true faith being taught as it should

[38] Csi 2.1.1; SBOp 3:410.

be. In both manuscripts, the beginning of this book is announced in red letters and the images shown within the initial *F(inis superioris libri huic principium ponit)*—'The preceding book concludes with a beginning for this one'.[39] The english manuscript (MA285) has the two figures standing, facing each other in the upper half of the initial, dressed as before. On the right Bernard raises his right hand towards the pope on the left, who holds the long piece of parchment with the treatise in his right hand while his left is raised, pointing to Bernard. The image in the italian manuscript (MA236) is also contained within the upper half of the initial, which is decorated with green and rosa leaves, but only Bernard is featured. He is nimbed and sitting at a desk against a gold ground and now has his hood over his head. Here he is looking down whereas in the other images he is looking straight ahead or at an open book. He is concentrating on sharpening his pen which he holds in his left hand while in his right he has a knife with which he is cutting the pen towards himself. It is the only known image in bernardine iconography depicting him performing this commonplace task.

Book 4 contains Bernard's famous criticism of the Roman Curia. Bernard enjoins the pope to set an example and to consider that the Holy Roman Church is the mother of churches, not the mistress. The opening initial *S(i mihi plenius innotuisset)*—'If I had been more fully aware of the manner in which you received the books previous to this one'[40]—has Bernard on the right in the earlier, english manuscript (MA286), looking towards Eugene who, on the left, is holding the parchment treatise in his left hand while raising his right hand towards Bernard. They are both dressed as before. The equivalent image in the later, italian, manuscript (MA237) shows, once again, only Bernard and not the pope. The half-figure of Bernard within the initial is nimbed and he holds a red book—his work—in his left hand while his right hand is raised.

While Bernard considers a variety of practical aspects of the papal office in the first four books, Book 5 is more metaphysical and directs consideration to God. It opens with the initial *L(ibri superiores, etsi De consideratione inscribantur)*—'The former books, although they are entitled "On Consideration", nevertheless contain many things which

[39] Csi 3.1.1; SBOp 3:431.
[40] Csi 4.1.1; SBOp 3:448.

pertain to action, for they teach or advise some things which must not only be considered but acted upon'.[41] In the York manuscript (MA287) the opening is again announced in red letters. Within the lower half of the large blue initial the half-figure of Bernard on the right bows down, with both hands raised in homage to Eugene who, on the left, holds the parchment scroll of the treatise in his left hand while raising his right hand to acknowledge Bernard. The background to the two figures is gold. The large initial in the Vatican manuscript (MA238) is blue with green and rosa decoration against a gold background. Here the half-figure of a nimbed Bernard with his hood of his white cowl over his head holds a red book—his work—in both hands.

In the York manuscript *De consideratione* is followed by what is headed *Bernardus super cantica* but, as we mentioned above, the work is in fact Origen's First Homily on the Song of Songs although it shows the image of Bernard writing under the inspiration of the Holy Spirit (MA288). In the Vatican manuscript (MA240) the *De consideratione* is followed by the famous treatise *Apologia ad Guillelmum Abbatem,* the opening of which is identified as *dictus Apologeticus,* the most frequently used title of the work. It has an image of Bernard almost identical to the four in the earlier work in which he is portrayed alone. Bernard is shown within the large blue and gold opening initial *V(enerabili Patri Guillelmo, frater Bernardus, fratrum qui in Claravalle sunt inutilis servus)*—'To the venerable Father William, from Brother Bernard, the unworthy servant of the brothers who are at Clairvaux'.[42] The three-quarter figure of Bernard with the hood of his white cowl over his head holds an open red book of the work in his left hand. He points to this with the index finger of his right hand in the same way as in the author portraits referred to above (MA319 and MA245).

Another example of a dedicatory image is found in a thirteenth-century composite manuscript in which Bernard is portrayed at the beginning of each of the three works it contains. The first is Bernard's main Marian text, the sermons *In laudibus Virginis Matris* (In Praise of the Virgin Mother) on the feasts of the Virgin. These are also known as *Sermones Missus est* from the opening words of Saint Luke's account of the Annunciation, *Missus est angelus Gabriel a Deo* (The angel

[41] Csi 5.1.1; SBOp 3:467.
[42] Apo 1.1; SBOp 3:81.

Gabriel was sent by God), the first of the four homilies.[43] The scene is evoked by a miniature in the second column of a folio, immediately before the text *Missus est*. It depicts an angel appearing to Mary holding a scroll with the words *AVE MARIA*. Preceding this is a tiny image of Bernard within the opening initial to the Preface *S(cribere me aliquid et devotio iubet, et prohibet occupatio)*—'My devotion demands that I write something but I am too busy to do so' (MA346). A bearded and nimbed Bernard in a white cowl has a red book in his left hand which he is presenting to the Virgin in front of him to whom he is pointing with his right hand. He is accompanied by a smaller monk who stands behind him. His crozier is just visible against the gold background. The miniature is, sadly, somewhat damaged but is of considerable interest as it celebrates Bernard's famous marian text. The other two texts in the manuscript are both pseudo-Bernardine works: *Lamentatio Sancto Bernardo super passione Christi* (Lamentation of Saint Bernard on the Passion of Christ) which is decorated with an image of Bernard kneeling before the half-figure of a cross-nimbed Christ who appears from a cloud displaying the wounds in his side and hands (MA347); and *Tractatus de revelatione facta Beato Bernardo a Beata Virgine super dolore quem sensit in passione filii sui* (Treatise on the Holy Revelation to the Blessed Bernard from the Blessed Virgin on the Pain which She Feels in the Passion of her Son) which has a miniature of Bernard kneeling before the Virgin who is holding a crucifix in her left hand to which she points with her right hand (MA343). Although the attribution to Bernard is erroneous, like so many pseudo-Bernard texts, both were widely accepted as genuine and contributed to the esteem in which Bernard was held.

One of the most common places to find his image adorning his work is at the beginning of his First Sermon for Advent. This is not surprising as Advent Sunday marks the commencement of the Church's liturgical year. Of the seventy-five recorded images decorating Bernard's works, six are contained within the opening initial of this sermon: *H(odie, fratres, adventus initium celebramus)*—'Today, my Brothers, we celebrate the beginning of Advent'.[44] Among the six are two early thirteenth-century images: one (MA039) comes from the cluniac priory of Saint-Martin des Champs in Paris and shows his burial, the first known image

[43] Luke 1:26; SBOp 4:13.
[44] SBOp 4:161.

illustrating a scene from his life, and the other, showing him seated in a frontal position with his hand raised in blessing, comes from the english abbey of Buildwas (MA061). A late thirteenth-century example from the abbey of Nizelles in Brabant (MA037) shows Bernard preaching to a group of nuns. It is almost identical to another image (MA036), also from Nizelles, which decorates the opening initial of his first sermon for Easter. Later examples from the fifteenth century include a single leaf from a german collection of Bernard's Sermons in which Bernard is depicted within a blue initial *H(odie)* on gold ground (MA281). He is seated in a vaulted chamber between two pillars dressed in a black cowl with the hood over his head and carrying a crozier in his right hand and a red book in his left. He is shown in much the same way in an early fifteenth-century manuscript (MA226) which was probably from the North Netherlands. Within a red initial *H(odie)* with white decoration on a gold background a nimbed standing Bernard in a dark brown habit has a crozier in his right hand and a book in his left. He stands on a white and black checkered floor. The head of the crozier and the halo are produced by needlepoint indentations on shiny gold.

The most common place of all in which to find bernardine images in his work is at the opening of Sermon One *on the Song of Songs,* the first of the eighty-six sermons which he began in 1135 and which were unfinished when he died eighteen years later. Altogether seven such images have been recorded, a testimony to Bernard's undoubted masterpiece. They include the manuscript from the benedictine monastery of Liesborn (MA025) which contains one of the earliest representations of Bernard. Dated *c.* 1180 it depicts Bernard within the opening initial *V(obis fratres)* as the teacher of a group of monks.

Another early example within the opening initial comes from the austrian abbey of Zwettl (MA342). In an early thirteenth-century manuscript a half-figure of a bearded Bernard is featured within the initial *V*, drawn in red ink with clasps decorated with nails. He is wearing a chasuble decorated with crosses on the orphreys which gives it the appearance of a pallium. Bernard, his hand raised in blessing, is drawn in brown ink against a red geometric background. The top of the initial is missing as is the top of Bernard's head and, on account of this, his tonsure cannot be seen.

This early example may be contrasted with three later italian examples within the same opening initial to the first sermon on the Song of Songs: one late thirteenth-century; one early fifteenth; and one late fifteenth. In a composite manuscript from Umbria dated *c.* 1290, which also contains Bernard's *De diligendo Deo,* a bearded Bernard in a white cowl is depicted sitting, an open book on a lectern before him, within the rosa initial *V* against a blue decorated background (MA230). His hand is raised and pointing to the text, thereby indicating that he is instructing the two tonsured monks in white cowls who are sitting in front of him and looking up at him in awe. The one in front holds an open book with both hands. The manuscript belonged to the franciscan convent of Santa Maria in Aracoeli.

The second image occurs in an early fifteenth-century manuscript of *De cantica canticorum* (MA060). It is said to have been copied by the camaldolese monks of Santa Maria degli Angeli in Florence.[45] As the six busts within the quatrefoils which decorate the border of the folio—one in each corner and one halfway down on each side—are of dominican friars, however, it would seem more likely that it originated at a house of Friars Preacher. Within the initial *V,* a nimbed and bearded Bernard is depicted sitting at a desk, pointing to an open book before him. Lying on the desk are his pen and knife. Four volumes—Bernard's works—are lying on the shelves of a castellated bookcase behind him. Two of the three monks before him are young, one with his hood over his head and the other with an open book at which he is pointing. They are both looking up at the preacher, avid for his words. A third monk is old and bearded and is absorbed by the text of the open book he is holding.

The third image is in a renaissance manuscript magnificently illustrated by Francesco d'Antonio del Chirico or his School and dated between 1475 and 1482 (MA244). It contains Bernard's eighty-six Sermons on the Canticle and their continuation by Gilbert of Hoyland. The half-figure of a nimbed Bernard sporting a long beard and wearing a white cowl is contained within the ornate initial *V* against a blue background. The work is introduced in gold letters against a black background within a frame above the initial and text; the multi-coloured border is elegantly decorated with stylized foliage, busts of figures, the arms of Federico di Montefeltro, duke of Urbino, and *putti*. The opposite folio has a magnificent full-page *Doctrina* image (MA243).

[45] Hassall 1976, 113–114.

Although most bernardine images adorning the *In cantica canticorum* sermons are found within the opening initial of Sermon 1,[46] there are two known exceptions, both from the thirteenth century. The first is a full-page miniature from the cistercian abbey of Altzelle (MA022). In this Bernard is depicted in a frontal position in the same authoritative way we saw in the early benedictine image from Liesborn (MA025). The other (MA168), from the german premonstratensian abbey of Weissenau, depicts Bernard, most unusually, in the opening initial to Sermon 64 and not to Sermon 1. He is shown standing behind the crossbar of the initial *A([d]sum meae promissioni. Capite nobis vulpes parvulas, quae demoliuntur vineas; nam vinea nostra floruit)*—'I stand by my promise: "catch us the little foxes that spoil the vines, for our vines are in flower"'.[47] In this chapter, considered to be of special importance, Bernard talks of different kinds of foxes (*de diversis generibus vulpium*), by which he means heretics who were ravaging various parts of Europe at the time, among them southern France and the Rhineland, and whom he was committed to counter by his preaching. He is identified by the inscription within the upper part of the initial *S(an)c(tu)s Bernhardus abbas.* He is bearded, his tonsure is broken showing a small tuft of hair at the front, he is wearing a blueish grey cowl and carrying a primitive crozier in his left hand while his right hand is raised in blessing.

AS TEACHER

Forty-seven examples depicting Bernard teaching or preaching have been recorded. An examination of these reveals two distinct types: images of him alone in which the teaching mode is suggested by a raised hand with the index finger pointing; and those in which he is addressing two or more of his disciples in which the difference in status between master and pupil is often indicated by a difference in scale or in the level in which they are portrayed.

An early example of the former is the standing figure of Bernard in a late twelfth-century manuscript of the *Vita Prima,* ▶ *Fig. 6* (MA026). In the office for his feast day in an early thirteenth-century antiphonary from

[46] Apart from those already mentioned, these are: MA262 and MA227.
[47] SBOp 2:166.

the catalan cistercian abbey of Poblet (MA104), Bernard adopts the same gesture, raising his right hand in a teaching mode in the three-quarter length figure within the initial *P(rima virtus viri sancti)*. The group teaching/preaching images are far more numerous, however. Images of Bernard teaching have already been noted in illustrations to his monastic writings (MA060, MA230) as well as elsewhere (for example MA024 and MA044). They include images of Bernard with his disciples in a Homiliary from the second half of the thirteenth century from the italian abbey of Morimondo (MA292), a very similar scene in another Antiphonary from the same monastery dated *c.*1300 (MA291), an Obituary from the nuns' abbey of Notre-Dame des Prés from the second half of the thirteenth century (MA318), a manuscript of the Golden Legend in French dated *c.* 1340 (MA161)—in which Bernard is shown seated on a high chair and wearing a mitre, and another fourteenth-century french Golden Legend (MA198) in which Bernard and all the monks are in black cowls, all with their hoods over their heads. Typical of the many images of Bernard instructing his monks is one in a 1455 manuscript of the *Speculum Historiale* by Vincent de Beauvais translated into French by Jean de Vignay (MA197). Nimbed and dressed in a white cowl, he sits on a high-backed chair raised two steps off a green floor on which six monks, also in white cowls, sit on benches listening to him. The scene is set in a chamber with a large window through which one sees a bright blue sky. The text below in red reads: *de la recommendacion du benoit bernard abbe de clervaux.*

In describing what kind of man should be abbot, Saint Benedict wrote that 'his commands and teaching should be infused into the minds of his disciples like the leaven of divine justice', and warned that 'at the dread Judgement of God there will be an examination of both these matters, of his teaching and of the obedience of his disciples'. He went on to say that the abbot should rule both by his words and by his example, and that he should observe the rule of Saint Paul who says 'Reprove, persuade, rebuke' (Rom 2:11).[48] This interpretation of the abbatial office is beautifully transmitted visually in the *De cantica canticorum* image from Liesborn (MA025). This expresses the authority of the abbot by the frontal position of the figure of Bernard, the key monastic virtue of obedience by the scroll he carries with the quotation from

[48] Rule Chapter 2, trans. McCann 1976, 6-9.

Hebrews 'Obey them that have rule over you' (*Obedite propositis vestris:* Heb 13:17), and the dependence of the monks on the abbot's discernment by the group of monks in the lower part of the miniature who look up at him in awe.

At the very beginning of his masterpiece, the sermons *De cantica canticorum,* Bernard makes a distinction between the kind of words suitable to a monastic audience and those appropriate to a wider public, saying: 'The instructions that I address to you, my brothers, will differ from those I should deliver to people in the world' (*Vobis fratres, alia quam aliis de saeculo, aut certe aliter sunt*). There is a parallel between this and his earlier distinction in his *Apologia* between the kind of embellishment appropriate in a monastic as against a secular context.[49]

The distinction between Bernard the writer and Bernard the teacher is, in a way, specious, for the overwhelming bulk of his writing was directed at the formation of his monks at Clairvaux and at the numerous monasteries of the Clairvaux filiation. The interdependence and inseparability of the two roles of writer and teacher is clearly indicated by two images of Bernard on the same folio decorating his sermons in the Hedwig Codex (MA024). Above, Bernard is depicted writing at an adjustable desk. The inscription in red ink above him reveals that the text is the first of his four Sermons *In laudibus Virginis Matris*. Below he points to an open book, representing his work, which he holds in his left hand while addressing a group of five monks at his feet. The inscription has: 'Here he reads the homily to his most beloved brethren'. As Jean Leclercq has pointed out,[50] it is in fact unlikely that this or his better-known *Sermons on the Song of Songs* were delivered as homilies to a monastic congregation. Bernard himself refers to the *marian* work as an *opusculum*.[51] The way he holds the book open and points to the text suggests that we are witnessing not a conventional homily with a preacher and his audience, but a kind of monastic tutorial involving reading, writing and private meditation. The monks are not just listening to him passively but, with their various postures, are indicating their active participation. This same distinction is particularly well illustrated by a scene in a Lectionary from the cistercian monastery

[49] SBOp 3:81.
[50] Leclercq 1962-9, 1:193-212.
[51] SBOp 4:58.

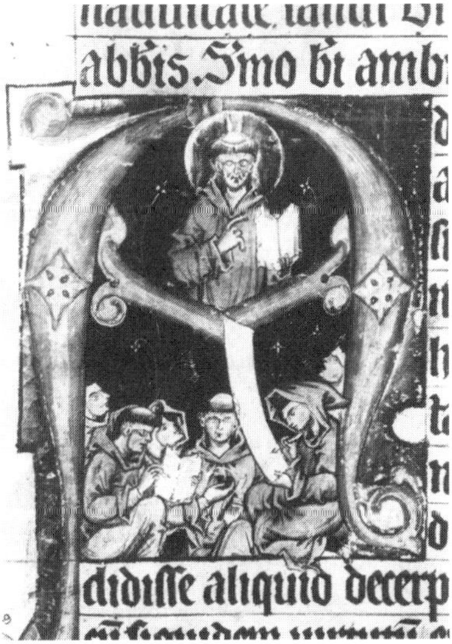

Figure 8

Marienstern in Saxony, ▶ *Fig. 8* (MA068). Dated *c.*1280, it is now lost, but was formerly in the National Library in Prague. Within the initial *A*(*c*) the half-figure of a nimbed Bernard in a frontal position, this time without crozier, points to an open book in his left hand. Below him sit six tonsured monks, three of them looking up and concentrating on what Bernard is saying, while on the left one of them is writing in a book, on the right another, with his hood over his head, is busy writing on a long scroll, and in the middle, between the two writing monks, the sixth monk is assisting them by holding an inkwell in one hand and a penknife in the other.

As a number of images indicate that his influence as a teacher was not confined to monks but also extended to nuns (MA035 and MA036) and spread beyond the Cistercians to other monastic Orders, as is testified by *De cantica canticorum* manuscripts from benedictine Liesborn (MA025), premonstratensian Weissenau (MA168), franciscan (MA230), and dominican (MA069) houses.

CONCLUSION

Just as the literary sources have little to say about how Bernard ruled Clairvaux, the visual evidence in his iconography, too, is meagre. It is confined to a small number of examples and, significantly, these come predominantly from the Altenberg cloister glass which, being unique in its comprehensiveness, is not a reliable guide in evaluating the data. Furthermore, while the earliest narrative images, those from the late twelfth and early thirteenth centuries, predominantly feature such key events in Bernard's life as his early formation (MA054, MA233), his conversion to monastic life (MA089, PA098), and his death (MA034,

MA039), the small number of pictures of him interacting with his monks are all late medieval (for example GL14, MA142).

In the perception of Bernard as a writer there is a distinct development from the earliest images—the author portraits in which he is depicted in profile at a desk, as it were *in vacuo* (MA006, MA040)—to the late medieval scenes (MA196, MA260) in which he appears as the learned scholar-author sitting in a gothic chamber surrounded by his books. A similar change may be detected by comparing the english thirteenth-century dedicatory image of Bernard handing Eugene III a copy of his *De consideratione* with the same scene in an italian manuscript two centuries later (MA283 and MA234). The informality of the former image suggests a meeting of near-equals: while Bernard fully acknowledged the plenitude of power (*plenitudo potestatis*) which was vested in the papal office, he laid stress on stewardship rather than supremacy. His relationship with the pope was complex; the pope was a former disciple while Bernard and the pope's subordinate. The dilemma is expressed in one of Bernard's letters to Eugene:

> I do not dare to call you a son any longer. You were my son, but now you have become my father. I was your father, but now I have become your son. You who came after me have been preferred before me.[52]

In the fifteenth-century image the relaxed atmosphere which, according to the twelfth-century literary sources, characterized their relations without in any way detracting from the difference in their status, has been replaced by a formal encounter between a subservient Bernard and the ornate figure of a late medieval successor to Eugene, perhaps someone whom Bernard had called a lord of his fellow-bishops rather than their brother.[53]

The change from the informality of earlier images to the formality of later ones may also be detected in portrayals of Bernard as a teacher. The intimate and familiar scene of Bernard surrounded by and engaged

[52] Ep 238; SBOp 8:116; trans. James 1953, 277: *Jam enim filium dicere non audeo, quia filius in patrem, pater est mutatus in filium. Qui post me venit, ante me factus est.*

[53] *De consideratione* 4:7:23; SBOp 3:466: *te vero non dominum episcoporum, sed unum ex ipsis, porro fratrem diligentium Deum et participem timentium eum.*

in dialogue with a small group of his monks (MA044, MA230, MA318), sometimes depicted sitting on the ground around him (MA024), is replaced by one in which Bernard is the master in the schools, sitting on a raised dais in a schoolroom with his students sitting in serried rows before him (MA197). The later depiction conjures up the image of a master with bright young monks selected to study scholastic theology at the College of Saint Bernard in Paris, a studium founded by the Clairvaux abbot Stephen Lexington in 1245, rather than that of an abbot engaged in the monastic formation of his charges.

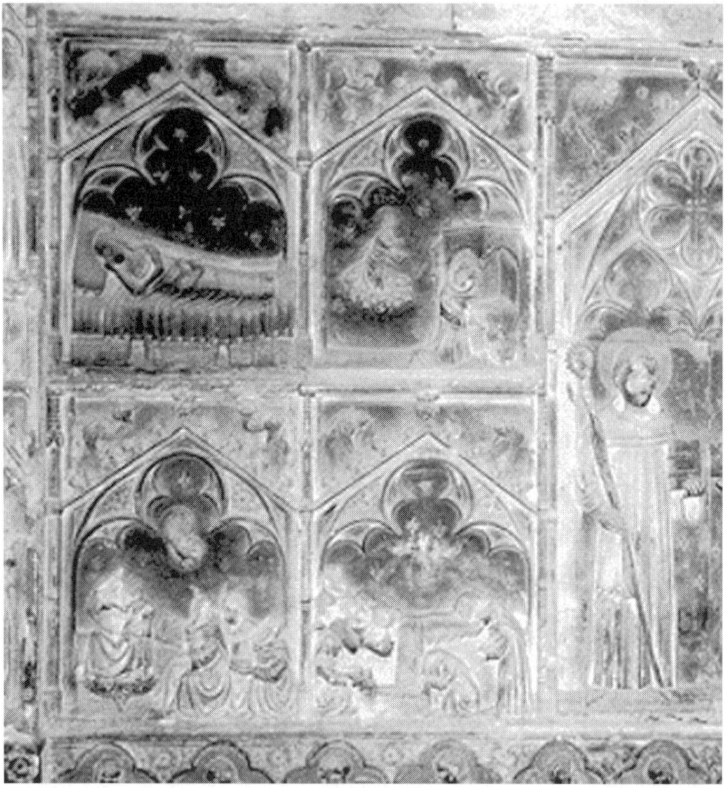

Figure 9: Carved stone retable from the Church of Saint Mary, Montblanch, 1348 (SC39-43).

FIVE

IMAGES FROM THE LIFE OF BERNARD

ONE HUNDRED SIXTY-ONE of the nine hundred sixty images of Bernard recorded here are narrative pictures featuring legends from his life, episodes which are either historical in the sense that their authenticity can be verified or supernatural phenomena which belong to the hagiological tradition.[1] The great majority refer to Bernard's life as monk and abbot, but they include three which deal with Bernard's involvement with the crusade, all three in non-cistercian manuscripts. A miniature in a Universal Chronicle in French (MA304), which goes up to 1220, shows Bernard preaching the crusade to Louis VII at Vezelay in 1146. He stands, wearing a grey cowl and holding a blue crozier with red volute on his left shoulder. His hands are raised to the seated king, who wears a red crown, a red dress, and over it a blue mantle. The event was recorded by the monk-bishop-historian Otto of Freising as follows: 'There [at Vezelay] Louis, the king of the Franks, with great eagerness of spirit received the cross from the aforesaid abbot [Bernard]

[1] The figure does not include the large number of *Amplexus* or *Lactatio* images. For these, see Chapters 7 and 8.

and volunteered for military service across the seas'.[2] In two crusader manuscripts known as the *History of Outremer*, both from *c.* 1295–1300 and in French, Bernard is depicted preaching the Crusade to a group of lay people who are listening attentively (MA030, MA031). The subject is indicated by the text in red ink above the miniature: *le sermon s. bernart par la surie.*

Of the one hundred sixty-one narrative images no fewer than sixty-nine are found in the extensive cycles of late medieval glass panels from the former cloisters of Altenberg and Saint Apern in Cologne. There are two distinct categories of narrative images: groups of images forming cycles, which are overwhelmingly late medieval and largely represented by altarpieces, stained glass, and wall painting; and single images featuring one episode from the life of Bernard, which are mostly found in manuscripts. There are also a small number of cycles in illuminated manuscripts. Their sources are the *Vitae*, particularly the *Vita Prima; exempla* and historical accounts in the Clairvaux tradition, notably the twenty chapters devoted to Bernard in the *Exordium Magnum;* and thirteenth-century legendaries, primarily the *Golden Legend.*

THE SOURCES

The Vitae

The chief source for the narrative depictions, both single scenes in manuscripts as well as the numerous Bernard cycles, are the five books of the *Vita Prima*—either directly or through later intermediary literary sources of which by far the most important is the *Legenda Aurea.*[3] The growing centralization of the post-gregorian-reform Church and the requirement of papal authorization of any saintly cult led to growing legal requirements. These hagiographical books, with all the inherent qualities associated with the genre, were chiefly designed to promote the cult of Bernard, and represent the dossier required in support of Bernard's canonization. As miracles were considered the surest sign of sainthood, large numbers were included. The emphasis on and exag-

[2] Mierow 1953, 72–74.

[3] For an examination of the sources and Bernard's canonization, see Bredero 1996.

geration of miracles and visions led to a one-sided view which tends to obscure the historic Bernard. Unlike many similar documents, however, four of the five books were written by those who knew Bernard well, and, in the words of a modern authority,[4] upon 'close reading' they manage to convey a picture not just of the conventional saint, but also of a real human being.

The writing of Bernard's *Life* was initiated by Bernard's secretary, Geoffrey of Auxerre. He gathered early biographical material and handed it to the former benedictine abbot, William of Saint Thierry. William's friendship with Bernard made him an ideal choice as Bernard's biographer. Born in Liège in the late eleventh century and therefore apparently somewhat older than Bernard, he became abbot of Saint Thierry about 1119, and met Bernard at roughly the same time. In 1135 he decided to become a Cistercian at Signy, where he remained until his death in 1147/1148. William describes the impact of Bernard's personality on him at their first meeting:

> how agreeable the affection arising in me for that person, how great the desire to share his lodging in that poverty and simplicity! Had a wish been offered me that day, nothing would I have so wished as to remain there with him and be his servant forever.[5]

William was to have his wish partially fulfilled. Some time later, when Bernard heard that William was sick, he sent his brother Gerard to invite and accompany him to Clairvaux. While both Bernard and William were ill they spent a good deal of time together, during which Bernard shared his thoughts and experiences with him. While at Clairvaux William also gathered much material from those around him, a debt he acknowledged in the Preface:

> Then too, I am egged on and greatly encouraged by the kindly goodwill of certain brothers, men constantly at the Man of

[4] Bredero 1996, 16.

[5] VP 1:7:33 (PL 185:246-7), trans. Guadelupe Translations 1990: *Tantaque affectus sum suavitate circa hominem illum, tantoque desiderio in paupertate illa et simplicitate cohabitandi ei, ut si optio illa die mihi data fuisset, nil tam optassem quam ibi cum eo semper manere ad serviendum ei.*

God's side and acquainted with his every concern. They it is who have been reporting to me materials obtained by diligent investigation and inquiry, reporting other episodes too that they were present for and saw and heard for themselves.[6]

One hundred and thirty manuscripts of the *Vita Prima* have survived,[7] and, among the only known twelfth-century representations of Bernard—twelve in total—two feature him at the opening of William's Preface and Book One. The first shows him wearing eucharistic vestments—an alb, blue chasuble with white spots, and stole—and carrying a simple crozier in his left hand and raising his right hand in blessing, ▶ *Fig.* 6 (MA026). He is placed below the words in red announcing the Preface to Book One and beside the opening initial *S*(*cripturus vitam servi tui ad honorem nominis tui prout dederis domine deus*) ('It is my aim to write the life of your servant to the honour of your name in so far as you have endowed me, O Lord God'). The manuscript was probably from a cistercian abbey, possibly german or flemish. Contemporary with this, and among the earliest of all representations of Bernard, is an image at the beginning of the first chapter of Book One in a composite manuscript made in the scriptorium of the austrian abbey Zwettl *c.* 1189 (MA001). The upper half of the opening initial *B*(*ernardus*), which goes on to announce Bernard's birth to illustrious parents at Chatillon in Burgundy, contains a half-figure of a youthful Bernard in a frontal position, nimbed and tonsured, a simple crozier in his right hand and his left hand raised in blessing as in the image from the Preface. Again, he seems to be wearing a chasuble. In the lower half of the initial a tonsured monk sits on a stool writing at a desk with a pen in his right hand and a knife in his left. This represents the author, William of Saint Thierry, and is the earliest known 'portrait' of him. The initial is in reddish-brown ink while the figures are in black. Another early *Vita Prima* manuscript (MA327) has an image of Bernard within the upper half of a very large initial *B* with the rest of the opening word—*ernardus*—in red ink vertically on the side. He is nimbed and bearded,

[6] VP 1:7:225 (PL 185:225-6): *Sed et me fratrum quorundam pia benevolentia plurimum ad hoc impellit et cohortatur, qui cum Viro Dei jugiter assistant, omnia ejus noverunt, ingerentes quaedam diligenti inquisitione vestigata, plura etiam, quibus, cum fierent, ipsi interfuerunt et viderunt, et audierunt.*

[7] Bredero 1996, 6.

and again has a simple crozier in his right hand while his left is raised in blessing. Above him, the text in red ink announces the beginning of Book One.

The only other known medieval image of William is found in another composite manuscript consisting of the *Vita Prima* and Bernard's Sermons (MA120). It dates from the late thirteenth century and belonged to the nuns at Loewenbrück, Trier, until 1468 when it came to the cistercian abbey of Himmerod. Within the opening initial of the Preface *S(cripturus)*, a small monk, in a dark brown cowl with his hood over his head and his hands clasped in prayer, kneels before the larger figure of Bernard, who is dressed in a grey cowl and holds a crozier in his left hand and his right hand raised in blessing. The identity of the monk is indicated by the text in red above, which announces the 'beginning of the Prologue of the Life of Saint Bernard, abbot of Clairvaux, by William, abbot of Saint Thierry' (*Incipit prologus domini Wilhelmi abbatis s. Theoderici in vita sancti Bernardi clarevallis abbatis*).

By the time William of Saint Thierry died in 1147/1148 he had described the events of Bernard's early life in Book One. Geoffrey of Auxerre then turned to another benedictine abbot, Arnold of Bonneval, to continue the story; he wrote Book Two.[8] He was considerably less close to Bernard than either William or Geoffrey and he wrote with much less feeling than Bernard's other biographers. Through his contacts he was able, however, to fill in information on the period 1130–1145, and to highlight Bernard's vital role in the papal schism of 1130–1138, an important factor in securing papal endorsement of Bernard's sainthood. Among other topics Arnold dealt with were Bernard's participation in the Council of Étampes, his visit to Milan, and, most important, his healing of the schism in Aquitaine by the conversion of the Duke of Aquitaine, a theme which caught the imagination of artists in a way that no other episode Arnold recorded has done (MA106, MA251, PA058, WA30).

Geoffrey of Auxerre, Bernard's secretary, who had accompanied Bernard on many of his journeys and knew him better than any of his other biographers, wrote the last three books of the *Vita Prima*.[9] He

[8] PL 185:267-302. See Bredero 1996, 102–108.
[9] PL 185:301-68. See Bredero 1996, 91–102.

was a disciple whose admiration for and veneration of his master knew virtually no bounds. To Geoffrey Bernard was

> the example of perfection, the model of virtue, the mirror of sanctity. . . . the pride of Israel, the joy of Jerusalem, the delight of your century, the only charm of your time. . . . the strongest pillar of the holy church, a resounding trumpet of God, a lovely lute of the Holy Spirit.[10]

Unlike William of Saint Thierry, Geoffrey's tone is always totally uncritical and he lays a strong emphasis on miracles and prophetic omens. The scene was already set by the enthusiastic words with which he chose to begin the first of his three books: 'Innumerable were the signs and miracles that the whole world gathered together by which God glorified his faithful servant, Bernard, abbot of Clairvaux'.[11] In the only known medieval miniature to adorn the last three books of the *Vita Prima,* the initial containing this phrase—*I(nnumeris quidem signis atque miraculis)*—contains an image of a standing cistercian monk, tonsured and bearded, in a white cowl with his hood partially over his head and both hands raised in prayer (MA119). It is found in a composite manuscript from the premonstratensian abbey of Windberg and is dated the last quarter of the twelfth century. The figure, whose hands are raised pointing to the text, may represent either Bernard, the subject of the work, or, as he is not nimbed and does not carry a crozier, may be a 'portrait' of the author, Geoffrey of Auxerre.

The *Vita Prima* was translated into several languages. A french version entitled *la vie de monseigneur saint Bernard et ses miracles,* translated at Clairvaux in 1396 and commissioned by the Duchess of Burgundy from Jacotin de Ramecourt, has a full-page miniature at the beginning (MA203). It depicts Bernard in a grey cowl seated on a chair holding a crozier and with an open book on his knees. The earliest printed edition,

[10] VP 5:2:11; PL 185:357: *Tu perfectionis exemplar, virtutis forma, speculum sanctitatis. Tu gloria Israel, tu laetitia Jerusalem, tu deliciae tui saeculi, et unicum tui temporis decus. . . . Tu Ecclesiae sanctae fortissima splendidissimaque columna, tu vehemens tuba Dei, tu dulcissimum sancti Spiritus organum.*

[11] VP 3:1:1; PL 185:303: *Innumeris quidem signis atque miraculis, ut Orbis comperit universus, fidelem famulum suum Bernardum Clarae-Vallensem Deus glorificavit abbatem.*

by the milanese humanist Boninus Mombritius, appeared *c.* 1480, and approximately fifty editions of the Latin text were printed before 1641, most of them appended to the *Works* of Bernard.[12]

After Geoffrey had been deposed as abbot of Clairvaux, the task of replacing the *Vita Prima* was given to Alan of Auxerre whose *Vita Secunda* repeats much of what had already appeared in the *Vita Prima*, some of it even *verbatim*.[13] While it is of secondary interest, it does contain an account of Bernard's death, something not found in the earlier *Vita*. According to Alan, Bernard

> tried to instill humility, patience and charity into the minds of his disciples, for he proposed to them to imitate these things not so much in word and speech as in act and reality.[14]

In the *Legenda Aurea* the same story appears, and there it is greatly strengthened by being put into the mouth of Bernard to become his own testimony: 'Thus I leave you these three: charity, humility and patience: these are my testament!'[15] In one of the eight scenes from the life of Bernard in the hungarian Legendary illustrated by Nicolas of Bologna in 1330–1340 (MA252), Bernard is depicted sitting up in bed. His top half is naked, and he is instructing approximately ten monks in three rows who listen to him attentively. Adapting Alan's words he tells them that he would leave them three things: 'charity, humility, and patience'. A lamp hangs above Bernard. The inscription reads: *Quomodo narrabat fratribus de morte sua* ('How he told his brethren of his death').

The most exaggerated claim for Bernard's sanctity comes in John the Hermit's *Vita Quarta*, written towards the end of the twelfth century. John records how Bernard revived a dead man, a story which later found its way into the *Exordium Magnum* and Caesarius of Heisterbach's *Dialogus Miraculorum*.[16] The miracle is depicted in one of nine

[12] Bredero 1996, 163.

[13] *Vita Secunda:* PL 185:469-524; see Bredero 1996, 53–55.

[14] *Vita Secunda* 30:82; PL 185:520: *humilitatem, patientiam, charitatemque, discipulorum mentibus inserere nitebatur, imitanda proponens eis non tam verbo et lingua, quam opere et veritate.*

[15] LA 220. For the adaption of the *Vita Secunda* story by James of Voragine, see McGuire 1994, 202–203.

[16] *Vita Quarta* 2:11; PL 185:546. EM 2:19 (Griesser 1961, 113–115). *Dialogus Miraculorum* 1:16.

frescos, dated 1482, showing scenes from the life of Bernard at the chapel of Saint Bernard in Pamparato (WA16). Bernard, accompanied by one of his monks, who is hooded, stands at the foot of a bed in which a man sits up, his hands clasped in prayer. Bernard has a red book in his left hand while his right hand is raised in blessing. The inscription reads: COMO S. BERNARDO RESOSITARE UNO OMO CHI ERA MORTO ('How Saint Bernard revived a man who was dead').

The Exordium Magnum

The *Exordium Magnum* is the source for one of the most widespread bernardine pictorial themes, the *Amplexus*,[17] in which Christ detaches his arms from the cross to embrace the kneeling Bernard. Apart from this, however, very few episodes from the life of Bernard as described by Conrad of Eberbach, in the twenty chapters he devoted to him, have provided artists with material for narrative scenes and some that may have done so may also be found in the *Vita Prima*. Yet as far as we know, one is unique to the *Exordium Magnum*. It tells of Bernard's vision of angels surrounding the monks during vigils and recording their varying degrees of devotion by writing in gold, silver, ink, or water (GL51). For those who were not singing, the angels recorded nothing at all. The Clairvaux choir is depicted with three monks on either side of facing choir stalls, each carrying a book; and in the background is the high altar. Furthest left stands Bernard, holding a crozier and with an *aspersorium* of holy water before him. In front of the other monks kneel five angels, each with a scroll on which their decision is recorded in one of the four media. While four of them have their heads bowed and are clearly writing, the fifth, facing Bernard, is looking up and her scroll is blank. The story had already occurred in the *Liber Visionum et Miraculorum* compiled by Prior John of Clairvaux (1171–1179). As his version has 'as we read' (*legitur*), it is quite likely that it was based on an earlier written tradition.[18]

[17] See Chapter Seven.
[18] For this, see McGuire 1983, 44–45.

LECTIONARIES

Manuscripts of the *Lives* of the saints in the form of a *Passionale, Vitae Sanctorum* or *Vitae Patrum* had long formed an essential requirement in the Church's liturgical celebration. The lesson or reading—*lectio*—formed part of the Divine Office. It also provided edifying reading during the otherwise silent meals in monastic refectories as well as reading of a more private kind.[19] Such readings were known as *Legenda* or 'Legends', meaning 'Readings in the Lives of the Saints' and not, as one might think, myths or fables, although they were often rich in both. A number of *Legenda* were written by Dominicans, members of the Order of Preachers, and used in the preparation of sermons and the training of preachers.

Much the most important and widely disseminated collection was the *Legenda Sanctorum* compiled around 1265 by the dominican friar James of Voragine, who eventually became archbishop of Genoa in 1292. It became one of the most popular books of the Middle Ages and later came to be known as the *Legenda Aurea*—the Golden Legend. It comprised a prologue and one hundred seventy-seven chapters devoted to the *Lives* of saints and the main liturgical feasts, arranged according to the calendar of the Church year. The chapters varied enormously in length, from just a few lines to many pages, according to the perceived importance of the saint and the source material available. The chapter on Bernard was among the longest of all, thanks to James having access to one of the most exhaustive of all 'biographies', the *Vita Prima,* which provided him with virtually all his material.[20] As a result, knowledge of Bernard and his life was disseminated throughout Europe in a way that would otherwise not have occurred and the *Golden Legend* provided material for artists in a late-medieval outburst of pictorial narrative. James opens his Legend by acknowledging his debt, saying 'His [Bernard's] life was written by William, Abbot of Saint Thierry, and by Abbot Ernaldus of Bonneval'.[21] Strangely, he omits to mention the third author, Geoffrey of Auxerre, who not only instigated the *Vita Prima* but himself wrote three of its five books, in spite of the fact that fifteen

[19] Wormald 1952, 248–266.
[20] For James of Voragine's use of the *Vita Prima,* see McGuire 1994, 179–211.
[21] Jacobus de Voragine 1941, 465.

of the forty-seven stories in the *Legenda Aurea* are taken from Geoffrey's work.[22]

Although unsurpassed as a treasure-house of stories and information on the saints, including Bernard, the *Legenda Aurea* was not the first such book of readings. For example, the wording alongside the historiated initial containing an image of Bernard in a Legendary made for the Dominican nuns of the Holy Cross in Regensburg *c.* 1267–1276 (MA003), is that of the opening of Book One of the *Vita Prima* and, because of its early date, is unlikely to have come via the *Golden Legend.* It was taken either straight from the *Vita Prima* itself or indirectly from the *Summary of the Deeds and Miracles of the Saints,* a collection compiled some thirty years earlier than the *Golden Legend* by another Dominican, Jean de Mailly. Mailly's work contained a chapter on Bernard which, like the *Golden Legend,* was based mainly on the *Vita Prima* and James may, in fact, have derived his information from it.[23]

Among Jean de Mailly's stories there is only one which cannot be traced to the *Vita Prima* and whose origin is not known: when Bernard was preaching his Homily Eighty-two on the Song of Songs he omitted, through lack of self-confidence and because he had decided to save it for another occasion, to say something which the Holy Spirit had inspired. As a result, he heard a voice saying: 'As long as you keep back that thought, you will not receive another'.[24] This story found its way into the *Legenda Aurea.*[25]

While Jean de Mailly's work reached only a modest audience, the *Golden Legend* was disseminated throughout Christendom to become one of the most widely read books of the Late Middle Ages. Whereas only some twenty manuscripts of Mailly's *Summary* have been preserved, over a thousand manuscripts of the *Golden Legend* are in existence, and within the first hundred years of printing it appeared in more than one hundred fifty known editions and translations, seventy-four of them from before 1500.[26] Its easy availability meant that it was no longer confined to clerical circles but reached a much wider audience in lay society.

[22] McGuire 1994, 205.
[23] Jean de Mailly 1947, 348–354.
[24] Jean de Mailly 1947, 353.
[25] LA 212.
[26] Flieth 1991 has a catalogue of over a thousand copies.

The great majority of *Golden Legend* manuscripts were not illustrated. Most of those that were contained only a few miniatures, and in only a handful were all the saints depicted.[27] A rare exception is a fully illustrated manuscript with one hundred seventy-eight miniatures, written in 1362, probably in Strassburg, in an alsatian dialect of German. The chapter on Bernard is headed *Von S. Bernhart* and has a miniature depicting him standing dressed in a grey cowl and carrying a red crozier with a gold volute (MA331). He is nimbed and bearded. The background is green with branches and the miniature is contained within a red frame. The text in red ink above reads *von dem namen B'nhardi* ('on the name of Bernard') and goes on to describe the etymology of the name and not, as is most common in the illustrated versions, the biographical information which follows. Many of the *Lives* begin similarly.[28] James' explanations are based largely on his fertile imagination, although, in the case of Bernard, he displays a knowledge of Bernard's own writings.[29] According to him:

> Bernard comes from *ber*, fountain or well, and *nardus*, spikenard, as we read in the Gloss on the Canticles, is a lowly herb, and warming and of a sweet odour. For Bernard was warm in his fervent love, lowly in his dealings with others, a fountain in the pouring forth of doctrine, a well in the depth of his knowledge, and of sweet odour in his good renown.[30]

Only thirty-six images of Bernard illustrating the chapter devoted to him in the *Golden Legend* have been recorded on this index. Fifteen of these are woodcuts in printed editions, many of them from southern Germany, with the earliest, dated 1472, coming from Augsburg. The oldest known miniature (MA149) is found in a late fifteenth-century *Legenda Aurea* manuscript in Latin written in France, perhaps in Paris.

[27] Details of illustrated *Legenda Aurea* manuscripts are given in Flieth 1991 and Williams-Krapp 1986.

[28] Other exceptions in which the image of Bernard precedes the etymology and not the biographical text are MA088, MA154, and MA345. The more common arrangement in which the image is placed between the two may be seen in MA153.

[29] McGuire 1994, 191.

[30] The etymology is not included in the recent translation of the Golden Legend, but is found in the earlier version by Ryan & Ripperger, Jacobus of Voragine 1941, 465.

Above the decorated initial *B(ernardus)* with which the text begins, Bernard is depicted in a dark grey cowl. Facing him is his friend Saint Malachy, wearing a chasuble and a mitre. Both are nimbed and bearded and carrying croziers. They are kneeling, their hands clasped in prayer, against a blue checkered background within a rosa and gold frame and, above them are nine stars in the sky. This is also the earliest known example in art of Bernard being linked with Malachy and testifies to the importance attached to their friendship, knowledge of which was based on Bernard's *Life of Malachy,* Bernard's letters to the irish bishop, and references in the *Vita Prima* and the *Exordium Magnum*.[31]

The most popular translations into French of the *Legenda Aurea* were made by Jean de Vignay. The earliest known illustrated version of it comes from the second quarter of the fourteenth century. Among a large number of miniatures and historiated initials is an image of Bernard (MA198) sitting with hands outstretched in teaching mode in front of two monks, the front one of whom holds out his hands in acknowledgement. Bernard has an orange halo, and all three figures are in black cowls with their hoods over their heads against a checkered red background within a gold and blue decorated border. Almost contemporary with this is another Jean de Vignay manuscript with a miniature (MA161) showing Bernard in a grey cowl preaching to a group of monks, also in grey cowls, with their hoods over their heads. Most unusually, Bernard is wearing a white mitre. Of the relatively few known images of Bernard in the *Golden Legend* no fewer than eight are in french translations by Jean de Vignay.[32]

In most of the *Golden Legend* images Bernard is depicted as a single figure, identified by the usual attributes; the images mentioned above—Bernard with Saint Malachy and the two in which he is shown teaching monks—are the exception. Surprisingly, there are also two *Amplexus* scenes (MA053 and MA152), both among the oldest *Amplexus* images.

Two others show Bernard trampling the devil underfoot. Both occur in translations of the *Legenda* into French by Jean de Vignay. One of these (MA305) is a large miniature in a manuscript from Bruges dated

[31] McGuire 1991, 75–106.

[32] In addition to the two mentioned, they are: MA088, MA152, MA153, MA154, MA174, and MA305.

between 1445 and 1460; in it a youthful-looking Bernard stands in a doorway. He is nimbed and is wearing a black cowl over a white tunic and black scapular. In his right hand he holds an open book from which he is reading. In his left hand he has a black crozier with sudarium attached and a gold volute. Trampled beneath his feet is a large devil. The other (MA154) can be dated a decade or two later and is similar in composition. Although both the *Amplexus* and Bernard trampling the devil are common bernardine iconographical themes, neither of them relate to James of Voragine's text.

One artist chose to illustrate a *Vita Prima* story which had found its way into the *Golden Legend*. Within the initial *B(ernardus)* at the opening of the chapter on Bernard in a manuscript from 1446 (MA142) is depicted a scene recorded by William of Saint Thierry, Bernard writing a letter to his cousin Robert. For security reasons, he had decided to take his secretary, William, later abbot of Rievaulx, outside to dictate the letter. It started to pour, but Bernard decided to continue dictating and, miraculously, the letter did not get wet. The initial is decorated with acanthus leaves. The figure on the left, wearing a cap, is writing and must therefore be Bernard's secretary; the smaller figure on the right, with his hood over his head, must be Bernard. The remoteness of the setting is indicated by the rocks in the background.

One interesting example, although it does not feature Bernard (and is therefore not included here), nevertheless belongs to his iconography. It is found in a *Legenda Aurea* manuscript written in England *c.* 1300 by a scribe called Alanus. A number of witty drawings appear in the margin, many of them clearly referring to the adjacent text. One of these occurs in the chapter on Bernard alongside a *Vita Prima* story in which Bernard turns down a canon regular who wanted to enter Clairvaux.[33] The rebuffed canon wondered why Bernard recommended the way of perfection of Clairvaux in his books if he then refused entry to those who want to follow it. To this Bernard retorted that he had only ever recommended 'an amendment of life, and not a change of scenery. The canon, in a fury, fell upon Bernard and hit him so hard on the jaw that it became red and swollen'. He was only saved by Bernard's intervention. The story is more powerful in the *Golden Legend* than in the *Vita Prima* in that James of Voragine omits the qualification, 'if I remember correctly'

[33] VP 3:7:25; PL 185:317-318; LA 213.

(*si bene memini*), inserted by Geoffrey of Auxerre.[34] This dramatic episode was captured in a marginal drawing of a tonsured figure with a clenched fist.[35] The only other known pictorial representation of this scene is found in one of the early sixteenth-century glass panels from the Altenberg cloister (GL37). Here the canon is depicted raising his arm, ready to strike Bernard. The canon's scroll has him saying 'If I had those books of yours with me I would tear them to shreds!' (*Si libros tuos tenerem, discerperem illos!*). To which Bernard replies: 'You have not read in any of my books that you cannot be perfect in your cloister!' (*In nullo eorum legisti, non posse te in claustro esse perfectum!*).

As virtually all the episodes and anecdotes from Bernard's life which found their way into his iconography are included in the early *Lives,* it is impossible to determine which were taken from the *Vitae* directly and which were taken indirectly by way of the *Golden Legend*. The great disparity between the relatively small number of surviving *Vita Prima* manuscripts and the much larger number of the *Legenda Aurea*—one hundred fifty as compared with over a thousand—suggests, however, that the latter was the more important source. Furthermore, whereas the *Vita Prima* was largely restricted to cistercian and other monastic libraries, the *Golden Legend* was not only far more widely disseminated, but was, particularly in its translations into many languages, available to a much more extensive audience, both clerical and lay. By the second half of the Middle Ages the *Golden Legend* had become the standard work for stories on the saints. Although there can be little doubt that knowledge of Bernard was greatly influenced by the *Legenda Aurea,* or that artists relied heavily on it for inspiration in portraying scenes from his life, their use of it can be proved beyond doubt only in those cases where they chose a motif which only occurs in the *Golden Legend,* and not in the earlier cistercian tradition.

Three such stories have been identified.[36] Two of them feature in the late medieval iconography of Bernard, both in glass panels from the Altenberg cloister. One (GL39) concerns a monk who, before entering Clairvaux, had been a gambler and whom Bernard could not prevent from abandoning the cloister. The two halves of the panel tell the story:

[34] McGuire 1994, 192.
[35] Illustrated in Sandler 1998, Fig. 25.
[36] See McGuire 1994, 196–197.

on the left, the monk's departure from Clairvaux, and on the right, his return. The scrolls above the figures say it all:

> *Bernard:* 'How will you keep yourself?' (*Unde uicturus est?*).
>
> *Monk:* 'I am good at throwing dice, and will be able to support myself' (*Ego taxillos ludere scio, et inde uivere potero*).
>
> *Bernard:* 'Now then, if I give you some capital, will you come back every year and hand over my share of the profit?' (*Si nunc capitale commisero, uis singulis annis ad me redire et lucrum meum diuidere?*).
>
> *Monk:* 'I do so with pleasure' (*Libenter hoc agam*).
>
> *Bernard:* 'Then we will share the profit!' (*Diuidamus lucrum*).

On the right Bernard holds out his cowl to receive his winnings from the kneeling monk, who has returned and says: 'I have won nothing and even lost your contribution' (*Nihil super lucratus sum, sed etiam capitali uestro nudatus sum*).

> *Bernard:* 'If that is how things are, it would be better for me to have you back than to lose you as well as the money' (*Si ita est: melius est, ut te benigne recipiam, quam utrumque perdam*).

The words are taken virtually *verbatim* from James of Voragine.[37] Another, slightly earlier, from *c.* 1480, depiction of this story, but no longer existing, is known to have adorned the cloister of another cistercian abbey, Heilsbronn.[38]

The other *Legenda Aurea* story which is not known from earlier sources is that of Bernard challenging a peasant to say the Lord's Prayer without distraction. Wishing thereby to curb the peasant's complacency, Bernard promised him his horse if he could recite it without his mind wandering. The peasant failed the test, for half-way through the prayer he wondered whether he would get the saddle as well as the horse. After that he was less inclined to feel superior.[39] The story is depicted in one

[37] LA 216.
[38] Paffrath 1984, 404–405.
[39] LA 216.

of the twelve images of the Bernard cycle of wall paintings from around 1400 in the chapel dedicated to Bernard in Owen in Württemberg (WA43). A nimbed Bernard is sitting on his horse looking down on the bearded peasant, who holds a stick in his left hand and a sickle, the tool of his trade, in his right hand. A purse or bag hangs from his belt. Only two other depictions of this are known: a glass panel from the Altenberg cloister (GL55), in which the composition is almost identical to that at Owen; and one of the eight engraved silver plates which formed the base of a bust-reliquary made in 1519 by Urs Graf the Elder for the swiss cistercian abbey of Saint Urban (VA04). Two of the plates show only one scene while six have two scenes each; one of them has the gambler monk on the left and the peasant who was unable to concentrate on the right. Here the gambler monk is dressed as a jester and is throwing two dice on to a table placed on a bridge. The inscription reads: TESSERA FISSA DOCET LVDOS CONTEMNERE MIMUM ('Losing at dice teaches the player to have contempt for betting games'). On the opposite side Bernard is shown with his horse and the peasant who failed the test of concentrating when saying the 'Our Father'. The inscription has: PACTO ALIUM VICIT DVM VULT ORARE SECVRUS ('By an agreement he wins over another person who wanted to pray without distraction').

THE CYCLES

In Manuscripts

The tradition of hagiological illustration in the form of a series of pictures featuring episodes or anecdotes from the lives of saints goes back a long way. Such pictorial narrative was found, for example, in a double cycle of the *Lives* of Saint Benedict and Saint Maur from Monte Cassino dating back to the late eleventh century.[40] The scenes were usually arranged in groups of four or six panels to a page, and were sometimes accompanied by a minimal text. Pictorial *Legenda* featuring Bernard were extremely rare. Only two have been recorded. One of them is the magnificent illuminated manuscript produced in 1330–1340 by Nicolas of Bologna and his disciples and was much influenced by the french

[40] Pächt 1962, 16.

Jean de Pucelle, famous painter to the Duke of Berry. It is known as the Hungarian Legendary as it was commissioned by King Charles I of Hungary for the religious instruction of his children. Although referred to as a *Legendary,* this is something of a misnomer as the visual content predominates. A series of illustrations covers episodes from the lives of fifty one saints, while the text is limited to a short caption explaining each picture. Eight pictures covering two folios are devoted to scenes from the life of Bernard, making it one of the earliest known Bernard cycles. Of these, seven refer to stories in the *Vita Prima:* Bernard's vision of the Nativity (MA246); one of three stories of sexual temptation (MA247); two scenes with Bernard's sister Humbeline (MA248, MA249); the letter written in the rain (MA241); the conversion of the Duke of Aquitaine (MA251); and Bernard's deathbed (MA253), one of the most popular scenes in Bernard cycles. The eighth scene (MA252), Bernard's 'testament', comes not from the *Vita Prima* but the *Vita Secunda,* but as all eight are found in the *Legenda Aurea* it is almost certain that the artist drew his inspiration from this source.

The other manuscript cycle is in a french *exemplum* collection consisting of seven-hundred eighty-one chapters and entitled *Ci nous dit* from the opening words of most of the chapters which stands for 'This [image] tells us . . .'[41] It was written between 1313 and 1330 by a mendicant friar in the region of Soissons in north-eastern France. Although the origin of the stories is not known, in the tradition of *exemplum* tales, elements of them can be traced back to twelfth-century sources.[42] Written in the vernacular, the collection devotes eight chapters to Bernard. The first of these occupies two whole folios and is illustrated by two long panels, each of which consists of two scenes. The first (MA042) has, on the left, a monk representing the abbot of Cîteaux, Stephen Harding, receiving Bernard, identified by his green halo and beard, whose hands he holds. Behind Bernard there is another monk representing the thirty-five referred to in the text as having entered Cîteaux at the same time as Bernard and closely corresponding to the 'more than thirty companions' mentioned in the *Vita Prima.*[43] Bernard has his hands raised in praise and thanksgiving. On the right is one of the earliest representations in

[41] Chantilly, Musée de Condé, MS 1078. For this, see Berlioz 1988, 270–283.
[42] For this, see McGuire 1991, 196–204.
[43] VP 1:1:4:19; PL 185:237: *cum sociis amplius quam triginta. . . .*

art of the *Lactation*. It is unique in that Bernard is depicted sucking the white breast of the standing Virgin. The second illustration (MA043) shows, on the left, Bernard preaching from a wooden platform to an audience consisting of a mitred bishop and two monks. The picture on the right features the construction of Clairvaux, with Bernard, accompanied by a monk, admiring a workman dressing a square stone with a mallet. In the scene on the right, part of the church is already built. In this manuscript text predominates and, unlike the Hungarian Legendary, the illustrations are of only secondary importance.

In Altarpieces

The altarpiece, also known as the retable or *retrotabulum*, denoting its position as a panel at the back of the altar, did not emerge until around the middle of the thirteenth century. Before that the priest had celebrated Mass standing behind the altar facing the people and a panel at the rear would not have been possible. Any altar decoration would have taken the form of an *antependium* or frontal, as its name implies, a cloth hanging over the front of the altar. Once the priest was standing before the altar with his back to the people a frontal image would no longer have been clearly visible, and the solution was to raise it and move it to the back. The early type of retable often consisted of a full-length depiction of a saint with scenes from his life in a number of separate compartments on either side in a style which reveals a strong Byzantine influence. A storiated cross, on which the crucified Christ is surrounded by scenes from his Passion, had preceded and may well have been the source of this compositional arrangement.[44] Among the earliest altarpieces are a large number featuring Saint Francis; they are often gabled and contain anything from four to twenty scenes from his life.[45] These, and similar ones featuring Saint Catherine and Saint Mary Magdalen, all date from the second half of the thirteenth century.

The two earliest known altarpieces dedicated to Bernard belong to this type. Although neither is found in a cistercian church, they are both within the sphere of influence of the wealthy catalan abbey of Poblet,

[44] Cole 1973, 244.
[45] van Marle 1923–1938, 1: Figs. 178–182.

founded in 1150–1151 from Fontfroide in the clairvaux filiation. The first is dated 1290 and was in the church of the Templars in Palma, Majorca, closely related to the Cistercians because the Templars were close neighbours of the abbey of La Real, a daughter-house of Poblet founded in 1236, and particularly close to Bernard because he had addressed his treatise *In Praise of the New Warfare* (*De laude novae militiae*) to them. ▶ *Colour plate 5* (PA011-15) It is the work of the Catalan painter known as The Palma Master, who may also have painted some of the mural decoration in the royal palace in Barcelona and the retable of Saint Ursula for the church of Saint Francis in Palma. The Bernard altarpiece consists of a large representation of a tonsured and nimbed Bernard in a white cowl, standing with a crozier with sudarium attached, a book in his left hand and his right hand raised in blessing. His frontal position presents him as someone with great authority, which is accentuated by the two tall candlesticks, one on each side. He has been referred to as bearded,[46] but the meticulously painted stubble on his chin is the same as the shaven top of his head above the tonsure. This image is flanked by two square pictures on either side, each half the size of the central picture in what is a very well-ordered composition. At the top, on the left, is the earliest known representation of the *Lactation* (PA012), and on the right an image of Bernard writing in a rocky landscape with his hood over his head (PA14). Below, on the left, Christ appears to Bernard to assure him that his friend Malachy is a saint (PA013), and on the right Bernard is exorcizing two women, from whose mouths the evil spirits are emanating like fire or smoke (PA015). The scene depicting Malachy is based on Geoffrey of Auxerre's account in the *Vita Prima*.[47] He refers to Bernard's authorship of Malachy's *Life*,[48] and tells of how Bernard, when he was celebrating Mass one day, became aware of Malachy's 'state of glory as a result of a revelation of the Lord' (*gloriam ejus Domino revelante*

[46] Schmitt 1990, 155.

[47] VP 4:4:21; PL 185:333. I am grateful to Brian McGuire for the identification of the source of this image, particularly as the authority on the iconography of Bernard in Spain, Raphael M. Durán, wrongly claimed that the figure appearing to Bernard is Malachy himself (Duran 1950, 56), a mistake which has since been repeated by a number of other scholars (for example, Dupeux 1993, 156; Paffrath 1984, 409; Schmitt 1990, 155–156; Paris 1990, 200; and Aurenhammer 1959–1967, 337). The fact that the figure in the sky is cross-nimbed, identifying it as Christ, Duran explains by claiming that it is a later alteration.

[48] Printed in SBOp 3:307-378.

cognovit). Because of this inspiration he changed the form of the prayer, adding the Collect which is used for saint-bishops—'God, who has made blessed Malachy bishop among the merits of your saints, we ask that he whose feast of an outstanding death we hold, we also may imitate the example of his life'—and not the one commending the dead. Geoffrey adds that Bernard reverently kissed Malachy's sacred remains, but did not record it in his *Life of Malachy*. Bernard is depicted in a white cowl with his hands clasped in prayer in very much the same position as in the *Lactation* scene, but this time he kneels before an altar on which were placed a crucifix and the book from which he had just read the Collect. Bernard is gazing up at the much smaller cross-nimbed half-figure of Christ in the clouds attended by two angels. On the left six tonsured monks, forming the *schola,* stand behind Bernard before a lectern on which an open book is placed. They are clearly amazed that Bernard's words do not correspond to the prayer for a departed brother in the open book before them, and to which the monk leading the *schola* is pointing with his index finger.

The other early Bernard altarpiece is a polychromed carved stone retable from 1348 in the Church of Saint Mary in Montblanch, close to the cistercian abbey of Poblet. It is a double altarpiece dedicated to Saint Barnabas and Saint Bernard, and has four scenes from the life of each flanking the dominant standing figures of the two saints in the centre. Bernard and the scenes from his life are on the left. ▶ *Fig. 9* (SC 39-43). Each scene is contained within a trifoliate arch. Remarkably, two of the four scenes are the same as those in the Palma retable: the *Lactatio* (bottom left) and the Revelation (top right) that Malachy is a saint. These are the first two examples of the first in the iconography of Bernard, and the *only* two known portrayals of the vision. On the right Bernard is shown kneeling at an altar with a canopy above it, against a red background. Turning round he sees a vision of a gold-nimbed Christ on a cloud, in this example identified by the monogram IHS in gold above. Although other details from the same scene in the Palma retable are missing—the book on the altar and the schola of six monks at the lectern with their text in the open book—no other vision of Christ by Bernard is recorded, and there can be no doubt that the scene represents the same occasion, when Bernard changed the Collect for a departed brother to that for a saint-bishop. The other two scenes depict the dream of Bernard's mother that she would give birth to a dog (top left), and Bernard on his deathbed (bottom right). With the exception of the *Lactation,* the other scenes in both these spanish altarpieces were drawn from the *Vita Prima.*

Just as the earliest portrayals of Bernard in manuscripts were not of cistercian origin, but were produced in benedictine *scriptoria,* so the earliest known bernardine altarpieces are not found in cistercian churches. Under Bernard's influence the exuberance of the first Cîteaux manuscripts was followed by a period of restraint. Regulations limiting manuscript illumination and stained glass were enacted.[49] In the same way legislation was passed during the abbacy of Bernard's disciple from Clairvaux, Raynard, who, after a short interregnum, succeeded Stephen Harding as abbot of Cîteaux in 1134/1135. Included in the codification known as the *Instituta* is the following injunction:

> We forbid sculptures and paintings in our churches or in any place in the monastery; because while one's attention is directed to such things, the advantage of good meditation or the discipline of monastic seriousness is often neglected.[50]

After a relatively short period of conformity to bernardine ideals, cistercian manuscript illumination became indistinguishable from that found elsewhere. In the same way, it proved impossible in the long run to enforce early legislation forbidding the decoration of cistercian churches, although an attempt to do so was made as late as 1240, when the General Chapter ordered 'all multi-coloured painted panels' (*omnes tabulae depictae diversis coloribus*) to be removed or painted over in white.[51] As all cistercian churches were dedicated to Mary, the earliest exceptions were undoubtedly images of the Virgin. Statues of her, gradually introduced, are known to have found their way into some cistercian churches at least by the early thirteenth century. Caesarius of Heisterbach records having celebrated Mass in a cistercian nuns' church near Gröningen in Friesland before an image that 'was well sculptured by angelic hands and represented the Blessed Virgin holding

[49] Waddell 1999, 491.

[50] Waddell 1999, 464: *Sculpturae vel picturae in ecclesiis nostris seu in officinis aliquibus monasterii ne fiant interdicimus, quia dum talibus intenditur, utilitas bonae meditationis vel disciplina religiosae gravitatis saepe negligitur.*

[51] *Statuta* 2:218 (1240:12).

her Son in her lap'.[52] Among the early ones, and certainly one of the finest, was that from the abbey of Fontenay from the late thirteenth century.[53]

The first known altarpiece image of Bernard in a cistercian church is a carving in low relief from the cistercian nuns' abbey of Santa Maria della Celestia (SC54). Dated to 1363, it shows the Virgin and Child flanked by Saint Benedict on the left and Bernard on the right, identified by his crozier and book and the inscription above: S. BERNARDUS.

Quite a number of the total of one hundred thirty-three recorded altarpiece images of Bernard consist of large 'portraits' accompanied by scenes from his life; they all belong to the late Middle Ages. A fine example is a florentine panel from *c.* 1430, with a majestic image of Bernard in a frontal position in the centre (PA114). Depicted against a gold ground, he is wearing the late medieval two-piece white cowl, with the hood over his head. In his right hand he has a gold crozier and in his left a red book with clasps. On each side are three scenes with episodes from his life: on the left, from the top, Bernard's entry into Cîteaux (PA115); then an unusual image in which Bernard, accompanied by two monks, acknowledges two kneeling nuns being presented to him by the standing figure of Hildegard of Bingen (PA118). There is no evidence that Bernard ever met Hildegard, although they corresponded. The scene is not historical but is an imagined situation representing his 'endorsement' of her and his symbolic blessing of her benedictine community. The crowns worn by the two nuns have been interpreted as signifying their royal status,[54] but are more likely to represent the tiaras worn by nuns on festive days, examples of which are also known from cistercian female houses.[55] Below this is an example of the favourite italian iconographic theme, the *Doctrina,* with the Virgin appearing to Bernard kneeling before a desk at which he is writing (PA119). On the right, from the top, are scenes of Bernard blessing the infant William de Montmirail (PA116); Bernard's vision of Mary when ill in bed (PA117); and Bernard's funeral (PA120). Bernard's entry to Cîteaux and

[52] Caesarius of Heisterbach 1929, 1:528-529.

[53] France 1998, 180.

[54] In Kaftal 1952, 180 & Dal Pra 1991, 8–10.

[55] I am grateful to Brian McGuire for this interpretation. Cistercian examples are given in France 1998, 154–155, including an illustration of the dedication of the church at Beaupré in which the nuns are seen wearing coronets for the occasion (ill. 102).

these last three scenes are all recorded in the *Vita Prima,* and as the story of Bernard blessing the infant is not found in the *Golden Legend,* the artist's source must have been the *Vita Prima.*[56]

The earlier altarpieces were rectangular, like the one at Palma, and sometimes gabled, like many of the Saint Francis retables and the florentine one of Bernard. These simple panels were gradually replaced by more complex ones, eventually taking the form of triptychs consisting of a central panel and two hinged wings, or even more elaborate polyptychs with more than two wings. The wings could be folded over the central panel and when the altarpiece was closed, usually displayed different images painted on the reverse. They lent themselves to being divided into sections, each portraying a scene from the life of the saint or saints to whom the altar was dedicated. Sometimes pinnacles were added.

In some cases the retables were supported on a wooden plinth at the back of the altar known as the *predella,* meaning step. Raised they could be better seen. They often contained small images showing episodes in the lives of the standing figures of the saints featured in the main part of the altarpiece itself. Thus, in the altarpiece painted by Giovanni da Milano *c.* 1360, the four saints represented—Catherine, Bernard, Bartholomew, and Barnabas—are shown in scenes depicting events which are then described in the inscription: DECOLACIO SANCTE KATERINE, DOCTRINA SANCTI BERNARDI CONFESSORIS, PASIO SANCTI BARTOLOMEI APOSTOLI, PASIO SANCTI BARNABE APOSTOLI. Bernard is shown (PA150) seated at a desk as the Virgin appears to him (the *Doctrina*). The Bernard altar, painted by the Master of the Rinuccini Chapel features Bernard's Vision of the Virgin—the *Doctrina*—as the central panel (PA155), and has a predella with six sections consisting of a scene from each of the lives of the four saints depicted on the side panels (Benedict, John the Evangelist, Quentin, and Galgano) and two from the life of Bernard in the centre. One has Bernard sitting on the right surrounded by a number of his monks (PA156). He greets his five brothers, who stand before him, from the left Nivard, Bartholomew, Andrew, Gerard, and Guy. Bernard holds the hand of Gerard, identified by the wound in his side which, according to the *Vita Prima,* Bernard had predicted he would receive and after receiving which he changed his mind and decided to join his brothers

[56] VP 1:4:19; PL 185:237-238. VP 1:9:56; PL 185:257. VP 1:12:58; PL 185:258-259. VP 5:2:13; PL 185:359.

at Clairvaux.[57] The other scene from the *Vita Prima* is that of Bernard in a high pulpit preaching against heresy in Sarlat (PA157).

A number of cistercian churches having the more elaborate types of altarpieces contained Bernard cycles. One of the side chapels built at Maulbronn in 1424 had an altarpiece, painted in 1432, with two wings showing eight scenes from the lives of saints, four of them on the inside and four on the outside. Five of these depicted Bernard, while the other three contained scenes from the *Lives* of Dominic, Leonard and Theodul (also known as Jodokus), and Francis. Two of the Bernard scenes illustrate *Vita Prima* stories. The first (PA059) is of the vision Bernard had on his sickbed of Mary, Laurence, and Benedict. Mary is shown on the left, beside Bernard, and behind him is Laurence in a dalmatic, being a deacon, and Benedict in his black cowl and holding a crozier. The small figure of the monk whom Bernard ordered to visit the church may be seen in the background, praying on his knees before an altar. This picture is more faithful in following the story in its detail than the same scene in the florentine altarpiece mentioned above (PA117), in which Mary is the only other figure depicted with Bernard. The other *Vita Prima* scene is of the conversion of the Duke of Aquitaine (PA058), one of the most popular bernardine narrative themes. The artist here has deviated from the literary account, which has Bernard outside the church, by showing Bernard in eucharistic vestments standing before an altar, upon which is a chalice and an open Missal, holding up the Host before the kneeling duke. The scroll above Bernard is very damaged, but it probably contained some words in Latin from the *Golden Legend:*

> Look! The Son of the Virgin has come to you, the Lord of the Church you are persecuting. Here is your judge, at whose name every knee is bowed. Here is your judge, into whose hands your soul will pass. Will you despise Him as you despise His servants? Resist Him if you can![58]

The other three bernardine scenes show the image of Christ detaching his arms from the cross to embrace Bernard (PA060)—the *Amplexus,* particularly popular in southern Germany—and two scenes which pay

[57] VP 1:3:11-12; PL 185:233-234.
[58] LA 218.

tribute to Bernard in a general way: as the abbot and teacher of his monks to whom he is preaching in the chapterhouse (PA057); and as a thaumaturge surrounded by the poor, sick, and crippled for whom he did so much by way of healing (PA061).

Another Bernard cycle altarpiece from a cistercian monastery is one commissioned by Abbot Wolfgang Oertl of Zwettl in Austria (1495 1508) for his private chapel and painted in 1500 by Jörg Breu on fig wood. The centre of the altarpiece consists of painted, mostly gilt, wood carvings showing the Virgin flanked by Bernard on the left and Benedict on the right below an elaborately carved canopy (SC05). The wings have two scenes from the life of Bernard on each side, eight altogether. The four scenes on the outer side are framed in red while those on the inner side (the ones visible when the wings are open) are framed in gold with foliate ornament on the lower border. The outer side (seen when the wings are closed) has, on the top left, Bernard taking leave of his family (PA038), and on the right his arrival with his brothers at Cîteaux being greeted at the gate by a corpulent Stephen Harding, accompanied by two monks, all in black cowls with their hoods over their heads (PA039). On the far right Bernard's sister, Humbeline, is being received at Jully by three nuns. There are two small dogs in the foreground, an allusion to Bernard's mother's dream when expecting him. Below are scenes of Bernard praying to be given the grace to become a competent harvester (PA040), and Bernard healing a crippled child (PA041). The inner side portrays Bernard healing a woman possessed by the devil, blessing a group of farm animals by scattering salt, a scene not warranted by any known literary source and in which the artist may have confused him with Francis, and finally, Bernard's deathbed and his burial (PA042-PA045).

Surprisingly, the most comprehensive Bernard cycle was not in a cistercian church but comes from the benedictine abbey of Essenbæk in Denmark. After the Reformation the altarpiece was moved to a nearby church. Only a few remnants, now in the local museum in the town of Randers, were saved when the church was demolished in the nineteenth century, but a full description previously made by a danish art historian has survived.[59] The altarpiece was a large, complex polyptych dedicated

[59] Laurits Høyen who visited the church in 1830 and 1833 and whose unpublished *Lommebøger* (notebooks) are preserved in the *Antikvarisk-Topografisk Arkiv* of the National Museum, Copenhagen.

to Laurence, the patron saint of the abbey, and Bernard, and there were twelve panels on each side devoted to scenes from the lives of the two saints. A study of the written description has made it possible to identify the majority of the bernardine scenes and to establish that the artist's most likely source was the *Golden Legend*.

In Wall Paintings

There are only very few Bernard cycles in wall paintings. The earliest known, and most extensive, is that on the east wall of a chapel dedicated to Bernard at Owen in Württemberg. It consists of twelve scenes, one of which is totally destroyed while most of the others have been preserved only in fragments (WA39-49). Although, as we mentioned above,[60] the source of one of the scenes (WA43) is the *Golden Legend*, there are strong indications of a familiarity with the *Vita Prima*. There is, for example, a scene of Bernard preaching (WA46) of which there is only a brief mention in the *Legenda Aurea* whereas the *Vita Prima* features him preaching outside the monastery on a number of occasions during his travels. Second, while his death is merely noted in the *Golden Legend*, Geoffrey of Auxerre in Book 5 of the *Vita Prima* refers extensively to Bernard's death and his burial three days later. The two events form the subject of the last two Owen scenes. The first (WA48) shows Bernard lying in bed, his head resting on a pillow. He is surrounded by his monks, as Geoffrey of Auxerre recorded, all holding candles except for the monk in front, who is identified by the stole he is wearing as the officiating priest. He is pointing to Bernard with one hand and sprinkling him with an aspergillum of holy water with the other hand. The funeral scene (WA49) has Bernard, with a halo, lying on a bier dressed in eucharistic vestments, a mitre on his head and a crozier in his hand. Again he is surrounded by a group of monks led by an officiating priest, again wearing a crossed stole. The monks are carrying candles, as before, and one of them has a ring-like object in his hand which may be the top of a thurible containing burning incense. The priest holds a large candle in his left hand and, as in the deathbed scene, an aspergillum in his right. A figure on the right is holding a processional cross. Under Bernard are two objects which are likely

[60] See pages 122–124.

the bands of cloth used to lower him into the ground. Comparable images are found in a late twelfth-century manuscript (MA039) showing Bernard being placed in a tomb by two clerics, and in one of the six scenes from a florentine altarpiece dated *c.* 1430 (PA120). Although the origin of the chapel is not known, there is documentary evidence from the sixteenth century of its dedication to Bernard, and the reliance of a number of the scenes on the *Vita Prima* as their source points to a connection with a cistercian abbey, perhaps Bebenhausen, which was not far away.

The identification of one of the Owen scenes (WA47) is problematical. It has Bernard with a halo sitting up in bed, the lower part of his body covered by a bedspread and with two pillows behind him. His hands are folded in prayer before another saint whose right hand appears to be raised in blessing Bernard. He (or she) is accompanied by two angels, one of whom is holding a chalice. Although it is hard to identify the scene, the most likely saint to be blessing Bernard is Mary, and it may therefore refer to the story of Bernard on his sickbed ordering one of his monks to visit the church and pray for him.[61] According to the *Vita Prima*, the monk prayed before the high altar—as always in cistercian churches dedicated to Mary—and at the altars of Saint Benedict and Saint Lawrence. As a result the three saints visited him, laid hands on him, and the pain went away. Even though Benedict and Lawrence are absent from the Owen image, another example—from which the two saints are similarly absent—exists in one of the six scenes in the florentine altarpiece of *c.* 1430 (PA117) and is thought to represent the story.

The most impressive of the Owen images (WA45) is not a scene from Bernard's life but an author 'portrait' parallel to that in the first of all Bernard cycles, the Palma altarpiece. (▶ *Colour plate 5*). A nimbed Bernard is sitting on a high elaborate chair writing with his right hand in an open book placed on an adjustable lectern in front of him. (▶ *Colour plate 6*). He is facing a church, that of Clairvaux. Remarkably, the rocks and trees in the background are somewhat similar to those in the Palma picture. The rural setting in a rocky, mountainous landscape is a visual expression of two themes: the cave imagery associated with Saint Benedict; and Bernard's predilection for meditating in the woods and fields.[62] Both themes were later to play a prominent role in the Italian *Doctrina* images.

[61] VP 1:12:58; PL 185:258-259.
[62] Ep 106; SBOp 7:266.

The only other known extensive wall painting cycle is that at another chapel dedicated to Bernard, at Pamparato in northern Italy.[63] It consists of nine frescos painted in 1482 with scenes drawn from the *Vita Prima* and the *Exordium Magnum*. These are much more easily identified than the Owen wall paintings as there is an inscription under each picture.

In Stained Glass Windows

The narrative pictorial stained glass panels from the Altenberg cloister were by far the most comprehensive of all Bernard cycles.[64] Originally there were one hundred fifteen panels made in a Cologne workshop in the first third of the sixteenth century. Approximately a third of them depicted Old Testament scenes, and about seventy had scenes from the life of Bernard. They were dispersed after the secularization of the abbey in 1803, when the cloister was demolished, but fifty-seven are known to have survived. Of these fifteen were destroyed in the 1939–1945 war, while the remaining forty-two are now in seven different locations. Of these, the largest number (nineteen) are in the redundant Anglican St Mary's Church in Shrewsbury, England.[65] A similar cycle at the dependent women's house of Saint Apern, which had moved to Cologne in 1436, is known to have consisted at the secularization of fifty-four panels, eleven of which still exist, nine of them in Cologne Cathedral, one in the church in Shrewsbury, and one in an english village church at Marston Bigot in Somerset.[66] They are dated 1525–1526 and were made in the same Cologne workshop as the Altenberg windows. Although the most comprehensive, the Altenberg and Saint Apern cycles were not the oldest Bernard cycles in stained glass. The cloister at Heilsbronn was rebuilt during the abbacy of Peter Wegel (1463–1479), following which panels depicting bernardine scenes were installed. It is not known how many there were, and some of them had already disappeared by 1600; none now remains, but details of sixteen are known from a description, and eleven of them correspond to Altenberg scenes.[67]

[63] See Dal Prà 1991, 21–35.
[64] For this, see Paffrath 1984, 22–227.
[65] See Hunt 1951.
[66] Paffrath 1984, 391.
[67] Paffrath 1984, 404–405.

The majority of the scenes in the Altenberg cycle refer to Bernard's life outside the cloister, some before he entered Cîteaux but most relating to his later interventions in the wider world. Only eighteen deal with his monastic career: his entry to Cîteaux, his founding of Clairvaux, and a number of the miracles he performed.

The narrative themes illustrated in the Altenberg were comprehensive and wide-ranging. They owed their origin to several sources, including stories which only appear in any one of the three literary sources: the *Vita Prima*, the *Exordium Magnum*, or the *Legenda Aurea*. Among them is the story—told by William of Saint Thierry and represented in both the Altenberg and Saint Apern cycles (GL08 & GL60)—of Bernard being reprimanded by his abbot for failing to recite the seven penitential psalms he had promised to say daily for his mother—a rare example in hagiography in which a saint is portrayed as less than perfect.

Three stories unique to the *Exordium Magnum* are represented in the Altenberg cycle: the vision of angels (GL51); the reprieve of a convicted prisoner whom Bernard brought with him to Clairvaux where he was transformed 'from wolf to lamb, from robber to lay brother' (GL20);[68] and of the monk who did not believe in the Real Presence (GL14).

Two stories which are found exclusively in the *Golden Legend* are included in the Altenberg cycle. One is of the gambler monk whose departure and return are featured in a panel as one half of a double scene (VA04). The other, also a double panel, illustrates the story, mentioned above,[69] of the peasant whom Bernard challenged to say the Lord's Prayer without distraction (GL55). In the background the peasant is shown kneeling before a wayside shrine while reciting the prayer. Having failed, he kneels before Bernard who is mounted on his horse and accompanied by a monk and a layman.

SIGNS OF DIVINE ELECTION

The problem of duality in the presentation of Bernard's life—what Bredero refers to as the 'cult and history' in the sub-title of his study—[70]

[68] EM 2:15 (Griesser 1961, 109).

[69] See page 124.

[70] Bredero 1996.

is nowhere better conveyed than in the *Vita Prima.* As in the recounting of all stories, the three authors made a careful selection of the material that was available to them to achieve the purposes for which they were writing: primarily to obtain the canonization of the subject and secondarily to edify generations of monks to come. As has been demonstrated, it was even necessary to make changes in order to succeed in the primary aim.[71] An interesting example of the selective use of events in the *Vita Prima* is contained in the hymn *Bernardus inclitis,* assigned to Compline on the feast of Bernard. Written anonymously, it is almost certainly of cistercian origin. The earliest known sources date back to the fourteenth century. The manuscript tradition is almost entirely italian and germanic, although there is one manuscript extant from Vadstena in Sweden.[72] Almost every line is a cameo containing a complete story. To the uninitiated it would make little sense, but to those versed in the *Vita Prima* or the *Golden Legend* it provided material for meditation in much the same way as did viewing the narrative pictures in the Bernard cycles. As a literary counterpart to Bernard's iconography, the choice of themes to celebrate Bernard's feast day is in itself revealing. Here is the text, with the reference to the *Vita Prima* stories alongside:

Bernard arose from noble parents VP1:1:1; PL 185:227
Noted for his merits, with his distinguished brothers
He fled into hidden places VP1:3:10-17; PL 185:232-236
Having rejected his parental riches
And the attractions of the world.

He was holy from the womb VP1:2:2; PL 185:227-228
He emerged as a loud barking dog
A distinguished teacher of heavenly sweetness
Unremitting at attending Vigils, he was shown
To his mother in the guise of a dog bringing salvation.

Vigils was late, he slept at the door. VP1:2:4; PL 185:228-229
Suddenly the womb of Mary produced her Son.
These events inspired his Homilies of Praise.
Secretly the boy dispenses alms. VP1:2:5; PL 185:229

[71] Bredero 1996, 46–52.
[72] I am grateful to Fr Chrysogonus Waddell for this information.

When a woman knocked on his bedroom VP1:3:7; PL 185:231
He cried out 'Thieves!'
They searched the house with lanterns
He threw himself into freezing water VP1:3:6 (PL 185:229-30)
He despised lewd songs
And relinquished displays of splendour
He turned away from the woman in
the bed. VP1:3:7; PL 185:230

He enters Cîteaux with
thirty companions VP1:4:19; PL 185:237-238
The Order releases the marriage
bond of his brother VP1:3:10-1; PL 185:232-233
Gerard, struck with the sword of an enemy, goes free
Goes free, bound by the chains of the Order.

He obeys the precepts of his local bishop VP1:7:1; PL 185:245
He drinks the oil from the chalice
instead of water VP3.1.2; PL 185:304-305
He stands as a prophet in the heart of truth
And he counts the hoe equal to the ring
of high office VP1:4:1; PL 185:239

He writes a letter in the middle of
the downpour VP1:11:50; PL 185:255-256
He caused the flies to fall to
their death VP1:11:52; PL 185:256
By the sign of the cross he healed
A poor woman possessed of
the devil. VP2:4:21-22; PL 185:280-281

He interprets the Scriptures as a Song of Mary
He breaks the bonds leading to hell
He brings the dead back to life V Quarta 2:11; PL 185:546
Foreign people acknowledge
his holiness VP3:3:7; PL 185:307
In his speech, in his style, in his works of wonder.

Praise, honour, and glory to God the Father
Let there be repentance to sinners from the Only Begotten
May the Holy Spirit give us joy unending. Amen.[73]

In the same way, artists later made selective use of whichever literary sources were at hand in order to satisfy those who had commissioned them. The narrative picture cycles were overwhelmingly drawn from a monastic context, and the relative popularity of the choice of topics from Bernard's life reflects this. Themes which displayed the characteristic

[73] *Breviarium Cisterciense, Pars Aestivalis*, Westmalle, 1903, 422 & 427:

Bernardus inclitis ortus natalibus,
Praeclarus meritis, cum claris fratribus
Fugit in abditis, paternis opibus
Spretis, et mundi flosculo.

Latrator strenuus, sanctus ex utero,
Doctor praecipuus nectare supero:
Vigil assiduus, sub salutifero
Monstratur matri catulo.

Tardant Vigilae, dormit ad ostium.
Mox venter Mariae producit Filium.
Laudis homiliae provocant studium.
Dat puer nummos clanculo.

Pulsante femina, latrones clamitat:
Defixa lumina stagno praecipitat,
Jactae cedit in lectulo.

Intrat Cistercium cum tricenario,
Fratris connubium solvit religio:
Gerardus hostium perfossus gladio
Liber exit cum vinculo.

Jussu Pontificis obedit rustico;
Oleum calicis bibit pro thetico:
Stat in veridicis corde prophetico,
Rastrum coaequat annulo.

Scribit epistolam in imbris medio
Muscae parabolam affert extinctio
Fœminam dyscolam plenam daemonio
Curat crucis signaculo.

Mariae cithara, Scripturas explicat,
Spoliat tartara, functos vivificat:
Necnon gens barbara hunc sanctum praedicat
Ore, stylo, miraculo.

Sit laus Ingenito, decus et gloria:
Ab Unigenito sit reis venia:
Nobis Paraclito praestante gaudia,
In infinito saeculo. Amen.

signs of sainthood were among the most popular. Although a large number of the stories from the *Lives* are represented among the total of one hundred sixty-one narrative images recorded, five stand out as occurring more frequently than all the others. Of these, three define the three key events in Bernard's life: his birth, with the story of his mother's dream; his *conversio*, with his entry to Cîteaux; and his death and burial. The other two celebrate his ministry to the Church outside the cloister in which he harnesses the power of the Sacrament to secure the conversion of the Duke of Aquitaine, and his role as a thaumaturge who has the ability to expel devils from those possessed. The choice was not arbitrary but reflects the perceived relative importance and appeal of the themes.

Aleth's Dream

It is not difficult to see why the story of the dream of Bernard's mother Aleth should be among the most frequently illustrated bernardine themes.[74] The importance attached to the special divine grace with which Bernard was born is testified by William of Saint Thierry in Book One of the *Vita Prima* when, dealing with the beginning of Bernard's preaching ministry outside the cloister, he reminds his readers that 'divine revelation had pointed him out while still in the womb', a parallel to the biblical references regarding Jeremiah and John the Baptist.[75] It was not a theme unique to Bernard: the same story formed part of the hagiographic tradition of Saint Dominic (see MA217). The immense influence of pious mothers in their formation, such as that of Aleth on Bernard and all her other children, is another characteristic of the *Lives* of saints.

The earliest known picture of Aleth's dream is in a late thirteenth-century cistercian breviary which belonged to the german abbey of Bebenhausen, where it was possibly written (MA054). According to information given on the first page, it was given on 28 September 1538, to the swiss cistercian abbey of Saint Urban. One of the twenty-seven

[74] For the story, see Chapter Two.

[75] VP 1:8:42; PL 185:251: *Jam tunc enim ad opus praedicationis divinitus aptabatur, ad quod, ut supra dictum est, ex utero matris suae cum testimonio divinae revelationis olim fuerat praesignatus.* The biblical references are: Jer 1:4-5: 'Before I formed you in the womb, I knew you. Before you came to birth, I consecrated you', and, on John the Baptist, Luke 1:15: 'Even from his mother's womb he will be filled with the Holy Spirit'.

miniatures shows Aleth lying in a bed, with a barking dog standing on top of her within the initial *A(d sancti ac beatissimi patris nostri cuius hodie festa celebramus laudes . . .)*, words ascribed to Saint Ambrose and used in the Bernard Office until 1656.[76] The theme is rare in illuminated manuscripts, but forms part of several Bernard cycles. One (VA10) is engraved on the early sixteenth-century silver reliquary from Saint Urban, but the earliest is the carved stone retable from Montblanch in which the top left of the four scenes shows Aleth in bed with a dog on top of her. (▶ *Fig. 9, top left*).

The late-medieval altarpiece from the benedictine abbey of Essenbæk in Denmark, now known only from the notes of a nineteenth-century art historian, had two of its twelve scenes dedicated to Aleth's dream. According to the description by Laurits Højen, one panel had 'a woman lying on a bed with a dog sitting on the roof barking', while the other had 'a monk with a book in his hands . . . he says something to the woman' of which the only two words which are legible are '*optimus . . . mater . . .*'.[77] These words are not entirely correctly quoted (they should have been *optimi catuli mater*—'the mother of a wonderful puppy'), but they are undoubtedly intended to be those of the *Vita Prima* story repeated in the *Golden Legend,* and identify the two scenes as representing Aleth's dream. The story is related in the same two parts, but within one panel, in one of the Altenberg windows, sadly destroyed during the 1939–1945 war (GL01). In a double scene, Aleth was shown on the left, asleep in bed with a small dog at the foot of the bed; on the right she is kneeling before an old man. The scroll emanating from his mouth has a paraphrase of the words of consolation from the story. In addition to the images of Aleth's dream, a further twenty-three images have been recorded in which the story is merely alluded to by the depiction of a small dog at Bernard's feet.

Bernard's Conversio

Bernard's *Conversio,* both in the more commonly used sense of turning to God and in the more technical monastic usage, the entry into reli-

[76] Paffrath 1990, 201 (note 348).

[77] From Laurits Højen's *Lommebøger,* now in the National Museum, Copenhagen—in *Antikvarisk-Topografisk Arkiv.*

gious life, was undoubtedly the key event of his life. It was recorded by William of Saint Thierry with unusual solemnity in terms reminiscent of an entry in ancient annals:

> In the year of the Lord's Incarnation 1113, the fifteenth year from the founding of Cîteaux, when he was twenty-three years old, the servant of God Bernard entered that house with more than thirty companions. Thus he submitted his neck to the gentle yoke of Christ, under abbot Stephen.[78]

It is therefore not surprising that there are a larger number of representations in art of this event than of most others in his life. In some he is depicted arriving in lay clothes, accompanied by his brothers and greeted at the gates of Cîteaux by his abbot, Stephen Harding. In the Altenberg cycle (GL07), for example, he appears in a red tunic with long reddish hair, kneeling before Stephen Harding who, in order that he may welcome him with both hands, has his crozier under his arm. Bernard's youngest brother, Nivard, is depicted in the corner as a small child playing with a bird. He is engaged in a dialogue in the form of scrolls with the eldest brother Guy, who informs him that he will now inherit all the family's lands. Wise beyond his years, Nivard retorts that while his brothers will gain heaven, all they left him with was earth, 'hardly a fair deal'.[79] He later joined them at Cîteaux. This small detail is more accurate than other scenes in which all the brothers, including Nivard, are depicted arriving at Cîteaux at the same time.

Bernard's arrival at Cîteaux forms one of the eight scenes from Jörg Breu's altarpiece at Zwettl, discussed above (PA039). Here he is depicted being greeted with all his five brothers, all dressed in their lay clothes, by a corpulent Stephen Harding. In these and most other examples, Bernard is shown, significantly, being received with his brothers and not with the 'more than thirty companions' referred to in the *Vita Prima*. The reason is undoubtedly to be found in the disparity between this single statement and the extensive coverage in the text of the conversion of his brothers,

[78] VP 1:4:19; PL 185:237: *Anno ab incarnatione Domini millesimo centesimo decimo tertio, a constitutione domus Cisterciensis quindecimo, servus Dei Bernardus annos natus circiter tres et viginti, Cistercium ingressus, cum sociis amplius quam triginta, sub abbate Stephano, suavi jugo Christi collum submisit.*

[79] VP 1:3:15; PL 185:236.

one after the other. In this way the iconography not only records the central event of Bernard's conversion but at the same time commemorates the important contribution of his entire family to Cistercian history.

This momentous event is also depicted on one of the engraved silver plates from the Saint Urban bust-reliquary, which has the inscription: 'He gave himself to God under the holy religion' (COLLA DEO SVBDIT SANCTA SUB RELIGIONE) (VA11). On it Stephen is shown on his own and not accompanied by any of his monks, as was usual, and Bernard is joined by only two companions. Bernard's entry is also known to have formed part of the former glass cycle from Heilsbronn,[80] and the former altarpiece from Essenbæk in Denmark.[81]

Another way of showing Bernard's submission to 'the gentle yoke of Christ' was by representing the occasion when he received the monastic habit. This could either be the 'clothing', that is, the ceremony shortly after entering when he became a novice, or his solemn profession when, a year later, according to the *Rule,* he made his vows, received the cowl, and became a full member of the monastic community. It is not always clear in Bernard's iconography which of these two ceremonies is represented. In one of four panels from an altarpiece painted in 1518 from the cistercian abbey of Neuberg in Styria (PA098), Bernard is kneeling before Stephen Harding, who is dressed in a black cowl and wears a large black cap. He is corpulent, in the way that abbots are so often depicted in late medieval art. He has a crozier in his left hand while his right hand is raised in blessing Bernard, who is putting on a white cowl over his white tunic with the help of another monk. The scene takes place in a vaulted chamber with columns, probably the chapter house, and therefore most likely represents Bernard's clothing and not his solemn profession, which would have taken place in the chapel. It is witnessed by a large group of monks, all in black cowls on one side, and on the other side a group of laymen, probably his brothers. The garment Bernard is putting on is definitely the monastic cowl and not the novice's sleeveless mantle, and yet he is all in white while the monks' cowls are black. The three other Neuberg altarpiece scenes are of the building of Clairvaux, the *Lactatio,* and the *Amplexus* (PA099, PA100, PA101).

[80] Paffrath 1984, 404.
[81] See pages 133–134.

Similar scenes of the clothing ceremony are found in two late fifteenth-century miniatures. A manuscript of Vincent de Beauvais' *Speculum Historiale* (MA089) has a scene with Stephen Harding, identified by his name above his head, receiving new recruits assisted by three of his monks. He is wearing a white cowl and black cap but is not nimbed, whereas Bernard, standing beside him, is. Bernard, identified by 's.bernard' above his head, has already received the habit. Another recruit kneels before the abbot, and a further three—Bernard's brothers—await their turn, one of them being helped out of his secular clothes by one of the monks. Bernard's father, Tescelin, identified by his name, is on the left. In a parallel scene on the far right his mother, Aleth, though long dead, is depicted assisting Bernard's sister, Humbeline, who is being received by the benedictine abbess of Jully and two of her nuns, all in black habits. Again there is some confusion as to what the scene represents: it is clearly a clothing ceremony, for the candidates are changing out of their ordinary clothes, and yet they are shown putting on, not the distinctive mantle of the novice, but the monastic cowl, which would have been conferred on them only at their profession. The other late fifteenth-century miniature (MA088) appears in a french translation of the *Golden Legend,* at the beginning of the section on Bernard and above the decorated initial *B(ernard est dit de ber cestadine)*—the prologue which deals with the etymology of his name. In a scene which appears to take place in a chapter house, the young Bernard kneels before abbot Stephen Harding, who is seated and places his left hand on Bernard's head and blesses him with his right. The act is witnessed by his parents, identified by their names on their backs, and his five brothers, the tiny figures kneeling on the left. The abbot is assisted by two monks sitting on either side of him. Most unusually, and contrary to the *Speculum Historiale* miniature, Stephen Harding is nimbed while Bernard is not.

Bernard's Death and Burial

Bernard's death on 20 August 1153, and subsequent burial is described in detail by Geoffrey of Auxerre in the *Vita Prima:*

> It was hardly the hour of Terce when, amidst a great number of brethren, and bishops and abbots, that great light of his age,

> holy (and indeed blessed) Bernard was led by Christ from the body of death into the land of the living. No longer with those who wept at his departure, he was now with the rejoicing throng of those who had gone before him into the dwelling of the saints in heaven and of the choirs of angels. . . . He had exchanged death for life, and the light of faith for the fulfilled vision. His pilgrimage was over, and he had gone from this world to the Father.[82]

His body was prepared in the mortuary chapel and the number of those who came to view him and touch his body was so great that it became difficult to maintain order and the monks decided to bury him earlier than was the custom. The interment took place early on 22 August, before the anticipated crowds arrived. In recognition of his sanctity, he was buried in the church and not in the chapter house, as was normal for abbots. According to common practice, when he was canonized in 1174, his feast day was set at 20 August, thought of not so much as the day he died as the day he was born into eternal life, identifying the event with the culmination of the life of Christ. Not surprisingly, more examples of it have been recorded in medieval art than of any other event in Bernard's life, altogether fifteen out of a total of one hundred sixty-one narrative scenes. In addition to these, death scenes of Bernard are also known to have formed part of the two cycles which no longer exist, the glass at Heilsbronn[83] and the altarpiece at Essenbæk in Denmark.

As we saw above the event merited two scenes in the Owen cycle (WA48 & WA49). It was also covered by two scenes in each of the two glass cycles at Altenberg (GL48, GL49) and Saint Apern (GL64, GL65). Two of the deathbed scenes have scrolls which paraphrase texts from the *Vita Prima*. One of the Saint Apern scenes has Bernard voicing his dilemma: 'I do not know what I shall choose. It is a hard choice. I would

[82] VP 5:2:13 (PL 185:359): *Hora autem diei pene tertia singularis lucerna suae generationis, sanctus et vere beatus abbas Bernardus, a corpore mortis in terram viventium feliciter Christo duce migravit, ex filiorum circumstantium et inter graves singultus ac lacrymas uberes utcumque psallentium choro ad multorum, quos ipse praemiserat, coetus transiens laetabundas, ad sanctorum cuneos gratulantes, ad obvia agmina angelorum. Felix transitus . . . de morte ad vitam, de fide ad notitiam, de peregrinatione ad patriam, de mundo ad Patrem!*

[83] Paffrath 1984, 405.

like to leave and be with Christ which would be better, but it is necessary to remain in the flesh in order to stay with you' (*Quid eligam ignoro, coarctor autem e duobus: desiderium habens dissolvi et esse cum christo multo magis melius; permanere autem in Carne necessarium propter vos*).[84] In one of the Altenberg panels, Bernard raises his hand to greet the bishop of Langres, standing at the foot of his bed wearing a mitre and carrying a crozier. Bernard's scroll says: 'Do not mourn, for now I am not of this world' (*Ne Miseris, jam enim non sum de hoc mundo*). Two monks kneel by Bernard's bed and a larger group stands in the background, saying: 'Why, O father, do you leave us, or to whom will you entrust us who are desolate?' (*Cur nos Pater deseris, aut cui nos desolatos relinquis?*).[85]

Two panels out of a total of eight are also devoted to Bernard's death and burial in the Zwettl altarpiece painted by Jörg Breu in 1500. In one (PA044) Bernard lies on a mat on the floor and is being handed a candle by one of the eight kneeling monks, all of them, like Bernard—and all the monks depicted in all eight panels—in black cowls; six of them have their hoods over their heads. An aspersorium with holy water and a candlestick with a candle are placed on the tiled floor in the foreground. On the left there is a view of a passage with two more monks, and beyond that, through a doorway, a man is carrying a coffin on his shoulder. Two angels, carrying a cloth with which they are preparing to receive Bernard's soul, are floating above the scene. The death scene is portrayed in one of two hundred forty-five miniatures in a manuscript in the *Concordantiae Caritatis* written between 1351 and 1358 by Abbot Ulrich of Lilienfeld (MA034). Here the death of Bernard is featured in a medallion which illustrates his feast on 20 August. Again, two angels are holding the ends of a cloth, but this time the soul of Bernard, which in true medieval style takes the form of a small naked figure, is already being carried to heaven on the cloth. The body of Bernard in a grey cowl with his hands crossed over his body lies watched over by five monks, two in white cowls and three in grey. Three of them have their hands raised. One is wiping tears

[84] VP 5:2:13; PL 185:359: 'Bernard wept with those who were weeping, and lifting up his eyes to heaven, and being straitened between the two alternatives, he knew not which to choose. . . . His fatherly love urged him to remain with his sons, and yet the desire for Christ drew him away'.

[85] VP 5:2:13; PL 185:359: 'Do not be surprised, I am no longer of this world', and 'Who will look after your work when you are gone from us?'.

from his eyes and one is pointing to Bernard with his left hand and holding a book in his right. The inscription around the circular border reads: 'The choir of angels sing a song pleasing in its sweetness which tells us that he is blessed' (*It Pater ad celos cui cantant agmina melos. Dulcedine gratum quod et hunc probat esse beatum*). The ascent of Bernard's soul to heaven appears in two other images. The first is one of the four scenes from the carved altarpiece from Montblanch dated 1348 (SC42). (▶ *Fig. 9, bottom left*). Bernard, on his deathbed, is accompanied by two monks standing, one sitting with a book and one kneeling with his hood over his head. Painted above them is a tiny figure representing his soul, which is being carried up to heaven by two small angels. The other is a miniature in a late thirteenth-century manuscript known as the Breviary of Philippe le Bel (MA183). Bernard is depicted within the rosa initial *A*(*nno*), the first of the four lessons taken from the *Vita Prima* for Vigils on the Octave of the Feast of Bernard, it describes his entry to Cîteaux, quoted above.[86] He lies, nimbed and in a black cowl, on a white bed at the end of which are three tonsured monks, also in black. A naked baby with gold nimbus, representing his soul, rises from Bernard's mouth to be received into heaven by an angel coming out of blue and white clouds.

Bernard's burial is represented in various ways. The second of the Zwettl panels (PA045) shows the funeral procession. In the front are two novices carrying a processional cross and an aspersorium. They are followed by four monks carrying Bernard's coffin draped with a black cloth and a white cross. On the left is a cemetery with a dug grave ready to receive the coffin. Beside it are two grave diggers and three more monks. Bernard's funeral procession also forms the subject of one of the miniatures (MA318) in an Obituary from the nuns' house of Notre-Dame-des-Près dated the second half of the thirteenth century. Here Bernard's remains, draped by a red cloth, are carried in procession by four white monks, preceded by another monk in a white cowl carrying a processional cross, and followed by a monk in rosa eucharistic vestments and carrying an open book from which he is reading prayers. Above this scene there is another miniature of Bernard standing in a frontal position with a red crozier in his left hand while with his right hand he blesses two smaller monks at his feet. A date is given in red ink—XIII Kalends September [20 August]—and the text under refers

[86] VP 1:4:19; PL 185:237.

to 'the burial of Blessed Bernard, abbot of Clairvaux, a man glorious in his way of life, in his teaching, and in his miracles'. In one of the eight scenes in the Hungarian Legendary from 1330–1340 (MA253) he is shown in his black cowl with the hood over his head, being placed on a bier. Behind him are four monks, and in the centre a cleric with a long beard and a blue chasuble or cope, perhaps a bishop, who is presiding. The inscription reads: 'The last one—how he was buried' (*Ultima: Quomodo fuit sepultus*). A similar scene is featured as one of the six lateral panels of the florentine altarpiece from *c.* 1430 (PA120). Here Bernard, with a gold halo and wearing a white cowl, is lying on a slab at the foot of the scene, while an officiating monk in a red cope is reading from a red book. Five other standing monks are present, one of them carrying a processional cross. The earliest known representation of Bernard's burial—indeed the first known narrative image of him (MA039)—occurs in a late twelfth- or early thirteenth-century manuscript of his *Sermons* from the cluniac priory of Saint-Martin des Champs in Paris. Within the initial *H*(*odie fratres*) from his sermon for the beginning of Advent,[87] a bearded and tonsured but not nimbed Bernard is being placed in a tomb by two prelates, who are wearing red vestments with white spots as well as greyish pallia with white crosses, denoting their ranks as metropolitan archbishops. Bernard is wearing eucharistic vestments—a white chasuble above a pale blue alb. Unlike all other portrayals of the scene, this early representation is in accord with the description in the *Exordium Magnum*, which states that he was wearing priestly vestments (*sacerdotalibus indumentis*).[88] Above Bernard and the archbishops are two rows of three tonsured monks; four of them carry candles, and the two in front swing censers over the tomb. The scene accords with Geoffrey of Auxerre's description of the event: 'After the sacrifice of the Mass was over, they celebrated Mass for two more days and continually recited psalms. They then committed the most pure balsam into its vessel, and in a stone they placed the most precious jewel'.[89]

[87] SBOp 4:161.

[88] EM 2:20 (Griesser 1961, 116).

[89] VP 5:2:14 (PL 185:360): *Sacrificia consummantes, sicut et biduum jam in celebratione Missarum et jugi fecerant psalmodia, purissimum illud balsamum suo vasculo commisere, in lapide reponentes lapidem pretiosum, optimam margaritam.*

The conversion of the Duke of Aquitaine

The conversion of the Duke of Aquitaine (PA058) was one of the five bernardine themes featured on the Maulbronn altarpiece painted in 1432, as we saw above.[90] Altogether six examples have been recorded, and a further two are known from the former Bernard cycles at Heilsbronn[91] and at Essenbæk in Denmark. Among the many themes covered by Arnold of Bonneval in Book Two of the *Vita Prima,* the miracle of William of Aquitaine's conversion was one of the most popular in the iconography of Bernard.[92]

At the bidding of Innocent II, Bernard visited Duke William of Aquitaine. As a result the peace of the Church was established in the territories under William's control. However, Bishop Gerard of Angoulême, the legate of Innocent's competitor for the papal see, Anacletus, imposed bishops loyal to Anacletus to replace the legitimate incumbents and succeeded in obtaining William's support, notwithstanding a pledge he had previously given to Bernard to support Innocent's claim. In a letter to the bishops of Aquitaine Bernard wrote: 'You know from your own experience how savage and cunning is the enemy'.[93] During a second visit, Bernard celebrated Mass. Being excommunicate, the duke remained outside the church. Immediately after the consecration Bernard placed the Host on the paten, took it outside and addressed the duke with these words:

> Your judge is present, in whose name every knee in heaven, on earth, below the earth is bowed. . . . Do you spurn him? Do you treat him with the contempt with which you treat his servants?[94]

At this William trembled and fell upon the ground. Bernard then invited William to be reconciled with the bishop of Poitiers, whom the duke

[90] See page 132.

[91] Paffrath 1984, 404.

[92] VP 2:6:37-38; PL 185:289-290.

[93] Ep 126; SBOp 7:319; trans. James 1953, 198: *Quam saevus et callidus hostis insurrexerit in vos, proprio certe agnoscitis experimento.*

[94] VP 2:6:38; PL 185:290: *Adest Judex tuus, in cujus nomine omne genu curvatur, caelestium, terrestrium, et infernorum. . . . Nunquid et ipsum spernes? Nunquid et ipsum, sicut servos ejus contemnes?*

had driven from his church, and ordered him to submit to Innocent II. Peace was thus restored. The action not only expressed Bernard's ascendancy over his adversary, but underlined in a most graphic way the power of the consecrated Host at a time when the Church's teaching on the Eucharist was under attack by the albigensian heretics.

The story was later popularized by its inclusion in the *Legenda Aurea*, but the scene had already found its way into cistercian iconography through the *Vita Prima*. It appears for the first time, as far as we know, in northern France in 1260–1270, in a fragment (MA106) of an Antiphonary which may have come from the cistercian abbey of Cambron and is now in the J. Paul Getty Museum in California. It consists of nineteen leaves with three cut-out initials. In one of these Bernard is depicted within the initial *P(rima virtus viri sancti)* from the first Responsory of the first Nocturn from Vigils on his feast. He is shown in eucharistic vestments—chasuble, stole, and maniple—coming out of a church after the kiss of peace towards the end of Mass. In his hands he holds a paten on which is placed the consecrated Host, which he displays to the Duke of Aquitaine. The duke falls to the ground before Bernard, looking up at the Host. Beside him is a soldier, carrying a lance, and Bernard has with him a monk who stands in the doorway of the church holding Bernard's crozier. Three other cut-out initials from the same manuscript are now in the National Library, Stockholm.

The same theme is featured in two early fourteenth-century frescos at Palambora Sabina in the Gulielmite church of Saint John in Argentella. The first (WA29) shows Duke William of Aquitaine on horseback pointing to Bernard, whom he is on the way to meet. With him are two other horsemen. The other (WA30) has a bearded Bernard, again in eucharistic vestments, holding up the Host to the duke who, having dismounted his white horse, lies prostrate on the ground before him. Bernard is accompanied by a small monk who stands behind him. This image forms part of a biographical cycle of Saint William of Maravalla, the founder of the Guilelmite Order of hermits, in one of whose churches it is found. Bernard was considered to have been responsible for the conversion of this William, who is not the same as the Duke of Aquitaine. In the Middle Ages the identity of the two was commonly confused.

One of the eight miniatures in the Hungarian Legendary dated 1330–1340 (MA251) portrays Bernard coming out of the church carrying the Host on a paten. The penitent William of Aquitaine lies prostrate at his feet with his hands clasped, begging for pardon. A doorway with roof above it symbolizes the church, and a tree behind indicates that the encounter takes place out of doors. The inscription reads: 'How he carried the Body of Christ on a paten to the count who, having seen this, fell at his [Bernard's] feet' (*Quomodo portaverat uno comitu corpus Christi sive unam patenam et hoc viso cecidit ad pedes eius*). Late medieval examples include the Altenberg cycle (GL25), and the silver reliquary from the abbey of St Urban (VA08) which has the inscription; 'By the Body of Christ he restrained the boldness of the unruly count' (CORPORE XPI AVSVS EFRENI COMITIS ARCET).

Bernard expels Demons

The ability to perform miracles was an essential prerequisite for sainthood, and it is only natural that Bernard the thaumaturge should be among the most popular subjects in his iconography. One of the most telling expressions of a saint possessing supernatural powers was his ability to deliver those possessed by the devil, and seven examples of Bernard the exorcist have been recorded. A further two are known to have been included in the former cycles from Heilsbronn[95] and the danish benedictine abbey of Essenbæk.

Two exorcisms are included by Arnold of Bonneval in Book Two of the *Vita Prima:* one in Pavia and the other in Aquitaine. James of Voragine chose to ignore the bulk of Arnold's text, which dealt with Bernard's political activities, but he included both stories of Bernard's miraculous powers.[96] The Pavia demon, who had possessed a woman, engaged Bernard in a lengthy dialogue, taunting him by claiming that 'no leek-eating cabbage-guzzler like him is going to drive me from my little old woman!'.[97] After Bernard had prayed, the demon eventually left, but as soon as Bernard was no longer there he returned and entered the woman again. Bernard instructed her husband to pin a note to the woman's neck forbidding the devil in the name of Christ to touch her again. After that, he never returned. In the second story the devil threat-

[95] Paffrath 1984, 404.
[96] LA 217 and LA 218. For this, see McGuire 1994, 199–200.
[97] VP 2:4:21-22; PL 185:280-281.

ened to do the same: even if Bernard succeeded, the devil would exact a terrible revenge as soon as he had left.[98] When Bernard returned, he gathered a large crowd who witnessed him banishing the devil and forbidding him ever to return, and the woman was completely freed from her possession.

The earliest known pictorial representation of Bernard expelling devils is one of the four lateral scenes by the Palma Master from the altarpiece from the Templars' Church in Palma painted in 1290 (▶ *Colour plate 5, bottom right*). The scene deviates from the two stories by Arnold of Bonneval in representing the exorcism of two women by Bernard, instead referring to yet another story, found in John the Hermit's *Vita Quarta*, about two women from Bar-sur-Aube who were troubled by two demons whom Bernard expelled. As a result those present exclaimed: 'This man is truly holy!'.[99] In the altarpiece Bernard stands on the right, the hood of his white cowl partially over his head. With his right hand he blesses the women, from whose mouths the evil spirits are emanating in the form of fire or smoke. The scene is witnessed by five men and women who are standing behind the kneeling women. The building in the background suggests an urban scene.

The theme is also represented (MA228) in one of seventy six historiated initials in an italian fourteenth-century treatise on deadly sins which also contains a collection of moral tales. The tonsured and bearded bust of Bernard in a brown habit, on the right, faces the bust of a woman (or man?) in pink, on the left. From her (or his) mouth issues a black dragon with a red flame. Alongside the miniature, text in red letters (*Miraculo scō bernar*) tells readers that of the many topics the artist might have chosen to represent Bernard the miracle-worker, he settled on the subject of him casting out a devil from a woman possessed in preference to other favourite stories such as, for example, the excommunication of flies (GL15) or Bernard's letter which did not get wet in the rain (MA142).

In the two examples provided by Arnold of Bonneval, the expulsion of the devil is depicted by fire and smoke or by a dragon emitting a

[98] VP 2:6:34-35; PL 185:287-288.

[99] Vita Quarta 2:15; PL 185:548: *Igitur apud Barrum super Albam erant duae feminae, quas duo daemones vexabant. Deinde parentes adduxerunt eas ad Hominem Dei in Claram-Vallem ut ab eo curarentur.*

flame from the mouths of the possessed. In one of the eight panels of the Jörg Breu Zwettl altarpiece (PA42), the evil spirit, in the form of a small black dragon, is not just coming out of the mouth of the woman but is already some distance away. As in all the Zwettl panels, Bernard wears a black cowl. He holds an open book with the prayers used for exorcisms in his left hand and his right hand is raised in blessing. The woman is being restrained by two men.

The most common way of portraying exorcisim was to show a tiny black devil being expelled. This is how it is depicted in one of the two remaining scenes from a catalan altarpiece painted by Ferrer Bassa (PA110). In this, a bearded and nimbed Bernard in a white cowl, accompanied by one of his monks, stretches out his hands towards a kneeling woman, who is supported by another woman behind her. A small black devil is seen coming out of the woman's mouth. The scene is witnessed by three other women. An almost identical composition is found in one of the nine bernardine scenes at the Chapel of Saint Bernard, Pamparato, painted in 1482 (WA17). Here Bernard, accompanied by two monks, has an open book with the appropriate prayers in his left hand, while his right hand is raised to exorcize the woman before him, who is held by a man. The evil spirit leaving her is again shown as a small black devil. The inscription reads: 'How Saint Bernard expelled the devil from the body of a lady' (COMO S. BERNARDO FESE FUSIRE DIAVOLI DE EL CORPO DI ONO DONA). The image probably refers to the exorcism at Pavia: not only is the wall-painting italian, but it shows the woman being held by a man; and Arnold of Bonneval had specifically mentioned a man from Milan who brought his wife who was possessed to Pavia to be cured by Bernard.

CONCLUSION: PATTERNS

For the first half century after his death—that is, from 1153 until the beginning of the next century—Bernard was portrayed exclusively as a great monastic figure: the teacher of his monks; the abbot of Clairvaux and father-abbot of numerous daughter-houses; and the author of important works of monastic theology. Although the *Vita Prima* was begun some years before his death and completed not many years afterwards, none of the stories relating to events in his life was represented in art until the end of the thirteenth century.

Narrative depictions of Bernard were slow to emerge. To begin with, they were not required—or allowed—for the decoration of cistercian churches. Painted altarpieces were at first forbidden in houses of the Order and the earliest known altarpiece (Palma, 1290) to include a Bernard cycle did not belong to a cistercian church. The grisaille windows of plain glass with geometric designs, for which the Cistercians were famous, were only gradually replaced in Cistercian churches by multi-coloured figurative glass which allowed stories to be told in glass. The stories from which artists drew their inspiration became widely known only after James of Voragine had compiled his *Golden Legend*, which became the most important source for the Bernard cycles.

Pre-dating these stories and to a large extent reflecting the cistercian interest in Bernard were individual narrative representations focusing on him as abbot and writer. With the emergence of the cycles there was a gradual development: Bernard was portrayed as much outside the monastery as within. Scenes showing him involved in the affairs of the world, in his travels across Europe, in meeting popes, kings, and bishops, in preaching, as well as in performing miracles often predominated. In the most comprehensive of all cycles, the late medieval Altenberg cloister glass, we find Bernard represented in all roles: child, novice, young monk, abbot, writer, preacher, churchman, politician, healer, and thaumaturge.

Only eleven of the one hundred sixty-one narrative images that have been recorded belong to the thirteenth century, and nine of these are individual representations. Of the latter, three—all in non-cistercian manuscripts—deal with Bernard's involvement with the second crusade (MA030, MA031, MA304).

Another three of the eleven thirteenth-century narrative images deal with Bernard's death and burial. First, a deathbed scene in which Bernard's soul is seen leaving his mouth in the form of a small naked figure is featured in the late thirteenth-century Breviary of Philippe le Bel (MA183); second, a funeral procession scene in a cistercian Obituary (MA318); and, third, the earliest of all, which may even belong to the end of the twelfth century, the wonderful depiction of his funeral from a benedictine manuscript of Bernard's sermons (MA039).

Only two of the images from the end of the thirteenth century were part of groups of images belonging to cycles which, in the form of altarpieces and stained glass, were to become popular in the last two centuries of the Middle Ages. They were the two narrative scenes—Christ revealing Malachy's sainthood and the exorcism of two women—in the wonderful Palma altarpiece from 1290. Of its altogether four panels the other two respectively looked backwards in depicting Bernard as a writer, and forwards in providing the earliest known representation of the most popular of all late medieval bernardine picture types, the *Lactatio* (*Colour plate 5*).

In one of the last three narrative scenes from the thirteenth century (MA058), Bernard is depicted in a monastic context as one of the first four abbots to be sent out by Stephen Harding to establish new houses. The two others provide the earliest examples of the most popular themes drawn either directly from the *Vita Prima,* or, perhaps, indirectly from the *Legenda Aurea:* his mother Aleth's dream (MA054) and the conversion of Duke William of Aquitaine (MA106).

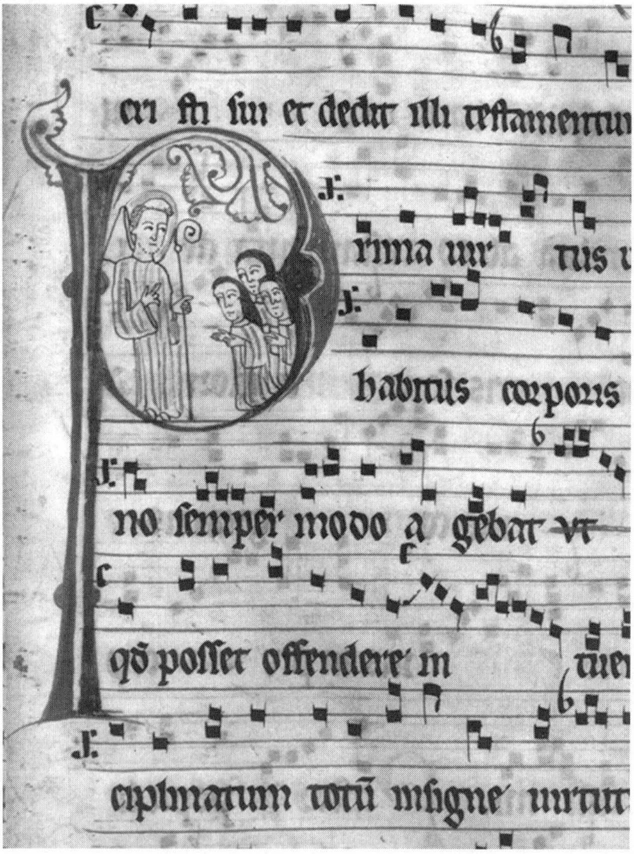

Figure 10: Bernard with nuns from a late twelfth-century antiphonary.
The earliest known image of cistercian nuns (MA 035).

SIX

NUNS AND THE ICONOGRAPHY OF BERNARD

TRADITIONALLY the first generation of cistercian monks has been seen as misogynist and hostile to nuns, and no one more so than Bernard, who, in the words of one biographer 'was hostile to any arrangement involving contact with women', a statement belied by the part he is known to have played in founding at least one house of nuns, Montreuil-sous-Laon,[1] and the extensive correspondence he is known to have conducted with laywomen, including several queens and other women of rank, as well as with at least three nuns.[2] Cistercian historians have traditionally ignored nuns altogether or, at best, relegated them to a final chapter almost as an afterthought,[3] and yet recent research has rendered this negative view no longer tenable.

[1] Bouton 1995, 1:15.

[2] Luddy 1959, 358. See Letters 114, 115, 120, 121, 289, 315, 366, 375, and 391; SBOp 7:291, 294, 300, 301, & SBOp 8:205, 248, 323, 338 & 391.

[3] Knowles 1940, 362, the standard work on english monasticism, for example, dismissed cistercian nuns in two lines. Lekai 1977, devoted one of the last chapters to nuns; and in a recent work, Williams 1998, they are relegated to the final chapter entitled 'The Nunneries'.

The monastic revival of the late eleventh and early twelfth centuries, with its emphasis on an ascetic and solitary way of life, was as appealing to women as it was to men, and it was not uncommon for entire families to leave the world. The cloistered life was also an option for large numbers of the wives of men who wanted to become monks; this followed the established practice according to which there was no obstacle to a married man entering a monastery if at the same time his wife agreed to take the veil. This would almost certainly explain the involvement of cistercian abbots in nuns' foundations.[4] Chief among these abbots was Bernard, for among the group of relatives and friends with whom he entered Cîteaux in the spring of 1113 were several married men.[5] The *Vita Prima* records Bernard's role in enlisting his eldest brother, Guy, a married man of some standing who at first hesitated, but then agreed provided he could obtain his wife's consent. At first she refused, but following a severe illness she relented and 'separated from her husband by the mutual vow of chastity according to the custom of the Church, she joined a group of religious women, and to this day she is serving God there as a nun'.[6] Her name was Elizabeth, and the 'there' was Jully, a monastery founded from Molesme by Robert's successor, Guy de Chastelcensoir, to whom the nuns were subject.

HUMBELINE IN THE ICONOGRAPHY OF BERNARD

The importance of Jully in the monastic vocation of Bernard is acknowledged by William of Saint Thierry in the *Vita Prima:*

> Some of his [Bernard's] companions had been married and the wives as well as their husbands had taken a religious vow. Through his solicitude, and with the help of God, a monastery of nuns was built which was called Jully, situated in the diocese of Langres.[7]

[4] Nichols & Shank 1995, 1:4.

[5] On the date of Bernard's entry to Cîteaux, see Bredero 1996, 201–204.

[6] VP 1:3:10; PL 185:233: *Denique juxta morem ecclesiasticum separata a viro, interveniente parili voto castitatis, in caetum sanctimonialium transiit feminarum, religiose usque hodie serviens Deo.*

[7] VP 1:4:19 (PL 185:237): *Quia vero ex praedictis sociis ejus uxorati aliqui fuerant, et uxores quoque cum viris idem votum sacrae conversationis inierant; per ipsius*

William may have exaggerated the part played by Bernard, although a recent historian refers to 'a close association between Bernard of Clairvaux and the nuns of Jully that belies most assertions that Bernard was opposed to women's communities'.[8] The closeness of his association may also be explained by the fact that his sister, Humbeline, became a nun there and succeeded his sister-in-law, Elizabeth, as prioress. Later he is known to have been consulted by the abbot of Molesme—together with three other cistercian abbots, Hugh of Pontigny, Gaucher of Morimond, and Godfrey of Fontenay—when he was drawing up new usages for the Jully nuns.[9]

The close family tie of Bernard with Jully may explain a remarkable similarity between the observance of the benedictine nuns there and that of Bernard's Clairvaux. In a recent article André Louf has pointed to the pivotal influence Jully had on the early cistercian agrarian economy in its transformation from the traditional feudal structures to a new economic system based on direct exploitation.[10] He draws attention to the similarity between the foundation charter of Jully, drawn up around 1113, and some of the primitive Cistercian documents with which Bernard must have been acquainted. Both the Jully charter and the Cistercian texts refer to simplicity in food and clothing, the work of their own hands, and the renunciation of churches and tithes, using almost identical wording.[11]

The story of Humbeline's visit to Clairvaux *c.* 1123 is recorded at some length in the *Vita Prima*.[12] From there it found its way into the *Legenda Aurea*, and thereafter became much more widely dispersed in monastic circles as well as reaching a broader clerical and, in translation, a lay audience. Along this route it eventually found expression in cistercian iconography.

---

sollicitudinem aedificatum eis caenobium sanctimonialium feminarum, quod Julleium dicitur, in Lingonensi parochia, Domino cooperante.

[8] Berman 2000, 14.

[9] Connor 1995, 1:38-39.

[10] Louf 1999, 40–78.

[11] Compare the Jully text in Bouton 1995, 1:14, with the *Exordium Parvum* in Waddell 1999, 434–435, 453. Bernard's involvement and the closeness of Jully with the cistercian family is acknowledged by Jean Leclercq in these words (quoted in Berman 2000, 40): 'If we consider the definition of Cistercian not in a juridical way, but as a way of life, then the women inspired by Bernard at Jully, or those fostered by Stephen Harding at Tart, were Cistercians just as much as were the men at Cîteaux or Pontigny or Poblet'.

[12] VP 1:6:30; PL 185:244-245.

All illustrations of Bernard connected with women—not just nuns but all women—are late. The twelfth-century stories found no pictorial expression until, at the earliest, the fourteenth century. The *Legenda Aurea* was undoubtedly the inspiration for the magnificent illuminated manuscript known as the Hungarian Legendary produced in the first half of the fourteenth century by Nicholas of Bologna, and containing eight illustrations devoted to the life of Bernard. The story of Humbeline is covered in two images, taking up the lower half of the first of two folios (f. 88v). In the first of these (MA248) she is depicted in her worldly finery with a crown on her head, arriving 'with a superb retinue' represented by three companions She extends her hands to her two brothers standing in the doorway of the monastery. Bernard, 'detesting and execrating her as a net of the devil to catch souls', is depicted turning round and fleeing. The caption reads 'How he fled before his sister' (*Quomodo fugebat ipse ante sororem suam*). The artist has changed the story: in the *Vita Prima* Bernard did not flee from her, but merely refused to see her. Her other brother, Andrew, did not mince his words, describing her as 'bundled dung',[13] at which she burst into tears. The story goes on to record Humbeline's reaction to her frosty reception:

> 'And if I am a sinner', she said, 'then it is for such that Christ died. It is precisely because I am a sinner that I need the advice and conversation of good men. If my brother despises my body, let not a servant of the Lord despise my soul. Let him come, let him command, whatever he commands I am ready to do'.[14]

Bernard relented and came out to greet her. He advised her to return to her husband but to model her style of life on that of their mother. After two years her husband 'released her according to the rite of the Church' and 'she went to the monastery of Jully where she vowed to God to live the rest of her life with the nuns serving him there'. In the second image (MA249), Bernard is depicted in a red cope, blessing

[13] *stercus involutum*. The translation is by Martinus Cawley who, in a footnote, explains that the 'dung' is her body and the 'bundling' is its trappings.

[14] VP 1:6:30; PL 185:244-245: *'Et si peccatrix sum,' inquit,'pro talibus Christus mortuus est. Quia enim peccatrix sum, idcirco consilium et colloquium bonorum requiro. Et so despicit frater meus carnem meam, ne despiciat servus Dei animam meam. Veniat, praecipiat: quidquid praeceperit, facere parata sum'.*

Humbeline with his right hand raised and his left hand on her head. She is depicted in a simple red dress and white veil kneeling before an altar. Her consecration is witnessed by three tonsured monks behind Bernard, one of them carrying a cross, and four nuns behind the altar. There is nothing in the literary sources to warrant Bernard's direct intervention in Humbeline's conversion or to suggest that he was present at her entry to Jully, and yet the caption reads: 'How he made his sister a nun' (*Quomodo ipse sororem suam fecit munialem*).

The second of the eight scenes (MA247), the one above the two featuring Humbeline, is devoted to the story from his youth in which he found his gaze dwelling on a young lady for rather too long. As a result he blushed, ashamed of himself, and leapt into a pool of freezing water until he 'was cooled down from the heat of that carnal longing'.[15] Bernard is shown lying in a bed looking at a woman asleep next to him. Below he is depicted naked, lying in flowing icy water. According to the caption these show 'How he lay with his sister and threw himself into the water to prevent fornication from taking place' (*Quomodo jacebat cum sorore sua et occulte surgens posuit se in aquam ut fornicationis sit non eventus*). This reference to a potentially incestuous relationship with his sister is not warranted by any of the literary sources. It is not to be found in any of the *Lives* or in the *Legenda Aurea* and appears to be the invention of the artist, perhaps inserted for dramatic effect.

Humbeline's story is also featured in the Owen cycle of wall paintings from the mid-fourteenth century. Here (WA44) Humbeline is seen riding in her finery and accompanied by other horses and riders. The small figure atop a castellated building does not appear to have a halo and is probably Bernard's brother Andrew, whose insult would reduce Humbeline to tears. It may, however, equally represent Bernard himself later in the story, after he had changed his mind and agreed to meet his sister.

The story is also depicted in one of the early sixteenth-century glass panels from the Altenberg cloister (GL13). It has three scenes that take place in three different locations, a parallel to those featured in the Legendary. The unfolding in time is handled by a sequence in which the chief characters reappear, an old device commonly used to illustrate the *Lives* of saints. On the left the fashionably-dressed Humbeline arrives at Clairvaux accompanied by a servant, who holds her horse. Her

[15] VP 1:3:6; PL 185:230: *a calore carnalis concupiscentiae totus refriguit.*

banderole has the words she spoke, quoted above, which made Bernard change his mind.[16] In the centre Bernard, in a white cowl with his hood over his head and wearing a black cap, and his brother Andrew are seen on their way to greet her. On the right Humbeline, in a plain red dress with a white veil, kneels before Bernard while wiping away tears with a white cloth. The viewer's ability to understand the story is aided by the use of a text-scroll, a more effective way of incorporating text with image than are the captions to the Legendary manuscript. A further aid to the viewer is an abbreviated version of the whole story written across the foot of the panel.

Humbeline features in several other medieval Bernard cycles, her entry as a nun at Jully being treated almost as an accompaniment to Bernard's own arrival at Cîteaux. She appears in one of the eight Jörg Breu panels formerly in the abbot's chapel at Zwettl in Austria (PA039). While Bernard and his brothers are being greeted by a corpulent Stephen Harding on the left, on their right the tiny figure of Humbeline in a red dress is being received by three nuns in black cowls over white tunics.

A fifteenth-century manuscript of Vincent de Beauvais' *Speculum Historiale* (MA089), like the Zwettl altarpiece, shows double scenes, erroneously also giving the impression that Humbeline's entry to Jully coincided with Bernard's to Cîteaux. This in fact happened only several years after her visit to Clairvaux, which itself took place some ten years after Bernard had been sent there. On the left Stephen Harding presides at the clothing of Bernard and his brothers, all in the white cistercian cowl, while on the right Humbeline is welcomed by three nuns in the black benedictine habit. Not only are chronology and location inaccurate, but one of the nuns is depicted as an abbess, carrying a crozier, despite the fact that Jully was only a priory. Once again accuracy of chronology and location is disregarded, but the more important point is made, that Aleth bore seven children 'to her husband, or rather to God: six boys and one girl, the boys all destined to become monks and the girl a nun'.[17] Humbeline's decision to become a nun served as an

[16] VP 1:6:30; PL 185:244: *Et si despecit frater meus carnem meam, ne despeciat servus Dei animam meam. Veniat, praecipiat: quidquid praeceperit, facere parata sum.*

[17] VP 1:1:1; PL 185:227: *septem quippe liberos genuit non tam viro suo quam Deo, sex mares, feminam unam: mares omnes monachos futuros, feminam sanctimonialium.*

inspiration and a model to future generations of cistercian nuns, even though, as a nun of Jully which was dependent on Molesme, she was a Benedictine and not a Cistercian.

IMAGES OF BERNARD IN NUNS' MANUSCRIPTS

A number of communities of nuns wishing to emulate the way of life of the monks of Cîteaux were established within two or three decades of the monks' arrival from Molesme. First among these was Tart, founded in 1120 with the daughter of the great benefactress of Cîteaux, Elizabeth de Vergy, at its head and with the active support of Stephen Harding.[18] Among these communities were groups of nuns already in existence who wished to become Cistercians, and nunneries attached to the congregations of Savigny and Obazine, which joined the Cistercian Order in 1147. Even so, Jacques de Vitry's famous remark, adapting the words of Genesis, that cistercian nuns' houses 'multiplied like the stars of heaven and grew tremendously'[19] applies only to the decades around the time when it was made, *c.* 1221. Whereas the expansion of men's houses reached its peak in the first half of the twelfth century, the growth of women's monasteries was at first very slow but accelerated enormously in the first decades of the thirteenth century. In German-speaking lands, for example, only fifteen cistercian nunneries were founded in the twelfth century, yet by the end of the Middle Ages a staggering total of three hundred seventy-seven had been founded, greatly outnumbering houses of monks.[20] Whereas cistercian monks are depicted in the earliest manuscripts produced in the scriptorium at Cîteaux—Stephen Harding's Bible and the *Moralia in Job*—little more than a decade after the arrival of the monks from Molesme, there are no known portrayals of cistercian nuns until towards the end of the twelfth century.[21]

[18] On Tart, see Bouton 1995, 1:15; Connor 1995, 1:38-46; and Dengler-Spengler 1995, 1:87-8.

[19] *Historia occidentalis,* in Hinnebusch 1972, 117.

[20] Kuhn-Rehfus 1995, 1:135-136. The final figure is taken from a list of all german houses is given in Schneider 1986, 710–726.

[21] For the Cîteaux manuscripts, see Zaluska 1989, and illustrations in France 1998 (ill 37, 45, 134, and colour plate 24).

There are, as one would expect, quite a number of medieval representations of Bernard in the company of nuns. These are not historical in the sense that there is evidence Bernard preached to nuns. They not so much reflect his contribution to the expansion of cistercian women's houses as pay tribute to the enormous debt the nuns owed to his spiritual teaching, not least in the later imagery of the Brautmystik and his emphasis on the approachability and nearness of God through the humanity of Christ and his Passion and his devotion to the Eucharist. Much of the nuns' spirituality can be traced to Bernard's inspiration. To them Bernard was, in the words of Hildegard of Bingen, 'as a man in the sun'.[22]

The earliest portrayal of Bernard with nuns (MA035) is, significantly, also the earliest known image of cistercian nuns (▶ *Fig. 10*). Found in a late twelfth-century antiphonary, in which nuns in white cowls and black veils are represented elsewhere (on f. 59v), it almost certainly originated in a flemish cistercian women's house—the identity of which is not known. The red and green initials with fine floral decoration as well as the habits of the nuns indicate its cistercian provenance. Bernard is featured within the initial *P(rima virtus viri sancti)*, the first Responsory of the first Nocturn from Vigils on his feast; it offers a visual celebration in the opening hours of the day dedicated to his commemoration. He is shown with a stubble beard, nimbed and carrying a simple crozier, blessing three kneeling nuns in white cowls with black veils. Another early example (MA414), dated to the first half of the thirteenth century, comes from the celebrated nuns' abbey of Arouca in Portugal, made famous by Mafalfa, daughter of King Sancho I of Portugal who married King Henrique of Castile and after his death in 1219 took the veil at Arouca. In this manuscript the feast of Bernard is marked by a large initial *P(rima virtus viri sancti)* within which the standing figure of a bearded Bernard in a greyish cowl with the hood partially over his head is pointing in a teaching mode (▶ *Colour plate 7*). As is quite common in early images, his halo is blue.

These two early unsophisticated images may be compared with the equivalent historiated initial in the magnificent antiphonary from another women's house (MA212), produced about a century later and altogether very much more accomplished. The antiphonary was written in three volumes for the nuns' abbey of Beaupré by a monk-scribe who

[22] James 1953, 460.

probably came from Beaupré's mother house, Cambron. This, and other comparable examples, reflect the disparity between the far more restricted opportunities of nuns as compared with those of monks.[23] The nuns' book collections were smaller, and accentuated liturgical and devotional works; the proportion of vernacular books was greater; and only a small number of scribes are known.[24] The identity of the Beaupré scribe is revealed at the beginning of the third volume. At the top the Visitation is depicted, with Mary and Elizabeth accompanied by a slightly smaller nun in a grey habit and black veil, by a scroll. In an ornamental bar in the lower margin a tiny monk is seated in a small gothic niche, writing at a desk, identified as the scribe by a scroll: 'I am John who wrote this book'.[25]

One of fourteen historiated initials in the second volume, which covers the period from the Assumption to Advent, shows Bernard in a frontal position within the initial *P(rima virtus viri sancti)* (MA212). He is depicted in a brown cowl, with a red nimbus, and carries a green book in his right hand and an orange crozier in his left. He is flanked by two smaller, kneeling nuns in grey habits, black veils and white wimples. The nun on the left looks straight ahead, the one on the right looks up. The three figures are on a gold ground. In the borders are two hybrid creatures, one with a musical instrument and one dancing, and the head of a beast with an orange cap. In another antiphonary, which comes from Mainz and is thought to be from one of the three cistercian nunneries in that city, the same historiated initial *P(rima virtus viri sancti)* from the first Responsary for Bernard's feast day, is green with acanthus decoration and has a nimbed standing Bernard holding a red crozier in his left hand and a grey book in his right (MA233). At his feet sits a dog, an allusion to his mother Aleth's dream when she was expecting him.

Another, almost contemporary, antiphonary from the abbey of Seligenthal is exceptional in that it was written at a women's house. A manuscript from the late thirteenth or early fourteenth century contains antiphons for the summer season and has four historiated initials. In the lower margin of one of the folios is a drawing of a nun in a

[23] For this, see France 1998, 161.

[24] See Bondeelle-Souchier 1994, and the nun scribe illustrated in France 1998, colour plate 17.

[25] Illustrated in France 1998, 161 (ill. 108).

blueish-grey cowl with black veil and white wimple, standing before a nimbed Bernard also in a blueish-grey cowl and carrying a red book with gold studs in his right hand and a primitive red crozier in his left (MA320). Both Bernard and the nun are identified by the text surrounding them: around the nun we read: 'Having arrived at the end of the work, I ask for the reward of my labour. She who writes me has the name of Adelhaid' (*Finis adest operis mercedem posco laboris. Et qui me scribebat Ahelhaidis nomen habebat*), and around the figure of Bernard his reply: 'Saint Bernard: Our Lord Jesus Christ will himself be your reward' (*Sanctus Bernhardus. Dominus noster Jhesus Christus ipse erit merces tua, fiat fiat*). Also from Seligenthal, and written there a little earlier by a nun named Elizabeth, is a Gradual. It is ornamented with large initial letters containing miniatures rudely executed. One of them (MA164) features Bernard with the inscription above *Sti Bernhardi abbis* on the left of an orange and rosa initial *I*(*n medio ecclesie*), the introit at the beginning of the Mass for the feast of Bernard. He is depicted with a blue halo and wearing a grey cowl with long but fairly tight sleeves. He holds a crozier and a book in his right hand and with his left hand he is acknowledging the figure of Saint John the Evangelist, who has a red halo and wears a green tunic and orange cloak. Both figures are on gold ground with a blue border decorated with a red line and blue dots. At the beginning of the manuscript is the following inscription: *1260, Bey erster Frau Abtissin Agnes, Graffin Preyssing, dis grosse Ambt-Buch gesch[r]iben worden von Kloster Frau Elizatha* ('This large Service Book was written by Sister Elizatha in 1260 for the first Lady Abbess Agnes, Countess of Preyssing').

Apart from folios devoted to his feast in liturgical tomes, the most likely place to find images of Bernard as the patron of nuns is in manuscripts of Bernard's own works. Among them are two historiated initials which feature Bernard preaching to nuns in two manuscripts of his sermons from the end of the thirteenth century. Like other images of Bernard with nuns, the scenes are not historical, for there is no evidence that Bernard ever preached to nuns; it intended to indicate the immense importance his teaching had on their spiritual lives. In one (MA036), now in the Belgian Royal Library, he is shown sitting on a stool, nimbed and in a brown habit, a crozier in his left hand, within the initial *V*(*icit leo de tribu Juda*) at the beginning of his sermon for Easter. With his right hand he blesses a group of seven kneeling nuns in brown habits and black veils. The other (MA037), from the Austrian National Library, shows Bernard within the initial *H(odie)* at the opening of his sermons for Advent. As in the belgian miniature, Bernard is nimbed, wears a brown habit, and carries a crozier in his left hand, with his right hand outstretched to a group of seven sitting nuns. The pictures in the two initials are almost identical, the main difference being that in one Bernard is sitting and the nuns kneeling, while in the other Bernard is standing and the nuns sitting. The style of the two manuscripts is very similar and indicates that they come from the same workshop in the diocese of Cambrai, and it is thought that they probably belonged to the famous abbey of Nizelles, near Nivelles in Brabant.[26] As the format of the two manuscripts is also the same, it may well be that they were originally the summer and winter halves of the same work.

A collection of Bernard's sermons dated *c.* 1300 has an opening full-page miniature (MA023) with Mary and the Christ Child as the central figures in a frontal position, nimbed and crowned, on an elaborate throne under a round trifoliate arch, with the Child, his right hand raised in blessing, on her knees. On the right is a tonsured and blue-nimbed Bernard with a short beard, wearing a dark brown cowl and holding a book in his left hand. In his right hand he holds a crozier and, with his index finger, points at himself, perhaps indicating that his work forms the subject of the manuscript. His gaze is fixed on the Child. On the left kneels the diminutive figure of a cistercian nun, gazing upwards at Mary and the Child. She is dressed in a brown habit with black veil and white wimple, and her hands are raised in adoration. In true medieval fashion, the artist has chosen to represent the figures in three quite distinct scales: in order of their importance the largest are the Virgin and Child, then Bernard, and then, smallest of all, the kneeling nun.

Very striking evidence of the cult of Bernard among cistercian nuns is provided by a magnificent miniature (MA312) in a manuscript entitled *Somme le roi,* a manual of moral and religious instruction composed at the behest of Philip III (1270–1285) by the Dominican Laurent d'Orleans. It was made in Paris in the 1290s and belonged to the nuns of Notre-Dame la Royale de Maubuisson, founded in 1236 by Blanche of Castile, the daughter of the founder of the royal house of nuns at Las Huelgas, King Alphonsus VIII of Castile, the wife of Louis VIII of

[26] Brussels 1990, 58.

France, who died in 1226, and the mother of another great benefactor of the Cistercians, Louis IX who became Saint Louis following his canonization in 1260. The frontispiece (folio 1v, not illustrated here) has an image of the *sainte abbaie* depicting saints, the persons of the Trinity, a novice mistress instructing novices, and an abbess and a nun adoring the Trinity above them. The second picture, on folio 6v (our MA 312), is a full-page miniature framed by a cut-away gothic monastic building. In the upper register a male tonsured saint wearing a yellow chasuble is celebrating Mass. He holds the Host while the chalice rests on the altar. He is assisted by two tonsured deacons. An angel carrying a scroll hovers above the altar. Behind the clergy a nun kneels, pulling the bell at the elevation of the Host. Behind her is the abbess, carrying a red crozier, and five more nuns, all holding red missals. Two more nuns—probably too old or infirm to take part in the church—witness the scene from a gallery above. The lower register has a procession of nuns, headed by a young acolyte carrying a processional cross, two small nuns—perhaps novices—carrying candles, a deacon with a book, a bearded and tonsured saint in a blue chasuble followed by five nuns carrying open processionals, and, at the rear an abbess, carrying a red crozier. In the open processionals can be read the words of Psalm 47:10: *Suscepimus, Deus, misericordiam tuam in medio templi tui* ('We have received your mercy, O God, in the midst of your temple'), the Introit for Candlemass. Candlemass—the feast of the Purification of the Blessed Virgin Mary—was marked by one of the most solemn processions of the liturgical year. All the nuns in both registers wear grey cowls over white tunics, and black veils and white wimples. There is little doubt that the two pictures of the tonsured saint on this folio represent Bernard even though there is nothing in the text or in any inscription to identify him. Although he does not carry a crozier in the traditional manner, its absence is not unusual when he is shown engaged in an activity where one would not be appropriate, as when saying Mass. In the oldest known image of him as a priest, in the late twelfth-century Missal from Zwettl in Austria (MA002), this is in fact how he is depicted.

Images of Bernard with nuns were not confined to manuscripts belonging to cistercian nuns. The dominican nuns of the Holy Cross in Regensburg had a *Legendary* made for them in *c.* 1267–1276, at the expense of Gebhard von Hierzpech and his wife. It contained a calendar, legends, and homilies for lessons at Matins. Among many fine miniatures is a historiated initial *B(ernardus)* (MA003) at the beginning of the section on Bernard, which opens with the usual sentence regarding his origin in the town of Fontaine in Burgundy of noble parentage, adapted from the *Legenda Aurea*. A nimbed and bearded Bernard is depicted in a blueish-grey cowl standing behind a blue initial with white decoration. He has a crozier in his left hand and a book in his right. In the margin is the small figure of a kneeling nun identified as *Mathildis*. She is dressed in the dominican habit consisting of a white tunic and scapular, black veil and white wimple. On another folio (63r) Saint Benedict is depicted in an almost identical way except for the colour of his cowl which is black.

An antiphonary dated *c.* 1500, which belonged to the benedictine nuns at Vorst near Brussels, marks the feast of Bernard with a very unusual historiated initial *P(rima virtus viri sancti)*, from the first Responsory from Vigils (MA015). Although not nimbed or carrying a book or crozier, the central figure can be identified as Bernard by his position at the introduction to his feast. He is shown standing in the middle of a room with a brocade hanging behind him, his black cowl lifted up to reveal a white tunic underneath. On the left is a group of four kneeling monks with their hands clasped in prayer, and on the right a similar group of four nuns. Both monks and nuns are in black cowls and, in view of the ownership of the manuscript, are probably Benedictines. Bernard has a bundle of myrrh in his left hand, which tells us that he was preaching on the *Song of Songs*, and more precisely on Sermon 43, which he begins with the quotation 'My beloved is to me a little bundle of myrrh that lies between my breasts' (*Fasciculus myrrhae dilectus meus mihi, inter ubera mea commorabitur*) (Song 1:12).[27] This detail tells us that either the artist or at least those who commissioned the work were well acquainted with Bernard's Sermons.

Bernard in Nuns' Devotional Books

The prominence of Bernard's image in the liturgical books used by cistercian nuns in their communal worship is matched by a similar emphasis in the iconography of their private devotional books. The

[27] SBOp 2:41.

bernardine tradition of affective meditation had played an important part in forming the devotional lives of nuns whose spirituality was marked by a special devotion to the Passion of Christ. In the words of the eminent art historian Emile Mâle, in the late Middle Ages 'the Passion became the chief concern of the Christian soul',[28] and this was nowhere more true than in communities of cistercian nuns. The chief iconographic vehicles used by nuns as an aid to identifying with Christ's suffering were devotional images, *Andachtsbilder,* and small books of private prayers. Produced by the nuns themselves these were therefore known as *Nonnenarbeiten*.[29] Primitive in the sense that they were the work of a marginalized group of untrained artists, they represent 'folk' art in contrast to the 'high' art of artists commissioned to paint the magnificent altarpieces which adorned the nuns' churches. Until quite recently they would have been considered the province of historians of folklore and dismissed as not warranting the attention of serious art historians. Now, however, they are regarded as what they are: images which had joined texts 'as recognized sources of religious authority and devotional authenticity and served as an integral, even indispensable, part of the experience of prayer'.[30]

Devotion to the Passion of Christ is perhaps most compellingly depicted in a highly expressionistic representation of the Crucifixion in which nothing has been spared in conveying Christ's suffering (DR10). In a pen and ink drawing dating from the first half of the fourteenth century, Bernard and a nun are witnesses to the bloody scene. They kneel at the foot of the cross, grasping it and the legs of Christ. Christ's emaciated, lifeless body hangs down, his cross-nimbed head droops. A green crown of thorns stands out against the bright red torrents of blood issuing from his hands and side and flowing down his body to form a pool on the ground between the two kneeling figures. The jets from his side testify to the strength of devotion to the Wounds of Christ. It is an *Andachtsbild* thought to be from a cistercian nuns' house in the Lower Rhineland, and it may be the work of the nun depicted. The highly expressive figures, almost reminiscent of Matisse, are boldly drawn. Both Bernard and the nun are demurely looking down and

[28] Mâle 1986, 83.
[29] For this, see Hamburger 1997.
[30] Hamburger 1997, XXI.

Bernard is too preoccupied to be carrying his crozier, which is there in the background to identify the saint.

This startling picture has sometimes been mistaken for an *Amplexus* image, but both Christ's arms are attached to the cross and there is no sign of an Embrace.[31] The *Amplexus* theme, however, reflected and acknowledged Bernard's immense contribution to late-medieval devotion to Christ's sufferings, death, and burial which formed such an important part of the nuns' spirituality. Not surprisingly, it was incorporated into the iconography of both their service books and their private prayer books. The earliest known representation of the *Amplexus* (MA059) is to be found, not insignificantly, in a Gradual from a cistercian nunnery, Wonnental in Breisgau. Elsewhere in this manuscript there is a historiated initial with a cistercian nun in a grey habit with black veil and white wimple kneeling before the standing figure of Saint Agnes.[32] The *Amplexus* motif also appears in a fine image in a Breviary dated 1472, from the nuns' monastery of Lichtenthal in which the Instruments of the Passion or *Arma Christi*, associated with the cult of the Wounds of Christ, are depicted (MA222).

A small Prayer Book written in 1513, probably by a cistercian nun in the region of Cologne, provides a typical example of *Nonnenarbeit*, and is comparable to the work produced at the benedictine abbey of Saint Walberg in Eichstätt, which has recently been extensively studied.[33] One of its eleven full-page miniatures (MA317) shows a nimbed Bernard in a dark brown cowl embracing the lifeless-looking and blood-stained body of Christ with his arms detached from the cross. The two large nails for the hands are still in place on the cross, which is surmounted by the traditional INRI inscription. On the ground around the cross are white and red flowers and a snail. Next to Bernard is the inscription in red *S bernard*. This *Amplexus* scene is framed by red, white, and blue bands and a border of red and green stylized flowers and leaves. Prayers to Bernard are found on three other folios as are the Eight Verses of Bernard.[34] One of the full-page miniatures shows a cistercian nun kneeling before Mary.

[31] For example in Dupeux 1993, 153. For this, see Chapter Seven.
[32] MS Cod. UH 1, fol. 147v.
[33] Hamburger 1997.
[34] On folios 127v, 228v, 251v and 54r respectively.

IMAGES OF BERNARD IN CISTERCIAN ABBEYS OF NUNS

The cult of Bernard among cistercian nuns naturally found expression as well in the variety of altarpieces, sculpture, wall paintings and stained glass which adorned the majority of their churches, cloisters, and conventual buildings. An *Amplexus* sculpture attributed to Michel Erhart and dated *c.* 1500/10 (SC32) embellishes the nuns' choir at the abbey of Oberschönenfeld in southern Germany. It is carved in two parts in limewood and painted. The upper part has Christ hanging on the wall, his arms outstretched to the separate figure of Bernard kneeling on the ground beneath. More common, however, were statues of Bernard with the traditional attributes of the monastic cowl, crozier, and book. These were usually carved in wood and painted, often close to one metre in height, and almost always date to the late fifteenth or early sixteenth century. An example from *c.* 1490 in painted wood and attributed to the Cologne workshop of Tilman van der Burch (SC28) belonged to the nuns who moved to Niederwerth from nearby Koblenz in 1580, and probably brought the statue with them then. Although the present colouring on the ninety-eight cm high statue is not original, Bernard is depicted, as he often is, in a black cowl which is held up on one side to reveal the white tunic underneath. He has a book with a clasp and decorative metal studs in his left hand. His right hand is raised in blessing, but this, however, is modern; originally he would have held a crozier in this hand. In the same church there was a grisaille window dated *c.* 1480 with another picture of a standing Bernard (GL89). Here he is portrayed with all the traditional attributes, including the nimbus which was usually omitted in the carved figures as it was too difficult to convey satisfactorily.

Other statues from nuns' abbeys include examples from Seligenthal (SC31) from the second quarter of the fifteenth century (80 cm high); Notre-Dame de Soleilmont (SC48), dated *c.* 1500 (89 cm high); Val-Notre-Dame, Antheit (SC 36), from the early sixteenth century (99 cm high); and Roermond (SC38), from *c.* 1525. At La Cambre, on the outskirts of Brussels, there is a stone carving (SC37) from the second half of the fourteenth century (139 cm high) which is now in the lavatorium niche in the cloister, but which was formerly in one of three niches on the west front of the church, the other two having contained carvings of Saint Mary Magdalene and Saint John Evangelist (?). Copies of the three figures are now in the original position.

Visual art played a vital part in the religious life of nuns. In the words of an authority on the iconography of nuns, they made works of art 'an integral, even indispensable, part of their piety'.[35] A fine example of this emphasis on the visual in their cultus of Bernard may be seen in a wall painting (WA07) in the former refectory (now the library) of the nuns' abbey of Seligenthal. (We have already referred to an Antiphonary, a Gradual, and a statue from this abbey.)[36] The wall painting is thought to have originated after re-building done in 1484, but it was extensively restored in the seventeenth century.[37] The painting is dominated by the large figures of Bernard on the left and Benedict on the right. Bernard is in a grey cowl with his right hand raised in blessing, his crozier under his right arm and a book in his left hand. He is facing Benedict, in a black cowl, with the traditional attributes of beaker and snake in his right hand and a crozier and book in his left. Between them a small nun kneels on Jacob's Ladder, a reference to Genesis 28:12 and the twelve-rung ladder of humility which is at the heart of the Rule in its longest chapter, Chapter 7,[38] and which was interpreted by Bernard in his first written work, the *Steps of Humility and Pride,* probably composed in 1118/1119.[39] This benedictine virtue occupied a central position in the teaching of Bernard, who argued that the journey to the goal which is Christ is a slow step-by-step process. The diminutive cistercian nun in a grey habit with black veil has reached the seventh rung of the ladder, which is held up by two angels, one on each side and surmounted by a cross and the monogram of Christ, IHS. She is more than half way there, but has still a long way to go! The ladder theme is also depicted in a magnificent full-page miniature (MA028) which contains one of the earliest images of Bernard and occurs in the oldest collection of his works, compiled at the benedictine abbey of Anchin *c.* 1165. In this, however, Bernard and Benedict are portrayed, not at the foot of the ladder, but at the top, on either side of Christ; Benedict in a brown habit is shown writing his Rule and Bernard in white carrying a book—either the Rule or his own treatise.

[35] Hamburger 1997, 4.
[36] See pages 167–168 and 174.
[37] Aachen 1981, 421–422.
[38] Rule 7, trans McCann 1976, 16-22.
[39] *Liber de Gradibus Humilitatis et Superbiae,* SBOp 3:13-59.

Although there were cistercian women's monasteries during Bernard's lifetime, their proliferation occurred later than that of men's houses, and the earliest image of nuns in the company of Bernard, ▶ *Fig. 10* (MA035), significantly also the earliest known portrayal of cistercian nuns, belongs to the late twelfth century. The nuns kept Bernard's memory alive first and foremost by a variety of works of art—statues, paintings, glass—which adorned their churches and conventual buildings. The cult of Bernard also found expression in the communal worship of the nuns, who regarded Bernard as the patron of nuns, as well as in their private devotional aids, in images in manuscripts of Bernard's own works, in small books of private prayers and in individual devotional images (*Andachtsbilder*). The place of small images, albeit not specifically bernardine, in the visual culture of female monasticism may be seen in the *Life* of the Cistercian Beatrice of Nazareth. Beside a wooden cross adorned with various pious texts, she 'also carried tied to her arm another image of the Lord's cross painted on a piece of parchment' as a constant reminder of the Lord's passion.[40] Alongside texts, images played an indispensable role in the cistercian nuns' cult of Bernard. As meditational aids images served as a vehicle for imitation and edification and formed an essential part of the distinctive spirituality of cistercian nuns.

[40] De Ganck 1991, 89.

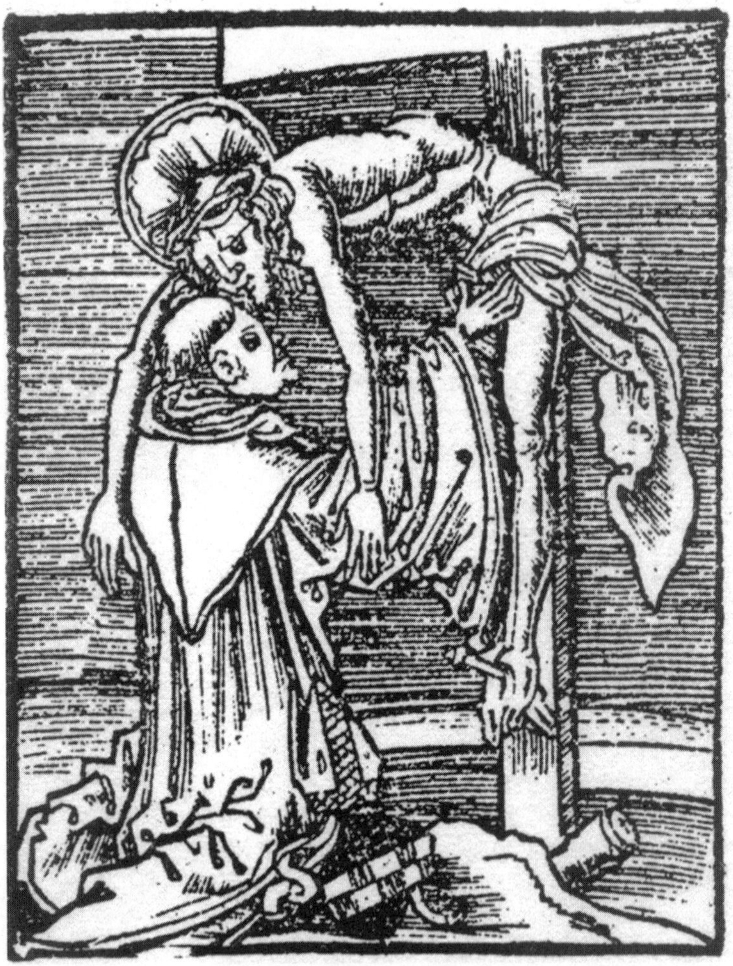

Figure 11: One of a number of woodcuts by Hans Baldung Grien in the *Hortulus animae,* printed at Strassbourg, 1511–1512 (EN85).

SEVEN

BERNARD RECEIVING THE EMBRACE OF CHRIST

CHRIST REMOVING HIS ARMS from the Cross, bending down, and embracing Bernard was to become one of the most popular bernardine representations in the later Middle Ages.[1] It was one of the four iconographical *topoi* which have been described as 'scene-attributes'[2]—scenes based on popular stories whereby Bernard may be identified as easily as he is by the traditional attributes of cowl, crozier and book, or by the halo which marks him as monk, abbot, and saint respectively. The other 'scene-attributes', we remember, are Bernard receiving Mary's Milk (the *Lactatio*), the related Vision of Mary (the *Doctrina*), and Bernard with the Devil on a chain.[3] With seventy-two *Amplexus* or *Amplexus Bernardi* images recorded, Christ's Embrace of Bernard was less popular than the *Lactatio,* represented by one hundred nineteen, but its literary source dates back considerably further. It may be traced back to the golden age of cistercian

[1] For the origin of this and its later interpretation, see McGuire 1991, 227–249; for its iconography, see Posset 1998, 289–314.

[2] A term first used referring to the *Lactatio* in Dupeux 1993, 157.

[3] For these, see Chapters 8, 9, and 11.

miracle stories and exemplum collections, particularly those associated with Clairvaux a generation or so after Bernard's death.[4]

The theme of Christ's Embrace is the more remarkable in that it is the only one of the four which is truly bernardine in origin. In one of his so-called *Sententiae,* Bernard talks of the

> cross of Christ—not that wooden cross on which he hung, but the cross of charity on which, then as now, he was outstretched as if to embrace us with his extended, loving arms.[5]

Although the origin of the *Sentences* is obscure, they are thought to consist of words spoken by Bernard, snippets of sermons written down by his monks. The origin of the picture-type which was later to become so popular may thus be sought in Bernard's own words.

The idea of Christ stretching out his arms from the Cross in a gesture of love predates Bernard by more than half a century. An anglo-norman *Manuel des Péchés,* a versified penitential treatise composed *c.* 1260, was intended to instruct the laity on the practice of penance and confession. In the discussion on anger, the second of the seven deadly sins,[6] it illustrates the story of a knight who spares the murderer who had slain his father in anger; Christ rewarded him by bending down from the cross and embracing him. The description closely resembles the account of the crusading knight in the *Dialogus Miraculorum.* The anglo-norman image has variously been interpreted as representing the embrace of Bernard and Saint John Gualbert, but the figure wears a blue cloak and does not have a halo or carry a crozier and is not tonsured; there is no doubt that it represents the knight of the story.[7] As the first known example

[4] See McGuire 1991, 153–187, and the introduction by Brian McGuire to the french edition of the *Exordium Magnum,* Conrad d'Eberbach 1998, XI-XXXV.

[5] SBOp 6/2:59: *Quattuor sint cruces diversa meritorum stipendia exspectantes. Prima est crux Christi, non linqua illa in qua perpebdit, sed crux caritatis in qua et tunc et nunc extensus quasi ad amplexandos nos amoris brachiis expansis.* The translation is from *Bernard of Clairvaux: The Parables & The Sentences,* 2000, 181.

[6] Bennett 1990, 170, illustrated as Fig. 10. It is found in MS 1 in the Robert H. Taylor Collection at Princeton University Library.

[7] The incorrect attribution to Bernard is found in Camille 1989, 213, where it is illustrated as Fig. 114, and in Wenzel 1995, 313 where the caption to Fig. 40 reads 'Christus umarmt St Bernhard'. In Posset 1998, 297 (illustrated as Fig. 1) it is also wrongly interpreted, this time as probably St John Gualbert.

of the *Amplexus* image traditionally associated with Bernard, it is nevertheless of considerable interest in bernardine iconography, pre-dating the earliest recorded *Amplexus Bernardi* by more than half a century.

A Middle English poem conveys the same image when it says that his arms were spread to 'love-clipping' as his head was bowed to 'sweet kissing'[8]—the word 'clip' being an archaic term meaning to 'clasp with the arms, embrace, hug'. The identification of Bernard with the theme is expressed in another english poem, from the thirteenth century, in which the reader is exhorted to look at Christ's face and to receive, like Bernard, the embrace of his arms, spread out upon the tree:

Man, folwe seintt Bernardes trace
And loke in Jhesu Cristes face,
How he lut his heved to the
Swetlike for to kessen the,
And sprat hise armes on the tre,
Sinful man, to klippen the.
In sygne of love ys open his syde:
Hiis feet ynayled with t'abyde.
Al his bodi is don on rode,
Senful man, for thyne goode.[9]

A literary version of the *Amplexus Bernardi,* the story of Bernard receiving the Embrace of Christ, is first found in a collection known as the *Liber Miraculorum,* compiled by Herbert of Clairvaux in the late 1170s.[10] Almost all the stories about Bernard in this, including that of the Embrace, appear again in Conrad of Eberbach's *Exordium Magnum,* in which it forms one of the twenty chapters devoted to Bernard. Entitled 'Of a devout monk who saw the image on the Cross embracing the holy father Bernard in prayer', it reads:

> The religious man, Lord Menard, former abbot of Mores[11] which is a monastery neighbouring on Clairvaux, told the

[8] Quoted in Bennett 1982, 71.

[9] Bennett 1982, 47.

[10] *De Miraculis* 3:2:19; PL 185:1328. It does *not* appear in the *Vita Prima,* as asserted in Posset 1998, 292, 293 (note 19), 302, 312.

[11] Founded from Clairvaux 1153. Menard was the second abbot.

> following miraculous story as if it had happened to someone else but which we believe referred to himself: I heard of a certain monk who once found the blessed abbot Bernard alone in the church deep in prayer. As he was prostrate before the altar, a cross with its Crucified appeared placed on the floor in front of him. This the most blessed man devoutly adored and kissed. Then that Majesty removed his arms from the branches of the cross and he seemed to embrace the servant of God and draw him to himself. The monk who witnessed this, having watched for a while, was beside himself with amazement. Afraid of offending his saintly father if seen observing so closely his secrets, he left in silence, for he knew that all the prayer and the life of this saintly man were beyond the human condition.[12]

Like accounts of the numerous miracles he performed, Bernard's vision was included to show the favour accorded to him by God and thus bolster the confidence of his monks, who had been under increasing attack in the second half of the twelfth century, not least by the black monks of Conrad's native Germany.[13] That Bernard, whose life, according to the monk who witnessed the scene, was 'beyond the human condition' had been embraced by the crucified Christ signalled divine approval of the cistercian way of life.

As well as inspiring the monks to persevere in the spirit of their founders, the *Amplexus* vision reflects and acknowledges Bernard's

[12] EM 2:7; Griesser 1961, 102–103: *Domnus Menardus, quondam abbas de Moris, quod est monasterium vicinum Claraevalli, vir religiosus, mirabilem quandam rem quasi de alio retulit familiaribus suis, quam tamen sibimet evenisse putamus, ita dicens: Notus est mihi monachus quidam, qui Bernardum abbatem aliquando reperit in ecclesia solum orantem. Qui cum prostratus esset ante altare, apparebat ibi quaedam crux cum suo crucifixo super pavimentum posita coram illo, quam isdem vir beatissimus devotissime adorabat ac deosculabatur. Porro ipsa maiestas separatis brachiis a cornibus crucis videbatur eundem Dei famulum amplecti atque astringere sibi. Quod dum monachus ille aliquandiu cerneret, prae nimia admiratione stupidus haerebat et quasi extra se erat. Tandem vero metuens, ne patrem sanctum offenderet, si eum veluti secretorum suorum exploratorem ita sibi de proximo imminere conspiceret, silenter acscessit, intelligens nimirum ac sciens de illo homine sancto, quod vere supra hominem esset tota ipsius oratio atque conversatio.*

[13] EM 1:10; Griesser 1961, 61: *Monachi namque nigri ordinis, maxime in provinciis Germaniae degentes, ubicumque vel apud quoscumque possunt, sacro ordini nostro derogare non cessant asserentes sanctos patres nostros cum scandalo et inobedientia contra voluntatem abbatis sui de molismensi coenobio egressos fuisse.*

immense contribution in a developing theology centred on Christ's sacrifice on the cross. By his focus on the Passion, Bernard had drawn attention to Christ's full participation in our humanity. The theme recurs time and again in his works. It is exemplified by his frequent choice of the quotation from Saint Paul, 'I would speak of nothing but Jesus Christ and him crucified' (1 Cor 2:2),[14] and he meditated on it at length in his famous Sermon 43 on the Song of Songs—known by the opening words *Fasciculus myrrhae* (a little bundle of myrrh—Sg 1:12). In it Bernard reminded his monks of the need to 'preserve without fail the memory of all those bitter things He endured for you'.[15]

The theme is also found in a famous twelfth-century pseudo-bernardine hymn of lamentation, the *Planctus ante nescia,* which was often sung at passion plays. It contains the line 'Rush to the embrace! While he hangs on the tree of the cross he offers himself with outstretched arms to the loving for a mutual embrace'.[16] The popularity of this hymn, probably enhanced by the prestige attaching to its attribution to Bernard, indicates that the Embrace was not confined to Bernard.[17] The imagery is used by Aelred of Rievaulx in the *Rule for A Recluse* which he wrote for his sister:

> On your altar let it be enough for you to have a representation of Our Saviour hanging on the cross; that will bring before your mind his Passion for you to imitate, his outspread arms will invite you to embrace him, his naked breasts will feed you with the milk of sweetness to console you.[18]

[14] For example, Sermon 43 on the Song of Songs (SBOp 2:43).

[15] SBOp 2:41. The phrase from the Song of Songs (*Fasciculus myrrhae dilectus meus mihi inter ubera mea comorabitur:* 'a little bundle of myrrh is my beloved who lies between my breasts') appears on a banderole above Bernard's head in a painting attributed to Martin Bellegambe in which Bernard is depicted kneeling before an altar and clutching a small crucifix. It was commissioned by Abbess Philippine of Flines. It is illustrated in Paris 1990, 279 (but in reverse). As it is dated 1562 it falls outside the period of this study and is not recorded. I am grateful to Andrea Pearson for the information.

[16] Quoted in Belting 1990, 75: *In amplexus ruite, dum pendet in stipite, mutuis amplexibus parat se amantibus manibus extensis.*

[17] For examples of others who experienced the *Amplexus,* see Posset 1998, 289–290.

[18] Aelred of Rievaulx, *Opera Omnia* 1971, 1:658: *Sufficiat tibi in altari tuo Salvatoris in cruce pendentis imago, quae passionem suam tibi prepresentet quam imiteris, expansis brachiis ad suos te invitet amplexus in quibus delecteris, nudatis uberibus lac tibi suavitatis infundat quo consoleris.* Translation from Aelred of Rievaulx, Treatises I 1971, 73.

Here Christ's gesture invites a response and this was reflected in the mutual embrace of most *Amplexus Bernardi* representations but goes beyond Bernard's passive role in the original literary source. As we shall see, the development from Christ's embrace in the story, to the mutual embrace in the hymn, and then to the invitation to embrace Christ in Aelred's text, is reflected in the development of the *Amplexus* iconography.

Caesarius of Heisterbach, in the *Dialogus Miraculorum,* records a number of visions of the Crucified in which the Embrace, instead of being a sign of sanctity, as in the case of Bernard, is represented as a safeguard against sin. Peter, a prayerful monk of Himmerod in the Rhineland, had once lain prostrate in the lay brothers' choir, imploring divine help that he might not fall into sin. Suddenly,

> there stood before him the Lord Jesus Himself, or rather as if he were hanging upon the cross. And He, withdrawing His most merciful arms from the cross, embraced his servant and drawing him to His breast as one being dear to Him, in sign of mutual friendship, He clasped him close and by that clasp destroyed his strongest temptations.[19]

Caesarius adds that 'he could not tell whether he received that revelation through his bodily eyes or through the spirit only'. He tells a similar story of a nun under temptation, who 'by His embrace changed all her trouble into the greatest peace'.[20] In another story a knight who had taken the cross was passing by the altar of the church of the Holy Sepulchre in Jerusalem when 'the image of the Lord's body bowed very plainly to him from the cross' because he had spared his enemy for the love of Christ.[21]

Just as *Christ's Embrace* is considered a reward for virtuous conduct in these stories Christ's wrath at sinful behaviour is depicted in two spanish manuscripts in what may be described as *Colaphus* images. They illustrate stories of nuns being chastised for planning to elope with men and subsequently repenting. One of these tales is found in the *Cantigas de Santa Maria,* a collection of over four hundred marian

[19] *Dialogus Miraculorum* 8:13; Caesarius of Heisterbach 1929, 2:15-16.
[20] *Dialogus Miraculorum* 8:16; Caesarius of Heisterbach 1929, 2:18.
[21] *Dialogus Miraculorum* 8:25; Caesarius of Heisterbach 1929, 2:26.

miracles and hymns in verse collected by King Alfonso X (1252–1284). It tells of a nun who takes leave of an image of Mary before running away. The image weeps, but the nun persists. As she passes a life-size crucifix the figure of Christ wrenches one of his arms from the cross and strikes her, driving a nail through her cheek. In the *Castigos e documentos para bien vivir* ('Counsel and instrument for right living') written by Alfonso's son, Pancho IV, Christ tears himself from the cross, strikes the nun and, again, drives a huge nail through her cheeks. In the illustration of this second version, Christ is shown having left the cross altogether; huge nails pierce his bleeding feet and left hand, while the nail from his right hand transfixes both sides of the nun's bloodied cheeks.[22] Although the source for these two images is not known, they may have been inspired by the inverse theme featured in the slightly earlier *Dialogus Miraculorum*. Caesarius of Heisterbach tells of a bell-man from the church of Saint George in Cologne who had no reverence for the cross and stole candles which devout women had placed before it. While he was in bed one night, the cross came to him and with a voice of rebuke smote him so that he was sick for many days.[23]

Passion imagery became increasingly common from the thirteenth century onwards. Bernard's writings on the sufferings of Christ made it only natural that, in time, he would also be featured in representations of the crucified Christ. A fragment of a Hymnal from *c.* 1480 has a miniature illustrating a long Passion poem ascribed to Bernard (MA007). He is depicted embracing the foot of the cross as is customary on Good Friday, surrounded by Mary, John, the two other Marys, Longinus, soldiers and lay men in a traditional Calvary scene.

Bernard also appears in a highly expressionistic, almost modern, pen and ink drawing of the Crucifixion to which the only other witness is a cistercian nun (DR10).[24] Like most *Amplexus* images, the scene is shared by the two figures alone, unencumbered by the presence of Mary and John or the usual crowd. They kneel at the foot of the cross, both grasping the legs of Christ with one hand and the cross with the other. The hanging, cross nimbed head of Christ and his body, bright red with streaming torrents of blood, are in keeping with the ecstatic visions of

[22] The two images are illustrated in France 1998, 159 and 160.
[23] *Dialogus Miraculorum* 8:25; Caesarius of Heisterbach 1929, 2:26.
[24] See pages 172–173 in Chaper Six.

the Crucified associated with mystics like Saint Lutgard of Aywières (1182–1246), who may possibly be the nun represented in the picture. The drawing is from the first half of the fourteenth century and is thought to be a devotional picture from a cistercian women's house in the Lower Rhineland. Like the previous image, it is not an *Amplexus;* Christ's lifeless body hangs on the cross with both arms attached and there is no indication of an Embrace. A Book of Hours made in the 1340s by a follower of Jean Pucelle contains a number of miniatures illustrating Passion prayers in French. One of them (MA087) depicts a kneeling saint-abbot, thought to be Bernard, praying in front of a crucifix on an altar. Although Christ's arms are again attached and make no contact with the kneeling figure, this has been erroneously identified as an *Amplexus* image.[25] These two pictures testify to Bernard's devotion to the Passion, but neither is an *Amplexus* image.

As we have seen, the genesis of the *Amplexus Bernardi* theme may be traced back to the twelfth century, although a century and a half passed before it found pictorial expression. The seventy-two recorded *Amplexus* images may be divided into two main groups: those that take place in a church—that of Clairvaux—in accordance with the literary source; and those that are sited out of doors, transferring the scene, with Bernard's presence, to Golgotha. In some cases (for example, images in sculpture form) the location is not clear. Of the fifty-one *Amplexus* images where the location may be discerned, however, thirty-five are set out of doors and only sixteen indoors, as described by the monk in the original story.

The great majority of the seventy-two images are represented in four media: twenty-four manuscript illuminations, which include the first three known representations of the Embrace and are strongly represented in the earlier period; twelve paintings—mostly altarpieces, beginning in 1432; six sculptures, some forming part of altarpieces; and seventeen woodcuts, also beginning around *c.* 1430–1434.

THE *AMPLEXUS* IN MANUSCRIPTS

The earliest known *Amplexus* image, dating to the first half of the fourteenth century, occurs in a Gradual from the cistercian women's

[25] In Schmitt 1990, 163.

abbey of Wonnental in Breisgau, Baden (MA059). Within the filigree initial *O(scintillans sidus celi)*, itself decorated with four intertwining hybrids—one of which appears to be a hooded monk—a kneeling Bernard is embraced by Christ, partially descended from the cross. A smaller kneeling monk with hands folded in prayer may represent the monk who witnessed the vision in the original story. Christ is cross-nimbed, Bernard nimbed with his crozier leaning on his left shoulder, his hands outstretched to receive Christ bending down from the cross, which is surmounted by the traditional INRI ('Jesus of Nazareth King of the Jews') inscription and in which the two nails for the hands are still attached. Two anomalies stand out between this image and the description in the *Exordium Magnum*. First, according to the original account, Bernard kissed the cross as a result of which Christ freed his arms to embrace Bernard and draw him to himself; here their heads touch in what has the makings of a mutual embrace. Secondly, the cross is embedded in uneven ground out of doors, thus transferring the scene from inside the church at Clairvaux to Calvary. While the initiative in the literary account is entirely with Christ, in the image Bernard's role is less passive; at the same time the change of location connects the action more closely with the actual Passion.

Approximately another century passed before the next known depiction of the *Amplexus*. A paper manuscript from 1419 of the *Lives of the Saints* in an Alsatian dialect of German derived from James of Voragine's *Golden Legend* has a pen and ink drawing of the traditional *Amplexus* picture. It is one of one hundred seventy-two images depicting saints. The opening of the chapter on Bernard has a large miniature of Christ embracing Bernard (MA053) which is headed 'von sant Bernhardus'. It is decorated using only three colours: green for Christ's loincloth and his crown of thorns, the grass on which the cross is placed and two trees in the background; yellow for the cross, Christ's and Bernard's halos and Bernard's crozier and tonsure; and pale brown for Bernard's cowl. As in the Wonnental miniature, the scene is set out of doors and there is the same mutuality of embraces. A comparable image (MA152) is found in an almost contemporary manuscript of a french version of the *Golden Legend* translated by Jean de Vignay, written in *c.*1420. An inscription on folio 312v reveals that it belonged to the nobleman Charles de Croy. In the same way as in the alsatian manuscript, the beginning of the section on Bernard has a large miniature depicting

Bernard before the figure of Christ whose two hands are detached from the cross and outstretched towards Bernard. Again the scene is set out of doors with the cross on grass. The background is chequered in gold, red, and blue with white dots. The pale emaciated body of Christ emphasizes his lifelessness even though he is reaching out to Bernard, but, in contrast to the two previous miniatures, the kneeling figure of Bernard in a dark cowl is some distance from Christ and his hands are clasped in prayer and not raised in response to Christ's gesture.

An unusual *Amplexus* depiction is a pen and ink drawing in a Missal from the cistercian abbey of Heilsbronn dated 1440/1450 (DR20). The blood-stained body of Christ has his arms outstretched from a T-cross to embrace the kneeling Bernard. The cross is set in the ground, supported by a number of rocks, and, in what is the only recorded example of the motif, the scene is witnessed by Mary and John. Above an angel is swinging a thurible.

The remaining twenty known examples in illuminated manuscripts are all from the last third of the fifteenth century, or later. Most of them were service books which belonged to cistercian monasteries of monks or nuns in German-speaking lands. Among the exceptions are the Prayerbook in Dutch of Beatrijs van Assendelft dated *c.* 1480, which probably came from the convent of Saint Agnes in Delft (MA257), two examples in a manuscript belonging to the dominican nuns in Nuremberg (EN 63, EN 64), and a Missal in German dated 1471 in which the *Amplexus* scene (MA191) is witnessed by a kneeling monk as in the Wonnental miniature, although in this case the figure may represent the donor or the abbot of a cistercian house whose arms are shown at the bottom and not the monk of the original story. In this Christ's arms are clasped round Bernard, who reciprocates in a mutual embrace, and their heads are touching each other. The scene takes place out of doors, with the figures standing on grass. A closed book with a mitre on it lies in the middle between the monk and the figures of Christ and Bernard. Above the mitre—one of the late medieval attributes by which Bernard was known—there seems to be a crozier, another of the more usual attributes associated with Bernard. Both Bernard and the monk are dressed in black cowls.

A cistercian Breviary dated 1472 from the nuns' monastery of Lichtenthal contains a similar image, but the witness is absent (MA222). The cross-nimbed Christ with the crown of thorns and a blood-stained body has his arms joined round the neck of a larger Bernard, who is nimbed and in a dark grey cowl. He grasps Christ round the body in a close embrace. Bernard's crozier rests behind him. On the left are the lance and pole with a sponge on top and a bucket in which are some of the other *Arma Christi*—the 'Instruments of the Passion' which serve as reminders of the Gospel narrative. Below is the text of the first Responsory from the first Noctern from Vigils on the feast of Bernard.

The same considerable difference in scale is found in the *Amplexus* image (MA135) in the magnificent Missal commissioned in 1492/1493 by the twenty-seventh abbot of Rein, near Graz in Austria, Wolfgang Schroetl (1481–1515), for his own use. Therefore known as the Wolfgang Missal, it was kept by the abbot himself and used regularly by succeeding abbots until the nineteenth century. Richly decorated, it contains one full-page miniature of the Crucifixion with a portrait of the abbot kneeling at the foot of the cross, as well as twenty-three other miniatures and forty historiated initials. Among these the scene of the Embrace adorns the opening of the Mass of the feast of Saint Bernard; within a pink initial *P(erfice quaesumus domine)* on a gold background within a green border, is a prayer to Bernard. Bernard is nimbed and wears a purplish-grey cowl. He kneels before Christ, whose arms are placed on Bernard's shoulders, while Bernard's arms are outstretched supporting Christ's body. The image of Bernard resembles the portrait of Abbot Wolfgang in the Missal's opening miniature. Featuring the abbot in the guise of Bernard—as was quite common in late medieval *Lactatio* images—makes the point that he is the successor of Bernard.[26] The scene is set indoors in a room that looks like a chapter house, making this the only fifteenth-century example of the motif in an illuminated manuscript not set out of doors. The small bullfinch—also known in German as 'Blutfinch' (bloodfinch)—refers to the legend according to which its beak was bent and its chest stained red on account of its attempt to pull the nails out of the hands and feet of Christ.[27]

In a full-page miniature in a Prayer Book from the cistercian abbey of Herrenalb (MA052), a corpulent Bernard kneels at the foot of the cross from which the arms of Christ are detached and placed round Bernard. Their two heads meet. Above the cross is the INRI inscription

[26] See PA073.
[27] Sieveking 1986, 57–59.

and the date 1484. Bernard's crozier, a book, and the arms of Herrenalb—very similar to that of Clairvaux but with a crozier added—lie on the ground. Two *Amplexus* images (MA219 and MA220) are also found in manuscripts from the cistercian abbey of Langheim: one in a Gradual dated 1496 with the arms of Clairvaux surmounted by a mitre placed on the ground; the other an historiated initial *P(rima virtus viri sancti)* in an Antiphonary—the first Responsory of the first Nocturn for the feast of Bernard. In the latter a much smaller Christ has his arms detached from a T-cross and placed around the shoulders of Bernard, who supports the lifeless-looking body of Christ, and their heads touch each other. A crozier and a mitre lie on the ground and a small white dog, alluding to Bernard's mother's dream, lies at his feet.

Of the twelve recorded sixteenth-century manuscript images only three are of cistercian origin (MA317, MA326, & MA389), while twelve were of lay ownership. Of the latter, one is a miniature in the *Hortulus animae*—a prayer collection for the laity—from the 1520's (MA016). The scene is set in a church in accordance with the original story, and the difference in scale is so great that there is no doubt it represents a crucifix which comes alive. The other is one of thirty-nine full-page miniatures in a slightly later german Book of Hours (▶ *Colour plate 8;* MA131). Set in a rocky landscape, the smaller lifeless-looking Christ is supported by a kneeling Bernard in a black cowl.

DEPICTIONS IN RETABLE PAINTINGS AND IN SCULPTURE

Eight out of the twelve altarpiece paintings featuring the *Amplexus* are thought to have come from cistercian churches, and out of the total the great majority (nine) were, like those in manuscript miniatures, set out of doors in a Golgotha scene. Almost all of them were secondary scenes from the wings of altarpieces with central panels featuring the Virgin and Child—as would be the case for high altars in cistercian churches, which were always dedicated to Mary—or other major biblical scenes. The incorporation of the *Amplexus* theme as one of the marginal retable scenes indicates its use as a kind of shorthand—the scene-attribute whereby Bernard would be recognized.

Sculptures and paintings were prohibited by early cistercian legislation and for a long time this restriction was strictly adhered to; there were no images of any kind in their churches, not even of Bernard.[28] The earliest known *Amplexus* depiction in a cistercian church (PA060) was one of eight from the lives of the saints painted for Maulbronn in 1432 by an anonymous artist known as the 'Master of the Maulbronn Altar'. The eight scenes adorn the wings of an altarpiece from the side chapel built in 1424, four of them on the inside and four on the outside, a parallel to the earliest known bernardine altar in the Templars' church in Palma from 1290, in which a *Lactatio* image and three scenes from Bernard's life flanked the central panel (▶ *Colour plate 5*). Five of the eight Maulbronn pictures feature Bernard: four scenes from his life and the *Amplexus* image (PA057-PA061). The lower picture on the left outside wing of the altarpiece (PA060) has Christ descending from the cross to embrace Bernard, their heads touching. As in the earliest manuscript image of the motif, the scene is witnessed by a small monk on the left, again perhaps the monk who saw the vision recorded in the *Exordium Magnum*.

The next five recorded altarpiece images of the Embrace belong to the last third of the fifteenth century. Johann Koerbecke's *Amplexus* painting from *c.* 1470 (PA008) was originally one of the wings of an altarpiece. His main work was the retable, which he finished in 1457 for the cistercian monastery of Marienfeld, where he also restored the great hanging crucifix. It is therefore possible that this *Amplexus* painting was also commissioned by Marienfeld. A nimbed Bernard in a flowing black cowl reaches up to the crucified figure of Christ on a T-cross who has his arms on Bernard's shoulders, ready to embrace him. The setting is a room with a tiled floor in what appears to be a monastery; a cloister can be seen through the window and, beyond this, a wall and some houses. An exchange between the two figures is indicated by the scrolls. Christ's scroll appears to say *In charitate perpetua dilexi te. h[e?]re. z* ('I have loved thee with perpetual love'), and Bernard's *Gloria, te dom.ie . . . mea* ('Glory to you Lord . . .').

In 1480/85 the Master of the Bonn Diptych painted a triptych of the Mass of Saint Gregory, one of the most popular late-medieval themes in religious iconography, for the benedictine nuns of Saint Agatha in

[28] For this, see Waddell 1999, 413: *Instituta XXVI. De sculpturis et picturis et cruce lignea* (Of sculptures and paintings, and of the wooden cross. Sculptures are never permitted; and the only paintings allowed were on the crosses, which had themselves to be of wood).

Cologne. The side panels consist of four scenes: on the right is Saint Agatha, naked to the waist and with both hands tied to a column above her head, with eight female figures kneeling at her feet; and, on the reverse, Saint Benedict in a black cowl, carrying a book and a crozier; on the left, the Virgin and Child stand on grass on which four donors are kneeling; and on the reverse is the *Amplexus* (PA017). Bernard, in a black or very dark brown cowl, is depicted larger in scale than Christ, whose emaciated body Bernard is supporting. Bernard is looking up at Christ whose hands are on Bernard's shoulders, but the initiative seems to be with Bernard and the picture resembles more a Deposition scene than that of the Embrace of the original story.

As we mentioned above, a considerable development had taken place between the time of the original twelfth-century literary source and the earliest known iconographical representation of the theme: not only had the siting been changed from the church at Clairvaux where the vision is said to have taken place, but Bernard's passivity in Herbert of Clairvaux's original account had also been replaced by what in most of the visual representations amounted to a mutual embrace.

A text from Arnold of Bonneval's *De Laudibus B. Mariae Virginis,* which was thought to have been written by Bernard, found its way into the *Golden Legend* and had a considerable influence on the iconographical theme of the *Lactatio*.[29] In the same way one of the two prayers in a popular compilation entitled the *Anthidotarius Animae* (Antidote for the Soul), first published in 1489 by the cistercian abbot of Baumgarten near Strassburg, is attributed to Bernard.[30] This prayer Bernard is said to have recited before the Crucifix when the image of Christ detached itself from the cross and embraced him. It contains effusive greetings to all parts of the body of Jesus; in it the biblical quotations with which all Bernard's authentic works are peppered are replaced by descriptive details and episodes in which physical contact is emphasized—images which are a far cry from twelfth-century bernardine spirituality. The other is a

[29] See MA117, MA133, and PA138.

[30] The full title of this work is *Liber meditationum ac orationum devotarum qui antidotarius anime dicitur*. It includes the prayer *Memorare* which was wrongly attributed to Bernard. Pfleger 1934, 120, lists nineteen editions prior to 1500 and a further eight from 1500 to 1523. For the importance of this work and what follows, see McGuire 1991, 238–247, and Chen 1994, 24–54, which also contains the Latin text and a translation into English.

prayer *to* Bernard which begins: 'He who loved you with such charity that He deigned to embrace you with the arms of his passion'.

In the original story Bernard was the passive recipient of Christ's Embrace in a vision which took place in the mind of the monk who related it. The next stage, which found expression visually in some of the early *Amplexus* images, was a mutual embrace in which the spiritual, visionary action became an intimate physical act which provided the ever-wider audience with material for meditation. The rendering of the mystical subject in strongly sensual and physical terms makes it comparable to the literary *Salutatio* poem. In some of the late medieval retable paintings Christ's life is depicted as ebbing away and the mutuality of embrace has been replaced by Bernard's active participation in what has the feel more of a Deposition than that of an *Amplexus*.

Bernard's more active role is featured in the *Amplexus* image in the retable for the nuns of Saint Agatha in Cologne (PA017) and, to an even greater extent, in the altarpiece for the augustinian church in Nuremberg painted in 1487 and attributed to Michael Wolgemut (PA009). This latter is one of the most important works from the Nuremberg School of the second half of the fifteenth century. Although it was made only for a side altar, it was a large retable with double wings and a central panel (which no longer exists) depicting Mary with Saint Augustine. Four saints are featured on the inner side of the inner wings: on the left Bernard in an *Amplexus* image (PA009) and Saint Christopher; on the right Saint Luke as a painter, and the martyrdom of Saint Sebastian. Here the *Amplexus* theme is used as the scene-attribute whereby Bernard may be easily identified. The composition of the picture with the falling figure of the lifeless Christ being supported by Bernard may be compared with that of Ugolino di Nerio's Deposition painted in *c.* 1325.[31] The position of the figure of Christ is almost identical in the two and the embrace and the anguished look of Mary in the one is very similar to that of Bernard in the other, as too is the manner in which they support Christ's dead body. The scene takes place in a rocky landscape with trees, a castle, a house, and a lake. The arms of Clairvaux are at Bernard's feet.

A very similar composition, also reminiscent of a Deposition, is a late fifteenth-century painting from the cistercian abbey of Bebenhausen in Württemberg (PA047). A nimbed Bernard in a brown cowl

[31] Illustrated in London 2000, 127.

receives the body of the dead Christ, his arms detached from the cross. Kneeling on the right is the smaller figure of a portly monk in a black cowl with his hands clasped in prayer, gazing up at the Crucified. He has a red book under his arm. His individualized features indicate that it may well be the portrait of the donor-abbot in the guise of the monk who had the vision. The scene is out of doors, but instead of it creating a traditional Golgotha picture, the artist has chosen the abbey of Bebenhausen as the setting. The monastery is surrounded by water in which some monks are fishing from an open boat. The landscape is rocky, with delicate flowers in the foreground and pheasants and grazing deer in the distance. On the ground at the front are an open book and a small white dog, alluding to Bernard's writings and his mother's dream. Bernard's crozier lies on the ground behind the cross.

The small white dog appears again in an *Amplexus* image which forms the upper half of retable wings painted around the same time for the cistercian abbey of Neuberg in Austria (PA124). The scene is again a rocky landscape. The very much smaller figure of a lifeless-appearing Christ slumps down on to the large Bernard. Again the scene resembles the Deposition more than an Embrace. Another altarpiece from Neuberg featured an *Amplexus* image (PA101). One of four panels with scenes from the life of Bernard painted in 1518, it has Bernard in a white cowl kneeling before the crucified Christ in yet another scene resembling the Deposition. The scene is again a rocky wooded landscape with a castle on a hill. Bernard's crozier lies on the rocky ground into which the cross with the usual INRI inscription is fixed with two wooden wedges.

Another triptych of the Mass of Saint Gregory, dated *c.* 1500, has an *Amplexus* image (PA020) on the inside of the right wing. It may originally have come from the abbey of Heisterbach. Set inside a church, it shows a living Christ with his hands detached from a raised T-crucifix, on Bernard's shoulders while Bernard's hands are supporting Christ's body. The scene is watched by a cistercian monk carrying an open book. The five mitres at the foot of the cross refer to the five bishoprics which Bernard refused. Bernard and the monk are in white cowls.

The Deposition variation is repeated in an unusual, perhaps unique, austrian *Amplexus* image (PA079) which forms the inner side of a retable wing painted in 1508 for the cistercian abbey of Lilienfeld by the Master of the 'Historia Friderici et Maximiliani'. The outer side of this wing features four saints: Barbara, Catherine, Pantaleon, and

Margaret. The *Amplexus* image on the inner side shows Christ slumped against the body of the kneeling Bernard, his head with a large crown of thorns resting against Bernard's and his arms falling down Bernard's back. Bernard is helped in supporting Christ's body by two hovering angels, one on either side, holding a long cloth with which they are helping to lower the body. Streams of blood may be seen running down Christ's body. Bernard is in a black cowl and has his crozier leaning against his right shoulder. A mitre rests on the ground next to the arms of Clairvaux.

Another unusual image is an early sixteenth-century painting by Jean van Eckele (PA091), perhaps unique in that it incorporates three iconographical themes. A central *Lactation* scene, with Bernard in a cope over his white cowl kneeling before the Virgin who bares her breast, is accompanied by two scene-attributes: in the middle background the Virgin appears to Bernard, who kneels before her out of doors; on the far right in a scene inside a church Bernard kneels before the crucified Christ, whose arms are detached in an embrace. The provenance of this is not known, but the subject matter suggests cistercian ownership.

An *Amplexus* painting forms part of a polyptych from Bartoszyce in Poland dated *c.* 1510 (PA053). Again the provenance is not known, but the coat of arms at the foot of the cross indicates that it came from a cistercian monastery and resembles that of Clairvaux, although the chequered pattern is green and yellow rather than red and white. Christ with his arms detached from a T-cross with the INRI inscription places his hands on the shoulders of the larger and youthful kneeling Bernard in a black cowl. Blood is running down Christ's body. The setting is indoors with the crucifix on a tiled floor; through a doorway on the left a gatehouse can be seen and through a window on the right a church. Bernard's crozier lies on the floor. One of the characteristics associated with a number of *Amplexus* representations—the larger figure of Bernard as compared with that of Christ—is here very noticeable. This serves as a reference to the original twelfth-century narrative of the vision of the Crucified removing his arms from the cross and embracing Bernard, that is, of a crucifix in a church coming alive.

The *Amplexus* motif also appears on a carved altarpiece, originally a pentatych, commissioned, probably from a north german workshop, for the high altar at the cistercian abbey of Esrum in Denmark by the abbot, Peder Andersen (SC51). He is represented kneeling at the foot of the central crowded Crucifixion scene, and identified by an inscription in gold letters against a red background running along the base of the altarpiece: *Memoria reverendi in Chri[s]to patris Petri abbatis in esrum an[n]o d[omi]ni mccccxcvi* ('In memory of the reverend father in Christ Abbot Peter in Esrum the year 1496').[32] Only fragments have been preserved of the two pairs of hinged wings and the carved figures these contained, including that of Bernard (SC52), but the *corpus* remains intact. The central Crucifixion scene is flanked by four panels with carvings of saints, two on each side. At the top left is an *Amplexus* showing Christ with his arms detached from the T-cross in an embrace of a larger Bernard kneeling before him. The difference in scale between them is particularly accentuated. The scene is set out of doors with a church in the background. Below is the inscription *Sant bernhardus ora pro n[obis]* ('Saint Bernard pray for us').

In addition to the Esrum altarpiece *Amplexus* there are a further five medieval examples of the theme in sculpted form, all from the first third of the sixteenth century and all formerly in cistercian monasteries of monks or nuns. It is likely that at least some of these formed parts of altarpieces. That this is true of a carved wooden figure of Bernard from the abbey of Heilsbronn (SC06) is suggested by the back being hollowed out. Both hands of Christ with the stigmata are still there, fixed to Bernard's shoulders, but the rest of Christ's body and the cross are missing. Christ's hands are smaller than Bernard's, indicating the difference in scale sometimes found in images of the motif. The hands and face are flesh-coloured, the rest gilt. A mitre rests at Bernard's feet.

The early prohibition against pictures and sculptures in cistercian churches had by then long been a dead letter, and the *Amplexus* theme lent itself particularly well to representation not only in altarpieces but also in a free-standing three-dimensional way, with the crucifix placed on the wall and the kneeling figure of Bernard before it. In the nuns' choir at the cistercian abbey of Oberschönenfeld, for example, the motif is represented by two separate figures attributed to Michel Erhart (SC32).[33] They are carved in limewood and painted and dated *c.* 1500/10. The cross with Christ's arms detached hangs on the wall and below it

[32] The whole altarpiece is illustrated in France 1998, colour plate 14.

[33] See page 174 in Chapter Six.

Bernard kneels, his hands outstretched to the smaller slumping body of Christ. Below Christ's feet are the arms of Clairvaux. Another two part polychrome *Amplexus* carved in wood in high relief and dated 1520/1530 came from the austrian abbey of Rein (SC25); a wood sculpture, attributed to Gregor Erhart, was probably from the cistercian abbey of Kaisheim (SC10). A relief from the nuns' abbey of Himmelkron (SC59) had the abbess kneeling before the *Amplexus* image, and a later painted wood relief from the second quarter of the sixteenth century (SC44) belonged to the cistercian nuns of Niederwerth. The Niederwerth *Amplexus* is unusual in that the crucifix, with Christ's arms detached, is placed on an altar and Bernard is standing, not kneeling. Although Bernard reaches out he is some distance from the crucifix and has no contact with Christ. There are two monks in the background.

THE *AMPLEXUS* MOTIF IN WOODCUTS

The *Amplexus* motif appeared in woodcuts in two different ways: as devotional images on single leaves (*Einblattdrücke*), which became particularly popular in late medieval lay circles; and in illustrations in books, especially as frontispieces.

The earliest known *Amplexus* depiction in the new medium of printing (EN16) comes from around the same time as the first recorded image of the motif in a cistercian altarpiece—that from Maulbronn dated 1432. The woodcut forms the frontispiece of Bernard's *Sermons for the Liturgical Year* and also originated in southern Germany. It was printed by Jerg Haspel from Biberach (identified at the bottom of the picture as *jerg haspel ze Bibrach*), who died between 1430 and 1440. It is more faithful to the original story of the vision than most *Amplexus* depictions in that it is set in a church, in front of an altar on which two candlesticks and a book are placed, but the heads of Christ and Bernard are virtually touching in a mutual embrace. Bernard's early role as the passive receiver of Christ's affection has been transformed in the way we have seen in the earliest manuscript images of the theme.

Another early *Amplexus* woodcut (EN63), this one from *c.* 1450, illustrates a book of the prayers of Bernard which belonged to the dominican nuns in Nuremberg, where it was printed. On the left a larger Bernard kneels before Christ, whose right arm is already detached from the cross while the left arm is just being removed. On the left is an upright crozier, on the right a lance and a pole with a sponge on the end. On the ground is a mitre and below this a closed book. The ground and the crown of thorns are coloured green, the mitre light purple, the cowl greyish-brown, the hair brown, the crozier, cross and frame are yellow, the sky and the three nails blue, the nimbus gold, and the point of the lance silver. A single print (EN13) from *c.* 1460, also from Nuremberg, has an *Amplexus* picture of almost identical design. Bernard in a grey cowl kneels before the crucifix with both arms outstretched, ready to embrace Christ who is leaning down from a bright red cross. The cross is on a green ground, placing the scene out of doors. A crozier with a green sudarium is on the left in an upright position, a lance and a pole with a sponge on the right. As in the previous example, a mitre and a book are on the ground. Red is used to indicate Christ's blood-stained body. The background is pale yellow. A further *Amplexus* image (EN64) is almost identical to the two previous examples; the only minor difference in the latter is that Bernard is not nimbed.

A number of the woodcut images mentioned so far came from Nuremberg, and this was once more the case in 1503, when one of the sixty-three designs of saints attributed to Albrecht Dürer in the *Salus Animae,* printed by Hieronymus Hoeltzel, depicted Bernard in an *Amplexus* scene which, once again, more resembles a Deposition. ▶ *Fig. 4* (EN36). The lifeless figure of Christ with arms hanging limply down slumps against Bernard, who prevents Christ from falling by supporting his body. At Bernard's feet are the arms of Clairvaux surmounted by a mitre. Although the basic design may be Dürer's, members of his workshop, in keeping with tradition, are bound to have collaborated in such an extensive work. The composition of a later *Amplexus* woodcut by Hans Baldung Grien was almost identical. ▶ *Fig. 11* (EN85).

Woodcuts were the earliest form of 'mass market' reproduction and their introduction made it possible to disseminate images more widely and to a much broader audience than had previously been the case. The rapid development of printmaking techniques in the fifteenth century had a profound effect on popular imagery, most of it religious. The ease of production meant that designs, such as of the *Amplexus,* were used as models for subsequent woodcut images, allowed for modifications, and also influenced the composition of images in other media; by the same token, such images in turn inspired other woodcut representations of the

Embrace.[34] Very similar compositions may be seen in a miniature in a Prayer Book belonging to Abbot Konrad Moerlin and painted in Augsburg in 1505 by Ulrich Taler which has an *Amplexus* scene within the initial *C(aritate vulneratus castitate dealbatus)* from the Alleluia for the Mass of Saint Bernard. (MA411) The composition was repeated in a full-page miniature in another early sixteenth century german prayerbook, also from the workshop of Ulrich Taler (MA131) ▶ *Colour plate 8*. Here the lifeless-looking Christ is depicted with his arms detached from the Cross and slumped round the shoulders of Bernard who is supporting him. As in most *Amplexus* images Bernard is wearing a black cowl and at his feet are a mitre and the arms of Clairvaux, as in the Dürer woodcut. Almost identical to this illumination and the earlier Dürer woodcut is a design by Hans Baldung Grien (EN23) in a *Hortulus Animae* printed in Strasbourg in 1512 by Martin Flach. Here, as in the Dürer woodcut (▶ *Fig. 4*), Bernard appears in one of a large number of woodcuts representing saints. Whereas all the other saints are depicted with halos, Bernard is not nimbed in either of these woodcuts, whereas the figure of Christ is. By the early sixteenth century the *Amplexus* scene-type was sufficiently well established in southern Germany to allow people to identify Bernard easily, just as they could identify him by a *Lactatio* image, or recognize Francis by the stigmata, Mary Magdalene by a jar of ointment, or Sebastian by arrows.

Woodcuts are also thought to have been the models for a number of *Amplexus* pictures in late-medieval illuminated manuscripts. Among these are a single leaf full-page miniature from a Prayer Book dated 1510/1520 (MA231) and two *Amplexus* images by the celebrated Nuremberg illuminator Nikolaus Glockendon: a historiated initial in the Missal of Cardinal Albrecht von Brandenburg from 1522–1524 (MA385), and a miniature in a Missal made for a cistercian abbey *c.* 1525 (MA326). These miniatures, the woodcuts on which they were modelled, and the woodcuts which in turn were modelled on yet other miniatures, have a number of features in common: the relative position of the two figures with the full weight of Christ's body being supported by Bernard; the way Christ's head is partially obscured by Bernard's; the larger body of Bernard in relation to Christ's; and the inclusion at the foot of the Cross of the arms of Clairvaux surmounted by a mitre.

[34] The same development may be observed in the case of *Lactatio* images. See EN19 and MA158.

THE DISSEMINATION OF A GERMAN CISTERCIAN MOTIF

With one notable exception, all known *Amplexus* depictions in media other than those already referred to—that is, manuscripts, altarpiece paintings, sculpture, and woodcuts—belong to the last few decades of the Middle Ages. The exception is a grisaille stained glass window from the north cloister walk of the swiss abbey of Wettingen (GL81). Christ's arms, detached from the cross, on which the nails remain and which is slightly raised from the ground, are stretched out towards a kneeling Bernard, whose arms are raised to receive the embrace. Unusually, Bernard is accompanied by a group of monks, one of whom has his hood over his head. Smaller in scale than Christ or Bernard is the kneeling figure on the right representing Abbot Rudolf Wuelfinger of Wettingen (1433–1445) and carrying a crozier. At his feet are his coat of arms, consisting of a wolf as a pun on his name, and next to it, at the feet of Bernard, the arms of Clairvaux. Although Wuelfinger was granted *pontificalia* in 1439 by the council fathers at Basel, his arms here are not surmounted by a mitre, which suggests that the glass panel must be dated between his election in 1433 and 1439. The scroll above him reads *d[omin]ne.miserere.mei* ('Lord, have mercy on me'). The glass is grisaille in the cistercian tradition with the cross-nimbus of Christ, Bernard's nimbus, the cross, and the abbot's arms in yellow and the rest a brownish grey. The background consists of stylistic branches and leaves. Both this and the composition are very similar to the earliest *Amplexus* representation from Wonnental (MA059), and the composition was repeated in a rhenish woodcut some years later (EN14). There are two more *Amplexus* windows in the Wettingen cloister (GL82 and GL83), both from 1521, as well as two other sixteenth-century windows depicting Bernard, but not in *Amplexus* scenes (GL84 and GL85). From another swiss cistercian abbey, Saint Urban, comes a reliquary with eight silver engravings by Urs Graf the Elder dated 1519 featuring scenes from the life of Bernard and an *Amplexus* image (VA09).

A stained glass window from a non-cistercian church comes from the cathedral of Freiburg-im-Breisgau (GL80). It is one of four windows designed by Hans Baldung Grien and executed by Hans Wechtlin in 1520 for the Locherer Chapel. The others feature Saints Anthony, John, and Martin of Tours. As in the woodcut series of saints by Baldung Grien, the artist chose the *Amplexus* motif as a means of identifying

Bernard. Christ reaches down from a T-crucifix to a kneeling Bernard. The crucifix is dug into the ground and held in place by stones around its base. It is set in a green field in a mountainous landscape with buildings in the background. The arms of Clairvaux are at the foot of the cross, and two angels are in the top corners.

The other cathedral church with an *Amplexus* image (WA02) is that of Roskilde in Denmark. The artist of an early sixteenth-century wall painting there may have been inspired by the carving of the *Amplexus* image not far away in the altarpiece at the abbey of Esrum (SC51).

The only known *Amplexus* image south of the Alps is an early sixteenth-century fresco in the Chapter House of the cistercian abbey of Cestello in Florence attributed to the School of Pietro Perugino (WA22). Christ's arms hang down from the cross in the direction of the kneeling figure of Bernard in a white cowl, whose hands are raised up to meet Christ's. The scene is set in a rocky landscape, with the towers and spires of a town in the background; a skull and bones are at the foot of the cross. It is modelled on Perugino's Crucifixion, which is a fresco in the same chapter house (WA28).[35]

Although the story of the vision originated at Clairvaux in Herbert's *Liber Miraculorum*, it was disseminated most widely after being included among the bernardine stories related by the German, Conrad of Eberbach. There was a long delay between the late twelfth-century burgundian story and its first known visualisation in the early fourteenth-century Gradual belonging to the nuns at Wonnental in southern Germany. In itself this seems puzzling. It is of course more than likely that earlier depictions may have been lost, but the long delay may also be explained by the fact that the only representations of Bernard at the time the story originated were author 'portraits' and that narrative pictures had not yet made their appearance. At any rate, the great majority of *Amplexus* images belong to the last century of the Middle Ages. In fact, well over half of all known *Amplexus* images (thirty-nine out of a total of seventy-two) belong to the first few decades of the sixteenth century. They reflect the growth in a devotion to Bernard consistent with the circulation of a wealth of manuscripts attributed to him from the middle of the fourteenth century onwards, which then accelerated from the middle of the fifteenth century with the appearance of his works in printed form. The

[35] There is also a preparatory drawing for the fresco (DR18).

popularity of Bernard's writings in the late Middle Ages reveals the extent to which the spirituality they represent lived on among the Cistercians and beyond. The ideas contained in them were subjected to a continuing process of re-evaluation and re-interpretation. By being adapted to a changing world, and especially to the laity and their devotional practices, they managed to retain a vitality and remain relevant.[36] Many of the works attributed to Bernard, but not written by him, enormously influenced religious thinking, not least on account of the authority attaching to them by their perceived bernardine origin.

By the time of the earliest known *Amplexus* images, twelfth-century cistercian spirituality had been left behind and an activity-centered and more intimate and physical interpretation of the spiritual vision had developed. As a consequence, over time, the initiative in the Embrace was transferred to Bernard and the encounter assumed the character of Deposition scenes.

Amplexus images were concentrated in German-speaking areas. The best-known of these images in manuscripts were miniatures in service books belonging to cistercian abbeys in German-speaking lands, either those of nuns like Wonnental and Lichtental (MA059, MA222) or of monks like Rein (MA135), Herrenalb (MA052), and Langheim (MA219 and MA220). The notable exceptions, however, are among the earliest: the two manuscripts in which the motif was chosen to represent Bernard in vernacular versions of the *Legenda Aurea* (MA053 and MA152). Through these and later *Legenda Aurea* images, knowledge of the theme extended out to non-cistercian and non-monastic circles, to clergy, for whom the theme provided material for preaching, and through which it passed to an even wider lay audience.

The great majority of *Amplexus* depictions in altarpieces, as in manuscripts, belonged to cistercian monasteries: Maulbronn (PA060), Marienfeld (?) (PA008), Bebenhausen (PA047), Neuberg (PA124, PA101), Heisterbach (?) (PA020), and Lilienfeld (PA079). Two that were not in cistercian churches were both located in Germany: in the south, in the augustinian church in Nuremberg (PA009), and in the Lower Rhine in the church of the benedictine nuns in Cologne (PA017). The carved

[36] Three strands, emphasized in varying degrees by different scholars, have been identified in McGuire 1991, 227–249: the 'decadence' of Huizinga, the 'forerunners' of Obermann, and the 'recycling' of Constable.

Amplexus image in the danish Esrum retable (SC51) was probably made in a north german workshop, and the five other known *Amplexus* sculptures were all from german cistercian houses: Heilsbronn (SC06), Oberschönenfeld (SC32), Rein (SC25), Himmelkron (SC59), and Niederwerth (SC44).

No examples of the motif have been found in the British Isles or the Iberian Peninsula, and, except for the Paris manuscript of the *Golden Legend* from *c.* 1420 (MA152) and the Prayerbook from Delft (MA257), none are known from outside German-speaking lands until the sixteenth century. Even then, the rare exceptions to the rule are found only in the polish altarpiece (PA053), the danish wall painting in Roskilde Cathedral (WA02), the wall painting in the dominican church in Zwolle (WA31), and the fresco in the cistercian abbey in Florence (WA22).

In view of the uniqueness of the *Amplexus* theme in being the only one of the four bernardine iconographical *topoi* to have its origin in Bernard's own words, it is remarkable both how little the image was disseminated outside cistercian walls and how confined it seems to have been, almost exclusively, to one part of Europe in spite of the fact that the literary source, the *Exordium Magnum*, was widely known throughout the cistercian world. Similar regional disparities were later to apply to the other bernardine scene-attributes, as we shall see.

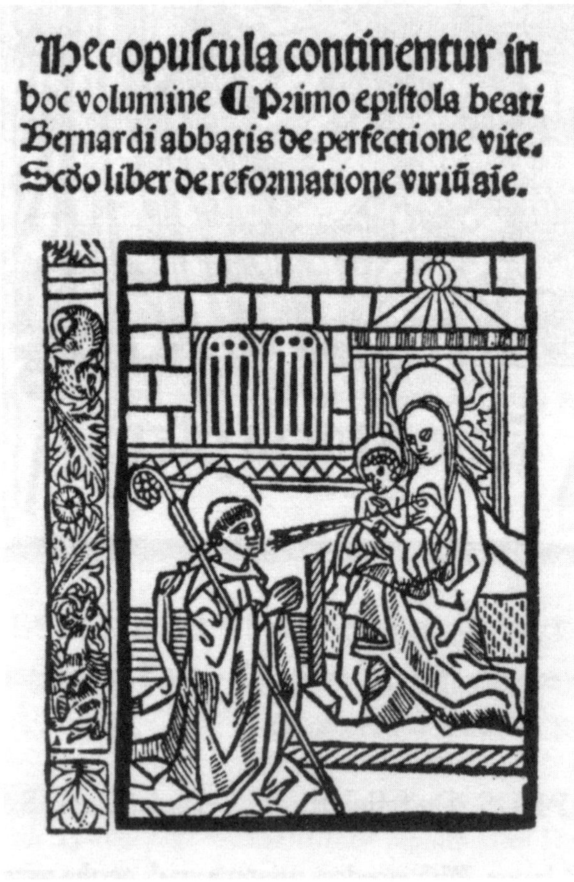

Figure 14: An early sixteenth-century woodcut on the title page of two pseudo-Bernard works (EN43).

EIGHT

MARY OFFERING BERNARD HER MILK

THE LITERARY SOURCES FOR THE THEME

BY FAR THE MOST POPULAR of all medieval images of Bernard, especially in the last century of the Middle Ages, was the so-called *Lactatio* or *Lactation*, Mary offering Bernard milk from her breast.[1] Very nearly twice as many *Lactation* as *Amplexus* images have been recorded (one hundred nineteen as compared with seventy-two), and yet it does not appear in any of the early *Vitae*, in the extensive cistercian *exemplum* literature, in the *Legenda Aurea*, or any of the other thirteenth century legendaries; nor, unlike the *Amplexus*, is it found in the *Exordium Magnum*.

The popularity of this medieval motif may seem surprising to us today: its mere mention usually evinces a reaction of embarrassed sniggering tinged with evident disgust. Medieval people, including monks, had no hang-ups about any of the bodily functions. The description one of Bernard's brothers gave of their sister in her extravagant finery as

[1] The first comprehensive study of the *Lactation* of Bernard is Dewez & Iterson 1956, 165–189. Others include Dupeux 1991 and Dupeux 1993.

'enveloped excrement' (*stercus involutum*),[2] may, for example, seem a little excessive to us, but was apparently quite acceptable at the time. The author of the *Life* of Abundus of Huy, a cistercian monk of Villers born *c.* 1189, refers to Mary kissing him and adds that anyone scandalized by this should remember the story of the cleric who had been healed by sucking the breast of Mary.[3] These examples tell us that such stories did not shock even monks who valued the image of the *Lactation,* of which twenty-five examples of cistercian origin have been recorded.[4] Suckling, the most basic and intimate of all physical acts, was widely represented in art; images of *Maria lactans*—the Virgin nursing her Child—can be traced back to the catacombs in Rome and remained popular throughout the Middle Ages.[5] The twin images of milk and honey in the Old Testament represent the perfect food which requires no preparation; pristine and pure in that they are untouched by man, they are rich in symbolising the transmission of life and wisdom. The image of a grown man receiving milk at a woman's breast may be shocking to moderns, but in its sheer physicality the symbolism was used to transmit a great spiritual truth, as we shall see. It was thought that by virtue of the milk he obtained from Mary's breast Bernard was enabled to become a great preacher and towards the end of the Middle Ages to earn the title of *Doctor mellifluus.*

Stories of the Virgin offering her milk to others than her Son as a reward for their faithfulness go back to the twelfth century. Whereas most visions of receiving milk at Mary's breast refer to men, it has been noted, women in contrast received visions of taking the Christ Child to their breasts.[6] William of Malmesbury in the *Gesta Regum Anglorum* refers to the noted theologian Fulbert of Chartres (d. 1028) whom 'Mary, the Mother of Our Lord, was seen to cure, when sick, by the milk of

[2] VP 1:6:30; PL 185:244.

[3] Quoted in McGuire 1995, 191. See below, note 12.

[4] This devotion was not to last. By the seventeenth century the Benedictine Jean Mabillon expressed his disdain for the legend in these words: 'There is no mention anywhere of this miraculous milk squeezed out by the Blessed Virgin in any of the books of Saint Bernard's miracles, and yet we see this miracle hawked around by painters and by other imprudent devotees of that holy Doctor at the expense of authentic ones' (*In omnibus S. Bernardi miraculorum libris nulla uspiam mentio de miraculoso illo lacte, a beatissima Virgine in Bernardum expresso: quod tamen miraculum prae aliis certissimis a pictoribus et ab incautis sancti Doctoris devotis nunc venditari cernimus*) PL 185:466, note 141.

[5] For this and the symbolism of milk, see the chapter 'The Milk of Paradise' in Warner 1985, 192–205. For examples, see Bynum 1987, figs. 14, 21–24.

[6] Bynum 1987, 270.

our Lord'.[7] The story was repeated by Alberic of Trois-Fontaines in his *Chronicle*, where he says that Fulbert was 'restored by the most holy milk'.[8] The healing power of Mary's milk was a very widespread theme in medieval collections of marian miracle stories. The twelfth-century Benedictine Gautier de Coincy records how Our Lady healed a gravely ill cleric by giving him her breast. The oldest known pictorial representation of this is a miniature in an early fourteenth-century manuscript from Soissons.[9] The cleric is lying on a bed behind which the Virgin stands, surrounded by angels. She places her breast in the cleric's mouth.[10] The scene is also illustrated in Alfonso X's (1252–1284) lavishly decorated marian miracle collection, *Cantigas de Santa Maria*.[11]

The *Lactation* theme seems to have filtered into the bernardine orbit through a pseudo-Caesarian exemplum collection which contains the story of an 'unlettered abbot who imbibed from the breast of the Blessed Virgin and was endowed with knowledge'.[12] The 'unlettered abbot' was Henry of Clairvaux (1176–1179), one of Bernard's successors who was ordered by the pope to preach a crusade, a task which 'would exceed the powers of his mind'. He therefore approached Mary who

> gave him sweetly her most sacred breast that he might suck it . . . and by means of that most holy liquid which he imbibed he was made so skilful at the knowledge of letters that he received at Rome the dignity of a cardinal.[13]

It was only a short step to attaching this story to Bernard himself. In the light of the role he played in the growing cult of Mary, one might say it was almost inevitable that the image of the *Lactation* should be incorporated into his iconography. Indeed, *Lactation* stories may be said to have been inspired both by information transmitted about him in the *Vita Prima*

[7] William of Malmesbury 1887–1889, 341, translated Giles 1968, 314.

[8] Alberic of Trois-Fontaines: *Florebat Fulbertus . . . qui etiam ab eadem Dei Genetricis in infirmitate sua visitatus, esse dicitur, et de ejus lacte sanctissimo recreatus*, quoted in Gripkey 1938, 19. For pre-Bernardine *Lactation* stories see also McGuire 1991, 191–196 and Berlioz 1988, 279–282.

[9] Quoted in Dewez & van Iterson 1956, 172.

[10] Illustrated in Dupeux 1993, ill. 3.

[11] Duran 1950, 39.

[12] Caesarius of Heisterbach 1937, 164: *De indocto abbate qui de uberibus beate Marie suxit et preditus est sciencia*. See also Berlioz 1988, 279–280 and McGuire 1991, 198–199.

[13] Caesarius of Heisterbach 1937, 164.

and later in the *Golden Legend,* and by his own writings. The connection between suckling and preaching is explicitly made by Geoffrey of Auxerre,[14] and, in his account of Bernard's infancy, William of Saint Thierry attached a great deal of importance to his mother's refusal to hand over her children to a wetnurse, as was customary in higher circles, and her insistence on suckling them herself.[15] William's story was repeated in the *Legenda Aurea,* for 'it was as if she hoped with her mother's milk to instil into her children something of her own goodness'.[16]

The importance of his mother's action was not lost on Bernard. In writing the *Life* of his friend Malachy, Bernard stressed the Irishman's debt to his mother when he says that Malachy 'drank the waters of saving wisdom as if milk from his mother's breast and day by day he gained in knowledge. Should I say more knowledgeable or rather holier?'.[17] Here Bernard makes it clear that the knowledge gained through mother's milk is 'science divine', sacred knowledge, and that its purpose is the service of the Church. In his teaching role as an abbot, Bernard used the image of milk in writing to his errant nephew Robert: 'I nourished you with milk when, while yet a child, it was all you could take'.[18] Yet another link with Mary *lactans* is provided by William of Saint Thierry's account of Bernard's childhood vision of the Nativity; as a result of it he is said to have gained in the understanding which later enabled him to write in praise of the Mother and Child, which he first did in his sermons on the Gospel passage: *The Angel Gabriel was sent.*[19] Bernard's devotion to Mary here links with his teaching on the Incarnation, the reality of the humanity of Christ—the Word made Flesh—and on Mary as the Mother of all believers, whom, in the Fourth Sermon on the Assumption, he describes as 'the fountain to which our thirsty souls hurry'.[20]

[14] See McGuire 1991, 200.

[15] VP 1:1:1 (PL 185:227): *Propter quod etiam alienis uberibus nutriendos committere illustris femina refugiebat quasi cum lacte materno materni quodammodo boni infundens eis naturam.*

[16] LA 209.

[17] *Vita Sancti Malachiae* 1:1; SBOp 3:310: *Bibebat autem pro lacte de pectore materno aquas sapientiae salutaris, et fiebat in dies seipso prudentior. Prudentior, dicam, an sanctior?*

[18] SBOp 7:8: *Nutrivi deinde lacte.* Cf. 1 Cor 3:2.

[19] VP 1:2:4; PL 185:229. Bernard's *De laudibus virginis matris,* Sermo 1:1; SBOp 4:13-58.

[20] SBOp 5:250: *ad hunc igitur fontem sitibunda properet anima nostra.*

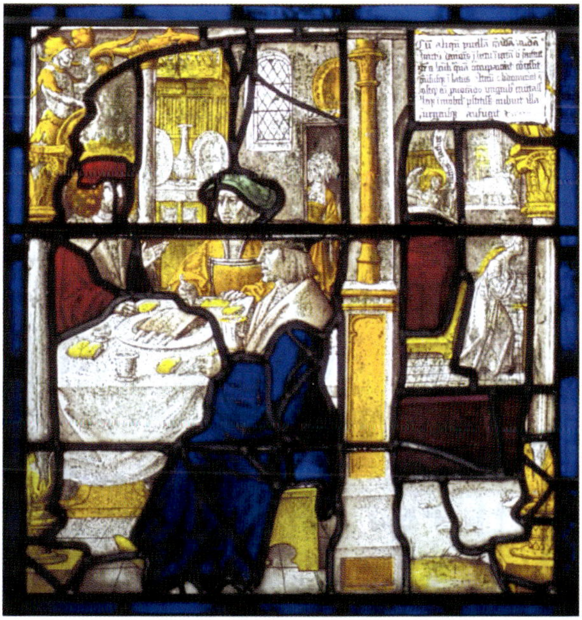

Plate 1: A glass panel from the Bernard cycle formerly in the cloister of the nuns' abbey of Saint Apern, Cologne (GL78). Photo by Tessa France. *Chapter One.*

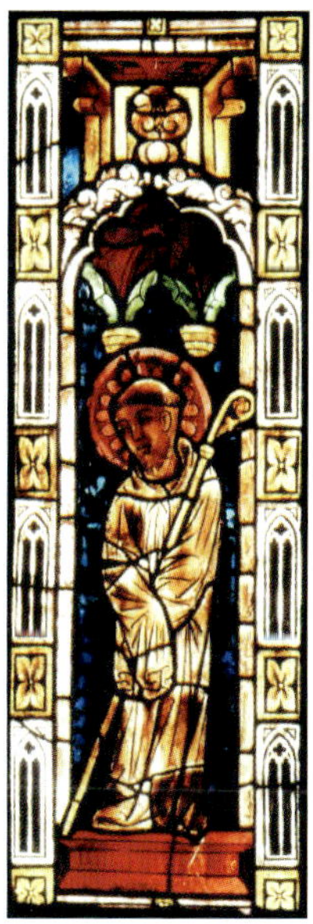

Plate 2: Stained glass window in the pilgrimage church at Strassengel, Austria (GL77). Used by permission of Corpus Vitrearum Deutschland. *Chapter Two.*

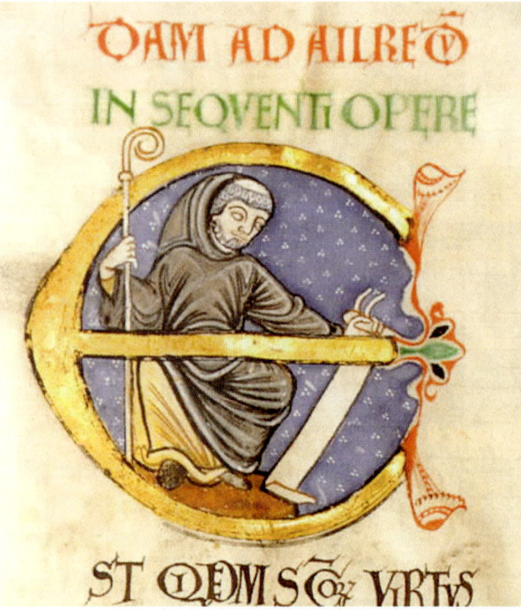

Plate 3: Bernard orders Aelred of Rievaulx to write *The Mirror of Charity.* A twelfth-century manuscript from the scriptorium of Anchin (MA004). Used by permission of the Bibliothèque municipale Douai. *Chapter Three.*

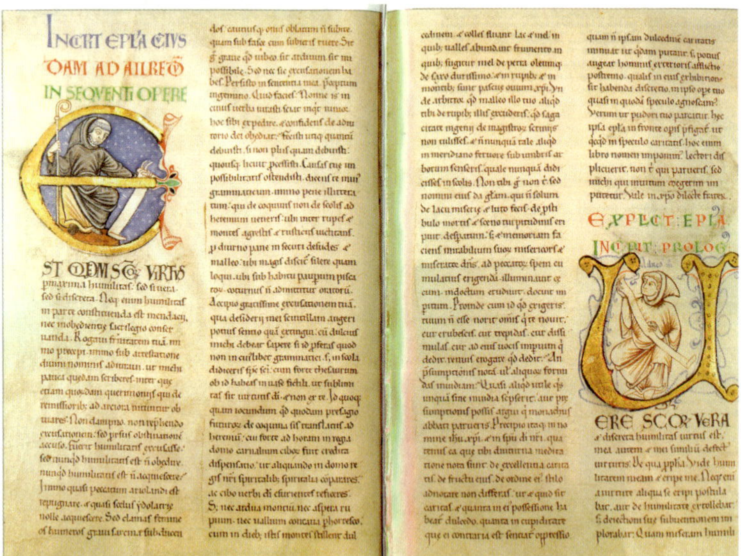

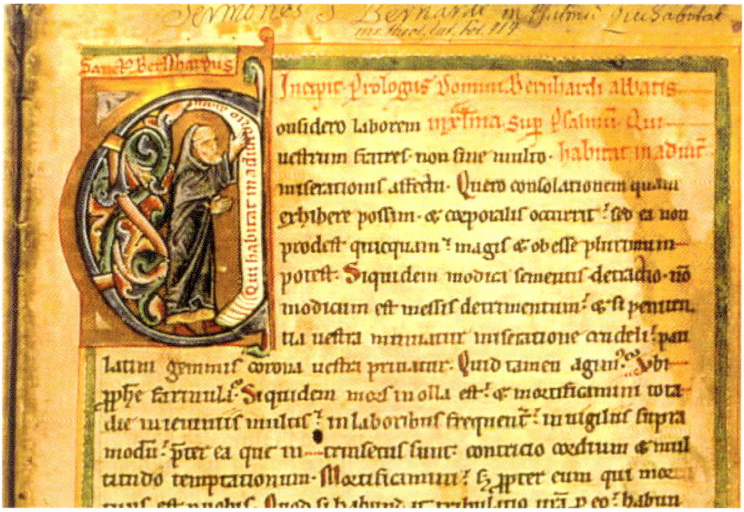

Plate 4: The opening of Bernard's sermon *Qui habitat,* from a late thirteenth-century manuscript from the polish abbey of Bledzow (MA319). Used by permission of the Staatsbibliothek zu Berlin—Preussischer Kulturbesitz. *Chapter Four.*

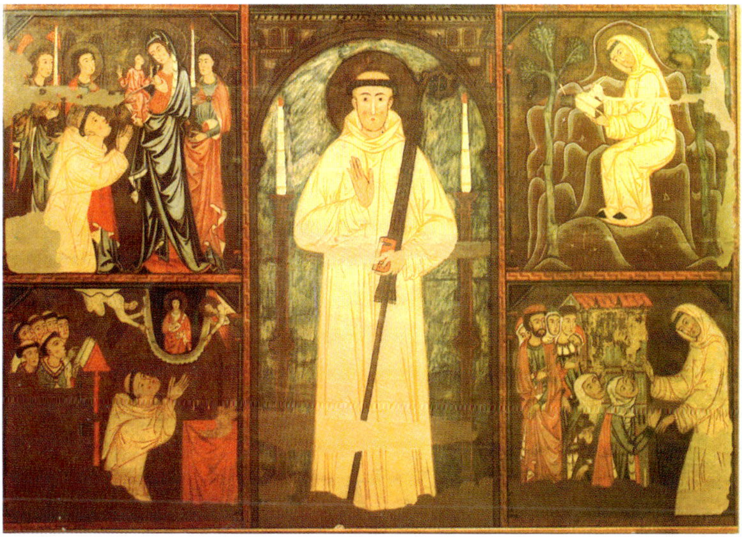

Plate 5: Retable from the church of the Knights Templar at Palma, Majorca, 1290 (PA11-15). Reproduced by permission of the Museu de Mallorca. *Chapter Five.*

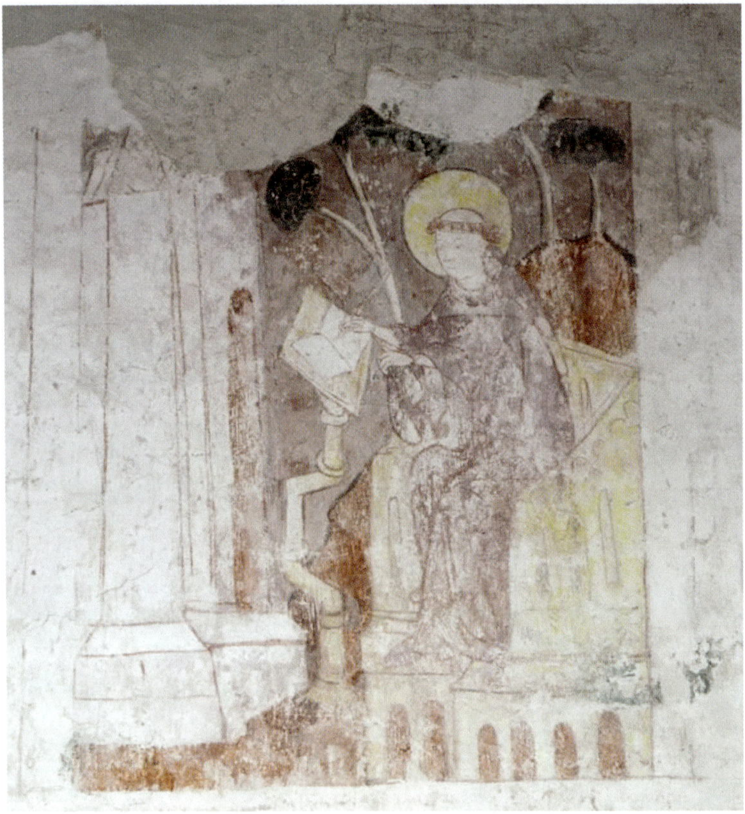

Plate 6: An author portrait of Bernard. One of twelve wall paintings illustrating the life of Bernard at Owen, Württemberg (WA45). Used by permission of the Landesamt für Denkmalpflege Baden-Württemberg. *Chapter Five.*

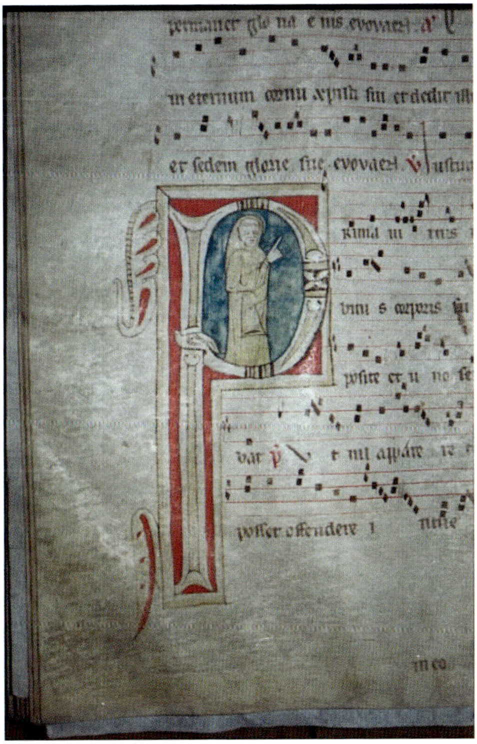

Left—Plate 7: Bernard within the initial *P* of *Prima virtus viri sancti* in an antiphonary from the cistercian nuns' abbey of Arouca, Portugal (MA414). Reproduced by permission of the Museu de Arte Sacra de Arouca. *Chapter Six.*

Below—Plate 8. *Amplexus* image in an early sixteenth-century german prayerbook (MA131). Photo by Tessa France. *Chapter Seven.*

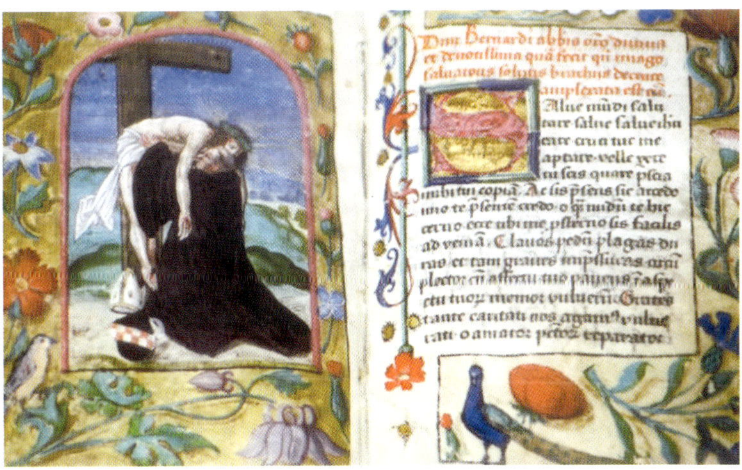

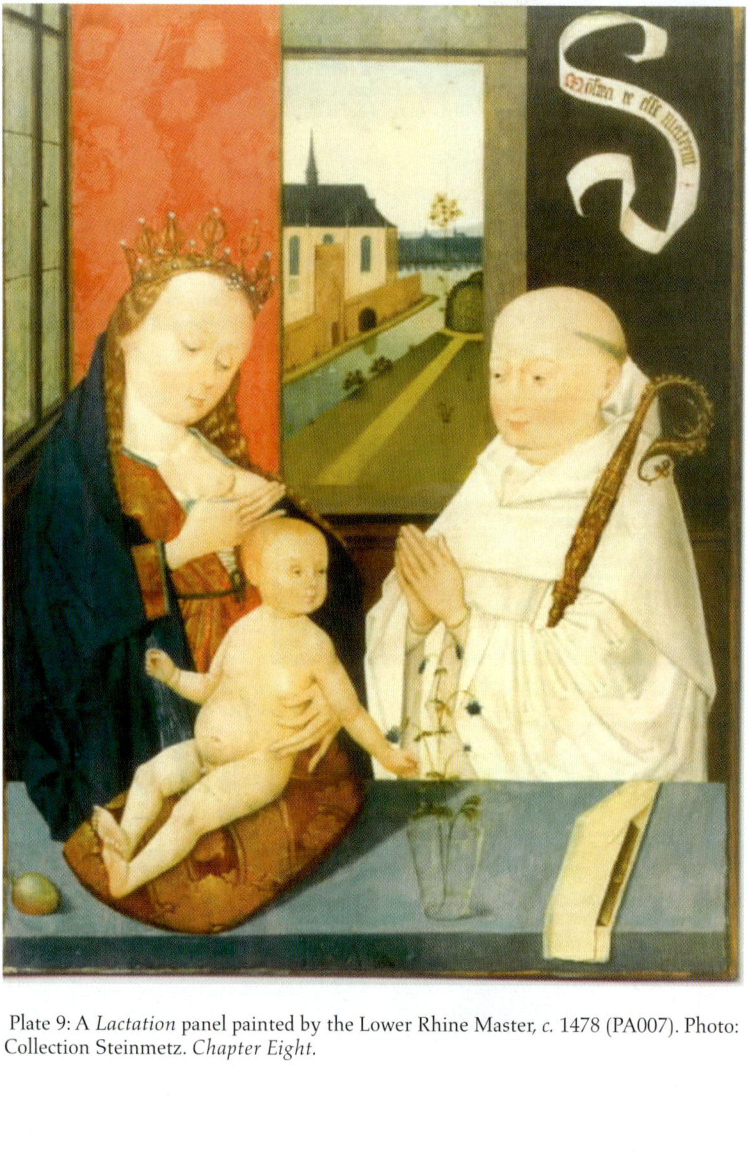

Plate 9: A *Lactation* panel painted by the Lower Rhine Master, *c.* 1478 (PA007). Photo: Collection Steinmetz. *Chapter Eight.*

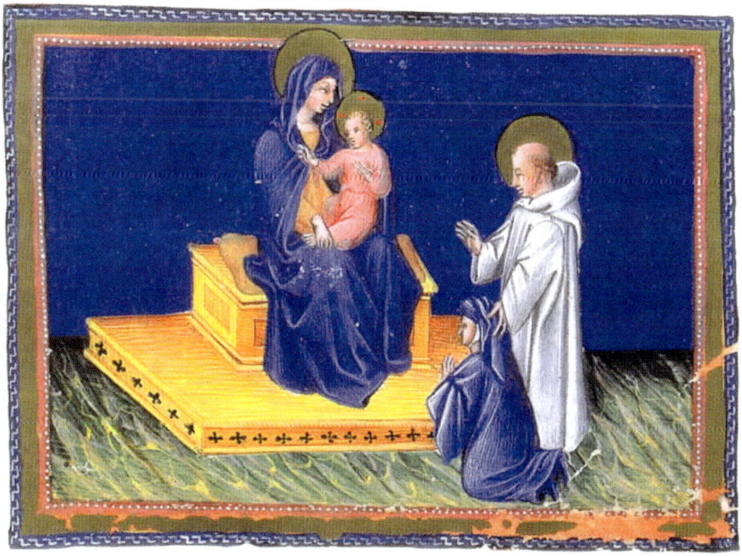

Plate 10: A miniature by Giovanni di Paolo illustrating Dante's *Commedia Divina, Paradiso,* Canto 33, dated to the mid-1440s (MA065). Reproduced by permission of the British Library. *Chapter Nine.*

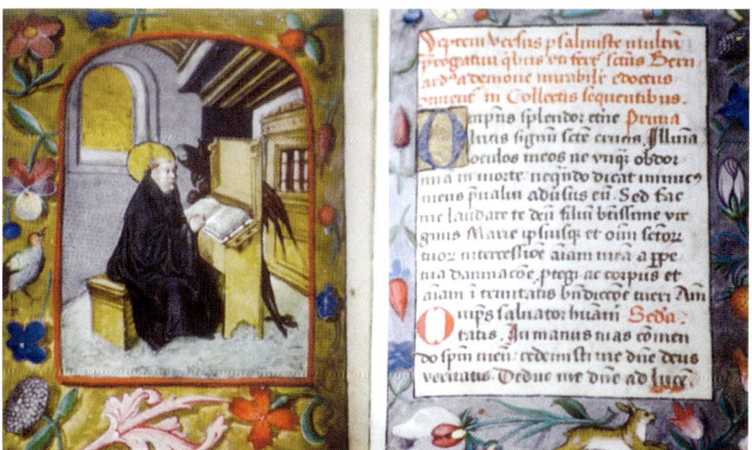

Plate 11: Bernard and the devil. An illustration of the *Seven Verses of Bernard* in an early sixteenth-century german prayerbook (MA137). Photo: Tessa France. *Chapter Eleven.*

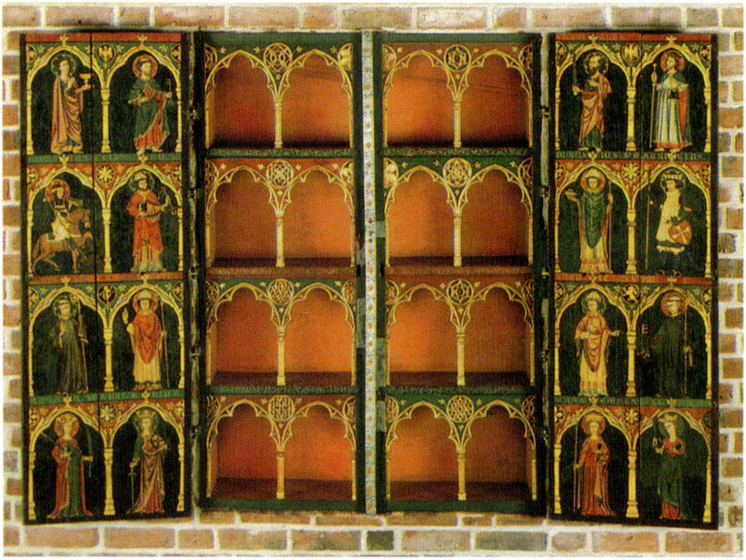

Plate 12: Reliquary cupboard from the former cistercian abbey of Løgum, Denmark. Saint Bernard appears among sixteen images of saints at the far left, third from the top (PA036). *Chapter Twelve.*

Although the *Lactatio* was generally the most popular bernardine iconographic theme, it was by no means so always or everywhere. Of the total of one hundred nineteen medieval images, thirty-eight come from the last quarter of the fifteenth century and a further sixty-four from the first three decades of the sixteenth century; in sum one hundred-two are post-1475 and only seventeen pre-date 1475—and of these only one belongs to the thirteenth century and only five to the fourteenth. The geographical distribution is as uneven as the chronological: approximately two-thirds (seventy out of one hundred nineteen) are found in the area of the Low Countries, Flanders, the Upper Rhine within the modern borders of Belgium and the Netherlands, and the regions of French Flanders and the German Rhineland. A further fifteen are from the iberian peninsula. The theme is scarcely represented in the iconography of southern France, England, central Europe, or Italy. What does a closer look at the different strands reveal about this glaring discrepancy?

THE CATALAN ICONOGRAPHIC TRADITION

Even though researchers may discern a retrospective source for the *Lactatio* in works by and about Bernard, the earliest known versions of the *Lactatio* are to be found, not in literary, but in pictorial form. The two earliest altarpieces dedicated to Bernard both consist of large central images surrounded by narrative scenes drawn from the legends of the saint, and each includes a *Lactation* scene. Both were painted within the orbit of the wealthy catalan abbey of Poblet, founded in 1150–1151, from Fontfroide in the clairvaux filiation.[21] The earlier is dated 1290, and was originally in the church of the Templars in Palma, Majorca, a close neighbour of the abbey of La Real, a daughter-house of Poblet founded in 1236.[22] The other, from 1348, is in the church of Saint Mary in Montblanch, only a short distance from Poblet.

The majorcan retable was painted by an artist known as the Palma Master and dated 1290. ▶ *Colour plate 5.* It features the large standing

[21] Dewez & Iterson 1956, 171, pointed to the Poblet connection and stressed that the *Lactatio* appeared first and foremost as an iconographical theme.

[22] As we noted above, page 127, the Templars were closely related to the Cistercians not only because Bernard addressed the famous treatise *In Praise of the New Knighthood* (*De laude novae militiae*) to them (SBOp 3:213-239).

figure of Bernard in a frontal position with crozier and red book in his left hand and his right hand raised in blessing. He is flanked by four scenes from his life: two that are referred to in the *Vita Prima*—the vision of Christ appearing to Bernard to assure him that his friend Malachy is a saint, and the exorcism of a woman[23]—; a traditional author image depicting Bernard writing; and, top left, the first appearance of the *Lactation* (PA012).[24] The standing Virgin holds a cross-nimbed Child on her right arm. She presses her bared breast with her left hand and a squirt of milk falls in a curved line into the mouth of the kneeling Bernard, whose head is raised and his hands clasped in prayer. Two nimbed angels hold the same type of candles as are featured in the central picture, and a third angel stands by. Whereas the fact that the Virgin and Bernard are depicted in the same scale gives the scene an air of reality, the presence of angels suggests the supernatural nature of the event.

The altarpiece in Montblanch (▶ *Fig. 9*) is dedicated to Saint Bernard and Saint Barnabas and is in polychrome stone carved by the english sculptor Reinard Fonnell, who is also responsible for the carvings in the cloister of the other neighbouring catalan abbey of Santes Creus. The central standing figures of the two saints are flanked by four scenes from the life of each. Bernard is depicted with the traditional attributes, a crozier in his right hand and a book in his left. As in the Palma retable, the other scenes, with the exception of the *Lactation*, are drawn from the *Vita Prima:* the dream of Bernard's mother that she would give birth to a dog; the vision of Christ assuring Bernard that Malachy is a saint; and Bernard on his deathbed.[25] Each scene is contained within a trifoliate arch. The *Lactation* image, at the bottom left, has the Virgin and Child raised up on a pedestal (SC41). The Virgin's hand is placed on her breast and Bernard kneels before them holding an open book. He is accompanied by two of his monks. The scene is blessed by the hand of God, appearing from above against a gold circular background. Above, two angels are swinging thuribles. Sadly, the heads of all the figures are missing. There are notable similarities between the two representations: the rare image of the vision of Christ confirming the sainthood of Malachy is found in both, and in

[23] VP 4:4:21; PL 185:303 and VP 2:6:34-35.

[24] Duran 1950, 43–44.

[25] VP 1:1:2 (PL 185:227-8); VP 4:4:21 (PL 185:333); VP 5:2:13 (PL 185:359). See SC39-43.

each case the figures of the Virgin and Child and Bernard are portrayed to the same scale. Both are equally represented in the iconographical tradition of the *Lactation*. And yet, the important difference whereby the Palma Virgin is a real person whereas the Montblanch figure is clearly a statue come alive, has been seen as evidence that the two versions do not owe their origin to a common archetype.[26]

Oddly enough, the first two known *Lactation* images are to be found in the earliest recorded Bernard altarpieces. They are early examples of the type of retable that emerged in Italy in the thirteenth century. The *antependium* which covered the front of the altar below the table and which derived from the byzantine *iconostasis* was their predecessor. They were originally feast-day images, when the legend recording the saint's miracles and virtues would be read out.[27] The Franciscans were at the forefront in introducing the retable and developed the iconography of Saint Francis soon after his canonization in 1228. A number of altarpieces were made featuring the cult image of Saint Francis as a new type of ascetic saint with emaciated face in a frontal position and flanked by between four and twenty scenes of him as the miracle worker.[28] The Palma retable is an early example of this 'franciscan' type and the first dedicated to Bernard. The scenes could be understood only by those who knew the stories that lay behind them and, perforce depended on either an oral or literary tradition. For this reason we must look beyond the images themselves for the inspiration behind these representations of the *Lactation*. Although texts are, as we saw above, perhaps the likely source, in a world which was predominantly a pre-literary world, the possibility of an oral origin cannot be excluded. Any notion that these visual representations appeared, as it were, *in vacuo* can be ruled out.

The *Lactation* motif later appeared on a number of other spanish altarpieces. The earliest of these is a panel of the Virgin and Child painted

[26] Depeux 1993, 156: *L'utilisation de schémas aussi différents montre l'absence d'une conception unique du phénomène et d'un archétype commun.* The author follows Duran in interpreting the Palma vision of Christ as that of Malachy himself, and the Montblanch vision as that of Bernard's vision of the Nativity whereas I believe that this is the same vision of Christ announcing Malachy's sainthood as at Palma. She goes on to contrast the scale of these two visions of the small figures in the sky with the greater reality of the *Lactation* image.

[27] For this, see Belting 1994, 377–382.

[28] For illustrations of some of the early Saint Francis retables, see van Marle 1923–1938, 1: figs. 178–182.

towards the end of the fourteenth century, which probably formed the centre of a larger retable (PA126). The Virgin sits on a high gothic chair with pinnacles, flanked by the kneeling figures of Bernard on the left and Benedict on the right, dressed in white and black cowls respectively. They each hold an open book with text showing, and they both carry croziers. The Virgin is turned in the direction of Bernard, her breast bare, and, with the assistance of the Child—an unusual detail—she sends a jet of milk into the mouth of Bernard, who looks up at her in awe. The altarpiece probably came from the abbey of Bonifaza, a daughter-house of Poblet. Another, slightly later, *Lactation* scene (PA128) formed part of a larger retable painted by Anton Peris *c.* 1415 for the convent of Saint Dominic, Valencia. A youthful Bernard, accompanied by one of his monks, who stands in a doorway behind him, kneels before the standing Virgin and Child, who are surrounded by a number of angels. The Virgin bares her breast which she squeezes with her right hand. As in the Palma retable, the figures are all in the same scale, which gives the event an air of reality, and the scene is set in a church with Bernard kneeling beside an altar on which an open book rests.

Unlike these two earliest examples, all later spanish *Lactation* portrayals did not form part of altarpieces dedicated to Bernard, but were merely one of the secondary scenes in marian retables. An altarpiece from the Hermitage of Our Lady of Hope at Albocacer (PA127), painted by Taller de Pedro Nicolau and also from the early fifteenth century, has the central figure of the Virgin enthroned with a smaller crucifixion scene above, and the lower half of the left-hand side has Bernard kneeling at a desk with an open book, looking up at the vision of the tiny figures of Mary and the Child in the sky surrounded by angels. Mary bares her breast in a typical *Lactation* pose, although the scene is very different from earlier images in that it clearly represents a vision. Another marian retable (PA034), known as Our Lady of the Milk, comes from the church of Sant Esteve de Canapost and is dated the second half of the fifteenth century. In the centre is the main scene of the Virgin lactating; on the left Saint Nicholas of Bari is depicted in two scenes; and on the right Bernard in two scenes. At the bottom is the main image of Bernard in a white cowl sitting and holding a red book on his lap, a crozier leaning on his left shoulder; above him, a smaller *Lactation* scene is taking place in a church, where he kneels before a cloth-covered altar on which a smaller Virgin and Child are seated. The Virgin bares her breast and three jets of milk are sent in the direction of Bernard. The scene is witnessed by two monks in the background, one of them with his hood over his head. Above the scene are two music-playing angels. Like the Montblanch image, the scene takes place in a church and also resembles a statue coming alive, but here the visionary nature of the scene is further accentuated by the difference in scale.

In the second half of the fifteenth century the theme appeared further east, in Aragon. The retable of San Ildefonso in Osma cathedral, painted by the Master of Osma in *c.* 1460, has a *Lactation* scene (PA129). Again, Bernard kneels before the much smaller figure of the Virgin, who, unusually, is without the Child and standing on an altar on which a candle is burning. She presses her right breast with her right hand and a jet of milk flows in a straight line to Bernard's mouth. The visionary aspect of the scene is heightened by the mandorla surrounding the Virgin. A fragment of an altarpiece painted by Martin Bernat *c.* 1493 in Tarazona cathedral has Bernard wearing a richly-embroidered cope and seated by a table or an altar upon which a tiny Virgin and Child within a mandorla are standing on a cloud (PA130). The Virgin bares her breast which she squeezes with her right hand. Again, the great difference in scale enhances the supernatural feel of the apparition. A painting from around the same period (PA083) by the Master of Castellnovo has Bernard standing on a decorated tile floor, wearing a white cowl with white tunic and black scapular showing underneath, his hands clasped in prayer and his crozier leaning on his right shoulder. He is looking up at a small painting on the wall representing the Virgin and Child. From the Virgin's bare breast a tiny jet of milk goes towards Bernard. Here it is not a statue but a painting that has come alive. There is a companion picture of the same size of Saint Benedict, also with a crozier but in a black cowl, but without the *Lactation* motif.

Even if the catalan abbey of Poblet was responsible for the pictorial introduction of the *Lactation*, it was not the first cistercian abbey to own a *Lactation* image. For this we must look to the other side of the iberian peninsula, to the great portuguese abbey of Alcobaça, founded in 1153. Like Poblet it was also in the clairvaux filiation, but as a daughter-house of Clairvaux itself, whereas Poblet was founded from Fontfroide, a grand-daughter of Clairvaux. Any connection between the two iberian abbeys seems therefore unlikely. This isolated image (MA084), enigmatically in the furthest south-western outpost of cistercian Europe, is not only the first known *Lactation* of cistercian ownership but also the first we know of in a manuscript. It appears in a cistercian missal from the beginning of the fourteenth century, contained within the initial *I(n medio ecclesie)* at the opening of the Introit of the Mass of the feast of Bernard. Unusually, the crowned and nimbed Virgin is standing. With her right hand she holds the cross-nimbed Child, whose right hand is raised in blessing. With her left hand she squeezes her breast and a jet of milk, only just visible, goes in the direction of the kneeling figure of Bernard. A *Lactatio Bernardi* scene was also depicted at Alcobaça on windows ordered in 1484 for the chapter house. Although they no longer exist, we know from an eighteenth-century description that they consisted of the central figure of Christ with Saint Benedict on the right and a *Lactatio Bernardi* on the left.[29]

How the theme reached Alcobaça is not known. We can only speculate that it may have been transmitted—as happened in the dispersal of *exemplum* stories as well as agricultural techniques and plant species—through exchanges between abbots visiting the General Chapter at Cîteaux or information gained by father-abbots during visitations to their daughter houses. This may also explain the origin of the only other known fourteenth-century example of a *Lactation* image. It is a full-page miniature (MA069) inserted into an eleventh-century manuscript of a Gospel Book from the Lower Rhineland. A crowned and nimbed Virgin with long golden hair sits on a raised throne with a high decorated back. She holds the naked Child on her lap. She looks down and holds her breast with her right hand in the direction of the kneeling figure of Bernard, who is nimbed, is in a white cowl, carries a crozier with sudarium attached under his left arm, and clasps his hands in prayer.[30] The scroll emanating from his mouth reads *Monstra te esse matrem,* the earliest known use of what was to become the standard inscription of *Lactation* scenes. The scene is a vaulted chamber with a green central column, rather like a chapter house. As with the Alcobaça image there is no ready explanation for this early isolated example of the theme, and, again, its transmission through the pan-european cistercian network must be a serious possibility.

[29] Barros 1983, 68.

[30] Bernard is described in the Bodleian Summary Catalogue (No 29127) as 'a saint kneeling'. Another possibility which cannot be ruled out is that the dating is erroneous and that the inserted folio is later than stated.

As we have seen, the emergence of the *Lactatio Bernardi* in the religious art of Catalonia was followed by a series of iconographical treatments of the theme in other parts of northern Spain. This regional dispersal of the theme was preceded further north in Europe by three known literary versions of the scene-attribute, none of which gave rise to a later pictorial tradition. All three belong to the first half of the fourteenth century, that is, a few decades after the Palma retable.

THREE FOURTEENTH-CENTURY LITERARY VERSIONS

The first known literary allusion to the miracle is found in a french manuscript of christian instruction, an *exemplum* collection entitled *Ci nous dit*.[31] Written in the vernacular between 1313 and 1330, it devotes eight chapters to Bernard. They are illustrated by two long panels, each of which consists of two scenes, including that of the *Lactation*.[32] The story it tells about Bernard is very similar to that of Henry of Clairvaux who, we remember, gained the ability to preach through Mary's milk. Bernard had been ordered by his abbot to preach before the bishop of Chalon but, feeling unworthy, he turned to Mary in prayer. In his sleep he had a vision that

> Our Lady placed her holy breast in his mouth and thereby taught him divine knowledge. From now on he became one of the most able preachers of his time and he preached before the bishop.[33]

The source of the story is not known, nor is the identity of the bishop, but, as with Henry of Clairvaux, Bernard turned to Mary for help, Mary placed her breast in his mouth, and as a result Bernard gained the ability to preach. The first illustration features Bernard's entry into Cîteaux and the *Lactation* scene (MA042). On the left a monk representing the abbot of Cîteaux, Stephen Harding, receives Bernard who is identified by his beard and green halo. The abbot holds Bernard's hands. Behind Bernard is another monk who represents the thirty-five referred to in the text as

[31] Chantilly, Musée de Condé, MS 26–27. For this, see Berlioz 1988, 270–283.
[32] Folios 178r and 178v.
[33] Quoted in Berlioz 1988, 273.

having entered at the same time. His hands are raised in praise and thanksgiving. On the right Bernard is sitting, covered by what looks like a blanket. His head is turned round and he is sucking the white breast of the standing and crowned Virgin. Behind her is an altar covered with a white cloth. The reverse of this folio (MA043) has the scene of Bernard preaching to the bishop on the left, and the construction of Clairvaux on the right. What distinguishes this *Lactation* image from the earlier catalan examples and from all subsequent representations of the theme is the greater physicality of Bernard obtaining Mary's milk directly by sucking her breast, in the same way as recorded in the Henry of Clairvaux *exemplum*. This illustrated literary version did not, however, mark the beginning of a new iconographical tradition of this popular scene-attribute of Bernard, and no other similar images of the subject are known.

There are two other near-contemporary literary versions of the *Lactation*. One of them is found in a Norse collection called *Mariu Jartegnir* (Mary's Miracles) which cannot be precisely dated but is thought to be from the first quarter of the fourteenth century. Although much of the material is taken from the *Vita Prima*, the source of part of it, including the *Lactation* scene, cannot be traced back, although it is likely to be an unidentified Latin text.[34] What distinguishes this nordic version from the others is that, in it, Mary's milk was needed not for its healing power or its property of transmitting 'science divine', but to quench the physical thirst of Bernard who, in the heat of the sun, had given up what little drink was left to the two brothers who accompanied him on a visitation. There are no known iconographical representations of this literary version.

The scene of Bernard's childhood vision of the Nativity,[35] the church of Saint Vorles at Châtillon-sur-Seine, was also the centre of a third *Lactation* legend. Literary evidence for it is based on an indulgence granted by five bishops to the faithful of Saint Vorles in 1340.[36] The original document was destroyed in a fire in 1475 and the story relies on a transcription from 1490, whose authenticity has been questioned. What cannot be contested is that the cult of Bernard which arose in his

[34] McGuire 1991, 189–225, and particularly 204–216.

[35] VP 1:2:4; PL 185:229.

[36] For this, see Arabeyre 1993, 173–197, and Berlioz 1990, 49–54, who says that the story was not 'invented' by the people of Châtillon but rather 'grafted' on to Châtillon.

own home territory centred around the story of the *Lactation* and that this was commemorated in a post-medieval wall painting in the chapel dedicated to him.[37] A similar tradition of the *Lactation* also arose in Afflighem in Belgium and Speyer in Germany.[38]

The Châtillon legend connects the *Lactation* with Bernard's Nativity vision. Marvelling at the mystery of the Incarnation and the motherhood of Mary, the story goes, Bernard was kneeling by the statue of Mary, meditating on the marian hymn, *Ave Maris Stella* ('Hail, star of the sea'). When he came to the fourth verse, which begins *Monstra te esse matrem* ('Show us that you are our mother') the image miraculously came alive and, with one hand on her breast, Mary placed three drops of milk into Bernard's mouth.[39] The trinitarian symbolism of the three drops matches that of the three jets of milk in a number of *Lactation* images.

Although there is no evidence that the Châtillon story gave rise to an iconographic tradition, a number of images follow in the related tradition of the Montblanch retable and several other spanish examples, which, like the Châtillon *Lactation*, represent a statue which miraculously came alive. This is how the monogrammist *I A M* represented the *Lactation* in his copper engraving dated *c.* 1480 (EN72). Bernard kneels, his hands clasped in prayer, an elaborate late medieval crozier with attached sudarium under his right arm, and he looks up at the Virgin and Child sitting on a high-backed chair surmounted by angels and raised high above the floor. A candle on either side suggests an altar. Mary squeezes her breast and, once again, three jets of milk, representing the Trinity, are sent in the direction of Bernard. Unusually, the *Monstra te esse matrem* inscription is here accompanied by the Virgin's response *ecce Bernarde* (Behold Bernard). This phrase is found in one other *Lactation* image, a woodcut printed by Pieter van Os at Zwolle in 1484 (EN19), but here the fragmentary inscription *'ecce.ber'* is contained on a scroll held by the Child.

In another *Lactation* image the difference in scale between Bernard and the statue of Mary before which he kneels emphasizes the supernatural character of the scene. In a fragment from an early sixteenth-century

[37] Illustrated in Arabeyre 1993, 197.

[38] Dewez & Iterson 1956, 167.

[39] This is how the story was handed down by the seventeenth-century Jesuit historian of Châtillon, Etienne Legrand, as quoted in Arabeyre 1993, 185.

Prayer Book thought to be from Brussels (MA210) a nimbed Bernard in a white cowl, with the traditional attributes of a crozier leaning against his left shoulder and red book lying on the ground, kneels on a tiled floor in a church. Before him is a much smaller statue of the Virgin and Child, supported on a pedestal attached to the wall. The Virgin bares her breast, which she squeezes with her right hand in a scene reminiscent of the Châtillon *Lactation* story. A similar version of the *Lactatio* is depicted in a late medieval oil painting by a Dutch Master dated *c.*1520 (PA019). The half-figure of Bernard, hands clasped in prayer and holding an elaborate crozier from which a sudarium with a triangular top is attached, kneels before an altar covered with a white cloth on which the Virgin and Child, very much smaller in scale, are seated. The Virgin, facing Bernard, squeezes her bared breast with her right hand. A candlestick and lighted candle, as well as an open so-called purse book, with its red purse ending with a tassle hanging down, are also on the altar. A mountain landscape with a walled town and two mountain-top castles may be seen through two arched windows. Again the miraculous nature of the vision is enhanced by the difference in scale. In yet another example (MA361), the *Virgo lactans* come to life is represented not by a statue but by an altarpiece. Found in a latin Book of Hours following the roman usage, originally from Ghent or Bruges and dated *c.* 1500, this image shows Bernard, wearing a black cowl with gold outlines, kneeling before a pink altar covered with a white cloth. Bernard's gold crozier with sudarium is in the background. Placed on the altar is a painting of a half-figure of the Virgin holding the Child. She presses her breast with her left hand and squirts three jets of milk towards Bernard. Here it is a painting, not a statue, which comes alive. The border around the miniature is decorated with flowers and fruit and golden crossed branches against a green ground. The miniature introduces the Suffrage to Bernard, as is indicated by the text above in red ink *de sancto bernardo.*

THE TRADITIONAL *LACTATION* INSCRIPTION

Monstra te esse matrem became the standard inscription on *Lactation* images. Whereas they are absent from all spanish *Lactation* pictures, both early and late, they occur in approximately a third of the thirty-eight *Lactation* images in manuscripts and of the forty-two in paintings.

They are usually found on a banderole emanating from Bernard's mouth, indicating that the vision occurred as Bernard was reciting the *Ave maris stella*. Many of the manuscripts which include the inscription are flemish, and among the paintings are a number of small devotional panels (PA025, PA051, PA075, PA076) and larger altarpieces (PA096, PA108) from the Low Countries, Flanders, and the Lower Rhine, along with one of the scenes from the early sixteenth-century retable from the Austrian abbey of Neuberg (PA100).

Sometimes the inscription is inserted below the picture, as in a single leaf from a Bruges manuscript dated *c*.1500 (MA013), where the words are written in white letters on a yellow scroll. In another example, the magnificent Rothschild Book of Hours from the beginning of the sixteenth century (MA204), in which the *Lactation* scene was probably painted by one of the most outstanding flemish miniaturists, Simon Bening, the inscription is below the picture in gold capital letters on a red ground. In some cases the words were inserted around Bernard's halo, as in an early sixteenth-century glass panel from a Cologne workshop (GL69). In one instance, a Dutch Book of Hours from *c*.1465, (MA258), the words in gold were arranged in a circle to form the halo itself.

The traditional *Lactation* text, but in an extended form, creates another variant. One of twenty-one leaves from a fragment of a Flemish Book of Hours in Latin from *c*.1510 (MA134), has this longer text. Letters in gold along the top and down the right hand side of a wide brown border read: MONSTRA TE ESSE MATREM SUMAT PER TE P(RECEM). Along the left-hand side and the bottom is the opening of the hymn: AVE MARIS STELLA DEI MATER A(LMA). Within the border, a miniature depicts the half-figures of Bernard in a white cowl kneeling before the Virgin and Child. The Virgin presses her bared breast and sends a jet of milk in the direction of Bernard. The main text, in white ink on a black background, is the *Alleluia* verse in the Mass for the feast of Bernard, introduced by the rubric *de sancto bernardo* in gold.

The extended version appears again in another late medieval Book of Hours (MA412) in which the *Lactation* scene is witnessed by a lady standing behind Bernard, the owner of the book. A similar arrangement of an extended version of the traditional *Lactation* inscription is also found in the so-called Book of Hours of Ferdinand and Isabella of Spain from *c.* 1492–1504, whose miniatures are attributed to Alexander Bening—father of the famous miniaturist Simon—and Gerard Horenbout, two of the best known painters of the Gent/Bruges School. In this, however, the artist has used a considerable degree of licence and let his imagination run riot in the arrangement of the words. One of forty-nine full-page miniatures has a *Lactation* scene (MA223) set in a church. In the background is an altar surmounted by a stone statue. On the facing folio is the text of the *Seven Verses of Bernard*. It is surrounded by a gold border containing a gold text on a blue ground. The top has the usual *Monstra te esse matrem* inscription. At the bottom the text is the beginning of the hymn *Ave Maris Stella Dei Mater Alma*. It is written in code, with a number of the letters transposed, in a way that makes it impossible to decipher the rest of the text. The first six words read BXF MBRKS STFLLB DFXS MBTER BLMB which form the opening of the hymn, if one makes the following substitutions: B=A, X=V, F=E, and K=I.

A full-page miniature in a Book of Hours from the North Netherlands dated *c.* 1470 has a *Lactation* scene (MA232) with the traditional inscription as well as another text and a response to it by the Virgin. A nimbed Bernard, with his hands clasped in prayer and his crozier leaning against his right shoulder, kneels before a crowned standing Virgin with Child. She stands on a black and gold tiled floor against a gold wall; the figures are all within a gold frame which is surrounded by a foliate decorated border. The Virgin presses her bared right breast with her right hand and milk is seen to flow towards Bernard. One banderole with the familiar *Te matrem* words goes from Bernard's mouth downwards, while another rises with the unusual text: *Cur tuo lacte pio madidas mea guttura virgo* ('O Virgin: why do you moisten my throat with your holy milk?'). The Virgin's reply, given on the scroll above her, is: *Omnibus ut populis lactea verba canas* ('So that the whole world may sing words like sweetened milk').

DISPERSION OF THE THEME IN NORTHWEST EUROPE

As we saw above,[40] the single isolated image chosen to illustrate the northern french *Ci nous dit* Lactation account followed the text faithfully. It represented contact between Mary and Bernard in a unique and

[40] See above, page 215.

more intimate and physical way than had previously been the case, and no other similar examples have been recorded. With the exception of this unique image, nearly two centuries were to pass before the *Lactation* theme made its appearance again outside the iberian peninsula. Beginning around 1470, it re-appeared in the area of northern Europe—the Low Countries, Flanders, and the Lower Rhineland—where it rapidly gained in popularity and was widely represented until the end of the Middle Ages and beyond. Whereas in earlier versions the legendary element of the theme had predominated, there was a shift in the later towards intercession as the primary purpose of the *topos*.

The image was in fact almost confined to the two regions of the Iberian peninsula and north-western Europe and only a handful of examples exist in other countries. Out of the total of one hundred-nineteen *Lactation* images, for example, only four from Italy have been recorded: a circular medallion at the foot of a folio of a cistercian Breviary from Padua or Venice dated *c.* 1500 (MA099); a Book of Hours in Latin dated 1500–1505 (MA299); a late fifteenth-century wall painting at the cistercian abbey of Rivalta Scrivia (WA34); and an early sixteenth-century painting of the Tuscan-Emilian School. This last (PA140) shows Bernard kneeling at a desk with an open book, looking up into the sky at Mary surrounded by small angels. The painting has all the characteristics of the similar but less physical variant of the theme known as the *Doctrina*[41] which became popular in Italy from the fourteenth century onwards, except that the Virgin is baring her breast which she squeezes, so it must be considered a *Lactation* image.

Only one example of a *Lactation* as been recorded from England (DR06). It is a faint sketch featuring the crowned Virgin with flowing hair underneath a canopy, holding the Child on her left arm. She presses her breast, looking to the left at the nimbed Bernard who carries a crozier, his hands clasped in prayer. It appears in a Model Book from the second half of the fifteenth century and probably came from a secular workshop. The book has twenty-four leaves, all covered in drawings, some in ink and others in pencil. Many of the subjects, including the *Lactation*, are those widely associated with Books of Hours. Although of only mediocre quality, it is of considerable importance in being unique, the only surviving english example, while at the same time indicating that the *Lactation* theme was

[41] For this, see Chapter Nine.

in fact known in England.[42] The artist is thought to have been either continental, working probably in Paris, or an Englishman who had worked there. The fact that no other examples apparently survived suggests that the *Lactation* theme was not in tune with the tradition of mystical spirituality that prevailed in England.[43] Similarly, in spite of the existence of a norse literary version of the theme, only one scandinavian *Lactation* image has been recorded: a woodcut (EN69) used as a frontispiece in a book printed in Copenhagen in 1493, with text totally different from the subject of the image. This time we know that the printer was a foreigner, the Dutchman Gotfred van Ghemen. He had worked in Leiden, where the theme would have been well known. During this same period hundreds of village churches in Denmark were being decorated with wall paintings which featured all the most popular biblical and religious subjects. Significantly, there is not among these a single example of the *Lactatio Bernardi,* although the other, generally less popular, bernardine scene-attribute of the *Amplexus* is represented both in a wall painting (WA02) and in an altarpiece (SC51).

Two main groups of late medieval images featuring the *Lactatio Bernardi* may be identified in addition to *Lactation* images. Some of them have already been mentioned in connection with the traditional *Monstra te esse matrem* legend. Both groups belong to the late fifteenth and early sixteenth centuries and to the northwest region of continental Europe.

The first and smaller group consists of visual aids to communal acts of worship in the form of altarpieces in cistercian churches. A triptych (PA065) painted at the end of the fifteenth century by Jan Provoost, who was active in Bruges until his death in 1529, has a central panel with the crowned Virgin sitting on a gold throne decorated with the images of four saints. She presses her left hand to her right breast and directs a jet of milk, now scarcely visible, to the mouth of the kneeling Bernard on the left. The figure of Bernard, in a white cowl and holding a crozier, is balanced by that of Saint Benedict on the right, holding a book—his Rule—and also a crozier. The left wing has Saint John the Baptist with the emblem of the Lamb bearing the Cross and a kneeling donor; and the right wing has Saint Martha with a female donor. Although the

[42] Scott 1996, 1:39-44.

[43] For example, although Julian of Norwich refers to all kinds of images in the *Revelations of Divine Love,* there is no mention of the *Lactatio Bernardi.*

provenance of the altarpiece is not known, the subject of the *Lactation*, with Mary glancing at Bernard and the Child turning towards Bernard to bless him with his right hand, strongly suggests a cistercian origin. The composition is a close parallel to that of a spanish painting from the cistercian abbey of Benefizá (PA126) which also featured Bernard and Benedict together in a *Lactation* scene. In both the attention is on Bernard, although in the spanish one the Child assists the Virgin in pressing the breast while Provoost depicts the Child blessing Bernard.

There are several examples of the use of the *Lactation* theme to decorate the reverse of the wings of large triptychs. The cistercian nuns' church at Roermond has a triptych of the Antwerp School dated *c.* 1500, with the Crucifixion in the centre. The reverse of the right wing has the Coronation of the Virgin while the left wing has the Virgin on the left, baring her breast which she squeezes, and Bernard, who kneels before her on the right (PA096). The scene is witnessed by two cistercian monks. Above Bernard is a banderole with the customary inscription. Two examples by Jean Bellegambe are more impressive in that the *Lactation* theme covers both outside wings. With the Virgin on one and Bernard on the other, they are seen together when the triptych is closed. One is found on the magnificent altarpiece which he painted *c.* 1509. It is known as the *Retable du Cellier*, because, although it was commissioned by Bellegambe's great patron, Abbess Jeanne de Boubais of Flines, and destined for Clairvaux, it eventually found its way to one of Clairvaux's granges of this name.[44] When open (PA087), it shows the Virgin and Child enthroned, with Bernard on the left wing and Saint Malachy on the right wing.[45] The outside wings (PA088) are painted in grisaille: on the left Bernard is holding his crozier (with sudarium attached) with both hands, which are clasped in prayer, and kneeling before a seated Virgin, who, on the right wing, holds the naked standing Child with her left hand while placing her right hand on her bared breast.

The reverse of the wings of a triptych of the Annunciation which Bellegambe painted in *c.* 1516, also in grisaille, is very similar but has the figures reversed. Here (PA108) the sitting Virgin and Child is on the left and kneeling figure of Bernard on the right, surmounted by the *Monstra te esse matrem* inscription which is missing in the Cellier

[44] For details of the triptych, see Stirling 1955.
[45] For this interpretation, see Genaille 1952, 99–108.

Retable. The placement of the subject is significant, for triptychs were displayed open only on special occasions, and the reverse of the wings would therefore have been viewed most of the time and would have had a greater impact. The choice of grisaille for the reverse of triptych wings emphasized the everyday aspect of the closed altarpiece, as against the 'red-letter' nature of the more colourful internal image, and was quite common at the time. These examples of large *Lactation* images intended for the monks' communal devotions indicate that the Cistercians maintained their own tradition of marian-lactation piety, parallel to what was going on in lay circles.

Another, much larger group of *Lactation* images is equally remarkable for its homogeneity and wide dispersal throughout the area. Nineteen examples of almost identical composition have been recorded.[46] It consists of small painted panels intended for the private devotional use of individuals as well as a few miniatures in manuscripts and engravings based on their design. The half-figures of the Virgin seated on the left, often under a baldachin, and Bernard, usually carrying a crozier and sometimes a book, on the right, are placed behind a sill or wall on which the naked Child is usually seated on a cushion. The figures are painted in the same scale. The *Te monstra* inscription is sometimes included. The Virgin caresses the Child with one hand while she places the other on her bared breast. The scene is usually a room with a window through which a landscape with a church or other building may be seen. The first known of these (PA021) was painted in 1470–1475 by the Master of the Life of Mary, the most important painter working in Cologne at the time. Bernard has his gaze on the Child, who is sitting on a cushion on a wall in the foreground. Bernard holds a red book in his left hand while his right hand is placed on the legs of the naked Child. Mary is presenting the Child, holding a carnation in her left hand while she is pressing her bared breast with her right hand. Bernard is identified by his name on the golden halo but he is not carrying a crozier. The usual inscription is missing, and the scene is outdoors in a landscape with a golden sky.

A panel (PA007) painted by the artist known variously as 'the Master of the Death of Saint Nicholas', on account of the altarpiece of this name which he painted, and the Lower Rhine Master followed shortly

[46] They are: EN02, 19, 21, 50; MA108, 158, 169; PA007, 021, 051, 052, 072, 073, 075, 076, 078, 095, 103, 105.

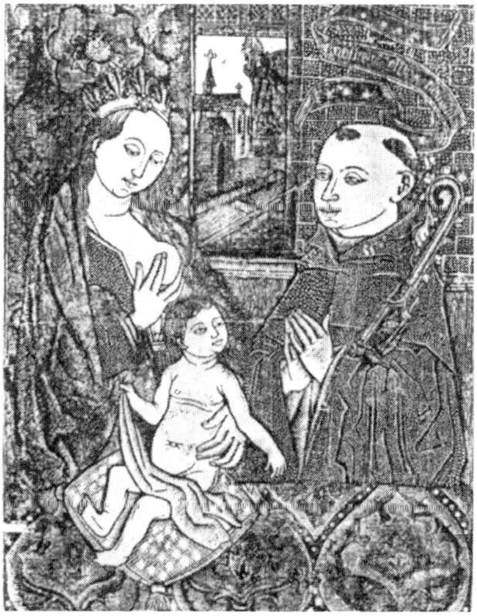

Figure 12

afterwards. ▶ *Colour plate 9* Dated *c.* 1478, the panel shows a youthful Bernard in a white cowl kneeling behind a sill with his hands folded in prayer and his crozier resting on his shoulder under his left arm. The crowned Virgin holds the naked Child with one hand and her breast with the other. The Child, placed on a cushion on the sill, turns to look at Bernard. The usual inscription is included, and the scene is a room with a window in the background and a landscape scene with a church thought to be that of Clairvaux. This panel was closely imitated in a metal engraving produced in a Cologne workshop *c.* 1480. ▶ *Fig. 12* (EN02). It is similar not just in its overall composition but even in such details as the cloth held by the Child, the scroll above Bernard, and the scene out of the window with the church and stream. Another variant (PA075) is a panel painted *c.* 1480 which has Mary sitting under a richly embroidered venetian velvet canopy, with the kneeling figure of Bernard depicted in a white tunic and black scapular and not a cowl, as was more usual in *Lactation* images. In this panel the sill is missing from the foreground, and the Child is held by Mary on her lap.

These *Lactation* panels and engravings—like the *Amplexus* images we examined earlier—formed the prototypes for a number of subsequent examples, both devotional images or *Andachtsbilder,* as well as other painted panels. These half-figure *Lactations* were undoubtedly the inspiration for the painting by Joos van Cleve (PA052), dated *c.* 1480, as well as for a lower rhenish example (PA051) dated *c.* 1500 which follows the earlier scenes in almost every detail, except that Bernard is unusually depicted in a violet-red cowl and there is an altar in the background.

With the advent of printing the theme in the form of woodcuts was also used for frontispieces in books. The best known of these is a woodcut (EN19) by an anonymous artist in a book of Bernard's sermons in the vernacular—*Dat boec van sinte Bernardus sermonen,* printed by Pieter van Os in Zwolle in 1484 and 1495. In this the figures are reversed from their usual positions, with the Virgin on the right and Bernard on the left.[47] The scene is a chamber in which Bernard stands with a crozier in his right hand. With his left hand he receives two flowers offered by the naked infant Christ, who is standing on a cushion on the sill and being supported by the Virgin with her right hand. With her left hand she presses her breast and the milk, which is indicated by a series of dots, squirts towards Bernard. The usual inscription is between their heads, while the Child holds an additional scroll with the fragmentary inscription *'ecce . ber'*. Bernard's book lies on the sill, and behind Bernard we look out through two round arches to a landscape with a castle. Such woodcut *Lactation* images, which had themselves originally been modelled on painted panels, in their turn served as the prototypes for illuminated manuscripts. In the early days of printing, books which were printed were not as highly esteemed or as valuable as manuscripts written by hand and illuminated. A full-page miniature (MA158) in a Book of Hours from *c.* 1480 clearly belongs to this category. Although primitively painted, its composition is based on the conventional half-figure *Lactation* images with the figures behind a sill in a room with windows, although in this instance the Child is not sitting on the sill but held by the Virgin and reaching out to a corpulent Bernard.[48]

DONOR *LACTATION* IMAGES

Closely related to the half-figure *Lactation* panels, and also intended for personal devotional use, are *Lactation* images showing the donor. These hinged double panels, known today as devotional portrait diptychs, show the kneeling donor on one side in adoration of the Virgin and Child on

[47] There are a few other examples of reversed positions: a single sheet woodcut from 1480–1500 (EN21), and a full-page miniature (MA108) painted by Simon Marmion in a manuscript which, although it does not follow the usual pattern in that the sill is missing and the scene is in a landscape outdoors, nevertheless belongs to this group of *Lactation* images.

[48] Another example of a different type of lactation image is the engraving (EN47) by Dirk Vellert from 1524, which was copied almost exactly but in reverse in another engraving (EN48), and was also the model for a fine full-page miniature in the devotional work *Manuale pietatis* from Antwerp (MA115).

the other. They were widespread in the same northern regions as the half-figure *Lactation* images.[49] Three portrait fragments which have been preserved are also *Lactation* images. The traditional *Monstra te esse matrem* inscription on a late fifteenth-century half-figure portrait of a monk in a white cowl with his hands clasped in prayer and his crozier leaning against his left shoulder tells us that the subject is Bernard and that we have one half of a *Lactation* diptych (PA089). The figure is turned to the left, where the other, now missing, half would have featured the Virgin and Child in the usual *Lactation* posture. The reverse is the case with another example: an early sixteenth-century panel (PA078), also with the *Lactation* inscription, has an abbot facing right, where the missing half of the diptych with the Virgin and Child would have been. The third example is also a fragment of a diptych, but of the other half: a small panel (PA161) from the School of Rogier van der Weyden has the Virgin baring her breast in what is probably a *Lactatio Bernardi* diptych, but the other half, which would have depicted Bernard, is missing. The naked Child turns away from Mary, presumably towards Bernard. Uniquely in a *Lactation* image, Christ holds a cross which is supported at the top by a small angel. This alludes to the coming Passion and links the two extremes of his life, thereby making the point that he came into the world to lay down his life for the world.

A closer look at the half-figure images and the diptych fragments reveals that while the general composition is in almost all cases almost identical, with only minor variants, there is a marked difference in the way Bernard is portrayed. He is sometimes depicted as an old man, often as rather portly, and his features are so individualized that there can be no doubt that they represent real contemporary people portrayed in the guise of Bernard, namely, the abbots who commissioned the paintings. The elaborate and precious croziers they hold correspond to those which late medieval abbots would have carried. An example may be seen in the *Lactation* painting by Joos van Cleeve from *c.* 1480 (PA052). Portraits of donor abbots include that of Denis van Zeverdonck of Villers (1521–1545) in the half-figure *Lactation* panel painted *c.* 1525–1535 (PA073). His identity is established by his coat of arms in the top right-hand corner. Two other examples, although not of the conventional half-figure images, may be cited: that of Jean van Deynse,

[49] I am grateful to Andrea Pearson for information regarding these.

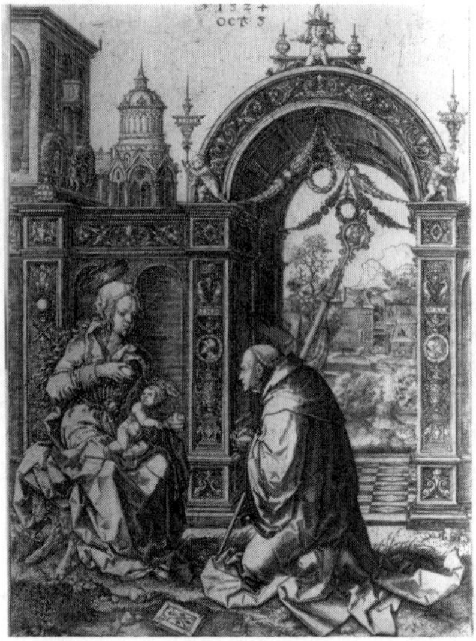

Figure 13

twenty-sixth abbot of Baudeloo, whose portrait was painted *c.* 1520 (PA132), and Peter van Onderberghen, abbot of les Dunes 1515–1519, who appears in the guise of Bernard in the altarpiece painted in the Bruges workshop of Simon Bening (PA077). The margin of the *Lactation* miniature (MA115) based on the Dirk Vellert engraving (▶ *Fig. 13;* EN47) has the figure of the small kneeling Abbot Marcus Cruyt of St Bernards-op-'t-Scheldt (Saint-Bernard-sur-l'Escaut), identified by his coat of arms. He may also have been the model for the Bernard depicted in the *Lactation* scene itself as well as for the *Lactation* image in the Missal belonging to the abbey (MA140). The very distinctive individualized features of these, and of many other representations of Bernard in half-figure panels, leave little doubt that they are portraits of their donors.[50] These abbots no doubt relished being portrayed as important prelates and were flattered at being identified with Saint Bernard. The popularity of the images also underlines their intercessional significance, the belief that the spiritual benefits which passed to Bernard through Mary's milk were also assimilated by these late medieval abbots.

The *Retable du Cellier,* mentioned above, which has a *Lactation* scene in grisaille on the reverse of the wings (PA088), depicts the central characters of the Virgin and Child enthroned with Bernard on the left wing and Saint Malachy on the right, together with portrayals of Bernard's parents, brothers, and sister (PA087). The historical figures may also be

[50] Other examples include PA072, PA075, PA095 (so close to that of Abbot van Zeverdonck that it may well be another portrait of him), PA103 and PA105 among the half-figure panels, and the two diptych fragments, PA078 and PA089.

viewed as the donor abbess, her confessor, and other contemporary figures associated with the abbey of Flines, who were portrayed as Bernard's father Tescelin, his mother Aleth, his five brothers, and his sister Humbeline. The same configuration is found in an earlier, late fifteenth-century, *Lactation* painting from the South Netherlands, unusual in the number of figures witnessing the event (PA082). The central scene in the background shows the Virgin with Child on a raised platform in an architectural setting and flanked by an angel on each side. She bares her breast with her right hand and looks in the direction of Bernard, who kneels on the platform on the right, his hands clasped in prayer and his crozier leaning against his right shoulder. His mouth is open, ready to receive the milk from Mary. Below the platform kneel members of the donor family: on the right two women, supported by their patron saints, Mary Magdalene with the ointment and Catherine with the crown and sword; on the left a man accompanied by five younger men, his sons, and supported by two saints, perhaps Saint Rochus with the pilgrim's staff and Saint Bavo, who was much revered in Ghent. The family's coat of arms (perhaps that of de Waele?) is at the top. Once again, by identifying the members of the donor family with Bernard's mother and sister on the right and his father and five brothers on the left, and thereby assimilating them into Bernard's family circle, they become partakers of and sharers of the grace bestowed on him by Mary's milk

BERNARD IN MARIAN INTERCESSION IMAGES

Mary is seen in these images as the *Mater omnium*—the Mother of all-and consequently also as the *nutrix omnium*—the nourisher of all. This sharing in Mary's outpouring was referred to by Richard of Saint Victor in his Commentary on the Song of Songs when he said, 'the Blessed Virgin pours out milk both for the reconciliation of sinners and for the benefit of believers'.[51] The same point was also made by the early thirteenth century cistercian writer Adam of Perseigne, who wrote that although Mary's first duty was to attend to the needs of her Son, she would not neglect her other children:

[51] PL 196:475: *Beata Virgo et peccactoribus reconciliationis et piis gratiae lac fundit.*

> Those breasts are full from heaven and they refresh with unfailing sweetness.They are not emptied by the many who drink from them and, although she preserves herself totally to one alone, she does not deny her mercy to those who drink of her milk. O, unfailing fruitfulness! How great is the sweetness of this milk which the famished children take from the breasts of this most tender Virgin.[52]

Bernard's role in fostering the cult of Mary is well-known and in his celebration of her powers of intercession. Quoting Jerome in one of his letters, Bernard had already referred to a mother baring her breast,[53] and, reflecting on the relationship between Christ and Mary, he talks of 'the sweetness of her milk', and adds: 'The Son will assuredly listen to the Mother and the Father will listen to the Son'.[54] The same reflection on the economy of salvation is expressed in his Second Advent Sermon: 'Through you we have access to the Son, O blessed provider of grace, begetter of life, mother of salvation'.[55] The idea was developed in a text attributed to Bernard, but in fact written by his friend, the benedictine abbot Arnold of Bonneval, the author of the second book of the *Vita Prima:*

> Man now has a secure access to God where he has the Son as a mediator of his cause before the Father, and the Mother before the Son. Christ with his naked side shows his wounds to the Father, while Mary shows her chest and breast. She cannot in any way be turned down, when these marks of clemency and signs of charity agree and pray eloquently in every tongue.[56]

[52] Ep 16; PL 211:636: *Ubera illa de caelo plena sunt et indeficienti suavitate reficiunt, nec lactentium multitudine vacuantur, sed nec mater illa se misericors negare solet lactentibus, licet totam illi unico se conservet. O ubertas indeficiens! O magna multitudo dulcedinis, quam de viscerosae Virginis uberibus sugit esuries parvulorum!*

[53] Ep 322, SBOp 8:256-8; trans. James 1953, 449.

[54] *In Nativitate Beatae Mariae;* SBOp 5:278-279: *Dulcedo lactis est. . . . Exaudiet utique Matrem Filium, et exaudiet Filium Pater.*

[55] Adv 2.5; SBOp 4:174: *Per te accessum habemus ad Filium, o benedicta inventrix gratiae, genitrix vitae, mater salutis.*

[56] *De Laudibus B. Mariae Virginis;* PL 189:1726: *Securum accessum jam habet homo ad Deum, ubi mediatorem causae suae Filium habet ante Patrem, et ante Filium matrem. Christus, nudato latere, Patri ostendit latus et vulnera; Maria Christo pectus et ubera;*

This motif, which has been described as a Double Intercession,[57] lent itself to visual representation and was frequently illustrated, sometimes also identifying Bernard as the supposed author of the phrase. The erroneous attribution may be seen in the inscription above a miniature featuring Bernard in the margin of the early sixteenth-century Choir Book in three volumes from the benedictine abbey of Lorch (MA103). Above the half figure of Bernard—in a black cowl with a gold crozier in his left hand, raised in blessing—a banderole has the text: 'O, man, it is not possible to be rejected where the Son shows his side and his wounds to the Father—the Mother shows to her Son her bosom and her breast. This according to Bernard, abbot of Clairvaux' (*O homo ibi non poterit esse repulse ubi filius ostendit patri latus et vulnera—Mater ostendit filio pectus et ubera: Hec bernardus abbas claraval[lensis]*). A full-page miniature in a Book of Hours dated *c.* 1480, probably from Macon or possibly from Lyons (MA117), shows a nimbed Bernard standing with a crozier in his left hand while his right hand is placed on a large scroll of parchment on which is a liberally-adapted version of Arnold's text which reads:

> O Man, you have secure recourse to God, where the Mother stands before the Son and the Son before the Father, the Mother showing the Son her bosom and her breasts, the Son showing the Father his side and his wounds! Nothing, therefore, can be denied you where there are so many signs of love![58]

The text is, in fact, taken *verbatim* from the lesson for the Ascension in the *Legenda Aurea,* where Jacobus de Voragine wrongly ascribes the words to Bernard.[59]

James of Voragine's error explains both the inclusion of Bernard in this and other images, as well as the perpetuation of the mistaken attribution and the popularity of the iconographical theme. Thus Bernard's authorship is assumed in the following text of a banderole above the half-figure of

nec potest ullo modo esse repulsa, ubi concurrent et orant omni lingua disertius haec clementiae monumenta et charitatis insignia.

[57] Bynum 1987, 272.

[58] *Securum accessum habes o homo apud deum ubi mater ante filium filius ante patrem. mater ostendit filio pectus et ubera. Filius Patri latus et vulnera. Ibi ergo nulla erit repulsa ubi tot occurrunt caritatis insignia.*

[59] Jacobus de Voragine 1941, 293.

Bernard in a manuscript from the benedictine abbey of Lorch (MA403): 'O, man, it is not possible to be rejected where the Son shows his side and his wounds to the Father—the Mother shows her bosom and her breast. This according to Bernard, abbot of Clairvaux'.[60] Above the figure of Bernard are the letters *IHS* (*Ihesus*) on one side and *MA* (*Maria*) on the other, and below them is a scroll with the words *Benyt soit Dieu a tous iours* (Blessed be God forever) and the initials *RG*, those of the owner. Arnold's text is illustrated by a full-page miniature on the opposite folio (f. 16v), at the opening of the Office of the Virgin. It contains portraits of the owners, a man of law and his wife presented by her guardian angel. The hands of both are clasped in prayer and holding a scroll with the *Monstra te esse matrem* inscription. Before them and between heaven and earth stands the Virgin accompanied by five angels, the intermediary between them and God. She intercedes for them with her Son in a very tender and maternal gesture, baring her breast to ensure that her request cannot be refused. The sequence to this takes place in heaven, where Christ, wearing the crown of thorns, transmits the request in a parallel way by baring his side to show his wound to the Father, represented in the traditional way as an old man wearing a tiara. The intercession of Mary with Christ and of Christ with the Father perfectly illustrates the words wrongly attributed to Bernard. Although not a *Lactation* image, the presence of Bernard, the baring of Mary's breast and the inclusion of the traditional *Lactation* inscription, nevertheless links it to the *Lactation* theme.

The same motif is found in a late fifteenth-century painting attributed to Gherardo di Giovanni (PA138). The half-figure of God the Father appears in the sky within circles of various colours with a yellow centre. He stretches his right hand out towards the figure of Christ, kneeling on a platform raised up from the ground, his hand pointing to the wound in his side. In the rays between the two is the dove representing the Holy Spirit. Also kneeling on the platform is the Virgin. Her left hand is placed on her naked breast and her right hand on the shoulder of a small man accompanied by his wife and two small children, all of them kneeling between the figures of Mary and Christ. On a tiled floor on the ground below the platform is the kneeling figure of Bernard. He looks out towards the viewer while pointing to the scene with his right

[60] *O homo ibi non potuit esse repulse ubi filius ostendit patri latus et vulnera—Mater ostendit filio pectus et ubera: Hec bernardus claraval[lensis].*

hand. With his left hand he holds a scroll containing another modified version of Arnold's words, also adapted from the *Legenda Aurea:* O HOMO SECURUM HABES ACCESSUM [. . .] ANTE PATREM MATREM HABES ANTE [. . .] OSTENDIT VULNERA. MATREM OSTENDIT FILIO PECTI UBERA. IBI VIDEO UBI TOT CARITATIS SUNT INSIGNIA. Once again, the association between Christ's wound and Mary's breast is made explicitly by the text accompanying the visual representation.

A similar composition is found in a full-page miniature (MA133) in another french Book of Hours from the beginning of the sixteenth century which, like the Macon Hours, also illustrates the Hours of the Virgin. Unlike the examples just given, this is a true *Lactation* image. The half-figure of God the Father appears at the top, encircled by the seraphim. He has an orb in his left hand while his right hand is raised in blessing. Below Him, in the centre Bernard kneels on the ground before the standing Virgin, who presses her bared breast with the right hand and sends a jet of milk towards Bernard. Standing to the left and slightly higher than the Virgin is Christ, looking up at the Father to whom, using his right hand, he shows the wound in his side. The inscription at the bottom has the opening words of Psalm 45 (Vulgate 44): 'My heart is stirred by a noble theme' (*Eructavit cor meum verbum bonum*). The scene is set in a green hilly landscape with two castles atop hills in the background. The composition of a zig-zag of glances from Bernard to Mary, Mary to Christ, Christ to the Father, and from the Father back to Christ perfectly illustrates the flow of grace; in what may be described as an extended *Lactatio Bernardi* scene, Bernard is not just a witness to the bestowal of divine favour on others, but is himself its beneficiary.

True *Lactation* images may be defined by the jet of milk, depicted either as a solid line or as a series of dots, issuing from Mary's bared breast, which she squeezes with one hand, in the direction of Bernard's face or even directly into his mouth. This is how artists conveyed the theme, from the earliest curved line of milk in the Palma altarpiece and the very faint straight line in the *Lactation* image in the Alcobaça Missal (MA084 and *Colour plate 5*) right up to the fifteenth and early sixteenth-century manuscripts and paintings.[61] The jet of milk may also be clearly seen in an early sixteenth-century Spanish woodcut on the title page of two pseudo-Bernard works. ▶ *Fig. 14* (EN43). The variant of three jets,

[61] For example MA097, PA126, and PA129.

representing the Trinity, is not infrequently found, as, for example in the Pieter van Os woodcut from 1484 (EN19) as well as in another woodcut, an engraving, and the altarpieces in the catalan church of Sant Esteve at Canapost and the austrian abbey of Neuberg.[62] The jet of milk is by no means always present, however. It is, for example, absent from the half-figure abbot donor portraits (for example PA052 & PA073). Perhaps it was considered too indelicate to be included in representations of actual living persons. And yet, the milk is also absent from a number of other images which show Mary baring her breast to Bernard and which must also be considered true *Lactatio Bernardi* images.[63]

This variation inevitably raises the question of the blurring between images of Mary the provider of sustenance, symbolized by the *Lactation,* and Mary the intercessor who bares her breast and thereby reminding her Son that it was she who nurtured him. The first is represented in art by the *Maria lactans* and the *Lactatio Bernardi;* the second by the Mother / Son / Father chain of intercession which, as we saw above, sometimes also included Bernard on account of the incorrect attribution to him of Arnold of Bonneval's text, and because of its similarity to the related iconographical theme of the *Deësis*.

Taking its name from the Greek for 'humble petition', the *Deësis* was a representation of the Last Judgment. It consisted of Christ seated in the centre, flanked by Mary baring her breast on his right and John the Baptist on his left.[64] The earliest known examples are from the seventh century, and by the tenth century it was commonly featured in the East on *iconostases*. Carvings of the composition can be seen in the cathedrals of Amiens and Mainz. In the late Middle Ages it became a popular iconographical *topos*. It is illustrated in a late fifteenth-century woodcut from the Low Countries in the *Speculum humanae salvationis,* and in a french translation of this in a manuscript from Bruges dated 1455.[65] It is also found in a number of late fifteenth-century and early sixteenth-century wall paintings in danish village churches. One of these, at Ottestrup on Zeeland, has a banderole above Mary with the words *Ecce ubera quae lactasti* ('Behold the breasts which you have

[62] EN26, EN72, PA034, PA100.

[63] They include MA013, 069, 115, 204, 211, and PA 007.

[64] For this and what follows, see Murray 1996, 134.

[65] Illustrated in Wilson 1984, 198 and 76 (the miniature is Glasgow, Hunterian Museum Library, MS 60, f 57v).

suckled'); another over the Baptist has *esto propicius* ('Look upon us with favour'), while the one over Christ proclaims *Salvator mundi, salva nos* ('Saviour of the world, save us').[66]

The Cistercians had a long tradition of associating Mary with Judgment Day. Caesarius of Heisterbach tells a story of how Mary, knowing that if the angel blew the trumpet a second time the world would come to an end, fell at the feet of Christ and begged him to wait 'at least for the sake of my friends, those of the Cistercian Order, that they may prepare themselves'. The story must have originated in the early thirteenth century for, according to Caesarius, 'our abbots returning this year from the General Chapter told us this'.[67] Although he makes no mention of Mary baring her breast, his story nevertheless has a clear connection with the popular *Deësis* image. And although Bernard does not feature in this, and there is nothing in his writings to suggest that he was in any way responsible for its promulgation, the confusion and overlapping of the four iconographical *topoi*—the *Maria lactans, Lactatio Bernardi, Intercessio,* and *Deësis*—is best shown by the way Martin Luther castigated Bernard for what he considered the 'shameful and blasphemous image of the Last Judgment . . . Saint John and Mary asking Christ for us on the Last Day. . . . This is taken from Saint Bernard's books, and it is not spoken or painted or done well by Saint Bernard, and one should put away these depictions'.[68] Luther was wrong in tracing the motif to a bernardine text; he—like many others—probably confused it with Arnold of Bonneval's intercessional chain. That confusion could easily arise is not surprising, for there was undoubtedly a strong similarity between the two types of *Lactatio* images (*Maria lactans* and *Lactatio Bernardi*) and between the two intercessional images (the *Intercessio* of Mother / Son / Father and the *Deësis* of the Last Judgment), and a blurring of the boundary between them. A contributing factor to the popularity of all four themes may well have been the opportunity it afforded artists to show a part of the female body not normally exposed in religious art.

[66] See Saxtorph 1967, 135–136, 176, and 306. All medieval wall paintings in Denmark may be seen on the internet: www.kalkmalerier.dk.

[67] *The Dialogue on Miracles,* Distinctio 12, Chapter 58: Caesarius of Heisterbach 1929, 2:344.

[68] Posset 1999, 320–323. Posset mentions that Luther may have known the theme from the stone sculpture in Erfurt cathedral where he was ordained and which is here illustrated as plate 24.

CONCLUSION

Two points in particular stand out as regards the *Lactatio Bernardi* image, both of them in contrast to other bernardine motifs. First, the theme seems to have been equally widespread in the iconography of the Cistercians and that of other religious orders, secular churches and among the laity in general. Its popularity among monastic as well as lay audiences is not paralleled by any of the other themes. It seems to have been favoured by the Cistercians. It owed its introduction in Catalonia to the influential abbey of Poblet (▶ *Colour plate* 5 and *Fig.* 9), and its first known appearance in a manuscript was in the Alcobaça Missal in the early fourteenth century (MA084). It was used again in missals at the low countries abbeys of Les Dunes in the late fifteenth century and at Sant Bernards-op-'t-Scheldt (Saint Bernard-sur-l'Escaut) in the early sixteenth century (MA145 & MA140). The latter monastery also possessed a Gradual in which the *Lactation* was featured (MA218), as did the abbey of Saint Salvator in Antwerp (MA130). Two of the only four known *Lactation* images in Italy are also of cistercian origin: a Breviary from Venice or Padua dated *c.* 1500 (MA099); and a wall painting from the monastery of Rivalta Scrivia (WA34). The image was used by the Cistercians in small devotional half-figure panels or diptychs portraying abbots in the guise of Bernard (e.g. PA078). The Cistercians also represented the image on altarpieces, as at Les Dunes and Neuberg (PA077, PA100), on the reverse of the wings at Roermond (PA096) and on the outside wings of the *Retable du Cellier* (PA088).

The *Lactation* theme was especially popular among the laity in the late Middle Ages in the northwest part of Europe, consisting of the Low Countries, Flanders, and the Upper Rhine. For the laity the *Lactation* theme satisfied a thirst for images which responded to their needs, and especially those of women. It reflected the late medieval emphasis on Christ's humanity, his vulnerability as a naked, defenceless baby, the mystery of the Incarnation, and it made a connection with the mysticism associated with Bernard and especially that of his *Sermons on the Song of Songs*. By accenting the interior life, private devotion and meditation, it was in tune with the spirituality of the *Brautmystik* of the Rhineland and of the later *Devotio moderna* associated with Thomas à Kempis. Although the transition in depicting the *Lactation* from early to later periods was less radical than with other iconographical *topoi*, there is nevertheless a discernible development in the way the Child is depicted. The rather characterless baby, who seems in the early images almost only to have been included to make the 'Virgin and Child' identification, is replaced by the thoroughly human baby whose presence becomes central. There is a tenderness in the way the relationship between the figures in the later *Lactation* images is depicted. In the half-figure painting by the Master of the Life of Mary (PA021), Bernard places his hand on the Child's legs, Jesus places his left hand on his mother's right hand, the hand with which she is holding her bared breast, thereby indicating his approval of his mother's action and bringing Bernard into their family relationship. In the late fifteenth-century altarpiece by Jan Provoost (PA065), as Mary presses her hand to her breast to send a stream of milk to Bernard's mouth, the Baby turns to Bernard to bless him with his right hand.

The late-medieval importance of women and the family is exemplified by the new themes of the so-called *Anna Selbdritt*—that is, Mary's mother Anne, Mary, and the baby Jesus—and that of the Holy Family, both of which gained in popularity towards the end of the Middle Ages. A combination of the *Lactatio* and *Anna Selbdritt* is found in a spanish painting by Rodrigo de Osona dated *c.* 1500 (PA131). Here, below an image of the Trinity, the Child sits on Mary's knee and tries to reach a small bird held by Saint Anne, who is sitting next to the Virgin. Mary squeezes her bared breast in the direction of Bernard, who kneels at her feet. In this painting, and especially in the crowded *Lactation* scene by the South Netherlands Master (PA082), we have evidence of the late medieval celebration of the Holy Family. Emphasis on the family may also be seen in the *Retable du Cellier* (PA087), in which a contemporary family substitutes for Bernard's family. In the course of the fifteenth century such scenes became more and more numerous with illustrations of the three Marys, their husbands and children, and they provide reflections of the bourgeois family of the new, urban merchant class in art and society.

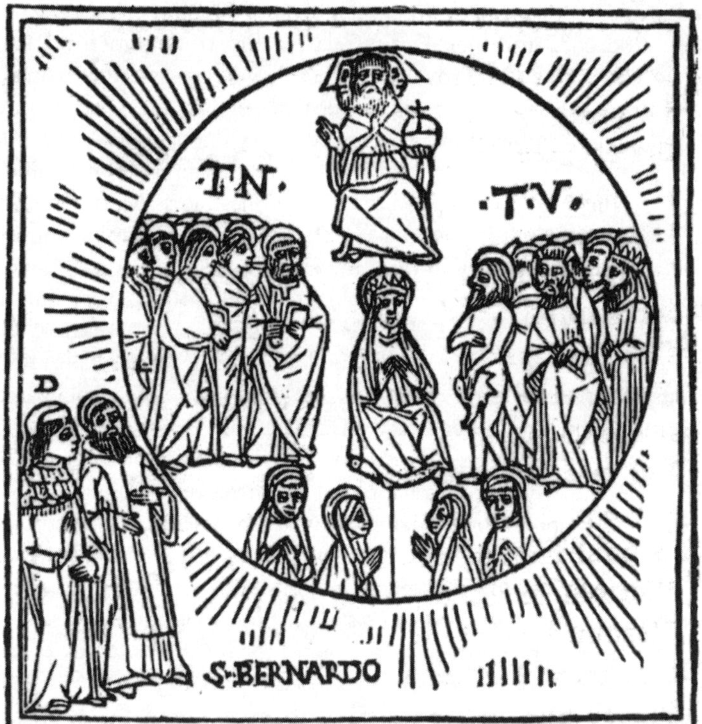

Figure 15: Woodcut in a Dante edition printed at Venice in 1491 (EN08).

NINE

BERNARD IN DANTE AND FLORENCE: THE *DOCTRINA*

BERNARD MAKES HIS APPEARANCE IN THE *COMMEDIA DIVINA*

> *Virgin Mother, daughter of thy Son, lowly and exalted more than any creature, fixed goal of the eternal counsel, thou art she who didst so ennoble human nature that its Maker did not disdain to be made its making.*[1]

BERNARD'S PRAYER to the Virgin, cited above, forms the last words spoken by any of the *dramatis personae* in the last canto of the last section of the *Commedia Divina* by Dante Alighieri (1265– *c.* 1321). It

[1] *Paradiso* 33, 1-3:
Vergine madre, figlia del tuo figlio,
umile e alta più che creatura,
termine fisso d'etterno consiglio,
tu se' colei che l'umana natura
nobilitasti si, che'l suo fattore
non disdegnò di farsi sua fattura.
This and later translations are from *The Divine Comedy of Dante Alighieri,* Italian text and trans. John D. Sinclair, London, 1939.

marks the climax of Bernard's role as Dante's final guide, after Virgil and his beloved Beatrice, on the last stage of Dante's journey to the vision of God.[2] So tenderly does it express Bernard's well-known devotion to Mary that—as we shall see—a number of the early commentators wrongly ascribed the prayer to Bernard himself.

Dante composed the last canto of his work, *Paradiso* 33, in the years immediately preceding his death. Some seventy years later Geoffrey Chaucer (*c.* 1345–1400) translated and adapted Dante's famous words:

> Thow Mayde and Mooder, doghter of thy Sone,
> Thow welle of mercy, synful soules cure,
> In whom that God for bountee chees to wone,
> Thow humble, and heigh over every creature,
> Thou nobledest so ferforth oure nature,
> That no desdeyn the Makere hadde of kynde
> His Sone in blood and fleesh to clothe and wynde.[3]

Chaucer's translation follows the original very closely and forms the second *Invocacio ad Mariam* introducing the Prologue to the *Second Nun's Tale.* The first invocation, in Chaucer's own words, begins: 'And thow that flour of virgines art alle, of whom that Bernard list so wel to write' ('And thou that art the flower of virgins all, of whom St Bernard had such skill to write'). It was precisely because of Bernard's dual reputation as a devotee of Mary and as an orator—both in the sense of his skill in the use of speech and in his renown as a man of prayer—that Dante chose him as his guide on the last stage of his journey to his final destination, Paradise. The intervention of Bernard would secure the

[2] For this and what follows, see Botterill 1994, the most exhaustive and authoritative study of Bernard's role in the *Commedia*.

[3] From *The Works of Geoffrey Chaucer,* ed. F. N. Robinson, 2nd Edition, Cambridge, 1957, 207. In a translation into modern English (*The Canterbury Tales,* trans. Nevill Coghill, Harmondsworth, 1951, 458) this reads:

> Thou maid and mother, daughter of thy Son,
> Thou well of mercy, balm to sinful nature,
> In whom God chose His dwelling as in one
> Humblest and highest over every creature,
> Who gav'st such nobleness to human feature
> That God had no disdain to clothe and wind
> His Son in flesh and blood of human kind.

intercession of Mary which was necessary to obtain the grace required to reach his goal. Dante's reliance on Bernard's guidance and his dependence on the intercessory 'ladder' echo the motif sometimes associated with the *Lactatio* (see MA117, PA138, MA133) and expressed in the bernardine idea developed in the *De laudibus beatae Mariae* attributed to Bernard, but in fact written by his friend and biographer, the benedictine abbot Arnold of Bonneval.[4]

The prayer which Dante put on Bernard's lips was in fact so apt that in the earliest surviving commentary on the *Commedia* (1324–1328), the earliest commentator on the *Commedia,* Jacopo della Lana (1324–1328), described the passage as Bernard's. This mistake was repeated by a number of later commentators, none of whom gave a reference as to where in Bernard's works it was to be found[5]—not surprisingly, for the passage is, of course, not to be found anywhere in Bernard's works. Significantly, Lana's adapted version was then used, virtually word by word, by Jacobus de Voragine in his lesson for the Ascension in the *Legenda Aurea,* where he also wrongly ascribed them to Bernard.[6] This then is the passage which appears on scrolls held by Bernard in some of the intercessory images (see MA117 and PA138), conveying the false impression that he was its author.

This is yet another example of the importance of the *Legenda Aurea* in transmitting knowledge of Bernard and, in this case, in fostering his reputation as a devotee of Mary. Its use by all the early Dantean commentators suggests that the *Legenda Aurea* was one of the primary sources in *trecento* Florence and undoubtedly also the basis for Bernard's reputation for Dante and his readers. Dante did not provide any biographical details for Bernard, as he did for such other saints as Francis and Dominic.[7] For the full significance of his choosing to appear at the climactic moment Dante relied on and assumed in his educated lay audience a prior knowledge similar to that which he himself possessed. We do not know whether Dante read Bernard or how much he relied on

[4] PL 189:1726. See above, Chapter Eight, pages 229–233.

[5] See Botterill 1994, 124–128.

[6] Lana's version is quoted in Botterill 1994, 124, and may be compared with those of the *Legenda Aurea* in Jacobus de Voragine 1941, 293. Botterill says that the passage occurs in the *Questiones de Assumptione* by the Franciscan Gualterus Cancellarius, but does not mention its origin in the Golden Legend (Botterill 1994, 126).

[7] *Paradiso* 11 and 12.

Bernard for his marian material. It is more likely that he drew on a common fund based on an amalgam of sources—first and foremost Scripture and biblical commentaries and sermons by Bernard as well as others, post-bernardine pious accretions, prayers, and such hymns as the *Ave Maria* and the *Salve Regina.*

'Bernard's' wonderful prayer at the opening of *Paradiso* 33 lent itself naturally to being illustrated. In the 1440s Giovanni di Paolo (*c.* 1399–1482) painted miniatures in a *Commedia* manuscript for the king of Naples, Alfonso V of Aragon. Bernard is depicted in the last four of these. The fourth and smallest of them (MA065)—► *Colour plate 10*—features the nimbed Virgin and Child sitting on a marble bench which rests on an inlaid marble platform against a blue background. On the right a standing Bernard, nimbed and wearing the white cistercian cowl, points with his right hand to the Virgin while he places his left hand on the head of the kneeling Dante, the suppliant before the Virgin's throne. The miniature illustrates the passage in which Bernard addresses Mary with the great prayer which begins with an eulogy, paying tribute to her place as Queen of Heaven and acknowledging her role as exemplar (*Paradiso* 33, 1-21), and continues with the invocation recognizing her power as 'Queen, who canst do what thou wilt' (*Paradiso* 33, 22-39). The importance of the prayer is underlined by the particularly elaborate initial on this folio. The same scene is depicted in a mid-fourteenth-century manuscript, in one of two miniatures featuring Bernard (MA080). In the lower part of the folio Dante kneels behind a standing Bernard, who holds Dante's hands in his right hand while pointing with his left to a circle at the top containing the Virgin enthroned between three angels.

In *The Divine Comedy* Bernard appears only in the last three out of a hundred cantos. The roman poet Virgil had been Dante's guide in his week-long visionary journey, which began on the eve of Good Friday 1300. Virgil had led him through *Inferno* to the mountain of *Purgatorio,* but as a pagan he had to give way and be replaced by Dante's beloved Beatrice, who accompanied him upwards towards the Empyrean. Shortly before reaching his destination, still expecting to see Beatrice, Dante instead caught sight of 'an old man, clothed like that glorious company' (*un sene, vestito con le genti gloriose*)[8] whom he identifies as Bernard only some forty lines later when he reveals himself as a devotee of

[8] *Paradiso* 31, 59-60.

Mary by his own famous words: 'and the Queen of Heaven, for whom I am all on fire with love, will grant us every grace, since I am her faithful Bernard' (*E la regina del cielo, ond' ïo ardo/ tutto d'amor, ne farà ogni grazia,/ però ch'ï sono il suo fedel Bernardo*)[9]. Bernard is there at the invitation of Beatrice to show Dante that to reach his goal, the vision of the Almighty, he must go beyond her. From then on Bernard dominates the scene. His qualifications are both his devotion to Mary and his fame as a contemplative.

Bernard's first appearance in this canto is illustrated in an italian manuscript from the second half of the fourteenth century (MA192), possibly from Florence, and including a commentary by Jacopo della Lana. A rather crude and unfinished pen and ink drawing shows two standing figures, on the right a nimbed and bearded Bernard pointing with his right hand to Dante on the left. The beard here, and in all *Commedia* illustrations of Bernard, corresponds to his first appearance as the 'senior' or *sane*. As well as being the most common way he is portrayed in italian art, this was also in line with the description given in the *Vita Prima* and the subsequent *Vera Effigies* tradition, and it corresponded as well to an ancient association of hairiness with holiness.[10]

Two miniatures, out of a total of five showing Bernard, illustrate Canto 31 in an emilian or paduan manuscript from the second quarter of the fourteenth century, the first known *Commedia* manuscript in which Bernard is depicted. One of these (MA073) has half figures at the bottom of a semi-circle of the Empyrean: Bernard on the right and Dante on the left are looking up at a bust of the crowned Virgin in glory between busts of saints, an angel, and Beatrice. The scene is that of Bernard urging Dante to look up:

> 'Child of grace', he began 'this joyful state will not be known to thee if thou keep thine eyes only down here at the foot; but look at the circles up to the farthest till thou see in her seat the Queen to whom this realm is subject and devoted.'.[11]

[9] *Paradiso* 31, 100-102.

[10] See, for example, Burchard of Balerne's discussion of the significance of different hair styles in his *Apologia de Barbis* (Burchard of Bellevaux 1985, 66).

[11] *Paradiso* 31, 112-117: *Figlioul di grazia, quest'esser giocondo', / cominciò elli, 'non ti sarà noto, / tenendo li occhi pur qua giù al fondo; / ma guarda I cerchi infino al più remoto, / tanto che veggi seder la regina / cui questo regno è suddito e devoto.*

The same scene occurs in one of three miniatures illustrating Canto 32 in a manuscript, dated 1456, from northern Italy with a commentary by Francesco da Buti (MA387). Here Dante and Bernard are standing on the left. Bernard is pointing up to the Virgin seated between Saint Peter and Moses in the Empyrean. Most unusually, Bernard is portrayed naked, as are Peter and Moses, following the medieval convention whereby the soul was distinguished by the absence, not of its body, but of its clothes. The only means of identification are the halo and the beard, but in the context we can be certain that the figure represents Bernard. By contrast with the many doubtful Bernard images despite the presence of all the usual attributes—cistercian cowl, crozier, halo, and book—here we have an example where the minimal clues to his identity are sufficient to establish positive identification. The model for this image is found in an early fifteenth-century paduan manuscript which contains only one miniature with Bernard (MA276). Here he is also naked. He turns to Dante, behind him, to show him the Virgin in the sky. Below her four souls—that is naked figures—are seated.

In Canto 32 Dante describes the arrangement of the *candida rosa* (white rose) of the Empyrean, the seating-plan of the celestial amphitheatre. There follows a long theological discussion, covering such issues as baptism, predestination, and grace, in which Bernard establishes his reputation as an eloquent teacher, the *dottore*. Giovanni di Paolo has two miniatures illustrating this canto, both of which show the rose, which is here, unlike other examples, depicted as a realistic flower. The first has the Virgin of Humility and the Child in the centre of the white rose, with the naked Eve prostrate beneath her feet (MA063). To the left of the Virgin is Peter with the keys, on the right John the Baptist pointing towards the Child. Clockwise after the Baptist are Francis, an unidentified male saint, Augustine, Bernard, and an unidentified female saint. Nestling on the petals beneath Mary are her mother Anne, and Lucy. Outside the rose Dante is kneeling, and Beatrice is still present, but to indicate that she is no longer real the artist has chosen to show her floating above him. She has one hand on Dante and the other on the halo of the unidentified female saint. Giovanni di Paolo's other miniature (MA064) again shows the white rose, but this time it has fewer but larger petals filled with larger saintly figures. Instead of the Virgin and Child, the centre now holds a representation of the Annunciation. Dante, still outside the rose, asks Bernard the name of the angel[12] and Bernard replies that it is Gabriel. We see Dante attracting Bernard's attention by tugging on his sleeve, while Bernard has turned his gaze away from Mary and fixed it on Dante. The position of Dante and Beatrice is identical to the previous picture but in this one Beatrice has her right hand on the kneeling Dante while her left rests on Bernard's halo. Although Dante arranged the seating within the rose in two groups—believers before and after the Incarnation—Giovanni di Paolo has only portrayed the New Testament saints. The two groups, however, are represented in the anonymous woodcut (EN08) which adorns this penultimate canto in the first fully-illustrated printed edition of Dante, printed by Bernardino Benali and Mattio da Parma from Venice dated March 1491. ▶ *Fig. 15* (EN08). In the bottom left corner Dante is identified by 'D' and Bernard, next to him, by the inscription S.BERNARDO. They are looking up at the heavenly circle, within which a number of figures are depicted: at the top the Trinity with three heads, seated and holding an orb; below the Virgin, and, divided into two choirs by a line running down the centre, on the right the Old Testament figures identified by superscript letters 'T.V.' and on the left those of the New Testament with the inscription 'T.N.' (TESTIMONIUM VETERUM / TESTIMONIUM NOVUM).

Towards the end of the journey, just before the climactic utterance of the prayer to the Virgin, Bernard uses the simile of a tailor:

> But since the time flies that holds thee sleeping we shall stop here, Like a good tailor that cuts his coat according to his cloth.[13]

This advice was heeded by the artists who illustrated the *Commedia*. Faced with one of the greatest poems of all time artists created miniatures to serve the text, with which it would have been foolish to try to compete. Furthermore, the poem contained some of the highest theological insights of the time, which by their very nature did not lend themselves to visual representation. The illustrations were not to be the centre of attraction and as a result relatively few *Commedia* manuscripts contain narrative miniatures. Their subsidiarity is indicated by

[12] *Paradiso* 32, 103-105.
[13] *Paradiso* 32, 139-141.

their humility, by most commonly being relegated to the margins. The restrictions also explain the relatively few medieval Dante manuscripts with illustrations. A recent landmark study of *The Divine Comedy* lists only thirty-six illustrated copies among the over six hundred fourteenth-century copies which have been preserved.[14] The great majority of those illustrated contain only a portrait of Dante, decorated initials, or a small number of narrative scenes. Some were never completed (for example, MA192-MA195). Furthermore, illustrations of the *Inferno* and *Purgatorio,* which lend themselves to the kind of grisly scenes which were so popular in the late Middle Ages, are far more frequent and numerous than those depicting the more ethereal and highly personal *Paradiso,* which was generally less popular than the two preceding *cantiche*. There are therefore relatively few pictures covering the last three cantos, those in which Bernard appears. The standard study of the illuminations in *The Divine Comedy* lists only ten manuscripts with images of Bernard, six of them from the fourteenth century, containing altogether twenty-six bernardine miniatures.[15] As is to be expected, many of these were florentine. The earliest dates to the second quarter of the fourteenth century and has five miniatures depicting Bernard (MA72-76). A magnificent and very comprehensive late medieval rendering by Sandro Botticelli (1446–1510), made for Lorenzo de Medici, contains ninety-three sketches with a soft silver-point and finished with a pen in black or brown ink, but has no image of Bernard. There is no drawing to Canto 31, and the design for Canto 32 has only small sketches of Christ and the Virgin and was never completed.[16]

Copper-plates were made from Botticelli's compositions and published in 1481. Six years later the first woodcut edition was published, but the first fully-illustrated edition by Bernardino Benali and Matthio da Parma from Venice did not appear until March 1491.[17] The first canto each of the *Inferno, Purgatorio,* and *Paradiso* had a full-page illustration while all others had smaller, square pictures (▶ *Fig. 15*). These same pictures were repeated over and over again in numerous later printed editions. Before 1529, there were altogether thirteen il-

[14] Roddewig 1984.

[15] Brieger, Meiss, and Singleton 1969, 219–230, 252–257, 262–269, 282–291, 300–306, 309–313, 332.

[16] Lippmann 1896, 80, and Volkmann 1899, 74–83.

[17] Lippmann 1896, 88–89, and Volkmann 1899, 84–91.

lustrated editions.[18] The reason for the poor quality of many of these editions has been interpreted as evidence that they were simply intended for readers looking for particular passages, as was the case with the *Biblia Pauperum*, and artistic considerations were of minor importance.[19] In terms of artistic merit they pale into insignificance alongside Dante's masterpiece.

SAINT BERNARD: PATRON SAINT OF FLORENCE

The first cistercian foundation outside the borders of modern France was made at Tiglieto in northern Italy in 1120. It was a daughter-house of La Ferté and itself became the mother-house of Staffarda in 1135 and of Barona in 1150. Locedio, also from La Ferté, was settled in 1124. Morimond was responsible for Morimondo in 1134/1135. Most numerous, however, were the houses settled from Clairvaux—as was only to be expected from the most prolific of the Cîteaux filiations. A number of existing monastic houses were absorbed into the cistercian family in the wake of Bernard's italian tours and others owed their initial foundation to his influence. The names of the two earliest indicate their close link with their burgundian mother-house: Chiaravalle Milanese (1135) and Chiaravalle della Columba (1136). In 1140 the ancient abbey of Saints Vincent and Anastasius near Rome, later known as Tre Fontane, became cistercian as did another former benedictine house, Casamari, itself to be the mother-house of numerous other abbeys. By the end of the Middle Ages the number of cistercian houses in Italy had grown to eighty-eight.[20] In spite of their early settlement and the relatively large number of houses compared with, for example, the seventy-five in England and Wales, the Cistercians were never an important force in the Italian church or society.

Only two individual Cistercians of note stand out in the initial period of settlement. One was the first cistercian abbot of SS Vincent and Anastasius, Bernard Paganelli of Pisa, a former novice at Clairvaux under Bernard who became the first cistercian pope as Eugene III (1145–1153). The other was Joachim of Fiore (*c.* 1135–1202), a calabrian

[18] Volkmann 1899, XIV.
[19] Lippmann 1896, 88–89.
[20] Lekai 1977, 36–37.

whose apocalyptic vision of the new kingdom of the Holy Spirit, with its concentration on the impending end of the world, led him to adopt extreme austerities inconsistent with the benedictine-cistercian tradition, to renounce his former way of life, and to found his own reformed Order. For him this was all part of an historical progression in the forms of religious life. For a time his monastery flourished; other houses were founded, but eventually these were absorbed back into the cistercian family.

Among the italian Cistercians there were no luminaries comparable to the french Bernard or William of Saint Thierry, the english Stephen Harding and Aelred of Rievaulx, or the german Conrad of Eberbach and Caesarius of Heisterbach. After his lifetime Bernard had less impact than did spiritual writers of other traditions, notably the Franciscans and later the Franciscan Spirituals, whose spirituality was influenced by Joachim of Fiore, and most especially the dominican scholastics.

Whether there is a connection between the relative paucity of early images of Bernard in Italy and the, apparently, lesser impact of his personality there as compared with his influence in countries to the North is impossible to say. It may just be that fewer have been preserved, although it is also possible that a lesser interest is responsible. At any rate, there are no known representations of Bernard in the peninsula in any media until the second quarter of the thirteenth century, and in all only seven thirteenth-century images have been recorded.[21] Five of these belonged to cistercian houses—Casamari, Tre Fontane, Badia a Settimo, and Morimondo—while the remaining two are found in manuscripts which were owned by the Franciscans.

The earliest of the bernardine images from the cistercian houses in Italy (VA01) is on a reliquary commissioned by the abbot of Casamari whose name is inscribed on it. One of a number of circular medallions painted on glass and set into the silver-gilt reliquary has a bust of Bernard as well as those of several other saints. He is bearded, his hood is over his head, he holds a simple crozier in his right hand and a book in his left. The inscription has 'S.BER'. The earliest of all known images of Bernard in an italian manuscript (MA292) occurs in a Homiliary from the second half of the thirteenth century which belonged to the abbey of Morimondo in Lombardy. It shows Bernard standing on the right, bearded, within the initial *A*(*d sancti ac beatissimi patris*), the beginning

[21] They are VA01, WA23, SC56, MA230, VA02, MA272, and MA292.

of a sermon by Saint Ambrose. He has a blue book in his left hand while his right hand is raised in blessing a group of seven kneeling tonsured monks dressed in white cowls, as is Bernard, their hands raised in acknowledgment. The composition is almost identical to that of another manuscript from the same abbey, an Antiphonary from *c.* 1300 (MA291). In both, the depiction is very much in the early tradition of bernardine monastic images, showing the saint as the teacher of his monks, comparable to the miniature in the *c.* 1180 manuscript of his *Sermons on the Song of Songs* (MA025) from the benedictine Liesborn, and to a Lectionary from Mariastern in Saxony (MA068), which was created a century later and is contemporary with the Morimondo image. The Casamari reliquary and the Morimondo manuscript represent two distinct iconographical strands. While the medallion with Bernard in a frontal position, bearded and with his hood over his head against a gold background, has great affinity with early images of Saint Francis and reveals a distinct byzantine influence, the Morimondo image follows the *praxis* which originated in monastic scriptoria north of the Alps.

The relatively low profile of Bernard in italian affairs generally did not apply in Florence. Here his *cultus* was very much alive and he is widely represented in art from around the time of Dante until the end of the Middle Ages.[22] A number of reasons have been advanced for his prominence in florentine society.[23] First, his early intervention on the side of the italian pope Innocent II during the anacletan schism—for which Bernard was rewarded by being given the roman abbey of Tre Fontane and being granted tithe privileges for Clairvaux—brought him into the very centre of the public life of the Church and established him as a figure of international repute for the first time.

Second, Bernard's reputation in Florence rested on a legend whose origin is not known but which circulated widely in Italy as early as the late twelfth century.[24] According to this, Bernard is supposed to have composed a letter entitled *Dottrina del vivere* (Teaching on how to live) or the *Lettera a Raimondo* (Letter to Raymond), named after the recipient, a

[22] It has, for example, been estimated that Bernard shared tenth place with Saint Michael on a list of most frequently depicted saints in italian painting in the period 1420–1540 (Burke 1972, 151). Among the known images which we recorded thirty-six are still preserved in Florence today.

[23] For this, see Lesher 1984, 258–267.

[24] Lesher 1984, 262.

young nobleman who sought Bernard's advice on how to reconcile his privileged position with the evangelical life. The legend lived on and was illustrated in one of three drawings in brown ink and water colour (DR15) by a florentine goldsmith, Marco di Bartolommeo Rustici. Two scenes drawn in the margin of a mid-fifteenth-century manuscript describing his visit to the Holy Land are explained by the text below them. On the left the seated Bernard hands a letter to a monk who stands in front of him. The text in red ink says: *Santo bernardo mando unapostola assignore ramondo* (Saint Bernard gives a letter to Signor Raymond). On the right Raymond, identified by the text below—*messer ramundo singnore*—, is seated on a high-backed chair on a dais and is being handed the letter by the kneeling monk. This pseudo-bernardine text enhanced Bernard's reputation as a very holy man and established him as an adviser to laypersons on the spiritual life, in the same way as his letters and treatises had made him the advisor of secular rulers who turned to him for guidance on public affairs.

Third, and connected with his role as a conciliator and adviser in church affairs, was his *De consideratione libri quinque,* the treatise he addressed towards the end of his life to his former disciple at Clairvaux Eugene III (see images MA234-240, MA245, and MA284-288). In these five books he tackled all the major problems connected with the exercise of papal authority, and established himself as someone whose reform credentials were unimpeachable. His role as counsellor to a succession of popes was established. The *De consideratione* became perhaps his best known work in Italy in the late Middle Ages, and was referred to by Dante, Petrarch, Marsilius of Padua, and Giles of Rome.[25] Its appeal was not confined to those involved in papal or ecclesiastical politics; much of the advice was equally applicable to secular rulers, dealing with topics of universal concern, such as the abuse of power through ambition and avarice, the importance of knowledge of self, and the relationship between temporal and spiritual power. The impact of Bernard's *De consideratione* was not confined to Florence, but could be read with profit by the ruler of any Italian city in the later Middle Ages anxious to maintain a certain distance from papal intervention. It contributed, nevertheless, to the reputation of its author and succeeding generations of Cistercians as reliable arbiters in the secular affairs of Florence.

[25] Lesher 1984, 264.

The fourth reason advanced for the civic cult of Bernard in Florence is the Cistercians themselves by virtue of the role they played in the government of Florence. Cistercian monks had settled near the city in 1236, when monks from the nearby abbey of San Galgano took over a former Vallombrosan abbey, the Badia of Settimo.[26] Of the four governing *Camarlinghi del Commune*, three were laymen while the fourth was a Cistercian from Settimo. It was an office held by the monks until the sixteenth century.[27] They were chosen for their reputation for impartiality and integrity and as a result they were entrusted with the care of the city's seal. The administration was centred on the Palazzo della Signoria (now called the Palazzo Vecchio) in which the Chapel of the Priors, the cornerstone of which had been laid in 1298 on the feast of Saint Bernard, was dedicated to Bernard.[28] Here morning prayers were said before each day's work. Bernard's role as the patron saint of the florentine commune was celebrated by works of art in his honour in the Palazzo, among them an altarpiece painted in 1486 by Filippino Lippi (1457–1504) (PA148). The Virgin is the central figure, enthroned with the Child on her knee, while two angels hold a crown over her head. She is flanked by John the Baptist and Victor on the left, and Bernard and Zenobius of Florence on the right, all patron saints of the city. The open book which Bernard holds has the words: TU PATRONA HUMANI GENERIS. TU AFFLICTIS MEDICA SINGULARIS ('You are the patroness and the supreme healer of the human race').[29]

In the fifteenth century Eugene IV (1431–1447) undertook a reform of Settimo and handed over the benedictine Badia in the city to the Cistercians. This gave them a base for their business and also facilitated their reform of the nuns at the abbey of Santa Maria Maddalena di Cestello (now Santa Maria dei Pazzi), whose direction the monks of Settimo took over. In the last two decades of the fifteenth and the first of the sixteenth century there was a remarkable surge of building and artistic activity at Cestello, perhaps unequalled by any other cistercian monastery anywhere. Works by a number of distinguished artists—including Ghirlandaio, Perugino, Botticelli, Lorenzo di Credi, Cosimo Rosselli, and

[26] For this, see Luchs 1977.

[27] Lesher 1984, 265.

[28] Clark 1981–1982, 175–187.

[29] According to Kaftal 1952, 177, this may be a paraphrase of the line *apotheca salutis hominum* in the pseudo-Bernard poem *Oratio devota ad Dominum Jesum et B. Matrem eius* (PL 184:1325).

Raffaellino del Garbo[30]—naturally included several representations of Bernard. Among them are three works by Pietro Perugino (*c.* 1450–1523) or his School: an altarpiece from *c.* 1489 of the Vision of Bernard with Saint Bartholomew and Saint Philip (PA151), commissioned for the Bernard Chapel by the brothers Nasi, one of whom was named Bernardo; an *Amplexus* fresco in the chapter house (WA22); and a magnificent Crucifixion fresco (WA28) commissioned by Dionisio and Giovanna Pucci and completed in 1496, also for the chapter house. The central of three arches has the Crucifixion itself with Saint Mary Magdalen, to whom the monastery was dedicated, kneeling at the foot of the Cross. In an arch on the right, Saint John the Evangelist stands with Saint Benedict, whose Rule the monks followed, kneeling beside him; and on the left stands the Virgin, and kneeling beside her is Bernard, her devoted admirer and the most celebrated saint of the Order.

These four reasons may have contributed to the civic cult of Bernard in Florence, but his practical influence was almost certainly eclipsed by his role as an exemplar of marian devotion in a city renowned for its veneration of the Virgin.[31] She had been acclaimed its protectress in 1296, when a new cathedral was constructed in her honour. This confluence of marian and bernardine affection may be seen as the point of departure for the specifically florentine motif of the *Doctrina*.

THE *DOCTRINA* OR *DOTTRINA*

In Italy, and especially in Florence, Bernard's intensely personal devotion to Mary found expression in an iconographical theme known as the *Doctrina* or *The Vision of Mary*. This scene-attribute is in many ways similar to the *Lactatio* in that the knowledge and the skill to preach and to write are, in a parallel way, in both transmitted from the Virgin to Bernard. In the *Doctrina* Bernard usually receives a visit or a vision of the Virgin as he sits at a desk writing; in quite a number of these images, he is shown in the unusual position of kneeling while at the same time writing (MA012, PA119, PA155, PA160, MA243, MA266). The physical nurture suggested by the *Lactation* is replaced in the

[30] Luchs 1977, 65–76.
[31] Janke 1974, 45–50.

Doctrina by verbal and intellectual sustenance. While the accent on mothering and motherhood in the *Lactatio* expresses itself by the presence of the Infant in Mary's arms, the *Doctrina* focusses on Mary, who is usually depicted on her own. Both themes originated around the same time—in the early fourteenth century—but, unlike the *Lactatio,* the *Doctrina* cannot be traced to any specific literary source.

The *Lactatio* was virtually unknown in Italy: only four exceptions have been recorded, all late medieval. One is in a Breviary from Venice or Padua dated *c.* 1500 (MA099), another in a Book of Hours from the beginning of the sixteenth century (MA299), the third a wall painting at the cistercian monastery of Rivalta Scrivia (WA34), and the fourth an early sixteenth-century painting of the tuscan/emilian School (PA140). The last has all the characteristics of a *Doctrina* image, but the Virgin is also baring her breast to Bernard, which makes it a unique combination of the two. Just as the *Lactatio* enjoyed popularity in only some places, so the *Doctrina* is unrecorded anywhere else in Europe, and to emphasize it as a uniquely Italian image it is often called the *Dottrina.* In view of limited distribution, the number of *Dottrina* images recorded—altogether thirty-two—is quite sizable. Of these only eight are from before the middle of the fifteenth century.

Dante's name inevitably springs to the mind of someone seeking a source for this new iconographic motif in early *trecento* Florence. He was one of the priors who governed the city and who daily attended the offices in the chapel dedicated to Bernard in the Palazzo della Signoria. He was well versed in, and contributed to, the cult of Bernard, whom he celebrated with the words: 'Such was I, gazing on the living charity of him who in this world tasted by contemplation of that peace'.[32] Although no direct influence of the *Doctrina* on Dante's treatment of Bernard in *Paradiso* can be demonstrated, the ideas and images they contain are derived from a common stock. For chronological reasons, however, the influence is more likely to be that of Dante on the iconography, than vice versa.[33]

The earliest known image which may be loosely described as belonging to the *Doctrina* category is a historiated initial *S(alve Virgo pretiosa)*

[32] *Paradiso,* Canto 31.

[33] The link has been made by David L Clark as regards Filippino Lippi's famous *Doctrina* image. Quoting Dante, he says: 'the scene probably comprises one source for the *istoria* in Lippi's painting and its prototypes' (Clark 1981–1982, 175–187).

marking the opening of a marian hymn in a tuscan Hymnal dated 1310–1315 (MA264).[34] Within the pale blue and rosa initial, a half-figure of the Virgin in red and blue against a red background is looking down from the upper half to a half–figure of a bearded and nimbed Bernard in a white habit against a blue background in the lower half. He is looking up, his hands are raised in awe, and his body is leaning backwards, perhaps to remind onlookers of Bernard's instruction to Dante to lift up his gaze to Mary: 'Look now on the face that most resembles Christ, for only its brightness can fit thee to see Christ'.[35] Before him a book is opened on a lectern, but there is no indication that Bernard has been writing; nor is there any gesture from the Virgin to suggest that she is dictating. In other respects, however, the image follows the convention associated with the *Doctrina* and it may be considered as a forerunner. The same manuscript contains another image of Bernard (MA263).

The name *Doctrina* may derive from the inscription on one of the best-known early examples of this type (PA149), a small predella scene of a polyptych painted by Giovanni da Milano in the 1350s. The main part of the altarpiece consists of the central figures of the Virgin and Child flanked by four saints: Catherine and Bernard on the left, and Bartholomew and Barnabas on the right. The lower predella shows biblical scenes and above these, conforming to the usual practice, are scenes from the lives of the saints featured on the main part of the altarpiece. Here they are described by an inscription which informs us of their subject matter: the decolation of Catherine, the passion of the apostles Bartholomew and Barnabas, and DOCTRINA SANCTI BERNARDI CONFESSORIS (PA150). Bernard, with a long beard and in a white cowl, is seated at a finely inlaid desk writing with a pen in his right hand. The knife in his left hand he holds against his chest. He is looking at the figure of Mary who stands in front of the desk, pointing to Bernard with her right hand while she directs her left hand towards his work, a

[34] In addition to the *Lactatio* and *Doctrina* there are a number of images of the Virgin appearing to Bernard in a general way which are not based on any particular literary source and do not belong to any specific iconographic tradition. In addition, a vision described in the *Vita Prima* is featured in a number of images recording events from Bernard's life. It is of Mary's visit, accompanied by Saint Lawrence and Saint Benedict, depicted on the altarpiece from the German abbey of Maulbronn (PA059), and two from the early sixteenth century—a bust-reliquary from the Swiss abbey of Saint Urban (VA06) and a glass panel from the Altenberg cloister (GL19).

[35] *Paradiso,* Canto 32.

clear indication of her dictation. Above Bernard is a lantern, and another open book is placed on a stand in the background, witnessing to his reputation as a writer. The title honours Bernard as a teacher, the dantean *dottore* who received his learning and who, in the words of an authority on Dante 'must be not only *doctus* (learned) but *docens* (a teacher)'.[36] The eloquence with which he carried out his mission under Mary's inspiration is what earned him the title of *Doctor Mellifluous*.

The altarpiece painted by the Master of the Rinuccini Chapel (PA155), dated to 1356–1359, was very similar in its composition to Giovanni da Milano's predella image. It has been described as its oldest extant prototype,[37] but, in reality, in 1335 the priors had commissioned Bernardo Daddi to paint a *Dottrina* picture, now lost, for the Saint Bernard chapel in the Palazzo della Signoria. The Master of the Rinuccini Chapel developed the theme in several respects. His *The Vision of Bernard* formed the central scene of the altarpiece which was made for the Cistercians of Settimo. It is flanked on the left by Saint Benedict, dressed in a white cowl (following the quite common italian tradition) and carrying a crozier and a bundle of sticks, and Saint John the Evangelist, and by Saints Quentin and Galgano on the right. In the usual way, the predella contained small scenes from the lives of the saints depicted above them. Two in the centre feature Bernard: one with his five brothers, in which Gerard may be identified by the wound in his side which he received as a soldier before entering Clairvaux (PA156)[38]; and the other (PA157) showing him preaching against heresy at Sarlat.[39] Unlike the earlier *Doctrina* image, this *Vision of Bernard* is set, not indoors but in a verdant landscape with flowers and trees. Bernard is kneeling at a *prie-dieu*, not sitting at a desk although he is still writing, and the Virgin is hovering before Bernard and not standing. She is accompanied by two angels, also raised above the ground. This accentuates the supernatural character of the scene, which is witnessed by two monks standing behind Bernard. The text on Bernard's book reads: *Regina Celi Mater Crucifixi dic Mater Domini si in Jerusalem eras quando captus fuit filius tuus . . . cui illa respondit* (Say, Queen of Heaven, Mother of the Crucified,

[36] Botterill 1994, 92.
[37] Clark 1981–1982, 175–187.
[38] VP 1:3:10-11; PL 185:232-233.
[39] VP 3:6:18; PL 185:313-314.

Mother of the Lord, whether you were in Jerusalem when your Son was captured . . . to which she replies), and the reply comes in the inscription issuing in gold letters from the mouth of Mary: *Jerusalem eram hoc audivi* (I was in Jerusalem when I heard this). The text is taken from the *Liber de passione Domini et doloribus et planctibus matris eius* (Book of the Passion of Christ and the Sorrows and Lamentations of his Mother), the work of the cistercian abbot Ogier of Locedio which for a long time was wrongly attributed to Bernard.[40] The same text, in a slightly modified form, was used in another image of Bernard. A small altarpiece from 1368–1370 attributed to Jacopo di Cione (PA030) has the Crucifixion as its central scene while the predella contains five roundels, each fifteen centimetres in diameter, featuring the Virgin and Child in the centre flanked by four saints. One of these is Bernard, who is carrying an open book in both hands, with the text turned outwards, displaying the same dialogue between the Virgin and himself in which the Virgin explains her suffering at the Passion.

Fifteenth-century *Dottrina* images incorporated some of the new elements introduced by the Master of the Rinuccini Chapel. One of them (PA119) is included among the six scenes from Bernard's life chosen to surround the central figure of Bernard in a florentine altarpiece from *c.* 1430. Here Bernard is kneeling, with an open book placed on a slanting desk before him. He is looking up to the sky at the Virgin, who is blessing him with her right hand. Together with two angels she is contained within a mandorla from which gold rays emanate. The considerable distance between them and the difference in scale has the effect of accentuating the visionary nature of the event, which here, as in the Settimo altarpiece, is also witnessed by one of Bernard's monks. Examples of *Doctrina* images in fifteenth-century manuscript illuminations in which the Virgin far away in the sky appears to a kneeling Bernard set in verdant landscapes include two small historiated initials (MA012 and MA266) and a stained glass window in the augustinian church of Santo Spirito in Florence (GL92). A variant to these outdoor *Doctrina* images is that of Bernard sitting indoors at a desk writing and looking out of the window at the Virgin, who appears in the sky. Three

[40] PL 182:1134-1135. On Ogier of Locedio and the *Planctus Mariae,* see Barré 1952, 243–266, and D. Martin Jenni, *Introduction* to *Ogier of Locedio: Homilies,* CF 70 (Kalamazoo, 2006) 1–21, esp. 14–15.

late fifteenth-century examples are the Sforza Book of Hours (MA132), a florentine manuscript of sermons (MA270), and a manuscript of Bernard's Sermons, also florentine (MA271).

The civic cult of Bernard continued into the fifteenth century and found artistic expression in the painting on wood of Bernard's *Vision of the Virgin* (PA032) by Fra Filippo Lippi (1406–1469), a carmelite friar much patronized by the Medici family. An irregular hexagon, the piece is thought to be the overdoor outside the chapel in the Palazzo della Signoria for which a payment is recorded in May 1447.[41] In it a youthful Bernard sits at a desk in a mountainous landscape next to some rocks, some of which form the base of his desk. His right hand is following the text of the open book before him while his left hand is raised towards the Virgin, on whom he is gazing. Her right hand is extended towards Bernard, indicating the dialogue between them. The disparity in scale—the smaller figure of the Virgin and of the three angels attending her—again underlines the visionary mode. Two further books on Bernard's desk, one of them open, denote Bernard's reputation as a writer. The heads of two small figures peer over the rocks in the background. Unlike the earlier images, these witnesses are not monks as they are not tonsured.

The rural setting in a rocky, mountainous landscape of a number of the later renaissance *Doctrina* images expresses visually two themes that go back to the time of Bernard and beyond. First, cave imagery was common among early monastic writers, and evokes memories of Saint Benedict in his cave at Subiaco.[42] William of Saint Thierry in the *Vita Prima* describes early Clairvaux as 'hidden away among impenetrable woods and within the narrow confines of adjacent mountains', a site 'reminiscent of that grotto of our Father Saint Benedict in which he was once discovered by shepherds'.[43] Secondly, the serenity of the rural scenes recalls William's testimony about Bernard, who 'by praying and meditating in the woods and fields discovered the deep meaning of Holy Scripture' and jokingly told his friends 'that it was only the oaks and beeches who were his masters in this subject'.[44] This corresponds with

[41] Davies 1961, 291.
[42] The connection is suggested in Clark 1981–1982, 175–187.
[43] VP 1:7:35; PL 185:248.
[44] VP 1:4:23; PL 185:240.

Bernard's own recommendation in a letter to Henry Murdac that 'you will find much more labouring amongst the woods than you ever will amongst books. Woods and stones will teach you what you can never hear from any master.'[45]

An outdoor setting among trees and rocks had already been chosen as being the most appropriate to the contemplative nature of the *Doctrina* theme by the fourteenth-century Master of the Rinuccini Chapel in his Settimo altarpiece (see above and PA155). In the second half of the fifteenth century the setting was not merely indicated by the inclusion of a few trees or rocks, as had hitherto been the case. The scenery became more realistic and thereby more prominent, and yet did not detract from the primarily spiritual character of the scene depicted. In fact, the opposite was the case; the meditative power of the Vision was enhanced. A good example is a full-page miniature in a magnificently illustrated manuscript of Bernard's *Sermons on the Song of Songs* and their continuation by Gilbert of Hoyland (MA243). The elegant decoration was provided by two artists of the Florentine School between 1475 and 1482. A nimbed and bearded Bernard in a white cowl is on his knees writing at a desk made of the same rock as the steep cliff behind him, much as in Filippo Lippi's overdoor (see above and PA032). Bernard is looking up at the smaller figure of the Virgin, who appears in a mandorla in the sky surrounded by a multitude of angels. The scene is witnessed by two monks in the foreground who are so dazzled by the supernatural light that they hold their hands over their eyes. The setting is a mountainous landscape with a river, a town in the background, and some peasants with a donkey in a field. In the background on the left the artist has depicted Clairvaux with a tall tower and spire, and, to make the identification certain three tiny figures of monks on a path leading to it.

The siting of the vision at Clairvaux had already been suggested by the inclusion of monks attending Bernard (for example, PA119); here it is made explicit by the depiction of the buildings themselves in the background. The first known example of the addition of this new element is found in the predella of the polyptych painted by Giovanni di Paolo (*c.* 1399–1482) a few years earlier—*c.* 1470—for the cistercian abbey of Saint Galgano. While the centre panel of this no longer exists, the side panels have the standing figures of Saints Benedict and Mary Magdalen

[45] Ep 106; SBOp 7:266-267; trans. James 1953, 156.

on the left and on the right Galgano and Bernard (PA163). The predella, decorated with the arms of the abbey of Saint Galgano and, following the usual practice, scenes relating to the lives of the saints depicted on the main panel, includes a *Doctrina* image of Bernard (PA160). The scene is a mountainous rocky landscape with fir trees and, at the top left Clairvaux, which is more faithfully depicted than in the other known *Doctrina* images (see MA243 and PA136). In the right foreground Bernard kneels at a gothic desk on which is an open book in which he has been writing with a pen in his right hand and a knife in his left. He looks up at the Virgin floating before him. Her right hand is raised in blessing Bernard and she is attended by two angels. Behind him are three monks, two of them in white cowls and with their hands raised in awe while the third, in a white tunic and grey scapular, clutches at a tree.

Sometime around 1486 Piero di Francesco del Pugliese commissioned Filippino Lippi to paint what is perhaps the most famous of all images of Bernard (PA136) for his family chapel, dedicated to Bernard, in the monastery of the Campora near the Porta Romagna. The donor is portrayed kneeling with his hands clasped in prayer in the lower right-hand corner. It has been entitled 'The Virgin Inspiring Saint Bernard's *Homilies in Praise of the Virgin Mother*'.[46] Bernard sits on a rock in an elaborate landscape. An open book in which he is writing is placed on a writing board supported by a gnarled tree stump. His status as a learned man of letters is indicated by a number of books untidily arranged on a rocky ledge behind him and on his seat. His arms rest on the board and his hands are raised in deference to the figure of the Virgin standing before him on whom his gaze is fixed. Mary looks down and places her right hand on Bernard's work. Bernard's inspiration is transmitted visually by the text in the book prominently open between them, which rests on Bernard's various manuscripts: the familiar words of Saint Luke, *Missus est angelus Gabriel a Deo in civitatem Galilaeae,* the account of the Annunciation with which Bernard begins his earliest sermons on the Virgin, *Homilies in Praise of the Virgin Mary*.[47] The artist may well have been inspired by his father, Filippo Lippi, whose *Doctrina*

[46] The title is suggested in Clark 1981–1982, 175–187.

[47] Luke 1:26: 'The angel Gabriel was sent by God into a city of Galilee whose name was Nazareth to a virgin espoused to a man whose name was Joseph of the house of David and her name was the Virgin Mary': *De laudibus Virginis Matris, Homilia* 1; SBOp 4:13.

overdoor (PA032), completed nearly forty years earlier, was displayed adjacent to a representation of the Annunciation in the Palazzo della Signoria.[48] He may also have known the passage in which Bernard himself referred to the moment the artist has captured:

> Here we must pause in order that we may contemplate awhile the splendour of so great a luminary as Mary. . . . I prefer the delight of gazing in silence upon that which no laboured eloquence can sufficiently describe.[49]

Other passages associated with Bernard also appear in the painting. Immediately above the saint's head is a small piece of paper with the motto SUBSTINE ET ABSTINE ('bear and forbear'), drawn from a passage in the pseudo-bernardine *Meditations on the Life of Christ:*

> I think it is a good life to bear evil, do good, and persevere in this till death . . . You must patiently bear what your neighbour causes you to suffer. Without complaint and rendering thanks, you must accept what you sustain from God.[50]

On the manuscript in front of Bernard appears a fragmented form of one of his most famous passages, known by its latin tag *respice stellam, voca Mariam* ('look to the star, call upon Mary):

> There is indeed a wonderful appropriateness in this comparison of her to a star, because as a star sends out its ray without detriment to itself, so did the Virgin bring forth her Child without injury to her integrity. And as the ray emitted does not diminish the brightness of the star, so neither did the Child born of her tarnish the beauty of Mary's virginity. She is therefore that glorious star which, according to prophesy, arose out of Jacob, whose ray illumines the entire earth, whose splendour shines out conspicuously in heaven and reaches even unto hell; a star which,

[48] Janke 1974, 45–50.

[49] *De laudibus Virginis Matris, Homilia* 2 (SBOp 4:35): *Sed iam modice pausandam est, ne et nos in transitu claritatem tanti luminis intueamur. . . . et libet dulciter contemplari in silentio, quod laboriosa nonb sufficit explicare locutio.*

[50] Quoted in Clark 1981–1982, 175–187.

> enlightening the universe, and communicating warmth rather to soul than to bodies, fosters virtue and extinguishes vice.[51]

Filippino Lippi chose not to capture the visionary nature of the theme by depicting the Virgin and her attendant angels smaller than Bernard or hovering before him or far away in the sky. The figures are all painted to the same scale, and the four angels are very lifelike, modelled on real florentine children. He has, however, in a very subtle way, achieved the same effect by brightening the front of Bernard's white cowl with light radiating from the Virgin. The same light also catches two monks with their hoods over their heads who are gazing in wonder at the scene, while two others, in their working clothes of white tunic and black scapular, are engaged in conversation outside the abbey buildings. A further group of monks may be seen in the distance. Discretely depicted in a small dark cave in the rocks behind Bernard is a chained devil denoting Bernard's ascendancy over the devil—a theme we shall discuss in more detail in Chapter 11. The first known example of this last detail in a *Doctrina* image occurs in a painting attributed to Paolo Uccello (PA135), dated *c.* 1460–1465, also depicting scenes from the lives of a number of other saints. Other *Doctrina* images also featuring the devil followed (DR09, EN42, MA132, MA270, PA141).

The sequence of large florentine altarpieces featuring the *Doctrina* theme continued. A few years later, in *c.* 1489–1490, the Nasi brothers, one of them called Bernardo, commissioned Pietro Perugino (*c.* 1450–1523) to paint the *Vision of Bernard* (PA151) for their family chapel in the cistercian Cestello. In 1507 the Dominican Fra Bartolommeo (1472–1517) completed an altarpiece for Bernardo del Bianco, the nephew of Filippino Lippi's patron Pugliese, for the family chapel in the Badia of Florence (PA026). The contract had called for a standing Virgin and Child with Saints Bernard, Francis, Benedict, and Barnabas in the form

[51] *De laudibus Virginis Matris, Homilia* 2; SBOp 4:34: *Loquamur pauca et super hoc nomine, quod interpretatum 'Maris stella' dicitur, et Matri Virgini valde convenienter aptatur. Ipsa namque aptissime sideri comparatur, quia sicut sine sui corruptione sidus suum emittit radium, sic apsque sui laesione Virgo parturit Filium. Nec sideri radius suam minuit claritatem, nec Virgini Filius suam integritatem. Ipsa ergo est nobilis illa stella ex Iacob orta, cuius radius universum orbem illuminat, cuius splendor et praefulget in supernis, et inferos penetrat, terras etaiam perlustrans, et, calefaciens magis mentes quam corpora, fovet virtutes, excoquit vitia.*

of a *Sacra Converzatione,* but what the artist instead produced was a *Vision of Bernard.* This explains the unusual presence of the other saints and the fact that the Virgin is carrying the Child, whereas she appears on her own in almost all other *Doctrina* images.[52] Bernard is kneeling at a desk with an open book before him, as in a number of earlier versions. Another open book is held up for him by an angel. Some years later, in *c.* 1520, one of Fra Bartolommeo's pupils, Domenico Puligo (1492–1527), painted yet another large *Vision* altarpiece (PA086). The Virgin, accompanied by two angels, appears to Bernard, seated at a desk, in a painting which is reminiscent more of Perugino and Filippino Lippi than of Fra Bartolommeo, although much simpler both in its composition and setting than that of Filippino Lippi.

The *Dottrina* continued to flourish as a florentine image until and beyond the end of the Middle Ages. A sixteenth-century woodcut used as the title page of Bernard's *Psalterium beate Marie virginis* (EN42) contains most of the elements which had become associated with the theme: a nimbed Bernard sitting at a desk writing, a smaller Virgin appearing in the sky on a cloud from which rays are emanating, a mountainous landscape, and a small demon lurking behind Bernard's stool.

CONCLUSION

Bernard's memory was kept alive in Florence and throughout Italy by a combination of factors: the official civic cult of the Florentine Republic, Dante's immortalization of his status as a holy man, and the presence in and around the city of monks of his Order. His reputation rested primarily on his devotion to Mary, which found its visual expression in the illustrations to the *Commedia Divina,* in altarpieces, and in woodcuts portraying his veneration for the Virgin, especially those illustrating the peculiarly italian legendary theme of the *Doctrina.* Like the *Lactatio,* the *Doctrina* grew out of the rapid increase of devotion to the Virgin Mary in the second half of the twelfth century, that is, shortly after Bernard's death. This mounting devotion spawned an iconography which incorporated Bernard's

[52] The few exceptions include the Sforza Book of Hours (MA132), a late fifteenth-century florentine manuscript of sermons (MA270), and the early sixteenth-century painting mentioned earlier which may also be classed as a *Lactatio* scene (PA140).

marian doctrine, real or imagined. His real contribution to the rise in the cult of Mary has been debated. A study of the relationship between Bernard and Dante has noted that marian themes form no more than 3.5% of the whole corpus of his works and that outside his specifically marian texts there are no more than a score of references to Mary.[53] The suggestion follows that the accretions of subsequent generations made up the Bernard of legend, who was the figure Dante chose to accompany him on the final stage of his journey heavenward. Bernard's reputation rests in part on the large number of works, among them marian texts which, up until modern times, have been wrongly attributed to him.

The iconography of Bernard in *trecento* and *quattrocento* florentine art is remarkable for the extent to which the artists relied on literary texts to convey their message. Bernard's role as a teacher (*dottore*) was celebrated in the inscription under the predella scene of Giovanni da Milano's altarpiece and gave the name *Doctrina* to what became a popular theme. The passage from Arnold of Bonneval's *De Laudibus B. Mariae Virginis*, erroneously attributed to Bernard, came to be used in a number of intercessional images associated with the *Lactation* (e.g. MA117, MA133, PA138), and deeply influenced Dante. In the mistaken belief that Bernard had written it, the Master of the Renuccini Chapel incorporated a quotation from the Cistercian Ogier of Locedio to convey the Virgin's grief at the time of the Passion (PA155). The same pseudo-bernardine text was used again in the predella roundel by Jacopo di Cione (PA030). While Filippino Lippi chose to represent in his famous Badia painting (PA136) the authentic and most celebrated of all Bernard's marian texts—the opening works of his sermons *In laudibus Virginis matris*—, the text he used in the book displayed by Bernard in his other altarpiece featuring the saint (PA148) is generally thought to be a paraphrase of a pseudo-Bernard hymn. The artists' choice of such disparate texts, both genuine and wrongly attributed to Bernard, as well as the great variety of sources which led to Dante's choice of Bernard as his final guide, highlight the great variety of ways in which the memory of Bernard was used and shaped and adapted by regional influences in various parts of Europe.

[53] Botterill 1994, 166.

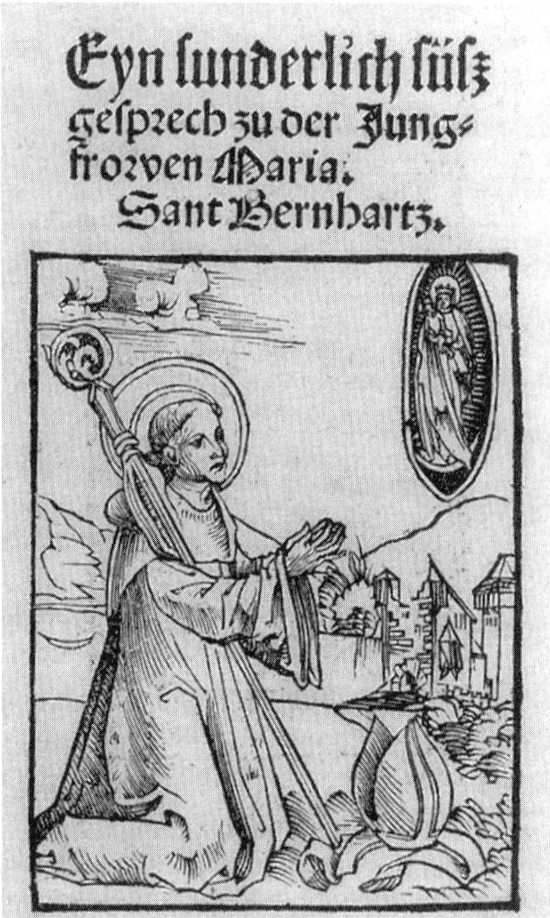

Figure 16: Title page of a pseudo-Bernard text printed in Basel *c.* 1506–1507 (EN45).

TEN

IMAGES OF BERNARD AS A DEVOTEE OF MARY

ANOTHER THEME resembles the two main marian picture-types just discussed but nevertheless represents a minor variant. As in the *Lactatio* and *Doctrina* images, so here Bernard is depicted on his knees before a vision of the Virgin in the sky; but the Virgin is not baring her breast, so it is not a *Lactatio* image, nor is Bernard sitting at a desk writing, so it is not a *Doctrina* scene, and there is no hint of the transmission of either physical or intellectual nourishment. Only eighteen examples of this picture-type have been recorded, and only two of these are found in illuminated manuscripts. The rest are woodcut illustrations, and therefore late medieval.

MANUSCRIPT IMAGES

One of the two manuscript images is featured in a Calendar with saints from a franciscan breviary, possibly from Milan, dated to the early fifteenth century. The image (MA184) is within the rosa initial *P(erfice quesumus domine . . .)* on a gold square ground with pointed corners, the beginning of the prayer to Bernard from the Office of his feast. A bearded and nimbed Bernard with a gold halo and wearing a white cowl kneels before the Virgin, whose half-figure in a blue dress, nimbed and surrounded by gold rays, appears in the sky. She raises her hand in blessing Bernard. The other (MA324) is found in an early sixteenth-century spanish missal produced approximately a century later in Toledo. The half-figure of Bernard, nimbed, his hands clasped in prayer and his crozier leaning on his right shoulder, looks up at Mary, whose tiny half-figure, this time carrying the naked Child, is suspended in the sky, again encircled by golden rays. Bernard stands in front of a low grey wall with a landscape of trees beyond. Next to the image is the decorated gold initial *I(n medio ecclesie)* on a red ground, marking the Introit of the Mass for Bernard's feast. Neither of these images have the characteristics associated with the *Lactatio* or the *Dottrina*.

WOODCUT IMAGES OF BERNARD'S VISION OF MARY

The sixteen known woodcuts, mostly from the 1480s and 1490s, are from southern Germany and are all, with one exception, used to illustrate the section on Bernard in german translations of the *Legenda Aurea*. The sole exception to the *Legenda Aurea* is a woodcut (EN45) which decorates the title page of a pseudo-Bernard work entitled *Eyn sunderlich suess gesprech zu der jungfrowen Maria* ('A wonderfully sweet talk with the Virgin Mary'). ► *Fig. 16* (EN45). This typically late medieval devotional tract is included in an anthology which also includes works by Bonaventure and Augustine, all translated into German by Ludwig Moser and printed in Basel by Michael Furter *c.* 1506–1507. Bernard is kneeling in prayer with his crozier under his right arm and a mitre at his feet before a vision of the tiny figure of the Virgin within a mandorla in the sky. The setting is a hilly landscape with buildings in the background.

The first known woodcut to adorn the section on Bernard in the *Golden Legend* (EN53) appeared as one of one hundred twenty-seven illustrations in a german version printed in Augsburg on 27 April 1472 by Guenther Zainer. A virtually identical design (EN54) appeared as one of one hundred twenty-four illustrations printed 12 August 1475, and again 4 October 1480, by Johann Baemler, also in Augsburg. In a crude outline without any shading or other detailing, a bearded and nimbed Bernard kneels before a smaller half-figure of the Virgin and Child on a crescent in the sky. The ground on which Bernard kneels is shown but there is otherwise no other indication of siting. Some of the later examples (EN55, EN59, EN60) are set in a landscape, usually with a building behind Bernard to suggest Clairvaux, and in some (EN52, EN56, EN58, EN62) Bernard is carrying a crozier and the arms of Clairvaux are at his feet. Six of the sixteen known *Legenda Aurea* woodcuts come from Augsburg. The last of these is far more accomplished than the earlier ones and the only one in which the artist is not anonymous. It is one of one hundred seventy-one illustrations by Hans Schaefelein published in an edition printed in two volumes by Johann Ottmar in 1513 (EN32). The image of the Virgin and Child in the heavens, surrounded by rays, appears to a nimbed Bernard kneeling with his hands clasped in prayer with a crozier leaning on his right shoulder. Behind him, set in a rocky landscape, is a church building, and the arms of Clairvaux are at his feet.

James of Voragine refers to Mary on only two occasions in connection with Bernard, both of which have featured in bernardine iconography. As the woodcuts are overwhelmingly used to denote the chapter on Bernard in the *Legenda Aurea,* one might expect the choice of subject to be dictated by one of the stories in the text.

Marian Visions in the Golden Legend

The first marian story *The Golden Legend* relates Bernard's vision of the Nativity as a child.[1] When all were getting ready on Christmas night for solemn Vigils Bernard fell asleep and in a dream saw the Infant Jesus revealing his Nativity. The experience inspired him to write in praise of the Mother and Child a passage which draws on the Annunciation passage in Saint Luke 'The angel was sent . . .'.[2] This story forms one of eight scenes (MA246) from Bernard's life in the Hungarian Legendary illustrated by Nicolas of Bologna between 1330–1340. In the top left Bernard is incorrectly depicted in a grey cowl as he was not yet a monk at the time of the vision. Below him are Mary and a bearded

[1] VP 1:2:4; PL 185:229.
[2] Lk 1:20.

Joseph while the cross-nimbed Child lies in a crib in front of Bernard. A donkey and a cow look into the crib and Bernard is blessed by the hand of God who appears from a cloud. The inscription reads: *Bernardus. Quomodo Christus manifestavit illi horam nativitatis sue* (Bernard. How Christ showed him the hour of his birth'). One of the early sixteenth-century glass panels from the cloister of the nuns' abbey of Saint Apern sets the scene in Bernard's parents' house (GL58). On the left Bernard's mother, Aleth, sits with a rosary in her hands. A young Bernard, this time correctly depicted in secular clothes, is sitting next to her, asleep. Bernard's halo is not the conventional round disc but a more restrained band of yellow surrounding his head. In front of him is an altar and in the background there are two men in a doorway. Above Bernard's head is a medallion which now contains a coat of arms but which would formerly have contained a Nativity scene, the subject of his dream, as we see in the corresponding scene from the Altenberg cloister (GL03).

The second marian motif in the *Golden Legend* is that of Bernard's vision during a serious illness.[3] When in great pain he ordered one of the monks looking after him to go into the church to pray. The monk went to each of the three altars, the main one honouring Mary, and those on either side dedicated to Lawrence and Benedict respectively. All three saints appeared to Bernard and laid their hands on him, and as a result the pain went away. The event is featured in one of the eight scenes depicting the lives of saints on an altarpiece painted in 1432 for a side chapel at the cistercian abbey of Maulbronn (PA059). Mary is shown on the left, sitting beside Bernard, who is lying on his sickbed. Behind him is Lawrence in a dalmatic—his usual attribute as a deacon—and Benedict in his black cowl, carrying a crozier. In the background is the small figure of the monk Bernard had sent to pray for him. He is wearing the cistercian white tunic and black scapular and kneeling before an altar. The same scene is depicted in a glass panel from the Altenberg cloister (GL19). In this version the three saints—Mary, Lawrence, and Benedict—are touching Bernard, and the monk who was sent into the church again appears in the background.

A florentine altarpiece of the same date also includes, as one of the six scenes from the life of Bernard, an illustration (PA117) of Bernard

[3] VP 1:12:58; PL 185:258-259.

lying on his sickbed comforted by Mary, who stands behind the bed and holds his left hand. The scene is witnessed by two monks in the background. Although Mary is not accompanied by Lawrence and Benedict and there are two monks instead of only one, the scene nevertheless likely refers to the same *Legenda Aurea* story. One of the wall paintings (WA47) from Owen in Württemberg, from which both Lawrence and Benedict are also absent, may likewise represent this story.

Neither of these two marian experiences in the *Golden Legend* seems sufficiently close to the *Vision of Bernard* woodcut image (e.g. EN53, EN54, EN45) of Bernard kneeling before the figure of the Virgin in the sky to have been its source. The choice of this image to decorate the opening of the chapter on Bernard in various editions of the *Golden Legend* therefore seems both strange and inappropriate. More fitting would have been narrative images depicting one of the episodes from his life described in the text by James of Voragine. A number of these stories, drawn from the *Vita Prima,* had been chosen by artists of earlier illuminated manuscripts to decorate the opening of the *Golden Legend* chapter on Bernard: his entry to Cîteaux (MA088), his preaching to his monks (MA161), and his dictating a letter in the rain (MA142). Yet other artists chose to identify Bernard by using the equally irrelevant and unsuitable motifs of the *Amplexus* (MA053) and of Bernard trampling on the devil (MA154), even though neither of these themes appear in James of Voragine's text. Their choices were dictated by what they apparently considered the best known attributes whereby Bernard would be readily recognized. By the end of the Middle Ages Bernard had become so closely associated with Mary that portraying him in her company had come to seem the surest means of identifying him.

THE DICHOTOMY BETWEEN MARY IN BERNARD'S LITERARY WORKS AND IN HIS ICONOGRAPHY

Mary's central and dominant role in the iconography of Bernard is in total contrast to the proportionately minor place of marian themes in Bernard's total literary output—which was very considerable. She appears in virtually a third of the total of nine hundred sixty recorded bernardine images—about two-thirds of them *Lactatio* and *Dottrina* images, while only a small part of the total corpus of his works, some sixty columns out of a total of 2200 in the *Patrologia Latina* edition, are dedicated to her.[4]

Of the approximately fifty testimonies to Bernard's influence and fame collected by Jean Mabillon, only two refer to his marian devotion.[5] Jean Leclercq noted the relatively small part Mariology played in Bernard's teaching in comparison, for example, to his Ecclesiology and his Christology.[6] Bernard's explicitly marian texts are limited to four sermons on the Annunciation (*Super missus est*)—which he himself titled *In laudibus Virginis Matris* (In Praise of the Virgin Mother); his sermons on the feasts of the Virgin (some of which have no Marian content); a few references in the sermons *De diversis;* and his famous letter to the Canons of Lyon. In Bernard's best-known work, the *Sermons on the Song of Songs,* on which he worked for over twenty years, Mary is mentioned only in passing some twenty times.[7] As we saw above, Mary appears in only two stories in the *Vita Prima,* both of which found their way into the *Legenda Aurea,* and she does not feature in any of the twenty chapters on Bernard in the *Exordium Magnum.*

BERNARD AND THE IMMACULATE CONCEPTION

Of all Bernard's writings his celebrated Letter 174 to the Canons of Lyon is the most controversial. For centuries it remained part of a heated debate which was resolved for Roman Catholics only in 1854, when the Immaculate Conception was pronounced a dogma of the Church by Pius IX in the Bull *Ineffabilis Deus.* The feast of the Conception of Mary had long been celebrated in the East, and in England it was observed in the eleventh century in some of the southern benedictine cathedral monasteries. From there it moved across the Channel to Normandy, and around 1136 it was adopted by the church of Lyon.[8] In 1139 Bernard

[4] Barré 1953, 96.

[5] PL 185:627-640.

[6] Leclercq 1954, 362: *La mariologie n'occupe point une grande place dans la doctrine de S. Bernard, en comparaison, par example, de son ecclésiologie et sa christologie.*

[7] Barré 1953, 97.

[8] Ep 174; SBOp 7:388-392; trans. James 1953, 289–293. On Bernard and the controversy, see Elder 2003, 423–448, Dessi & Lamy 1993, 229–251, and Luddy 1950, 695–713.

wrote to the Canons of Lyon, expressing surprise that the church 'well known to be pre-eminent for its dignity, sound learning, and praiseworthy customs' should have introduced a new feast, 'a rite of which the Church knows nothing, of which reason cannot approve, and for which there is no authority in tradition'.[9]

That the only known historiated initial in a manuscript of Bernard's Letters, other than those introducing Letter One and the collection as a whole, indicates the importance of this letter. The initial is found in a late thirteenth-century french manuscript (MA186), decorating the opening of Letter 174. The subject of the letter is given in red ink: *Ad canonicos Lugdunenses de conceptione sancte Marie* ('To the Canons of Lyon on the Conception of Saint Mary'). Bernard is depicted in a white cowl within the initial *I(nter ecclesias . . .)*, the opening of the letter: 'Among all the churches of France the church of Lyon is well known . . .'. He stands under a trilobe arch with his right hand raised and his index finger points in admonishment at the two tonsured figures representing the canons.

In opposing the introduction of the feast Bernard argued that Mary needed no more honours added to her, that the marian feasts already celebrated were sufficient, and, above all, that no change should be made without first seeking the authority of the Holy See, a course preferable to following the 'simplicity of the uneducated'.[10] Both here and elsewhere he maintained that Rome must be the arbiter in matters of faith and liturgical practice. His motivation has been described as virtually political.[11] For him the unity of the Church, challenged from within by the menace of schism and heresy—as he knew from his own experience—, was of paramount importance, not least in view of the threat posed by the infidel from without. The theological niceties of the argument seem to have been largely a matter of semantics, but the controversy continued with Saint Thomas Aquinas and the Dominicans taking Bernard's side in opposing the doctrine, and with the Franciscans ranged

[9] Ep 174:1; SBOp 7:388; trans. James 1953, 289–290: *quam ritus Ecclesiae nescit, non probat ratio, non commendat antiqua traditio.*

[10] Ep 174:9; SBOp 7:392; trans. James 1953, 293: *simplicitas paucorum imperitorum . . . .*

[11] Dessi & Lami 1993, 233: *'il ne faudrait pas ignorer les motivations presque 'politiques' qui ont amené Bernard à prendre position'.*

against them in its support; the opposing sides came to be referred to as 'maculists and immaculists'.[12]

The polemics surrounding the issue gave rise to a story, the purpose of which was to besmirch Bernard's reputation for opposing the feast. In a letter to Peter of Celle, abbot of Saint Remi in Reims, Nicolas, the prior of the benedictine abbey of Saint Albans in England, defended the celebration of the feast at his abbey by relating that 'at the convent of Clairvaux there was a devout lay brother who in a vision at night saw Abbot Bernard clad in a habit white as snow but with a dark stain on his chest',[13] a mark of his opposition to the feast. Bernard explained that the stain was the result of his having written about the Conception in a way he should not have done: 'The brother reported the vision to the community and one of the monks took it down in writing and it was related at the Cistercian General Chapter'. Although the authenticity of the letter from Nicolas of Saint Albans is uncertain, the legend lived on in a number of versions and was widely used by William of Ware and Duns Scotus among others in defence of the doctrine. The stain on the chest has been seen as a kind of 'inversion' of the most popular of all bernardine motifs, the *Lactatio*.[14]

Although Sixtus IV approved the liturgical office in honour of the Immaculate Conception in 1476 and again in 1482, while at the same time granting freedom to those who opposed it, the controversy continued. Bernard's reputation as a devotee of Mary had by then grown to such an extent that his name, which had hitherto been associated with his famous Letter 174 opposing the feast, was by a strange irony now used in support of the Immaculist cause. It has been suggested that this may be due to Bernard's equally strong identification with the Song of Songs; the quotation from it, 'Thou are all beautiful, my love, and there is no spot in thee' (Sg 4.7: *Tota pulchra es, amica mea, et macula non est in te*) became identified with the Immaculate Conception of Mary, even though it occurs at a point beyond where Bernard got to in

[12] In Elder 2003, 424.

[13] PL 202:623-624: *In Clarevallensi collegio quidam bene religiosus in visu noctis vidit abbatem Bernardum niveis indutum vestibus, quasi ad mamillam pectoris furvam habere maculam. . . . Frater visa conventui innotuit, et aliquis fratrum in scriptum redegit. Relatum est in generali Cisterciensi capitulo.*

[14] For this and the arguments challenging the origin of the legend, see Dessi & Lamy 1993, 248–251.

his sermons.[15] In Sermon 45 Bernard does comment on the phrase from earlier in the Song, 'Thou art beautiful' (Sg 1.14: *tu pulchra est*), but without referring to a 'spot' (*macula*). The assumption that Bernard was referring to Mary as the 'beautiful one' ignores that it is, in fact, quite clear that he was referring to the relationship between the soul and Christ. As time passed Bernard was used by the protagonists of the feast in what may be described as a case of collective amnesia, a common enough occurrence in medieval polemics.

In *quattrocento* Tuscany the doctrine of the Immaculate Conception was seized on by protagonists who commissioned works affirming it. The church of Saint Francis in Lucca, for example, had a painting in which the Virgin was depicted free from original sin, in the figure of Esther before King Ahasuerus.[16] According to the Book of Esther[17] Esther pleaded with the king to spare her jewish co-religionists. As she approached him the guards seized her, but Ahasuerus intervened and saved her. With his sceptre he said 'This law was made for all human beings but not for you' (*Non enim pro te, sed pro omnibus haec lex consituta est*). As Esther had been exempted from human law, so Mary was exempted from the divine law that applied to all others; and as Esther had pleaded for her people, Mary intercedes for all humankind. The upper 'heavenly' part of the painting shows God the Father with the sceptre and Mary kneeling, while below, in the 'earthly' part, prophets and saints hold scrolls with texts of marian devotion. In Florence so great was the prestige of Bernard, both as a civic patron saint and on account of the reputation as a devotee of Mary given him by Dante,[18] that his opposition to the feast had been forgotten and he was cited by the adherents in support of their cause. In *c.* 1510 the Franciscans in Fiesole commissioned a painting of the Immaculate Conception from Piero di Cosimo (PA152). Its composition was almost identical to that at Lucca, with the minor modification that various saints, Bernard among them, replaced the Old Testament figures.[19] Below the 'heavenly' scene, the most prominent figures are Saint Francis and Saint Jerome

[15] The theory is advanced in d'Ancona 1957, 8–9.

[16] For this, see d'Ancona 1957, 30. The painting in the Pinacoteca, Lucca, by a Follower of Ghirlandaio, is illustrated in d'Ancona, ill. 14.

[17] Esther 5:12-16.

[18] See Chapter Nine.

[19] See Florence 1990, 69.

kneeling on a raised platform in the centre. They are flanked by, on the left, Saint Augustine and Bernard and, on the right, Saint Thomas Aquinas and Saint Anselm. Saint Augustine is writing on a tablet while the other saints are holding tablets or scrolls containing texts affirming the sinlessness of Mary. The inclusion of these saints with texts from their works suggested that the doctrine had been defended for centuries by all the Fathers of the Church.

BERNARD—*CYTHARISTA MARIAE*

As we have already mentioned, Bernard in fact spoke relatively little about Mary. Scholars agree that he was a traditionalist in his marian doctrine and was not an innovator,[20] and yet it is often claimed that Mary occupies a privileged position in his work.[21] How do we explain this paradox? As Jean Leclercq has pointed out, Bernard was less concerned with intellectual speculation on the mystery of Mary's place in salvation history than he was with her cult. He admired her humility and praised her obedience—hence the title *In Praise of the Virgin Mother (In laudibus Virginis Matris)* he himself provided in the preface to the sermons *Super missus est*.[22] Bernard's view of Mary was dictated more by the heart than by the head, in keeping with his famous recommendation in his letter to Aelred of Rievaulx that he

> be able to strike something out of those rocks that you have not got by your own wits from the bookshelves of the schoolmen, and that you will have experienced sometimes under the shade of a tree during the heats of midday what you would never have learned in the schools.[23]

[20] The point is made both in Leclercq 1954, and Barré 1953.

[21] For example, Pranger 1989, 120: 'It is a well-known fact that the Virgin Mary occupies a privileged position in Bernard's work'.

[22] *In Laudibus Virginis Matris, Praefatio;* SBOp 4:13.

[23] Ep 523; SBOp 8:487; trans. James 1953, 247: *Unde arbitror quod malleo illo tuo aliquid tibi de rupibus illis excuderis, quod sagitate ingenii de magistorum scriniis non tulisses, et nonnumquam tale aliquid in meridiano fervore, sub umbris arborum senseris quale numquam didicisses in scholis.*

In much the same way Bernard had advised his friend Henry Murdac, abbot of Fountains and later archbishop of York, that 'woods and stones will teach you what you can never hear from any master'.[24] Considering the power of Bernard's eloquence, which earned him the title *Doctor mellifluous*—the teacher whose words flow like sweet honey—and the intensity of his devotion, one can begin to understand Dante's portrayal of him as Mary's *fedel Bernardo*.[25] The fervour of his feelings is revealed even in his celebrated Letter 174, which, while written to oppose the celebration of the feast of the Immaculate Conception, contains all Bernard's marian doctrine:

> Let us honour her for the purity of her body, the holiness of her life. Let us marvel at her fruitful virginity, and venerate her divine Son. Let us extol her freedom from concupiscence in conceiving, and from all pain in bearing. Let us proclaim her to be reverenced by the angels, desired by the nations, foretold by the patriarchs and prophets, chosen out of all and preferred by all. Let us magnify her as the channel of grace, the mediatrix of salvation, the restorer of the ages, and as exalted above the choirs of angels to the very heights of heaven. All this the Church sings in her praise and teaches me too to sing.[26]

Bernard celebrated Mary as mediatrix by the masterful metaphor of the aquaduct. She is the channel through which grace flows like water from the mountains, a vital conduit but not its source. He used this image in his sermon *In nativitate Virginis* (The Nativity of the Virgin) and gave it the title by which it is better known: *De aquaductu*.[27] As the bridge between heaven and earth, between God and man, Mary played

[24] Ep 106, SBOp 7:266-267; trans. James 1953, 156: *Ligna et lapides docebunt te, quod a magistris audire non possis.*

[25] *Paradiso* 31:102.

[26] Ep 174, SBOp 7:388-9; trans. James 1953, 290: *Honora sane integritatem carnis, vitae sanctitatem; mirare fecunditatem in Virgine, Prolem venerare divinam. Extolle nescientem vel in concipiendo concupiscentiam, vel in pariendo dolorem. Praedica reverendam angelis, desideratum gentibus, patrarchis prophetisque praecognitam, electam ex omnibus, praelatam omnibus. Magnifica gratiae invectricem, mediatricem salutis, restauratricem saeculorum; exalta denique exaltatam super choros angelorum ad caelestia regna. Haec mihi de illa cantat Ecclesia et me eadem docuit decantare.*

[27] SBOp 5:275-299.

an essential but, nevertheless, secondary role in the economy of salvation. The motif of Mary's intercessional role was frequently illustrated and was sometimes merged with *Lactation* images (see, for example, MA117, MA133, & PA138).

Bernard's eloquence and the intensity of feeling of his marian writings led Jean Leclercq to write: 'by his pen, this theme becomes inspired music',[28] the sweetness of its sound earned him the title *Cytharista Mariae*.[29] Bernard's marian works were widely copied and inspired a number of writers even outside the Cistercian Order, among them Arnold of Bonneval, Peter of Celle, Ekbert of Schönau, and Philip of Harvengt.[30] We have already mentioned a text in Arnold of Bonneval's *De laudibus B. Mariae Virginis* which was later wrongly attributed to Bernard and used in marian intercession images (e.g. MA117 & PA138).[31] Testimonials to his marian devotion were showered on him. Even during Bernard's lifetime he was credited with advancing the cult of Mary in a way unwarranted by historical fact. Peter of Celle, referring to Bernard as 'Our Lady's most intimate pupil', mistakenly attributed to Bernard the initiative of dedicating all the churches of the Order to her.[32] One of his biographers noted that he was buried before the altar of the Virgin 'whose most devoted priest he was'.[33] Before long, exaggerations, modifications, and apocryphal stories emerged. A generation or so after his death the author of the *Vita Quarta,* John the Hermit, mistakenly claimed that Bernard had been responsible for the introduction of the marian hymn *Salve Regina* throughout the Church:

> Walking as it were at the right hand of the glorious Virgin the holy man approached the altar where he heard the voice of an angel singing the *Salve Regina* from beginning to end. He remembered it by heart and later wrote it down and sent it to the Lord Pope Eugenius. By command of his apostolic authority

[28] Leclercq 1954, 368: *Sous sa plume, ce thème devient une musique inspirée.*

[29] The title may derive from the reference to *Mariae cithara* in the hymn *Bernardus inclitis*. See above, Chapter 5.

[30] Barré 1953, 92.

[31] PL 189:1726.

[32] PL 185:630: *Alumnus familiarissimus fuit Dominae nostrae, cui non unum tantum basilicam, sed totius ordinis Cisterciensis basilicas dedicavit.*

[33] VP 5:2:15;PL 185:360: . . . *cuius fuerat devotissimus ipse sacerdos.*

> it was to be solemnly sung throughout all the churches in honour of the blessed and glorious Virgin Mother of God Mary. This came about so that many witnessed it.[34]

Later still the real Bernard became hidden by the reputation which rests both on unauthentic works and on legends which bear little resemblance to historic fact. As both the quantity and the content of the images depicting him in the presence of Mary indicate, this is nowhere more true than in his iconography. Although he may be widely regarded as the quintessential *Docteur Marial*, Jean Leclercq has pointed to the role played by iconography and the invention of printing in creating a false image of Bernard.[35] Bernard's reputation as a devotee of Mary has more to do with the late medieval surge in the cult of Mary than it has with Bernard himself. As devotion to Mary flourished, Bernard was co-opted into playing a leading role in her cult.

[34] *Vita Quarta* 2:7; PL 185:544: *Horum altero eum deducente, Vir sanctus quasi a dextris gloriosae virginis incedens, ad altare usque pervenit; ubi voce angelica audivit decantari antiphonum, 'Salve Regina', ex integro usque ad finem. Quam corde tenus retinens, et postea scripsisse, atque Domino papae Eugenio transmisisse refertur, ut ex praecepto auctoritatis apostolicae per ecclesias solemnis haberetur, in honore beatae et gloriosae virginis Dei genetricis Mariae: quod et factum est, ut adhuc plerique testatur.*

[35] Leclercq 1954, 374.

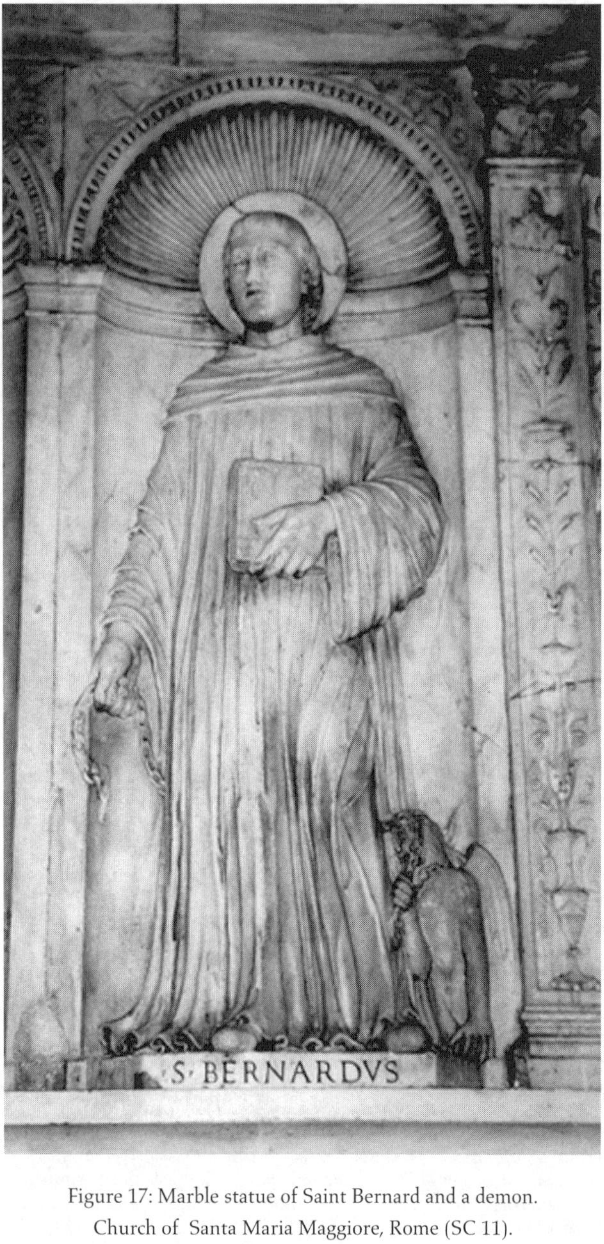

Figure 17: Marble statue of Saint Bernard and a demon.
Church of Santa Maria Maggiore, Rome (SC 11).

ELEVEN

BERNARD AND THE DEVIL

DEMONS WERE ALL-PERVASIVE in medieval society. They were held responsible for misfortunes of every sort—natural disasters, failing health, accidents, and all kinds of adversity. Monks, intent on waging spiritual warfare, were thought to be particularly at risk. According to Conrad of Eberbach, when Saint Bernard was told of how demons had afflicted a dying lay brother, he said: 'The evil directed at all Christians by demons is very great, but greater still is that which they aim at those who have made their monastic profession'.[1] The more sacred the place, the greater the risk of their attack. Cistercian literature abounds in anecdotes of their exploits: Caesarius of Heisterbach records how monks in choir, and especially during the night office, were particularly at risk. He devotes the whole of Book 5 of his *Dialogue on Miracles*—altogether fifty-six chapters—to demons. The title of the very first chapter is 'Of demons, their numbers, their malice and their hostility to man'.[2] One of his stories refers to 'hideous dogs [who] went in such a way that the

[1] EM 2:2; Griesser 1961, 99: *Multam esse malitiam daemonum erga omnes christianos, tamen praecipue contra monasticae religionis professores affirmans.*

[2] *Dialogue* 5:1-56; Caesarius of Heisterbach 1929, 1:313-390.

chains which could be seen round their necks passed round the necks of the monks also'.[3] In the *Exordium Magnum* the devil is time and again held responsible for the misfortunes of monks and lay brothers. One of Bernard's monks who doubted the real presence of Christ in the Eucharist is said to have been 'misled by the cunning of the devil',[4] and the evil spirits saw to it that a lay brother of Esrum in Denmark, who had fathered a son, lost his power of speech so that he was unable to confess his sin. By the intercession of Bernard and other saints interred at Clairvaux, however, he regained his voice and exclaimed: 'Lord, I believe that even if I found myself engulfed in the depths of hell, your mercy would have the power to deliver me'.[5] Conrad of Eberbach in another chapter refers to how Bernard, in his Sermon 48 on the Song of Songs, had exhorted his monks to apply themselves to the divine praises with great devotion 'not only to obtain the grace of Our Lord and Creator, but also to avoid the deceptive traps of the evil spirits'.[6]

The concentration of demonic activity around a cistercian monastery features in a story in an *exemplum* collection from Beaupré: a novice was sent home to try to overcome his father's opposition to him becoming a monk.[7] When he arrives he finds two devils sitting on the top of the local church. He takes fright and decides to return to his monastery, but when he gets there he finds to his horror that it is surrounded by a swarm of devils. He therefore decides to return home again. When the abbot subsequently comes to visit him, he explains that all the troops of devils were needed to besiege such a powerful fortress. The novice's mind is set at rest and he again returns to the monastery.

Although none of these episodes recorded in the twelfth-century cistercian sources found their way into early bernardine iconography, a number of confrontations of monks with the devil were depicted in medieval art. In a french chronicle a monk is shown wielding a large

[3] *Dialogue* 2:50; Caesarius of Heisterbach 1929, 1:384.

[4] EM 2:6; Griesser 1961, 102: *per fallacias daemonum. . . .*

[5] EM 2:31; Griesser 1961, 138–140: *Credo, Domine, quia, si etiam in profundum inferni demersus fuero, inde me potens est misericordia tua liberare.*

[6] EM 5:19 (Griesser 1961, 333): *Porro quam timoratos, quam alacres quamque sollicitos nos in exsequendis divinis laudibus esse oporteat, non solum ut Domini et creatoris nostri gratiam consequamur, verum etiam ut malignorum spirituum inextricabiles fallacias evadere valeamus, isdem venerabilis pater in sermone super Cantica canticorum quadragesimo octavo docet ita dicens.*

[7] McGuire 1983, 253.

sword before a horned demon of equal size.[8] A carved capital from the pomeranian abbey of Kolbacz dated *c.* 1330–1340 has a devil attacking a monk during Mass by tugging at his hood, and in a manuscript from the english abbey Dore, a winged devil with long pointed ears catches hold of a monk's hood from behind using a long rod with a hook.[9]

BERNARD'S ENCOUNTERS WITH THE DEVIL IN THE CISTERCIAN TRADITION

That the saintly abbot of Clairvaux should have been at still greater risk of demonic onslaughts than anyone else, that a number of his encounters with demons are recorded in his *vitae,* and that these gave rise later to one of the most widespread themes associated with his iconography comes as no surprise.

One of the three diabolic onslaughts on his chastity recorded in the *Vita Prima* has Bernard being tempted by the devil—that of the naked girl who invaded his bed but whose advances Bernard managed to withstand. This is described as having been 'at the instigation of the demon'.[10] In another Bernard challenges the devil and defeats him: 'leaving the enemy completely confounded, he left the gathering and the man of God came to himself'.[11]

Thanks largely to their incorporation by James of Voragine in his *Golden Legend* many of the original cistercian stories were not forgotten and made a much later appearance in the iconography of Bernard. Among the pictorial scenes is one (CL62) of Bernard on his sickbed surrounded by the community and attended by William of Saint Thierry on whose account in the *Vita Prima* the image is based. That is followed by Bernard's vision of appearing before the tribunal of the Lord. Satan was also there. After he had pressed his accusations, Bernard had his say:

[8] Paris, Bibliothèque nationale MS fr. 2813, fol. 329r, illustrated on the dust-cover of the french translation of the *Exordium Magnum, Le Grande Exorde de Cîteaux,* ed. J. Berlioz, Turnhout, 1998.

[9] Illustrated in France 1998, 216 and 217.

[10] VP 1:3:7; PL 185:230: *circa idem tempus instinctu daemonis in lectum dormientis injecta est puella nuda. . . .*

[11] VP 1:12:57; PL 185:258: *In hoc verbo confusus inimicus, conventus ille solutus, et Homo Dei in se reversus est.*

> I admit that I am not myself worthy; nor can I, by any merit of my own, lay claim to the kingdom of heaven. But I have gained heaven by a double right, by inheritance from the Father and by the merit of his passion, of which he is content with the one and gives me the other.[12]

Here, as in a nutshell, is the kernel of Bernard's unswerving faith in the power of Christ's passion, the very essence of the christian faith. His concern here is primarily with his duty as abbot in securing the salvation of his monks, but it is equally apposite as regards the redemption of all Christians. The message of the vision was considered of sufficient importance to be included in several later texts—for example, in a greatly expanded version in the *Liber Visionum et Miraculorum* by Prior John of Clairvaux,[13] and also in James of Voragine's *Golden Legend*.[14] Bernard's vision is depicted in one of the 1525 glass panels from Saint Apern in Cologne, now in Cologne Cathedral (GL63). A rare representation of the Trinity in the form of three human figures is flanked by Bernard kneeling on the left and the grey bearded figure of the devil on the right, making his claim to Bernard. An equivalent panel in the Altenberg cloister is now lost.[15]

The devil came in many guises. John the Hermit in the *Vita Quarta* chose to portray him as a black monk, alluding to the rivalry between the black and white monks immortalized in the best known of all of Bernard's treatises, the *Apologia,* and in later works like the *Exordium Magnum*. According to John, the devil said to Bernard:

> Father, what are you doing? I have come from a distant land to see you, and here you are polishing your boots. You should not be doing this, but you should let your servants and ministers do it for you'. The man of God replied: 'I haven't got any servants, and I do not want ever to have any. I have sons whom

[12] VP 1:12:57; PL 185:258: *Fateor, non sum dignus ego, nec propriis possum meritis regnum obtinere caelorum. Caeterum duplici jure illud obtinens Dominus meus, haereditate scilicet Patris, et merito passionis, altero ipse contentus, alterum mihi donat, ea cujus dono jure illud mihi vindicans, non confundur.*

[13] For this, see McGuire 1991, 161–163.

[14] LA 214.

[15] Paffrath 1984, 66–90.

> I have begotten for Christ through the Gospel. They minister to me with great charity and meekness, and I love them in the truth and I teach them the way to the kingdom of heaven.[16]

Having got nowhere with Bernard, the devil transformed himself into the likeness of a small animal and vanished. The story was repeated by Caesarius of Heisterbach. Here, the demon's outburst of ridicule, 'Oh, what an abbot' (*Vach qualis abbas*), in contrast to his assertive response to the challenge by the devil at the judgment seat of God, uncharacteristically met with no riposte from Bernard.[17] In this way the point of the story, his alleged humility, was emphasized.

The successful confrontation of saints with the devil formed part of the stock in trade of hagiological literature, and these bernardine examples are part and parcel of this tradition. The encounters were first recorded during Bernard's lifetime and formed an integral part of the cistercian *exemplum* literature of the late twelfth and early thirteenth centuries. Bernard's triumph over the devil made of him a paradigm to his monks. According to the *Exordium Magnum* both he and his abbot at Cîteaux, Stephen Harding, provided a safeguard against the challenge of the devil:

> . . . their teaching and example continued to remove innumerable captives from the grasp of the king of pride, that is the devil, and incorporate them to Christ, true king of humility.[18]

Bernard's victory over the devil also expressed itself in his ability to cure those possessed by the devil. In the second book of the *Vita Prima* Arnold of Bonneval has two stories of Bernard expelling demons, one in Pavia and the other in Aquitaine. Both found their way into the

[16] *Vita Quarta* 2:16; PL 185:549: *'Abba, quomodo te habes? Ego de longinquis terris veni ut te viderum, et te calceos angentum invenio. Non debuisses hoc facere, sed servi et ministri tui'. Cui respondit Vir Dei: 'Ego, inquit, servos non habeo, nec volui unquam habere, Filios habere, quos genui Christo per evangelium, qui mihi ministrant cum magna charitate et mansuetudine; et ego illos in veritate diligo, et viam regni caelorum doceo.*

[17] *Dialogue* 4:7; see McGuire 1991, 177.

[18] EM 1:27; Griesser 1961, 84: *quorum doctrina et exemplis usque hodie innumera captivitatis vasa regi superbiae, id est diabolo, auferuntur Christo Domino, vero regi humilitatis, incorporantur.*

Golden Legend.[19] Bernard also cured a man whose adulterous wife tormented him with evil spells. When the man's head was placed on the vessel that contained the Eucharist, the 'ancient foe' departed, and he was restored to perfect health.[20]

The earliest pictorial representations to be based on the cistercian literary sources appear on the altarpiece in Palma de Mallorca, dated 1290 (▶ *Colour plate 5*). One of its four cycle scenes shows two ladies kneeling before Bernard, who frees them from their possession by the devil, indicated by the fire emanating from their mouths. In another version—a fragment from another spanish altarpiece cycle painted by Ferrer Bassa in the first half of the fourteenth century (PA110)—two women, accompanied by four others standing behind them, are again depicted kneeling before Bernard who stands before them with his hands raised over them. One of the women has a tiny devil coming out of her mouth while the other woman is supporting her.

BERNARD WITH THE DEVIL ON A CHAIN

As we have seen several times already, in the second half of the thirteenth century many of the cistercian primary stories were incorporated into the legendary literature represented by the *Golden Legend*. Through this medium they were ever more widely dispersed, especially outside monastic circles. Not surprisingly, the theme entered the iconography of Bernard, although this seems to have happened only in the first half of the fifteenth century and in a form which cannot be directly attributed to any specific literary source though the motif is clearly analogous to them and refers in a general way to Bernard's triumph over the devil.

The most common forms of portraying Bernard's ascendancy over the devil were to show him standing, usually carrying his crozier and sometimes also a book, and either holding the much smaller figure of the devil on a leash or a chain or else trampling on the devil lying on the ground, or a combination of the two. The theme was perhaps derived

[19] LA 217 for the woman from Pavia, and LA 218 the one from Aquitaine.
[20] VP 1:10:49; PL 185:255: . . . *antiqui hostis*. . . .

from the angel in the Apocalypse who, with a great chain in his hand, took hold of the dragon serpent and held the key of the abyss.[21]

In *exemplum* stories devils usually appeared in the guise of some animal. They were commonly represented, by Caesarius of Heisterbach for example, as asses, pigs, apes, and dogs. Medieval people commonly regarded animals as the most common objects of demonic possession. In bernardine iconography, however, the devil appears not as an individual animal but as a composite creature with features drawn from a variety of beasts: birds' beaks and claws, dark and hairy crops, bats' wings, hooves, tails, goats' beards and horns, antlers. Examples include a miniature in a french translation of the *Golden Legend* from the South Netherlands, dated 1470–1477 (MA154). In it Bernard is shown in a white cowl with a gold crozier in his right hand and a book in his left hand. He stands on a dark grey horned devil with claws on hands and feet whom he is crushing. A flemish Book of Hours from about the same time depicts Bernard with a crozier in his left hand and a chained devil, which he crushes with his feet, in his right hand (MA100).

One of thirty-eight full-page miniatures in an italian manuscript, also from the last quarter of the fifteenth century, depicts Bernard bearded and in a white cowl (MA138). With the left hand he holds a chain, at the end of which is a standing, small, horned devil, while the other end of the chain is wound round a red column. With his right hand he is pointing at the demon. In the two former examples, as well as in most others, Bernard is shown standing upright and, although he is trampling on the devil, he does not appear to be interacting with him in any other way. In this italian miniature, however, an almost humourous exchange between them is taking place. Another more lively scene (MA353) is depicted in a Book of Hours made in the workshop of the famous illuminator Jean Colombe *c.* 1480 for a widow in the region of Tours. Here Bernard has caught a large brown and grey demon and is holding him with a red and yellow stole or scarf which he has placed round the demon's neck. Bernard is standing, nimbed and in a white tunic and black scapular. The scene is a landscape with mountains in the background and a large rock immediately behind Bernard.

By the second half of the fifteenth century *Bernard and the Devil* had become sufficiently well known to be used as a means of easy

[21] Apocalypse 20:1.

identification in the same way as the other favourite scene-attributes, the *Lactatio* and the *Amplexus* and the basic attributes of monastic habit, crozier, and halo.

It is as a means of identification that the motif was already being used in manuscripts. Three manuscripts of the *Golden Legend* in French begin the chapter on Bernard with the Bernard/devil miniature, even though it has no relationship to James of Voragine's text: the south-netherlandish one mentioned above (MA154); another from Bruges, dated between 1445 and 1460 (MA305), in which the figure of Bernard wearing a black cowl over white tunic and black scapular stands in a doorway astride the devil; and yet another (MA345) in a flemish manuscript in which the miniature decorates the etymology of Bernard which precedes the biographical text proper. Similarly, Bernard is depicted with the devil on a chain in an anonymous 1473 work entitled *de imitatione Christi et contemptu omnia vanitatu mundi,* an illustration (MA182) again quite unrelated to the subject of the text.

The motif was not confined to illuminated manuscripts but was also adopted by other media—paintings, sculpture and stained glass. It appears, for example, in the same unrelated way in the famous Erasmus altarpiece by Dieric Bouts in the Sint Pieterskerk in Louvain, commissioned sometime before 1466 by Ghert de Smet, a member of the Confraternity of the Blessed Sacrament, who is known to have requested that Mass be said for his soul on the feasts of Saints Jerome, Erasmus, and Bernard. The centre of the altarpiece shows Saint Erasmus being tortured by having his intestines wound round a rod. Saint Jerome, on the left wing, is identified by the usual attribute of a red cardinal's hat, while Bernard on the right (PA006) is depicted facing left in a three-quarter view in a rocky landscape. He is dressed in a black cowl over his white tunic and black scapular, and a red cap. In his right hand he holds a beautifully crafted golden crozier with a white plaited sudarium with fringes attached, while he holds a book in his left hand. A tiny hairy demon with pointed ears and four horns lurks behind him at his feet.

Three other examples of the Bernard/devil in paintings motif may be mentioned: first, a polyptych from the dominican church in Taggia, Italy, in which Saints Erasmus and Vincent are depicted in the centre, flanked by six smaller figures of other saints, three on each side. Among these is Bernard, bearded and in a white cowl, also with the hood over his head, a book in his right hand, and a crozier under his left arm

(PA046). With his right hand he holds a chain at the end of which is a tiny devil at his feet. Second, an altarpiece in the florentine church of Santo Spirito painted by Raffaele dei Carli in 1505 in the form of a *sacra conversazione* (PA112). The enthroned Virgin is flanked by four seated saints, two on each side: on the left Saint Laurence with the standard attribute of a grill, Saint John the Evangelist holding an open book with the opening words of his Gospel clearly readable (*In principio erat verbum . . .*); on the right Saint Stephen holding the martyr's palms and with a stone balanced on his head referring to his martyrdom by stoning, and Saint Bernard with an open book on his lap and holding a chain at the end of which is a small demon. Unusually, this has a human face with beard and horns. Bernard is gazing up at Laurence, perhaps alluding to the vision on his sickbed of the Virgin accompanied by Laurence and Benedict which William of Saint Thierry recorded in the *Vita Prima* (PA059 and PA117).[22] It is interesting to note that in this italian example the devil on a chain is used as the attribute whereby Bernard is recognized in the same way as the three other saints are identified by their traditional attributes. Here, as in several of the other examples from Italy mentioned (MA138 & PA066), Bernard is not shown carrying a crozier, and, apart from the halo and his Cistercian habit, the devil on a chain forms the chief means of identification. Third, in a painting from the workshop of Fra Filippo Lippi, one of the greatest florentine painters from the middle of the fifteenth century, Bernard is featured, wearing a white cowl with the hood over the head (PA066), as one of a group of eighteen saints which is thought to have adorned a sacristy cupboard. Bernard is depicted full-length on a pink marble platform before a rounded niche. His right hand rests on a green book held on his left forearm. Twisted round his left hand is a leash attached to the collar of a tiny demon at his feet.

In the north walk of the cloister of Cadouin in south-west France a carving which was completed in 1468 under Abbot Peter de Gaing depicts a monk holding a staff (SC07). The top of what was probably originally a crozier has been broken off but as the monk is holding a long chain at the end of which stands a horned devil of approximately the same size, the figure is likely meant to represent Saint Bernard. A marble statue of Bernard (SC12) made in 1480/1484 in Cremona by

[22] VP 1:12:59; PL 185:258-259.

Antonio Amadeo, a prominent architect as well as a leading lombard sculptor, unusually has him holding the devil by the hair instead of on a chain. These images may be compared with two other representations of Bernard in sculpture: a marble statue in Santa Maria Maggiore in Rome, in which he is also featured carrying a book but where he holds the devil on a chain, ▶ *Fig. 17* (SC11); and a sculpture carved in oak in the Rhineland around 1500 in which Bernard's asceticism is accentuated by the lean face and bony hands with veins showing (SC24). In his right hand he holds a crozier, relatively simple in design for the late Middle Ages, while with his left hand he clasps an open book to his body. A chain is attached to a ring around his left wrist at the end of which is a small demon at his feet.

The motif is also found in stained glass: a window in the Certosa (Charterhouse) in Pavia (GL70) has the inscription below 'Opus Cristofori de Motis 1477'. Bernard is shown with a crozier in his left hand while holding the devil, lying at his feet, on a long chain in his right hand.

The peculiarity of the Italian iconography of Bernard of linking the saint with the devil as the principal means of identification accounts for the inclusion of the devil on a chain in a number, although by no means all, representations of the *Doctrina*. Among these is one of the most famous of all paintings of Bernard, Filippino Lippi's from 1486 in the Florentine Badia (PA136) in which—almost unnoticeably—a small demon is perched in a cave under a rock immediately behind Bernard and next to an owl. Influenced by this is a late fifteenth century pen and ink drawing by Raffaellino de Garbo in which the Virgin on the left points to Bernard who is seated with an open book at a desk on a stool with the inscription 'SCO. BERNARD'. A partly visible demon entering a doorway behind Bernard is chained to Bernard's stool (DR09). Also from the late fifteenth century is a *Doctrina* picture, one of twenty-five miniatures decorating the suffrages of the saints in the magnificent Sforza Book of Hours (MA132). Here Bernard is shown sitting at an elaborate desk which is raised from the floor and to which a demon is attached by a chain. Next to the demon is another bernardine attribute, a small dog, which also appears jointly with the demon in the Isabella Breviary (MA118). Although the devil is often featured in *Doctrina* images he is by no means always included: he is, for example, not found in Filippino Lippi's from *c.* 1486 (PA032) or Perugino's from *c.* 1489–1490 (PA151).

BERNARD IN BOOKS OF HOURS

Virtually all examples of the devil theme in manuscripts so far mentioned are found in Books of Hours. In fact, of the one hundred fifteen Bernard images recorded in Books of Hours no less than fifty show Bernard with the devil, a considerably larger percentage than that of any other bernardine scene-attribute. By comparison, the *Lactatio* is featured in only twenty-one books of hours, and the *Amplexus* has been recorded in only three (MA306, MA416, & MA417). The devil theme was therefore by far the most popular pictorial image of Bernard in what was the most highly decorated of all books and a number-one best seller for over two hundred years, from the late thirteenth to the early sixteenth century. At the end of this period printed Books of Hours appeared in even greater numbers than the Bible.[23] Their popularity and wide distribution was responsible for greatly influencing lay religious devotion in the Late Middle Ages. At the same time ownership of a Book of Hours was a status symbol. They were commissioned by royal and noble patrons, and often included their coats of arms and portraits. A number of the foremost craftsmen of the time contributed to the rich decoration of these books. Among those which include images of Bernard are the *Belles Heures* of Jean, Duke of Berry, one of the foremost patrons of art, which was decorated by the three Limbourg brothers in Paris (MA033); the Utrecht Hours of the Master of Catherine of Cleves (MA029), the Book of Hours of Pope Leo X, dated *c.* 1470, illuminated by the Master of Rolin II (MA045); Jean Fouquet's masterpiece *Heures d'Etienne Chevalier,* executed just after the middle of the fifteenth century, and including one of the best known of all Bernard images, a two-tier scene of him preaching in the chapter house above and, below, with the devil (MA093); and the Hours of Simon de Varie, also illuminated by Jean Fouquet as well as by other artists (MA109).

The best of these Books of Hours are among the finest examples of medieval works of art. The great authority on medieval books of devotion, the Abbé Leroquais, said of them that they were 'at one and the same time very rich and very poor: very rich as regards the decoration

[23] On the Book of Hours, see Leroquais 1927, 1:I-LXXXV, Harthan 1977, Wieck 1983, and Backhouse 1985.

of the manuscripts, very poor as regards the text itself',[24] a description also most apt of the Bernard/devil theme in Books of Hours, in which the poverty of the devotional content is often accompanied by glorious illuminated miniatures. The majority of these devotion books, however, belonged to the lesser nobility or emergent middle class and were far from matching either the quality or the lavishness of decoration of the best. Among them are many which were crudely executed and illustrated with only a few miniatures of indifferent quality or even none at all.

The Book of Hours was designed specifically for the private devotions of individuals and its widespread popularity derived from the growing literacy of laypeople which expressed itself in a desire to imitate the routine pattern of worship of the clergy, the eight Offices or canonical hours of Matins, Lauds, Prime, Terce, Sext, None, Vespers, and Compline. Among the laity this took the form of the *Hours of the Virgin,* which was a simplified version of the Divine Office, a late medieval addition to the breviary. The appeal of these books was greatly enhanced by rich visual decoration, for which a tradition of standard sets of illustrations emerged. Such Books of Hours usually began with a Calendar displaying the appropriate signs of the zodiac and illustrated with pictures denoting the labours of the month. Then followed the Hours of the Virgin, introduced by miniatures featuring events from the life of the Virgin, the sequence beginning with the Annunciation at Matins. Other standard contents included the lesser Hours of the Cross and of the Holy Spirit, prayers to the Virgin known as *Obsecro te* and *O intemerata,* the seven penitential psalms (Psalms 6, 31, 37, 50, 101, 129, and 142 vulgate), the Office of the Dead, and, usually at the end, numerous Suffrages, also known as Memorials (*Memoriae*). These short prayers addressed to the saints asked for their intercession and consisted of three short elements—an antiphon, a versicle, and a response, followed by a longer prayer. The saints invoked might be local favourites—like Saint Bernardino in Italy—or they might be chosen for their special powers of intercession in one particular area—for example, Margaret of Antioch for childbirth and Roch in warding off plague—and, although they were not always depicted, when they were, they were shown standing with their attributes in their hands. Among the most popular were

[24] Leroquais 1927, 1:I.

Saint George with the Dragon, the stigmatization of Saint Francis, the crucifixion of Saint Andrew, the lapidation of Saint Stephen, and the martyrdom of Saint Thomas Becket. It is in this section that Bernard sometimes appears, although much less often than do a large number of other saints, including those just listed. He is identified either by the standard attributes of habit, crozier and book, and halo, or by the Bernard/devil motif. The *Memoriae* images include a Book of Hours dated *c.* 1440, which belonged to Catherine of Cleves, Duchess of Guelders. Bernard (MA029) is nimbed, carries a crozier and a book, and is wearing a brown cowl with the white tunic showing underneath. The prayer to Bernard is taken from the fourth antiphon of the first nocturn from Vigils on his feast. An early sixteenth-century Book of Hours has a standing Bernard holding a black horned demon in a miniature below the heading in red ink *de sancto Bernardo memoria* (MA159). In the Sforza Hours the suffrages form the finest cycle of decoration in what is a masterpiece of medieval illumination by the leading miniaturist of the Sforza court, Giovan Pietro Birago. In it a composite *Doctrina*-Devil picture shows Bernard, seated with the devil chained to his desk, gazing up at the Virgin (MA132).

THE VERSES OF BERNARD

To the *Suffrages* were added in the fifteenth century a number of supplementary prayers reflecting the devotional preference of the patron as well as the repertoire of the illuminator. Among these late medieval additions, along with the commemoration of the Fifteen Joys of the Virgin and the Seven Prayers of Saint Gregory, accompanied by a miniature depicting the Mass of Saint Gregory, were the so-called *Verses of Bernard*, consisting of parts of a number of psalm verses. The origin of these *Verses* goes back to a humorous legend which is sometimes included in the introduction to them.[25] The most detailed version is contained in a late fifteenth-century german prayer book which belonged to the daughter of a merchant from Constance who later became a dominican nun in Saint Gallen:

[25] Chevalier 1892–1921, 3:no 27912.

> One reads in the Life of Saint Bernard that the evil spirit once told him that he knew the eight verses in the psalter and that anyone who recited them daily would never be damned. And when Bernard requested to be told which they were the evil spirit refused to say. Saint Bernard then said: 'I know how I can say these verses, namely, if I daily recite the whole psalter'. When the evil spirit heard that Bernard would thereby achieve so much good he divulged the verses in question which are herewith given.[26]

Almost exactly the same introduction appears in Latin in one of the earliest examples, a Book of Hours from Ghent dated *c.* 1430–1440. Here the inaccurate claim that the story was derived from the *Life* of Bernard (*legitur in vita bernardi*) is also repeated. Similarly, it is said that when the devil heard that Bernard intended to recite the whole psalter the devil wished to prevent even greater spiritual advantage ensuing and decided to reveal them (*ne tantum bonum faceret revelavit sibi et dixit istos octo versus sequentes*).[27] The Verses were introduced in much the same way in a number of other manuscripts, either in Latin or in the vernacular.[28] Most common were abridged versions such as one which appears in an early sixteenth-century french manuscript: 'Here follow the seven verses which the devil taught Saint Bernard that anyone who recited them daily would not be damned' (*S'ensuit les sept vers saint Bernard que le dyable lui enseigna que quiconques les dyra tous les jours, qu'il ne seroit point dampne*) (MA178). The great majority were known either as the Seven or the Eight Verses of Bernard. The original seven verses—or parts of verses sometimes referred to as ver-

[26] Ochsenbein 1994, 213: *Man liset an sant Bernhartz leben, daz der boess gaist aines mauls zue im sprach, er wiste acht verss in dem psalter, wer die all tag spraech, der wert niemer verdamnot. Und do sant bernhart von im die selben verss begeret ze wissen, do antwort der boess, daz er die niemer saite. Sant Bernhard sprach: 'Ich waiss wol, wie ich die verss wirt sprechen, wenn ich all tag ainen gantzen psalter sprech'. Do daz der boess gaist hort, daz er [Bernhard] ain soellich gross guet wolt und daz es nit beschaeche, do offnet er im die versaiten verss [die geheim gehaltenen Psalmverse], die his nach geschriben stond.*

[27] Baltimore, The Walters Art Gallery, MS W 170, f 177 (Randall 1997, 126).

[28] For example, Baltimore Walters Art Gallery MSS W 166 and 169, and Paris Bibliothèque Nationale MSS lat 1400 and lat 18026.

sicles (*versiculi*), were, using the Vulgate numbering: Ps 12: 4b-5; 30:6; 38:5; 115:16b-17; 141:5b; 141:6; and 85:17:

> Ps 12:4b-5 Lighten my eyes, lest I sleep the sleep of death,
> lest my enemy say, 'I have prevailed over him'.
>
> Ps 30:6 Into thy hand I commit my spirit;
> Thou hast redeemed me, O Lord, faithful God.
>
> Ps 38:5 Then I spoke with my tongue: 'Lord, let me know my end.
> And what is the measure of my days; let me know how fleeting my life is!'
>
> Ps 115:16b-17 Thou hast loosed my bonds.
> I will offer to thee the sacrifice of thanksgiving
> and call on the name of the Lord.
>
> Ps 141:5b No refuge remains to me, No man cares for me.
>
> Ps 141:6 I cry to thee, O Lord;
> I say, thou art my refuge, My portion in the land of the living.
>
> Ps 85:17 Show me a sign of your favour
> That those who hate me may see and be put to shame
> because thou, Lord, hast helped me and comforted me.

The Seven Verses, consisting of the same magical number of components as the Mass of Saint Gregory and the Seven Last Words of Our Lord, represent approximately two–thirds of all known miniatures of the Verses of Bernard, while almost all others contain the Eight Verses. These were the same psalm verses, but with the third verse split into two: 38:5a (Then I spoke with my tongue: 'Lord, let me know my end') and 38:5b ('And what is the measure of my days; let me know how fleeting my life is!').

The Seven, or Eight, Verses usually took up two or three folios, but in one example all eight verses are contained on one folio: a Dutch Book of Hours in Latin dated 1460–1465 (MA095). It begins with a historiated initial 'I', which serves as the first letter of the first two verses: *I(llumina oculos meos)* and *I(n manus tuas)*. The verses are introduced by the words: *Incipiunt octo versus sancti bernardi abbatis* ('Here begin the eight verses of St Bernard the abbot') in red. Similar introductory headings, either in Latin or the vernacular, were usual.[29] The sequence of the verses was usually the same, and as listed above, although in some German manuscripts the order in which they appeared changed after the first four verses.[30]

There are also a few examples of Nine Verses, and one single of Ten Verses, all late medieval. Of the total of fifty-nine manuscripts with the Verses illustrated, only four contain nine verses: a german prayer book dated *c.* 1490 (MA048); a flemish Book of Hours from *c.* 1500 (MA365); a french Book of Hours from the end of the fifteenth century (MA185); and another french manuscript dated 1510 (MA296). In the last named, a miniature at the opening of the Verses, preceded by the introduction *sensuivent les ditz vers* ('Here follow the said verses'), has a nimbed Bernard garbed in a strange habit consisting of a white alb and a veil with tassels over his head. He has an open book in his left hand; in his right hand he holds a chain tethering the devil whose head appears in the lower left corner. An unusually full version of the Verses is begun in red on the previous folio and ends on the folio with the miniature. It opens by repeating the inaccurate claim that the story was based on his *vita:* 'We read in the life of Saint Bernard that the devil said to him one day that he knew in the psalter nine verses which whoever he or she recited them daily would be saved'.[31] The ninth verse is Ps 137:7:

[29] They include: *De VIII verse van sente bernaerde* (Brussels, Bibl.Royale MS 10606, f 54v); *VIII versus beati bernardi* (London, British Library MS Add. 17280, f 21v); *VIII versus beati bernardi* (London, British Library Add. 39761, f 95v); *septem versiculi sancto bernardi* (unknown, private ownership, f 132); *octo versus sancti bernardi* (Oxford, Bodleian Library MS Lat. Liturg. g.5, p 151); *s'ensuivent les sept vers saint bernard* (San Marino, Huntington Library MS HM 1147, f 17); *VIII vers saint bernard* (Baltimore, Walters Art Gallery MS W 218, f 68v); *les VIII vers saint bernars* (Baltimore, Walters Art Gallery MS W 173, f 103v); *octo versiculi sancti bernardi* (Baltimore, Walters Art Gallery MS W 195, f 106v); *die acht vers S.Bernharts* (Munich, Staatsbibl. MS Cod. germ. 97, f 76v); *Acht Verse des hl. Bernhart* (Munich, Staatsbibl. MS Cod. germ. 165, f 98v).

[30] See Stammler 1965, 13–14, which has the medieval German version of the eight verses.

[31] The text reads: *On list en la vie de saint bernard que le diable lui dist un yours quil savoit en psaultier neuf vers les quelz celuy ou celle qui les decrit . . . chaque jours ne*

> Though I walk in the midst of trouble,
> thou dost preserve my life;
> thou dost stretch out thy hand against
> the wrath of my enemies,
> and thy right hand delivers me.

The one example of Ten Verses occurs in a Book of Hours from West Flanders dated 1470–1480 and has the following introduction: *isti sunt decem versus sancti bernardi* ('These are the ten verses of Saint Bernard'). The tenth verse was formed by splitting psalm verse 137:7 into two. Although the ninth verse was the last to be added it was reckoned as number seven, and, in the one example of ten verses, the ninth and tenth were placed as numbers seven and eight.

A small and unusual variant to the text of the Verses was the insertion between them in red ink of the so-called 'O' Antiphons, the *Magnificat* antiphons sung at Vespers on the last seven days before Christmas. They are an acrostic in reverse of *ero cras* (I will be tomorrow), a typical example of the medieval predilection for word plays: *O Sapientia, O Adonai, O Radix, O Clavis, O Oriens, O Rex gentium,* and *O Emmanuel.* The antiphons are included in eight of the sixty-seven illustrated *Verses of Bernard,* six of them flemish or french and two of them italian (MA256, MA395). They do not always appear in the liturgical, or even in the same, order. In a french Book of Hours from the second half of the fifteenth century, for example, the first of the 'O' antiphons to appear is *O, Adonay* which can be clearly seen in red ink below the miniature (MA355). A nimbed Bernard in a white tunic and black scapular is depicted against a rocky landscape within the square opening initial *I(llumina oculos meos).* He holds a large grey demon on a chain in his left hand while his right hand is raised in a gesture of exorcism. The text is contained within a gold frame, and there is a full border of stylized leaves and flowers.

The Verses do not appear in Books of Hours until the second quarter of the fifteenth century and their origin is not known. In spite of the claim made in the introduction to some of the manuscripts, they certainly

fust en la fin sauve. Et saint Bernard luy demanda quelz estoyent ses neuf vers mais le dyable ne luy voulut dire. Alors saint Bernard luy repondit quil devait chaque jours tout le psaultier quil ne les dist. Pourtant le diable lui dist quelz estoient a celle fait quil nest plus grand merite en disant tout le psaultier.

do not go back to Bernard's *Vitae* or have their roots in the cistercian *exemplum* tradition following Bernard's lifetime. Unlike the other scene-attributes, the Verses, significantly, are not found in a single manuscript of cistercian origin or ownership. The legend savours more of late medieval lay devotional taste than of monastic spirituality, and it almost certainly originated outside the Cistercian Order. Although the theme is suggested by a line in the hymn for Compline *Te lucis ante terminum* which goes 'tread underfoot our foe' (*hostemque nostrum comprime*), one cannot allege that this was its source. The only clue we have comes in a fifteenth-century german Book of Hours in which the Eight Verses are preceded by the statement that 'the devil had taught them to Saint Bernard. That happened in the year of Our Lord 1389' (*die der teufel Sant Bernhartt gelertt hatt. Das geschah anno domini MCCCLXXXIX*).[32] But what exactly this means is not clear.

By no means all Verses of Bernard in Books of Hours were introduced by an illuminated miniature. Of the sixty-seven such illustrations recorded, the great majority are from the second half of the fifteenth century and the early sixteenth; only four (MA005, MA157, MA256, MA392) come from before 1450. They all feature Bernard; many of them begin with the opening initial *I(llumina oculos meos)* and are decorated with the figure of Bernard (e.g. MA095, MA100, MA315). Some show Bernard alone, nimbed and holding a crozier and a book (e.g. MA095), but the great majority show him trampling on the devil while usually also holding him on a chain, a general reference to the legend of the Verses.

In four cases the totally inappropriate *Lactatio* was chosen to accompany the Verses: two in flemish Books of Hours and two in French. One of the latter (MA097) belonged to the Scapeaux family of Rouen and dates to the early sixteenth century. At the beginning of the Verses of Bernard, quoted in Latin but introduced in French, is a full-page miniature *Lactation* scene within a richly decorated border. On the right is the crowned figure of the Virgin in a blue garment, sitting on a throne with her feet on a red velvet cushion. She holds the Child with her left hand and with her right hand she expresses from her breast a jet of milk in the direction of a kneeling Bernard, hands clasped and a crozier under his right arm. He looks up at the Virgin in an exchange of glances,

[32] Munich, Staatsbibl. MS Clm Cod. germ. 80, f 78.

and the scroll above him has him saying the traditional words *Monstra te esse matrem*. A green book with two clasps lies on the floor. In another exception, a Book of Hours painted in 1531 in Antwerp by Antonius van Damme (MA306), the *Seven Verses* are preceded by a full-page miniature *Amplexus* image set in a church with an altar in the background and enclosed within a golden frame.

Several examples may be cited of manuscripts in which the *Verses* have been graphically introduced by a miniature depicting the legend in a more faithful way than the standard devil-on-a-chain image. A manuscript from Augsburg, dated 1508, (MA137) has a full-page miniature with a corpulent Bernard, nimbed and wearing a black cowl, seated on a stool at a desk with a high back upon which an open book is lying. ▶ *Colour plate 11*. Lurking behind the desk and peering round at Bernard is a large demon with horns and a beak, bat's wings, and bird's claws. The scene is contained within a frame with a curved top and surrounded by a border with stylized flowers and leaves on a gold ground. The opposite folio introduces the *Verses* with a somewhat unusual text in red ink: 'The Seven Verses much favoured which Saint Bernard was accustomed to use and which the devil had wonderfully selected from the following collection'. The first two verses are preceded by a short prayer and identified by their numbers, PRIMA and SE[CUN]DA, also in red ink. An earlier example is a french Book of Hours of Pope Leo X, dated *c.* 1470, in which Bernard is depicted in his study, seated in a gilt canopied chair inscribing the opening words *Illumina oculos meos* on a scroll across his lap (MA045). In the background an open psalter is propped up on a hexagonal gold table topped by a lectern, while three closed books in red bindings are placed on a similar stand at the front on the right. In Jean Fouquet's famous full-page miniature in the Hours of Jean Chevalier, which shows Bernard preaching to his monks in the chapter house in the upper half page, the legend is depicted in the lower half (MA093). A brown horned devil with a tail and bat-like wings creeps up behind Bernard, who is sitting at a desk wearing a white tunic and black scapular with a red cap. Bernard turns round and with his left index finger he points to an open psalter on the desk before him. The devil here is of approximately the same size as Bernard unlike the smaller chained devils with which he is usually depicted.

An almost identical picture appears in a full-page miniature in a german prayer book from Augsburg or Salzburg dated *c.* 1490, which illustrates one of the few manuscripts with *Nine Verses* (MA048). Here Bernard, dressed in a black cowl, is sitting at a desk and turns round to the man-sized devil behind him while pointing to an open psalter. An hourglass is placed on top of the desk and a closed book lies on a shelf beneath the desk. In an early sixteenth-century french Book of Hours Bernard is also shown sitting at a desk in a large miniature under an arch supported by two columns (MA146). He is wearing a white tunic and black scapular, and on his head he has a red cap similar to the one he is shown wearing in the famous *Heures d'Etienne Chevalier* image (MA093). Behind the desk is a red-horned devil who, with a metal hook in his left hand, is stealing Bernard's inkwell. The text alongside announces the beginning of the *Seven Verses* in French: *S'ensuivent les sept vers saint bernad.* Another miniature (MA170) in a late fifteenth-century Book of Hours shows Bernard standing, dressed also in a white tunic and black scapular. He holds an open book with both hands and shows it to a black horned devil who is walking away. Here, as in the many images of him with the devil, the open book he holds represents, not the *Rule,* with which he is otherwise usually depicted, one of his traditional attributes, but the psalter to which the legend refers.

The *Verses of Bernard* occur in many netherlandish and german prayer books in the last century of the Middle Ages, not only in manuscripts but also in printed books, including some of the best-known pre-Reformation devotional works such as the *Antidotarius* of Nicholas Salicetus (from 1489 onwards) and the *Hortulas animae* (from 1498 onwards) in both latin and vernacular editions.[33] Despite the popularity of the *Verses* and of the Bernard/devil image in Books of Hours, however, other saints and other images outnumbered both. Infinitely more widespread, for example, was the Mass of Saint Gregory, an affirmation of the Real Presence of Christ in the consecrated bread and wine at a time in the Late Middle Ages when the doctrine was being challenged. Saints with timely powers—as Saint Sebastian in times of plague[34]—were more frequently pictured.

The key third verse of the eight (Ps 38:5a), with its request 'O Lord, make me know my end', formed an important part of the late medieval

[33] Ochsenbein 1994, 214.

[34] For the principal patronages of saints, see Farmer 1992, 515–516.

ars moriendi. It is hard to exaggerate the importance medieval people attached to making the necessary preparation for a good death and especially to seizing the opportunity for confession which prior knowledge of the hour gave them. In an age when death was everywhere and unpredictable, people feared not so much death as the horror of dying without the comfort of the sacraments, without making bequests to the poor and to the church, and thus obtaining the necessary suffrages.[35] Albrecht Dürer, in his *Gedenkbuch,* wrote that at the sudden fatal illness of her husband in 1502, his mother recited the *Verses* of 'Sant Pernhartz' with the request that he be granted a holy death.[36]

Although the *Lactatio* and the *Amplexus*—the other scene-attributes of Bernard—were more numerous and more widely diffused than the Bernard/devil theme, both generally as well as in a cistercian context, the devil theme was nevertheless the commonest way Bernard was represented in Books of Hours in the late Middle Ages—in most instances in connection with the *Verses.*

The Verses and Late Medieval Criticism

The hold which the recitation of the *Verses* and of similar pious devotions had over the minds of late medieval laypersons tells us a good deal about the spirituality of the society of the time. A german Prayerbook dated *c.* 1515, for example, has a full-page miniature (MA415) with Bernard trampling on a devil with a prayer in German on the facing page preceded by text claiming that a devout recital of the prayer would gain three hundred days' indulgence. The Abbé Leroquais lists the *Verses* among those compositions which were considered to have miraculous powers by virtue of their origin and the efficacy superstitiously attributed to them, and, not least, for the number of years of indulgence attached to them.[37] The *Eight Verses* were, for example, among the prayers in a german Book of Hours from *c.* 1480 to which a grant of indulgence specifically refers.[38]

[35] Vauchez 1993, 86.
[36] Rupprich 1956, 36–37.
[37] Leroquais 1927, 1:xxx.
[38] Plotzek 1987, 208–210.

The *Verses of Bernard* had been denounced as early as 1382 by Bishop Gerhard von dem Berg of Hildesheim specifically for the indulgences attached to them, but it was not until the early sixteenth century that they came under widespread assault.[39] The most virulent attack occurred in the satirical work *Encomium Moriae* (*The Praise of Folly*), written by Erasmus of Rotterdam for, and dedicated to, Thomas More.[40] Printed in 1511 and written shortly before then, it caused a great sensation for its trenchant and satirical comment on many of the abuses of the time and appeared in forty editions during Erasmus' lifetime. Erasmus ridiculed the *magicos versiculos* ('magical versicles') of Bernard as 'happy delusions' in the following words:

> But without any doubt those who love to hear about miracles and ghosts are especially grist for Folly's mill, for this sport not only makes the time pass quickly but also brings in revenue for the priests. Akin to these are the men who believe that the day they look at a Saint Christopher they are invulnerable against death; or that if they salute a sculptured Barbara they will return safely from battle. Among them also we include those who believe in the efficacy of indulgence,[41] of magic texts or of the miraculous verses which it is said a devil revealed to Saint Bernard. In this category of happy delusions we include the belief that every locality has its own saint and that each saint has his special duties and that votive pictures must be dedicated to them in order to induce them to exert their skill.[42]

In a 1515 edition published in Basel, and probably supervised by Erasmus himself, a commentary by the Dutchman Gerhard Lister was printed alongside the text. At the point where Erasmus refers to the efficacy of indulgences, Lister relates the story of the devil and the *Seven Verses*. In the margin alongside this passage one of a number of marginal drawings by Hans Holbein the Younger shows Bernard on the

[39] Ochsenbein 1994, 218.
[40] Erasmi Roterrodami 1931 (facsimile edition).
[41] Here Lister relates an anecdote about indulgences.
[42] Erasmi Roterrodami 1931, 2:23.

right, nimbed and with the hood of his cowl over his head, holding an open book (the psalter), which is also being held by a devil on the left. The devil is of equal size to Bernard, has antlers, pointed ears, the beak of a bird, thin arms and legs with claws (DR01).

Some years later the *Verses* were criticised in much the same terms in a Book of Hours in English printed in London by John Byddell on 16 June 1535. 'The verses, as they be called, of St Barnard' are included but are referred to in an admonition to the reader as among "blasphemies and vain promises"'.[43]

Opposition to the theme is suggested in a Book of Hours from Valenciennes or Cambrai dated *c.* 1480, in which Bernard is depicted within the initial *I(llumina oculos meos)* at the opening of the text of the *Eight Verses* (MA370). He is shown standing dressed in a white tunic and black scapular, as was not uncommon in late medieval Books of Hours (e.g. MA011, MA148, MA206). In the lower left-hand quarter, a miniature has been defaced, but there had undoubtedly been a devil at his feet as was usual in illustrations of the *Verses*. Although it is not possible to know when the damage was done, it is tempting to speculate that it may have occurred during the last decades of the Middle Ages and that it reflects an abhorrence of the theme. If so, it provides an interesting example of a form of iconoclasm directed, not at the cult of saints—as was becoming common at the time of the Reformation, but at the distortion of the cult; that it was viewed as a late medieval corruption of the traditional teaching on saints as models and intercessors.

The criticism to which Bernard was subjected by Lister and Erasmus is significantly balanced later in *The Praise of Folly* by the picture Erasmus gives of the real Bernard of monastic tradition, and that text is accompanied by the only other illustration of Bernard in the text. Without mentioning Bernard by name, Erasmus draws on one of the stories from the *Vita Prima* to demonstrate the contrast between the obsession of 'the masses' with material things and the disregard of the pious for them.[44]

> The masses regard the concrete as the only reality. The pious, on the other hand, whose highest goal is Christ, neglect the care of their body. Money they regard as rubbish; they reject

[43] Hoskins 1901, 201.
[44] VP 3:1:2; PL 185:304.

> it or flee from it. Or, if they are forced to handle anything so base, they do so most unwillingly. Since the pious strive toward the heights where the senses are not touched by trivial matters they soon degenerate. Thus it came about, so we are told, that some holy man drank oil instead of wine without becoming aware of what they had done.[45]

Lister reveals in his commentary that Erasmus is referring to the story in the *Vita Prima* about Bernard being so absorbed in his study of the scriptures that he was unaware of what he was drinking. The importance attached to this story of how Bernard neglected his body while concentrating on the things of the spirit is highlighted by the marginal drawing (DR02), which shows him sitting at his desk absorbed by the open book of the scriptures before him, while taking hold of a flask with his right hand. Unlike the other drawing this one is almost certainly not by Holbein.

The juxtaposition by Erasmus in the *Praise of Folly* of the two references to Bernard—the 'delusions' of the 'magic texts' with which his name is associated on the one hand, and his being counted among 'the pious whose highest goal is Christ' on the other—tells us a good deal about the late medieval perceptions of Bernard, and how his reputation was exploited in the late Middle Ages—what in German is referred to as his *Rezeption*.[46]

Shortly after Erasmus's criticism the young Martin Luther referred twice to the *Octo Versus sancti Bernardi* in his Exposition of the Psalms (1513–1516). Of the fifth of the eight *Verses* (Ps 115:16), he commented that it has so much power that a threefold repetition of it would remove sins; the sixth (Ps 141:5b) he referred to as 'this error . . . concerning the eight verses of the whole psalter as revealed to Saint Bernard by the devil'.[47] The 'error', as he saw it, was the reliance of the faithful on the superstitious and mechanical recitation of snippets of Scripture and especially the sale of indulgences designed to relieve the pain of souls in purgatory. It was examples of this kind that led him further along

[45] Erasmi Roterrodami 1931, 2:32.

[46] Elm 1994; part of the title is: *Bernhard von Clairvaux–Rezeption und Wirkung im Mittelalter und in der Neuzeit.*

[47] Martin Luther's *Werke* 1886, 4:267 and 442.

the road of defiance and to his gradual discovery of justification by faith and his conviction that good works are to no avail. Although Luther's theology owed much to Bernard,[48] a fact he himself freely acknowledged, in dividing faith from good works, this crucial alienation from what the church had theretofore taught, he was totally at variance with bernardine teaching. In one of the sermons *On the Song of Songs* Bernard had used the metaphor of the flower to represent faith and its fruit good works, stating that

> Just as the flower by necessity precedes the fruit, so faith ought to come before good works. Without faith, moreover, it is impossible to please God, as Paul attests. . . . But then, faith without good works is dead, just as a flower seems vain where no fruit follows.[49]

In spite of the misgivings of many humanist theologians, the efficacy of the *Verses* devotion was still acclaimed on the eve of the Reformation in an English Book of Hours printed in 1536. The *Horae Eboracenses. The Prymer or Hours of the Blessed Virgin Mary according to the use of the Illustrious Church of York* refers to the origin of the *Verses* in these terms:

> This prayer was shewyd to saynt Bernarde by the messanger of God, saynge that as golde is moste precyous of al other metell, so excedeth thys prayer all other prayers; and hoo that deuoutly sayth hyt scall haue a synglane rewarde of our blessyd lady and her swete son Jesus.[50]

The power of the prayer was described as

> Hoo that sayth deuowtely thys shorte prayer dayly, shalle nott depart owte of thys worlde wytheowt penannce mynystrayyon

[48] For Luther's attitude to Bernard, see Bell 1993, and Posset 1999.

[49] SC 51:2; SBOp 2:84-85: *Si ad instar floris necessario praecedentis fructum, bonum quoque fide oporteat praeveniri. Alioquin sine fide impossibile est placere Deo, Paulo attestante. . . . Itaque nec sine flore fructus, nec sine fide opus bonum.* Translation from Bernard of Clairvaux 1973–1981, 3:41.

[50] *Horae Eboracenses* 1920, 137.

> of the holy sacramente: the whyche was showed by an angelle onto saynt Bernarde.[51]

Shakespeare testifies that the memory of the *Verses of Bernard* lived on in England by putting into the mouth of Antonio in *The Merchant of Venice* the line 'the devil can cite Scripture for his purpose'[52]—undoubtedly a reference to the devil's altercation with Bernard.

In Luther's works there was, as with those of Erasmus, a dissonance between his generally positive perception of Bernard and Bernard's monastic theology, and his condemnation of the late medieval *Rezeption,* as expressed in the *Verses of Bernard*. The depictions of Bernard in some Books of Hours signals the chasm between what remained of the authentic monastic traditions and the later caricature in the *Verses*. Some of the extraordinary portrayals which appropriately match the spiritual bankruptcy of the *Verses* betray a lack of knowledge of his conventional iconography. Among them is the crude image we saw earlier in a french Book of Hours dated 1510, in which Bernard is wearing what looks like a grey shawl or veil over his head (MA296). He is shown in virtually identical garb in another french Book of Hours from the turn of the sixteenth century (MA147). Elsewhere he appears in a kind of pink cowl with a white scapular and carrying a curious crozier (MA185). In yet another, Bernard is dressed in a red tunic with a white hoodless scapular (MA187). These crude and historically inaccurate images stand as graphic tokens of the sharp contrast between the late medieval lay mentality and the cistercian monastic heritage.

[51] *Ibid.*

[52] *Merchant of Venice* 1:3.

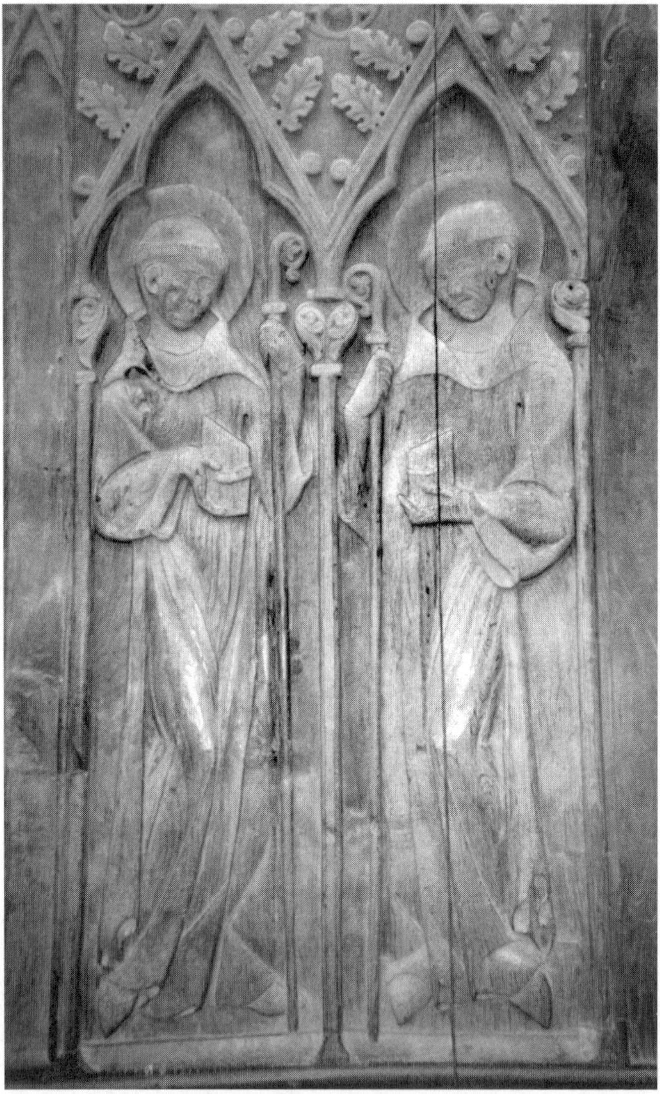

Figure 18: SS Benedict and Bernard.
Carvings on the choir stalls of the abbey of Doberan, *c.* 1310 (SC15).

TWELVE

BERNARD IN THE CONSTELLATION OF SAINTS

THE NEAR UNANIMITY with which Bernard's contemporaries acknowledged his saintliness is quite extraordinary. He received the accolade *venerabilis* from Orderic Vitalis, who was writing as early as 1135.[1] Even those who were not close to him, or did not always agree with him, did not fail to recognize in him the qualities of a saint. Otto of Freising (*c.* 1110–1158), the author of *The Deeds of Frederick Barbarossa,* although himself a Cistercian, never came under Bernard's influence and in fact criticized him for his stand against Gilbert de la Porrée and Abelard under whom Otto had studied in Paris. Yet he referred to Bernard as 'venerable in life and character, conspicuous in his religious order, endowed with wisdom and a knowledge of letters, renowned for signs and wonders . . . who was looked upon by all the peoples of France and Germany as a prophet and apostle'.[2] Peter the Venerable, abbot of Cluny, whose strained relationship with Bernard resulted from the rivalry between Cîteaux and Cluny as well as their

[1] Chibnall 1969–1980, 3:340.
[2] Mierow 1953, 70–71.

opposing views of Abelard, referred to Bernard as the 'fellow-citizen of the angels' (*concivis angelorum*),[3] a description which elicited from Bernard the following response: 'O you good man, what have you done? You have praised a sinner, you have numbered a good-for-nothing amongst the blessed!'.[4] William of Saint Thierry claimed that Bernard 'lived an angelic life on earth' (*tam angelicam gerens in terris vixit*).[5] John of Salisbury acclaimed him as 'a man of great sanctity and weighty influence'.[6] Aelred refers to the monks who founded Rievaulx as coming from 'the most noble monastery of Clairvaux at the hand of the saintly and by God beloved abbot, Bernard' (*de nobilissimo monasterio Clarevallis per manum sancti ac Deo dilecti abbatis Bernardi*).[7] All three authors of the *Vita Prima* described Bernard as a man of God (*vir Dei*), as did Conrad of Eberbach in the *Exordium Magnum*.[8] Most telling of all is the fact that already eight years before his death Geoffrey of Auxerre initiated the preparations for the writing of the *Vita Prima*, the dossier required for a canonization procedure and the papal authorisation of his cult. In the Preface William of Saint Thierry indicated that he had already had the idea of bearing witness to Bernard's sainthood, but that he considered himself unworthy and that 'the subject was too wonderful or holy for me to attempt', and so had decided to wait until Bernard's death. He needed little convincing to change his mind, for Bernard's 'doings are common knowledge to the whole world, and the entire church of the saints is telling the tale of all his virtuous, powerful deeds',[9] and in 1147 he wrote the first book. John of Clairvaux invoked the dead but as yet uncanonized Bernard in a prayer of intercession, calling on 'Our Lord Jesus Christ, Blessed Mary Mother of God, Saint

[3] Letter 175 to Bernard; Constable 1967, 1:416. For the relationship between Peter the Venerable and Bernard, see Bredero 1996, 227–239.

[4] Ep 265, SBOp 8:174; trans. James 1953, 377: *'Qui facis, o bone vir? Laudas peccatorem, miserum beatifica!'*

[5] VP 1:4:19; PL 185:237.

[6] *Memoirs of the Papal Court;* Chibnall 1956, 14.

[7] Howlett 1884–1889, 3:183.

[8] William of St Thierry, VP 1:4:19; PL 185:237. Arnold of Bonneval, VP 2:2:10; PL 185:274. Geoffrey of Auxerre, VP 4:3:12; PL 185:328. Conrad of Eberbach: EM 2:6; Griesser 1961, 102.

[9] VP 1: Preface; PL 185:226: *Quanquam id superfluo dixerim, cum totus ea noverit mundus, et virtutes ejus narret omnis ecclesia sanctorum.*

Benedict and the Lord Abbot Bernard of Clairvaux', as if he had already been declared a saint.[10]

In the same way that Bernard had anticipated the later formal canonization of his friend Malachy of Armagh by substituting the traditional collect for a bishop saint for that of a deceased bishop at his funeral Mass and then kissing the feet of the deceased in a gesture akin to venerating relics[11] (▶ *Colour plate 5* and *Fig. 9*), so his own sainthood was treated as an established fact some years before it was officially recognized.

Bernard's brethren at Clairvaux knew that his reputation for sanctity was well deserved, and Geoffrey of Auxerre's account of his passing is deeply touching. With streaming tears and a heavy heart the monks all wondered how they would manage without him. As he lay dying, they said to him, 'Have you then no compassion for this monastery? Have you no pity for us, your poor children, whom like a mother you suckled at the breast, whom you fostered with fatherly affection? How can you then abandon the fruit of your lifework in this valley?'[12] Bernard replied, weeping, that he did not know which to choose, to remain or to depart. Quoting the words of the apostle in Philippians 1:22-23, 'and what to choose I know not', Bernard chose to leave the decision to the Lord.

Shortly before the third hour on Thursday 20 August, within the octave of the Assumption, Bernard died. He was stripped of his garments and the ritual washing of the corpse from head to toe followed. This symbolic act of cleansing and primitive autopsy whereby the cause of death might be established took place in the death-chamber at Clairvaux on a stone slab.[13] The monks' decision to bury Bernard in the church at Clairvaux was in itself testimony to the veneration in which he was held at his death, for, according to cistercian usage, burial in the church was restricted to bishops and royal and princely families. Abbots were usually buried in the chapter house and their tombs in due course became objects of veneration. Almost immediately further signs of his sanctity appeared. It was claimed much later that Bernard's body had

[10] In the exemplum collection *Liber Visionum et Miraculorum* by John of Clairvaux quoted in McGuire 1998, 116.

[11] VP 4:4:21; PL 185:333.

[12] VP 5:2:12; PL 185:358: *Nunquid non misereris huic monasterio, Pater? Nunquid non compateris nobis, quos tanto pietatis affectu maternis lactasti uberibus, paterna consolatione fovisti? Quomodo sic exponis labores tuos, quos in loco hoc laborasti?*

[13] Lekai 1977, 376.

left an imprint or *umbra* on the stone on which it had been washed. The story, almost certainly post-medieval, has its roots in depictions of the Ascension in medieval art; while the legs of Christ disappear into a cloud his footprints can be seen on the rocks below. Saints were believed to be rewarded with the same force which continued to act in Christ's body after his death,[14] and the visible signs of this *virtus* had the effect of arousing in the faithful the memory of Christ's death.

A number of examples of this may be seen, including a wall painting in the danish church Førslev dated *c.* 1380.[15] Other parallels are the Shroud of Turin and the Veronica's Veil. The imprint of Bernard's body was mentioned by Joseph Meglinger in his *Iter Cisterciense,* published in 1667, in which he refers to pilgrims to Clairvaux being shown the miraculous image.[16] A fifteenth-century martyrology from the catalan abbey of Poblet contains a circular miniature of Bernard lying on a slab similar to that on which his body would have been washed after his death (MA 316). His bearded figure is dressed in a black cowl and a gold crozier has been placed in his left hand. His head rests on a yellow cushion. The scene is witnessed by a group of monks in cowls with their heads covered by their hoods. Their cowls are also black, except for one which is brown. The background has gold leaves on a red ground.

THE EARLY CULT OF BERNARD

As the news of Bernard's death spread a great crowd which, according to Geoffrey of Auxerre, 'filled the whole valley' gathered at Clairvaux. The sanctity which in life Geoffrey had described as an 'inner beauty' which 'revealed itself in his outward appearance'[17] was now, in death, enhanced, and Geoffrey found that 'his dear countenance lost none of its old appeal. Rather, it gained the more, for it gripped the eye, drew the attention, enfolded the attention of all'.[18] There is a remarkable

[14] For this, see Vauchez 1997, 425–427.

[15] Illustrated in Saxtorph 1967, 163.

[16] Quoted in Vacandard 1927, 2:52.

[17] VP 3:1:1; PL 185:303.

[18] VP 5:2:14; PL 185:360: *dum pristina illa dulcissimi gratia vultus nil minorata, sed aucta, magis omnium in se figeret oculos, animos traheret, sepeleret affectus.*

similarity between this and Walter Daniel's fuller description of Aelred's body after his death:

> When his body was laid naked before us to be washed, we saw how the glory to come had been revealed in the father. His flesh was clearer than glass, whiter than snow, as though his members were those of a boy five years old, without a trace of stain, but altogether sweet, and composed and pleasant. . . . Perfect in every part of his body, the dead father shone like a carbuncle, was fragrant as incense, pure and immaculate in the radiance of his flesh as a child.[19]

Both biographers knew their subjects intimately, but in this description they followed the conventions of hagiography. Their model was probably the *Life of Saint Martin* by Sulpicius Severus, which had its own roots in Saint Matthew's description of Christ's transfigured body (Mt 17:2) as well as in literary parallels in antiquity.[20] By these descriptions, both Bernard and Aelred became a second Martin, evoking the memory of Christ himself.

The crowd that descended on Clairvaux was eager to witness the burial and to touch his clothes and kiss his hands and feet, and to secure some tangible memento of the great man. The primary relic was his body, but such secondary relics as items of clothing or objects he had used were also venerated, for it was believed that holiness clung to everything the saint had touched. Among these objects the matting upon which Bernard lay and the cup from which he drank have been preserved.[21] The main opportunities for removing parts of Bernard's body for dispersal as relics came when his body was exhumed following his canonization in 1174 and moved to its new shrine, and again in 1178 when the third Clairvaux church was completed and the shrine was again translated. Because Henry II of England had contributed to the building of Clairvaux III, the abbot of Clairvaux sent him one of Bernard's fingers.[22]

[19] Powicke 1950, 62.

[20] For this, see Heffernan 1988, 101–118.

[21] Illustrated in Waddell 1990, 143, and Berlioz 1990, 124, respectively.

[22] On the dispersal of Bernard's relics, see Waddell 1990, 141–146, and Berlioz 1990, 121–125.

The process of collecting Bernard's relics had already been begun during his lifetime. Bernard's friend, Archbishop Eskil of Lund, had taken back to Denmark some hairs from Bernard's beard and one of his teeth and given them to the monks at the cistercian foundation of Esrum. Geoffrey of Auxerre records how these relics had then produced a miraculous cure. Eskil had taken a troublesome young relative who had become ill, but there his health deteriorated. A demon, resenting the monks' success in securing the young man's salvation, invaded one of the monks, causing him to become boisterous and violent. When Bernard's relics were placed on him, he shouted in German: 'Take it away, take it away, get Bernard away . . . . Oh, how heavy you have become, Bernard, how intolerably hard you are on me.'[23] He then opened his eyes and recovered his former health. The story gently implies that Eskil had some small share in the power of the relics to effect a cure.

Small bernardine relics—such as those at Esrum or others belonging to the Augustinians at Cambrai, the Premonstratensians at Floreffe, or the cathedral at Tournai—were usually kept in a metal chasse, often in the shape of a house or a church. A miniature in an early fifteenth-century manuscript of Vincent de Beauvais' *Speculum Historiale* by the Parisian Master of the Cité des Dames (MA127) depicts the veneration of Bernard's relics by four monks in black cowls. The scene is a chapel. A golden reliquary is placed on a green altar, above which hangs a lamp above. One of the monks is sitting, reading from a book on his knees, his hood over his head. Two others are kneeling, one of them with his hands clasped in prayer, and one is prostrating himself on the tiled floor.

Bernard's Miracles

Veneration of Bernard was focussed, however, on the shrine of the saint at Clairvaux, where most of his remains were preserved. Saints were believed to be especially responsive to prayers said in the vicinity of their relics, and such shrines attracted pilgrims who came both for

[23] VP 4:4:26; PL 185:335-336: *'Tollite, tollite, amovete Bernardum'. Et dicebat:'Heu, quam ponderosus factus es, Bernarde! Quam gravis, quam intolerabilis factus es mihi'.* See also McGuire 1982, 53.

spiritual comfort and frequently also in the hope of cures. The cult of saints flourished in medieval popular religion and interest in their relics and the miracles they performed at times loomed even larger than did the glorious deeds on which their sainthood rested.[24] The problem these pilgrims posed to monastic discipline became obvious almost immediately following Bernard's death. The cost to the regular routine of worship and work, and the concomitant financial advantage, may be seen by the later examples of the cistercian pilgrimage sites of Pontigny, with its shrine of Saint Edmund of Abingdon, and the english abbey of Hailes, which had in 1270 received the Blood of Christ preserved in a phial from Edmund, the son of Henry III. As a result, the monks at these two abbeys were able to build magnificent churches. Conrad of Eberbach records the cures of an epileptic monk in the presence of the body of Bernard and of a boy whose withered arm was healed on the eve of Bernard's funeral when he placed it on the saint's arm. When a third person seeking a cure prostrated himself before Bernard's coffin in front of the monks who were singing psalms, the abbot of Cîteaux, who had come to assist at the funeral

> Was greatly worried that the increase in miracles would attract a large multitude whose unruly behaviour might compromise the discipline of the order which might be destroyed by the unruly nature of such crowds, and that the religious fervour would slacken in that place. He therefore, having first considered the matter carefully, reverently approached the body and forbade it, in the name of obedience, to perform any further miracles . . . and the soul of our father continued his obedience to a mortal human being even after his physical death. . . . and from that day until now he has never been seen to perform any miracles in public'.[25]

[24] See Vauchez 1993, and Finucane 1995.

[25] EM 2:20; Griesser 1961, 116–118: *considerans tantam importunitatem tumultuantis populi et ex praesentibus futura coniciens vehementer timere coepit, ne, si crebrescentibus signis tam intolerabilis illuc populorum turba concurreret, earum improbitate disciplina periret ordinis et sanctae religionis fervor in eodem loco tepesceret. Quapropter habita super hoc deliberatione reverenter accedens per virtutem obedientiae, ne signa ulterius faceret, inhibuit. . . . sancta et vere humilis anima patris nostri mortali homini etiam post mortem carnis obediens fuit . . . ex illa die et deinceps nunquam publica miracula facere visus sit.*

Conrad goes on to record how, some years later, an abbot in Italy failed in an attempt to cure a woman possessed by a demon. When he exposed her to a relic of hair from Bernard's beard, the demon in her reacted violently, shouting at the abbot: 'Hey, little abbot, what are you attempting to do? What are you scheming against me under your habit? You are wasting your time. Keep your little Bernard. He won't be of any help to you'. The abbot then remembered that Bernard had been ordered by the abbot of Cîteaux not to do any more miracles.[26]

According to some, the story of the abbot's injunction against new miracles was a pious invention to cover the lack of posthumous miracles at Bernard's tomb.[27] Bredero has shown, however, that, while miracles featured prominently in Alexander III's other canonizations—Edward the Confessor in 1161, Knud Lavard in 1169, and Thomas Becket in 1173—there was no mention of them among the testimonials to sainthood in the pope's letter in January 1174 sanctioning the veneration of Bernard.[28] The shortage of miracles was seized upon by those who had not admired Bernard in life. Towards the end of the twelfth century the english satirist Walter Map in his *Courtiers' Trifles* told of miracles Bernard had intended, but had failed, to perform. One of them was narrated by an abbot and as a result of which 'he blushed and many left the room laughing'.[29] There is, however, little doubt that fear of commercial exploitation was responsible for the abbot's curtailment of further posthumous miracles. Furthermore, this restraint was consistent with Bernard's own teaching, expressed in his famous *Apologia ad Guillelmum Abbatem*. In the chapter 'On paintings and sculptures and silver and gold in monasteries' he posed the question, 'Tell me, priests, what is gold doing in the holy place?'[30]

Although miracles were central in establishing a claim for sanctity, the danger which an exaggerated interest in them, and in the relics of the saints, posed at the expense of an imitation of their virtuous lives,

[26] EM 2:20; Griesser 1961, 117: *Eia, inquit, abbatule, quid vis facere? Quid modo mali contra me sub illa veste tua machinaris? Frustra niteris, in cassum laboras; serva Bernardulum tuum, nec enim proficies quidquam.*

[27] Ward 1982, 180.

[28] Bredero 1996, 70–72.

[29] James 1983, 73–80.

[30] *Apologia* 28; SBOp 3:104: *Dicite, ait ille, pontifices, in sancto quid facit aurum?*

did not escape the early Cistercians. Bernard himself warned in his Sermon on the feast of Saint Martin:

> Does the word of God then pronounce those blessed who raise the dead, give sight to the blind, cure the sick, cleanse the lepers, heal the paralysed, cast out demons, foresee the future, shine out with miracles, or is it rather those who are poor in spirit, gentle, sorrowful, hungering and thirsting for righteousness, merciful, pure of heart, peacemakers, persecuted for righteousness' sake?[31]

The primacy of charity was also evoked by Aelred of Rievaulx's biographer, Walter Daniel, in his Letter to Maurice, when he sets out to put Aelred's miracles in perspective:

> Our father's are great miracles. But bad men can work miracles, even great miracles. . . . I marvel at the charity of Aelred more than I should marvel if he had raised four men from the dead. My hearers may laugh, they may mock at my words, they may throw my letter in the fire, they may do as they please, I hold fast and I hope I may hold fast to this, that Aelred's charity, 'out of a pure heart, and of a good conscience and of faith unfeigned' (1 Cor 13:4-5), exceeded every novelty of miracle.[32]

Bernard and Other Cistercian Saints

The example of Bernard may have been responsible for the reticence of the early Cistercians in promoting the cult of saintly members of the Order. Bernard himself had referred to 'festivals beyond count' as distractions from the core obligations of the faith in these terms: 'This repetition of joys would be more fitting for heaven than for here below,

[31] SBOp 5:410: *Nisi forte beatus predicat sermo divinus, qui mortuos suscitant, caecos illuminant, morbidos sanant, leprosos mundant, paralyticos curant, daemonibus imperant, futura praemunciant, miraculis coruscant, et non margis pauperes spiritu, mites, lugentes, esurientes et sitientes iustitiam, misericordes, mundicordes, pacificos, persecutionem propter iustitiam sustinentes?*

[32] Powicke 1950, 78.

for citizens than for exiles'.[33] Fear of the consequences of a proliferation of feastdays caused the General Chapter of 1194 to rule that the remains of Hugh of Bonnevaux, who had died 'in the odour of sanctity', be left where they had been buried and not moved to a grander shrine.[34] The indifference the Cistercians showed in seeking official recognition of the merits of their saintly members during the twelfth and early thirteenth centuries was inevitably seized on by their detractors as evidence of a shortage of saints in their ranks. Caesarius of Heisterbach told of a nobleman who exclaimed: 'The grey monks! Have they ever seen any saints there? On Sundays, when the priest reads his calendar, I've yet to hear him name a single grey monk'.[35] Although he was hardly an impartial observer, the english chronicler Matthew Paris nevertheless made the extravagant statement in his *Life of Saint Edmund of Abingdon* that 'virtually all glorious saints rest in houses belonging to monks of the black order while only a few, if any, lie in cistercian dwellings'.[36]

In the early days of the Cistercians the *Exordium Parvum* had promised those monks who emulated the holy lives of the founding fathers would 'repose happily in everlasting rest'.[37] The optimism and unswerving faith in their cause which had characterized the early monks in the first few decades after the foundation of Cîteaux was gradually replaced by a certain *angst* among the monks, brought on by a partial failure to live up to the demands they had set for themselves, and this inevitably led to a degree of mockery among the laity around their monasteries. This growing anxiety expressed itself in a story made famous by Caesarius of Heisterbach in the early thirteenth century, although it had previously appeared in an english manuscript of marian miracles and had been repeated in a collection of *exempla* from the cistercian abbey of Beaupré in northern France around 1200.[38] In a vision of heaven a terrified monk

[33] Ep 174; SBOp 7:391; PL 185:335: *patriae est, non exsilii, frequentia haec gaudiorum, et numerositas festivitatum cives decet, non exsules.*

[34] *Statuta* 1:176 (1194:33): *Abbas Bonaevallis* [B. Hugh of Bonnevaux] *qui sepultus est in oratorio pro religiosis suae opinione ibi sic remaneat. De iis vere qui contra ordinis formam hoc facere praesumpserunt, dominus abbas Cistercii inquirat et digne corrigat.*

[35] Quoted in Vauchez 1997, 124.

[36] Lawrence 1960, 276: *Omnes fere sancti gloriosi in domibus iacent nigri ordinis monachorum, pauci vel nulli in Cisterciensium domiciliis.*

[37] Waddell 1999, 417.

[38] McGuire 1983, 227–229.

could find no Cistercian, but he was comforted when he encountered Mary, who opened her cloak and revealed an 'innumerable multitude of monks, lay brothers, and nuns' of the Order.[39] Although the main purpose of the story was to highlight the central role of Mary among the Cistercians, it reveals an uncharacteristic disquiet in one of its members.

The story gave rise to a popular motif in cistercian iconography: Our Lady of Mercy—in German the *Schutzmantelmadonna,* Our Lady of the Protecting Mantle. The most famous example of it features Bernard.[40] It is an early sixteenth-century painting (PA182). from the nuns' house of Flines in french Flanders attributed to Jean Bellegambe (*c.* 1470–1535). A crowned Virgin sits on a throne with a high delicately traceried back. Her voluminous cloak is held up by two angels. Beneath it, on the left, is a nimbed and tonsured Bernard carrying a crozier and accompanied by a large group of monks, all of them in white cowls. On the right, a community of nuns, in white habits and black veils, is headed by the painting's donor, Ysabel de Maléfiance, and not by the abbess, Jeanne de Boubais, whose portrait appears on the reverse in a scene of the Last Judgment.

Early cistercian reserve in seeking the official canonization of saintly monks was not to last. 'In the space of a few decades', according to Vauchez, 'indifference and even negligence gave way to an active positive policy'.[41] In 1220 the General Chapter ordered the abbot of Cîteaux to petition the pope to canonize Hugh of Bonnevaux and Robert of Molesme, and in 1222 the chapter fathers decreed that Robert's feast be celebrated on 17 April with an office of twelve lessons and one Mass, the same way as Benedict was honoured (*sicut de beato Benedicto*).[42] The first half of the thirteenth century saw a proliferation of cistercian *vitae,* especially of nuns and lay brothers in the Low Countries, but although a multitude of members of the Order are recorded in the Cistercians' Menology and venerated in their cloisters, they apparently felt there was no need for their recognition in the wider Church and only a small number of Cistercians were ever officially canonized.

[39] *Dialogus Miraculorum* 7:64. Caesarius of Heisterbach 1929, 1:546.

[40] Other examples include a wood engraving in the Cîteaux collection of privileges printed in 1491, a miniature in a manuscript from Leubus (Lubiaz) dated *c.* 1320–1330, and the conventual seal of the danish abbey of Esrum, illustrated in France 1998, ills. 78, 79, and 129 respectively. On Cistercians under Mary's Mantle, see also France 2002.

[41] Vauchez 1997, 126.

[42] See *Statuta* 1:526-7 (1220:48); 1:527 (1220:53); and 2.15-6 (1222:13).

THE CULT OF THE SAINTS

The cult of the saints goes back to the early Church.[43] It emerged as a grassroots desire of the young churches to celebrate and honour those whose sanctity was universally recognized and to seek their intercession. This spontaneous proclamation of an exalted status, *vox populi, vox Dei,* has continued to find expression in the Church throughout history down to modern times, as can be seen recently in the reverence accorded Pope John XXIII and Mother Teresa. The imposition of specific criteria as to the indications of sanctity and the nature and content of the devotions gradually evolved into the process of papal recognition known as canonization from the tenth century onwards.[44] One of the ways in which growing papal prestige expressed itself following the Gregorian Reform was in regulating the expanding cult of saints. Twelve causes, i.e. candidates, for canonization were introduced during the pontificate of Alexander III (1159–1181), five of which were completed. Among them were Thomas Becket, in 1173, and Bernard, in 1174. The rules were further refined under Innocent III (1198–1216). Although minor changes have subsequently been made, the teaching of the Roman Church remains much the same today. According to the recent Catechism, 'by solemnly proclaiming that [the saints] practised heroic virtue and lived in fidelity to God's grace, the Church recognizes the power of the Spirit of holiness within her and sustains the hope of believers by proposing the saints to them as models and intercessors'.[45]

Throughout the history of the Church the qualities perceived as holy have received various emphases according to the varying needs of the times. Pointing to the example of luminaries has long been a powerful tool in teaching the faith. The young churches emerged from the era of persecution gained strength by celebrating the heroic lives of their martyred leaders and bishops. Military virtues were prized in the time of the Crusades and so therefore were warrior saints like George, Maurice, and Theodore. Saint Sebastian and other saints who were invoked against diseases became increasingly popular as plague swept through Europe in the fourteenth century. Many local patron saints were in-

[43] Brown 1981.
[44] For this, see Vauchez 1997.
[45] Catholic Catechism 1994, 192.

voked in rivalries between neighbouring communities. Renewed monastic life, both at Cîteaux and elsewhere, played an important part in the Gregorian Reform of the late eleventh and early twelfth century, providing a model of christian living based on the evangelical simplicity and poverty of the early Church. Its leaders therefore formed the majority and the most prestigious of the new saints of the period. Among them was Bernard, along with Hugh of Cluny, Bruno, the founder of the Carthusians, Stephen of Muret, and John Gualbert. By the thirteenth century canonizations among members of the old Orders gradually decreased, while those of friars of the new Orders increased. While regulars formed 40.8% of canonizations in the period 1198 to 1304, this group fell to 27.4% in the years from 1305 to 1431. As european society became thoroughly, and often literately, permeated by Christianity, sanctity, which had predominantly been a clerical and monastic phenomenon, came to be perceived as well in lay saints, among them married men and women.

The Hierarchy of Saints

The medieval predeliction, amounting almost to an obsession, for enumerating and tabulating everything expressed itself in arranging the company of heaven in order of precedence. As the Mother of Christ Mary is also Queen of Heaven and stands indisputably at the pinnacle of all the saints. The choice of saints to be portrayed in the company of Mary always carried a special significance. She played a central role in the iconography of Bernard, as we have seen, appearing most commonly in the two picture-types, the *Lactatio* and the *Doctrina*,[46] and cistercian churches were dedicated to her.[47]

Monks, from the Desert Fathers onwards, featured prominently among the saints portrayed in early medieval art. As the influence of the monastic Orders beyond their cloisters gradually waned from the early thirteenth century onwards, their saints still remained role models for members of the newer Orders. Sometimes agreement was reached between the various Orders whereby they adopted the feasts of their

[46] See Chapters 8 and 9.
[47] *Statuta* 1:17 (1134:18).

respective saints. In 1255 the Cistercian General Chapter introduced the feasts of Saint Dominic and Saint Peter Martyr and in return the Dominicans adopted the feast of Saint Bernard.[48] Saints belonging to the various religious families were usually grouped together, and the names of the founder saints—Anthony, Benedict, Dominic, and Francis—were invoked in the Roman Litany. As Bernard was not the founder of the Cistercians and, as the Cistercians were part of the family of Saint Benedict, he was not included, nor were any other cistercian saints.

BERNARD IN THE HIERARCHY OF SAINTS

While the Litany, a series of prayers in which the names of the saints were called out and entreated one by one to 'pray for us', represented the literary form of this hierarchy in the liturgy of the Church and in devotional books, a visual counterpart may be found in illuminated manuscripts and altarpieces. We see this visual litany in a fourteenth-century image depicting two hundred seventy-one saints, including Bernard and Benedict (MA177). Almost contemporary with it is an altarpiece of the *Coronation of the Virgin with Adoring Saints* attributed to Jacopo di Cione and his workshop and painted in 1370–1371 for the church of S Pier Maggiore, Florence (PA029). The central panel features the Virgin being crowned Queen of Heaven by her Son in the presence of choirs of angels with musical instruments. The scene is witnessed by a large number of kneeling saints on the side panels on either side, all turning inwards towards the central scene. Altogether there are twenty-four saints on each side, arranged in five rows. The saints on the left include Peter, Bartholomew, Stephen, John the Evangelist, Francis, Mary Magdalen, Philip, Blaise, Gregory, Benedict, Lucy, Luke, and Ambrose; on the right Paul, Matthew, Lawrence, John the Baptist, Julian, Nicholas, Dominic, Catherine of Alexandria, James the Greater, Ivo of Brittany, Bernard, Anthony Abbot, Agnes, Mark, Augustine, Jerome, Scholastica, and Ursula. The conventional order has been observed: the most important saints have been placed nearest the central scene, and, in the usual way, Bernard and Benedict have been paired on opposite sides. Other saints are 'balanced' in the same

[48] *Statuta* 2:410 (1255:4); *Statuta* 2:450 (1259:9).

traditional fashion: John the Baptist with John the Evangelist; Peter with Paul; and Francis with Dominic.

Another example of grouping saints into various categories may be seen on the inside of the painted doors, or wings, of the reliquary cabinet in the cistercian church of Løgum in Denmark dated *c.* 1325. ▶ *Colour plate 12.* This consists of sixteen 'portraits' of saints, eight on each wing, corresponding to the sixteen compartments of the cupboard, four across and four down, which, it is thought, originally contained relics of the saints. The overall size of the cabinet is 181 cm x 133 cm, the width with the doors/wings when open being 266 cm. That the overall width of the cabinet corresponds to a magnificent frontal now preserved in the National Museum, Copenhagen, allows the conjecture that the cabinet matched the altar in size, and that originally the cabinet was likely placed on or at the back of the altar, even though it is now set into a wall elsewhere in the church. The outside of the doors are now painted plain green but were almost certainly decorated in the Middle Ages, and the effect would have been very much like that of an altarpiece. In the same way, the cabinet would ordinarily have been closed and only on special occasions opened to reveal the relics and the images of the saints. A number of similar cabinets are found in Schleswig Holstein and Mecklenburg, including an earlier example—dated *c.* 1275—at the cistercian Doberan consisting of twenty compartments.[49] Further south, at the cistercian abbey of Marienstatt, there was a variant in the form of a reliquary retable dated *c.* 1300. At Løgum the saints, from left to right, are: on the top row, the apostles, two on each side (John, Peter, Paul, and James the Greater, thus Peter and Paul nearest the centre); second row, martyrs (George, Clement, Dennis, and Maurice); third row, confessors (Bernard, Ambrose, Augustine, and Benedict); and bottom row, virgins (Barbara, Catherine of Alexandria, Margaret, and Ursula). Once again Bernard is 'paired' with Benedict in the same way as Peter is with Paul. The name of each is inscribed above against a red or green background in alternate rows, and they all carry the traditional attributes. The halos are red and green alternatively, with gold outline. Each figure is painted against a deep green background and placed within a golden trifoliate arcade supported by golden columns and corresponding to the decoration around the sixteen reliquary compartments. Above

[49] Illustrated in Erdmann 1995, 16.

Bernard (PA036) is the inscription BERNARDUS in gold letters on a red background. He is wearing a dark grey cowl with gold edges, and has a crozier in his right hand while his left hand is raised in blessing. Benedict is depicted in much the same way, but in a black cowl and is also carrying a book (the *Rule*). Five of the saints included across the categories of martyrs and virgins (George, Dennis, Barbara, Catherine of Alexandria, and Margaret) were part of the group of saints known as the Fourteen Holy Helpers (or Fourteen Auxiliary Helpers—*Vierzehnheiligen*) whose cult arose in the Rhineland in the fourteenth century and spread both southwards and northwards to Scandinavia. Their popularity was based on the perceived efficacy of their intercession against a variety of diseases and especially at the hour of death.

A more usual way of keeping relics of the saints was to place them in small metal reliquaries of architectural design, such as the one illustrated in the early fifteenth-century manuscript of the *Speculum Historiale* (MA127). These were sometimes decorated with images of the saints they contained, as we see in an early fourteenth-century engraved silver gilt reliquary decorated with enamel plates from the cistercian nuns' abbey of Lichtental (VA14). On the side the saints are depicted under six trefoiled canopies; the four central ones contain the crowned Virgin and Child and the Three Kings, on the left is the donor nun, Margaret of Speyer, and on the right the standing figure of a youthful-looking nimbed Bernard with a crozier in his right hand and his name inscribed above. Two thirteenth-century silver gilt reliquaries from the cistercian abbey of Grandselve in southern France (VA29, VA 30), probably created in a goldsmith's workshop in nearby Toulouse, are made in the form of a church. Central biblical scenes are flanked by saints, including Bernard in eucharistic vestments, carrying a book and a crozier. Images of Bernard to indicate the presence of one of his relics are also found on reliquaries which did not belong to the Cistercians. A triptych reliquary (PA143) commissioned by the Dominican Fra Francesco da Montebelluna in 1352 has Saint Benedict and Saint Catherine with the donor kneeling on the central panel, on the left wing Saint Dominic and on the right wing Bernard with a crozier in his left hand and a book in his right, all on a green background. The small nun who kneels at the feet of Saint Dominic suggests the probable provenance as the Convent of Saint Paolo in Treviso. The text at the base reads: ANNO DOMINI MCCCLII FR FRANCESC' D MOTEBELU / ORDIS FRM PDICATO-

RUM FECIT FIERI HAC ANCONA AD HONOREM DEI / . . . SCM QUORUM RELQE SUT HIC POSITE.

Bernard and the Virgin Mary

By the time the early injunction forbidding sculptures and paintings had become a dead letter,[50] an image of the Virgin held the place of honour behind the high altar, and most monasteries would also have had a statue of her to which the community turned during the singing of the *Salve Regina* at the end of Compline. As altarpieces became more elaborate Mary came to be depicted on them, and one of the chief marian *topoi*—such as the Annunciation or her Coronation by Christ—often dominated the *corpus* or central panel in a triptych. Very often she is flanked by a number of saints or depicted in a so-called *Sacra converzatione,* in which saints from different periods, often numbering four, meet with the central figures of the Virgin and Child, usually seated. Examples in which only Bernard and Benedict are featured in the company of the Virgin and Child have already been mentioned. The inclusion of Bernard as one of a larger number of saints is often, but not always, indicative of cistercian provenance. A magnificent polyptych (PA149) painted in 1360–1361 by Giovanni da Milano for the Hospital of Saint Barnabas in Prato was commissioned by Frater Francesco da Tieri, prior of the hospital 1334–1363. The central panel shows the Virgin and Child enthroned, flanked by Saint Catherine of Alexandria and Bernard on the left and Saint Bartholomew and Saint Barnabas on the right. Bernard is bearded and carries a red book. The upper predella has scenes from the lives of the saints, including the Vision of Bernard (PA150), and the lower predella has biblical scenes. The medallions in the pinnacles contain busts of five prophets. The inscription reads: EGO JOHANNES DE MEDIOLANO PINXI HOC OPUS FRATE FRANCESCO FECI DEPINGERE QUESTA TAVOLA SOTTO LE STORIE DEI SANTI: DECOLACIO SANCTE KATERINE, DOCTRINA SANCTI BERNARDI CONFESSORIS, PASIO SANCTI BARTOLAMEI APOSTOLI, PASIO SANCTI BARNABE APOSTOLI.

A similar but somewhat less complex and later triptych of the Madonna Enthroned with Saints and Angels (PA070) was painted by Agnolo

[50] Waddell 1999, 464.

Gaddi of the Florentine School, who was active from 1369 to 1396 and who studied under Giovanni da Milano. The book held by the naked Child is inscribed EGO SUM A & O ('I am the Alpha and Omega'), and below the Virgin are the opening words of the angelic salutation. The names of the four saints are given under each one: from left Andrew (*S Andreas Apps*), Benedict (*S Benedictus Abbas*) in a white cowl (as was quite common in italian iconography) holding a book with the opening words of his Rule *Ausculta o Fili precepta . . .*, Bernard (*S Bernardus Doctor*) holding an open book from which he is reading, and Catherine of Alexandria (*S Katherina Virgo*). The positions of three of the saints—Benedict, Bernard, and Catherine—are almost identical to those in another work by Gaddi (PA80).

The choice of saints in the company of Mary always carried a special significance. The saint sometimes represented the patron of the church—such as Saint Galgano in the altarpiece by Giovanni di Paolo painted *c.* 1470 for the cistercian abbey of Saint Galgano, sometimes the founder of the religious Order to which the church belonged—such as Saint Dominic in a triptych reliquary from the dominican convent in Treviso dated 1352 (PA143), and sometimes the patrons of the donor or donors—such as Saint John the Baptist and Saint Martha depicted with the kneeling donors in the late fifteenth-century triptych by Jan Provoost (PA065). Although it is not always possible to ascertain the reason for the inclusion of certain saints in these composite images, the choice was never arbitrary. Occasionally, it is both clear and poignant with meaning. On a triptych painted by Jean Bellegambe in *c.* 1516 (PA107), for example, the wings are decorated with the saints as a kind of visual biography of the donor. The central panel (not illustrated) has a most unusual Annunciation scene in which a kneeling benedictine donor abbot is placed between his intercessor, the angel Gabriel, and the Virgin to whom he is presented. He is in fact Guillaume of Bruxelles, a former Cistercian who had been the reformer of Flines and the nuns' confessor under the abbess, Jeanne de Boubais, the great patron of the artist. In 1513 Guillaume became the sixty-ninth abbot of the ancient benedictine monastery of Saint Amand near Valenciennes. In 1516 he resigned, moved to another benedictine house, Saint Trond, as abbot in 1517, and in 1532 he died. He had appeared earlier in the guise of one of Bernard's brothers in another triptych, also by Bellegambe, known as the Retable of Le Cellier (PA087), painted *c.* 1509. There Abbess Jeanne is portrayed as Bernard's sister. A portrait of Guillaume, also attributed to

Bellegambe, is found on a small diptych on which he is depicted being presented to the Virgin by Bernard (PA084); on the reverse is a portrait of the abbess. The wings of the Annunciation triptych (PA 107 and PA 108) feature a number of saints: on the left Saint Amand in his episcopal vestments with crozier and mitre carries a model of the church he founded. Behind him, recognizable by his name and the crest above him, are the Cistercian Saint William (Guillaume), archbishop of Bourges, with mitre and archbishop's cross, and Saint Benedict in a black cowl and with the usual attributes of book and crozier. On the right wing, identified by their names and crests, are Bernard, in a white cowl and also carrying a book and crozier, and Saint William of Aquitaine in armour and a black coat, carrying a standard with *fleurs de lys* corresponding to his crest below. Before them is Saint Trond in a green chasuble, carrying a model of his church. The reverse of the wings has Bernard in a grisaille *Lactation* scene (PA108) similar to the one in the Retable of Le Cellier (PA088). The triptych celebrates the donor abbot's devotion to Mary and to his patron saint, while the presence of other saints commemorates his tenure of the abbacy of the two ancient benedictine houses, and the appearance of Bernard twice—on the right wing and on the reverse—proclaims both his debt to his own cistercian formation and the veneration in which Bernard was held in the late Middle Ages in the wider benedictine family.

Bernard and Benedict

Bernard is portrayed with Benedict more frequently than with any other saint. Of the total of nine hundred sixty-four bernardine images recorded, the two appear together in no less than seventy-four, in most of them alone, although in some cases also in the company of other saints.

The prominence of Benedict in cistercian iconography is scarcely surprising. According to the *Exordium Parvum* Robert and his companions while still at Molesme 'often used to speak of, complain about, grieve over the transgression of the Rule of the most blessed Benedict, Father of monks'.[51] They promised to 'carry out their profession by observing

[51] *Exordium Parvum* 3, Waddell 1999, 421: *Nam viri isti apud Molismum positi saepius inter se, Dei gratia aspirati, de trangressione Regulae beati Benedicti patris monachorum loquebantur, conquerebantur, contristabantur.*

the Holy Rule'.[52] Contemporary observers acknowledged the centrality of the Rule in the cistercian reform. Writing in 1130, Orderic Vitalis described the monks as endeavouring to 'carry out a literal observance of the Rule of Saint Benedict', William of Malmesbury asserted that 'so intent are they on their Rule, that they think no jot or tittle of it should be disregarded', and Philip of Harvengt writing in the 1140s noted that 'the Rule of Benedict recovered in our times the truth of the letter'.[53]

According to tradition Cîteaux was founded on 21 March, the day the feast of Saint Benedict was celebrated.[54] As followers of the Rule the monks who settled at Cîteaux were Benedictines, although this name, notwithstanding its accuracy, is normally reserved to describe the 'black' monks in order to avoid confusion between them and the 'white' monks of Cîteaux. The Rule was one of those books which every cistercian abbey was bound to possess and a number of these are adorned with images of Benedict within the opening initial *A(usculta o fili precepta magistri)*—'Hearken, my son, to the precepts of the master and incline the ear of thy heart . . .'.[55] Examples survive from Zwettl and Altzelle.[56] Benedict is also sometimes depicted within the initial *O(s justi meditabitur)*, the Introit of the Mass for his feast. This can be seen in a Missal from *c.* 1270 from the silesian abbey of Kamenz in which he holds a scroll with the opening words of the Rule while at his feet a young novice has his own scroll which reads *Loquere Domine* ('Speak, O Lord') taken from 1 Kgs 3:9, 10.[57]

Most unusual is a miniature (MA354) in the Sanctoral at the same abbey introducing the feast of Saint Benedict alongside the usual opening words *Os justi*. On the left is the standing figure of Benedict in a black cowl. He holds an open book—the Rule—in his left hand while his right hand is raised with the index finger pointing in a teaching mode to two cistercian monks in white habits. Benedict's teaching is endorsed by the figure in a brown habit standing behind him, who

[52] *Exordium Parvum* 3, Waddell 1999, 421: *ut professionem suam observantia sanctae Regulae adimplerent.*

[53] Chibnall 1969–1980, 3:338-339; William of Malmesbury 1847, 349; Philip of Harvengt, *De institutione clericorum,* 4:125, PL 203:836-837.

[54] His feast has since been moved to 11 July.

[55] Rule Prologue, trans. McCann 1976, 1.

[56] Illustrated in France 1998, ill. 1 & 2.

[57] Illustrated in France 1998, ill. 3.

represents Bernard. The figures are identified by the inscription *sanctus bernardus abbas et sanctus benedictus abbas*. That Bernard should feature in a miniature celebrating the feast of Benedict is in itself amazing, but that he should be mentioned first in the inscription is even more astounding. It therefore comes as no surprise that the image appears in a Missal which belonged to the cistercian nuns of Lorvão in Portugal and is dated 1305–1314.

Although the Lorvão example is exceptional, Benedict is frequently portrayed together with Bernard in cistercian iconography. Together they not only symbolize the two great branches of the benedictine family, but also represent the Lawgiver and the Mystic, Moses and Elijah, who were present at the Transfiguration of the Lord, united in leading their disciples to the heights of the union of love. When linked to Benedict, Bernard is to be understood as interpreting the Rule of the Father of Monks, and the book he is most frequently depicted carrying may safely be considered to represent the Rule upon which he based his teaching.

Bernard's role in these dual images is that of *alter Benedictus*—the 'other Benedict'—as he was described by Burchard of Balerne.[58] Among these is one of the earliest bernardine images, the manuscript of Bernard's *The Steps of Humility and Pride* from the benedictine abbey of Anchin, dated c. 1165 (MA028), showing two figures flanking that of Christ at the summit of Jacob's Ladder. Drawn little more than a decade after Bernard's death, it depicts Benedict in a brown cowl writing his Rule while Bernard is in a white cowl and holds a book, presumably the Rule or in this case perhaps a copy of his own work which the image illustrates.

A comparable composition in a plaster relief from the second half of the thirteenth century (SC56) had a central figure of a seated Christ in Majesty—Christ Pantocrater—in a frontal position in a niche under a trifoliate arch with the figures of Benedict and Bernard on either side, each holding a long scroll. Originally polychromed, it had belonged to the Cistercians in Florence, but, sadly, was destroyed in 1944.

Benedict and Bernard are more commonly depicted wearing the traditional black and white cowls of their Orders, as we see in the two standing figures in a full-page miniature in a Book of Hours from around 1500 (MA083). Sometimes Bernard is depicted in a grey cowl with Benedict in black because the Cistercians were also known as 'grey' monks from

[58] PL 185:267.

the colour of their habit, which was made of undyed wool and therefore not always pure white. This is how they appear in the opening folio of the Property Register of the cistercian abbey of Tennenbach from 1341–1347, which meticulously records all the belongings of the monastery. Folio one contains two historiated initials. Within the initial *O(Dee paratum sit opus*) are two layered images (MA019): above is a very unusual representation of the Trinity consisting of an abnormally large one-eyed dove, representing the Holy Spirit, with its wings enveloping the Father and the Son on either side and two beaks pointing left and right. Beneath it are the kneeling figures of Benedict in black on the left and Bernard in grey on the right, both nimbed, tonsured, and carrying croziers.[59] Occasionally, Bernard is also shown wearing a black cowl, as was not uncommon in the later Middle Ages, but with the white cistercian tunic showing underneath. The two figures in black on the late fifteenth-century cupboard doors from Sweden (PA035), in which the two are identified by the inscription of their names, provides an example of this.

Dual representations were most commonly found in cistercian monasteries, where the two saints appear together in a variety of media. Many formed part of altarpieces, were carved on choir stalls, adorned the windows of the churches or cloisters, or decorated their service books. Frequently Benedict and Bernard flanked the central figure of Mary. At Santes Creus in Catalonia statues of the two saints were placed at either end of an elaborate altarpiece carved by Taller de Padro Sanglada in *c.* 1420 (SC45); the carved golden centre of an altar from 1500 at Zwettl in Austria has the Virgin flanked by Benedict and Bernard (SC05); and at Lehnin in Brandenburg the two saints were depicted on the wings on either side of the central figure of the Virgin (PA067). A painting by Paolo de Sancto Leocadio (PA178), dated *c.* 1500, has the Virgin and naked Child seated in the centre with the standing figures of Benedict in black looking at an open book (his Rule) on the left and Bernard in white with his hand on the shoulder of the small figure of the donor knight of Montesa on the right. Two spanish paintings of Our Lady of Mercy, both from the first half of the fifteenth century (PA170 and PA173), show kneeling under her mantle two groups of figures led by Benedict in black on the left and Bernard in white on the right; they are by the Master of Olleria and Bernardo Martorell respectively. Another

[59] Illustrated in France 1998, colour plate 23.

version of the enthroned Virgin and Child flanked by the two saints is a fresco dated 1515 (WA32) and attributed to Bernardino Luini in the cistercian church of Morimondo near Milan. This is most unusual in that the figures are joined by the small figure of John the Baptist as a child who is standing at the foot of the throne holding out his hand to the Child who is reciprocating. On the left is Benedict with a long beard and wearing a black cowl; on the right the younger figure of Bernard in white. They are both carrying open books and croziers.

On the end of one of the rows of oak choir stalls from *c.* 1310 in the abbey church of Doberan in Mecklenburg are the two saints carved almost identically. ▶ *Fig. 18* (SC15). Both are nimbed and, to preserve the symmetry of the composition, they each carry a crozier and a book but in opposite hands. Being carved in natural oak makes it impossible to distinguish the colour of their habits, usually the only way of telling them apart. Perhaps the broken tonsure and central tuft of hair of the figure on the right is meant to indicate that this represents Bernard. Other choir stalls with carvings of Benedict and Bernard are found in later examples from the german abbey of Zinna (SC23) and the swiss abbey of Hauterive (SC18). The two saints are depicted in two adjacent pointed stained glass windows from *c.* 1340 in the upper cloister of the nuns' abbey of Wienhausen. Bernard is in a greyish blue habit (GL75), while Benedict is in greyish violet;[60] each of them carries a book in the right hand and a white crozier in the left. Glass panels with the two saints are also found in the churches of the austrian Walpurgiskapelle at Sankt Michael bei Leoben from *c.* 1290 (GL71), the german nuns' abbey of Heiligkreuztal from *c.* 1300 (GL90), the swiss abbey of Hauterive dated 1327 (GL72), and, included among a number of other saints, in the great west window at the german Altenberg from *c.* 1400 (GL76).

Manuscripts depicting the two together include an early fourteenth-century antiphonary from the czech nuns' abbey of Stare Brno (MA082) which shows Benedict in black and Bernard in white. An english manuscript from the second half of the fourteenth century which takes the form of an extensive pictorial litany of two hundred seventy-one saints goes one step further and represents the two saints by just one figure (MA177). The dual identity is signalled by the inscription above the figure and the usual pleas for intercession: *Sancte bernarde ora pro*

[60] The two together are illustrated in France 1998, colour plate 2.

nobis, Sancte benedicte ora pro nobis ('Saint Bernard, pray for us, Saint Benedict, pray for us'). The red book the figure holds stands out in contrast to the pale colour of the rest, and its prominent position at the centre of the figure points to the importance attached to the Rule in the iconography of both saints.

The book which Benedict holds can always be identified as his Rule. Similarly, the book which Bernard is traditionally depicted carrying is almost always the Rule. Exceptions to this are most often the images of Bernard with the devil illustrating the *Verses of Bernard,* when the book, almost always open, represents the psalter (e.g. MA048, MA296). When Bernard is portrayed instructing a group of monks the book may be either the Rule or one of his own works, on which he is presumably commenting. In the full-page miniature in a fourteenth-century manuscript of William of Tournai's *Flores Sancti Bernardi* (MA094) two saints are again shown looking like identical twins, each with a crozier in the right hand and a book in the left. Virtually the only difference besides the black habit with long sleeves on Benedict on the left and the white with narrow sleeves on Bernard on the right, is the text in the two open books: Benedict's book shows the familiar opening words of the Rule—*Ausculta o fili precepta magistri* ('Hearken, my son, to the precepts of the master'); Bernard's displays those of his commentary on the Rule, the treatise *On Precepts and Dispensation.*[61] In a late fourteenth-century spanish *Lactation* painting (PA126) the text of Bernard's book is taken from his First Sermon for the Vigil of Christmas while Benedict's, instead of being the usual opening words of his Rule, are nevertheless from the Prologue to it: IN EIUS DOCTRINA USQUE AD MORTEM IN MONASTERIO [PERSEVERANTES] ('. . . persevering in his teaching in the monastery until death'). Depicting Benedict and Bernard as virtual twins emphasised the link they had in observing the Rule.

Bernard with Other Saints

As the precursor of Christ, John the Baptist, the bridge between the Old and the New Testament, was at the summit of the hierarchy saints. His

[61] *De praecepto et dispensatione* 9:21 (SBOp 3:269): *Praelatum tamquam Deum in his que non sunt contra Deum audire debemus.*

name was invoked in the litany immediately after that of Mary and the archangels. Of him Christ remarked that 'of all the children born of women, a greater than John the Baptist has never been seen' (Mt 11:11). As the prototype of ascetics, he occurs with the two monastic saints, Benedict and Bernard, in an italian polyptych (PA158) painted 1438 by Dominico di Bartolo for the cistercian nuns of Saint Giuliana in Perugia, which had been founded in 1253 by the english cistercian cardinal John of Toledo. In the centre the enthroned Virgin sits with the Child, her left hand on the head of the small kneeling figure of the cistercian nun in a white habit and a black veil who commissioned the painting. On either side of her are, on the left Saint Benedict, in a black cowl and carrying a crozier and a book, and Saint John the Baptist, and, on the right, Saint Giuliana and Bernard in a white cowl, also with crozier and book. The inscription reads: DOMINICUS BARTOLI—DE SENIS. ME PINXIT. HOC OPUS FECIT FIERI DOMINA ANTONIA FILIA FRA[N]CISCI DE DOMO BUCCHOLIS ABBATISSA ISTIUS MONASTERII IN ANNO D[OMIN]I MCCCCXXXVIII. The name of each saint is given at the base of the panels.

Next after Mary and Saint John the Baptist in the hierarchy of the saints came the apostles. Benedict and Bernard are featured together with six of the apostles on the two wings of the magnificent Heisterbach retable painted *c.* 1450 by an important pupil of Stephen Lochner, the great master of the Cologne School. Together with them are six of the apostles, while the six other apostles were probably represented in the central panel which is now lost. Bernard (PA010) holds an elaborate gold crozier in his right hand and with his left hand he holds up his dark grey cowl revealing the white tunic underneath. In his left hand he also has a so-called purse book, another example of which, out of its purse and open, may be seen in a somewhat later *Lactation* image (PA019). Around the edge of the gold nimbus is the inscription *sanctus bernardus.* Bernard appears again with the apostles in the pentatych commissioned in 1496 by Abbot Peder Andersen for the high altar at Esrum in Denmark. The central part of this consisted of a Crucifixion scene which was flanked by four panels with saints, one of them Bernard in an *Amplexus* image (SC51). The inner wings contained sixteen carved oak figures, the twelve apostles together with the two deacon saints, Vincent and Lawrence, as well as Benedict and Bernard (SC52).

A rare, perhaps unique, full-page miniature in a late medieval breviary illustrating All Saints' Day with a multitude of the company of heaven gives an unusually prominent position to the saints belonging to the various religious orders, and Bernard has the pride of place (MA217). At the top the Holy Spirit appears beneath a flaming sky and a bust of God the Father. Around a great gathering of saints is a border consisting of stylized leaves in a diamond pattern. Various categories of saints are easy to recognize—popes by tiaras, bishops by mitres, monks by tonsures, hermits by unkempt hair, kings by crowns. In the centre are two popes and behind them several other bishops. A number of the other prominent figures can be identified: on the left is Saint Dominic, founder of the black friars or Dominicans, in white tunic and black mantle, with the traditional attribute of a dog at his feet, a reference to the nickname given his disciples—the *Domini canes* (the Lord's hounds). Next to him is Saint Francis, founder of the grey friars, in a grey habit with his hands raised showing the stigmata. The figure behind him with his white hood over his head probably represents Saint Bruno, founder of the Carthusians. On the right, and somewhat larger than any of the other figures, is the corpulent figure of Bernard in a white cowl. He is kneeling, his hands clasped in prayer and his elaborate late medieval crozier leaning on his left shoulder. He is further identified by the demon he tramples underfoot, a parallel to the many images illustrating the *Verses of Bernard* in Books of Hours (e.g. MA100, MA146, MA353). Unlike the remarkably similar faces of other saints depicted, the features of his full face are quite distinctive and individualized. This is undoubtedly a portrait of a real contemporary person, most likely a cistercian abbot, as was not uncommon in late medieval images of Bernard, especially in *Lactatio* images (e.g. PA072). Behind Bernard is a figure in a black cowl also carrying a crozier, Saint Benedict; and next to him in a grey habit with a long beard and untidy hair is probably Saint Anthony. One could be forgiven for assuming that this image is in a manuscript commissioned by a cistercian monastery, but in fact it belongs to a manuscript known as the Mayer van den Bergh Breviary and was made in Ghent or Bruges *c.* 1510 and is thought to have belonged to Manuel I of Portugal (1495–1521). On it at least four of the most outstanding illuminators worked: Master of the Older Prayerbook of Maximilian, Gerard Horenbout, Jan Provoost, and Simon Bening. It is, however, safe to conclude that there must have been a cistercian connection, even if the particulars are not known. Don Manuel I is known to have commissioned the magnificent new sacristy at the cistercian abbey at Alcobaça, which had originally been founded in 1153 by a grant to Saint Bernard from his predecessor, Don Alfonso, founder of the portuguese dynasty, following the expulsion of the Moors from the region.[62]

BERNARD'S POPULARITY IN RELIGIOUS ART AND LITURGY

The large number of images of Bernard in the company of other saints inevitably raises the question of the extent of his cult, his relative popularity in various social groups and particular regions, and the fluctuation of this in the course of the medieval centuries. How was he ranked in the 'great multitude, past all counting, taken from all nations and tribes and peoples and languages'? (Rev 7:9).

The cult of Bernard was, and remains, of supreme importance within the cistercian family. To a lesser degree he was also celebrated in the wider monastic and religious world.[63] But to what extent, if at all, can he be described as a 'popular' saint? If 'popular saints' are defined as 'those whose cult was born and developed at the lowest levels of society'[64] the answer must be a resounding 'No'. His cult did not arise from popular lay devotion which was subsequently sanctioned by the official Church, but resulted from the initiative of his own monks, most noticeably that of his friend and secretary Geoffrey of Auxerre. It was gladly endorsed by the papacy in recognition both of the contribution of reformed monasticism to papal policy generally and of the decisive role Bernard played in the anacletan schism of 1130–1138.

Just as Bernard had been greeted by throngs on his travels to places like Milan and Speyer during his lifetime,[65] so, according to Geoffrey of Auxerre, a great crowd gathered at Clairvaux as word of his death spread.[66] This may, admittedly, be an example of the hyperbole for which the genre of hagiography is noted. Even if it is accurate, evidence of a later cult in the region is totally lacking. A rough indicator is provided by an analysis of christian names in Châtillon-sur-Loire in the *département* of the Côte d'Or, in which Cîteaux is situated and which is adjacent to

[62] Cocheril 1978, 263.
[63] See Chapter Four.
[64] Vauchez 1997, 142.
[65] VP 2:2:9; PL 185:273-274. VP 4:5:31; PL 185:338-339. VP 6:4:15; PL 185:381-382.
[66] VP 5:2:14; PL 185:360.

the *department* in which Clairvaux is located. Out of a total of 1693 military personnel in 1414, there were only two mentions of Bernard, a mere 0.1% of the total or practically only one per thousand.[67] A similar result emerges from a survey of names in Beaune in the Côte-d'Or in the fifteenth century: a list of 2640 names in 1400 only has two Bernards, while the name occurs only once in the list totalling 2560 for the year 1470. The name does not appear at all in other lists for the years 1391, 1431, 1433, 1442, and 1450. Furthermore, the name Bernard appears to have been more popular in Burgundy in the ninth and tenth centuries than it was after the death of the saint.[68]

A different picture emerges from the jewish community of the Rhineland. In a letter Bernard stated that 'the Jews are not to be persecuted, killed or even put to flight',[69] and in the Rhineland he had condemned the anti-semitic rantings of a certain monk.[70] As a token of gratitude, 'Bernard' became a popular name among Jews in that region and was perpetuated through future generations.

Another guide to the popularity of Bernard in relation to other saints is provided by a study of church dedications. A survey of the two hundred–sixteen parish churches dedicated to one hundred sixteen different saints in the *département* of Saône-et-Loire in southern Burgundy shows that, only one was named after Bernard, and that none of the other four hundred-one chapters, collegiate or monastic churches, or chapels bore his name.[71] If this was the situation in the cradleland of the Cistercian Order, it is perhaps less surprising that it was repeated in more distant lands. One study of church dedications in England lists three hundred twenty-five different saints' names.[72] The list is headed by the Virgin, followed by All Saints and Saint Peter. Eighty churches are named after Saint Thomas of Canterbury, twenty after Saint Benedict, and one each after Saint Francis and Saint Dominic.

[67] Berlioz 1990, 128. The most popular names were Jehan (John) representing 23%, followed by Guillaume (William) and Pierre (Peter) with 12% and 11% respectively, then Etienne (Stephen), Jacques (James), and Hugues (Hugh), accounting for 4.7%, 3.5%, and 3.4%.

[68] *Ibid.*

[69] Ep 363:6; SBOp 8:316: *Non sunt persequendi Iudaei, non sunt trucidandi, sed nec effugandi quidem.*

[70] Ep 365; SBOp 8:320-322.

[71] Berlioz 1990, 127.

[72] Bond 1914, 17–25.

Bernard is not represented at all. Another study lists one english parish dedicated to Bernard—Stanton-Saint Bernard in Wiltshire in the diocese of Salisbury—while the number named after Saint Benedict is again twenty.[73]

Evidence based on a catalogue of surviving and dated italian paintings for the period 1420 to 1539 reveals a different picture, however.[74] First of all, the all pervasive place of religion in renaissance society is revealed by the fact that 87% (or 1796 out of a total of 2229 paintings) represent religious subjects. Of these, approximately half are concerned mainly with the Virgin or the Virgin and Child, and a quarter each with Christ or the saints. There are exactly one hundred identified saints, of whom twenty-two occur seven or more times. The list is headed by John the Baptist (51 examples), then Sebastian (34), Francis (30), Catherine of Alexandria (22), Jerome (22), Anthony of Padua (21), Rocco (19), Peter (18), Bernardino (17), and, most remarkably, Bernard (15) who ties for tenth place with Michael the Archangel (15). The pre-eminence of John the Baptist is understandable in view of his place in the hierarchy of saints. A number of the other saints had important local cults: Sebastian, as well as being the patron saint of Rome, was also invoked against the plague; Francis was important throughout Italy. But the burgundian Bernard is not an obvious choice. His popularity seems the more remarkable in the context of the next ten saints after him on the list: Christopher, James, Martin, Nicholas, Paul, Mary Magdalene, Stephen, George, and Mark, all of whom were generally more celebrated than Bernard. These figures must, of course, be treated with a certain caution, for they are based only on paintings which have survived and which are dated. Not all artists dated their work, and more material survives from the later part of the period than from the earlier. In addition, many of the paintings are found in monasteries and other religious houses and this may account for the relatively large number of bernardine images. The striking relative popularity of Bernard in late medieval italian painting can only be explained by his perceived devotion to Mary, exemplified by his role in Dante's *Commedia Divina*, and by the iconographical theme known as the *Doctrina* or the *Vision of Mary*.[75]

[73] Arnold-Forster 1899, 3:263 & 343.
[74] Burke 1972, 145–152.
[75] See Chapter Nine.

Another indicator of Bernard's popularity in lay devotional life may be found in Books of Hours. The names of saints occur mainly in two sections of these devotional books: the Calendar, and the Suffrages. Although Bernard's name is sometimes entered in Calendars on 20 August, his feast day, and although his name occasionally appears among the Suffrages, he is not mentioned in the great majority of Books of Hours. The names and images of many other saints appear more frequently than those of Bernard in these two sections. In the fifteenth century a number of supplementary prayers were added, among them the *Verses of Bernard*, and these were usually accompanied by an image of Bernard holding the devil on a chain and trampling on him underfoot.[76] This late medieval iconographical theme was found almost only in Books of Hours, and then only in a small minority of them. The devotion which it illustrated was exclusively lay and largely female, and women formed the greater part of the audience of these prayerbooks.

Another test of the popularity of late medieval saints, and of other religious devotions, is provided by pilgrim souvenirs that have survived. These were not only cherished as tangible evidence of journeys, much as, for example, car stickers are today, but, if they had touched a saint's relic or shrine, the badges became in themselves a form of minor relic and were considered to have a potency as wonder-working objects. The most common form of these small badges was made by pouring a moulten tin-alloy into a form. They were sometimes produced by seal engravers or goldsmiths, and their manufacture ran into millions. Thousands of examples have been found throughout Europe with the largest concentration in the floodlands of the prov-

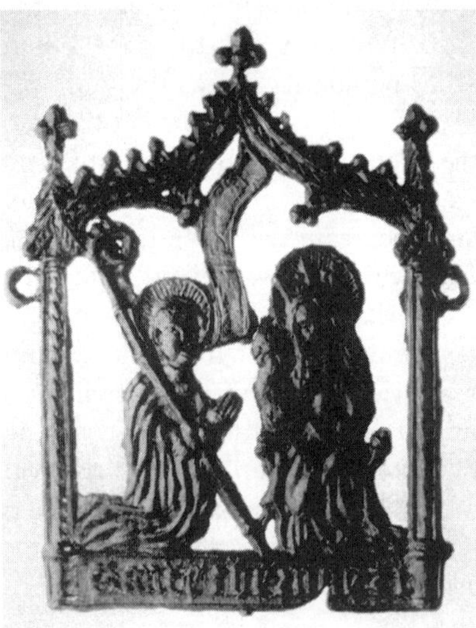

Figure 19

[76] See Chapter Eleven.

ince of Zeeland in the Netherlands, by the banks of the Seine in Paris, and by the Thames in London. They were designed to be worn on a cap or a cloak, nailed up at home or attached to a rosary, and were fitted with pins and clasps. A badge with the image of Bernard has been preserved. ► *Fig. 19* (VA18). It is one of a large number of badges found at the former town of Nieuwlande, which was inundated in 1530 and thereafter formed part of the flooded land of the Oosterschelde in the province of Zeeland. Within an architectural setting a nimbed Bernard kneels before a standing Virgin, nimbed and crowned, and Child. Bernard's hands are clasped in prayer and his crozier leans on his right shoulder. Between them is a banderole which would have had the traditional *Lactation* text *Monstra te esse matrem*. It is probably from the first quarter of the sixteenth century. Although the exact provenance is not known, it almost certainly originated in the southern Netherlands or French Flanders, probably at a bernardine shrine with a devotional panel or sculpture representing the *Lactatio* and one important enough that pilgrims would have wanted a souvenir by which to remember it. Places in the area known to have possessed relics of Bernard were the Augustinians in Cambrai, the Premonstratensians at Floreffe, and the cathedral at Tournai.[77] This bernardine badge presents undoubted evidence of a popular cult, but, equally significant is the fact that among the thousands of surviving badges featuring Thomas Becket, the shell of Saint James of Compostella, the Three Kings of Cologne, and Our Lady of Rocamadour, only one example has been found portraying Bernard.

Bernard was already acknowledged as a saint during his lifetime, but, even before he was canonized, the fear of an exaggerated preoccupation with miracles and relics made the Cistercians wary of promoting his cult. Alongside other leaders of the monastic reform movement Bernard was accorded a place in the hierarchy of saints after the Virgin Mary, Saint John the Baptist, and the apostles. While he was never a 'popular' saint and was not as extensively represented in medieval art as some other saints, the late fifteenth and early sixteenth centuries saw a surge in bernardine depictions. These occurred notably in illustrations in Books of Hours of the *Verses of Bernard* and showed him trampling the devil underfoot, a 'popular' theme in an age of rising insecurity.

[77] Waddell 1990, 143.

CONCLUSIONS

BERNARD THE WRITER, THE TEACHER, AND THE SAINT

THE GREATEST MODERN AUTHORITY on Bernard, Jean Leclercq, has claimed that 'St Bernard was and still is a master of the spiritual life'.[1] That reputation rests on the quality of his writing, which spans the best part of his years as abbot of Clairvaux. He wrote his first treatise *The Steps of Humility and Pride* in 1119 and his last, his treatise of advice to the pope, *On Consideration,* a few years before his death.[2] Best known of all were the eighty-six *Sermons on the Song of Songs* which he began in 1135 and left unfinished when he died in 1153. It is Bernard the writer who is celebrated in the earliest images. The way he is depicted—as an author in profile writing at a desk with pen and knife in his hands—links him with the evangelists and a long line of spiritual writers, especially the Fathers of the Church (a title he was himself given when proclaimed by the pope in 1830). An exception to this general rule is his early seal, in which he is shown holding a writing-tablet and stylus of the kind his secretaries would have used as he dictated letters to them.

[1] Leclercq 1976, 9.
[2] Holdsworth 1994, 21–56.

Apart from placing Bernard in the tradition of the Fathers and showing something of writing methods, as a source of information these early images do not compare with later ones in which the setting is depicted or Bernard is portrayed in the company of others. The earliest example of a pairing occurs in the twin images of Bernard and Aelred of Rievaulx (▶ *Colour plate 3;* MA004) illustrating Aelred's *Mirror of Charity,* in which the composition of the two within historiated initials speaks volumes about their relationship as master and disciple. Similarly, the portrayal of Bernard with his hand raised in admonishment at the figures of two canons at the beginning of his Letter 174 to the canons of Lyons (MA186) indicates the importance attached to his opposition to the introduction of the feast of the Immaculate Conception.

A good deal of information may be gleaned from presentation miniatures, particularly when a comparison is possible of the same theme in two manuscripts separated by several centuries. A thirteenth-century english manuscript portraying an informal encounter of two simple figures, Bernard and Pope Eugene III, sitting at the same level facing each other (MA283), may be compared with a picture of the same event in an italian manuscript commissioned by Pope Nicholas V in 1452 (MA234). In the later manuscript Bernard kneels subserviently before the pope to receive the pope's blessing. The pope, wearing a rich cope and the triple tiara and accompanied by his curial officials, reflects the growing authority and prestige of the papacy in the later medieval centuries. The earlier scene has an informality which is consistent with the way Bernard in his treatise enjoins the pope to set an example, and is in sharp contrast to the pomp and protocol of the later image, in which the pope is portrayed, using Bernard's description, as the head of the mistress of churches, not their mother.

Bernard the Teacher

A similar change took place in the related image of Bernard the teacher between the twelfth and the early sixteenth century. Numerous manuscripts and later printed editions and translations testify to a continuing and ever-increasing interest in his work. By the end of the fifteenth century two hundred ninety-one editions of his works had appeared in print, and by 1530 this had risen to 465. There was, however, a discernible development in the way he was portrayed as a writer and teacher over these centuries. According to the *Vita Prima* Bernard lived apart from the community in a primitive hut much of the time, and yet in late medieval manuscripts he is usually depicted sitting on a high-backed chair in a well-furnished panelled gothic chamber surrounded by shelves containing his books. In earlier images he is shown engaged in an intimate dialogue with a group of his monks, who are sometimes depicted squatting at his feet or sitting informally in a circle around him. These earlier images conjure up his affective and experiential approach to teaching, an approach he expressed in his letter to Aelred when he talked of imparting 'knowledge that comes from the school of the Holy Spirit rather than the schools of rhetoric'[3], or, when in a letter to Henry Murdac, he says that 'woods and stones will teach you what you can never hear from any master'[4]. And again, in *On Consideration* he says: 'We search in a worthier manner, we discover with greater facility through prayer than through disputation'—*orando quam disputando.*[5]

While the early images of Bernard teaching convey the intimate spirit contained in Bernard's own statements, the later ones portray him as a master engaged in the dialectic pedagogy of the schools. He is raised up on a dais in a schoolroom, sitting on a high-backed chair lecturing to his students who are seated below in formal serried rows, facing him. Bernard's academic status is suggested by the red cap he is shown wearing in, among other pictures, Jean Fouquet's famous miniature of him preaching to his monks (MA093). Just as late medieval artists were happy to portray Bernard's contemporaries dressed as renaissance figures, so too they used the College of Saint Bernard in Paris of their day and not the novitiate of twelfth-century Clairvaux as their setting to depict Bernard as a teacher of his monks. Late medieval artists have transformed the monastic formation of twelfth-century Clairvaux to the method of teaching theology in fifteenth-century schools. He appears as a master involved in the question-and-answer method of scholastic disputations, the very kind of teaching he opposed because of the danger it presented to the monastic virtue *par excellence* of humility.

[3] Ep 523; SBOp 8:487.
[4] Ep 106:2; SBOp 7:266-267.
[5] *De consideratione* V.32: SBOp 3:493.

A similar transgression against this key monastic virtue is discernable in a large number of late medieval bernardine images in which artists have painted true portraits of contemporary abbots in the guise of Bernard. Many, although not all, such portraits occur in *Lactation* scenes in which the abbots who commissioned the works associated themselves with the intercessional channel of grace flowing from Mary to Bernard and, at the same time, flattered themselves as models of monastic leadership on a par with Bernard. The thin austere figure of Bernard portrayed in the *Vita Prima* and other early literary sources as wearing a simple cowl and carrying a primitive pastoral staff, has, paradoxically, been transformed into a well-fed prelate in an ample cowl and carrying an elaborate golden crozier who gives every sign of a life of plenty, prosperity and even luxury. The scandal of using contemporary models to portray biblical and saintly characters had been criticized by Savonarola and was later condemned by the Counter Reformation.[6] Although such strictures were undoubtedly directed on the likes of Fra Filippo Lippi, who used as his model for the Virgin the nun Lucrezia Buti, who became his mistress; or of Jean Fouquet, whose Virgin was almost certainly a portrait of Agnès Sorel, mistress of Charles VII of France, the practice would almost certainly have been denounced by Bernard himself. By the end of the Middle Ages the Cistercians were in no position to take this stance. The general relaxation of early austerity and adaptation over the centuries was to a large extent symbolized by the evolution of the abbatial office from the spiritual father—*abba*—of his monks—to the *grand seigneur* on a social level with other leading landowners.

THE INCREASE OF BERNARDINE IMAGES

The following table shows how the number of bernardine images rose in almost geometric progression as the medieval centuries unfurled. From a modest thirteen in the twelfth century they increased to a staggering four hundred nineteen in the fifteenth century and then levelled off to three hundred sixteen in the first three decades of the sixteenth century. As no less than sixty-nine of the three hundred sixteen sixteenth-century images are the late medieval glass panels from the former cloisters of

[6] Campbell 1990, 2–3.

Altenberg and Saint Apern in Cologne, these have been deducted as they would otherwise unduly distort the figures. For the purposes of a chronological breakdown the total is therefore eight hundred ninety-one and not the full nine hundred sixty images recorded.

Century	TOTAL	MA	PA	EN	SC	WA	VA	GL	DR
12C	13	12	-	-	-	-	1	-	-
13C	65	50	5	-	3	1	5	1	-
14C	147	79	27	-	13	17	4	6	1
15C	419	197	93	49	31	25	8	7	9
16C (to 1530)	247	81	66	37	22	7	12	11	11
TOTAL	891	419	191	86	69	50	30	25	21

The total is broken down into the various media, beginning with the most numerous by far, illuminations in manuscripts (MA), and then in decreasing order according to the total in each medium: paintings (PA), engravings (EN), sculpture (SC), wall paintings (WA), various, representing metalwork, embroidery, seals, and pilgrim badges (VA), glass (GL), and drawings (DR).

The first things that strike one are that the only medium which is represented in all the medieval centuries is manuscript illumination and that there is only one other twelfth-century image, namely, Bernard's own seal—assuming that it is genuine and not, as has been suggested, a post-medieval falsification. The sharp rise in the number of bernardine images in manuscripts in the course of the medieval centuries may be attributed to a number of factors. First, and most obvious, is that the further back one goes the less likelihood there is of the survival of manuscripts. Second, manuscripts were both rare and costly to produce and, until the about the thirteenth century, they belonged almost exclusively to monasteries and churches. Third, the small number of twelfth-century images of Bernard may paradoxically be linked to

Bernard's own opposition to figural representations and explain why the earliest examples were produced in benedictine and not in cistercian *scriptoria.* Bernard's celebrated diatribe in his *Apologia* to William of Saint Thierry against 'a fantastic conglomeration of beauty misbegotten and ugliness transmogrified'[7] has traditionally been viewed as directed against the excesses of cluniac cloister carvings, but a recent study[8] has interpreted it as having been aimed at the exuberance of the Cîteaux manuscript illuminations under Bernard's former abbot, Stephen Harding. In Bernard's opinion both types of decoration were inappropriate for monks because of both their extravagance and distractive influence.[9] Visual imagery was inconsistent with the spirituality characterized by simplicity and inner meditation. Significantly, legislation decreeing that manuscripts were to be in one colour and without illuminations[10] was passed when, following a short interregnum, Stephen Harding was succeeded at Cîteaux by one of Bernard's disciples from Clairvaux, Raynald de Bar. Paradoxically, Bernard possessed a lavishly illuminated Bible (not produced at Clairvaux, but a gift), and, most unusually, he chose to be represented by his own image in his second, 1151, seal. For some decades cistercian manuscripts were noted for their lack of decoration, but the use of images as a spiritual aid was too strong to be resisted and, although the General Chapter attempted to enforce the legislation, it soon became a dead letter. Cistercian manuscripts became indistinguishable from those of other monastic *scriptoria* and, significantly, the earliest known examples of deviation from the bernardine ideal come from abbeys far removed from the cradle lands of the Order, Zwettl and Heiligenkreuz in Austria and Stična in Slovenia.

Simplicity and austerity were not only mandated for manuscripts but characterized cistercian art in all media. The policy formulated during Reynard's abbacy is contained in the following injunction:

> We forbid sculptures and paintings in our churches or in any place in the monastery, because while one's attention is directed

[7] *Apologia* 29: SBOp 3:106; trans. Matarasso 1993, 57.
[8] Rudolph 1990.
[9] *Apologia* 12:28; SBOp 3:104-6.
[10] For legislation on art and architecture, see Norton 1986.

> to such things, the advantage of good meditation or the discipline of monastic seriousness is often neglected.[11]

Under Bernard's influence abstract symbols were universally adopted by the Cistercians as aids to contemplation in what the art historian Jeffrey Hamburger has described as an 'ideal of imageless devotion'.[12] Geometric patterns and interlace, sometimes accompanied by simple vegetative designs, not only adorned the modest initials in their manuscript but also decorated the corbels and capitals and the grisaille glass in their churches, and became the tell-tale sign of cistercian art. As the above table shows, there are only a handful of images of Bernard from the late thirteenth century in media other than manuscript illumination; after that there was a gradual increase which gathered momentum in the fifteenth century. In the words of another modern authority, Patrik Reutersward: 'Had it been fully implemented, the Cistercian church reform would have been one of the most radical manifestations of abstinence and restraint in history'.[13] But it was not to be, and, paradoxically, the iconography of Bernard blossomed. As time passed, the importance of art in medieval devotional life, even among monastics, increased, not least perhaps as a result of the influence of female spirituality.

Although cistercian restrictions no doubt contributed to the early dearth of bernardine images in media other than illuminated manuscripts, it was not the only reason. The fragility of glass and the iconoclasm of the Wars of Religion and the French Revolution are, for example, responsible for the fact that there are virtually no surviving medieval stained glass representations of Bernard in France. For the same reasons, many statues have been mutilated or destroyed. Upheavals elsewhere in Europe had the same effect. Also to be factored in is that the great majority of paintings were created as altarpieces and these did not emerge until around the middle of the thirteenth century. The panels, known as the retables or *retrotabula,* were only introduced after the priest no longer celebrated Mass facing the people but stood in front of it with his back to the congregation. The first known bernardine example is the retable from the Templars' church in Palma dated 1290

[11] Waddell 1999, 464.
[12] Hamburger 1989, 163.
[13] Reuterswärd 1986, 99.

(▶ *Colour plate 5*), and the first in a cistercian church belongs to the first half of the fourteenth century.

NARRATIVE IMAGES OF BERNARD

The function of narrative imagery was both didactic and mnemonic. It depended on a literary text as its source and some knowledge of the text was required for its visual interpretation. In Bernard's case the most important source by far was the *Vita Prima,* initiated during his lifetime by his friend William of Saint Thierry, continued by the benedictine abbot Arnold of Bonneval, and completed by Bernard's secretary Geoffrey of Auxerre. The twenty chapters of the thirteenth-century *Exordium Magnum* devoted to Bernard by Conrad of Eberbach provided another source. But most important of all were the *Legendaries* or collections of readings—*lectiones*—which formed part of the Office and provided edifying reading during the otherwise silent meals in monastic refectories. The most important and widely disseminated of these was the so-called *Legenda Aurea—Golden Legend*—compiled by the Dominican James of Voragine around 1265. James had access to the *Vita Prima,* from which he obtained virtually all his material, and as a result the chapter on Bernard was one of the longest in the collection. In a recent edition, for example, twelve pages are devoted to Bernard while only a few are given to some of the most popular saints, among them Saint Sebastian (four pages), Saint Margaret of Antioch (three pages), and Saint Thomas Becket (only two pages). One of the most widely copied and read of all medieval books, translated into a number of languages and later frequently printed, it was available to a lay audience as well as being used extensively by preachers. Furthermore, it provided artists with material upon which to base their pictorial narrative in a way that would not previously have been possible. The restricted availability of the *Vita Prima,* of which only some one hundred fifty manuscripts have survived, for example, contrasts with over a thousand of the latin text of the *Golden Legend* alone. As virtually all the *Legend's* material was drawn from the *Vita Prima,* it is not normally possible to be certain about the artists' source, but it is probably no coincidence that, of the large number of bernardine narrative images, there are only three known examples of individual representations that pre-date the

Legenda Aurea, and that the earliest cycle, the Palma retable, was painted several decades after its publication. Furthermore, there are three known cases in which artists chose a motif based on stories which only occur in the *Golden Legend* and are not found in the earlier cistercian tradition.

As a prior knowledge of the text was a pre-condition for understanding narrative images, such images were particularly suitable for monastics who were most likely to have access to the *Vita Prima* or the *Legenda Aurea* and to have heard or read them. The viewers' ability to understand the story depicted was sometimes aided by captions or by banderoles on which the dialogue between the figures represented was inscribed.

The selective choice of stories in the *Vita Prima* was determined by the purpose for which it was written, the cause for Bernard's canonization. A closer look at which episodes from the life of Bernard were most commonly chosen by artists, or those who commissioned them, similarly gives us an insight into the nature of his cult. While three of the five most popular narrative themes in bernardine iconography marked the defining moments in the saint's life—his mother's prenatal dream, his entry into the monastery, and his death—two were devoted to his role as a thaumaturge. One of the essential marks of sanctity was the ability to perform miracles, and this was widely illustrated by scenes of exorcisms. The other most popular motif was the conversion of the Duke of Aquitaine, proof of the power of the Sacrament at a time when this was under attack by the Albigensians.

THE 'SCENE ATTRIBUTES'

Bernard the miracle worker and the mystic given to having visions came to dominate his medieval iconography. Four principal themes emerged at different periods, beginning in the early fourteenth century, and in different countries: the Embrace of Christ (*Amplexus*); Bernard receiving Mary's Milk (the *Lactatio* or *Lactation*); the related *Vision of Mary* (*Doctrina* or *Dottrina*); and Bernard's encounter with the devil. Together these account for the tremendous increase in the number of bernardine images in the last century of the Middle Ages. Their popularity was so widespread that they have been described as 'scene-attributes', that is themes whereby Bernard may be identified as easily as he is recognized by the principal attributes of monastic habit, crozier, halo, and book as monk, abbot, saint, and writer. The use of the four themes as a means of recognition, rather than as conveying a message, may be seen in a number of examples in which they occur totally out of context.

The Embrace of Christ

Of the four iconographical *topoi* Christ's Embrace is the only one which goes back to Bernard's lifetime. Its origin in Bernard's so-called *Sententiae,*[14] was expanded into the story of Christ embracing Bernard, first found in Herbert's *Liber Miraculorum* from the 1170s and again in the *Exordium Magnum* at the turn of the thirteenth century. Although the theme may be traced back to the twelfth century, one and a half centuries were to pass before it found a pictorial expression in a gradual from the women's abbey of Wonnental (MA059), and approximately another century passed before the next known depiction, a manuscript of the Lives of the Saints in an alsatian dialect of German dated 1419 (MA053). The question *why* inevitably arises. The early cistercian rejection of imagery in their churches, and the late development of altarpieces, both already mentioned, may have played a part, and, in any case, narrative depictions were slow to emerge. Of central importance, however, was undoubtedly the increasing popularity in the later Middle Ages of imagery based on Christ's sacrifice on the Cross and an acknowledgement of Bernard's contribution to the theology of the Passion, particularly as expressed in his Sermon 43 on the Song of Songs.

A development of the theme may be detected in two respects. First, while the initiative in the original story rests entirely with Christ, who embraces Bernard, there was a gradual shift whereby in most depictions there is either a mutuality of embrace or the action has shifted entirely to Bernard, who is shown supporting Christ's lifeless body in what has the feel more of a Deposition than that of an *Amplexus,* marking the growth in the role of Bernard. Second, while the story of the vision takes place in a church—that of Clairvaux—there are more examples of *Amplexus* pictures sited out of doors, transferring the scene to Gol-

[14] Bernard of Clairvaux 2000, 181; SBOp 6.2, 59: *crux Christi . . . in qua et tunc et nunc extensus quasi ad amplexandos nos amoris brachiis expansis.*

gotha and thus linking Bernard with the biblical account of the crucifixion more than with the Clairvaux miracle story. The very physical and almost sensual presentation of many late medieval *Amplexus* scenes has a parallel in the detailed literary rendering of the suffering of Christ in the poem known as *Salutatio*.

A disproportionately large number of *Amplexus* images belonged to cistercian monasteries—whether in manuscripts, as part of altarpieces, or as sculptures—perhaps reflecting the greater availability there of their source, the *Exordium Magnum*. No examples of the motif have been found in the British Isles or the Iberian Peninsula, and only a handful in France and Italy; the vast majority belong to German-speaking lands where there was a late medieval concentration on the Passion of Christ—the *Jesusminne* or memory of Jesus.

The Lactation

By far the most popular of the four major bernardine themes, and the one that more than any other helped to foster popular devotion to the saint, was that of Mary offering Bernard milk from her bared breast, the so-called *Lactatio Bernardi* or *Lactation*. It represents a medieval archetype: the transmission of a great spiritual truth by way of an intimate physical act. By virtue of Mary's milk Bernard became a great preacher. There are over a hundred known *Lactation* images, almost twice as many as of the *Amplexus*. Unlike the *Amplexus*, the earliest known versions are to be found not in a literary but in a pictorial form. The two earliest known examples occurred in the late thirteenth century within the orbit of influence of two iberian cistercian monasteries: the cistercian abbey of Poblet in Catalonia. These were followed in the early fourteenth century by a manuscript from the great Cistercian abbey of Alcobaça in Portugal. Three literary versions appeared a few decades after the first known image. One occurs in a french *exemplum* collection in the vernacular, according to which Mary placed her breast in Bernard's mouth. Another version appears in a norse collection of marian miracle stories. The third belongs to a legend from Châtillon according to which Mary placed three drops of milk into Bernard's mouth as he was meditating on the fourth verse of the marian hymn, *Ave maris stella* ('Hail, star of the sea'): *Monstra te esse matrem* ('Show us that you are our mother'). As a result these words became the standard inscription on *Lactation* images, usually found on a banderole emanating from Bernard's mouth.

Nearly two centuries were to pass from the appearance of the *Lactation* scene in the iberian peninsula before it made its appearance, around 1470, in the area of the Low Countries, Flanders, and the Lower Rhineland. Here it rapidly gained in popularity and was equally widespread in the iconography of the Cistercians, of other Orders, in secular churches and among the laity in general. These were the most fervent religious centres of the age, associated with a spirituality that accented private devotion and meditation and the interior life, and it was in tune with the *Brautmystik* of the Lower Rhineland and the *Devotio moderna* of the Low Countries.

It was in this setting that we find many cistercian donor images in which abbots associated themselves with the intercessional power of Bernard through Mary's milk, while at the same time allowing the artist to flatter them by portraying them in the guise of Bernard.

There was a discernible transition from early to late *Lactation* images: stiff, formal 'Virgin and Child' figures are replaced by a thoroughly human baby, gently and tenderly cradled in his mother's arms. The increasing importance of women and the medieval appreciation of the family, exemplified by the celebration of the Holy Family, is reflected in some of the crowded late medieval *Lactation* scenes. Growing prosperity, especially in this northwestern region of Europe, gave rise to an urban bourgeois merchant class, influenced the religious culture and art of the time and found expression in the iconography of Bernard in which earthly families were substituted for Bernard's own family.

The Doctrina

In Italy Bernard's devotion to Mary found expression chiefly in the iconographical theme known as the *Doctrina*. Originated at around the same time as the *Lactatio*, it too implies that the skill to write and preach were transmitted to Bernard from Mary but the physical nurture through Mary's milk is replaced by the more verbal and intellectual exchange between them. The *Lactatio* was virtually unknown in Italy and the *Doctrina* outside Italy.

Bernard and the Devil

A number of stories of Bernard's encounters with the devil recorded in the *Vita Prima* were later more widely dispersed by being incorporated into the legendary literature, especially the *Golden Legend*. Yet the theme did not enter Bernard's iconography until the first half of the fifteenth century and when it did it referred, not to any specific anecdote in the *Vitae* but in a general way to Bernard's triumph over the forces of evil. The ability of saints to control the devil was a common hagiographical theme in the later Middle Ages, and Bernard's ascendancy over the ancient foe is most commonly depicted by showing him either holding a smaller figure of the devil on a leash or a chain or trampling on the devil underfoot, or a combination of the two.

In Italy the motif was sometimes incorporated into *Doctrina* images by showing the devil chained to Bernard's desk, and a number of italian statues portray Bernard standing with a small chained demon at his feet. The absence of the usual attributes of crozier and book indicates that the theme was widely substituted as a means of identification. The largest number of Bernard/devil images, however, are found in manu scripts, virtually all of them in Books of Hours. The Bernard/devil theme occurs much more frequently than the other bernardine scene-attributes, even though these were generally more popular. A number of images of Bernard appear in the Suffrages in these Books of Hours and ask for his intercession.

More frequently, however, Bernard appears in supplementary prayers added in the fifteenth century known as the *Verses of Bernard*, usually introduced by a Bernard/devil image.

Unlike other bernardine scene-attributes, the Bernard/devil images illustrating the *Verses* are not found in a single manuscript of cistercian origin or ownership. The legend is more in tune with late medieval lay devotional taste than with monastic spirituality. The contrast between late medieval lay mentality, exemplified by the miraculous powers attributed to the recital of the *Verses*, and the cistercian heritage of *lectio divina* and meditation is underscored by the images of Bernard in each tradition. Indulgences attached to the *Verses* were denounced at the end of the fourteenth century, but it was not until the early sixteenth century that they came under widespread attack, first by Erasmus of

Rotterdam in *The Praise of Folly* and then by Luther, who referred to the *Verses of Bernard* as an 'error'.

A miniature in a *c.* 1480 Book of Hours in which the devil at Bernard's feet has been defaced suggests that a form of late medieval iconoclasm was directed, not at the cult of the saints, but at the distortion of the cult on the eve of the Reformation.

BERNARD AS A PRINCE TO THE QUEEN OF HEAVEN

The most striking of all the bernardine images is the portrayal—in large numbers—of Bernard in the company of the Virgin. They are featured together in two of Bernard's four scene-attributes—the *Lactatio* and the *Doctrina*—and Bernard appears in many marian altarpieces, either alone with the Virgin or together with Saint Benedict. As altarpieces became more elaborate, Bernard appeared in the company of a number of saints in a so-called *Sacra converzatione* in which saints from various periods flanked the central figures of the seated Virgin and Child. An alternative was the triptych with a marian theme dominating the central panel or *corpus* with images of saints on the wings. In cistercian churches, once early injunctions against paintings and images had come to be ignored, a number of *Lactation* images in grisaille were painted on the back of the wings of triptychs, where they would have been seen most of the time during ferial seasons when the wings were closed.

Marian themes occur approximately ten times more frequently in Bernard's iconography than they do in his writings. Although Bernard makes much of Mary's intercessional powers, calling her both aquaduct of grace and mediatrix, in his writings her role is nevertheless secondary in the economy of salvation. Furthermore, Mary only appears in two stories in the *Vita Prima* and is not referred to in any of the twenty chapters devoted to Bernard in the *Exordium Magnum.* The most popular Bernard image, the *Lactation,* was developed in a text attributed to Bernard, but in fact written by the benedictine abbot Arnold of Bonneval.

Paradoxically, Bernard was credited with advancing the cult of Mary in a way that was not warranted by historical fact but based on exaggerations and often on apocryphal stories. The dichotomy between Bernard's teaching and his iconography in the company of Mary can only be explained by the considerable growth in the cult of the Virgin in the late Middle Ages—of which Bernard was a beneficiary. It explains the disproportionately large number of bernardine images in relation to other saints. With a few notable exceptions, among them Saint Francis of Assisi, hardly any other medieval saint was as extensively represented in art as Bernard. Yet Bernard was not a popular saint in the sense that his cult arose from widespread lay devotion and was subsequently sanctioned by the official Church. His canonization took place on the initiative of his own monks and his cult arose primarily to fulfil the needs of his own cistercian family. To them his holiness was of supreme importance, as it was to a lesser degree, to the wider monastic and religious world. At the time of his canonization, however, the renewal of monastic life was modelled on the evangelical simplicity and poverty of the early Church, and its leaders, among them Bernard, formed the majority of the new saints whose holy lives were believed to make them role models well beyond the cloister.

Two other indicators of Bernard's relative popularity—the analysis of christian names and of church dedications (although only available for certain regions)—again indicate a variance between the relative dearth of his cult and the wealth of his iconography. Bernard's association with the Virgin was, for example, responsible for Dante's choice of Bernard as his final guide in the *Divine Comedy*. In Dante's judgment Bernard's intervention would secure the intercession of Mary which was necessary to obtain the grace required to reach the beatific vision. These dantean pictures and later bernardine images in a marian context reflect the growth in the role of Bernard which resulted directly from his perceived association with the Virgin. His iconography was constantly evolving and being adapted to a changing world. As spirituality came to reflect the greater involvement of the laity and their devotional practices, Bernard's reputation and visual representation retained a freshness and remained relevant.

Bernard once called himself the 'chimaera of my age', referring to the conflict between his life as a monk and his activities in the wider Church. The title he chose, of the fire-breathing monster of greek mythology whose body was made up of three parts from different animals, allows us to identify, in a parallel way, three divergent and conflicting elements in the iconography of Bernard: the monastic, the miracle-worker, and the ecclesiastical politician. They do not always appear in isolation, but often overlap. Similarly, the great profusion of images of

Bernard, visual as well as literary, reflect and highlight the great variety of ways in which his memory was used. Among the many Bernards are the historical figure—the monk and abbot, writer and teacher of his monks as well as the man of action; the legendary—imbued with the traditional themes of hagiography and issuing in devotional themes like the *Amplexus* and the *Lactatio*;, and the apocryphal—based on texts wrongly attributed to Bernard or on legends with no basis whatever in the bernardine tradition, such as his *Verses*. Parallel to the development of the images of Saint Bernard, from the earliest in monasteries to serve a monastic audience, to the popularized apocryphal *topoi* which were later to dominate the way he was portrayed, we note the transition from an earlier allegorical age with its emphasis on symbols with moral messages to a more literal epoch when everything had to have a precise explanation. The various pictures that emerge represent one of the most influential characters in medieval history, a man who was at the same time one of the most complex, and they reflect his own words in a letter to the Carthusians of the Grande Chartreuse: 'I am not as I am believed or said to be'—*Non sum talis qualis putor vel dicor*.[15]

The Catalogue of Bernardine Images has provided visual evidence upon which tentatively to draw conclusions on the place of Bernard in the life of monastic, clerical, and lay audiences with a degree of accuracy which it has hitherto not been possible to achieve. Although comprehensive, it is not exhaustive: further images of Bernard, mostly in privately-owned Books of Hours or late medieval paintings in obscure or remote collections, will undoubtedly be located in future.[16] Nor is the study definitive: I hope that it may open a window to yet further study and it invites a yet broader interpretation on perceptions of sanctity itself by those more qualified than I. In the final words of Saint Bernard at the end of his last written work: 'Therefore, let this be the end of the book but not the end of the search'.[17]

[15] Ep 11:10; SBOp 7:60.

[16] A number of such images in private ownership that have recently been offered for sale in auction rooms have been included. They have been photographed and recorded during their short sojourns at the auction houses before being again 'lost' into private ownership.

[17] *De consideratione* V.32: SBOp 3:493: *Proinde is sit finis libri, sed non finis quaerendi.*

APPENDIX ONE

PRESENT LOCATION OF IMAGES

AUSTRALIA

Sydney	State Library of New South Wales	MA308 MS Mitchell 1/7a, f 9r

AUSTRIA

Graz	Holy Ghost Hospital	SC25
	Landesmuseum Joanneum	PA124
	Universitätsbibliothek	MA141 MS 1289, f 190r
Heiligenkreuz	Stiftsbibliothek	MA021 MS 20, f 1r
Herzogenburg	Stiftsgalerie	PA102
Lilienfeld	Stiftsbibliothek	MA034 MS 151, f 205v
Neuberg	Abbey Church	PA098
	-	PA099
	-	PA100
	-	PA101
Rein	Stiftsbibliothek	MA135 MS 206, f 56v
Stams	Stiftsbibliotehk	MA057 MS 12, f 19v

Strassengel	Pilgrimage Church	GL77
Vienna	Albertina, Graphische Sammlung	EN16
	-	EN20
	Österr. Galerie Belvedere	PA079
	Österreichischer Nationalbibliothek	EN12 Inv No 323
	-	MA016 MS 2706, f 273v
	-	MA037 Ser.n.12771, f 1r
	-	MA048 MS 2738, f 1118v
	-	MA142 MS 326, f 169v
	-	MA275 MS 3085, f 130v
	-	MA372 MS 1840, f 230r
	-	MA398 MS 1254, f 574v
	-	MA399 MS Ser.n. 3308, f 119r
	Schottenstift	MA327 MS 189, f 40v
Zwettl	Abbey Church	PA38
	-	PA39
	-	PA40
	-	PA41
	-	PA42
	-	PA43
	-	PA44
	-	PA45
	-	SC05
	Stiftsbibliothek	MA001 MS 144, f 26v
	-	MA002 MS 194, f 3r
	-	MA342 MS 171, f 2r

BELGIUM

Antheit	Val-Notre-Dame	SC36
Anthisnes	Church of Saint-Maximin	WA37
Antwerp	Koninklijk Museum	PA082 Inv No 976
	Museum Mayer van den Bergh	PA105
	-	MA217 Inv. 946, f 562v
Averbode	Premonstratensian Abbey	VA20

Bornem	Sint-Bernardusabdij	MA115 MS 9, f 1v
	-	MA116 MS 9, f 31v
Bruges	Archief Grootseminarie	MA114 MS 49/18, f 9v
	-	MA144 MS 49/18, f 302r
	-	MA145 MS 50/66, f 106r
	Church of Saint-Sauveur	PA153
	Groeningemuseum	PA050 Inv No 0.91.1
Brussels	Bibliothèque Royale Albert 1er	MA018 MS 11053/4, f 241r
	-	MA035 MS 268, f 86r
	-	MA036 MS 1787, f 8r
	-	MA038 MS 12166, f 28
	-	MA134 MS FS 9 No 7, f 12v
	-	MA150 MS IV 438, f 131r
	-	MA151 MS IV 736, f 49r
	-	MA152 MS 9226, f 195v
	-	MA153 MS 9228, f 210
	-	MA154 MS 9282-5, f 198r
	-	MA155 MS IV 414, f 46r
	-	MA156 MS II 2207, f 1v
	-	MA157 MS 10,606, f 54v
	-	MA158 MS IV 497, f 70v
	-	MA159 MS IV 280, f 225v
	-	MA218 MS II 3633, f 4
	La Cambre Nuns' Abbey	SC37
	Musées Royaux d'Art et d'Histoire	GL94
	-	SC34 Inv No V 2635
	Musées Royaux des Beaux-Arts	PA072 Inv No 370
Gent	Musée des Beaux-Arts	PA132
	Universiteits-bibliotheek	MA110 MS 74, f 148v
	-	MA111 MS 74, 243r
	-	MA112 MS 74, 268v
	-	MA113 MS186, 136v
Liége	Collections artistiques de l'Univ.	PA073 Inv No 12046

	Musee Curtius	PA104
	Musee d'Art Religieux et Mosan	PA075
	-	SC24 Inv C15
	University Library	EN44 MS 310 frontispiece
	-	EN 68
Louvain	St Pieterskerk	PA006
	Stedelijk Mus.Vanderkelen-Mertens	SC63
Namur	Musee Regional d'Art et d'Histoire	SC33
Soleilmont	Nuns' Abbey of Notre Dame	SC48
Tournai	Bibliothèque du Séminaire	MA396 MS 43, f 7v
	Bibliothèque de la Ville	MA345 MS 21, f 232r
	Cathedral	GL88
	Musee des Beaux-Arts	PA091
Val Dieu	Cistercian Abbey	SC20
Westmalle	Cistercian Abbey	MA015 MS 9, Vol IV, f 244r

CANADA

Montreal	Museum of Fine Art	PA138 Inv No 1084

CZECH REPUBLIC

Brno	Mestsky Archiv	MA082 MS F.M. 7, f 69v
Ossek	Cistercian Abbey	PA093

DENMARK

Copenhagen	Royal Library	EN59
	-	EN69
	-	MA192 MS Thott 411 fol, f 237r
	-	MA193 MS Thott 411 fol, f 239v

	-	MA194 MS Thott 411 fol, f 241r
	-	MA195 MS Thott 411 fol, f 243r
	-	MA259 MS Thott 129 oct, f 28v
	National Museum	SC51
Løgumkloster	Cistercian Abbey	PA036
	-	SC13
	-	SC67
Rislev	Parish Church	SC52
Roskilde	Cathedral	WA02
Skive	Old Church	WA01

FRANCE

Amiens	Bibliothèques d'Amiens Métropole	MA397 MS 200, f 163r
Bar sur Aube	Médiathèque Municipale	SC04
Besancon	Museum	SC61
Blany	Chateau	MA117 MS no number f 17r
Bouillac Church		VA29
	-	VA30
Bussiere, La	Cistercian Abbey	SC22
Cadouin	Cistercian Abbey	SC07
Chambery	Bibliothèque Municipale	MA329 MS 4, f 594r
Chantilly	Musée Condé	MA042 MS 1078, f 178r
	-	MA043 MS 1078, f 178v
	-	MA089 MS 722, f 209v
	-	MA093 MS 71, f 36
	-	MA260 MS 722, f 295r
	-	MA371 MS 604, f 95v
Chateauroux	Mediathèque Municipale	MA363 MS 2, f 304r
Chaumont	Bibliothèque Municipale	MA085 MS 33, f 365v
Clermont-Ferrand	Bibliothèque Municipale	MA394 MS 76, f 1v
Cordes (Tarn)	Parish Church	SC10
Dijon	Bibliothèque Municipale	MA027 MS 598, f 1r

	Musée des Beaux-Arts	PA055
	-	PA092 Inv No CA 142
	-	SC21 Inv No 408
Douai	Bibliothèque Municipale	MA004 MS 392, f 2v
	-	MA028 MS 372, f 2v
	Musée de la Chartreuse	PA165 Inv No 1070
	-	PA182 Inv No 408
Epinal	Bibliothèque Municipale	MA030 MS 45, f 140r
Fontaine-les-Dijon	Church	SC26
Hautecombe	Cistercian Abbey	PA184
Labessiere-Candeil	Chateau of Serres	WA50
Laon	Bibliothèque Municipale	MA334 MS 168, f 1r
Lille	Bibliothèque Municipale	MA335 MS 705, f 42v
	Musée des Beaux Arts	DR12 Inv No 473
Lyon	Bibliothèque Municipale	MA289 MS 5999, f 96v
	-	MA290 MS 1351, f 75r
Mans, Le	Musée de Tessé	MA355 MS 688, f 9r
Metz	Musée d'Art	PA002 Inv No 550
Nantes	Musée Dobrée	MA040 MS 5, f 1v
Paris	Bibliothèque de l'Arsenal	MA039 MS 268, f 2v
	-	MA079 MS 8530, f 170r
	-	MA080 MS 8530, f 172r
	-	MA185 MS 438, f 13r
	-	MA189 MS 600, f 201v
	-	MA190 MS 619, f 176r
	Bibliothèque Mazarine	MA400 MS 507, f 159v
	Bibliothèque Nationale	MA041 MS Lat 1142, f 1r
	-	MA086 MS Fra 17115, f 156r
	-	MA088 MS Fra 245, f 55r
	-	MA090 MS Roth. 2529, f 374
	-	MA105 MS Lat 10532, p 330
	-	MA171 MS Lat 1188, f 70r
	-	MA172 MS Roth. 2530, f 134r

	-	MA173 MS Lat 1052, f 478r
	-	MA174 MS Fra 242, f 182r
	-	MA175 MS Fra 376, f 95r
	-	MA176 MS Fra 52, f 188r
	-	MA177 MS Fra 400, f 35r
	-	MA178 MS Fra 2224, f 41v
	-	MA179 MS Lat 10555, f 315r
	-	MA180 MS Lat 1182, f 118r
	-	MA181 MS nal 688, f 151r
	-	MA182 MS nal 1134, f 1r
	-	MA183 MS Lat 1023, f 409r
	-	MA184 MS Lat 760, f 500r
	-	MA186 MS Lat 2924, f 2r
	-	MA187 MS Lat 1404, f 110v
	-	MA188 MS Lat 4900, f 184r
	-	MA196 MS Fra 311, f 206v
	-	MA197 MS Fra 311, f 208r
	-	MA198 MS Fra 241, f 214r
	-	MA199 MS nal 392, f 129r
	-	MA200 MS Fra 298, f 76r
	-	MA201 MS Fra 916, f 13r
	-	MA202 MS Fra 5594, f 138r
	-	MA203 MS Fra 917, f 15r
	-	MA406 MS Fra 314, f 117v
	-	MA407 MS Fra 314, f 210r
	-	MA412 MS nal 83, f 37v
	-	MA413 MS 4915, f 361r
	Bibliothèque Ste-Geneviève	MA349 MS 2704, f 139v
	Musée du Louvre	EN25
	-	PA052 RF 2230
	-	PA056 RF 590
Perigueux	Cathedral	PA083
Pralon	Church	SC27
Rouen	Musée des Antiquités	VA17
Sens	Bibliothèque Municipale	MA422 MS 49
Sept Fons	Cistercian Abbey	MA051 MS no number, f 26r
Tours	Bibliothèque Municipale	MA405 MS 2104, f 149r
Valenciennes	Bibliothèque Multimédia	MA318 MS 838, f 103r

GERMANY

Aachen	Ludwig Collection	GL06
	-	GL14
	-	GL17
	-	GL26
	-	GL27
	-	GL29
Altenberg	Cistercian Abbey	GL45
	-	GL48
	-	GL76
Altenburg	Staatliches Lindenau-Museum	PA125 Inv No 16
Amelungsborn	Cistercian Abbey	SC08
Aschaffenburg	Hofbibliothek	MA385 MS10, f 421v
Bamberg	Staatsbibliothek	MA219 MS Lit 15, f295r
	-	MA220 MS Lit 30, f 14v
	Staatsgalerie	EN17
	-	PA017 Inv 10644
Bebenhausen	Cistercian Abbey	PA047
Berchtesgarten	Schloss	PA024
Berlin	Bode-Museum	PA114 Inv 1066
	-	PA115 Inv 1066
	-	PA116 Inv 1066
	-	PA117 Inv 1066
	-	PA118 Inv 1066
	-	PA119 Inv 1066
	-	PA120 Inv 1066
	Gemäldegalerie	PA063 Inv 1 071 A
	Kunstgewerbemuseum	VA19 Inv K 9223
	Staatl. Museen Gemäldegalerie	PA005 Inv GG 1156C
	-	PA048 Inv GG 183
	-	PA183 Inv GG 12
	-	PA191 Inv GG 69
	Staatl. Museen – Kupferstickkab.	EN33
	-	EN65
	-	MA221, Inv No 671

	Staatsbibliothek	
	Preuss. Kulturbes.	MA025 MS theol lat f. 347, f 1v
	-	MA046 MS germ. qu. 42, f 230r
	-	MA052 MS theol lat f. 409, f 72v
	-	MA120 MS lat.fol. 754, f 1r
	-	MA191 MS germ fol 1287, f 106r
	-	MA 319 MS theol.lat.fol 414, f 2r
	-	MA326 MS theol lat f.148, f 174r
Bonn	Rheinischen	
	Landesmuseum	PA016 Inv No 21 910 (GK 65)
Brandenburg	Cathedral	PA067
Breitscheid	Chapel of St Anne	SC19
	-	SC29
Bretzenheim	Church of St Bernard	SC30
Cologne	Cathedral	GL59
	-	GL60
	-	GL61
	-	GL62
	-	GL63
	-	GL65
	-	GL66
	Diocesanmuseum	MA415 MS Sigmaring, f 44v
	Historisches Archiv	MA023 MS W 255, f 1v
	Museum für	
	Angewandte Kunst	PA069 Inv A 1063
	Schnütgen Museum	DR10
	-	GL05
	-	GL16
	-	GL18
	-	GL31
	-	GL34
	-	GL37
	-	GL39
	-	GL40
	-	GL41
	-	GL42
	-	GL44
	-	GL53
	-	GL64
	-	GL67
	-	GL68

Wallraf-Richartz	Museum	PA021 Inv No WRM 128
	-	PA022 Inv No WRM 170
	-	PA023 Inv No WRM 359
	-	PA025 Inv No WRM 415
	-	PA051 Inv No WRM 3167
	-	PA054 Inv No WRM 166
	-	PA074 Inv No WRM 119
Darmstadt	Univ.- und Landesbibliothek	MA348 MS 975, f 298v
	-	MA369 MS 975, f 321v
Doberan	Cistercian Abbey	SC15
Dresden	Sächsische Landesbibliothek	MA066, MS A 311, f 94v
Düsseldorf	Maxkirche	VA28
	Universitätsbibliothek	MA055 MS D 5, f 1r
Eberbach	Cistercian Abbey	SC09
Eberstein	Schloss	SC65
Erlangen	Universitätsbibliothek	DR20 MS 107, f 43v
	-	MA071 MS 308, f 1r
Frankfurt/M	Cathedral	VA16 Inv No 152
	Museum für Angewandte Kunst	MA328 MS11, f114v
	Stadt- und Universitätsbibliothek	MA049 MS lat oct 4, f 1r
	-	MA050 MS lat oct 4, f 4r
Freiburg/B	Augustinermuseum	PA018 Inv No M 39/3
	-	SC58 Inv No 11546
	Cathedral	GL80
	-	SC01
	-	SC35
Hamburg	Staats- u. Universitätsbibliothek	MA421 MS Scrin. 210, f 122r
Hannover	Kestner-Museum	VA21 Inv No WM XXII, 8
	-	VA22 Inv No WM XXII, 29a
	Niedersächsisches Landesmuseum	PA095 Inv No KM 139
Heidelberg	Universitätsbibliothek	MA053, MS Pal Germ 144, f 76r
	-	MA330 MS Cod Sal XI 4, f 1r
	-	MA404 MS Cod Sal IX d, f 290r
Heiligkreuztal	Cistercian Nuns' Abbey	GL90

Himmelkron	Cistercian Nuns' Abbey	SC59
Isenhagen	Cistercian Nuns' Abbey	SC69
Karlsruhe	Badische Landesbibliothek	MA059 MS Cod U H 1, f 195r
	-	MA222 MS Lichtental 20, f 220v
	Generallandesarchiv	MA019 Cod Berain 66/8553, f 1v
	Staatliche Kunsthalle	PA062
Koblenz (near)	Schloss Stolzenfels	GL54
	-	GL57
Leipzig	Universitätsbibliothek	MA022 MS 375, f 1v
Lichtenthal	Cistercian Nuns' Abbey	PA186
Lieding	Church of St Margaret	GL93
Lübeck	St Anne Museum	PA019 Inv No 1960/1
Marienstatt	Abbey Church	SC68
Maulbronn	Cistercian Abbey	SC17
	-	WA04
Münster	Westfälisches Landesmuseum	SC03 Inv No E-365 LM
Munich	Alte Pinakothek	PA008 Inv No 10644
	-	PA010 Inv No WAF 588
	-	PA020 Inv No WAF 663
	-	PA151 Inv No WAF 764
	Bayerische National Museum	SC62
	Bayerische Staatsbibliothek	EN13
	-	EN15 MS Clm 20020, f 45r
	-	MA020 MS Clm 7950, f 2v
	-	MA032 MS Clm 23056, f 258v
	-	MA119 MS Clm 22253, f 160v
	-	MA320 MS Clm 23046, f 144r
	-	MA331 MS Cgm 6, f 143r
	-	MA389 MS Clm 28150, f 199v
	-	MA402 MS Clm 30080, f 1v
Niederwerth	Cistercian Nuns' Abbey	GL89
	-	SC28
	-	SC44

Nuremberg	Germanisches Nationalmuseum	EN02
	-	GL71
	-	MA231 Inv No Hz 5197
	-	PA009
	-	VA27
	Landeskirchliches Archiv	SC06
	Stadtbibliothek	EN63 MS Cent V 81, f 77v
	-	EN64 MS Cent V 81, f 121v
Oberschönenfeld	Cistercian Nuns' Abbey	SC32
Owen	Chapel of St Bernard	WA39
	-	WA40
	-	WA41
	-	WA42
	-	WA43
	-	WA44
	-	WA45
	-	WA46
	-	WA47
	-	WA48
	-	WA49
Rastatt	Church	WA38
Seligenthal	Cistercian Nuns' Abbey	SC31
	-	WA07
Stuttgart	Staatsgalerie	PA057
	-	PA058
	-	PA059
	-	PA060
	-	PA061
	Württembergische Landesbibl.	MA403 Cod.mus.fol.I 64, f 144v
Thyrnau	Cistercian Nuns' Abbey	EN84
Wienhausen	Cistercian Nuns' Abbey	GL75
Zinna	Cistercian Abbey	GL79
	-	SC23
	-	WA09

HUNGARY

Budapest	National Széchényi Library	MA411 MS Cod.lat. 309, f 127r
	Nemzeti Muzeum	MA091

IRELAND

Bective	Cistercian Abbey	SC66

ITALY

Avio (Trento)	Church of Our Lady of the Snow	SC55
Bologna	Pinacoteca Nazionale	PA159 Inv No 166
Chiarano d'Arco	Church of St Anthony Abbot	WA26
Faenza	Pinacoteca Comunale	PA140
Ferrara	Pinacoteca Nazionale	PA154
Fiesole	Badia Fiosolana	PA167 Inv dep n 10
	Church of St Francis	PA152
Florence	Accademia	PA122
	-	PA134 Inv No 3462
	-	PA135 Inv No 5381
	-	PA155 Inv No 8463
	-	PA156 Inv No 8463
	-	PA157 Inv No 8463
	Badia Fiorentina	PA136
	Badia a Settimo	PA142
	Biblioteca Medicea Laurenziana	MA077 MS Ashb. 960, f 10v
	-	MA078 MS Plut. 21 d.1, f 335v
	-	MA081 MS Ashb. 572, f 1
	-	MA267 MS Conv Sopp 268, f 1r
	-	MA268 MS Gaddi 134, f 1r
	-	MA271 MS Ac e Doni 54, f 111r
	-	MA272 MS Pluteo XXV 3, f 183v
	-	MA386 MS Lau Plut XL1, f 325v
	-	MA387 MS Lau Plut XL1, f 328v

	-	MA388 MS Lau Plut XL1, f 333r
	-	MA401 MS Ashb. 961, f 1v
	Biblioteca Nazionale Centrale	MA262 MS Con Sop J VI 22, f 1
	-	MA263 MS Banco Rari 18, f 110
	-	MA264 MS Banco Rari 18, f 114v
	-	MA269 MS Con S B 1 2568, f 3r
	-	MA270 MS Palatino 50, f 1r
	Biblioteca Riccardiana	MA391 MS Ricc. 372, f 358r
	-	MA392 MS Ricc. 429, f 163v
	Cestello Major Seminary	DR14 MS Cod Rustici, f 19v
	-	DR15 MS Cod Rustici, f 20r
	-	DR16 MS Cod Rustici, f 21v
	Dominican Convent of St Mark	WA27
	Galleria Corsini	PA137
	Galleria Palatina	PA123 Inv No 1912, n. 165
	-	PA147
	S. Maria del Carmine Church	WA08
	S. Maria Maddelena Cist. Abbey	DR18
	-	WA22
	-	WA28
	S. Spirito Church	GL92
	-	PA112
	Serristori Collection	PA097
	Uffizi Gallery	PA026 Inv No 1890 n. 8455
	-	PA133 Inv No 9258
	-	PA148 Inv No 1468
	Gabinetto Stampe	DR07
	-	DR11 Inv No n. 1328 F
	Corridoio Vasariano	DR17
Genoa	Accademia Ligustica	PA113
Milan	Cistercian Abbey of Chiaravalle	WA21
Modena	Biblioteca Estense Universitaria	MA374 MS It. 474, f 137v
	-	MA375 MS Est. 116, f 166v
	-	MA376 MS V.G. 11, f 212v
	-	MA377 MS V.G. 11, f 407v

	-	MA378 MS Lat. 873, f 78r
	-	MA379 MS Lat. 1021, f 128v
	-	MA380 MS Lat. 889, f 107v
Morimondo	Cistercian Abbey	WA32
Orvieto	Church of St Giovenale	WA05
Padua	Biblioteca Capitolare	MA384 MS A 58, f 1r
	Biblioteca del Seminario	MA276 MS 67, f 303v
	University Library	MA362 MS 687, f 2r
Palombara Sabina	St John of Argentella Abbey	WA29
	-	WA30
Pamparato	Chapel of St Bernard	WA11
	-	WA12
	-	WA13
	-	WA14
	-	WA15
	-	WA16
	-	WA17
	-	WA18
	-	WA19
	-	WA20
Parma	Baptistry	WA25
Pavia	Certosa	GL70
Perugia	Galeria Nazionale dell'Umbria	PA158
Pesaro	S. Maria dell'Anzilla Church	PA174
Prato	Antichita Moretti	PA139
	Galleria Comunale	PA150
	Pinacoteca Comunale	PA149 Inv No 5
Rivalta Scrivia	Cistercian Abbey	WA34
	-	WA35
Rome	Biblioteca Apostolica Vaticana	MA234 MS 658, f 1r
	-	MA235 MS 658, f 11v
	-	MA236 MS 658, f 25r
	-	MA237 MS 658, f 38r
	-	MA238 MS 658, f 51r
	-	MA239 MS 658, f 71r
	-	MA240 MS 658, f 113r

	-	MA241 MS Vat.lat. 5493, f 272v
	-	MA242 MS Urbin.lat. 92, f 2r
	-	MA243 MS Urbin.lat. 93, f 7v
	-	MA244 MS Urbin.lat. 93, f 8r
	-	MA245 MS Vat.lat. 5095, f 1r
	-	MA246 MS Vat.lat. 8541, f 88v
	-	MA247 MS Vat.lat. 8541, f 88v
	-	MA248 MS Vat.lat. 8541, f 88v
	-	MA249 MS Vat.lat. 8541, f 88v
	-	MA250 MS Vat.lat. 8541, f 89r
	-	MA251 MS Vat.lat. 8541, f 89r
	-	MA252 MS Vat.lat. 8541, f 89r
	-	MA253 MS Vat.lat. 8541, f 89r
	-	MA314 MS Rossiana, f 167v
	-	MA410 MS Vat.lat. 3768, f 140r
	Pinacoteca Vaticana	PA090 Inv No 243
	Biblioteca Casanatense	MA230 MS 970, f 2r
	Palazzo Venezia, Pinacoteca	PA141
	S.Croce in Gerusalemme Cistercian Abbey	MA265 MS Cod D, f 18r
	-	MA266 MS Archivio, f 1r
	S. Maria Maggiore Church	SC11
	Tre Fontane	WA23
San Galgano	Oratory	WA03
San Ginesio	Pinacoteca Comunale	PA145
Siena	Archivio di Stato	PA166
	Biblioteca Comunale Intronati	MA332 MS F.V.10, f 1r
	-	MA333 MS F.V.13, f 1r
	Church of St Cristoforo	PA190
	Pinacoteca Nazionale	PA160
	-	PA163
	-	PA188 Inv No 437
Staffarda	Cistercian Abbey	WA36
Taggia	Church of St Dominic	PA046
Tortona	Episcopal Palace	PA146
Treviso	Museo Civico	PA143
Turin	Galleria Sabauda	PA168 Inv No 186

Venice	Biblioteca Nazionale Marciana	MA381 MS Marc. It. IX, f 75r
	-	MA382 MS Marc. It. IX, f 75v
	-	MA383 MS Marc. It. IX, f 76r
	-	MA409 MS Marc. It. I 35, f 108
	Patriarchal Seminary, Museum	SC54
Vercelli	Museo Borgogna	PA189
Veroli	Cathedral	VA01
	-	VA02
Viboldone	Abbey of Sts Peter & Paul	WA24
Vicenza	Museo Civico	PA049 Inv No A 297
Viterbo	Church of St Mark	PA144

NETHERLANDS

Amsterdam	Bibl. Philosophica Hermetica	MA257 MS BPH 158, f 63r
	-	MA258 MS BPH 151, f 129r
	Free University Library	MA360 MS XV05502, f 157r
	Print Cabinet	EN72
	Rijksmuseum	DR03 Inv No 13:55
Cothen	Van Beuningen Collection	VA18 Inv No 2360
The Hague	Koninklijke Bibliotheek	EN34 Inv No 171 E 21
	-	EN35 Inv No 1084 D 5
	-	MA122 MS 128 C 1 (III), f 203v
	-	MA123 MS 135 E 22, f 140v
	-	MA124 MS 135 J 10, f 97v
	-	MA125 MS 133 E 17, f 184r
	-	MA126 MS 135 G 19, f 126r
	-	MA127 MS 72 A 24, f 175r
	-	MA128 MS 135 E 19, f 9v
	-	MA129 MS 76 F 2, f 267r
	-	MA273 MS 135 E 18, f 41r
	Mus. Meermanno-Westreenianum	MA280 MS MMW 10A16, f 211v

Roermond	Munsterkerk	PA096
	-	SC38
Rotterdam	Mus. Boijmans Van Beuningen	DR04 Vol M 193
	-	DR05 Vol N 49
Utrecht	Museum Catharijneconvent	MA007 MS ABM h3
	-	MA232 MS ABM h9, f 16v
	-	PA001 Inv No ABM h59
	-	PA003 Inv No ABM h60
	-	SC02 Inv No BMH bh227
	University Library	MA 224 MS 157 (2.C.6), f 2r
	-	MA 226 MS 153 (3.F.7), f 1r
	-	MA 227 MS 155 (3.B.8), f 1r
Venray	Parish Church of St Peter	SC60
Zwolle	Dominican Church	WA31

POLAND

Olsztyn	Warmia & Mazury Museum	PA053 Inv No W 1274
Wroclaw	University Library	MA070 MS IF 401, f 193r

PORTUGAL

Arouca	Museu de Arte Sacra	MA414 MS D, f 66v
	-	SC50
Celas	Cistercian Nuns' Abbey	SC14
Lisbon	Biblioteca Nacional	MA084 MS ALC 26, f 254v
	Calouste Gulbenkian Museum	MA143 Inv M35, f 56r
	Instituto dos Arquivos Nacionais	MA354 MS ANTT Lorvao 42
	Jerominos Abbey of Sante Maria	SC64
Vile Real	Church of Vial Marim	WA33

RUSSIA

St Petersburg	The State Hermitage Museum	PA107 Inv No GE-5574
	-	PA108 Inv No GE-5574

SPAIN

Albocacer		PA127
Barcelona	Cathedral	PA177
	Losbishler Collection	PA131
	Museu Nac.d'Art de Catalunuya	PA169 MNAC/MAC 15855
	-	PA170 MNAC/MAC 15797
	-	PA171 MNAC/MAC 15927
	-	SC57 MNAC/MAC 9883
Burgo de Osma	Cathedral	PA129
Cordoba		PA172
Girona	Museo Diocesano de Girona	MA316 Inv No MDG 273
	-	PA034 Inv No MDG 293
Lonja, Mallorca		PA179
Madrid	Biblioteca Nacional	MA315 MS 1545, f 235r
	-	MA321 MS Vitr.24-3, f 131r
	-	MA322 MS Vitr.24-3, f 325
	-	MA323 MS Vitr.24-3, f 326
	-	MA324 MS Vitr.18-5, f 360r
	Garnelo Collection	PA126
	Museo Arqueologico Nacional	GL91
	Museo Nacional del Prado	PA173
	-	PA176
	-	PA178 Inv No 1335
Montblanch	Church of St Mary	SC39
	-	SC40
	-	SC41
	-	SC42
	-	SC43
Palencia	Cathedral	SC53

Palma, Mallorca	Museu de Mallorca	PA011
	-	PA012
	-	PA013
	-	PA014
	-	PA015
Poblet	Cistercian Abbey	MA104 MS M 3
Tarazona	Cathedral	PA130
Tarragona	Cathedral, Corpus Christi Chapel	SC46
	Diocesan Museum, Cathedral	PA027
	-	PA028
	-	SC45
Torrente	Parish Church	PA181
Valencia	Julio Iranzo Collection	PA180
	Museo Provincial of San Carlos	PA128
Vic	Cathedral	SC47
	Museu Episcopal	PA094
	-	PA110
	-	PA111

SWEDEN

Risinge	Old Church	WA10
Stockholm	Antikvariska-topografiska arkivet	PA035 Inv No 4001:4
	-	VA25 Inv No 170
	State Archives	VA23 RAperg 1477 3/2
	-	VA24 RAperg 1424 15/8
	-	VA26 RAperg 1506 1/6

SWITZERLAND

Basel	Öffentliche Kunstsammlung	DR01 Inv 1662.166, f K 2v
	-	DR02 Inv 1662.166, f X 2v
	-	EN14 Inv X.1874
Bern	Burgerbibliothek	MA341 MS 801, f 167r

	-	MA343 MS 43, f 18r
	-	MA346 MS 43, f 3r
	-	MA347 MS 43, f 16v
	Historical Museum	GL74
Geneva	Bibliothèque publique & univ.	MA353 MS lat. 35, f 162r
Hauterive	Cistercian Abbey	GL72
	-	SC18
Kappel	Cistercian Abbey	GL73
Luzerne	Kantonsbibliothek	MA047 St Urban P15 fol, f 128v
	-	MA054 MS P. Msc 4, p 314
Ramsen	Heribert Tenschert Collection	MA370 MS, f 24v
Wettingen	Cistercian Abbey, Cloister	GL81
	-	GL82
	-	GL83
	-	GL84
	-	GL85
Zofingen	Church	GL86
Zürich	Schweizerisches Landesmuseum	MA008 MS Gradual, f 189v
	-	VA07
	-	VA08
	-	VA09
	-	VA11

UNITED KINGDOM

Cambridge	Fitzwilliam Museum	MA291 MS CFM 6, f 125r
	-	MA292 MS McClean 114, f 119r
	-	MA293 MS CFM 3-1954, f 247v
	-	MA294 MS CFM 39-1950, 229v
	-	MA295 MS CFM 167, f 173v
		MA296 MS CFM 133, f 137r
	-	MA297 MS CFM 128, f 112r
	-	MA298 MS CFM 118, f 187v
	-	MA299 MS CFM 116, f 157r
	-	MA300 MS CFM 8, f 252v
	-	MA301 MS Marley Cutting Fl 7a
	-	MA336 MS CFM 22, f 1v

	-	MA337 MS CFM 22, f 5r
	-	MA338 MS CFM 22, f 40r
	-	MA339 MS CFM 22, f 40r
	-	MA340 MS CFM 22, f 107v
	-	MA364 MS CFM 36-1950, f 144r
	-	MA365 MS CFM 1058, f 161v
	-	MA366 MS CFM 334, f 425v
	-	MA367 MS Marley Cutting It 42
	-	MA368 MS Marley Cutting, Fl 6
	-	PA081 Inv No 0557
	Magdalene College, Pepys Library	DR06 MS 1916, p 18b
	University Library	MA058 MS Mn 150, f 2v
	-	MA390 MS Add 4100, f 117r
Chatsworth	Devonshire Collection	DR13 Inv No 733
Eton	College Library	MA307 MS 96, f 22v
Glasgow	University Library	MA261 MS Gen. 1111, f 150r
Hampton Court	Royal Collection	PA065 Inv No 405816
	-	PA106 Inv No 404758
Lincoln	Cathedral Library	MA418 MS 218, f 47
	-	MA419 MS 218, f 79
London	British Library	MA062 MS Yates Th. 36, f 186
	-	MA063 MS Yates Th. 36, f 187
	-	MA064 MS Yates Th. 36, f 188
	-	MA065 MS Yates Th. 36, f 189
	-	MA072 MS Egerton 943, f 181v
	-	MA073 MS Egerton 943, f 183v
	-	MA074 MS Egerton 943, f 182r
	-	MA075 MS Egerton 943, f 184v
	-	MA076 MS Egerton 943, f 185r
	-	MA092 MS Yates Th. 32, f 9v
	-	MA118 MS Add 18,851, f 441r
	-	MA132 MS Add 34,294, f 200v
	-	MA160 MS Royal 19 C 1, f 94v
	-	MA161 MS Royal 19 B17, f 220v
	-	MA162 MS Add 17,280, f 21v
	-	MA163 MS Add 15,677, f 143v
	-	MA164 MS Add 16,950, f 168v
	-	MA165 MS Add 39,761, f 95v
	-	MA166 MS Add 35,313, f 228v
	-	MA167 MS Add 20,729, f 145v
	-	MA168 MS Add 24,077, f 37r

	-	MA169 MS Add 17,353, f 146v
	-	MA225 MS Add 29,433, f 211v
	-	MA228 MS Add 22,557, f 24r
	-	MA229 MS Add 15,815, f 52v
	-	MA312 MS Add 39,843, f 6v
	-	MA359 MS Yates Th. 86, f 6v
	British Museum	DR08
	-	DR09
	-	DR19 Inv No SI 5226.61
	-	EN11 Inv No 1865-7-8-90
	-	EN24
	-	VA04
	-	VA05
	-	VA06
	-	VA10
	-	VA13
	Lambeth Palace Library	EN66 (ZZ)1494.6
	National Gallery	PA029 Inv No NG 569
	-	PA030 Inv No NG 1468
	-	PA031 Inv No NG 580
	-	PA032 Inv No NG 218
	-	PA033 Inv No NG 250
	-	PA037 Inv No NG 663.2
	Victoria & Albert Museum	MA233 MS 593/1107.31
	-	MA254 MS KRP.B.10, f 38r
	-	MA255 MS KRP.A.1, f 88r
	-	MA256 MS KRP.C.10, f 223v
	-	MA281 MS 1.70.250.1
	-	VA03
Marston Bigot	Church of St Leonard	GL78
Mount St Bernard	Abbey	MA026 MS MSB, f 1r
Oxford	Ashmolean Museum	EN50
	Balliol College	MA061 MS150, f 2v
	Bodleian Library	MA006 MS Bodley 530, f 15r
	-	MA044 MS Laud M.385, f 41v
	-	MA060 MS Can.Pat.Lat 156, f 1r
	-	MA069 MS Lat Liturg e.3, f 2v
	-	MA094 MS Lyell 85, f 1v
	-	MA095 MS Douce 93, f 90v
	-	MA096 MS Douce 373, f 19r

	-	MA097 MS Douce 264, f 38v
	-	MA098 MS Lat Liturg g.5, p 156
	-	MA099 MS Can.Lit. 343, f 193r
	-	MA100 MS Buchanan E.8, f 143r
	-	MA101 MS Lyell 77, f 1r
	-	MA102 MS Laud Misc 7, f 160r
	-	MA103 MS Can.Lit. 206, f 251r
	-	MA278 MS Holkham 48, p 145
	-	MA279 MS Holkham 48, p 147
	-	MA393 MS Lat Liturg f.4, f 138r
	-	MA408 MS Can.it. 108, f 64r
	Keble College	MA003 MS 49, f 162r
Penshurst	de l'Isle & Dudley Collection	VA15
Shrewsbury	St Mary's Church	GL02
	-	GL07
	-	GL08
	-	GL09
	-	GL10
	-	GL12
	-	GL13
	-	GL15
	-	GL20
	-	GL22
	-	GL25
	-	GL32
	-	GL36
	-	GL43
	-	GL47
	-	GL51
	-	GL55
	-	GL56
	-	GL58

UNITED STATES

Austin, Texas	Univ. of Texas Mus. of Art	PA089 Inv No 1984.105
Baltimore, MD	Walters Art Gallery	MA031 MS W 137, f 180v
	-	MA045 MS W 285, f 100
	-	MA083 MS 420, f 252v

	-	MA205 MS W 256, f 166v
	-	MA206 MS W 280, f 141r
	-	MA207 MS W 214, f 136r
	-	MA208 MS W 131, f 63r
	-	MA209 MS W 163, f 38r
	-	MA210 MS W 425, f 30v
	-	MA211 MS W 182, f 37v
	-	MA212 MS W 760, f 113v
	-	MA213 MS W 436, f 90v
	-	MA214 MS W 432, f 21v
	-	MA215 MS W 333, f 474v
	-	MA216 MS W 412B
	-	PA004 Inv No 37.729
	-	PA085 Inv No 37.700
		PA086 Inv No 37.652
Cambridge, MA	Houghton Library	MA350 MS Richardson 9, f 149r
	-	MA351 MS Ital 116, f 1r
	-	MA352 MS Lat 249, f 1r
Cleveland, OH	Museum of Art	MA223 MS 1963.256, f 266v
	-	MA274 MS 1964.40, f 588r
Greenville, SC	Bob Jones University	PA103
Indianapolis, IN	Museum of Art Clowes Collection	PA080
Kalamazoo, MI	Institute of Cistercian Studies.	MA344 MS 20, f 1r
Malibu, CA	The J Paul Getty Museum	MA005 MS 83.ML.105, f 137r
	-	MA024 MS 83.MN.126, f 167r
	-	MA106 MS 92.MH.22, p. 135
	-	MA107 MS 83.ML.109, f 183v
	-	MA108 MS 88.MS.14, recto
	-	MA109 MS 85.ML.27, f 72r
New Haven, CO	Beinecke Library, Yale Univ.	MA133 MS 411, f 62v
	Yale University Collection	PA068 Inv 1871.26
New York, NY	Metropolitan Museum of Art	EN22 Inv 1992.1038
	-	GL11 Inv 59.183.2
	-	GL46 Inv 59.183.1
	-	GL69 Inv 41.170.105
	-	MA033 MS Berry Hours, f 175v

	-	MA087 MS 1969 (69.36), f 295
	-	PA066 Inv No 1975.1.70B
	-	PA071 Inv No 50.229.2
	-	PA087 Inv No 32.100.102
	-	PA088 Inv No 32.100.102
	-	PA175
	Pierpont Morgan Library	MA029 MS M, f 286
	-	MA302 MS M 26, f 24r
	-	MA303 MS G 1, f 291r
	-	MA304 MS M 751, f 98v
	-	MA305 MS M 675, II, f 10v
	-	MA306 MS M 451, f 118v
	-	MA309 MS M 215, f 4r
	-	MA310 MS M 854, f 199v
	-	MA325 MS M 463, f 499v
	-	MA416 MS 399, f 301v
	-	MA417 MS 307, f 145v
	-	VA14
	Alex P Rosenberg Collection	MA311 MS 8, f 50r
Oberlin, OH	Allen Memorial Art Museum	PA109 61.78 (Kress Coll. K254)
Pittsburgh, PA	The Frick Art Museum	PA084
San Marino, CA	Huntington Library	MA146 MS HM 1147, f 17r
	-	MA147 MS HM 1181, f 69v
	-	MA148 MS HM 1143, f 140v
	-	MA149 MS HM 3027, f 106r
Washington, DC	National Gallery of Art	PA070 Inv No 4

IMAGES IN PRIVATE COLLECTIONS. PRESENT LOCATION NOT KNOWN

DR21
GL52
GL87
MA009
MA010
MA011
MA012
MA013
MA014
MA017
MA056
MA067
MA121
MA130
MA131
MA136
MA137
MA138
MA139
MA140
MA170
MA204
MA277
MA282
MA283
MA284
MA285
MA286
MA287
MA288
MA313
MA317
MA356
MA357
MA358
MA361
MA373
MA395
MA420
PA007
PA064
PA076
PA077
PA078
PA121
PA162
PA164
PA185
PA187
SC12
SC49

NO LONGER EXTANT – MOSTLY WAR LOSS 1939–1945

GL01	GL33
GL03	GL35
GL04	GL38
GL19	GL49
GL21	GL50
GL23	MA068
GL24	SC16
GL28	SC56
GL30	WA06

APPENDIX TWO

IMAGE CATEGORIES

1. THE EARLIEST IMAGES—THE TWELFTH AND THIRTEENTH CENTURIES (78 images)

Twelfth Century (13 images):
MA001, MA002, MA004, MA006, MA020, MA025, MA026, MA028, MA035, MA040, MA119, MA327, VA17

Thirteenth Century (65 images):
GL71, MA003, MA021, MA022, MA023, MA030, MA031, MA036, MA037, MA039, MA044, MA047, MA049, MA050, MA051, MA054, MA058, MA061, MA068, MA070, MA104, MA106, MA120, MA149, MA164, MA168, MA183, MA186, MA208, MA212, MA230, MA272, MA283, MA284, MA285, MA286, MA287, MA288, MA292, MA304, MA307, MA312, MA318, MA319, MA320, MA342, MA343, MA346, MA347, MA364, MA414, PA011, PA012, PA13, PA14, PA15, SC01, SC14, SC56, VA01, VA02,VA13,VA30, VA31, WA23

2. IMAGES FROM THE LIFE OF BERNARD (161 images)

DR02, DR14, EN29, EN71, GL01, GL02, GL03, GL04, GL05, GL06, GL07, GL08, GL09, GL10, GL11, GL12, GL13, GL14, GL15, GL16, GL17, GL18, GL19, GL20, GL21, GL22, GL23, GL24, GL25, GL26, GL27, GL28, GL29, GL30, GL31, GL32, GL33, GL34, GL35, GL36, GL37, GL38, GL39, GL40, GL41, GL42, GL43, GL44, GL45, GL46, GL47, GL48, GL49, GL51, GL53, GL54, GL55, GL58, GL59, GL60, GL61, GL62, GL63, GL64, GL65, GL66, GL67, GL88, GL95, MA030, MA031, MA034, MA039, MA042, MA043, MA054, MA058, MA088, MA089, MA106, MA142, MA176, MA183, MA188, MA202, MA228, MA246, MA247, MA248, MA249, MA250, MA251, MA252, MA253, MA304, MA316, MA318, MA407, MA413, PA13, PA15, PA018, PA022, PA023, PA024, PA038, PA039, PA040, PA041, PA042, PA043, PA044, PA045, PA055, PA057, PA058, PA059, PA061, PA098, PA099, PA110, PA111, PA115, PA116, PA117, PA118, PA120, PA156, PA157, SC39, SC40, SC42, VA04, VA05, VA06, VA07, VA08, VA10, VA11, WA12, WA13, WA14, WA15, WA16, WA17, WA18, WA19, WA20, WA29, WA30, WA39, WA40, WA41, WA42, WA43, WA44, WA45, WA46, WA47, WA48, WA49

3. *AMPLEXUS* IMAGES (72 images)

DR18, DR20, EN03, EN13, EN14, EN15, EN16, EN17, EN20, EN23, EN33, EN36, EN51, EN63, EN64, EN65, EN78, EN84, EN85, GL50, GL80, GL81, GL82, GL83, MA016, MA052, MA053, MA059, MA131, MA135, MA152, MA191, MA219, MA220, MA222, MA231, MA257, MA306, MA317, MA368, MA373, MA385, MA389, MA402, MA404, MA411, MA416, PA008, PA009, PA017, PA020, PA047, PA053, PA060, PA079, PA091, PA101, PA124, PA187, SC06, SC25, SC32, SC51, SC59, VA03, VA09, WA02, WA22, WA31, WA38

4. *LACTATIO* IMAGES (119 images)

DR03,DR06, DR19, EN02, EN04, EN06, EN11, EN19, EN21, EN26, EN27, EN28, EN35, EN41, EN43, EN44, EN46, EN47, EN48, EN49, EN50, EN66, EN69, EN72, EN73, EN74, EN77, EN80, EN81, GL69, GL91, MA013, MA042, MA069, MA084, MA097, MA099, MA108, MA115, MA128, MA130, MA133, MA134, MA140, MA145, MA158, MA167, MA169, MA199, MA204, MA210, MA211, MA218, MA223, MA232, MA258,

MA273, MA289, MA299, MA301, MA308, MA311, MA313, MA352, MA361, MA378, MA402, MA409, MA410, MA412, PA001, PA007, PA019, PA021, PA025, PA034, PA051, PA052, PA065, PA069, PA072, PA073, PA075, PA076, PA077, PA078, PA082, PA083, PA088, PA089, PA091, PA095, PA096, PA100, PA102, PA103, PA105, PA106, PA108, PA126, PA127, PA128, PA129, PA130, PA131, PA132, PA140, PA153, PA161, PA184, PA186, SC33, SC41, SC53, VA08,VA16, VA18, WA34

5. *DOCTRINA* IMAGES (32 images)

DR04, DR07, DR08, DR09, DR16, EN42, EN70, GL92, MA012, MA077, MA132, MA184, MA241, MA243, MA264, MA266, MA270, MA271, MA391, PA026, PA032, PA086, PA119, PA135, PA136, PA140, PA141, PA150, PA151, PA155, PA160, PA184

6. BERNARD AND THE DEVIL (98 images)

DR01, DR09, DR21, EN22, EN42, EN90, GL63, GL70, GL94, MA010, MA011, MA017, MA018, MA066, MA067, MA081, MA093, MA098, MA100, MA102, MA105, MA109, MA118, MA126, MA132, MA137, MA138, MA146, MA147, MA154, MA155, MA157, MA159, MA162, MA163, MA170, MA171, MA172, MA178, MA179, MA180, MA182, MA185, MA187, MA189, MA200, MA201, MA213, MA217, MA241, MA254, MA255, MA256, MA261, MA270, MA277, MA296, MA297, MA298, MA302, MA303, MA305, MA310, MA314, MA315, MA322, MA323, MA345, MA349, MA350, MA353, MA355, MA357, MA360, MA365, MA370, MA376, MA390, MA394, MA405, MA415, MA422, PA006, PA046, PA066, PA110, PA112, PA113, PA135, PA136, PA141, PA190, SC07, SC11, SC12, SC24, SC55, WA11

7. IMAGES OF BERNARD IN BOOKS OF HOURS (116 images)

MA005, MA009, MA010, MA011, MA017, MA029, MA033, MA045, MA066, MA067, MA083, MA087, MA093, MA095, MA100, MA102, MA105, MA107, MA108, MA109, MA113, MA117, MA118, MA123, MA124, MA125, MA126, MA128, MA129, MA132, MA133, MA134, MA136, MA138, MA146, MA147, MA148, MA151, MA157, MA158, MA159, MA162, MA163, MA165, MA166, MA169, MA170, MA171,

MA172, MA178, MA179, MA180, MA185, MA187, MA199, MA204, MA205, MA206, MA207, MA211, MA223, MA225, MA232, MA241, MA254, MA255, MA256, MA258, MA259, MA273, MA274, MA277, MA289, MA293, MA294, MA296, MA297, MA298, MA299, MA302, MA303, MA306, MA310, MA313, MA314, MA321, MA322, MA323, MA328, MA349, MA350, MA352, MA353, MA355, MA356, MA357, MA358, MA359, MA361, MA365, MA370, MA372, MA378, MA390, MA392, MA394, MA395, MA397, MA400, MA405, MA409, MA410, MA412, MA416, MA417, MA422

8. THE *VERSES OF BERNARD* ILLUSTRATIONS (69 images)

DR01, MA005, MA009, MA010, MA017, MA045, MA048, MA066, MA067, MA093, MA095, MA097, MA098, MA100, MA102, MA109, MA124, MA126, MA137, MA146, MA147, MA157, MA162, MA163, MA165, MA169, MA170, MA171, MA172, MA178, MA179, MA180, MA185, MA187, MA206, MA207, MA223, MA241, MA254, MA255, MA256, MA296, MA297, MA302, MA303, MA306, MA311, MA313, MA314, MA322, MA323, MA349, MA350, MA353, MA355, MA356, MA357, MA365, MA379, MA378, MA385, MA390, MA392, MA394, MA397, MA400, MA405, MA420, MA422

9. BERNARD IN DANTE'S '*DIVINE COMEDY*' ILLUSTRATIONS (32 images)

EN07, EN08, EN09, EN10, EN75, EN87, MA062, MA063, MA064, MA065, MA072, MA073, MA074, MA075, MA076, MA079, MA080, MA192, MA193, MA194, MA195, MA276, MA278, MA279, MA374, MA381, MA382, MA383, MA386, MA387, MA388, MA408

BIBLIOGRAPHY

Exhibition Catalogues
are listed under the city where the exhibition was held.

Aachen. *Die Zisterzienser,* Katalog zur Ausstellung des Landschaftsverbandes Rheinland, Rheinisches Museumsamt, Brauweiler, Exhibition Catalogue, Cologne, 1981.

Aelred of Rievaulx. *Opera Omnia 1. Opera ascetica.* Corpus Christianorum Continuatio Mediaevalis 1. Edd. Anselme Hoste & C. H.Talbot. Turnhout: Brepols, 1971.

Ainsworth, Maryan W. and Keith Christiansen, edd. *From Van Eyck to Bruegel –Early Netherlandish Painting in the Metropolitan Museum of Art,* New York, 1999

Alexander, J. J. G. and E. Temple. *Illustrated Manuscripts in Oxford Colleges, The University Archives and the Taylor Institution,* Oxford: OUP, 1985.

Amsterdam. *Mitteleewse kunst der noorelijke Nederlanden,* Exhibition Catalogue, Amsterdam, 1958.

Anderes, Bernhard and Peter Hoegger. *Die Glasgemälde im Kloster Wettingen,* Baden-Schweiz: Baden Verlag, 1989.

Andorfer, Eduard. 'Zwei bemerkenswerte Skulpturen im Grazer Bürgerspital', *Zeitschrift des historischen Vereines für Steirmark,* 1938. P. 122.

Arabeyre, Patrick. 'La lactation de saint Bernard (Châtillon-sur-Seine): données et problèmes', *Vies et légendes de Saint Bernard,* ed. Patrick Arabeyre, Jacques Berlioz and Philippe Poirrier, Cîteaux: Commentarii Cistercienses 1993, 173–197.

Arndt, Gerda. 'Aus dem Brandenburger Dom: Der Lehniner Altar', *Kulturspiegel Brandenburg,* 1992, 27–32.
Arnold-Forster, Frances. *Studies in Church Dedications or England's Patron Saints,* 3 vols. London, 1899.
Aubel. *Abbaye Notre-Dame du Val-Dieu, Trésors d'Art.* Exhibition Catalogue, Aubel 1966.
Augsburg. *Hans Holbein der Ältere und die Kunst der Spätgotik,* Ehhibition Catalogue, Augsburg, 1965.
Aurenhammer, H. *Lexikon der Christlichen Ikonographie,* Vienna, 1959–1967.
Avril, François. 'Le destinataire des Heures Vie à mon desir: Simon de Varie', *Revue de l'Art* 67 (1985) 33–44.
——— and Patricia Danz Stirnemann, *Manuscrits Enluminés d'Origines Insulaire VIIe-Xe Siècle,* Paris: Bibliothèque nationale, 1987.

Bacher, Ernst. *Die Mittelalterlichen Glasgemälde in der Steirmark,* 1 Teil, Graz und Strassengel, Vienna/Cologne/Graz, 1979.
Backhouse, Janet. *Books of Hours,* London: British Library, 1985.
———. *The Isabella Breviary,* London: British Library, 1993.
Baker, Christopher and Tom Henry, edd. *The National Gallery. Complete Illustrated Catalogue,* London, 1995.
Baldass, Ludwig. *Joos van Cleve–Der Meister des Todes Maria,* Vienna, 1925.
Ballhorn, Jesper. 'Løgumkloster kirkes middelalderlige udsmykning', *Løgumkloster-Studier* 4 (1984) 60–85.
Baltimore. *The International Style. The Arts in Europe Around 1400,* Exhibition Catalogue, Walters Art Gallery, Baltimore, 1962.
Barbey, M. Stanislas. *Vision de Paix. L'Abbaye Cistercienne d'Hauterive dans son cadre historique et spirituel,* Fribourg, 1951.
Barré, Henri. 'Le *Planctus Mariae* attribué a Saint Bernard', *Revue Ascétique et de Mystique* 28 (1952) 243–266.
———. 'Saint Bernard, Docteur Marial', *Analecta Sacri Ordinis Cisterciensis* 9:3-4 (1953) 92–113.
Barros, Carlos Vitorino da Silva. *O Vitral em Portugal.* Lisbon, 1983.
Barth, Medard. 'Die illustrierte Strassburger Uebersetzung der Legenda aurea von 1362, Cgm 6 in München', *Archiv für Elsässische Kirchengeschichte* 9 (1934) 137–162.
Bartsch, Adam. *Le peintre Graveur,* 21 volumes, Vienna 1803–1821.
Bartsch, The Illustrated, ed. Walter L. Strauss *et al.,* 48 volumes. New York, 1978–1988.
Batselier, P. ed. *Benedictus Pater Europae.* Antwerp: Mercatorfonds, 1980.
Becksmann, Rüdiger. 'Fensterstiftungen und Stifterbilder in der deutschen Glasmalerei des Mittelalter', *Vitrea Dedicata–Das Stifterbild in der deutschen*

Glasmalerei des Mittelalters. Hannover-Berlin: Stiftung Volkswagenwerk, 1995, 65–85.

——— and Ulf-Dietrich Korn. *Die Mittelalterichen Glasmalereien in Lüneburg und den Heidenklöstern,* CVMA Deutschland 2, Berlin, 1979.

Beer, Ellen J. *Beitrage zur oberrheinischen Buchmalerei.* Basel–Stuttgart, 1959.

———. *Die Glasmalereien der Schweiz aus dem 14. Und 15. Jahrhundert,* CVMA Schweiz Band III. Basel, 1965.

Bell, David N. *An Index of Authors and Works in Cistercian Libraries in Great Britain,* CS 130. Kalamazoo, Michigan, 1992.

Bellosi, Luciano. *Francesco di Giorgio e il Rinascimento a Siena 1450–1500.* Milan, 1993.

Belting, Hans. *The Image and its Public in the Middle Ages.* New York, 1990.

———. *Likeness & Presence—A History of the Image before the Era of Art,* trans. Edmund Jephcott. Chicago-London: University of Chicago Press, 1994.

Bennett, Adelaide. 'A Book Designed for a Noblewoman: An Illustrated *Manuel des Péchés* of the Thirteenth Century', *Medieval Book Production, Assessing the Evidence,* ed. Linda L. Brownrigg. Los Altos Hills: Anderson-Lovelace, 1990. Pages 163–181.

Bennett, J. A. W. *Poetry of the Passion. Studies in Twelve Centuries.* Oxford: Clarendon Press, 1982.

Berenson, Bernard. *The Italian Painters of the Renaissance,* London, 1932.

———. 'Ristudiando i Desegni di Cosimo Rosselli', *Bolletino d'Arte* 26 (1933) 537–547.

———. *Italian Pictures of the Renaissance . . . Florentine School,* Volume 1. London: Phaidon, 1963.

———. *The Italian Painters of the Renaissance,* London: Phaidon, 1952.

———. *Italian Pictures of the Renaissance . . . Central Italian and North Italian Schools.* 3 vols, London: Phaidon, 1968.

———. *Homeless Paintings of the Renaissance,* London-[Bloomington], 1969.

Bergau, R. ed. *Inventar der Bau- und Kunst-Denkmäler in der Provinz Brandenburg.* Berlin, 1885.

Berlin. *Das Christliche Gebetbuch im Mittelalter. Staatsbibliothek Preussischer Kukturbesitz,* Exhibition Catalogue, Berlin, 1987.

Berlin, Gemäldegalerie. Gesamtverzeichnis der Gemälde, Berlin, 1986.

Berlioz, Jacques. 'La lactation de saint Bernard dans un exemplum du "Ci nous dit" début du XIVe siècle', *Cîteaux* 39 (1988) 270–283.

———. *Saint Bernard en Bourgogne. Lieux et mémoire.* Dijon: Les Éditions du Bien Public, 1990.

Berman, Constance Hoffman. *The Cistercian Evolution.* Philadelphia: University of Pennsylvania, 2000.

Bernard de Clairvaux (Commission d'Histoire de l'Ordre de Cîteaux). Paris: Éditions Alsatia, 1953.

Bernard de Clairvaux. Histoire, Mentalités, Spiritualité. Colloque de Lyon–Cîteaux–Dijon, Paris: Les Éditions du Cerf, 1992.

Bernard of Clairvaux. *On the Song of Songs,* trans. Kilian Walsh and Irene M. Edmonds, 4 volumes. CF 4, 7, 31, 40. Spencer, Massachusetts–Kalamazoo, Michigan. 1971–1983.

———. *Five Books on Consideration,* trans. John D. Anderson and Elizabeth T. Kennan. CF 37. Kalamazoo, 1976.

———. *The Life and Death of Saint Malachy the Irishman,* trans. Robert T. Meyer. CF 10. Kalamazoo, Michigan, 1978.

———. *The Steps of Humility and Pride,* trans. Ambrose Conway. CF 13A. Kalamazoo, Michigan, 1980. Originally published in *Bernard of Clairvaux: Treatises 2,* CF 13. 1974. Pp. 25–82.

———. *The Parables* and *The Sentences,* trans. Michael Casey and Francis R. Swietek. CF 55. Kalamazoo, 2000.

Beseran, Pere and Rosa Alcoy. 'Notícia sobre procedència del retaule de santa Úrsulla de Joan Reixac', *Bulletí del Museu Nacional d'Art de Catalunya* 2 (1994), 145–150.

Bibliotheca Sanctorum, Volume 3. Rome: Istituto Giovanni XXIII nella Pontificia Universita lateranense 1963.

Biedermann, Gottfried. *Katalog Alte Galerie am Landesmuseum Joanneum. Mittelalterliche Kunst.* Graz, 1982.

Biermann, Alfons W. 'Die Miniaturenhandschriften des Kardinals Albrecht von Brandenburg (1514–1545)', in Peter Ludwig, ed., *Aachener Kunstblätter,* 46 (1975) 15–310.

Birch, W. de Grey. *Catalogue of Seals in the department of manuscripts in the British Museum,* 6 volumes. London, 1887–1900.

Blum, Shirley Neilsen. *Early Netherlandish Triptychs. A Study in Patronage.* Berkeley–Los Angeles: University of California Press, 1969.

Bob Jones University. Supplement to the Catalogue of the Art Collection, Paintings Acquired 1963-8, Greenville, North Carolina, 1968.

Boeren, P. C., ed. *Catalogus van de handschriften van het Rijksmuseum Meermanno-Westreenianum,* The Hague, 1979.

Bond, Francis. *Dedications and Patron Saints of English Churches.* Oxford, 1914.

Bondeelle-Souchier, Anne. *Bibliothèques Cisterciennes dans la France Médiévale.* Paris: CNRS, 1991.

———. 'Les Moniales Cisterciennes et leurs Livres Manuscrits dans la France', *Cîteaux* 43 (1994) 193–337.

Bonn-Bad Godesberg. *Das Christliche Gebetbuch im Mittelalter–Andachts- und Stundenbücher in Handschrift und Frühdruck,* Exhibition Catalogue, ed. Gerard Achten, Berlin, 1987.

Boon, K. G. *Netherlandish Drawings of the Fifteenth and Sixteenth Centuries,* 2 volumes. The Hague: Government Publishing Office, 1978.

Borchgrave d'Altena, Joseph de. 'Les Sculptures du pignon de l'église Notre-Dame de la Cambre', *Annales de la Sociéte royale d'Archéologie de Bruxelles* 40 (1936) 226–229.

Borsi, Franco and Stefano. *Paolo Uccello.* Paris, 1992.

Borsook, Eve. *Gli affreschi di Montesiepi.* 1968.

Boskovits, Miklos ed. *Frühe Italienische Malerei–Gemäldegalerie Berlin,* Berlin: Staatliche Museen Preussischer Kulturbesitz, 1987.

Botterill, Steven. *Dante and the Mystical Tradition. Bernard of Clairvaux in the* Commedia. Cambridge-New York: Cambridge University Press, 1994.

Bouton, Jean de la Croix. 'The Life of the Twelfth and Thirteenth Century Nuns of Cîteaux', *Hidden Springs,* edd. John A. Nichols and Lillian Thomas Shank, CS 113/1:11-27. Kalamazoo, 1995.

Bouyer, Louis. *The Cistercian Heritage,* London: A. R. Mowbray, 1958.

Brandis, Tilo ed. *Zimelien–Abendländische Handschriften des Mittelalters aus den Sammlungen der Stiftung Preussischer Kulturbesitz,* Berlin-Wiesbaden, 1975.

Braun, Joseph. *Tracht und Attribute der heiligen in der Deutschen Kunst.* Stuttgart, 1943.

Bredero, Adriaan H. *Bernard of Clairvaux: Between Cult und History,* Edinburgh-Grand Rapids: T & T Clark, 1996.

Brieger, Peter, Millard Meiss, and Charles S. Singleton. *Illuminated Manuscripts of the Divine Comedy.* 2 volumes. London: Routledge & Kegan Paul, 1969.

Brinkmann, Bodo. *Die Flämische Buchmalerei am Ende des Burgunderreichs.* 2 volumes. Turnhout: Brepols, 1997.

Brown, Peter. *The Cult of the Saints.* London: SCM Press, 1981

Bruch, Robert. *Die Malereien in den Handschriften des Königreichs Sachsen.* Dresden, 1906.

Bruckner, A. ed. *Scriptoria Medii Aevi Helvetica,* Vol. 9. Geneva, 1964.

Bruges. *Tentoonstelling van Miniaturen en Boekbanden.* Exhibition Catalogue, Bruges, 1927.

Bruges. *Vlaamse kunst op perkament. Handschriften en miniaturen te Brugge van de 12de tot de 16de eeuw.* Exhibition Catalogue, Gruuthusemuseum Bruges, 1981.

Brussels. *Manuscrits Cisterciens de la Bibliothèque royale de Belgique,* ed. Thérèse Glorieux-De Gand, Exhibition Catalogue, Brussels: Bibliothèque Royale, 1990.

Buberl, Paul. *Die Kunstdenkmäler des Zisterzienserklosters Zwettl.* Baden bei Wien, 1940.

Burchard of Balerne (*Burchardi, ut videtur Abbatis Bellevallis*). *Apologia de Barbis,* ed. Giles Constable. Corpus Christianorum Continuatio Medievalis 62. Turnhout: Brepols, 1985.

Buren, Anne Hagopian van. 'Jan van Eych in the Hours of Turin and Milan approached through the Fashions of Dress', in Koert van der Horst and Johann-Christian Klamt, edd., *Masters and Miniatures.* Doornspijk : Davaco, 1991. Pp. 221–243.

Burke, Peter. *Culture and Society in Renaissance Italy 1420–1540.* London, 1972.

Burlington Magazine, Volume 2, 1903.

Bushart, Bruno. 'Der Meister des Maulbronner Altars von 1432', *Münchner Jahrbuch der Bildenden Kunst,* Series 3, Vol. 8 (1957) 81–100.

Büttner, F. O. Imitatio pietatis: *Motive der christlichen Ikonographie als Modele der Verähnlichung.* Berlin: G. Mann, 1983.

Bynum, Caroline Walker. *Holy Feast and Holy Fast. The Religious Significance of Food to Medieval Women.* Berkeley-Los Angeles-London: University of California Press, 1987.

———. *Fragmentation and Redemption. Essays on Gender and the Human Body in Medieval Religion.* New York: Zone, 1991.

Byvanck, A. W. *Les Principaux manuscrits a Peintures de la Bibliothèque Royale des Pays-Bas et du Musée Meermanno-Westreenianum.* Paris, 1924.

Byvanck, A.W. And G. J. Hoogewerff, edd. *Noord-Nederlandsche Miniaturen in Handschriften der 14e, 15e, en 16e eeuwen.* The Hague, 1925.

Caesarius of Heisterbach. *The Dialogue on Miracles,* trans. H. von E. Scott and C. C. Swinton Bland. 2 volumes. London, 1929.

———. *Die Wundergeschichten des Caesarius von Heisterbach,* ed. Alfons Hilka, Volume 3. Bonn, 1937.

Calabuig, Ignazio M. ed. *Respice Stellam. Maria in San Bernardo e nella Tradizione Cistercense.* Rome, 1993.

Calkins, Robert G. *The Illustrated Books of the Middle Ages.* London, 1983.

Camille, Michael. *The Gothic Idol: Ideology and Image-making in Medieval Art.* Cambridge-New York: Cambridge University Press, 1989.

Campbell, Lorne. *The Early Flemish Pictures in the Collection of Her Majesty the Queen.* Cambridge: University Press, 1985.

———. *Renaissance Portraits: European portrait painting in the 14th, 15th, and 16th Centuries.* New Haven & London: Yale University Press, 1990.

Cataldi, Riccardo, ed. *Melliflui Doctoris Opera.* Casamari, 1992.

Catalogue Général des Manuscrits des Bibliothèques Publiques des Départements, Vol. 1. Paris, 1899.

Cavadini, Luigi. *Giovanni da Milano.* Valmorea: Comune di Valmorea, 1980.

Chauvin, Benoît, 'À travers les sources illustrées de quatre abbayes cisterciennes féminines de Flandre francaise', in Benoît Chauvin, ed., *Cîteaux et les femmes*. Paris, 2001.

Chen, Frances Sheryl. 'Bernard's Prayer Before the Crucifix that Embraced Him: Cistercians and Devotion to the Wounds of Christ', *Cistercian Studies Quarterly* 29 (1994) 24–54.

Chevalier, U. *Repertorium Hymnologicum,* Louvain, 1892–1921.

Chiarini, Marco and Serena Padovani, edd. *La Galleria Palatina e gli Appartimenti Reali di Palazzo Pitti, Catalogo dei* Dipinti, Volume 1. Florence, 2003.

Chibnall, Marjorie, trans. [John of Salisbury], *Memoirs of the Papal Court,* London: Thomas Nelson, 1956.

———. ed. and trans. *The Ecclesiastical History of Orderic Vitalis.* 6 volumes. Oxford: Clarendon, 1969–1980.

Christie. *Works of Art from the Collection of the Barons Nathaniel and Albert Rothschild,* Sale 8/7/1999.

Clark, David L. 'Filippino Lippi's *The Virgin Inspiring St. Bernard* and Florentine Humanism', *Studies in Iconography* 7–8 (1981–1982) 175–187.

Clay, C. 'The Seals of the Religious Houses of Yorkshire', *Archaeologia* 78 (1928) 1–36.

Cleveland. A Handbook. The Cleveland Museum of Art. Cleveland, Ohio, 1978.

Cocheril, Maur. *Notes sur l'Architecture et le Décor dans les Abbayes Cisterciennes du Portugal.* Paris, 1972.

———. *Routier des Abbayes Cisterciennes du Portugal.* Paris, 1978.

Cockerell, S. C. *The Book of Hours of Yolande of Flanders.* London, 1905.

Coelho Dias, Geraldo J. A., ed. *Cister No Vale Do Douro.* Porto, 1999.

Cole, Bruce. 'Old in New in the Early Trecento', *Mitteilungen des Kunsthistorischen Institutes in Florenz* 17 (1973), 229–248.

Cole, Bruce. *Agnolo Gaddi.* Oxford-New York: Clarendon, 1977.

Colin, Georges, Marie-Thérèse Lenger, and Louis Rouzet. *Bibliothèque de Madame Louis Solvay.* Brussels, 1969.

Cologne. *Das Schnütgen Museum. Eine Auswahl.* Exhibition Catalogue. Cologne, 1968.

———. *Herbst des Mittelalters. Spätgotik in Köln und am Niederrhein.* Exhibition Catalogue, 1970.

———. *Die Parler und der schöne Stil 1350–1400.* 3 volumes. Exhibition Catalogue. Cologne, 1978.

———. *Andachtsbücher des Milttelalters aus Privatbesitz,* ed. Joachim M. Plotzek. Exhibition Catalogue. Cologne, 1987.

———. *Genie ohne Namen / Der Meister des Bartholomäus Altars.* Wallraf-Richartz-Museum, Exhibition Catalogue. Cologne, 2001.

———. *Ars Vivendi – Ars Moriendi.* Exhibition Catalogue. Cologne, 2002.

Comblen-Sonkes, Micheline. *The Collegiate Church of Saint Peter Louvain,* Corpus of Fifteenth-Century Painting in the Southern Netherlands and the Principality of Liége, 18. 2 volumes. Brussels, 1996.

Connor, Elizabeth, trans. *Aelred of Rievaulx: The Mirror of Charity.* CF 17. Kalamazoo, 1990.

Connor, Elizabeth. 'The Abbeys of Las Huelgas and Tart and their Filiations', in John A. Nichols and Lilian Thomas Shanks, edd. *Hidden Springs* 1:29-48. CS 113. Kalamazoo, 1995.

Conrad of Eberbach. *Le Grand Exorde de Cîteaux,* ed. Jacques Berlioz. Turnhout, 1998.

———. *The Great Beginnings of Cîteaux,* trans. Benedicta Ward & Paul Savage. CF72. Kalamazoo, 2006.

Constable, Giles, ed. *The Letters of Peter the Venerable.* 2 volumes. Cambridge, Massachusetts-London: Harvard University Press, 1967.

Coo, Jos de. *Museum Mayer van den Bergh Catalogus I.* Antwerp, 1960.

Coomans, Thomas. *L'Abbaye de Villers-en-Brabant. Construction, configuration et sigification d'une abbaye cistercienne gothique.* Brussels: Racine and Brecht: Cîteaux: Commentarii Cistercienses, 2000.

Copenhagen. *Levende Ord og Lysende Billeder,* Exhibition Catalogue, Copenhagen, 1999.

Coppack, Glyn. *Fountains Abbey.* London: Batsford, 1993.

Couderc, Camille. *Catalogue des Manuscrits de la Bibliothèque de la Ville de Clermont-Ferrand.* Paris, 1890.

Coulton G. G. *Five Centuries of Religion.* 4 volumes. Cambridge: University Press, 1923–1950.

Dal Prà, Laura. 'L'immagine di Bernardo nell'arte italiana (secc. XIII–XVII)', *Bernardo Cistercense – Atti del XXVI Convegne storico internazionale, Todi, 8–11 ottobre 1989.* Spoleto, 1990.

———. *Iconografia di San Bernardo di Clairvaux in Italia,* II, 1 La Vita, Biblioteca Cisterciensis 8/2: Corpus Iconographicum Bernardinum. Rome: Editiones Cistercienses, 1991.

D'Ancona, Mirella Levi. *The Iconography of the Immaculate Conception in the Middle Ages and Early Renaissance.* New York, 1957.

Daniel-Rops, Henri. *Bernard of Clairvaux.* New York-London: Hawthorn Books, 1964.

Danmarks Kirker, Vol. VI (1), Præstø Amt, edd. Chr. Axel Jensen and Victor Hermansen. Copenhagen, 1933.

Dante, Aligheri. *La Divina Commedia,* ed. Karl Witte for G. Daelli & Co (Biblioteca Rara). 3 volumes. Milan, 1864.

———. *La Divina Commedia, Paradiso,* Vol. 6 (illustrated edition). Milan: Fratelli Fabbri, 1965.

Datini, Giulio. *Musei di Prato.* Bologna, 1972.

David, Henri. 'Une Statue de Saint Bernard', *Saint Bernard et Son Temps.,* Vol. 1: 130-138. Dijon, 1928.

———. *De Sluter a Sambin,* Vol. 2. Paris, 1932.

Davies, Hugh William. *Catalogue of a Collection of Early French Books in the Library of C. Fairfax Murray.* 2 volumes. London, 1910.

Davies, Martin. *National Gallery Catalogues: Earlier Italian Schools.* Plates, Vol. 2. London, 1953.

———. *National Gallery Catalogues: The Earlier Italian Schools* (Second edition revised). London, 1961.

De Gray Birch, Walter. *Early Drawings and Illuminations in the British Museum.* London, 1879.

Defoer, Henri L.M., Anne S. Korteweg, and Wilhelmina C.M.Wüstefeld, *Golden Age of Dutch Manuscript Painting.* New York: George Braziller, 1990.

Degler-Spengler, Brigitte. 'The Incorporation of Cistercian Nuns into the Order in the Twelfth and Thirteenth Century', *Hidden Springs,* 1:85-134, edd. John A. Nichols & Lillian Thomas Shank. CS 113. Kalamazoo, 1995.

Dehio, Georg. *Handbuch der Deutschen Kunstdenkmäler: Rheinland-Pfalz Saarland,* ed. Hans Caspary, Wolfgang Götz and Ekhart Klinge. Munich/ Berlin, 1972.

Del Bravo, Carlo. *Liberale da Verona.* Florence: Edizioni d'arte Il Fiorino, 1966.

Del Vita, Alessandro. 'La Pinacoteca d'Arezzo', *Rassegna d'Arte* 1915, 75–88.

Delen, A. J. J. *De Grafische Kunsten door de eeuwen heen.* Antwerp/Amsterdam, 1956.

Delluc, Brigitte & Gilles, Jacques Lagrange, and Jean Secret. *Cadouin. Une aventure cistercienne en Périgord.* Le Bugue: PLB éditeur, 1990.

Dessi, R. M. and M. Lamy, 'Saint Bernard et les Controverses Mariales au Moyen-Âge', *Vies et Légendes de Saint Bernard de Clairvaux,* edd. P. Arabeyre, J. Berlioz, and P. Poirrier. Cîteaux, 1993. Pp. 229–260.

Deutchler, Florens. 'Looking at Bonne of Luxembourg's Prayer Book', *Metropolitan Museum Bulletin* N.S. 29 (1971) 267–278.

Dewez, L. and A. van Iterson. 'La Lactation de Saint Bernard: Légende et Iconographie', *Cîteaux in de Nederlanden* 7 (1956) 165–189

Dijon, *Saint Bernard et l'art des Cisterciens* (Musée de Dijon). Exhibition Catalogue. Dijon: Musée de Dijon, 1953.

Dodgson, Campbell. *Catalogue of Early German and Flemish Woodcuts preserved in the Department of Prints and Drawings in the British Museum,* Vol. 1. London, 1903.

———. *Woodcuts of the Fifteenth Century in the Ashmolean Museum, Oxford.* Oxford, 1929.

———. *Woodcuts of the XV Century in the Department of Prints and Drawings British Museum,* 2 volumes. London, 1934.

Dodwell, C. R. *The Canterbury School of Illumination 1066-1200* Cambridge: University Press, 1954.

Domaslowski, Jerzy. 'Znaczenie Klasztorów Cysterskich dla Sredniowiecznej Sztuki Pomarza Wschodniego', *Cystersi w Kulturze Sredniowiecznej Europy,* ed. Jerzy Strzelczyk. Poznan 1992. Pp. 241–265.

Donkin, R. A. *The Cistercians: Studies in the Geography of Medieval England and Wales,* Studies and Texts 38. Toronto: Pontifical Institute of Mediaeval Studies, 1978.

Douët-d'Arcq, Louis-Claude. *Collection de Sceaux,* Vol. 3. Paris, 1868.

Duchet-Suchaux, Gaston and Monique. *Les Ordres Religieux. Guide historique.* Paris, 1993.

——— and M. Pastoureau. *The Bible and the Saints.* Paris/New York: Flammarion, 1994.

Dunkerton, Jill, Susan Foister, Dillian Gordon and Nicholas Penny. *Giotto to Dürer.* London: National Gallery – New Haven: Yale University Press, 1991.

Dupeux, Cécile. 'La Lactation de Saint Bernard de Clairvaux. Genèse et Évolution d'une Image', *l'Image et la Production du Sacré,* ed. F. Dunand, J-M Spieser, & Jean Wirth, Paris, 1991, 165–193.

———. 'Saint Bernard dans l'iconographie médiévale: l'example de la lactation', *Vies et légendes de Saint Bernard de Clairvaux* edd. Patrick Arabeyre, Jacques Berlioz et Philippe Poirrier. Cîteaux: Commentarii Cistercienses, 1993. Pp. 152–166.

Durán, Rafael M. *Iconografía Española de San Bernardo.* Poblet, 1953 (second edition 1990).

Dürer Scriftlicher Nachlass, ed. Hans Rupprich. Berlin, 1956.

Durville, G. *Catalogue de la Bibliothèque du Musée Thomas Dobrée,* Vol. 1. Nantes, 1904.

Dutschke, C. W. *Guide to Medieval and Renaissance Manuscripts in the Huntington Library.* San Marino: Huntington Library, 1989.

Eales, Samuel J. *Life and Works of Saint Bernard,* 2 volumes. London: John Hodges, 1889.

Eberbach. *Bernhard von Clairvaux. Der Zisterzienserheilige zur und in der Kunst.* Exhibition Catalogue. Eberbach, 2003.

Eckert, K. *Sankt Bernhard von Clairvaux Glasmalereien aus dem Kreuzgang von Altenberg bei Köln.* Wuppertal: Abendland Verlag, 1953.

Edinburgh. *Treasures of Belgian Libraries. National Library of Scotland.* Exhibition Catalogue. Edinburgh, 1963.

Eirwen Jones, Mary. *A History of Western Embroidery.* London: Studio Vista, 1969.

Eisler, Colin. *Masterworks in Berlin.* Boston-New York-Toronto-/London: Little Brown, 1996.

Eizenhöfer, Leo and Hermann Knaus. *Die Liturgischen Handschriften der hessischen Landes- und Hochschulbibliothek Darmstadt.* Wiesbaden, 1968.

Elder, E. Rozanne. '*Macula nigra et virgo immaculata:* Bernard's Tests for True Doctrine', *Cistercian Studies Quarterly* 38 (2003) 423–438.

Elm, Kaspar, ed. *Bernhard von Clairvaux. Rezeption und Wirkung im Mittelalter und in der Neuzeit.* Wiesbaden: Harrassowitz, 1994.

Erasmus, Desiderius. *Encomium Moriae–Praise of Folly,* published at Basle 1515 and decorated with the marginal drawings of Hans Holbein the Younger–in facsimile, with introduction by H. A. Schmid, trans. Helen H. Tanzer, 2 volumes. Basle, 1931.

Erdmann, Wolfgang. *Zisterzienser-Abtei Doberan.* Königstein im Taunus: Hans Köster, 1995.

Escallier, E. A. *l'Abbaye d'Anchin 1079–1792.* Lille, 1852.

Essling, Prince d'. *Les Livres a Figures Vénitiens.* Florence-Paris, 1907.

Euw, Anton von and Joachim M. Plotzek. *Die Handschriften der Sammlung Ludwig,* 4 volumes. Cologne: Ludwig Museum, 1979–1985.

Evans, Mark. *The Sforza Hours.* London, 1992.

Faider, P. and P van Sint Jan, edd. *Catalogue Général des Manuscrits des Bibliothèques de Belgique,* Vol. VI: *Catalogue des Manuscrits conservés a Tournai.* Gembloux, 1950.

Falkenburg, Reindert L. *The Fruit of Devotion.* Amsterdam-Philadelphia: John Benjamin, 1994.

Ferrari, Bruce P. *Catalogue No 1 – Important Western Medieval Illuminated Manuscripts and Illuminated Leaves.* Akron, Ohio, 1987.

Ferras, Vincent. 'Matériaux pour une Iconographie Bernardine Méridionale', *Mélanges à la Mémoire du Père Anselme Dimier,* ed. Benoît Chauvin, Vol. II/3: 285-323. Pupillin, 1984.

Finucane, Ronald C. *Miracles and Pilgrims: Popular Beliefs in Medieval England.* Basingstoke-Totowa: Macmillan, 1995.

Fischer, Chris. *Fra Bartolommeo. Master Draughtsman of the High Renaissance.* Rotterdam. Museum Boymans van Beuningen, 1990.

Fleith, Barbara. *Studien zur Überlieferungsgeschichte der Lateinischen Legenda Aurea.* Brussels, 1991.

Florence. *Cataloghi dei Manoscritti della R. Biblioteca Nazionale Centrale di Firenze,* Vol. 1. Rome, 1889.

———. *Raffaello a Firenze. Dipinti e desegni delle collezioni fiorentine.* Exhibition Catalogue. Palazzo Pitti, Florence, 1984.

———. *Bernardo di Chiaravalle nell'arte italiana dal seculo XIV ai seculo XVIII*, ed. Laura Dal Prà. Exhibition Catalogue. Florence (Certosa di Firenze). Rome, 1990.

———. *L'Eta di Savonarola; Fra Bartolommeo e la Scuola di San Marco.* Exhibition Catalogue. Florence, 1996.

———. *I Colori del divino,* ed. Giovanna Lazzi. Exhibition Catalogue. Biblioteca Riccardiana, Florence 2001.

Folda, Jaroslav. *Crusader Manuscript Illumination at Saint-Jean d'Acre, 1275–1291.* Princeton, New Jersey: Princeton University Press, 1976.

France, James. *The Cistercians in Medieval Art.* Stroud-Kalamazoo, 1998.

———. 'Cistercians Under Our Lady's Mantle', *Cistercian Studies Quarterly* 37 (2002) 393–414.

Fraser, A. Ian. *A Catalogue of the Clowes Collection.* Indianapolis: Museum of Art, 1973.

Frati, C. and A. Segarizzi. *Catalogo dei codici Marciana Italiani.* Venice, 1909.

Frederickson, Burton B. and Federico Zeri. *Census of Pre-Nineteenth Century Italian Paintings in North American Public Collections.* Cambridge, Mass.: Harvard University Press, 1972.

Fremantle, Richard. *Florentine Gothic Painters from Giotto to Masaccio. A Guide to Painting in and near Florence 1300–1450.* London, 1975.

Friedländer, Max J. trans. Norden, H. *Early Netherlandish Painting,* 14 volumes (in 16). Leyden: Sitjhoff, 1967–1976.

———. *Die altniederländische Malerei,* 14 volumes. Berlin 1924–1937.

Fruchard, Marie-Francoise and Guy Ahlsell de Toulza. 'La Chapelle du Chateau de Serres', *Revue du Tarn* 100 (1980) 508–511.

Fründt, Edith. *Das Kloster Doberan.* Berlin: Union Verlag, 1987.

Gad, Tue. *Helgener–Legender fortalt i Norden.* Copenhagen, 1971.

Gagnebin, Bernard. *L'enluminure de Charlemagne à Francois 1er.* Geneva: Bibliothèque publique, 1976.

Galob, Natasa. *Twelfth-Century Cistercian Manuscripts: The Sitticum Collection.* Ljubljana – London: Slovenska Knjiga in conjunction with H. Miller, 1996.

Gariboldi, Vittoria. *Perugino. Catalogo completo.* Florence: Octavo, 1999.

Garnier, J. *Catalogue des Manuscrits de la Bibliothèque de la Ville d'Amiens.* Amiens, 1843.

Gaspar, Camille & Lyna, Frédéric. *Les Principaux Manuscrits à Peintures de la Bibliothèque Royale de Belgique,* 3 volumes. Brussels: Leberte-Delcour, 1984–1989.

Gazzelli, Annarosa. *Miniatura Fiorentina des Rinascimento 1440–1525,* 2 volumes. Florence: Giunta regionale toscana, 1985.

Geldern 2001. *Das Goldene Zeitalter des Herzogtums Geldern.* Exhibition Catalogue. Geldern, 2001.

Genaille, Robert. 'L'Énigme du Retable du Cellier–Recherches sur l'art de Jean Bellegambe', *Révue des Arts* 1952, 99–108.

———. 'L'Annonciation de Jean Bellegambe', *Gazette des Beaux-Arts* 57 (1961) 5–16.

Gevers, A. J. and A. J. Mensema, eds. *De Broerenkerk te Zwolle.* Zwolle, 1989.

Gheyn, J. van den. *Catalogue des Manuscrits de la Bibliothèque royale,* 6 vol., Bruxelles, 1901–1906.

Gibbs, Robert. *Tomaso da Modena. Painting in Emilia and the March of Treviso, 1340–80.* Cambridge-New York: Cambridge University Press, 1989.

Giraud-Badin L. *Manuscrits et Incunables provenant de la Bibliothèque du Chateau de la R.-G.* Sale Catalogue. Paris, 1927.

Glaser, Curt. *Gotische Holzschnitt.* Berlin, 1924.

Goff, Frederick R. *Incunabula in American Libraries.* New York: Bibliographical Society of America, 1964.

Goldberg, Gisela and Gisela Scheffler. *Altdeutsche Gemälde–Köln und Nordwestdeutschland–Bayerische Staatsgemäldesammlungen Alte Pinakothek,* 2 volumes. Munich: Bayerische Staatsgemäldesammlungen, 1972.

Goodison, J. W. and G. H. Robertson. *Fitzwilliam Museum Catalogue,* 3 volumes. Cambridge, 1967.

Gordon, Dillian. *National Gallery Catalogues: The Fifteenth Century Italian Paintings* Vol. 1. London: National Gallery, 2003.

Gothic Art Guide. Catalogue of *Museu Nacional d'Art de Catalunya.* Barcelona: MNAC, 2000.

Gottschalk, Joseph. 'Die älteste Bilderhandschrift mit den Quellen zum Leben der hl. Hedwig', *Aachener Kunstblätter* 34 (1967) 61–161.

Griesser, Bruno ed. 'Die *Ecclesiastica Officia Cisterciensis Ordinis* des Cod. 1711 von Trent', *Analecta Sacri Ordinis Cisterciensis* 12 (1956) 153–288.

Gripkey, Mary Vincentine. *The Blessed Virgin Mary as Mediatrix in the Latin and old French Legend prior to the Fourteenth Century.* Washington: Catholic University of America, 1938.

Grönwoldt, Ruth ed. *Webereien und Stickereien des Mittelalters–Kestner-Museum Hannover – Textilien I.* Hannover, 1964.

Guidotti, Allesandro. 'Il Maestro Daddesco in Codici della Badia a Settimo', in Grazia Vailati Schoenburg Waldenburg, ed., *Miniatura Italiana in Età Romanica e Gotica.* Florence, 1979.

Günther, Jörn and Bruce P. Ferrini. *Overlooking the Ages.* Dealers' Catalogue, 1999.

Guth-Dreyfus, Katia.*Transluzides Email–in der ersten Hälfte des 14. Jahrhunderts am Ober-, Mittel- und Niederrhein.* Basel: Birkhäuser, 1954.

Gyldendal og Politikens Danmarkshistorie, Vol. 7. Copenhagen: Gyldendal, 1989.

Haberditzl, Franz Martin. *Die Einblattdrucke des XV. Jahrhunderts in der Kupferstichsammlung der Hofbibliothek zu Wien,* 2 volumes. Vienna, 1920.

Hain, L. *Repertorium bibliographicum.* Stuttgart/Paris, 1826–1838.

Hall, Marcia B. *Color and Meaning: Practice and Theory in Renaissance Painting.* Cambridge: University Press, 1992.

Hallberg S., R. Norberg, and O. Odenius. 'Benediktinarnes, cluniacensernas och cisterciensernas ämbetssigill I det medeltida Sverige', *Kyrkohistorisk årsskrift* 65 (1965) 57–114.

Hamburger, Jeffrey F. 'The Visual and the Visionary: The Image in Late Medieval Monastic Devotions', *Viator* 20 (1989) 161–182.

———. *Nuns as Artists. The Visual Culture of a Medieval Convent.* Berkeley/Los Angeles/London: University of California Press, 1997.

Hannover. *Die deutschen und niederländischen Gemälde bis 1550.* Exhibition Catalogue. Niedersächsisches Landesmuseum, Hannover Landesgalerie, Hannover, 1992.

Harthan, John. *Books of Hours and their Owners.* London: Thames & Hudson, 1977.

Hassall, A. G. and W. O. *Treasures from the Bodleian Library.* London: G Fraser, 1976.

Hayward, Jane. *Painted Windows.* Metropolitan Museum of Art. Vol 30. New York, 1971–1972.

Heck,Christian ed. *L'art flamand et hollandais: le siècle des Primitifs 1380–1520.* Paris: Citadelles & Mazenod, 2003.

Heffernan, Thomas J. *Sacred Biography.* Oxford-New York: Oxford University Press, 1988.

Heid-Guillaume, Caroline and Anne Ritz. *Manuscrits Médiévaux de Chambery.* Paris: Brepols, 1998.

Heilsbronn/Erlangen. *Das Zisterzienserkloster Heilsbronn und seine Bibliothek. Ausstellung des Landeskirchlicher Archivs,* ed. Svetozar Sprusansky. Exhibition Catalogue, 1991.

Heitz, Paul ed. *Einblattdrücke des fünfzehnten Jahrhunderts.* Strassburg, 1899–1924.

Helbig, Jean. *Les Vitraux Médiévaux Conservés en Belgique 1200–1500,* CVMA Belgique vol. Brussels: Weissenbruch, 1961.

Heller, Elizabeth. *Das altniederländische Stifterbild.* Munich, 1976.

Hellinga, Lotte and Wytze. 'Gotfred af Ghemens færden ca. 1486–1510. En typologisk undersøgelse', *Fund og Forskning* 15 (1968) 7–38.

Helms, Hans Jørgen. *Næstved St. Peders Kloster.* Næstved: Haase & Søn, 1940.

Hendrix, Guido. *Bernardina en Cisterciensia in de Universiteitsbibliotkek-Leesboek – Kataloog.* Gent, 1990.

Hermann, Hermann Julius. *Die Westeuropäischen Handschriften und Inkunabeln der Gotik und der Renaissance 3 – Französische und Iberische Handschriften.* Beschreibendes Verzeichnis der Illuminierten Handschriften in Österreich Band VIII, VII Teil. Leipzig, 1938.

Hernad, Béatrice. *Die Gotischen Handschriften Deutscher Herkunft in der Bayerischen Staatsbibliothek – Teil 1, von Später 13. Bis zur Mitte des 14. Jahrhunderts.* Wiesbaden: L Reichert, 2000.

Heslop, T. A. 'Cistercian Seals in England and Wales', in Christopher Norton and David Park, edd., *Cistercian Art and Architecture in the British Isles.* Cambridge-New York: Cambridge University Press, 1986. Pp. 266–283.

Himmelein, Volker. 'Beiträge zur Herrenalber Kunstgeschichte', in Peter Rückert and Hansmartin Schwarzmaier, edd., *850 Jahre Kloster Herrenalb.* Stuttgart, 2001. Pp. 45–60.

Hind, Arthur M. *Early Italian Engraving,* 7 volumes. New York-London: B. Quaritch, 1938–1948.

———. *An Introduction to a History of Woodcut,* 2 volumes. New York: Dover, 1963.

Hinnebusch, Frederick ed. *Jacques de Vitry: Historia occidentalis.* Fribourg: The University Press, 1972.

Hockey, S. F., ed. *The Account-Book of Beaulieu Abbey.* London. Royal Historical Society, 1975.

Hodnett, Edward. *English Woodcuts 1480-1535.* Oxford: University Press, 1973.

Hoegger, Peter. *Die Kunstdenkmäler des Kantons Aargau,* Band VIII: *Das Ehemalige Zisterzienserkloster Marisstella in Wettingen.* Basel, 1998.

. *Galsmalerei im Kanton Aargau: Kloster Wettingen* Aargau: Baden-Verlag, 2002.

Holdsworth, Christopher. 'Saint Bernard: What Kind of Saint?', in Judith Loades, ed., *Monastic Studies.* Bangor, 1990, 86–101.

———. 'The Early Writings of Bernard of Clairvaux', *Cîteaux* 45 (1994), 21–61.

———. 'The Reception of St Bernard in England', in Kaspar Elm, ed., *Bernhard von Clairvaux – Rezeption und Wirkung im Mittelalter und der Neuzeit.* Wiesbaden, 1994.

Hollstein's *Dutch and Flemish Etchings, Engravings and Woodcuts c 1450–1700,* 46 volumes. Amsterdam: M Hertzberger, 1949–1994.

Hollstein's *German Engravings, Etchings and Woodcuts 1400-1700,* 43 volumes. Amsterdam: M. Hertzberger, 1954–1996.

Holmes, Megan. *Fra Filippo Lippi. The Carmelite Painter.* New Haven-London: Yale University Press, 1999.

Horae Eboracenses. The Prymer or Hours of the Blessed Virgin Mary according to the use of the Illustrious Church of York, Surtees Society 132. London, 1920.

Horst, Koert van der. *Illuminated and Decorated Medieval Manuscripts in the University Library, Utrecht*– an illustrated catalogue. Cambridge-New York: Cambridge University Press, 1989.

Hoskins, Edgar. *Horae Beatae Mariae Virginis.* London, 1901.

Hoste, Anselm. 'De iconografie van Bernardus van Clairvaux in Vlaanderen. Een korte inleiding', in M. Sabbe, M. Lamberigts and F. Gistelinck, edd., *Bernardus en de Cistercienzerfamilie in Belgie 1090-1990.* Leuven, 1990. Pp. 171–179.

Howlett, Richard, ed. *Chronicles of the Reigns of Stephen, Henry II and Richard I,* 4 volumes. Rolls Series, 1884–1889.

Hübl, Albertus. *Catalogus Codicum Manu Scriptorum qui in Bibliotheca Monasterii B.M.V. ad Scotos Vindobonae.* Vienna, 1899.

Hümpfner, Tiburtius. *Ikonographia S. Bernardi Abbatis Claravallensis.* Augsburg-Cologne-Vienna: Benno Filser Verlag, 1927.

Hunt, J. Eric. *The Glass in St. Mary's Church Shrewsbury.* Shrewsbury, 1951.

Huy 1990. *Filles de Cîteaux au pays mosan. Catalogue de l'exposition,* ed. M. Él. Montulet-Henneau. Huy, 1990.

Iconografia di San Benedetto nella Pittura della Toscana. Immagini e Aspetti Culturali ino al XVI Seculo Florence, 1982.

Jacobi, Franz. *Studien zur Geschichte der Bayerischen Miniatur des XIV Jahrhunderts.* Strassburg, 1908.

Jacobus de Voragine. *The Golden Legend of.* Trans. Grange Ryan and Helmut Ripperger. New York-London-Toronto: Longmans, Green & Co, 1941.

———. *The Golden Legend,* selected and translated by Christopher Stace. Harmondsworth: Penguin, 1998.

Jaffé, Michael. *The Devonshire Collection of Italian Drawings. Roman and Neapolitan Schools.* London: Phaidon, 1994.

Jakobs, Dörthe and James France. 'Bie Bernhardszyklus auf der Ostwand – Ikonographie und Datierung', in Dörthe Jakobs, ed. *Bernhardskapelle Owen.* Esslingen am Neckar: Kunstverlag Josef Fink, 2005.

James, B. Scott, trans. *The Letters of St Bernard of Clairvaux.* London: Burns Oates, 1953; revised edition. Stroud-Kalamazoo, 1998.

James, M. R. *The Descriptive Catalogue of the Manuscripts in the Fitzwilliam Museum.* Cambridge: University Press, 1895.

———. *A Descriptive Catalogue of the Manuscripts in the Library of Eton College.* Cambridge: University Press, 1895.

———. *A Descriptive Catalogue of the McClean Collection of Manuscripts in the Fitzwilliam Museum.* Cambridge: University Press, 1912.

———. 'An English Medieval Sketch-book, No. 1916 in the Pepysian Library, Magdalene College, Cambridge', *The Walpole Society* 13 (1925) 1–17.

———. ed. & trans. *Walter Map. De Nugis Curialium–Courtiers' Trifles*, revised by C. N. L. Brooke and R. A. B. Mynors. Oxford: University Press, 1983.

Janauschek, Leopold. *Xenia Bernardina, pars quarta, Bibliographia Bernardina*. Vienna, 1891.

Janini, José and José Serrano. *Manuscritos liturgicos de la Biblioteca Nacional*. Madrid: Direcion General de Archivos y Bibliotecas, 1969.

Janke, R. Stephen. 'The Vision of St. Bernard: A Study in Florentine Iconography', in Robert Enggass and Marilyn Stokstad, edd., *Hortus Imaginum*. Lawrence, Kansas, 1974. Pp. 45–50.

Jaritz, Gerhard. 'Religiöse Bildbotschaften und ihre Entwicklungsmuster im Mittelalter: Bernhard von Clairvaux im Kontext', *Festschrift Gerhard Pferschy zum 70. Geburtstag*. Graz, 2000. Pp. 105–116.

Jazdzewski, Konstanty Klemens. *Lubiaz – Losy I kultura unyslowa slaskiego opactwa Cystersow (1163-1642)*, (with German summary 242–245). Wroclaw, 1992.

Jöckle, Clemens. *Encyclopedia of Saints*. London: Parkgate, 1997.

Kaftal, George. *Iconography of the Saints in Tuscan Painting*. Florence: Sansoni, 1952.

———. *Iconography of the Saints in Central and South Italian Schools of Painting*. Florence: Sansoni, 1965.

———. *Iconography of the Saints in the Painting of North East Italy*. Florence: Sansoni, 1978.

———. *Iconography of the Saints in the Painting of North West Italy*. Florence: Sansoni, 1985.

Kamp. *Buchmalerei der Zisterzienser–Kulturelle Schätze aus sechs Jahrhunderten*. Katalog zur Ausstellung 'Libri Cistercienses' in Ordensmuseum Kamp. Stuttgart, 1998.

Karl, Louis. 'Les Vies des Saints par l'Image', *Gazette des Beaux-Arts* 71:2 (1929) 185–205.

Karlowska-Kamzowa, Alicja, 'Znaczenie Ilumina Torstwa Cysterskiego', in Jerzy Strzelczyk, ed., *Historia I Kultura Cystersow w Dawney Polsce*. Poznan: Universytet im. Adama Mickiewicza w Poznaniu, 1987. Pp. 380–383.

Karlsruhe. *Hans Baldung–Buchholzschnitte*. Exhibition Catalogue. Karlsruhe, 1959.

———. *Initial und Miniatur: Buchmalerei aus 9 Jahrhunderten in Handschriften der Badischen Landesbibliothek*. Exhibition Catalogue by Ellen J. Beer, ed. Franz Anselm Schmitt. Karlsruhe, 1965.

———. *Staatliche Kunsthalle–Katalog Alte Meister bis 1800*. Karlsruhe, 1966.

———. *Spätmittelalter am Oberrhein–Maler und Werkstätten 1450–1525.* Exhibition Catalogue. Staatliche Kunsthalle. Stuttgart, 2001.

Ker, N. R. *Medieval Manuscripts in British Libraries,* Vol. 2. Oxford: Clarendon Press, 1977.

Kinder, Terryl N. 'Les églises médiévales de Clairvaux–Probabilités et fiction', *Histoire de Clairvaux,* Actes du Colloque Juin 1990, Bar-sur-Aube, 1991, 205–229.

Kirschbaum, E. and W. Braunfels. *Lexikon der Christlichen Ikonographie,* 8 volumes. Rome-Freiburg- Basel-Vienna: Herder, 1968–1976.

Klemm, Elizabeth. *Die Romanischen Handschriften der Bayerischen Staatsbibliothek,* Teil 1: Die Bistümer Regensburg, Passau und Salzburg. Wiesbaden: Reichert, 1980.

Kline, Francis. 'Saint Bernard and the *Rule* of Saint Benedict: An Introduction', in John R. Sommerfeldt, ed. *Bernardus Magister,* CS 135. Kalamazoo, 1992. Pp. 169–183.

Kloss, Ernst. *Die Schlesische Buchmalerei des Mittelalters.* Berlin: Deutscher Verein für Kunstwissenshaft, 1942.

Knapp, Ulrich. *Das Kloster Maulbronn.* Stuttgart: Theiss, 1997.

Knipping, John B. *Iconography of the Counter Reformation in the Netherlands,* 2 volumes. Leiden: De Graff, 1974.

Knowles, David. *The Monastic Order in England.* Cambridge: University Press, 1940.

———. *Christian Monasticism.* London: Weidenfeld & Nicolson, 1969.

Kofod-Hansen, Elizabeth & Scharff, Mikkel *Løgumskabet.* Padborg: Forlaget de Unges Kunstkreds, 1985.

Kohler, Ch. *Catalogue des Manuscrits de la Bibliothèque Sainte-Geneviève,* Vol. 2. Paris, 1896.

König, Eberhard. *Leuchtendes Mittelalter,* Neue Folge II. Ramsen, 1998.

———. *Französische Buchmalerei um 1450.* Berlin: Gebr. Mann, 1982.

Köpf, Ulrich. 'Bernhard von Clairvaux in der Frauenmystik', in Peter Dinzelbacher and Dieter R. Bauer, edd. *Frauenmystik im Mittelalter.* Ostfildern, 1985. Pp. 48–77.

———. 'Die Rezeptions- und Wirkungsgeschichte Bernhards von Clairvaux–Forschungsstand und Forschungsaufgaben', in Kaspar Elm, ed., *Bernhard von Clairvaux.* Wiesbaden: Harrassowitz, 1994. Pp. 5–58.

Korn, Ulf-Dietrich. *Kloster Wienhausen – Die Glasmalereien.* Wienhausen: Ulf-Dietrich Korn, 1975.

Kraus, H. P. Catalogue 121*: Illustrated Books.* New York, no date.

_____. Catalogue 88*: Fifty Medieval and Renaissance Manuscripts.* New York, 1958.

———. Catalogue 95: *Twenty-Five Manuscripts.* New York, no date.

Kren, Thomas and Roger S.Wieck. *The Visions of Tondal from the Library of Margaret of York.* Malibu: Getty, 1990.

Kristeller, Paul. *Early Florentine Woodcuts.* London, 1987.

Kubach, Hans Erich, Fritz, Michel, and Hermann Schnitzler. *Die Kunstdenkmäler des Landkreises Koblenz.* Düsseldorf, 1944.

Kubes, Karl and Joachim Rössl. *Stift Zwettl.* St Pöltern-Vienna, 1897.

Kuhn-Rehfus, Maren. 'Cistercian Nuns in Germany in the Thirteenth Century', in Nichols and Shank, edd., *Hidden Springs,* CS 113. Kalamazoo, 1995. 1:135-58.

Künstle, Karl. *Ikonographie der Heiligen.* Freiburg im Breisgau, 1926.

Kvet, Jan. *Iluminované Rukopisy Královny Rejcky* (Résumé in French, 250–256). Prague, 1931.

Ladner, Gerhart B. 'Das älteste Bild des hl. Franziskus von Assisi–ein Beitrag zur mittelalterlichen Porträtikonographie', in Peter Classen and Peter Scheibert, edd., *Festschrift Percy Ernst Schramm zu seinem siebzigsten Geburtstag von Schülern und Freunden zugeeignet,* 2 volumes. Wiesbaden, 1964. 1:449-460.

Lage, Maria Augusta and Pablo da Trindade Ferreira. *Mosteiro de Santa Maria de Alcobaça.* Lisbon, 1987.

Latham, Robert ed. *Catalogue of the Pepys Library at Magdalene College, Cambridge,* Vol 5: Manuscripts, Part 1: Medieval. Woodbridge: D. S. Brewer, 1992.

Lawrence, C.H. *St. Edmund of Abingdon.* Oxford: Clarendon Press, 1960.

Leclercq, Jean. 'Études sur Saint Bernard et le Textes de ses Écrits', *Analecta Sacri Ordinis Cisterciensis* 9 (1953) 1–245.

———. 'Saint Bernard et la dévotion médiévale envers Marie', *Revue d'Ascétique et de Mystique* 30 (1954) 361–375.

———. 'Pour l'Iconographie de S. Bernard', *Analecta Sacri Ordinis Cisterciensis* 11 (1955) 145–146.

———. L'*Amour des Lettres et le Désir de Dieu.* Paris, 1957. English translation by Catherine Misrahi, *The Love of Learning and the Desire for God.* New York: Fordham, 1961.

———. 'Aspects littéraire de l'oeuvre de Saint Bernard', *Cahiers de Civilisation Médiévale* 1 (1958) 425–450.

———. *Recueil d'études sur saint Bernard et ses ecrits,* 3 volumes. Rome: Sacri Ordinis Cisterciensis, 1962–1969.

———. *Saint Bernard et l'Esprit Cistercien,* Paris, 1966. English translation: *St Bernard and the Cistercian Spirit,* CS 16. Kalamazoo, 1976.

———. 'Le portrait de saint Bernard dans la littérature des 'exempla' du bas Moyen Age', *Collectanea Cisterciensia* 50 (1988) 256–267.

———. 'L'écrvain', *Bernard de Clairvaux: Histoire, Mentalités, Spiritualité.* Paris: Les Éditions du Cerf, 1992. Pp. 529–556.

———. 'Toward a Sociological Interpretation of the Various Saint Bernards', in John R. Sommerfeldt, ed., *Bernardus Magister,* CS 35. Kalamazoo: Cistercian Publications-Cîteaux: Commentarii Cistercienses, 1992. Pp. 19–33.

Lekai, L. J. *The Cistercians. Ideals and Reality.* Kent, Ohio: Kent State University Press, 1977.

Lemeunier, Albert. 'La statue de saint Bernard', *Notre-Dame du Val-Dieu.* Exhibition Catalogue,.Val-Dieu, 1998. Pp. 126–128.

Leroquais, V. *Les Sacrementaires et les Missels Manuscrits des Bibliothèques de France.* Paris: Protat, 1924.

———. *Les Livres d'Heures Manuscrits de la Bibliothèque Nationale,* 2 volumes. Paris: Protat, 1927.

———. *Les Bréviaires Manuscrits des Bibliothèques Publiques de France,* Vol. 4. Paris: Protat, 1934.

———. *Un Livre d'Heures Manuscrit a l'Usage de Mâcon.* Mâcon: Protat, 1935.

———. *Les Psautiers Manuscrits Latins des Bibliotheques Publiques de France,* 2 volumes. Macon: Protat, 1940–1941.

Leroux, Gérard. *São Bernardo (1090–1153). Catálogo bibliográfico e iiconográfico.* Lisbon: Biblioteca Nacional, 1991.

Lesher, Melinda Kay. 'St. Bernard of Clairvaux and the Republic of Florence in the Late Middle Ages', *Cîteaux* 35 (1984) 258–267.

Leuven 1998. *Dirk Bouts–een Vlaams primitief te Leuven, ed. Maurits Smeyers.* Exhibition Catalogue. Leuven, 1998.

Levi d'Ancona, Mirella. *The Choir Books of santa Maria degli Angeli in Florence,* Vol. 1: *The Illuminators and Illuminations.* Florence: Maria Pacini Fazzi, 1994.

Lexikon der Marienkunde, ed. Konrad Algermissen *et. al.,* Vol. 1. Regensburg: F. Pustet, 1967.

Libor, Reinhard Maria. *Ars Cisterciensis. Buchmalereien aus mittel- und ostdeutschen Klosterbibliotheken.* Würzburg: Holzner, 1967.

Lippman, Friedrich. *The Art of Wood-Engraving in Italy in the Fifteenth Century.* London, 1888.

———. Introduction and commentary. *Drawings by Sandro Botticelli for Dante's Divina Commedia,* reduced facsimiles. London, 1896.

Lisbon. *A iluminura em Portugal–Identidade e Influências.* Exhibition Catalogue. Biblioteca Nacional, Lisbon, 1999.

London. *Burlington Fine Arts Club–Exhibition of Illuminated Manuscripts.* London, 1908.

———. Hayward Gallery. *Frescos from Florence.* Exhibition Catalogue. London, 1969.

———. *The Image of Christ.* Catalogue of the Exhibition 'Seeing Salvation', ed. Gabriele Finaldi. National Gallery. London, 2000.

Los Angeles. *The Renaissance–The Triumph of Flemish Manuscript Painting in Europe,* ed. Thomas Kren and Scot McKendrick. Exhibition Catalogue. Los Angeles, 2003.

Louf, André. 'Un Triptyque de Simon Bening, commandite par Pierre van Onderberghen, abbé des Dunes (1515–1519)', *Cîteaux* 43 (1992) 221–237.

———. 'Le Cîteaux de Saint Bernard', *Collectanea Cisterciensia* 61 (1999) 40–78.

Louvre, *Catalogue sommaire illustré des peintures du Musée du,* I: Ecoles flamande et hollandaise, ed. Arnauld Brejou de Lavergnée, Jacques Foucart, and Nicole Reynard. Paris, 1979.

Luchs, Alison. *Cestello–A Cistercian Church of the Italian Renaissance.* New York-London, 1977.

———. 'Saint Bernard in the Wilderness', in Benoît Chauvin, ed., *Mélanges à la Mémoire du Père Anselme Dimier,* II:3. Pupillin, 1984. Pp. 348–354.

Luddy, Ailbe J. *Life and Teaching of St Bernard.* 3rd impression, Dublin: M. H. Gill & Son, 1959.

Lutze, Eberhard. *Katalog der Handschriften der Universitätsbibliothek Erlangen, VI Band: Die Bilderhandschriften.* Erlangen: Universitätsbibliothek, 1936.

Lymant, Brigitte. *Die Mittelalterlichen Glasmalereien der Ehemaligen Zisterzienserkirche Altenberg.* Bergisch Gladbach: Altenberger Domverein, 1979.

Maddalo, Silvia, 'Momenti dell'iconografia di Bernardo', *Arte medievale,* II Serie, VIII/2 (1994) 123–135.

Maggs Bros. *Early Presses and Monastic Libraries of North-West Europe.* Catalogue No. 890. London, 1964.

Mailly, Jean de. *Abrégé des Gestes et Miracles des Saints,* trans. to French by Antoine Dondaine. Paris: Les Éditions du Cerf, 1947.

Mainz. *Cîteaux 1098–1998: Rheinische Zisterzienser im Spiegel der Buchkunst.* Exhibition Catalogue. Landesmuseum Mainz, Wiesbaden: Reichert, 1998.

Mâle, Émile. *Religious Art in France: The Late Middle Ages: A Study of Medieval Iconography and its Sources.* Princeton: Princeton University Press, 1986.

Manion, Margaret M and F. Vines. *Medieval and Renaissance Illuminated Manuscripts in Australian Collections.* Melbourne–London–New York: Thames & Hudson, 1984.

Mann, Jill ed. *Ysengrinus–Text with Translation,* Mittelalterliche Studien und Texte, Band 12. Leiden: Brill, 1987.

Mannini, Maria Pia and Marco Fagioli. *Filippo Lippi Catalogo completo.* Florence: Octavo, 1997.

Manuscrits Enluminés de la Péninsule Ibérique dans la Bibliothèque Nationale. Paris: Bibliothèque nationale, 1982.

Marabottini, Alessandro. *Giovanni da Milano.* Florence, 1950.

Marchi, Andrea De and Tiziana Franco. 'Il Gotico Internazionale: da Nicolò di Pietro a Michele Giambono', in Valter Curzi, ed., *Pittura Veneta Nelle Marche.* Milan, 2000.

Marchini, Guiseppe. *Filippo Lippi.* Milan: Electa, 1975.

Marcucci, Luisa. *Gallerie Nazionali di Firenze –I Dipinti Toscani del Secolo XIV.* Rome: Istituto poligrafico dello Stato, 1965.

Marle, Raimond van. 'La Scuola Pittorica Orvietana del '300', *Bolletino d'Arte,* Anno 3, Serie 2, Vol. 2 (1923–24) 305–335.

———. *The Development of the Italian School of Painting,* 19 volumes. The Hague, 1923–1938.

Marlier, G. 'Le Mâitre de la Légende de Sainte Ursule', *Jaarboek Koninklijk Museum voor Schone Kunsten* (1964) 5–51.

Marrow, James H. 'Miniatures inédites de Jean Fouquet: Les Heures de Simon de Varie', *Revue de l'Art* 67 (1985) 7–32.

———. *The Hours of Simon de Varie.* Malibu: Getty, 1994.

Martin, André. *Saint Bernard.* Paris, 1925.

Martin, Henry. *Catalogue Général des Manuscrits des Bibliothèques Publiques de France. Catalogue des Manuscrits de la Bibliothèque de l'Arsenal.* Paris, 1885.

Masai, François. 'Un Missel Cistercien de Baudeloo', *Scriptorium* 6 (1952) 279–284.

Masseron, Alexandre. *Dante et Saint Bernard.* Paris: A. Michel, 1953.

Matalon, S. *Affreschi Lombardi del Trecento.* Milan, 1964.

Matalon, S. and F. Mazzini. *Affreschi del Tre e Quattrocento in Lombardia.* Milan: Edizioni del Milione, 1958.

Matarasso, Pauline. *The Cistercian World.* Harmondsworth: Penguin, 1993.

Mavarelli, Cristina Guoni. *I Libri d'Ore della Biblioteca Riccardiana,* Vol. 1: *I Libri d'Ore francesi e fiamminghi.* Rome: Istituto poligrafico dello Stato, 1986.

Mayer, Bettina. *Bildschnitzerpersönlichkeit und Regionale Stilausprägung im Spätmittelalter.* Augsburg, 2002.

Mazal, Otto and F. Unterkircher. *Katalog der Abendländischen Handschriften der Österreichischen Nationalbibliothek.* Series Nova, Teil 2/1. Vienna: G. Prachner, 1963.

McCann, Justin, trans. *The Rule of St Benedict* (second edition). London: Sheed & Ward, 1976.

McGuire, Brian Patrick. 'A Lost Clairvaux Exemplum Collection Found: The *Liber Visionum et Miraculorum* compiled by Prior John of Clairvaux (1171–1179)', *Analecta Cisterciensia* 39 (1983) 26–62.

———. 'A Saint's Afterlife. Bernard in the Golden Legend and in Other Medieval Collections', in Elm, ed., *Bernhard von Clairvaux*. Wiesbaden, 1994. Pp. 179–211.

———. *The Cistercians in Denmark*, CS 35, Kalamazoo, Michigan, 1982,

———. *The Difficult Saint*, CS 126. Kalamazoo, Michigan, 1991.

———. *Brother and Lover–Aelred of Rievaulx*. New York: Crossroad, 1994.

———. 'Introduction', *Conrad d'Eberbach, Le Grand Exorde de Cîteaux*. Turnhout: Brepols, 1998. Pp. xi–xxxv.

———. 'Les Mentalités des Cisterciens dans les Receuils d'*Exempla* du XIIe Siècle', in Jacques Berlioz and Marie Anne Polo de Beaulieu, edd. *Les* Exempla *Médiévaux: Nouvelles Perspectives*. Geneva, 1998.

Meer, Frederic van der. *Atlas de l'Ordre Cistercien*. Amsterdam-Brussels: Elsevier, 1965.

Meiss, Millard. *Painting in Florence and Siena after the Black Death*. Princeton, New Jersey: Princeton University Press, 1951.

———. *French Painting in the Time of Jean de Berry; The Late Fourteenth Century and the Patronage of the Duke*. London: Phaidon, 1967.

———. *The Great Age of Fresco*. London: Phaidon, 1970.

——— and Elizabeth H. Beatson. *The Belles Heures of Jean, Duke of Berry*. New York: G Braziller, 1974.

Meissner, Helmuth. *Himmelkron–Geschichte und Geschichten, Namen und Daten*. Himmelkron, 1979.

Mende, Matthias. *Hans Baldung Grien: Vollständiger Bildkatalog der Einzelholzschnitte, Buchillustrationen und Kupferstiche*. Unterschneidheim: A. Uhl, 1978.

Merkl, Ulrich. *Buchmalerei in Bayern in der ersten Hälfte des 16. Jahrhunderts*. Regensburg: Schnell & Steiner, 1999.

Mierow, Charles, trans. *Otto of Freising. The Deeds of Frederick Barbarossa*. New York: Norton, 1953.

Modena. *Legenda Aurea–Iconografia religiosa nelle miniature delle Biblioteca Estense Universitaria*. Exhibition Catalogue. Modena, 2001.

Mons. *Tresors d'Art du Hainaut*. Exhibition Catalogue. Mons, 1953.

Montreal. *Catalogue of Paintings–Montreal Museum of Fine Art*. Montreal, 1960.

Morson, John. 'A Newly Found Bernardine Manuscript', *Collectanea Ordinis Cisterciensium Reformatorum* 16 (1954), 30–34, 214–221.

Müller, Christian ed. *Katalog der Zeichnungen des 15. und 16. Jahrhunderts–Öffentliche Kunstsammlung Basel*,Kupferstichkabinett, Teil 2A: Die Zeichnungen von Hans Holbein. Basel, 1996.

Muller, *Frederick & Cie, Catalogue de Dessins Anciens,* Auction Catalogue. Amsterdam, 11–14 June, 1912.

Mund, Hélène, Cyriel Stroo and Nicole Goetghebeur. *The Mayer van den Bergh Museum, Antwerp.* Brussels: Centre d'Étude de la Peinture dans les Pays Bas, 2003.

Munich, *Alte Pinakothek, Katalog II: Altdeutsche Malerei.* Munich, 1963.

Munich. *Catalogus Codicum Manu Scriptorum Bibliothecae Monacensis,* Tome V, pars 1: *Codices Germanicos Complectans.* Munich, 1920.

———. *Bayerns Kirche im Mittelalter–Handschriften und Urkunden.* Exhibition Catalogue. 1960.

Murray, Peter and Linda. *The Oxford Companion to Christian Art and Architecture.* Oxford-New York: Oxford University Press, 1996.

Musées royaux des Beaux-Arts de Belgique–Département d'Art Ancien. Catalogue Inventaire de la Peinture Ancienne. Bruxelles, 1984.

New York. *Treasures from The Pierpont Morgan Library.* New York, 1957.

———. *The Golden Age of Dutch Manuscript Painting.* Exhibition Catalogue by Henri L. M. Defoer, Anne S. Korteweg and Wilhemina C. M. Wustefeld. New York: Pierpont Morgan Library, 1989.

———. *Painting and Illumination in Early Renaissance Florence 1300–1450.* Exhibition Catalogue. Metropolitan Museum of Art, New York, 1994.

Nichols, John A. and Lillian Thomas Shank, edd. *Hidden Springs. Cistercian Monastic Women,* CS 113. 2 volumes. Kalamazoo, 1995.

Nikulin, Nikolai N. *The Hermitage. Catalogue of Western European Painting: Netherlandish Painting, Fifteenth and Sixteenth Centuries.* Moscow, 1989.

Nilsen, Lauritz. *Dansk Bibliografi 1482-1550,* Copenhagen, 1919.

Norton, Christopher. 'Table of Cistercian legislation on art and architecture', in Norton and Park, edd., *Cistercian Art and Architecture in the British Isles.* Cambridge: University Press, 1986. Pp. 315–393.

Oberlin College, Ohio. *Catalogue of European and American Paintings and Sculpture in the Allen Memorial Museum–Oberlin College.* Oberlin, Ohio, 1967.

Ochsenbein, Peter. 'Bernhard von Clairvaux im spätmittelalterlichen Gebetbüchern', in Elm, ed., *Bernhard von Clairvaux.* Wiesbaden: Harrassowitz, 1994. Pp. 213–232.

Oertel, Robert. *Frühe Italienische Malerei in Altenburg,* Beschreibender Katalog der Gemälde des 13. bis 16. Jahrhunderts im Staatlichen Lindenau-Museum. Berlin: Henschel Verlag, 1961.

Offner, Richard. *Bernardo Daddi and his Circle. A Corpus of Florentine Painting.* Florence: Giunti, 2001.

——— with Klara Steinweg, continued under the direction of Miklos Boskovits and Mina Gregori. *A Critical and Historical Corpus of Florentine Painting,* Section III, Volume II. Florence, 1987.

Oldenbourg, M. Consuelo. *Hortulus animae 1494–1523–Bibliographie und Illustration.* Hamburg: Hanswedell, 1973.

Olivar, Marcial. *Museo d'Arte di Catalogna.* Barcelona: Istituto geografico de Agostini, 1963.

Paatz, Walter and Elizabeth. *Die Kirchen von Florenz,* 6 volumes. Frankfurt-am-Main: V. Klostermann, 1940–1954.

Pächt, Otto. *The Rise of Pictorial Narrative in Twelfth-Century England.* Oxford: Clarendon Press, 1962.

———. *Altniederländische Malerei.* Munich: Prestel, 1994. Translated as *Early Netherlandish Painting.* London: Harvey Miller, 1997.

——— and J. J. G. Alexander. *Illustrated Manuscripts in the Bodleian Library,* 3 volumes. Oxford: Clarendon Press, 1966–1973.

——— and Dagmar Thoss. *Die Illuminierten Handschriften und Inkunabeln der Österreichischen Nationalbibliothek, Französische Schule 1.* Vienna: Österreichische Akademie der Wissenschaften 1974.

———, Ulrike Jenni, Dagmar Thoss. *Die Illuminierten Handschriften und Inkunabeln der Österreichischen Nationalbibliothek, Flämische Schule 1.* Vienna, 1983.

Padua. *I Manoscritti della Biblioteca del Seminario Vescovile di Padova.* Tarvanuzze, 1998.

Paffrath, Arno. *Bernhard von Clairvaux–Leben und Wirken–dargestellt in den Bilderzyklen von Altenberg bis Zwettl.* Bergisch Gladbach: Altenberger Dom-Verein, 1984.

———. *Bernhard von Clairvaux 2.* Bergisch Gladbach: Altenberger Dom-Verein, 1990.

Palmer, Nigel F. *Zizterzienser und ihre Bücher.* Regensburg: Schnell & Steiner, 1998.

Panofsky, Erwin. *Early Netherlandish Painting,* 2 volumes. Cambridge, Massachusetts, 1966; New York: Harper & Row, 1971.

Paris: Arsenal, Bibliothèque de l'. *Catalogue des Manuscrits de la Bibliothèque de l'Arsenal,* 8 volumes. Paris, 1885–1999.

———. Bibliothèque Nationale *Catalogue des Manuscrits Francais: Bibliothèque Impériale–Département des Manuscrits.* Paris, 1868–1892.

———. Bibliothèque Nationale. *Catalogue Général des Manuscrits Latins,* Vols. 1–3. Paris: Bibliothèque nationale, 1939–1952.

———. Bibliothèque Nationale. *Inventaire des nouvelles acquisitions latines,* 2 volumes. Paris, n.d.

———. *Manuscrits a Peintures du VIIe au XIIe siècle.* Bibliothèque Nationale. Exhibition Catalogue. Paris, 1954.

———. *Saint Bernard & le Monde Cistercien,* Exhibition Catalogue. Edd. L. Pressouyre & T. N. Kinder. Paris, 1990.

———. *Joos van Cleve au Louvre.* Exhibition Catalogue. Paris, 1991.

———. *Les Manuscrits à Peintures en France.* Exhibition Catalogue. Edd. Francois Avril et Nicole Reynaud. Paris, 1993.

Parkes, M. B. *The Medieval Manuscripts of Keble College, Oxford.* London: Scolar Press, 1979.

Patoul, Brigitte de and Roger van Schoute, edd. *Les Primitifs flamands et leur temps.* Wesmael: La Renaissance du Livre, 1994.

Pearson, Andrea G. 'Nuns, Images, and the Ideals of Women's Monasticism: Two Paintings from the Cistercian Convent of Flines', *Renaissance Quarterly* 54 (2001) 1356–1402.

Pedrick, Gale. *Monastic Seals of the XIIIth Century.* London: The de la More Press, 1902.

Pereira, Paulo. *Jerónimos Abbey of Santa Maria.* London, 2002.

Pfleger, L. 'Abt Nicolaus Salicetus von Baumgarten, ein gelehrter Cisterzienser der 15 Jahrhunderts', *Archiv für Elsässische Kirchengeschichte* 9 (1934) 107–122.

Piazonni, Ambrogio M. 'Le premier biographe de Saint Bernard, Guillaume de Saint-Thierry', in Patrick Arabeyre, Jacques Berlioz, et Philippe Poirrier, edd., *Vies et Légendes de Saint Bernard.* 1993. Pp. 3–18.

Pierpont Morgan Library. Medieval & Renaissance Manuscripts–Major Acquisitions 1924-1974. New York, 1974.

Pittura a Genova e in Liguria, La. 2 volumes. Genoa, 1970.

Plathe, Sissel F. 'Altertavlen I Esrum klosterkirke', *Bogen om Esrum Kloster,* eds. Søren Frandsen, Jens Anker Jørgensen and Chr. Gorm Tortzen. Hillerød, Frederiksborg Amt, 1997. Pp. 150–167.

Plummer, John. *The Hours of Catherine of Cleves.* London-New York: Barrie & Rockcliff, 1966.

———. *The Last Flowering. French Painting in Manuscripts 1420–1530 from American Collections.* New York-London: Pierpont-Morgan and Oxford University Press, 1982.

Polo, Claudio de. 'Un Codice della Seconda metà del Trecento', in Grazia Vailati Schoenburg Waldenburg, ed., *La Miniatura Italiana in Èta Romanica e Gotica.* Florence, 1979.

Pontigny. *Les Cisterciens dans l'Yonne,* ed. Terryl N. Kinder. Exhibition Catalogue. Beernem, 1999.

Pope-Hennessy, John, ed. *A Sienese Codex of the Divine Comedy.* Oxford-London: Phaidon, 1947.

———. *The Complete Works of Paolo Uccello.* London: Phaidon, 1950.

———. *The Robert Lehmann Collection*, I: Italian Paintings. New York: Princeton University Press, 1987.

———. *Paradiso. The Illuminations to Dante's Divine Comedy by Giovanni di Paolo.* London: Thames & Hudson, 1993.

Popham, A. E. and Philip Pouncey. *Italian Drawings in the Department of Prints in the British Museum.* Catalogue, 2 volumes. London: British Museum, 1950.

Porcher, Jean. *Le Bréviaire de Martin d'Aragon.* Paris, 1950.

———. *Les Belles Heures de Jean de France Duc de Berry.* Paris: Bibliothèque nationale, 1953.

Portsmann, Gisbert and Dirk Schumannk. 'Überlegungen zum Chorgestühl der Zisterzienserklosterkirche Zinna', in Oliver H. Schmidt and Dirk Schumann, edd., *Zisterzienser in Brandenburg.* Berlin, 1996. Pp. 136–156.

Posset, Franz. 'Saint Bernard of Clairvaux in the Devotion, Theology, and Art of the Sixteenth Century', *Lutheran Quarterly* 11 (1997) 308–352.

———. 'The Crucified Embraces Saint Bernard: The Beginnings of the *Amplexus Bernardi*', *Cistercian Studies Quarterly* 33 (1998) 289–314.

———. *Pater Bernhardus,* CS 168. Kalamazoo, 1999.

———. 'The 'Double Right to heaven': Saint Bernard's Impact in the Sixteenth Century', *Cistercian Studies Quarterly* 38 (2003), 263–273.

———. '*Amplexus Bernardi.* The Dissemination of a Cistercian Motif in the Later Middle Ages', *Cîteaux* 54 (2003) 251–400.

Post, Chandler Rathfon. *A History of Spanish Painting,* Vol. 3. Cambridge, Massachusetts, 1930.

Powicke, F. M. ed. and trans. *The Life of Aelred of Rievaulx by Walter Daniel.* Nelson's Medieval Texts. London, 1950; new edition *Walter Daniel: The Life of Aelred of Rievaulx with the Letter to Maurice.* Kalamazoo, 1994.

Prado, Museo del. *Inventario General de Pinturas I: La Colección Real.* Madrid, 1990.

———. *Catálogo de las Pinturas.* Madrid, 1996.

Procacci, Ugo. *La R. Galleria dell'Accademia di Firenze.* Rome: Libreria dello Stato, 1936.

———. *The Gallery of the Academy of Florence.* Rome: Libreria dello Stato, 1951.

Provinzialmuseum in Bonn. *Katalog der Gemäldegalerie,* 2nd edition. Bonn, 1927.

Quarré, Pierre. 'Saint Bernard et l'Art des Cisterciens', *Revue des Arts* (1953) 251–255.

———. 'L'Iconographie de Saint Bernard à Clairvaux et les Origines de la *Vera Effigies*', *Mélanges Saint Bernard.* Dijon, 1954. Pp. 342–349.

Raguin, V. C. and H. J. & Zakin. *Stained Glass before 1700 in the Collections of the Midwest States,*2 volumes. London-Turnhout: Harvey Miller, 2001.

Randall, Lillian M. C.'From Cîteaux Onwards: Cistercian-Related Manuscripts in the Walters Art Gallery', in Meredith Parsons Lillich, ed., *Studies in Cistercian Art and Architecture,* Vol. 3, CS 89. Kalamazoo, 1987. Pp.111–136.

———. *Medieval and Renaissance Manuscripts in the Walters Art Gallery,* 3 volumes. Baltimore- London, 1989–1997.

Réau, Louis. *Iconographie de l'Art Chrétien,* 3 volumes. Paris: Presses universitaires de France, 1955–1959.

Reutersward, Patrik. *The Forgotten Symbols of God,* Stockholm Studies in Art History 35. Uppsala: Almquist & Wiksell, 1986.

Reyniès, Nicole de. *Principes d'analyse scientifique: le mobilier domestique, vocabulaire typologique,* Vol. 1. Paris, 1987.

Rheinisches Landesmuseum Bonn. *Gemälde bis 1900,* ed. Fritz Goldkuhle, Ingeborg Krueger and Hans M. Schmidt. Cologne, 1982.

Ricci, Elisa. *Mille Santi nell'Arte.* Milan, 1931.

Ricci, S. De, and W. J. Wilson. *Census of Medieval and Renaissance Manuscripts in the United States and Canada,* Vol. 1. New York, 1935.

Riedl, Peter Anselm and Max Seidel. *Die Kirchen von Siena,* 2 volumes. Munich: Bruckmann, 1992.

Ringbom, Sixten. *Icon to Narrative.* Åbo: Åbo Akademi, 1965.

Roddewig, Marcella. *Dante Alighieri Die göttliche Komödie–vergleichende Bestandsaufnahme der Commedia-Handschriften.* Stuttgart: A. Hirsemann, 1984.

Rode, Herbert. *Die Mittelalterlicher Glasmalereien des Kölner Domes.* Berlin: Deutscher Verlag für Kunstwissenschaft, 1974.

Rodriguez, Ann Dominguez. *Libros de Horas del Siglo XV en la Biblioteca Nacional,* Madrid: Fundacion Universitaria Espanola, 1979.

Rome. *Maria, Vergine Madre Regina.* Exhibition Catalogue. Biblioteca Vallicelliana, ed. Claudio Leonardi and Antonella Degl' Innocenti. Rome, 2000.

Rouse, Richard H. and Mary A. *Manuscripts and their Makers. Commercial Book-Producers in Medieval Paris 1200-1500,* 2 volumes. London: Harvey Miller, 2000.

Rowley, George. 'The Gothic Frescos at Monte Siepi', *Art Studies* (1929) 107–127.

Rückert, Peter and Dieter Planck, edd. *Anfänge der Zisterzienser in Südwestdeutschland.* Stuttgart: J. Thorbecke, 1999.

Rückert, Peter and Hansmartin Schwarzmaier, edd. *850 Jahre Kloster Herrenalb.* Stuttgart, 2001.

Rudolph, Conrad. *The 'Things of Greater Importance'. Bernard of Clairvaux's* Apologia *and the Medieval Attitude Toward Art.* Philadelphia: University of Pennsylvania Press, 1990.

Sabbe, M., M. Lamberigts, and F. Gistelinck, edd. *Bernardus en de Cistercienzerfamilie in Belgie, 1090–1990.* Louvain, 1990.

Samek-Ludovici, Sergio, trans. Peter J. Tallon. *Dante's Divine Comedy: 15th Century Manuscript*, Fribourg-Geneva, 1979.

Sánchez, Alfonso E. Pérez. *Spanish Painting in the Prado Museum.* Madrid, 1966.

Sander, Max. *Le Livre a Figures Italien depuis 1467 jusqu'a 1530*, 6 volumes. Milan: U Hoepli, 1942.

Sandler, Lucy Freeman. 'Pictorial and Verbal Play in the Margins: the Case of British Library, Stowe MS 49, in Michelle P. Brown & Scot McKendrick, edd., *Illuminating the Book*, London: British Library, 1998.

Saxtorph, Niels M. *Jeg ser på Kalkmalerier.* Copenhagen: Politikens Forlag, 1967.

Scarpellini, Pietro. *Perugino.* Milan: Electa, 1984.

Schaefer, Claude. 'Autour des Heures de Laval: les activités de l'atelier de Jean Colombe après 1470', in Peter Rolfe Monks and D. D. R. Owen, edd., *Medieval Codicology, Iconography, Literature, and Translation. Studies for Keith Val Sinclair.* Leiden, 1994.

Schaeffer, Claude. *Jean Fouquet: The Hours of Etienne Chevalier.* London, 1972.

Scharf, Alfred. *Filippino Lippi.* Vienna: A. Schroll, 1935.

Schmidt, Hans Martin. *Der Meister des Marienlebens und sein Kreis.* Düsseldorf: Schwann, 1978.

Schmidt, Peter. *Gedruckte Bilder in Handgeschriebenen Büchern.* Cologne-Weimar-Vienna: Bühlau, 2003.

Schmitt, Jean-Claude. '*Imago:* de l'Image à l'Imaginaire', in Jérôme Baschet and Jean-Claude Schmitt, edd., *L'Image- Fonctions et usages des images dans l'Occident médiéval. Actes du 6e International Workshop on Medieval Societies 1992.* Paris, 1996. Pp. 29–37.

———. 'Le Culte de Saint Bernard et ses Images', in Preyssouyre and Kinder, edd., *Saint Bernard et le Monde Cistercien.* Paris, 1990. Pp. 149–163.

———. 'Saint Bernard et son Image', *Bernard de Clairvaux–Histoire, Mentalités, Spiritualité.* Paris, 1992. Pp. 639–657.

Schneider, Ambrosius *et al. Die Cistercienser – Geschichte, Geist, Kunst.* Cologne: Wienand Verlag, 1986 (third enlarged edition).

Schneider, Karin, ed. *Die Handschriften der Stadtbibliothek Nürnberg:Die Deutschen Mittelalterlichen Handschriften*, 2 volumes. Wiesbaden, 1965–1967.

Schramm, Albert. *Der Bilderschmuck der Frühdrücke*, 23 volumes. Leipzig: Deutsches Museum für Buch und Schrift, 1920–1943.

Schreiber, W. L. *Handbuch der Holz- und Metallschnitte des XV. Jahrhunderts*, 8 volumes. Leipzig: Hiersemann, 1927.

Schuba, Ludwig. 'Leben und Denken der Salemer Mönchsgemeinde im Spiegel der liturgischen Handschriften', *Salem–850 Jahre Reichsabtei und Schloss*. Constance, 1984.

Schwenk, Wilfried. *Das Herrenalber Gebetbuch 1482–84. Seine Wiederentdeckung 1980*. Bad Herrenalb, 1983.

Scott, Kathleen L. *Later Gothic Manuscripts 1390-1490*, 2 volumes. London: Harvey Miller, 1996.

Scriptoria medii aevi helvetica. Geneva: Roto-Sadag, 1935–1971.

Seidel, Max. 'Studien zur Skulptur der Frührenaissance: Francesco di Giorgio, Giovanni Antonio Amadeo', *Pantheon* 49 (1991) 55–73.

Shailor, Barbara A. *Catalogue of Medieval and Renaissance Manuscripts in the Beinecke Rare Book and Manuscript Library, Yale University*, 3 volumes. New Haven: Yale University Press, 1984–1992.

Shapley, Fern Rusk. *Paintings from the Samuel H. Kress Collection. Italian Schools XIII-XV Century*. London: Phaidon, 1966.

———. ed. *National Gallery of Art Washington: Catalogue of the Italian Paintings*, 2 volumes. Washington, D.C.: National Gallery of Art, 1979.

Sheppard, Jennifer M. 'The Twelfth Century Library and Scriptorium at Buildwas: Assessing the Evidence', in D. Williams, ed., *England in the Twelfth Century*. Woodbridge: Boydell, 1990. Pp. 193–204.

———. *The Buildwas Books*, Oxford Bibliographical Society Publications, Vol. 3. Oxford: Oxford Bibliographical Society, 1997.

Sieveking, Hinrich. *Der Meister des Wolfgang-Missale von Rein*. Munich, 1986.

Sirén, Osvald. *A Descriptive Catalogue of the Pictures in the Jarves Collection belonging to Yale University*. New Haven, 1916.

Slenders, F. P. J. and M. K. J. Smets. *Waar het koepeldragend Munster rijst: Historisch overzicht betreffende de Onze Lieve Vrouwe Munsterkerk*. Roermond, 1984.

Smeyers, K. 'A Pre-Eyckian *Legenda Aurea* (Glasgow, U. L. MS Gen. 1111): Tradition and Innovation', in M. Smeyers and Bert Cardon, edd., *Flanders in a European Perspective*. Leuven: Peeters, 1995. Pp. 237–249.

Smeyers, Maurits and Jan Van der Stock. *Flemish Illuminated Manuscripts 1475–1550*. Ghent: Ludion Press, 1996.

———. *Dirk Bouts: Peintre du silence*, Leuven: Peeters, 1998.

Sobré, Judith Berg. *Behind the Altar Table. The Development of the Painted Retable in Spain, 1350–1500*. Columbia, Missouri: University of Missouri Press, 1989.

Spencer, Brian. *Pilgrim Souvenirs and Secular Badges*. London: Stationery Office, 1998.

Squire, Aelred. *Aelred of Rievaulx. A Study*. London: SPCK, 1969-Kalamazoo: Cistercian Publications 1981.

Stadlober, Margot. 'Die Vision des Heiligen Bernhard vom Meister der Historia Friderici et Maximiliani, ein Werk der frühen Donauschule', in G. G. Brücker, W. T. Müller, H. Schweigert, and B. Wagner, edd., *Orient und Okzident im Spiegel der Kunst -Festschrift Heinrich Gerhard Franz zum 70. Geburtstag.* Graz, 1986. Pp. 365–379.

Stalley, Roger. *The Cistercian Monasteries of Ireland.* London -New Haven: Yale University Press, 1987.

Stammler, Wolfgang ed. *Spätlese des Mittelalters II–Religiöses Schrifttum.* Berlin: Erich Schmidt, 1965.

Stange, Alfred. 'Beitrage zur Kaisheimer Buchmalerei', *Festschrift für Georg Leidinger,* Munich, 1930, 277–281.

———. *Deutsche Malerei der Gotik,* 10 volumes. Munich-Berlin, 1951–1961.

———. *Kritisches Verzeichnis der deutschen Tafelbilder vor Dürer,* 2 volumes. Munich: Bruckmann, 1967–1970.

Steffen, Stephan. 'Gemälde des hl. Bernhard im städtlichen Wallraf Richartz Museum zu Köln', *Cisterzienser-Chronik* 33 (1921) 97–99.

Stercal, Claudio. *Il'Medius Adventus'–saggio di Lettura degli Scritti di Bernardo di Clairvaux,* Bibliotheca Cisterciensis 9. Rome: Editiones Cistercienses 1992.

Sterling, Charles. *The Metropolitan Museum of Art. A Catalogue of French Paintings XV–XVIII Centuries.* Cambridge, Mass.: Harvard University Press, 1955.

———. *The Master of Claude, Queen of France.* New York: H. P. Krauss, 1975.

Stockholm. *Gyllene Böcker–Nationalmuseum, Stockholm.* Exhibition Catalogue. Stockholm, 1952.

Stolleis, Karen ed. *Frankfurther Domschatz Band I: Die Paramente.* Frankfurt am Main, 1992.

Studies in the History of Art, Vol. 15: Stained Glass before 1700 in American Collections. New England and New York (CV Checklist). Washington, 1985

Stuttgart, Staatsgalerie. Alte Meister. Stuttgart, 1992.

Swarzenski, Georg and Rosy Schilling, edd. *Die illuminierten Handschriften und Einzelminiaturen des Mittelalters und der Renaissance in Frankfurter Besitz.* 2 volumes. Frankfurt, 1929.

Swarzenski, Hanns. *Die lateinischen illuminierten Handschriften des XIII Jahrhunderts in den Ländern am Rhein, Main und Donau,* 2 volumes. Berlin: Deutscher Verein für Kunstwissenschaft, 1936.

Thieme, Ulrich and Felix Becker. *Allgemeines Lexikon der Bildenden Künstler,* 37 volumes. Leipzig 1907–1950; reprinted Zwickau, 1964.

Thompson, Henry Yates-Illustrations from the Hundred Manuscripts in the Library of Henry Yates Thompson. London: Chiswick Press, 1915.

Thomson, R. M. *Catalogue of the manuscripts of Lincoln Cathedral Chapter Library.* Cambridge, 1989.

Toesca, Pietro. *La pittura e la miniatura nella Lombardia.* Turin, 1966.

Toledano, Ralph. *Francesco di Giorgio Martini.* Milan: Electa, 1987.

Tomaschek, Johann. *Zisterzienserstift Zwettl.* Vienna: C Brandstätter, 1989.

Tomea, Paolo. *Chiaravalle–Arte e storia di un'abbazia cisterciense.* Milan: Electa, 1992.

Torriti, Piero. *La Quadreria dell' Accademia Ligustica.* Genoa: Casa di risparmio di Genova, 1963.

———. *La Pinoteca Nazionale di Siena I dipinti dal XII al XV secolo.* Genoa: Sagep, 1977.

Toussaint, Jacques, ed. *Les Cisterciens en Namurois XIIIe–XXe Siècle.* Namur, 1998.

Trenkler, Ernst. *Rothschild-Gebetbuch* (Facsimile Edition and Commentary), 2 volumes. Graz: Akademische Druck- u. Verlagsanstalt, 1979.

Treviso. *Tomaso da Modena.* Exhibition Catalogue, ed. Luigi Menegazzi. Treviso, 1979.

Turin. *Tra Gotico e Rinascinto–Scultura in Piemonte.* Exhibition Catalogue. Museo Civico d'Arte Antica a Palazzo Madama. Turin, 2001.

Unterkircher, Franz. *Abendländische Buchmalerei–Miniaturen aus Handschriften der Österreichischen Nationalbibliothek.* Graz-Wien-Köln: Styria, 1967.

———. *Das Rothschild-Gebetbuch: die schönsten Miniaturen eines flämischen Stundenbuches.* Graz, 1984.

———. *Das Stundenbuch des Mittelalters.* Graz: Akademische Druck- u. Verlagsanstalt, 1985.

Utrecht. *Handschriften en Oude Drukken van de Utrechtse Universiteitsbibliotheek.* Exhibition Catalogue. Utrecht, 1984.

Val Dieu. Lemeunier, Albert. 'La statue de saint Bernard', *Notre-Dame du Val Dieu.* Exhibition Catalogue. Val Dieu, 1998. Pp. 126–128.

Van Beuningen, H. J. E. and A. M. Koldeweij. *Heilig en Profaan–1000 Laatmiddeleeuwse Insignes uit de collectie H. J. E. van Beuningen,* Rotterdam Papers VIII, Cothen: Middeleeuwse religieuze en profane insignes, 1993.

Vandenbroeck, Paul. *Catalogue Schilderijen 14e en 15e Eeuw–Koninklijk Museum voor Schoone Kunsten, Antwerpen.* Antwerp, 1985.

Vatasso, M. and P. F. de Cavalieri. *Codices Vaticani Latina.* Rome, 1902.

Väth, Paula. *Die Illuminierten Lateinischen Handschriften Deutscher Provenienz der Staatsbibliothek zu Berlin Preussischer Kulturbesitz 1200–1350,* 2 volumes. Wiesbaden: Harrassowitz, 2001.

———. 'Das Herrenalber Gebetbuch', in Peter Rückert & Hansmartin Schwarzmaier, edd., *850 Jahre Kloster Herrenalb.* Stuttgart, 2001. Pp. 89–107.

Vatican. *Miniatures of the Renaissance.* Exhibition Catalogue. Vatican, 1950.

———. *Quinto centenario della Biblioteca Apostolica Vaticana 1475–1975.* Exhibition Catalogue. Biblioteca Apostolica, 1975.

———. *XV Centenario della Nascita di S. Benedetto 480–1980.* Exhibition Catalogue. Biblioteca Apostolica, 1980.

———. *Vaticanae, Bibliothecae Apostolicae–Codices Urbinates Latini,* 3 volumes. Rome, 1902–1921.

Vauchez, André. *The Laity in the Middle Ages.* Notre Dame, Indiana: University of Notre Dame Press, 1993.

———. *Sainthood in the Later Middle Ages.*, Cambridge, 1997. A translation of *Ls Sainteté en Occident aux derniers siècles du Moyen Age; d'après les process de canonisation et les documents hagiographiques.* Rome-Paris, 1988.

Vavalà, Evelyn Sandberg. 'Vitale della Madonne e Simone dei Crocifissi', *Revista d'Arte* 12 (1930) 1–49.

Venturini, Lisa. *Francesco Botticini.* Florence: Edifir, 1994.

Vetter, Ewald M. 'Iconografia del *Varon de Dolores*', *Archivo Español de Arte* 36 (1963) 197–231.

Veyssière, Laurent. 'Le personnal de l'abbaye de Clairvaux au XIIe siècle', *Cîteaux* 51 (2000) 17–89.

Viale, Vittorio. *Civico Museo Francesco Borgogna Vercelli, I* Dipinti. Vercelli, 1969.

Victoria & Albert Museum. Catalogue of Miniatures, Leaves, and Cuttings from Illuminated Manuscripts, Catalogue I. London, 1923.

Virdis, Caterina Limentani & Mari, Pietrogiovanna. *Gothic and Renaissance Altarpieces.* London: Thames & Hudson, 2002.

Vloberg, Maurice. *La Vierge Notre Médiatrice.* Grenoble, 1938.

Voelkle, William M., ed. *The Pierpont Morgan Library Masterpieces of Medieval Painting– The Art of Illumination.* Oxford, 1980.

Volkmann, Ludwig. *Iconografia Dantesca. The Pictorial Representations to Dante's Divine Comedy.* London, 1899.

Vos, Dirk de. *Hans Memling.* Ghent: Ludion, 1994.

———. *Hans Memling –The Complete Works.* London: Thames & Hudson, 1994.

Vsetecková, Zuzana. 'Some remarks on the Osek Lectionary', *Umeni* 43 (1995) 219–223.

———. 'The Cistercian Origin of the Osek Lectionary and the Mural Paintings in the Royal Chapel of the Cistercian Monastery in Plasy', *Cîteaux* 47 (1996) 285–300.

Wachtel, Alois, ed. *Monumenta Germaniae Historica,* Quellen zur Geistesgeschichte des Mittelalters 1. Weimar, 1955.

Waddell, Chrysogonus. 'Le Culte et les Reliques de Saint Bernard de Clairvaux', in Leon Pressoyre & Terryl N. Kinder, edd., *Saint Bernard et le Monde Cistercien.* Paris: CNHMS/Sand, 1990. Pp. 141–146.

———. 'The Clairvaux Saint Bernard Office: Ikon of a Saint', in John R. Sommerfeldt, ed., *Bernardus Magister,* Cistercian Studies Series 135. Kalamazoo, 1992. Pp. 381–427.

———. *Narrative and Legislative Texts from Early Cîteaux,* Studia et documenta 9. Cîteaux: Commentarii Cistercienses, 1999.

Walford, Weston S. and Albert Way. 'Examples of Medieval Seals', *The Archaeological Journal* 14 (1857) 48–57.

Walliser, Franz. *Cistercienser Buchkunst–Heiligenkreuzer Skriptorium in seinen ersten Jahrhundert.* Heiligenkreuz: Heiligenkreuzer Verlag, 1969.

Wallraf-Richartz Museum und Kunstgewerbemuseum der Stadt Köln. Katalog der Deutschen und Niederländischen Gemälde bis 1550 (mit Ausnahme der Kölner Malerei), ed. Irmgard Hiller and Horst Vey. Cologne, 1969.

Wallraf-Richartz-Museum Köln. Vollständiges Verzeichnis der Gemäldesammlung. Catalogue. Cologne, 1986.

Ward, Benedicta, ed. *The Influence of Saint Bernard: Anglican Essays.* Oxford: Fairacres Press, 1976.

———. *Miracles and the Medieval Mind.* Aldershot: Scolar Press, 1982.

Warner, Marina. *Alone of all her Sex. The Myth and Cult of the Virgin Mary.* New York-London: Vintage, 1985.

Washington and New Haven. *Hans Baldung Grien Prints and Drawings.* Exhibition Catalogue. National Gallery of Art and the Yale University Art Gallery. Washington & New Haven, 1981.

Weber, Max. *Das Tennenbacher Güterbuch (1317–1341).* Stuttgart, 1969.

Weigel, T. O. And A. D. Zestermann. *Die Anfänge im Bild und Schrift,* 2 volumes. Leipzig, 1866.

Weis, Gustav. *Die Leonhardskirche und die Hospitalkirche zu Stuttgart- eine Darstellung der beiden gotischen Kirchen und kunstgeschichtliche Erläuterungen.* Stuttgart, 1956.

Wentzel, Hans. *Meisterwerke der Glasmalerei.* Berlin: Deutscher Verein für Kunstwissenshaft, 1954.

———. *Die Glasmalereien in Schwaben von 1200–1350.* Berlin: Deutscher Verein für Kunstwissenshaft, 1958.

Wenzel, Horst. *Hören und Sehen Schrift und Bild. Kultur und Gedächtnis im Mittelalter.* Munich: Beck, 1995.

Werner, W. *Cimelia Heidelbergensia.* Wiesbaden: Reichert, 1975.

Wescher, Paul. *Beschreibendes Verzeichnis der Miniaturen–Handschriften und Einzelblätter–des Kupferstickkabinetts der Staatlichen Museen Berlin.* Leipzig: J. J. Weber, 1931.

Wetesko, Leszek. 'Rekopisy Iluminowane', *Cystersi w Sredniowiecznej Polsce. Kultura I Sztuka*, ed. Krystyn Sobkowicz. Warsaw, 1991.

Whitaker, Thomas Dunham. *An History of the Original Parish of Whalley.* 1806 (2nd edition).

White, Helen C. *Tudor Books of Saints and Martyrs.* Madison, Wisconsin: University of Wisconsin Press, 1967.

Wieck, Roger S. *Late Medieval and Renaissance Illuminated Manuscripts 1350-1525 in the Houghton Library.* Cambridge, Massachusetts: Harvard University Press, 1983.

———. *Time Sanctified. The Book of Hours in Medieval Art and Life.* New York: Braziller, 1988.

———. *Painted Prayers. The Book of Hours in Medieval and Renaissance Art.* New York: Braziller, 1997.

Wiesbaden. *Rheinische Zisterzienser im Spiegel der Buchkunst, Landesmuseum Mainz.* Exhibition Catalogue. Wiesbaden: Reichert, 1998

Will, Robert. 'Une peinture Murale, Datée de 1504, se trouvant jadis en l'Église Saint-Guillaume de Strasbourg–Contribution à l'Iconographie de saint Bernard', *Cahiers Alsaciens d'Archéologie a'Art et d'Histoire* [Strasbourg] 24 (1981) 121–129.

William of Malmesbury. *Chronicle of the Kings of England,* trans. J. A. Giles. London, 1847, reprinted New York, 1968.

Williams, David H. *The Cistercians in the Early Middle Ages.* Leominster: Gracewing, 1998.

Williams, Ulla and Werner Williams-Krapp, edd. *Die 'Elsässische Legenda Aurea'*, 3 volumes. Tübingen: M. Niemeyer, 1980–1990.

Williams-Krapp, Werner. *Die deutschen und niederländischen Legendare des Mittelalters.* Tübingen: M. Niemeyer, 1986.

Williams, Watkin. *Saint Bernard of Clairvaux.* Manchester: Manchester University Press, 1935.

Wilson, Adrian and Joyce Lancaster. *A Medieval Mirror–Speculum humanae salvationis 1324-1500.* Berkeley: University of California Press, 1984.

Winkler, Erich. *Die Buchmalerei im Niederösterreich von 1150–1250.* Vienna, 1923.

Winkler, Gerhard. *Der Hl. Bernhard von Clairvaux.* Regensburg, 2000.

Wixom, William D. 'Twelve Masterpieces of Medieval and Renaissance Book Illumination-A Catalogue to the Exhibition March 17–May 17 1964', *The Bulletin of the Cleveland Museum of Art* 51, No 3 (1964) 43–63.

Woolley, R. M. *Catalogue of the Manuscripts of Lincoln Cathedral Chapter Library.* Oxford: N. Milford, 1927.

Wormald, Francis. 'Some Illustrated manuscripts of the Lives of the saints', *Bulletin of the John Rylands Library* 35, No 1 (1952) 248–266.

——— and Phyllis M. Giles. *A Descriptive Catalogue of the Additional Illuminated Manuscripts in the Fitzwilliam Museum,* 2 volumes. Cambridge: University Press, 1982.

Zafran, Eric M. *Fifty Old Master Paintings from the Walters Art Gallery.* Baltimore: Trustees of the Walters Art Gallery, 1988.

Załuska, Yolanta. *L'Enluminure de la Scriptorium de Cîteaux au XIIe Siècle.* Cîteaux: Cîteaux – Commentarii Cistercienses, 1989.

———. *Manuscrits Enluminée de Dijon,* Paris: Éditions du Centre national de la Recherche scientifique, 1991.

Zampetti, Pietro. *Carlo Crivelli.* Florence: Nardini, 1986.

Zappella, Giuseppina. *Il ritratto nel libro italiano del Cinquecento,* 2 volumes. Milan: Editrice Bibliografica, 1988.

Zehnder, F. G. *Katalog der Altkölner Malerei.* Cologne: Stadt Köln, 1990.

Zeri, Federico & Gardner, Elizabeth E. *Italian Paintings. A Catalogue of the Collection of the Metropolitan Museum of Art Florentine School.* New York: New York Graphic Society, 1971.

Zeri, Federico. *Italian Paintings in the Walters Art Gallery,* 2 volumes. Baltimore, 1976.

Ziegler, Charlotte, ed. *Zisterzienserstift Zwettl–Katalog der Handschriften des Mittelalters,* 3 volumes. Zwettl, 1985–1992.

Zinke, Detlef. *Bildwerke des Mittelalters und der Renaissance 1100–1530.* Munich: Hirmer, 1995.

Zürich. *Himmel, Hölle, Fegefeuer–Das Jenseits im Mittelalter.* Exhibition Catalogue. Schweizerischen Landesmuseum, Zürich, ed. Peter Jezler. Zürich, 1994.

Zwettl. *Die Kuenringer–Das Werden des Landes Niederösterreich (Niederösterreichische Landesausstellung – Zwettl).* Exhibition Catalogue. Vienna, 1981.

INDEX

Colour plate numbers are in **bold** type, black and white illustration numbers in *italics*

Abbreviations: archbp. = archbishop, bp. = bishop
M = Cistercian monasteries for men, W = Cistercian monasteries for women